How to use your Connected Casebook

Step 1: Go to **www.CasebookConnect.com** and redeem your access code to get started.

Access Code: SWhSaLe852105434

Step 2: Go to your **BOOKSHELF** and select your Connected Casebook to start reading, highlighting, and taking notes in the margins of your e-book.

Step 3: Select the **STUDY** tab in your toolbar to access a variety of practice materials designed to help you master the course material. These materials may include explanations, videos, multiple-choice questions, flashcards, short answer, essays, and issue spotting.

Step 4: Select the **OUTLINE** tab in your toolbar to access chapter outlines that automatically incorporate your highlights and annotations from the e-book. Use the My Notes area for copying, pasting, and editing your book notes or creating new notes.

Step 5: If your professor has enrolled your class, you can select the **CLASS INSIGHTS** tab and compare your own study center results against the average of your classmates.

Is this a used casebook? Access code already scratched off?

You can purchase the Digital Version and still access all of the powerful tools listed above.
Please visit CasebookConnect.com and select Catalog to learn more.

ASPEN CASEBOOK SERIES

Problems and Materials on the Sale and Lease of Goods

Eighth Edition

Douglas J. Whaley
Professor Emeritus
Moritz College of Law
The Ohio State University

Stephen M. McJohn
Professor of Law
Suffolk University Law School

Wolters Kluwer

Published by Wolters Kluwer in New York.

Wolters Kluwer Legal & Regulatory U.S. serves customers worldwide with CCH, Aspen Publishers, and Kluwer Law International products. (www.WKLegaledu.com)

To contact Customer Service, e-mail customer.service@wolterskluwer.com, call 1-800-234-1660, fax 1-800-901-9075, or mail correspondence to:

Wolters Kluwer
Attn: Order Department
PO Box 990
Frederick, MD 21705

Printed in the United States of America.

2 3 4 5 6 7 8 9 0

ISBN 978-1-5438-0463-8

Library of Congress Cataloging-in-Publication Data

Names: Whaley, Douglas J., author. | McJohn, Stephen M., 1959- author.
Title: Problems and materials on the sale and lease of goods / Douglas J.
    Whaley, Professor Emeritus, Moritz College of Law, The Ohio State
    University; Stephen M. McJohn, Professor of Law, Suffolk University Law
    School.
Description: Eighth edition. | New York : Wolters Kluwer, [2019] | Series:
    Aspen casebook series | Includes bibliographical references and index.
Identifiers: LCCN 2018055486 | ISBN 9781543804638 (hard cover : alk. paper)
Subjects: LCSH: Sales—United States. | Leases—United States.
Classification: LCC KF915.W445 2019 | DDC 346.7307/2—dc23
LC record available at https://lccn.loc.gov/2018055486

About Wolters Kluwer Legal & Regulatory U.S.

Wolters Kluwer Legal & Regulatory U.S. delivers expert content and solutions in the areas of law, corporate compliance, health compliance, reimbursement, and legal education. Its practical solutions help customers successfully navigate the demands of a changing environment to drive their daily activities, enhance decision quality and inspire confident outcomes.

Serving customers worldwide, its legal and regulatory portfolio includes products under the Aspen Publishers, CCH Incorporated, Kluwer Law International, ftwilliam.com, and MediRegs names. They are regarded as exceptional and trusted resources for general legal and practice-specific knowledge, compliance and risk management, dynamic workflow solutions, and expert commentary.

For Mary Bush, Tim Ihle, and Pamela Maggied

DJW

To Lorie and Ian

SMM

Summary of Contents

Contents

This book explores the law of the sale and lease of goods and licenses primarily by focusing on a series of Problems designed to encourage the student to concentrate on the exact statutory language of the Uniform Commercial Code and related statutes. Representative cases and textual notes are also included.

Unfortunately, students reared on the case method sometimes have trouble concentrating on Problem after Problem. Such an attitude here can be academically fatal. As a guide to the degree of concentration required, we have used a hierarchy of signals. When the Problem states "Read §2-302," we mean "Put down this book, pick up the Uniform Commercial Code, and study §2-302 carefully." When the instruction is "See §2-302," the reader need look at the cited section only if unsure of the answer. "Cf. §2-302" or simply "§2-302" are lesser references, included as a guide for the curious.

We have edited many of the footnotes out of the cases; the ones that remain have been stripped of their original numbering and have been consecutively numbered with our other textual footnotes. Unless clearly indicated otherwise, all footnotes in the cases are the court's own.

Whaley co-authored the first edition of this book with Professor Rhonda Rivera, then his colleague at The Ohio State University College of Law. Due to other commitments she declined to participate in subsequent editions, so he reluctantly went on alone. Nonetheless, much of her work on the first edition is still reflected in this one, and he is, as always, in her debt.

Finally, we would like to thank all the good people at Aspen Publishers for the assistance they have given us through the years in the production of this and other books. It is a pleasure to work with true professionals. We would also like to express gratitude to our students who suffered through these materials in earlier forms, spotted errors, made suggestions, and helped shape the final version. Our students have always taught us as much about commercial law as we have taught them, and we thank them for it.

Douglas J. Whaley
Columbus, OH

Stephen M. McJohn
Boston, MA

January 2019

PROBLEMS AND MATERIALS ON THE SALE AND LEASE OF GOODS

CHAPTER 1

INTRODUCTION TO THE UNIFORM COMMERCIAL CODE AND SALES LAW

I. A BIT OF HISTORY

During medieval times, commercial law varied widely from place to place throughout the trading world, and the statutes of the various countries either didn't address the relevant issues that traders cared about or reached results that were at odds with what those traders thought either realistic or fair. During much of English history, for example, the common law courts were lumbered by such arcane rules of procedure that justice was either unavailable or so slow as to come far too late.

To solve this dilemma the traders developed their own legal system, the so-called law merchant (or *lex mercatoria* in Latin). By agreement they created their own courts, chose their own judges, and developed mercantile understandings that made trade efficient and fair (in their own eyes). At some point the real courts became aware that they were being bypassed and began to incorporate the law merchant into their own rules. During the time of the American Revolution, the English court system had as its Chief Justice the great jurist Lord Mansfield. He believed in pragmatism in his courtroom, and during his tenure the law merchant was given much influence in English decisions. Lord Mansfield would call merchants into court

1

to testify as to what mercantile understandings were in the matter before the court, and was not above putting merchants on the jury and then asking them questions as cases proceeded.

Lord Mansfield

II.   THE CREATION OF THE UNIFORM COMMERCIAL CODE

Starting in the 1940s, two private bodies, the American Law Institute (ALI) and the National Conference of Commissioners on Uniform State Law (NCCUSL), decided it was time to modernize the state laws on commercial matters. Over the coming years, they gathered together the greatest commercial experts in the country to draft a new giant statute that would supersede existing ones for the areas that were covered. Chief draftsman was Professor Karl N. Llewellyn, the leading voice for the "legal realism" school of jurisprudence (very much in Lord Mansfield's tradition), and he led a drafting team that by 1952 produced the first version of what was called the "Uniform Commercial Code."

Karl Llewellyn

The Uniform Commercial Code went through various versions from that day to this (though Article 2 on "Sales" has remained largely unchanged). The UCC (or, in this course, simply "the Code") is divided into "Articles" covering different aspects of commercial law. The chief Articles we will study are those in Article 2 (Sales), Article 2A (Leases), Article 5 (Letters of Credit), and Article 7 (Documents of Title), though references will be made to other parts of the Code, particularly Article 1, which deals with general provisions applicable throughout the rest of the statute.

It is important to appreciate that the UCC is not federal law. Instead, the two drafting bodies submitted it for adoption to the states, and it had to be individually enacted into law state by state. The idea was that if commercial law were uniform throughout the country, commerce would be more certain and efficient (the same goals animating the law merchant centuries before). Most states did adopt the Code with few changes (though some have sneaked in through the years, and you, budding lawyer, should always check your own state's enactment to make sure some evil alteration hasn't muddled what you've learned in this course). By the end of the last quarter of the twentieth century, all states, most U.S. territories, and a number of Native American tribes had adopted the UCC, though most importantly for this course, Louisiana, with its French law, Napoleonic Code, tradition did not enact Article 2 on the Sale of Goods, but has its own civil law version thereof.

III.   FEDERAL LAW

The federal government, of course, has a great interest in commercial matters, and thus has enacted a wide number of statutes that exist alongside the states' UCC mandates. Federal law supersedes inconsistent state laws, and in this book we will explore these collisions as they occur.

IV.   ARTICLE 1 OF THE CODE

The first Article of the UCC covers "General Provisions," and it applies to all UCC matters unless a more specific section elsewhere in the Code says otherwise. Article 1's most recent rewrite occurred in 2001, and that version, now adopted by most of the states, is the one referred to in this book.

Look at §1-103 and let's highlight some of what it says. Subsection 1-103(a)(1) tells us that the UCC shall be "liberally construed." This is not a political statement, but instead is meant to combat the old presumption that the common law (meaning the law as created by precedent with no statutory guidance) was thought so wise that a rule of statutory construction arose stating that "statutes in derogation of the common law are to be *strictly* construed" so as to change the common law result as little as possible. Karl Llewellyn was having none of that: the UCC is to be read broadly, the common law be damned.

Subsection 1-103(a)(3) commands the courts of the various states to work to make the law "uniform" throughout the country. This gives the attorney finding a favorable ruling in one state a strong argument that it's a good precedent in another — a valuable thing to remember.

Finally §1-103(b) preserves all of the common law rules (including the rules of equity and even the law merchant) to the extent that they do not contradict the statutory rules contained in the UCC. If the UCC doesn't speak to an issue, then attorneys must look to other laws to find the desired result.

One of the most important sections in the Code is §1-201, which is a huge definition section containing definitions for 43 different words and phrases. You will consult it often when exploring the matters we'll discuss in later chapters. Section 1-202 has complicated definitions of *notice* and *knowledge* that answer important questions such as what the two terms mean and at what moment a notice is effective (when sent? when received?). Section 1-204 defines *value* and §1-205 explores the issues of *reasonable time* and *seasonable*.

P. 321 tangible forming
P. 322 own definition
P. 302 *1-103 ( )(2) unless this place
supplement provision
began w/

IV.   Article 1 of the Code   5

There's a choice of law provision in §1-301 that generally applies the law of the enacting state if "appropriate," but allows the parties by agreement to choose the law of any state having a "reasonable relation" to the transaction.

Another important section, often referred to in this book and the case law, is §1-303, which explains what are sometimes called "construction" terms: the items that make up the understanding of the parties as to what the contract means. Section 1-303(c) explains that a *usage of trade* is a *custom* within the industry (sort of a throwback to the law merchant) and this custom binds all of those who should know about it, sometimes including even consumers. Ask yourself this: is it the "usage of trade" that car dealers can lie about the attributes of the vehicle being sold and therefore get away with that? (Of course not — a usage of trade can't violate the law, and such lies would be fraud.) *Course of dealing* in §1-303(b) refers to what the parties did in their *past* contacts with one another. If the parties have dealt with each other in prior dealings, that history creates an expectation of what will happen in this contract, and the Code thusly recognizes it. Finally *course of performance* in §1-303(a) means what the parties do in performing this one particular contract, especially important where the contract goes on over a period of time and creates its own history and expectations. The common law called *course of performance* by the term *practical construction* and found that it gave great guidance to the true boundaries of the contract. Then, in §1-303(e), there is a hierarchy of importance of these construction terms, with the more relevant ones beating out the less relevant. Under this idea, express terms control course of performance, but course of performance is more important than both course of dealing or usage of trade, and course of dealing beats out an inconsistent usage of trade. One caveat to this little list: §1-303(f) explains that an express term in a contract ("deliveries must be made on time or the contract is breached") can be *waived* by course of performance (accepting late deliveries without protest means one cannot suddenly call a breach for this reason — a result codified by §2-209 for the sale of goods).

Section 1-304 provides that "[e]very contract or duty within the Uniform Commercial Code imposes an obligation of good faith in its performance and enforcement." The definition of *good faith* is "honesty in fact and the observance of reasonable commercial standards of fair dealing." §1-201(b)(20). Note that good faith has both a subjective component (honesty in fact) and an objective component (observance of reasonable commercial standards of fair dealing). This standard has changed over time. Some states have kept to the old definition of good faith, which required only "honesty in fact." Failure to act in good faith, by itself, "does not support an independent cause of action." Official Comment to §1-304; see, e.g., Brooklyn Bagel Boys, Inc. v. Earthgrains Refrigerated Dough Products, Inc, 212 F.3d 373 (7th Cir. 2000). Courts have held that failure to act in good faith, by itself, does not make a party liable, but a party that has performed in bad faith may be unable to assert rights under the Code. In one case, for example, a creditor who behaved in a blatantly evil manner had the usual Article 9 priorities reversed and ended up losing its collateral; see Ninth Dist. Prod. Credit Assn. v. Ed Duggan, Inc., 821 P.2d 788 (Colo. 1991).

V.   THE OFFICIAL COMMENTS

All of the sections of the Code are followed by the Official Comments (such as the one quoted in the previous paragraph), which explain how the drafters wanted the sections to be interpreted. These Comments, the courts have said clearly, are not the law, but they are important to in understanding the meaning of the relevant section and are to be studied in that light. If in a future case you have an Official Comment in your favor, you will of course call it to the court's attention and remind the court that this Comment was written by the very experts who wrote the statute and therefore it should be given great weight. If the relevant Comment hurts your case and has, annoyingly, been raised by the other side, remind the court that the Comment are not the law, and that sometimes these Comments have the look of "Oops, we meant to say this, but knew we couldn't get it through the legislature so we're trying to amend the law through a more devious channel."

CHAPTER 1 REVIEW QUESTIONS

Who developed the law merchant and why?
How did the law merchant affect the development of commercial law in the courts?
Who drafted the Uniform Commercial Code and why?
How does the UCC become law?
How does the UCC define "good faith"?

Chapter 2

BASIC CONCEPTS

I. INTRODUCTION

Disputes about sales have always been with us. In what has been called the earliest documented customer service complaint, a Babylonian clay tablet from 1750 B.C. bears a letter from an aggrieved buyer, Nanni, to the seller, Ea-nasir. Nanni complains that the wrong grade of copper ore was delivered, that goods were misdirected after a gulf voyage, and that the seller was guilty of further delays and failures to respect the buyer as a merchant.[1] Nanni further protests that the buyer wrongfully retained money bags and forced Nanni's messengers to return home empty-handed through enemy territory. We will see the same concerns arise today in sales of goods as diverse as smart home systems, thoroughbred racehorses, diving boards, uranium stockpiles, diamond rings, paintings, stock cars, grass seed, truckloads of seafood, communications satellites, and more. Nanni's concerns echo in the cases in this book: A seller promises to create web application software but delivers it late

---

1. See description of clay tablet, Museum number 131236, at the site of the British Museum, https://www.britishmuseum.org/research/collection_online/collection_object_details/collection_image_gallery.aspx?assetId=141562001&objectId=277770&partId=1.

and full of bugs. A corn seller complains that a buyer has refused to honor their custom of meeting each month to confirm sales. A seller of merchandise ships boxes filled with garbage and uses the shipping receipt to draw on a letter of credit (today's equivalent of money bags carried by messengers). A clothing shopper tries on a pair of slacks and is bitten by a poisonous spider. Enemy territory problems for seller's servants do not come up much in the 21st century.

From the beginning of civilization buyers and sellers have traded things across great distances, even in very primitive times. Over 14,000 years ago Native American peoples living in the middle of the continent possessed items such as beads and weapons that could only have originated on the east coast, demonstrating that tribal merchants were at work moving goods around even then. The need to trade and the desire to acquire goods both for necessities and more luxurious purposes has fueled much of the development of our world. During times of major international wars, trade still flourished (and sometimes thrived, as in the sale of weapons), and in countries where private bargains have been severely regulated or even forbidden (as in some communist regimes), black markets arise to slide deals past the eyes of the authorities.

In all transactions there is a commonality of expectations: the parties must agree on the terms of the bargain, those terms must be honored, the product being sold must meet some standard of quality or suitability, and if the transaction hits snags, the parties must have recourse to a viable remedy. In the materials that follow we will explore how the Uniform Commercial Code provides a legal framework to resolve these matters.

II. SCOPE OF ARTICLE 2

A. *"Transactions in Goods"*

Article 2 of the Uniform Commercial Code applies to *transactions in goods*. Read §2-102. The word *transactions* is not defined in the Code. Look at §2-106(1); does that help? Much is encompassed within these parameters. Both the delivery of a multibillion-dollar space craft to the U.S. government and the purchase of a package of chewing gum at a local store trigger the application of Article 2 of the Code. *Goods* is defined in §2-105. Read it, and work through the following materials.

PROBLEM 1

Whether Article 2 applies may determine the outcome of a case. If Article 2 applies, its rules may favor one party (such as the implied warranty of merchantability that automatically is given to many buyers by §2-314). Does Article 2 of the Code apply to the following matters?

(a) The sale of an insurance policy? See Call v. Czaplicki, 2010 WL 3724275 (D.N.J. 2010). *contract*

(b) The sale of real property? What about the sale of a house apart from the realty? See §2-107. *X*

(c) The sale of building materials as part of a construction project? See the case following this Problem. *X*

movable (d) The sale of standing timber? Crops? See §2-107. *if they are sold by seller*

(e) A defective spinal plate given a patient in a hospital operating room? See Brandt v. Boston Scientific Corp., 204 Ill. 2d 640, 792 N.E.2d 296 (2003). The preparation of false teeth by a dentist? See Carroll v. Grabavoy, 77 Ill. App. 3d 895, 396 N.E.2d 836 (1977). The injection of a drug (for which the patient was separately billed) into a patient's eye as part of an operation? See Providence Hospital v. Truly, 611 S.W.2d 127 (Tex. Civ. App. 1980). *one person uses / to service*

(f) The sale of membership in a health spa? *X not a movable. contract to service*

(g) The sale of electricity? See GFI Wisconsin, Inc. v. Reedsbury Utility Commn., 440 B.R. 791 (W.D. Wis. 2010). *X*

(h) Devices signed a distribution agreement giving Detail Retail the exclusive right to sell Gooseberry phones in the Midwest. Is this an Article 2 transaction? Same result if Detail Retail also agreed to buy 1 million Gooseberry phones directly from Devices? See MidAmerican Distribution, Inc. v. Clarification Technology, Inc., 807 F. Supp. 2d 646 (E.D. Ky. 2011); Franklin Publications, Inc. v. General Nutrition Corp., 2007 WL 2071914 (S.D. Ohio 2007).

(i) Specially manufacturing and supplying a yacht? See §2-105(1); Fed. Ins. Co. v. Mathews Bros., LLC, 2015 WL 4879194 (D. Md. 2015).

(j) When a customer paid for groceries at the counter she was given a plastic bag to put them in. The bag proved defective such that the groceries spilled and she suffered serious injuries from broken glass in the bag. Is there a sale of goods as to the plastic grocery bag by the grocery store? See Fuller v. Winn-Dixie Montgomery, LLC, 2017 WL 3098104 (S.D. Ala. 2017).

(k) You go online to Amazon.com and buy a product there. Is Amazon the seller who will be responsible if the product is defective? See Milo & Gabby, LLC v. Amazon.com, Inc., 693 Fed. Appx. 879, 2017 WL 2258605 (Fed. Cir. 2017). *No doesn't have titled to produc.*

Audio Visual Artistry v. Tanzer

Court of Appeals of Tennessee, 2012, 403 S.W.3d 789

J. STEVEN STAFFORD, J.

This is a breach of contract case. Appellant/Homeowner contracted with Appellee for the installation of a "smart home" system. After myriad problems arose, Appellant fired Appellee, who filed the instant lawsuit to collect the unpaid balance for equipment and installation. The trial court determined that the primary purpose of the parties' agreement was the sale of goods and applied Article 2 of the Uniform Commercial Code. The court granted judgment in favor of Appellee, but allowed certain offsets for items rejected by Appellant. Appellant appeals, arguing that the trial court erred in applying the UCC, and in its calculation of damages. Appellant also appeals the trial court's determination that the Tennessee Consumer Protection Act does not apply. Discerning no error, we affirm.

On or about March 26, 2004, Appellant Stephen Tanzer and Appellee Audio Video Artistry ("AVA") entered into discussions for the sale and installation of electronic and entertainment equipment in Mr. Tanzer's home. AVA is a residential entertainment and communications firm specializing in custom design projects. AVA is a general partnership; its partners, Chris Rogers and Brad Parsley, founded the firm in 1999 to offer state-of-the-art home theater, multi-room music and television, lighting control and phone/intercom systems. The sale, installation, and integration of these systems for the creation of a "smart home" (also known as "domotics") is AVA's specialty.

In March 2004, Chris Rogers met with Mr. Tanzer to discuss Mr. Tanzer's desires for the home he was building. Based upon their discussion, AVA submitted a proposal to Mr. Tanzer for components, parts, and installation, totaling $78,567.13. The written proposal specifically provided for the following work:

- 6 "independent" zones of music consisting of 13 rooms and related equipment to switch, power, and control the music system;
- phone system throughout the house with door communications;
- lighting control system throughout the house to include 64 standard wattage (600w) loads;
- network wiring for television, phone, music, and computers throughout the home.

The systems pricing for this work (i.e., the total price of $78,567.13) was broken out in the original proposal as follows:

- Equipment: $56,375.00
- Labor/Programming: $9,880.00

- Cable: Misc. Parts: $5,660.00
- Total: $71,915.00
- Tax: $6,652.13

On September 22, 2004, AVA and Mr. Tanzer entered into a written contract, which incorporates the original proposal, adding an additional "seventh zone" for music, and also adding seven automated shades. These shades were included as a "purchase incentive" at no cost to Mr. Tanzer. The contract provides that, in the event the shades do not work in an acceptable fashion, Mr. Tanzer would receive an additional $8,400 credit. The contract further contemplates that Mr. Tanzer's needs and desires for the "smart system" would likely evolve during the course of the project; therefore, the contract specifically provides that "[v]erbal agreements throughout the life of the project may also be honored as part of this contract and will be documented by AVA."

As originally contemplated, the contract called for a Concierge whole-house audio system. The audio/visual items were to be integrated via the Crestron system, which would allow Mr. Tanzer to play music in the seven, independently controlled music "zones." Remote control "touch-panels" would control and integrate DVD, television, music, and other smart home functions. The contract further included a Lutron automated lighting system, which would be integrated into the Crestron system, along with an intercom/phone/whole house networking system.

At the time the parties entered their contract, construction had just commenced on Mr. Tanzer's home. The home is not a usual residence; rather, it is an approximately 15,000 square foot, $3.5 million dollar build. Because of the size and scope of the project, AVA was to install certain wiring and equipment during the construction process. Pre-wiring began on the house as the framing went in, but equipment installation and programming of the smart system did not begin in earnest until March, 2006. Mr. Tanzer and his family moved into the home in April, 2006.

During the project, and as contemplated in the contract, the original scope of work was changed and AVA performed additional work. One significant change was the decision to use an Escient music system in lieu of the Concierge music system. Mr. Rogers allegedly represented to Mr. Tanzer, after the job had begun, that the Escient system was better able to do what Mr. Tanzer wanted, i.e., stream music from his PC, which was not a function that the Concierge system offered. AVA agreed to sell and install the Escient system for the same price as the Concierge system. Later, an art frame and shade were also added to conceal the television in the sitting room. The "art shade" is a custom-painted, frame-mounted piece of artwork on canvas, which can be rolled down to conceal a television at the push of a button. Other changes related to the Crestron touch panels, which were changed from radio-frequency panels to Wi-Fi panels (Crestron came out with a Wi-Fi product before installation commenced). The Wi-Fi panels were changed at the same cost as that previously quoted for the radio-frequency panels. Another change was the switch in the music distribution equipment, which would allow for future expansion of the system. Further changes included equipment for the media room and five additional pairs of speakers. AVA also integrated the pool system, the alarm system, and the HVAC system with the Crestron control system.

Mr. Tanzer eventually became unsatisfied with AVA's work. Mr. Tanzer contends that, based upon Mr. Parsley's statements, he thought that the installation, programming, and debugging of the "smart home" system would take less than three months. However, Mr. Tanzer claims that, after fifteen months, he was still having significant problems with the functionality of the system. Specifically, Mr. Tanzer states, in his brief, that: (1) the punch list ebbed and flowed; (2) [t]he programming was unstable; (3) "[i]t seemed every time AVA would come out to resolve one problem, two or three new problems would crop up in its place"; (4) [t]hings that AVA fixed didn't stay fixed. As a result, Mr. Tanzer became "extremely frustrated and inconven[ienced]." To compound these alleged issues, in July, 2006, the basement of the house flooded, damaging the media room. A year later, in July of 2007, while AVA was allegedly still trying to "debug" the system, the home was struck by lightning. The power surge from the lightning caused damage to the Crestron processor and Ethernet card. Although the damaged components had no warranty against "Acts of God," it is not disputed that AVA replaced them without additional charge. In August 2007, Mr. Tanzer fired AVA and requested a final billing.

Both the original equipment and work and the additional work, equipment, and changes were set out in Invoice #3036, which was presented by AVA to Mr. Tanzer. This Invoice shows a total project cost of $119,402.15, and reflects an outstanding balance of $43,824.55. Mr. Tanzer disputed this balance and the instant lawsuit ensued.

On November 19, 2007, AVA filed suit against Mr. Tanzer for breach of contract. On December 31, 2007, Mr. Tanzer filed his answer, in which he denies any liability. Concurrent with the answer, Mr. Tanzer filed a counter-complaint against AVA, alleging that AVA breached the contract and seeking damages for the breach. AVA answered the counter-complaint, denying any liability.

After the lawsuit had commenced, in February or March of 2008, a second lightning strike to the house shut down the entire "smart home" system. Mr. Tanzer then hired Marquis Home Solutions ("Marquis") to make repairs. Tom Brown, an employee of Marquis, testified that there were numerous problems with AVA's installation of the systems, including: (1) improper power source to the Lutron processor; (2) improper surge protection; (3) failure to install the Lutron processor in a proper recessed and covered enclosure; (4) failure to label wiring and improper wiring; (5) instability of the Wi-Fi handles for the Crestron system. Marquis charged Mr. Tanzer $67,587 for the repairs. Mr. Tanzer avers that the amount Marquis charged includes only the cost of repairs to the systems that AVA installed, and does not include the price of any upgrades.

The parties filed various trial briefs, which are incorrectly included in this record. Tenn. R. App. P. 24(b) ("The following papers filed in the trial court are excluded from the record … (4) trial briefs.…"). Regardless, on May 19, 2011, the trial court entered its preliminary findings of fact and conclusions of law, which were based upon the parties' briefs. Therein, the court states, in relevant part, that:

> [T]he Court finds that the parties' agreement in this matter involved the sale of consumer goods governed by the Uniform Commercial Code found at T.C.A. §47-2-101 et seq. Although the parties' agreement involved some provision of labor and services, an examination of the entire transaction and application of the "predominant factor" test, leads the Court to the conclusion that this was simply an agreement for the sale and installation of electronic equipment. The labor and services provided under the terms of the parties' agreement was insignificant in comparison to the cost of equipment provided. As such, the Uniform Commercial Code is applicable to this transaction and the Court is required to consider its provisions in determining the rights and remedies afforded the parties under the agreement in this case.

The trial court then allowed additional time for the parties to prepare and present supplemental evidence on the issue of remedies under the Uniform Commercial Code ("UCC"). In addition, the preliminary findings of fact include a specific finding that the Tennessee Consumer Protection Act ("TCPA") is not applicable to the case. Specifically, the court found that there was insufficient proof to show that AVA had "engaged in any unfair or deceptive acts or practices," and that there was "insufficient proof that Chris Rogers held himself out to [Mr. Tanzer] as an electrical engineer."

In response to the trial court's preliminary findings, Mr. Tanzer filed a motion for reconsideration on June 14, 2011. AVA opposed the motion, which was ultimately denied by the trial court's July 22, 2011 order. By order of October 17, 2011, the trial court granted judgment in favor of AVA. The order includes the following, relevant, findings:

> 1. That within a reasonable time after delivery and installation of the equipment involved in the parties' contract, AVA had actual knowledge and

notice that the Escient music system and phone system did not perform properly even after repeated attempts by AVA to fix the problems complained of by Tanzer. As such, the Court finds from the proof that these items were never accepted by Tanzer and were rejected in accordance with the requirements of the UCC.

2. That, under the facts in this case, Tanzer is entitled to an offset for these items in the amounts indicated below:

      a. Escient Music System $14,098.00
      b. Phone System $3,825.00

3. That in addition to these offsets against the balance owed AVA, Tanzer is entitled to the following credits for items that were improperly charged:

      a. 5 Sonance volume controls $400.00
      b. 4 Lutron switches $1,200.00
      c. Overcharge on wire run $330.00

4. That the charges paid to Marquis Solutions by Tanzer are not appropriate for a consequential damage claim under the facts here. Marquis made extensive upgrades and changes to Tanzer's whole house system and there was insufficient detail in Mr. Brown's testimony regarding the specific work performed and the amount charged for each specific item for the Court to make an award for consequential damages. Additionally, the Court has offset the amount owed by Tanzer for the items that were rejected. Tanzer is not entitled to an offset for the rejected items and to receive an award for repairs to these items. It is also noted that Marquis' repair bill is unreasonably high and grossly exceeds the amount charged by AVA for these items in its contract with Tanzer.

5. That HVAC integration was not included in AVA's original proposal to Tanzer. I further find from the proof that AVA completed this additional work at Tanzer's request and is entitled to the amount charged for this work. Tanzer also failed to prove that the HVAC integration was not functioning properly when AVA completed its work.

6. That Tanzer failed to establish through his proof that AVA had any responsibility for the lightning strike which damaged some of the components installed by AVA and which was later repaired by Marquis. As such, Tanzer is not entitled to recover for the amount charged by Marquis for such repairs.

7. That AVA is entitled to the equipment rejected by Tanzer which is in his possession. Tanzer is hereby ordered to make these items available to AVA if requested by AVA.

Based upon the foregoing findings, the court awarded offsets and credits to Mr. Tanzer in the total amount of $19,842.00. Accordingly, AVA was awarded judgment in the amount of $23,982.55. On October 31, 2011,

AVA filed a motion to alter or amend the judgment under Tennessee Rule of Civil Procedure 59. The motion was granted and, on December 12, 2011, the trial court amended its previous order.... AVA's total judgment was increased from $23,982.55 to $35,580.55. Upon Mr. Tanzer's motion, the judgment was stayed pending appeal. By separate order, entered on February 23, 2012, the trial court also denied both parties' requests for attorney's fees and costs.

Mr. Tanzer appeals. He raises four issues for review as stated in his brief:

> I. The trial court erred in finding that the UCC applied to the services rendered by AVA.
>
> II. The Court erred in not declaring the failure to complete its work a material breach on the part of AVA and denying damages to [Tanzer].
>
> III. The trial court erred in not awarding Tanzer the cost incurred to make the system work properly and get the benefit of his bargain.
>
> IV. The trial court erred in finding that AVA did not violate the Tennessee Consumer Protection Act....

I. Applicability of UCC Article 2

In his first issue, Mr. Tanzer asserts that the trial court erred in applying UCC Article 2 to his contract with AVA. Specifically, Mr. Tanzer argues that thrust of the contract is for services and not for the sale of goods such that common law breach of contract principles apply. We begin our analysis with 67 Am. Jur. 2d Sales §37, which provides:

> Article 2 [of the UCC] applies to transactions in goods but does not apply to construction contracts or contracts for the rendition of services. However, the existence of a sale in and of itself does not automatically implicate the Uniform Commercial Code. In many cases, a contract or transaction may involve both the transaction of a sale and the rendition of services, presenting a "mixed" or hybrid transaction or contract. To determine whether such "mixed" or "hybrid" contracts are governed by Article 2, a court must examine the whole transaction and look to the essence or main objective of the parties' agreement or the primary or overall purpose of the transaction.
>
> Ordinarily, a court determines whether a mixed contract for goods and services is subject to Article 2 by considering whether the contract, reasonably stated, is for goods with labor incidentally involved or for services with goods incidentally involved. The question is generally one of fact, involving a consideration of the contract in its entirety. Depending upon whether the contract or transaction is predominantly for the sale of goods or the rendition of services, Article 2 applies to the entire contract or not at all.

Id. (footnotes omitted). As further discussed in 1 Stephen W. Ramp & Katherine Simpson Allen, Tennessee Practice: Uniform Commercial Code Forms §2-106 (2d ed. 2002):

> A sale is the passing of title from the seller to the buyer for a price. Courts will consider the substance of the transaction rather than how the parties chose to label the transaction. Where the service component of a contract for sale overrides the goods aspect of the transaction it will not fall within Article 2 once the transaction is determined to be a service and not a sale.

The question of whether UCC Article 2 or common law contract principles apply is important in terms of available warranties and the measure of damages. As discussed in R. Alan Pritchard, The Predominant Factor Test Under the Uniform Commercial Code, Tenn. B. J., July, 2001, at 23:

> Article 2 of the Uniform Commercial Code (UCC) sets forth the provisions that govern certain sales transactions involving goods. The provisions establish the terms that will govern such a transaction including, among other items, warranty provisions, remedies provisions for both the buyer and the seller, and damages provisions. Section 2-313 establishes the express warranty that governs the sales transaction, and §§2-314 and 2-315 establish the implied warranties of merchantability and fitness for a particular purpose. All of these warranties are subject to exclusion under the sales contract between the parties; however, such exclusions must be in accordance with the specific provisions of the Uniform Commercial Code. In the event there is a breach of these warranties, the Uniform Commercial Code sets forth the remedies that are available for such breach. A claim for breach must be brought within four years from the date the cause of action accrues. See UCC 2-725. The cause of action accrues at the time the breach occurs, which is at the time the tender of delivery is made. See 2-725.

As noted above in 67 Am. Jur. 2d Sales §37, many transactions are neither pure sale of goods nor pure service transactions, but a combination of the two, i.e., a hybrid contract. As discussed in Barkley Clark and Christopher Smith, The Law of Product Warranties §2:19 (2012):

> When faced with these hybrids, the courts have generally employed a predominant element test: If the service aspect predominates, tort theories must control (even as to defective goods), but if the goods aspect predominates, Article 2 warranties come into play (sometimes even with respect to the service component). This is a rather mechanical approach, but the courts favor it. Sometimes they are swayed by the wording of the contract, as when the plaintiff is denominated as an "owner" rather than a "buyer," and the defendant is denominated as the "contractor" rather than the "seller." Sometimes the courts look at the price factor, attempting to analyze the billing, and

sometimes the decision is based on nothing more than a judicial hunch as to which element predominates. In the usual case, the plaintiff will push to persuade the court that the goods element predominates, so the more lenient standard of the Article 2 implied warranties can be used to measure liability, and the defendant will shove in the opposite direction in a real tug-of-war.

Id. (footnotes omitted). One of the earliest cases to adopt the predominant purpose test was Bonebrake v. Cox, 499 F.2d 951 (8th Cir. 1974), which involved a contract for the sale and installation of pre-fabricated bowling equipment. The *Bonebrake* Court noted that such hybrid contracts are legion and then proposed its test:

The test for inclusion or exclusion is not whether they are mixed, but granting that they are mixed, whether their predominant factor, their thrust, their purpose, reasonably stated, is the rendition of service, with goods incidentally involved (e.g., contract with artist for painting), or is a transaction of sale, with labor incidentally involved (e.g., installation of a water heater in a bathroom).

Id. at 960. In *Bonebrake,* the court concluded that the goods element predominated, thus invoking the rules of Article 2, including the warranty provisions. Id.

In the case of Pass v. Shelby Aviation, No. W1999-00018-COA-R9-CV, 2000 WL 388775 (Tenn. Ct. App. April 13, 2000), Tennessee adopted and applied the *Bonebrake* predominant purpose test. Applying the test, the *Pass* Court determined that a mixed transaction of goods and services was "predominantly the provision of a service, not subject to the warranty provisions of the UCC." Id. at *6. In that case, Max E. Pass, Jr., and his wife, Martha N. Pass, were both killed when their aircraft, piloted by Mr. Pass, crashed outside of Opelika, Alabama. Approximately four-and-one-half months prior to the fatal flight, Mr. Pass had taken the aircraft to defendant, Shelby Aviation, Inc., for inspection and service. During the servicing, Shelby Aviation replaced both rear wing attach point brackets on the plane.

After the crash, the administrators of the Pass's estates filed a lawsuit against Shelby Aviation. The suit alleged that the rear wing brackets, which were sold and installed by Shelby Aviation, were defective and asserted claims for breach of common law warranties, and for breach of express and implied warranties under Article 2 of the UCC. Shelby Aviation filed a motion to dismiss for failure to state a claim, contending that, because the contract was primarily for services, Article 2 did not apply. The motion was denied, and Shelby Aviation requested, and was granted, permission to file an interlocutory appeal to this Court. The main issue on appeal was whether the transaction between Mr. Pass and Shelby Aviation was governed by Article 2.

This Court determined that the predominant purpose test was the appropriate test to apply because it looks at the transaction as a whole. In applying the test, the Court stated:

> In order to determine whether the predominant purpose of a mixed transaction is the sale of goods or the provision of a service, we examine the language of the parties' contract, the nature of the business of the supplier of the goods and services, the reason the parties entered into the contract (i.e., what each bargained to receive), and the respective amounts charged under the contract for goods and for services. [Citations omitted.]. None of these factors alone is dispositive. BMC Industries, Inc. v. Barth Industries, Inc., 160 F.3d 1322, 1330 (11th Cir. 1998). The party seeking application of the UCC bears the burden of proof to show that the predominant purpose of the contract was the sale of goods. *Insul-Mark*, 612 N.E.2d at 555; Northwestern Equipment, Inc. v. Cudmore, 312 N.W.2d 347, 351 (N.D. 1981).

Pass, 2000 WL 388775, at *4. In concluding that the foregoing relevant factors should be considered in determining the choice of law for mixed contracts for sales of goods and service, the *Pass* Court relied upon an Indiana Supreme Court Case, Insul-Mark Midwest, Inc. v. Modern Materials, Inc., 612 N.E.2d 550 (Ind. 1993), wherein the Indiana Court stated:

> To determine whether the predominant thrust of a mixed contract is to provide services or goods, one looks first to the language of the contract, in light of the situation of the parties and the surrounding circumstances. Specifically one looks to the terms describing the performance of the parties, and the words used to describe the relationship between the parties.
>
> Beyond the contractual terms themselves, one looks to the circumstances of the parties, and the primary reason they entered into the contract. One also considers the final product the purchaser bargained to receive, and whether it may be described as a good or a service.
>
> Finally, one examines the costs involved for the goods and services, and whether the purchaser was charged only for a good, or a price based on both goods and services. If the cost of the goods is but a small portion of the overall contract price, such fact would increase the likelihood that the services portion predominates.

Pass, 2000 WL 388775, at *4 (citing *Insul-Mark,* 612 N.E.2d at 555 (citations omitted)).

Applying the foregoing principles, the *Pass* Court determined that "the invoice clearly emphasizes the repair and inspection aspects of the transaction, indicating that the predominant purpose was the sale of service, with the sale of goods incidental to that service." *Pass,* 2000 WL 388775, at *4. Further, the overall nature of Shelby Aviation's business was service rather than the sale of parts, and "Mr. Pass took the plane to Shelby Aviation primarily to have a service performed, i.e., the annual inspection." Id. at *5. Finally, the court looked to allocation of costs between goods and services. Id. The court indicated that it did not favor adding the labor charges for installing the parts to the cost of the parts as was proposed by the plaintiffs, and then the court stated that:

> Regardless of how the percentage of the cost of goods is calculated, viewing the transaction as a whole, we must conclude that the predominant purpose of the transaction was the provision of a service rather than the sale of goods.... As such, it is not subject to the warranty provisions of Article 2 of the UCC. Shelby Aviation is entitled to judgment as a matter of law on the [p]laintiffs' UCC breach of warranty claims.

Id. at *6. The decision denying Shelby Aviation's motion for summary judgment on the UCC breach of warranty claims was reversed, and the case was remanded for further proceedings. *Id.*

From *Pass,* we understand that, in applying the predominant purpose test, the court looks to four factors:

(1) the language of the contract;
(2) the nature of the business of the supplier of goods and services;
(3) the reason the parties entered into the contract, and
(4) the amounts paid for the rendition of the services and goods, respectively.

We now turn to address each of these factors based on the evidence contained in the record to determine whether the trial court correctly found that the contract at issue in this case predominantly involves the sale of goods such that UCC Article 2 is applicable.

A.   LANGUAGE OF THE CONTRACT

The first factor set out by the *Pass* Court requires us to look "to the language of the contract, in light of the situation of the parties and the surrounding circumstances. Specifically, [the court] looks to the terms describing the performance of the parties, and the words used to describe the relationship between the parties." *Pass,* 2000 WL 388775, at *4 (quoting *Insul-Mark,* 612 N.E.2d at 555). Contractual language that refers to the transaction as a "purchase," for example, or identifies the parties as the "buyer" and "seller," indicates that the transaction is for goods rather than services. See *Bonebrake,* 499 F.2d at 958 (stating that language referring to "equipment" is peculiar to goods rather than services); Bailey v. Montgomery Ward & Co., 690 P.2d 1280, 1282 (Colo. Ct. App. 1984) (holding that a contract that identifies the transaction as a "purchase" and one of the parties as the "customer" signals a transaction in goods); Meeker v. Hamilton Grain Elevator Co., 110 Ill. App. 3d 668, 66 Ill. Dec. 360, 442 N.E.2d 921, 923 (1982) (stating that a contract that calls the parties "seller" and "purchaser" indicates a contract for goods).

Turning to the contract between Mr. Tanzer and AVA, we first note that it is titled "Systems Sale and Installation Contract." From the plain language, it is clear that this is a hybrid contract, contemplating both the sale of goods and the installation of the goods. The question, then, is whether the language, when viewed in context, indicates the predominant purpose of the contract.

Throughout the contract, Mr. Tanzer is referred to as the "purchaser," a term that connotes a sale of goods contract. *Bonebrake,* 499 F.2d at 958. In various sections, the contract states that: (1) "[p]er this contract, AVA agrees to deliver and install **equipment** included in the proposal"; (2) "AVA retains ownership of the equipment until contract is paid in full"; (3) "Delays . . . by parties other than AVA that prohibit proper installation of **delivered equipment** shall not delay payment . . .;" (4) "Prices are subject to change on items . . . between the time of execution of this contract and the **delivery of goods**"; (5) "All **pre-paid goods** shall be delivered at the price agreed"; (6) "Model numbers may change . . . therefore Product delivered may not . . . be the same model number agreed to in the Proposal"; and (7) "Final installation of most **electronic hardware** corresponds with purchaser['s] actual move-in date. . . ." (Emphases added). As noted in *Bonebrake,* "equipment" is a term of art, which is "peculiar [to the sale of goods.]" *Bonebrake,* 499 F.2d at 958. Furthermore, the contract incorporates, by reference, the earlier proposal, which sets out the specific equipment that AVA would install in the Tanzer home.

In his brief, Mr. Tanzer urges this Court to read the disputed contract as a construction or building contract based, *inter alia,* upon the fact that the equipment and installation occurred during the building process and the items installed allegedly became part of the completed home. In support of his argument, Mr. Tanzer relies upon the case of Aluminum Vinyl Sales Company v. Woerz, No. 03A01-9304-CV-00172, 1993 WL 367125 (Tenn. Ct. App. Sept. 20, 1993). *Woerz* involved a contract for the installation of vinyl siding on a home. In pertinent part, the *Woerz* Court stated:

> "The Uniform Commercial Code does not apply to a contract for the rendition of services or to construction contracts." The subject matter of the contract before us is to furnish "all the materials and labor necessary for" the installation of vinyl siding to the entire exterior of Defendant's house.
>
> A contract to furnish a movable thing and affix it to the freehold is not a contract for the sale of goods, but one to furnish materials and affix them to the freehold by work and labor, and, until the materials are affixed, title to the materials does not pass.

1993 WL 367125, at *3 (citing 67 Am. Jur. 2d, Sales, §39 (1985); 77 C.J.S., Sales, §2, p. 585). Despite Mr. Tanzer's reading of *Woerz,* we cannot extend its holding so far as to conclude that it stands for the proposition that any and all contracts that contemplate the sale of goods, which are installed in a home or affixed to realty, are to be construed as predominantly service contracts. Rather, as noted in 1 Barkley Clark and Christopher Smith, The Law of Product Warranties §2:22 (2012):

> Contracts for the installation of products that were identifiable goods before installation and that, when installed, constitute only a small portion of a total building, are covered by Article 2. ... As long as the transaction involves defective products that were moveable before installation and thus once qualified as "goods" under §2-105(1), the courts assume that the service elements are also covered.

Id. Accordingly, cases have held that the installation of the following are all sale of goods: (1) carpet, *Snyder v. Herbert Greenbaum & Associates, Inc.,* 38 Md. App. 144, 380 A.2d 618 (1977), *Colorado Carpet Installation, Inc. v. Palermo,* 668 P.2d 1384 (Colo. 1983); (2) electrical equipment, *E.C. Ernst, Inc. v. Manhattan Const. Co. of Texas,* 551 F.2d 1026 (5th Cir. 1977); (3) trees, shrubs and sod, *Burton v. Artery Co., Inc.,* 279 Md. 94, 367 A.2d 935 (1977); (4) steel lockers, *Anderson Const. Co., Inc. v. Lyon Metal Products, Inc.,* 370 So. 2d 935 (Miss. 1979); (5) overhead doors, *Meyers v. Henderson Const. Co.,* 147 N.J. Super. 77, 370 A.2d 547 (1977); (6) water heaters, *Shapiro v. Long Island Lighting Co.,* 71 A.D.2d 671, 418 N.Y.S.2d 948 (1979); (7) a furnace, *O'Laughlin v. Minnesota Natural Gas Co.,* 253 N.W.2d 826 (Minn. 1977); (8) an air-conditioning system, *B & B Refrigeration & Air Conditioning Service, Inc. v. Haifley,* 1978 WL 23510 (D.C. Super. Ct. Nov. 6, 1978); and (9) interior window panels, *The Plantation Shutter Co. v. Ezell,* 328 S.C. 475, 492 S.E.2d 404 (1997).

In *Glazer, et ux v. Tri-State Tile and Marble Co., Inc.,* 1985 Tenn. App. LEXIS 2767 (Tenn. Ct. App. March 22, 1985), a suit for breach of express warranty in connection with the resurfacing of plaintiffs' patio with "prairie film," which is "a mixture of epoxy and very fine gravel," Id. at *1, this Court noted that, in cases "involving building useful improvements out of raw materials," courts have held that these contracts are "outside the scope of the U.C.C." Id. at *3. Such cases involved: (1) the sale and installation of blacktop, *Rose Acre Farms v. L.P. Cavett Co.,* 151 Ind. App. 268, 279 N.E.2d 280 (1972); (2) construction of a house with a builder furnishing all materials and labor, *Vernali v. Centrella,* 28 Conn. Supp. 476, 266 A.2d 200 (1970); and (3) construction of electrical equipment, *Mainland v. Alfred Brown Co.,* 85 Nev. 654, 461 P.2d 862 (Nev. Sup. Ct. 1969). On the other hand, in cases where the courts have found the contract to be one for the sale of goods, and thus governed by the UCC, "the items therein involved have been tangible things, movable at the time they are identified to the contract and where installation has not been a major or predominant factor in the contract." *Glazer*, 1985 Tenn. App. LEXIS 2767, at *3. Such cases involved: (1) installation of water tank, Pittsburgh-Des Moines Steel Co. v. Brookhaven Manor Water Co., 532 F.2d 572 (7th Cir. 1976); (2) installation of a bowling alley and equipment, *Bonebrake*, 499 F.2d at 951; and (3) installation of a liner for the bottom of a swimming pool, Riffe v. Black, 548 S.W.2d 175 (Ky. Ct. App. 1977). The *Glazer* Court applied the foregoing principles in reaching its conclusion that the installation of "prairie film" is not a sale of goods. In reaching its holding, the Court noted:

> [T]his is clearly not a sale of "goods," but is closely akin to some of the cases cited above, such as, the sale and installation of a blacktop driveway, or building or painting a house. We see no difference between installing a Prairie Film system over a patio and overlaying the patio with concrete or quarry tile. Plaintiffs were contracting to obtain a service from the defendant, not to purchase a quantity of gravel.
>
> By the same token, materials, such as the Prairie Film, when attached to realty, such as a patio cover, lose their character as goods. See T.C.A. §47-9-313. Once the patio was resurfaced by defendant the resurfacing lost any characteristics of personalty and became part of an improvement of the real estate, not severable therefrom.

Glazer, 1985 Tenn. App. LEXIS 2767, at *3.

Tennessee Code Annotated Section 47-2-105 sets out the current definition of "goods" under the UCC. The statute provides, in relevant part, that: "'Goods' means all things (including specially manufactured goods) which are movable at the time of identification to the contract for sale. . . ." The comments to the code section clarify that: "The definition of goods is based on the concept of movability. . . . It is not intended to deal with things which are not fairly identifiable as movables before the contract is performed." The comment goes on to explain that:

> The use of the word "fixtures" is avoided in view of the diversity of definitions of that term. This Article in including within its scope "things attached to realty" adds the further test that they must be capable of severance without material harm thereto. As between the parties any identified things which fall within that definition becomes "goods" upon the making of the contract for sale.

In light of the foregoing statutory provisions, the holding in *Glazer* is still applicable. Because the "prairie film" became "attached to the realty," such that it could not be removed "without material harm" to the structure, the Court correctly held that the contract was one for service, thus excluding application of the UCC. By contrast, in Highland Rim Contractors v. Atlantic Software Corp., No. 01-A-01-9104CV00147, 1992 WL 184872 (Tenn. Ct. App. Aug. 5, 1992), this Court held that a contract involving the sale of a computer system to a construction company was a sale of goods contract. The Court noted that the contract was a hybrid contract, involving both sale of goods and service. The Court then applied the predominant purpose test to determine that the UCC applied to the transaction; in so holding, the Court stated:

> Other courts, using the predominant [purpose] test, have found that contracts for the sale of computer systems or related components, including hardware, software, training, and support services, are contracts for the sale of goods governed by Article 2. RRX Indus., Inc. v. Lab-Con, Inc., 772 F.2d 543, 546 (9th Cir. 1985) (software, training, systems repairs, and upgrades); Triangle Underwriters, Inc. v. Honeywell, Inc., 604 F.2d 737, 742-43 (2d Cir. 1979) (hardware and software); Neilson Business Equip. Ctr., Inc. v. Monteleone, 524 A.2d 1172, 1174 (Del. 1987) (computer system); USM Corp. v. Arthur D. Little Sys., Inc., 28 Mass. App. Ct. 108, 546 N.E.2d 888, 894 (1989) (computer system); Communications Group, Inc. v. Warner Communications, Inc., 138 Misc. 2d 80, 527 N.Y.S.2d 341, 344 (N.Y. Civ. Ct. 1988) (software); Camara v. Hill, 157 Vt. 156, 596 A.2d 349, 351 (1991) (computer system).
>
> We agree with the reasoning of these precedents. Atlantic's agreement with Highland Rim was predominately for the sale of an integrated computer system. Its obligation to provide training in the use of the system was incidental to the purchase of the system itself. Accordingly, the transaction is one involving goods, and the parties' rights are governed by Article 2.

Highland Rim Constructors, 1992 WL 184872, at *6. We find the reasoning and cited cases in *Highland Rim* persuasive in the instant appeal. As set out in the contract, and in the incorporated proposal, it is clear that the contract contemplates the sale of various, moveable components, which were to be integrated via a control system. Unlike the *Glazer* case, the fact that the components were installed in the home did not result in an attachment that would change the movability of the goods sold. Accordingly, we are not persuaded by Mr. Tanzer's argument that the integration of the components constitutes a "construction" contract. The plain language of the contract simply does not support such a finding.

B. NATURE OF AVA'S BUSINESS

In addition to the plain language of the contract, the court may also consider the nature of the seller's business. *Pass*, 2000 WL 388775, at *4. It is not disputed in the record that AVA is in the business of design and sale of custom, state-of-the-art, home theater, multi-room music/television/

lighting control, and phone/intercom systems. AVA does not manufacture or promote one brand of product; rather, it sells and installs products from various manufacturers. From our review of the record, it appears that AVA's "design" role really constitutes a determination of what goods the customer needs and what integration system(s) will work to link the various components. In this sense, the "integration" of the whole system is done by the controlling system, i.e., Escient, Concierge, Crestron, Lutron. The sale of these respective systems is, in the opinion of this Court, similar to the sale of an integrated computer system. *See Highland Rim Constructors,* 1992 WL 184872, at *6-7. The installation and service that AVA performs is incidental to the overarching purpose of its business, which is to sell "smart home" components.

C.   REASON FOR THE CONTRACT

The third factor instructs the court to "consider the final product the purchaser bargained to receive, and whether it may be described as a good or a service." *Pass,* 2000 WL 388775, at *12 (quoting *Insul-Mark,* 612 N.E.2d at 555). Whether the purchaser sought to procure a good or a service by entering into the subject contract is "a strong indication of the predominant purpose of the contract." Id. at *15 (citing Stafford v. Int'l Harvester Co., 668 F.2d 142, 147 (2d Cir. 1981) ("underlying nature of a hybrid transaction is determined by reference to the purpose with which the customer contracted with the defendant")); NW Equip. Inc. v. Cudmore, 312 N.W.2d 347, 349 (N.D. 1981) ("*Bonebrake* test looks to the predominant purpose or thrust of the contract as it would exist in the minds of reasonable parties."). In analyzing this factor, the *Pass* Court found guidance from the Michigan Supreme Court, in Neibarger v. Universal Cooperatives, Inc., 439 Mich. 512, 486 N.W.2d 612 (1992), wherein the Michigan court described its analysis of the purpose of the parties' dealings as follows:

> If the purchaser's ultimate goal is to acquire a product, the contract should be considered a transaction in goods, even though service is incidentally required. Conversely, if the purchaser's ultimate goal is to procure a service, the contract is not governed by the UCC, even though goods are incidentally required in the provision of this service.

Id. at 622.

As discussed above, even in cases where labor and services were contemplated by the parties to be an integral part of the contract, courts have still held that Article 2 applies. See, e.g., *Highland Rim Constructors,* 1992 WL 184872, at *7 (noting that the seller's "obligation to provide training in the use of the system was incidental to the purchase of the system itself."); see also IBP, Inc. v. HK Sys., No. 98cv00480, 2000 WL 35725320 (D. Neb. Sept. 21, 2000) (holding that contract for purchase of a computer system was a sale of goods, with rendition of services such as design, construction, manufacturing and installation incidental); *Bonebrake*, 499 F.2d at 958 (holding that installation of pre-fabricated bowling lanes incidental to the contract because the lanes remained "movable"); Meyers v. Henderson Constr. Co., 147 N.J. Super. 77, 370 A.2d 547, 549 (1977) (holding that installation of pre-fabricated disassembled doors was incidental to the contract for sale of the tangible goods).

Turning to the record in the instant case, in his answer, Mr. Tanzer admits that he contracted for electronic equipment. It is not disputed that AVA orders all of the equipment it sells from the manufacturer or from the distributor. In other words, none of the equipment was "constructed" at Tanzer's home; it was merely installed there. The record further indicates that the equipment maintained its characteristics as personalty and was never rendered immovable from the residence. In support of this conclusion, Mr. Tanzer presented a spreadsheet at trial, which indicated all of the equipment he was willing to return to AVA. The fact that Mr. Tanzer could return this equipment supports a finding that it had not become a permanent improvement to his realty. The fact that the original proposal, which was incorporated into the contract, breaks apart the costs of the "equipment," i.e., tangible goods, from the cost of "cable/misc. parts," i.e., materials also supports a finding that Mr. Tanzer bargained for the purchase of equipment, and that the services rendered by AVA in connection with that sale, including delivery and installation, were necessary but incidental to the ultimate purpose of the contract, i.e., to obtain the various components and the integration system that would link them.

D. AMOUNTS PAID FOR SERVICES AND GOODS, RESPECTIVELY

The final factor to be considered is the respective amounts charged under the contract for the goods and services. *Pass*, 2000 WL 388775, at *4. "If the cost of the goods is but a small portion of the overall contract price, such fact would increase the likelihood that the services portion predominates." Id. at *12 (quoting *Insul-Mark*, 612 N.E.2d at 555). Conversely, where "the charge for goods exceeds that for services, the contract is more likely to be for goods." *BMC Indus.*, 160 F.3d at 1330 (citations omitted).

In this case, the trial court found that the costs of labor and services were "insignificant" compared to the cost of the equipment. As set out above, under the original contract, equipment sales constituted $56,375 of the total price of $71,915 (before taxes); on the other hand, labor accounted for only $9,880. In the final invoice, equipment totaled $89,640.03 of the total contract price of $109,830.03 (before taxes), with labor constituting only $13,260.00. Viewed as a percentage, equipment constitutes roughly 82% of the final contract price. Accordingly, this factor weighs heavily in favor of a finding that the contract was predominantly for the sale of goods.

Based upon the foregoing, we conclude that all four of the *Pass* factors favor the trial court's conclusion that the instant contract was predominantly for the sale of goods. Accordingly, we conclude that the trial court did not err in applying UCC Article 2 to this transaction.

[The court then concluded that Mr. Tanzer had accepted the system and could only offset the amount of damages he could prove AVA's breaches of warranty caused him, but that, with some exceptions, his proof was inadequate due to complication caused by the lightning strike, extra work done by the new contractor, and the excessive size of that contractor's bill.]

For the foregoing reasons, we affirm the judgment of the trial court. The case is remanded for all further proceedings as may be necessary and are consistent with this opinion. Costs of this appeal are assessed against the Appellant, Stephen Tanzer, and his surety.

One thorny area that is much litigated concerns the extent to which contracts for the sale of software are governed by Article 2 of the Uniform Commercial Code. This was briefly discussed in the last case, and the next one considers the issue in more depth.

Simulados Software, Ltd. v. Photon Infotech Private, Ltd.

United States District Court, Northern District of California,
2014, 40 F. Supp. 3d 1191

EDWARD J. DAVILA, United States District Judge
Presently before the Court is Defendant Photon Infotech Private, Ltd.'s ("Photon" or "Defendant") Motion to Dismiss Plaintiff Simulados Software, Ltd.'s ("Simulados" or "Plaintiff") Amended Complaint ("AC"). See Docket Item No. 46. Federal jurisdiction arises under 28 U.S.C. §1332(a). This case is proceeding in this Court because of the parties' venue selection clause in their contract. See Docket Item No. 15. Having fully reviewed the parties' papers, the Court will GRANT Defendant's motion for the reasons stated below.

I. BACKGROUND

Simulados is a Texas software development company based in Houston, Texas. Photon is a technology consulting corporation incorporated in New Jersey with its principal place of business in Chennai, India, and a virtual office in San Jose, California. See AC, Docket Item No. 44 ¶¶1-2. Simulados developed a program called Certify Teacher, which is a test simulation program used by educators to prepare for the Texas Examinations of Educator Standards ("TExES") certification exam. Simulados decided to produce a version of its product compatible with Apple Macintosh ("Mac") computers as well as an internet web application. *Id.* ¶¶3-4.

In early 2009, Photon called Simulados, representing Photon's ability to create a Mac-compatible product and develop a web application. *Id.* ¶¶6-7. Simulados and Photon entered into a contract ("Contract") on March 31, 2009, which consisted of a Statement of Work ("SOW") and a Master Professional Services Agreement ("MPSA"). See Docket Item No. 1-1 (the SOW incorporates all the terms and conditions of the MPSA). In the Contract, Photon represented that the project would start on May 20, 2009, and finish on September 17, 2009. The Contract provided that Photon would complete: CD mastering, migrating the existing source code to Real Basic, convert VB project, add Mac specific BASIC code, add support for New DB format, address performance bottlenecks in product, customize for Mac operating systems, add platform specific paths, tweak for Mac Human Interface Guidelines, provide license key generation and key validation, create a web application, create website authentication certification for downloads, upgrade to database content creator, provide support for reading the content, provide support for modifying content, migrate up to three sample products, and code review. Simulados agreed to pay $23,560 in four installments, the final of which was to be made upon delivery of a complete workable product. Id. at 10-12. The Contract contained the following choice-of-law and forum selection provision: "[t]his Agreement shall be governed by and construed and enforce [sic] in accordance with the laws of the State of California." Id. at 23.

Simulados contends that Photon never fulfilled its obligations under the Contract. On June 9, 2009, Photon communicated to Simulados that it was initiating the project, and represented that there would not be any outstanding serious or critical defects at the time of the site launch, with fewer than five medium defects and fewer than ten low defects. On August 14, 2009, Photon requested that Simulados approve completion of the project's development phase. A teleconference demonstration was held on August 19, 2009 and on September 24, 2009 Simulados received an access link for user testing and approval. During the review, Simulados found 38 low level and 8 critical issues. Simulados requested a status update on the web application and expressed dissatisfaction that the product was not complete. On May 3, 2010, Simulados gave Photon a deadline of June 3, 2012, to correct an additional 17 errors. On May 17, 2010, Photon responded to Simulados' notice, providing a link to incomplete software. To date, Photon has not provided Simulados with fully functioning web application. Dkt. No. 44 ¶¶12-16.

Simulados filed a complaint on May 11, 2012 in the District Court for the Southern District of Texas. See Docket Item No. 1. The case was transferred to this Court on August 20, 2012, based on the choice-of-law provision in the Contract. See Docket Item No. 16. Simulados filed an Amended Complaint ("AC") on December 11, 2012. Dkt. No. 44. On December 24, 2012, Photon filed a Motion to Dismiss, which is presently before the Court. Dkt. No. 46. Plaintiffs have filed written opposition to this motion. See Docket Item No. 51. The parties engaged in mediation, but failed to reach an agreement regarding arbitration. See Docket Item No. 63. Photon re-noticed its Motion on July 23, 2013. See Docket Item No. 67. Pursuant to Civil Local Rule 7-1(b), the Court took the motion under submission without oral argument....

C.   CLAIMS ARISING UNDER THE UNIFORM COMMERCIAL CODE

Photon contends that Simulados' claim that it is entitled to remedies outside the contract by virtue of the UCC is implausible and must be dismissed because Article 2 of the UCC applies only to contracts for the sale of goods, not services, and the Contract between the parties is for services. Simulados argues that the Contract is for sale of software, which is considered a good, and thus the UCC applies. For the reasons outlined below, the Court will dismiss any claims arising from the UCC.

The UCC applies to the transaction of goods. Cal. Com. Code §2102. The UCC defines goods as "all things (including specially manufactured goods) which are movable at the time of identification to the contract for sale ..." Cal. Com. Code § 2105. Applying the UCC to software poses a complex issue because transactions for software often combine elements of both goods and services. As such, courts have arrived at different decisions concerning whether software transactions are covered by the UCC.

The primary test used by courts to determine whether software is a good under the UCC is the predominant factor test, where courts look to the "essence of the agreement" on a case-by-case basis to decide how to characterize the transaction. Gross v. Symantec Corp., No. C-12-00154-CRB, 2012 WL 3116158, at *8 (N.D. Cal. July 31, 2012) (citing RRX Indus., Inc. v. Lab-Con, Inc., 772 F.2d 543, 546 (9th Cir. 1985)). Courts determine whether the predominant factor or purpose of the contract is rendition of services, with goods incidentally involved, or is rendition of goods, with labor incidentally involved.

Generally, courts have found that mass-produced, standardized, or generally available software, even with modifications and ancillary services included in the agreement, is a good that is covered by the UCC. In RRX Industries, Inc. v. Lab-Con, Inc., the Ninth Circuit found that a license for mass-produced software for use in medical laboratories was covered by the

UCC, even when the software contract also provided for ancillary services such as training, repair, and system upgrading. *RRX Indus.*, 772 F.2d 543 (9th Cir. 1985). The court noted, "[h]ere, the sales aspect of the transaction predominates. The [services] were incidental to sale of the software package and did not defeat characterization of the system as a good." Id. at 546. See also *Gross*, 2012 WL 3116158, at *8-9 (where a user purchased and downloaded Symantec's pre-existing software from the internet, this court determined that the "essence of the agreement" was the sale of a good); Olcott Intern v. Micro Data, 793 N.E.2d 1063 (Ind. Ct. App. 2003) ("generally-available standardized software" was found to be a good under the UCC); Rottner v. AVG Tech. USA, Inc., 943 F. Supp. 2d 222, 230 (D. Mass. 2013) (noting that the sale of a downloadable computer software is like a sale of tangible goods and that courts nationally have consistently classified the sale of a software package as the sale of a good for UCC purposes); Advent Sys. Ltd. v. Unisys Corp., 925 F.2d 670, 675-76 (3d Cir. 1991) (noting that the majority of academic commentary supports the view that software fits with the definition of a good under the UCC).

Software may still be considered a good even when accompanied by ancillary services, which "are not substantially different from those generally accompanying package sales of computer systems consisting of hardware and software." *Advent Sys.*, 925 F.2d at 676. Such ancillary services include installation, training, and technical support. See Dahlmann v. Sulcus Hosp. Tech. Corp., 63 F. Supp. 2d 772, 775 (E.D. Mich. 1999) (a contract for property management systems incorporating hardware, software, installation, training, and technical support services for plaintiffs' hotels was a contract for goods because the provisions for services were incidental to the agreements for the system); ePresence v. Evolve, 190 F. Supp. 2d 159 (D. Mass. 2002) (a contract for software licensing which also included services was determined to be a transaction for goods, as the software programs themselves were the essence of the parties' agreement); Wachter Mgmt. Co. v. Dexter & Chaney, Inc., 282 Kan. 365, 369, 144 P.3d 747 (2006) (even when incidental services such as modifications, corrections, maintenance, training, and consulting were provided with software, the services would have been unnecessary if the software had not been purchased, so the transaction is predominantly for a good).

Even software adapted for specific needs has been considered a good. In Micro Data Base Systems, Inc. v. Dharma Systems, Inc., 148 F.3d 649 (7th Cir. 1998), the Seventh Circuit determined that the UCC governed a contract for software where one party agreed to adapt its software program for use in the other party's system. The court noted that "labor is a service" that is part of the manufacture of every good and opined, "we can think of no reason why the UCC is not suitable to govern disputes arising from the sale of custom software." Id. 654-55. Similarly, the Third Circuit found that the software contracted for was a good where one party planned to modify its existing software and hardware interfaces for the other party's use. *Advent Sys.*, 925 F.2d 670. The court noted, "[t]he fact that some programs may be tailored for specific purposes need not alter their status as 'goods' because the Code definition includes 'specially manufactured goods.'" Id. at 675. The Third Circuit found that the advantages of applying the UCC to software transactions (namely uniformity on a range of questions) and the importance of software to the commercial world were strong policy arguments favoring the application of the UCC and that the majority of academic commentary espoused the view that software falls under the UCC. Id. at 675-76. See also Commc'ns Groups, Inc. v. Warner Commc'ns, 138 Misc. 2d 80, 83, 527 N.Y.S.2d 341 (N.Y. Civ. Ct. 1988) (determining that a contract which provided for the installation of specially designed software equipment for one party's telephone and computer systems, including recording, accounting and traffic analysis and optimizations, modules, buffer, directories and an operational user guide was a transaction of software equipment involving movable, tangible and identifiable products or goods); Waterfront Properties v. Xerox Connect, 58 U.C.C. Rep. Serv. 2d 809, 2006 WL 266581 (W.D.N.C. 2006) (agreements for the provision of custom adapted preexisting computer software and attendant hardware were contracts predominately for goods, which are governed by the UCC).

On the other end of the spectrum, courts in this district and beyond have determined that certain software transactions are better defined as services and therefore are not covered by the UCC. Where software is designed from scratch, or the transaction is mainly for one party's knowledge and skills in creating software, the software is often found to be a service rather than a good.

In Systems America, Inc. v. Rockwell Software, Inc., No. C-03-2232, 2007 WL 218242 (N.D. Cal. Jan. 26, 2007), the agreement entered into between the parties called for development of a final software product for reproduction and distribution to one party's customers. The developing party developed new software to supplement existing software, provided the source code to an escrow agent, and retained all ownership rights to the software. The court determined that the contract was for services, not goods, because the essence of the contract was the development of software from scratch and the granting of a license for use of the software. Id. at *4. Where a contract required a party to design, develop, and implement a tailored, highly complex automated software system, that contract was deemed to be for services, not goods. State v. Lockheed Martin, No. C-036815, 2002 WL 99554, at *18 (Cal. Ct. App., Jan. 25, 2002). This district found that even in a situation where an agreement was made for production of physical prototypes, since most of the price paid was for the other party's "knowledge, skill, and ability" to develop software code and test prototypes, the agreement was for services rather than goods. TK Power v. Textron, 433 F. Supp. 2d 1058, 1062 (N.D. Cal. 2006). See also Data Processing Serv. v. L.H. Smith Oil Corp., 492 N.E.2d 314, 318-19 (Ind. Ct. App. 1986) (custom-designed accounting software is not a good because no hardware was involved and the contract bargained for the programmer's "knowledge, skill, and ability" rather than standardized software); Pearl Inv. v. Standard I/O, 257 F. Supp. 2d 326 (D. Me. 2003) (custom-made software is distinguishable from pre-existing software — even with custom modifications and upgrades — and is a service); Multi-Tech Sys. v. Floreat, No. Civ-01-1320, 2002 WL 432016, at *3 (D. Minn. March 18, 2002) ("work" toward "jointly developing" a new product is a service … the UCC does not apply to an agreement to design and develop a product, even if compensation under that agreement is based in part on later sales of that product"); Wharton Mgmt. Grp. v. Sigma Consultants, Inc., 50 U.C.C. Rep. Serv. 2d 678, 1990 WL 18360 (Del. Super. Ct. 1990) (software contract is for services where a party was hired for its skills to "design, develop, and install computer software which would meet … specific needs and objectives …").

In this instance, Photon was meant to produce a Mac-compliant version of Simulados' existing Windows-based software and an internet web application. Based on an analysis of the cases concerning the application of the UCC to software transactions, this Court determines that in this particular case, Simulados contracted for a service and the UCC does not apply to this software transaction. Following other courts, this Court uses the predominance test on a case-by-case basis to analyze a transaction that involves elements of both a good and a service. The Contract between the parties calls for Photon to provide services, skills, and knowledge to customize Simulados' existing product for sale to Simulados' customers. Although customized software may still be considered a good, here Simulados was not purchasing any software from Photon. Rather, Photon was only providing services to modify Simulados' already-existing software. As such, Simulados was contracting only for the modifications, a service, and not for software as a separate good. Thus, the UCC does not apply to this transaction and any claims arising from it are dismissed....

IT IS SO ORDERED.

———————————

The "predominate purpose" test doesn't entirely carry the day. It's wildly unpredictable, and that instability has caused other courts to look for a test that will lead to more predictable outcomes. Maryland's highest court led the way in the following case.

Anthony Pools v. Sheehan

Maryland Court of Appeals, 1983, 295 Md. 285, 455 A.2d 434

RODOWSKY, J.

This products liability case presents questions of implied warranty and of defense to strict liability in tort involving an in-ground, gunite swimming pool and its diving board. Analysis of whether there is any implied warranty and, if so, whether it can be excluded takes us into the problem of hybrid transactions and into Md. Code (1975), §2-316.1(1) and (2) of the Commercial Law Article (C.L.).[1]

Plaintiffs, John B. Sheehan (Sheehan) and his wife, Pilar E. Sheehan, of Potomac Woods, Maryland, sued Anthony Pools, a division of Anthony Industries, Inc. (Anthony) in the Circuit Court for Montgomery County. Sheehan sustained bodily injuries when he fell from the side of the diving board of the plaintiffs' new, backyard swimming pool. The swimming pool had been designed and built by Anthony. Anthony also designed and manufactured the diving board which it installed as part of the swimming pool transaction.

The swimming pool is 16 feet by 40 feet, with a depth from 3 feet to 8 feet. Its style is "Grecian," which means that there is a curved alcove in the center of each of the 16 foot sides. The 6-foot-long diving board in question was installed over an imaginary centerline bisecting the alcove at the deep end of the pool. Anthony had completed its work by mid-June of 1976. On August 21, 1976, the plaintiffs entertained at a pool party. Sheehan testified that he had not previously used the diving board. He said that on that evening he emerged from swimming in the pool, stepped up onto the diving board, and, while walking toward the pool end of the diving board, slipped and fell from the right side of the diving board and struck the coping of the pool.

Plaintiffs advanced two theories of liability. First, skid resistant material built into the surface of the top of the diving board did not extend to the very edge of the board on each side. It stopped approximately one inch short of each edge. This condition, it was claimed, breached an implied warranty of merchantability. Plaintiffs also presented testimony directed toward

---

1. C.L. §2-316.1 in relevant part provides:

"(1) The provisions of §2-316 do not apply to sales of consumer goods, as defined by §9-109, services, or both.

"(2) Any oral or written language used by a seller of consumer goods and services, which attempts to exclude or modify any implied warranties of merchantability and fitness for a particular purpose or to exclude or modify the consumer's remedies for breach of those warranties, is unenforceable. However, the seller may recover from the manufacturer any damages resulting from breach of the implied warranty of merchantability or fitness for a particular purpose." [This is a nonuniform addition to the UCC, and is not the law in most other states.—Ed.]

proving that use of the "defective" diving board, particularly as positioned in the alcove, was unreasonably dangerous.

At the end of the plaintiffs' case, the trial court directed a verdict for Anthony as to liability founded on warranty, because the written contract between the parties conspicuously provided that the express warranties which it contained were in lieu of any other warranties, express or implied. The case went to the jury on a strict liability in tort theory. Verdict was in favor of the defendant, and judgment was so entered.

Plaintiffs appealed to the Court of Special Appeals which reversed and remanded for a new trial. That court said that "the swimming pool package purchased by the Sheehans constitute[d] 'consumer goods'" so that C.L. §2-316.1 rendered ineffective Anthony's attempt to limit the implied warranty of merchantability. Sheehan v. Anthony Pools, 50 Md. App. 614, 619, 440 A.2d 1085, 1088 (1982). The granting of the directed verdict based on the contractual limitation was held to be error. Judgment based on the jury verdict was reversed because of error in the instructions. As to that issue, Judge Moore, writing for the court, concluded:

> In the instant case, it is our view that while the trial court was eminently correct in rejecting the defendant's request for a contributory negligence instruction, the matter should not have ended there. On the basis of the facts involved and of the Sheehans' specific request, an instruction should have been granted that Mr. Sheehan's inadvertent or careless use of the diving board and the pool would not bar his recovery. On the other hand, giving such an instruction would also have required an appropriate instruction on assumption of risk, i.e., that the defendant was entitled to prevail if Mr. Sheehan had discovered the defect, was aware of the danger, and then proceeded unreasonably to use the diving board and pool. [Id. at 625-626, 440 A.2d at 1092.]

We granted Anthony's petition for certiorari which raised three questions. In essence, the petition asks us to review (1) the implied warranty issue; (2) the inadvertent use instruction issue; and (3) whether the Court of Special Appeals erred "in holding, as dictum that contributory negligence is not a defense in a strict liability case."

1

The warranty issue, as presented here, involves only the implied warranty of merchantability under C.L. §2-314. Plaintiffs do not argue that their warranty claim is based upon any express warranty or that the diving board was to be used for other than its ordinary purpose. Anthony contends that the Sheehans' swimming pool is not "goods," that exclusion of implied warranties is allowed, and that a directed verdict on the plaintiffs' warranty count was proper. We agree with the Court of Special Appeals that the directed verdict was improper in this case, but we reach that conclusion by a somewhat different route.

Title 2 of the Commercial Law Article is the Maryland Uniform Commercial Code Sales. C.L. §2-101. Unless the context otherwise requires, that title "applies to transactions in goods. . . ." C.L. §2-102. For purposes of title 2, and with certain exclusions not here relevant, "goods" means "all things (including specially manufactured goods) which are movable at the time of identification to the contract for sale. . . ." C.L. §2-105(1). C.L. §2-314(1) in part provides that "[u]nless excluded or modified (§2-316), a warranty that the goods shall be merchantable is implied in a contract for their sale if the seller is a merchant with respect to goods of that kind." C.L. §2-316(2) permits the exclusion or modification of the implied warranty of merchantability by language which mentions merchantability and which, in the case of a writing, is conspicuous. The Maryland UCC, in §2-316.1, then states that the "provisions of §2-316 do not apply to sales of consumer goods, as defined by §9-109, services, or both," and that any "language used by a seller of consumer goods and services, which attempts to exclude or modify any implied warranties . . . is unenforceable." C.L. §9-109(1) provides that goods are " '[c]onsumer goods' if they are used or bought for use primarily for personal, family or household purposes."

The May 25, 1976 contract between Anthony and the plaintiffs is a printed form designed for use in Anthony's Washington, D.C., region. It is a single sheet of paper, approximately 15" by 20," with printing on both sides. The face of the document is three columns wide. The lefthand column on the face is headed "Retail Installment Contract." Under that column are set forth Anthony's contractor license numbers in Virginia, Maryland and the District of Columbia, a statement of the buyer's right to cancel a home solicitation contract, federal truth-in-lending disclosures and a detachable notice of cancellation. The next two columns on the face are entitled "Swimming Pool Construction Agreement." Anthony "agrees to construct for and sell to" the plaintiffs, called " 'Buyer,' " the "swimming pool and related equipment described below (herein collectively called the 'work') to be installed at" the plaintiffs' home for a fixed cash price. Below this covenant, under the heading "Plans and Specifications," are two columns listing 47 items, some of which are automatically included and some of which are optional. These items appear under the headings, "General Construction Specifications," "Hydraulic and Filtering Specifications," "Color-Coordinated Exclusive Deck Equip.," "Automatic Pool Equipment" and "Other Anthony Features." In the subject contract Anthony's obligations included pool layout, structural engineering, obtaining construction permits, excavation, use of engineered steel reinforcing throughout the pool structure, guniting the pool structure, finishing the pool interior with hand troweled, waterproof plaster, installation both of a six-inch band of water-line tile and of coping and installation of a filter, a pump, a skimmer and a specified model of six foot diving board. The reverse side of the contract contains two columns of terms and conditions, including the implied warranty exclusion. The subject contract presents a mixed or hybrid transaction. It is in part a contract for the rendering of services and in part a contract for the sale of goods.

Burton v. Artery Company, 279 Md. 94, 367 A.2d 935 (1977) addressed the applicability vel non of the Maryland UCC Sales to hybrid contracts. The issue presented was whether the four-year statute of limitations under §2-725(1), or the general three-year statute, applied to a contract to landscape around a construction project of 13 buildings. The contract called for the furnishing and planting of hundreds of trees, of hundreds of shrubs, and of sod. We there adopted the test enunciated in Bonebrake v. Cox, 499 F.2d 951 (8th Cir. 1974), a case holding that the sale and installation of bowling lanes, with associated equipment, is a contract of sale and not of services. That test is whether "the predominant factor ..., the thrust, the purpose, reasonably stated, is a transaction of sale with labor incidentally involved," or vice versa. 279 Md. at 114-115, 367 A.2d at 946. Applying that test, the court held the contract in *Burton* to be predominantly a transaction in goods. See also Snyder v. Herbert Greenbaum & Associates, 38 Md. App. 144, 380 A.2d 618 (1977) (contract to furnish and install over 17,000 yards of carpet in 228 apartments was predominantly a sale of goods).

G. Wallach, The Law of Sales Under the Uniform Commercial Code (1981), §11.05[3] at 11-28 describes the current state of the law concerning implied warranties in hybrid transactions to be as follows:

> The general pre-Code approach to this issue was to examine the transaction to see whether the goods aspect or the service aspect of the transaction predominated. If the service aspect predominated, no warranties of quality were imposed in the transaction, not even if the defect or complaint related to the goods that were involved rather than to the services. This mechanical approach remains the most popular method of resolving the issue.[2]

The few reported holdings concerning whether Article 2 of the UCC applies to swimming pool installations have involved a variety of types of pools and are not uniform. A Connecticut trial court decision dealt with the alleged breach of the implied warranty of merchantability in the installation

---

2. Among recent decisions applying the predominant purpose test are: White v. Peabody Construction Co., Inc., 386 Mass. 121, 434 N.E.2d 1015 (1982) (contract for the construction of a housing project was one for services so that there was no warranty implied under the UCC on the windows or frames, which leaked); Milau Associates v. North Avenue Development Corp., 42 N.Y.2d 482, 368 N.E.2d 1247, 398 N.Y.S.2d 882 (1977) (there is no warranty of merchantability on a section of pipe which ruptured and which had been installed as part of a sprinkler system in the course of construction of a new building); Northwestern Equipment, Inc. v. Cudmore, 312 N.W.2d 347 (N.D. 1981) (contract for the repair of the transmission in a used bulldozer is a contract for services and carries no implied warranty of fitness for a particular purpose, even though the charges for parts exceeded the charges for labor).

of an aboveground swimming pool. Its sides were plywood panels, braced by a 29×4' support. A vinyl liner was laid within the sides. That court applied the predominant purpose test. It held that the owners did not offer any adequate evidence on the apportionment between labor and material and equipment, and so they failed to meet the burden of establishing the existence of a warranty under the UCC. Gulash v. Stylarama, Inc., 33 Conn. Supp. 108, 364 A.2d 1221 (1975). A vinyl liner pool was also involved in Riffe v. Black, 548 S.W.2d 175 (Ky. App. 1977). The walls of that pool consisted of prefabricated steel which was set into an excavated site. Sand was troweled for the bottom of the pool. Leaking had resulted from the contractor's failure both to reseal the liner after a wrinkle had developed during installation and to repair the hole which developed later. The Kentucky court applied a predominant purpose test and necessarily classified the contract as one for the sale of goods. It was held that the warranty provisions of that state's UCC "apply to services when the sale is primarily one of goods and the services are necessary to insure that those goods are merchantable and fit for the ordinary purpose." Id. at 177. Judgment for the pool owners was affirmed. Ben Construction Corp. v. Ventre, 23 A.D.2d 44, 257 N.Y.S.2d 988 (1965) is not a UCC case, but it is analogous. It presented the claim of the pool owners for return of moneys paid, based on a section of the New York Personal Property Law. The pool is described in the opinion only as "installed." Judgment for the defendant contractor was affirmed, 3-2. In the majority's view, the contract was for work, labor and services and was not a sale, while the dissent viewed the transaction as primarily a sale of a swimming pool with an incidental agreement to install.

The Court of Special Appeals has recently held that C.L. §2-601's "perfect tender" provisions do not apply to a contract for the installation of an in-ground, concrete swimming pool. There was no transaction in goods because the pool was not movable. Chlan v. KDI Sylvan Pools, Inc., 53 Md. App. 123, 452 A.2d 1279 (1982) [No. 192, September Term, 1982, decided December 7, 1982].

Here, Anthony undertook the construction of an in-ground, steel reinforced, gunite swimming pool with hand finished plaster surfacing, tile trim, and coping. The Sheehans were not buying steel rods, or gunite, or plaster or tiles. The predominant factor, the thrust, the purpose of the contract was the furnishing of labor and service by Anthony, while the sale of the diving board was incidental to the construction of the pool itself. The question thus resolves itself into whether the predominant purpose test, which we applied in *Burton* for the purpose of determining whether the UCC statute of limitations governed that transaction, should be applied to determine whether the sale of the diving board, included in the Anthony-Sheehans transaction, carries an implied warranty of merchantability under §2-314.

Were the predominant purpose test mechanically to be applied to the facts of this case, there would be no quality warranty implied as to the diving board. But here the contract expressly states that Anthony agrees not only to construct the swimming pool, but also to sell the related equipment selected by the Sheehans. The Sheehans are described as "'Buyer.' "The diving board itself is not structurally integrated into the swimming pool. Anthony offered the board as an optional accessory, just as Anthony offered the options of purchasing a pool ladder or a sliding board. When identified to the contract, the diving board was movable. See C.L. §2-105. The board itself remains detachable from its support, as reflected by a photograph in evidence. The diving board, considered alone, is goods. Had it been purchased by the Sheehans in a transaction distinct from the pool construction agreement with Anthony, there would have been an implied warranty of merchantability.

A number of commentators have advocated a more policy-oriented approach to determining whether warranties of quality and fitness are implied with respect to goods sold as part of a hybrid transaction in which service predominates. See Farnsworth, Implied Warranties of Quality in Non-Sales Cases, 57 Colum. L. Rev. 653 (1957); Comment, Sale of Goods in Service-Predominated Transactions, 37 Fordham L. Rev. 115 (1968); Note, Products and the Professional: Strict Liability in the Sale-Service Hybrid Transaction, 24 Hastings L.J. 111 (1972); Note, Contracts for Goods and Services and Article 2 of the Uniform Commercial Code, 9 Rut.-Cam. L.J. 303 (1978); Comment, Sales-Service Hybrid Transactions: A Policy Approach, 28 Sw. L.J. 575 (1974). To support their position, these commentators in general emphasize loss shifting, risk distribution, consumer reliance and difficulties in the proof of negligence. These concepts underlie strict liability in tort. See Phipps v. General Motors Corp., 278 Md. 337, 363 A.2d 955 (1976).

A leading case applying a policy approach in this problem area is Newmark v. Gimbel's Incorporated, 54 N.J. 585, 258 A.2d 697 (1969). There the patron of a beauty parlor sued for injury to her hair and scalp allegedly resulting from a lotion used in giving her a permanent wave. Because the transaction was viewed as the rendering of a service, the trial court had ruled that there could be no warranty liability. The intermediate appellate court's reversal was affirmed by the Supreme Court of New Jersey which reasoned in part as follows (id., at 593, 258 A.2d at 701):

> The transaction, in our judgment, is a hybrid partaking of incidents of a sale and a service. It is really partly the rendering of service, and partly the supplying of goods for a consideration. Accordingly, we agree with the Appellate Division that an implied warranty of fitness of the products used in giving the permanent wave exists with no less force than it would have in the case of a simple sale. Obviously in permanent wave operations the product is taken into consideration in fixing the price of the service. The no-separate-charge

argument puts excessive emphasis on form and downgrades the overall substance of the transaction. If the beauty parlor operator bought and applied
the permanent wave solution to her own hair and suffered injury thereby, her
action in warranty or strict liability in tort against the manufacturer-seller of
the product clearly would be maintainable because the basic transaction would
have arisen from a conventional type of sale. It does not accord with logic to
deny a similar right to a patron against the beauty parlor operator or the manufacturer when the purchase and sale were made in anticipation of and for the
purpose of use of the product on the patron who would be charged for its use.
Common sense demands that such patron be deemed a customer as to both
manufacturer and beauty parlor operator. [Citations omitted.]

The court was careful to limit its holding to commercial transactions, as
opposed to those predominantly involving professional services. Id. at 596-
597, 258 A.2d at 702-703.

1 R. Anderson, Uniform Commercial Code (1970), §2-102:5 at 209
refers to *Newmark* as illustrative of a possible trend in the law and states:

It is probable that a goods-services transaction will come to be subjected to
Article 2 of the Code insofar as the contractor's obligations with respect to the
goods themselves are involved, at least where the goods involved could have
been purchased in the general market and used by the plaintiff-customer.

A warranty of fitness for particular purpose under §2-315 of the UCC
was implied in Worrell v. Barnes, 87 Nev. 204, 484 P.2d 573 (1971). In that
case a contractor was engaged to do some carpentry work and to connect
various appliances in the plaintiff's home to an existing liquefied petroleum
gas system. The appliances were not supplied by the contractor. Suit was
for damage to the plaintiff's home resulting from a fire. The plaintiff produced evidence that the fire was caused by a defective fitting installed by the
contractor which had allowed propane to escape. Dismissal of the plaintiff's
claims, based on the Nevada version of strict liability in tort and based on
implied warranty, was reversed. The court reasoned that, because it had held
that the contractor had sold a product so as to bring into operation the doctrine of strict liability, "so also must we deem this case to involve 'goods' within
the purview of the Uniform Commercial Code." Id. at 208, 484 P.2d at 576.

1 W. Hawkland, Uniform Commercial Code Series (1982), §2-102:04, at
Art. 2, p. 12 has suggested what might be called a "gravamen" test in light of
the decision in *Worrell.* He writes:

Unless uniformity would be impaired thereby, it might be more sensible and
facilitate administration, at least in this grey area, to abandon the "predominant factor" test and focus instead on whether the gravamen of the action
involves goods or services. For example, in Worrell v. Barnes, if the gas escaped
because of a defective fitting or connector, the case might be characterized as

one involving the sale of goods. On the other hand, if the gas escaped because of poor work by Barnes the case might be characterized as one involving services, outside the scope of the UCC.

In this state, the provisions of C.L. §2-316.1(1) and (2) reflect an implicit policy judgment by the General Assembly which prevents the mechanical application of the predominant purpose test to cases like the one under consideration. Subsection (1) states that §2-316, dealing in part with the manner in which an implied warranty of merchantability may be excluded or modified, does not apply to "consumer goods ... services, or both." Under subsection (2) language "used by a seller of consumer goods and services" to exclude or modify implied warranties is unenforceable. The hybrid transaction is covered by, or at least embraced within, those terms.

Under the predominant purpose test, as applied by a majority of the courts, a hybrid transaction must first be classified as a sale of goods in order for there to be UCC-based, implied warranties on the goods included in the transaction. If goods predominate and they are consumer goods, §2-316.1 would render contractual disclaimers of implied warranties ineffective because that section applies to a seller of consumer goods. In such cases the result of applying the predominant purpose test is consistent with §2-316.1. If, however, the predominant purpose test results in classifying the transaction as a contract for services there would, under the majority approach, be no UCC-based, implied warranties on goods included in the transaction. But, §2-316.1 declares that a seller of consumer services may not contractually disclaim implied warranties. In the hybrid transaction, at least one effect of §2-316.1 is to render ineffective contractual disclaimers of implied warranties on consumer goods included in a consumer service transaction. Section 2-316.1 is at least partially predicated on a legislative understanding that warranties under the UCC are implied as to the goods included in such transactions. An all or nothing classification of the instant transaction under the predominant purpose test would mean there could be no UCC-based, implied warranties on the diving board and would be contrary to the legislative policy implicit in §2-316.1. Consequently, we cannot use that test in order to determine whether UCC-based warranties are implied as to consumer goods in a transaction that is predominantly for the rendering of consumer services.

The gravamen test of Dean Hawkland suggests the vehicle for satisfying the legislative policy. Accordingly, we hold that where, as part of a commercial transaction, consumer goods are sold which retain their character as consumer goods after completion of the performance promised to the consumer, and where monetary loss or personal injury is claimed to have resulted from a defect in the consumer goods, the provisions of the Maryland UCC dealing with implied warranties apply to the consumer goods, even if the transaction is predominantly one for the rendering of consumer services. The facts of the instant case, however, make it unnecessary for us presently to decide whether §2-316.1 would require that UCC-based, implied warranties also extend to consumer goods which are used up in the course of rendering the consumer service to the consumer.

Thus the diving board which Anthony sold to the Sheehans as part of the swimming pool construction contract carried an implied warranty of merchantability under C.L. §2-314. Anthony's contractual disclaimer of that warranty was ineffective under C.L. §2-316.1. As a result, the trial court erred in relying on the disclaimer as a basis for directing a verdict in favor of Anthony on the warranty count....

Judgment of the court of special appeals affirmed. Costs to be paid by Anthony Industries, Inc.

PROBLEM 2

Boswell Consultants purchased a Hawking 2020 printer from Ganges Devices. For the contract price, Ganges Devices agreed to deliver the internet-enabled printer along with its software, to store printed files in Ganges's cloud, to provide remote diagnostic and maintenance, and to provide software updates tailored to Boswell Consultants' pattern of use. Is the transaction covered by Article 2? See §2-105(1); Stacy-Ann Elvy, Hybrid Transactions and the Internet of Things: Goods, Services or Software?, 34 Wash. & Lee L. Rev. 77, 134 (2017) (citing Douglas J. Whaley & Stephen M. McJohn, Problems and Materials on Commercial Law 32 (11th ed. 2016)).

B.   Merchants

PROBLEM 3

Portia Moot, a third-year law student, sold her car to a fellow student. Does Article 2 of the UCC apply to this transaction? Would §2-314 apply to the sale?

Frix v. Integrity Medical Systems, Inc.
United States District Court, Western District of Tennessee,
Eastern Division, 2017, 2017 WL 4171987

S. Thomas Anderson, Chief United States District Judge

...

Plaintiff, as the owner and operator of several medical clinics throughout west Tennessee, wanted to expand the services at his clinics to include mammography. In order to do so, Plaintiff specifically sought to place a

64-slice CT scanner, then located at his Henderson clinic, inside a mobile trailer with the new mammography equipment. Plaintiff owned the mobile trailer, but it was currently occupied by a 4-slice CT scanner. Plaintiff sought to solve all of these issues at once and solicited bids from three medical equipment companies (1) to uninstall and remove the four-slice CT scanner from his trailer, (2) to transport and install the 64-slice CT scanner inside that same trailer, and (3) for new mammography equipment that would also be installed in the trailer. Defendant ultimately submitted the lowest bid to Plaintiff. Though the parties disagree on the legal results of what occurred next, they do not dispute that informal discussions took place. Nor do they dispute that the discussions eventually resulted in a contract between the parties (the "Contract"). Plaintiff alleges he simply accepted Defendant's bid and e-mailed David Denholtz, owner of Defendant, to confirm the terms of the deal....

For section 2-207 to have the effect that Defendant desires upon the Contract—the addition of the terms of the Purchase Agreement to the Contract despite the lack of evidence of Plaintiff ever having seen or agreed to them—the Contract must be "between merchants." Tenn. Code Ann. §47-2-207(2)(c). "Between merchants," in the UCC, "means in any transaction with respect to which both parties are chargeable with the knowledge or skill of merchants." Id. §47-2-104(3). Defendant relies on the statutory definition of merchant and Official Comment 1 to this provision in its assertion that Plaintiff is a merchant under the UCC. Def.'s Resp., at 12 n.2 (citing Fla. Stat. Ann. §672.104, cmt. 1) ("This Article assumes that transactions between professionals in a given field require special and clear rules which may not apply to a casual or inexperienced seller or buyer."). Plaintiff argues that Defendant has offered no evidence that Plaintiff is a merchant within the meaning of the statute. Indeed, Plaintiff points out that he does not deal in medical equipment and lacks particular knowledge or skill with respect to such equipment. Reply, at 2 n.3. Plaintiff relies on two Florida cases in support of his position. Id. at 2-3 n.3. Neither the Tennessee Supreme Court nor the Sixth Circuit has spoken to the issue of whether a physician that purchases equipment for his practice constitutes a merchant under the UCC. As there is no binding authority upon the Court as to this issue, it begins its analysis with the statutory language of the definition.

The UCC defines "[m]erchant" as "a person who deals in goods of the kind or otherwise by his occupation holds himself out as having knowledge or skill peculiar to the practices or goods involved in the transaction...." Tenn. Code Ann. §47-2-104(1). No evidence before the Court suggests that Plaintiff is a seller of CT scanners or mammography equipment, so it will restrict its analysis to the latter portion of the definition. To discern whether Plaintiff is a merchant under the UCC, the Court must decide whether Plaintiff is "a person who ... by his occupation holds himself out as having knowledge or skill peculiar to the practices or goods involved in the transaction."

Id. Plaintiff insists that he does not hold himself out as having such knowledge or skill. Pl.'s Reply, at 2 n.3. But that is not the relevant inquiry. The definition does not require a person who holds himself out as having a particular knowledge or skill but who does so "*by his occupation.*" Tenn. Code Ann. §47-2-104(1) (emphasis added); see also Loeb & Co. v. Schreiner, 321 So. 2d 199, 202 (Ala. 1975) ("[A] person cannot be considered a 'merchant' [under section 2-104] simply because he is a braggart or has a high opinion of his knowledge in a particular area.").

To Plaintiff's credit, the Tennessee Court of Appeals has adopted an individualized approach for farmers. Brooks Cotton Co. v. Williams, 381 S.W.3d 414 (Tenn. Ct. App. 2012). The test adopted by the court provides a nonexhaustive list of four factors for use in determining whether a *particular* farmer is a merchant based upon his own personal business sophistication. Id. at 425. While the decisions of the Tennessee Court of Appeals are not binding upon this Court, and this particular analysis seems applicable only to farmers, the departure in reasoning between the Court of Appeals and this Court is worth highlighting nonetheless. An individualized approach stands in stark contrast to the occupation-based approach that the language of the statute plainly calls for. The court seems to ultimately distinguish between a regular farmer and an "experienced commercial farmer[]." Id. at 427-28. The Tennessee Court of Appeals was faced with persuasive authority that ranged from "It is inconceivable that the drafters of the [UCC] intended to place the average farmer, who merely grows his yearly crop and sells it to the local elevator, etc., on equal footing with the professional commodities dealer whose sole business is the buying and selling of farm commodities," Pierson v. Arnst, 534 F. Supp. 360, 362 (D. Mont. 1982), to "This court does not believe that anyone in this day and age looks upon any person or corporation who conducts a farming operation as a simple tiller of the soil," Rush Johnson Farms, Inc. v. Mo. Farmers Ass'n, 555 S.W.2d 64 (Mo. Ct. App. 1977). *Brooks Cotton Co.*, 381 S.W.3d at 423-26. The court ultimately adopted its test from the Colorado Court of Appeals, which noted an evolution in the general sophistication of the farmer. Id. at 425 (quoting Colo.-Kan. Grain Co. v. Reifschneider, 817 P.2d 637 (Colo. Ct. App. 1991)). Unless experience and sophistication are capable of dividing farmers into distinguishable occupations, however, this Court cannot reconcile an individualized test with the clear dictates of the statute. According to section 47-2-104(1), the person must hold himself out with the peculiar knowledge by his occupation rather than by his individual experience or level of sophistication. A person's occupation is his or her "usual or principal work or business, esp[ecially] as a means of earning a living." Occupation, *The Random House Dictionary of the English Language* (2d unabridged ed. 1987). The novice that manages to make his living from the smallest patch of earth may call himself a farmer as much as any agricultural corporate giant. Any distinction is therefore immaterial to this Court's analysis of section 47-2-104(1). What changes from case to case are the goods or practices involved in transactions. Thus, the issue then becomes whether a physician inherently holds himself out as having knowledge or skills peculiar to medical equipment or the installation thereof.

This is of course a much narrower reading of "merchant" than Defendant argues for. But Defendant's apparent assertion that the UCC envisions merchants as encompassing all professionals is inconsistent with the statutory language, which significantly restricts the knowledge or skill that would trigger the merchant provisions to such "knowledge or skill *peculiar to the practices or goods involved in the transaction.*" Tenn. Code Ann. §47-2-104(1) (emphasis added). The Tennessee General Assembly did not include the Official Comments in the provisions of 47-2-104. United Foods, Inc. v. Hadley-Peoples Mfg. Co., 1994 Tenn. App. LEXIS 277, at *13, 1994 WL 228773 (Tenn. Ct. App. May 20, 1994) (citing Tenn. Code Ann. §47-2-207(2) & cmt. 3) (rejecting the argument that the use by Official Comment 3 to section 47-2-207 of "additional or different terms" was applicable when section 47-2-207(2) only called for "additional terms" because "the drafters could easily have included 'or different' in [section] 47-2-207(2) if they had so intended"). Defendant would perhaps be correct in relying on the legislature's use of "practices" in hopes that "practice" is meant in the sense of "the business of a professional person." Practice, *The Random House Dictionary of the English Language* (2d unabridged ed. 1987). Defendant could then argue that Plaintiff, by virtue of being a doctor, is charged with the requisite knowledge and skill peculiar to the practice of medicine, and this is sufficient to constitute a merchant under the UCC. It is true that one such rule, known as the last-reasonable-referent canon, provides that subsequent modifying language usually only modifies the closest reasonable word. Carroll v. Sanders (In re Sanders), 551 F.3d 397, 399 (6th Cir. 2008) (quoting Bryan A. Garner, *Garner's Modern American Usage* 523-24 (2003)) ("[W]hen a word … points back to a [] … referent, the true referent should generally be the closest appropriate word."); see also Lockhart v. United States, 136 S. Ct. 958, 962 (2016) (citing Barnhart v. Thomas, 540 U.S. 20, 26 (2003); Rule of the last antecedent, *Black's Law Dictionary* 1532-33 (10th ed. 2014); Scalia & Garner, supra note 8, at 144) ("The rule provides that 'a limiting clause or phrase … should ordinarily be read as modifying only the noun or phrase that it immediately follows.'"). Under that rule, it would not be unreasonable to suggest that the modifier "involved in the transaction" modifies the word "goods" but not "practices." But the rule of the last reasonable referent "can assuredly be overcome by other indicia of meaning." *Barnhart*, 540 U.S. at 26. For example, "the … rule does not generally apply … when '[t]he modifying clause appear[s] … at the end of a single, integrated list.' " *Lockhart*, 136 S. Ct. at 970 (Kagan, J., dissenting) (quoting Jama v. Immigration and Customs Enforcement, 543 U.S. 335, 344 n.4 (2005)). " 'When there is a straightforward, parallel construction that involves all nouns or verbs in a series,' a modifier at the end of the list 'normally applies to the entire series.'" Id. (quoting Scalia & Garner, supra note 8, at 147). Here, the phrase "the practices or goods" is written in a parallel construction. Both words are plural, and the definite article "the" is carried over to both words. See Scalia & Garner, supra note 8, at 147 (citations omitted) ("The typical way in which syntax would suggest no carryover modification is that a determiner (*a, the, some*, etc.) will be repeated before the second element."). Thus, "involved in the transaction" modifies both "practices" and "goods," restricting the meaning of practices in the instant case to the "business of a professional person" involved in the sale or installation of medical equipment. The Court now turns to resolving whether a physician inherently holds himself out as having knowledge or skills peculiar to medical equipment or the installation thereof.

In response to Defendant's assertion that Plaintiff is a merchant under the UCC, Plaintiff cites two cases: first, Czarnecki v. Roller, 726 F. Supp. 832, 843 (S.D. Fla. 1989), for the proposition that a "a party who engages in only a handful of transactions with respect to a particular good is not a 'merchant'"; and, second, Porter v. Rosenberg, 650 So. 2d 79, 81-82 (Fla. Dist. Ct. App. 1995), for the proposition that physicians are "more akin to the consumer or user of the product, especially where the product is not transferred to the patient but utilized incidental [sic] to the provision of medical services." Pl.'s Reply, at 2-3. The Court finds the first case irrelevant to its analysis. How often a person engages in the sales for a particular good goes to whether he is a "deal[er] in goods of the kind," a portion of the definition that clearly does not apply to Plaintiff. See Tenn. Code Ann. §47-2-104(1). A person's occupation can present that person to the world as having certain knowledge regardless of how many times they actually enter into a transaction so long as the knowledge is distinctive to the practices or goods involved in the disputed transaction. See id. The proposition Plaintiff draws from the second case certainly makes a lot of sense, but it speaks more to a common understanding of merchant rather than the UCC's definition. Common sense and understanding, however, are what must finally decide this dispute lest the Court and the parties remain forever more entangled in the UCC's provisions. A physician, put simply, is "a person qualified to practice medicine." Physician, *New Oxford American Dictionary* (3d ed. 2010). And medicine is "the science or practice of the diagnosis, treatment, or prevention of disease." Medicine, supra. This practice necessarily includes the ability to use various types of medical equipment, but the ability to use a machine is not a skill peculiar to one's practice.

> Physicians, like hospitals, are providers of medical services. The physician's expertise lies in the diagnosis, treatment and cure of illness, not in the research or development of prosthetics or devices used to aid medical diagnosis or treatment.... Products ... case are supplied and utilized only as needed to deliver the professional medical service. They are incidental, or integral, to a physician's service, but they are not the focus of the physician's delivery of health care.

Porter v. Rosenberg, 650 So. 2d 79, 81-82 (Pa. Super. Ct. 1995) (discussing health care providers in a strict liability context). Yes, the physician is more like the consumer in these transactions. But the reason that physicians are not merchants under the UCC is that physicians are not experts in the equipment itself. There is nothing peculiar about being able to use a machine for its intended purpose. And there is no indication that physicians generally know how to take apart, put back together, install, or repair complicated pieces of machinery. Nor is there an indication that physicians can converse easily about the market for medical equipment. Cf. Brooks Cotton Co. v. Williams, 381 S.W.3d 414, 424-25 (Tenn. Ct. App. 2012) (holding that farmers could constitute merchants under the UCC because of their "extensive knowledge and sophistication regarding the purchase and sale of crops on the various agricultural markets"). The Court finds that a physician, by mere virtue of being a physician, does not hold himself out as having skills or knowledge peculiar to the sale or installation of medical equipment. Accordingly, the Court must conclude that Plaintiff is not a merchant under the UCC, and, therefore, the Purchase Agreement cannot be part of the Contract under section 2-207.

Plaintiff's Motion for Partial Summary Judgment is hereby GRANTED.

Notice that the definition of *merchant* in §2-104(1) refers not only to those who deal in the goods involved, but also those merchants who deal in the *practices* of the kind involved in the transaction. Official Comment 2 explains:

> The special provisions as to merchants appear only in this Article and they are of three kinds. Sections 2-201(2), 2-205, 2-207 and 2-209 dealing with the statute of frauds, firm offers, confirmatory memoranda and modification rest on normal business practices which are or ought to be typical of and familiar to any person in business. For purposes of these sections almost every person in business would, therefore, be deemed to be a "merchant" under the language "who ... by his occupation holds himself out as having knowledge or skill peculiar to the practices ... involved in the transaction ..." since the practices involved in the transaction are non-specialized business practices such as answering mail. In this type of provision, banks or even universities, for example, well may be "merchants." But even these sections only apply to a merchant in his mercantile capacity; a lawyer or bank president buying fishing tackle for his own use is not a merchant.
>
> On the other hand, in Section 2-314 on the warranty of merchantability, such warranty is implied only "if the seller is a merchant with respect to goods of that kind." Obviously this qualification restricts the implied warranty to a

much smaller group than everyone who is engaged in business and requires a professional status as to particular kinds of goods. The exception in Section 2-402(2) for retention of possession by a merchant-seller falls in the same class; as does Section 2-403(2) on entrusting of possession to a merchant "who deals in goods of that kind."

A third group of sections includes 2-103(1)(b), which provides that in the case of a merchant "good faith" includes observance of reasonable commercial standards of fair dealing in trade; 2-327(1)(c), 2-603, and 2-605 dealing with responsibilities of merchant buyers to follow seller's instructions, etc.; 2-509 on risk of loss; and 2-609 on adequate assurance of performance. This group of sections applies to persons who are merchants under either the "practices" or the "goods" aspect of the definition of merchant.

PROBLEM 4

Are the following persons merchants?

(a) Amanda, who quit her teaching job on Friday and on Monday opened a clothing store?

(b) Tom Tiller, a farmer selling his produce to a wholesaler? Compare Loeb & Co. v. Schreiner, 294 Ala. 722, 321 So. 2d 199 (1975) ("Although a farmer might sell his cotton every year, we do not think that this should take him out of the category of a 'casual seller' and place him in the category with 'professionals.' ") with Continental Grain Co. v. Brown (W.D. Wis. 1976) ("A sale of 75,000 bushels of corn for a total price in excess of $212,000 is not a 'casual' sale."). See also Vince v. Broome, 443 So. 2d 23 (Miss. 1983) ("Some farming operations are worth millions of dollars. . . . It would stretch the imagination to conclude that all these operations were exempt from coverage under the Commercial Code."); Ohio Grain Co. v. Swisshelm, 40 Ohio App. 2d 203, 318 N.E.2d 428 (1973) (the modern farmer is more than "a simple tiller of the soil, unaccustomed to the affairs of business and the marketplace. . . . Only an agribusinessman may hope to survive."); Harvest States Cooperatives v. Anderson, 217 Wis. 2d 154, 577 N.W.2d 381 (1998) (man who had some cows and made occasional sales of corn not a merchant).

III.   SCOPE OF ARTICLE 2A

In recent years equipment leasing has become big business. In 2018, industry analysts expect it to account for over $400 billion in outstanding contracts in the United States alone. Leasing goods (as opposed to purchasing them with cash or on credit) has certain advantages. It may be desirable for accounting reasons because the lease obligation is not reflected as an asset/liability, thus improving the balance sheet ratios. At various times there have been tax advantages to leasing goods, though the tax laws have fluctuated on this through the years.[3]

A major problem with all this is that the law of personal property leasing has not been clearly defined. It originally developed from the law of bailments and, by analogy, from the law governing the lease of real property, though it fit comfortably into neither. Where the law was unfavorable or nonexistent, model equipment leases were promulgated by various bodies. See, e.g., Antin, An Equipment Lease Form, 8 A.L.I.-A.B.A. Course Materials J. 117 (1983). Since the adoption of the Uniform Commercial Code, many courts have applied Article 2 to leases, either stating that this was the intention of the drafters — see §2-102, stating that Article 2 applies to "transactions" in goods — or using Article 2 by analogy. Since many of Article 2's sections apply only if a "sale" occurs — defined in §2-106(1) to require the passing of title from the seller to the buyer — the Code's rules have to be stretched a great deal to encompass a true lease of goods.

In 1987, the last of the various bodies involved approved for adoption a new version of the Uniform Commercial Code containing Article 2A, entitled "Leases." It is modeled in large part (some say too much)[4] on Article 2. Throughout the rest of this book, reference will be made to sections of Article 2A, particularly where those sections deviate from the similar rules in Article 2.

It is important to appreciate the kind of leases to which Article 2A applies. Sometimes a transaction is called a "lease" when it is in reality a sale of goods. This is done for various reasons: the bookkeeping and tax considerations mentioned above, plus the desire to escape from the necessity of complying with either Article 2 or the secured transaction rules of Article 9. If a so-called lease does not pass the tests described therein, Article 2A is not triggered. Instead, the "lease" will be governed by those Articles and treated as a disguised sale on credit, with the "lessor's" interest in reality being nothing

---

3. It has always been malpractice for the authors to say the word *tax* out loud, and this book therefore expresses no opinion on the current position of the Internal Revenue Code on this or any other subject.

4. "The Article 2A draftsmen's desire to follow the Article 2 model on occasion resulted in virtual unintelligibility to all but the most experienced and knowledgeable." Report of the Uniform Commercial Code Committee of the Business Law Section of the State Bar of California on Proposed California Commercial Code Division 10 (Article 2A) (1987), reprinted in 39 Ala. L. Rev. at 979, 984 (1988). California has adopted Article 2A with major overhauls to some of its sections. See also Kripke, Some Dissonant Notes About Article 2A, 39 Ala. L. Rev. 791 (1988).

more than the "reservation of a security interest."[5] If the so-called lease is really a sale disguised as a lease, then it qualifies as what Article 9 of the UCC calls a "secured transaction," meaning, in this case, a sale on credit, with the seller having the right to repossess the goods if payment is not made by using its "security interest" (i.e., a lien on the goods) to reclaim them (and being also required to follow the formidable rules of Article 9). If the "lease" is really a "sale," and the seller did not follow the Article 9 rules, it runs the substantial risk of losing the ability to repossess the goods and/or having junior priority in them to other creditors (or to the buyer's bankruptcy trustee). It is therefore very important for the so-called lessor to prevail in this argument, or (the smart thing) to take the precautionary step of complying with the rules of Article 9 in case it has to battle other Article 9 claimants to the goods; see §9-505 (allowing a filing without it necessarily being an admission of a disguised sale). Read the very complicated definition of *security interest* in §1-203, concentrating on the major part of it that attempts to distinguish between a true lease and a security interest (that is, a sale on credit disguised as a lease). What are we to make of this definition? The happiest thing about it (despite its formidable size) is that it does draw some bright lines to help attorneys tell leases from secured transactions:

(1) As under the original definition, if at the end of the lease period the lessee becomes the owner of the property for little or no consideration, a secured transaction and not a lease has been created.
(2) If the contract contains a clause that permits the lessee to terminate the lease at any time and return the leased goods (the so-called walk away test), a true lease has resulted. Such a right of termination is not an attribute of a sale of goods.
(3) If the lease is for the entire economic life of the leased goods, with or without renewal, a disguised sale has occurred.

Other than that, each lease must be evaluated on its own. It does not necessarily answer the central question if the lessee pays consideration equal to or even greater than the fair market value of the leased goods as long as the lease does not cover the total economic life of the goods. Nor does the lessee's assumption of major duties (taxes, risk of loss, etc.) necessarily indicate a lease or a sale of goods.

Use the definition and the above tests to answer the following Problem.

5. Professors James White and Robert Summers deal with Article 2A in their splendid treatise on the Uniform Commercial Code: see Chapters 15 and 16 in Volume 2 (6th ed. Practitioner Treatise Series 2014). This work is published in two editions: a multi-volume work for practitioners and a one-volume student edition. All further citations, unless noted, are to the student edition: J. White & R. Summers, Uniform Commercial Code (6th ed. 2010) [hereinafter White & Summers].

PROBLEM 5

BIG Machines, Inc., leased a computer to Helen's Flower Shoppe for a five-year period. The machine was new and had cost BIG Machines $10,000. Helen's Flower Shoppe promised to pay $225 a month as rent. Is this a lease or a disguised sale? Is your answer affected by the following considerations?

(a) The lease provided that the lessee could terminate the lease at any time and return the computer to the lessor.

(b) Assume there was no such option as described in (a), but the goods had no value at the end of the five-year period.

(c) Assume instead that the rental amount is only $150 a month and the computer will be worth $3,500 at the end of the five-year period. The lease has a clause giving Helen's Flower Shoppe the option to purchase the computer for that amount at that time. Is this a true lease? What if the lease *requires* the lessee to renew this lease at the end of the five-year period for another five years?

IV.   INTERNATIONAL SALES

Effective January 1, 1988, the United States became bound by a treaty: the United Nations Convention on Contracts for the International Sale of Goods (hereinafter CISG). The Convention covers only issues of contract formation and the rights and duties of the parties thereto. It excludes coverage of products liability issues; it does not address matters touching on contract validity, such as fraud, illegality, etc. As of this writing, 89 countries, including most of the important trading states, are parties.[6] The leading text on the CISG is J. Honnold, Uniform Law for International Sales Under the 1980 United Nations Convention (4th ed. 2009).

PROBLEM 6

Hegemony Enterprises, headquartered in New York, is about to sign a contract for the sale of men's clothing to Cosas Americana, a retailer in Mexico City. You are the lawyer for Hegemony Enterprises, and a company official calls you with the following questions:

---

6. As of 2018, the largest trading states not parties to the CISG were India, South Africa, Taiwan, and the United Kingdom. See http://www.uncitral.org/uncitral/en/uncitral_texts/sale_goods/1980CISG_status.html.

(a) Will the CISG apply to this transaction? See CISG Articles 1 and 2.

(b) If Hegemony Enterprises wants the law of New York to apply, can the parties so stipulate in the contract and avoid the CISG? See Article 6.

(c) If Hegemony Enterprises were selling toys to Cosas Americana, would the CISG apply? See Article 2(a).

CHAPTER 2 REVIEW QUESTIONS

What difference does it make if a transaction is a transaction in goods?
What law governs transactions in services?
How do courts differentiate between transactions in goods versus services?
What difference does it make if someone is a merchant, for purposes of
   Article 2 of the UCC?
How do courts distinguish between a sale of goods and a lease? Why?
When does the CISG apply to a transaction?

ASSESSMENT: MULTIPLE CHOICE QUESTIONS

1. Which of the following cases would most likely be governed by Article 2?
   a. Gately Construction provided detailed specifications for inventory control software. Van Dyne Apps agreed to design, develop, and test software to meet those specifications.
   b. Van Dyne Apps agreed to provide inventory control software, update the software periodically, make any adaptations necessary to run it on Gately Construction's system, and train Gately Construction's employees to use the software.
   c. Van Dyne Apps sold Gately Construction a standard software package, identical to the package Van Dyne Apps sold to many small businesses.
   d. All of the above.

2. Incandenza liked a Marconi sedan offered at Pemulis Auto for $14,000, but wished to keep options open. Incandenza and Pemulis Auto signed a "Sales Contract," under which Incandenza would pay $400 per month to Pemulis Auto to use the car. Incandenza could at any time return the car and be obliged to make no more payments. Incandenza may also keep the car forever, as long as he makes the monthly payment. Does Article 2 apply to the transaction?
   a. Yes. The contract clearly states that it is a sales contract.
   b. No. The transaction is governed by UCC Article 2A, Leases.

c. Article 2 will apply until Incandenza returns the car.

d. Yes. The subject of the contract is a car, which falls into the category of goods, not services.

3. Avril agreed to design and build a custom wheelchair for Mario. The contract specified capabilities and dimensions of the chair and provided for Avril to determine the design and build the chair. Upon completion and delivery, Avril would be entitled to a lump-sum payment based on her time and other specified costs. Does Article 2 apply to the transaction?

a. Yes, because Article 2 applies to specially made goods.

b. No, because the predominant purpose of the contract is services in designing and building the chair.

c. No, because Avril is not a merchant.

d. Yes, because Avril is a merchant.

4. Steeply runs an art gallery in Baldwinsville, New York. She signs a contract to purchase a security system from Marathe Prevention of Montreal, Quebec. The contract provides that it is governed by Article 2 of the UCC. Is the contract governed by Article 2 of the UCC or by the Convention on Contracts for the International Sale of Goods (CISG)?

a. CISG, because the parties live in two countries that are party to the CISG.

b. UCC Article 2, because the CISG allows the parties to choose the law to govern their transaction.

c. Conduct in Quebec is governed by the CISG and conduct in the United States by UCC Article 2.

d. The parties must comply with all provisions of both the UCC and the CISG. Citizens do not choose the law.

5. Van Dyne Apps sold Gately Construction some software that would run its inventory control systems. What difference would it make if the transaction is governed by Article 2 of the UCC, rather than the common law of contracts?

a. Article 2 provides an implied warranty of merchantability, even if Van Dyne Apps did not make any specific promises about the software.

b. Article 2's rules on contract formation are more flexible, finding an enforceable contract even where there is no matching offer and acceptance.

c. Article 2's perfect tender rule may require the seller to deliver exactly the software agreed upon to be entitled to the price. Common law contract may only require substantial performance.

d. Article 2 will readily fill in gaps that the parties did not address, such as price or time for performance.

e. All of the above.

ANSWERS

1. *C* is the best answer. Courts routinely hold that the sale of standard software is a transaction in goods, subject to Article 2. *B* is at the other end of the goods/services spectrum. The contract not only requires the design and coding of software, but continued services to update and adapt the software, not to mention training employees. This would be predominantly services, not subject to Article 2. Answer *A* is a little more in the middle. As the cases in the chapter indicate, courts are somewhat split on whether a contract to design, develop, and implement software is a contract for services or for goods. So the case most likely to be governed by Article 2 is *C*.

2. *B* is the best answer. The parties called it a sale, but this is a lease: Incandenza may keep the car only as long as he pays for it, may terminate at any time, and never becomes the owner. The fact that the parties call it a sale has little weight, contrary to *A*. Both leases and sales may apply to goods, so *D* is misguided. *C* would give strange results.

3. *A* is the best answer. The contract calls for some services, but all geared toward providing the wheelchair, a specially made item of goods. All goods require services to be made, so any transaction in goods necessarily will require performance of services. This contract ultimately requires Avril to deliver goods, not to perform associated services such as training or maintenance. *C* and *D* are red herrings. They should remind us that Article 2 applies to transactions in goods, whether the parties are merchants or not. Some of the rules within Article 2 apply only to merchants.

4. *B* is the best answer. The CISG would apply to the contract, because the parties are residents of different CISG states. But Article 6 of the CISG allows parties to choose governing law. They chose Article 2, so Article 2 will provide the rules that govern their duties and rights under the contract. So parties can choose the law, sometimes, contrary to *D*. *C* is not the law, and would be strange to enforce.

5. *E* is the best answer. This question (instructive if not really fair, because it previews material ahead in the book) collects some of the biggest differences between UCC Article 2 and the common law of contracts. In the cases on the scope of Article 2, one party may be arguing that Article 2 applies so that the party gets an implied warranty of merchantability (answer *A*), or so that there will be an enforceable contract where the parties' forms or conduct show an agreement, even though there is no offer and acceptance (answer *B*), or so that the buyer can reject goods that did not match the contract, even if the seller substantially performed (answer *D*) or to use some other gap-filler in Article 2, such as finding a price where the parties did not specifically agree on price (answer *D*). That's really a lot of preview of what later chapters will cover. But that look ahead is helpful to show why it matters whether Article 2 applies to a transaction.

CONTRACT
FORMATION

The bargain of the parties to a sales contract must conform to most of the usual rules you learned in the course on Contracts, though Article 2 of the Uniform Commercial Code does change some of them. Thus the basics of contract formation should be reassuringly familiar to you already. Perhaps the UCC's approach to the Statute of Frauds, the parol evidence rule, and offer and acceptance were covered in the Contracts course. If not, as you learn these rules, rather than review them, contrast the UCC approach with the common law result and ask yourself why the drafters of the Code would have made these changes.

I. *THE STATUTE OF FRAUDS*

Read §2-201, which is quite a change from the original English Statute of Frauds from which it is descended. Passed in 1677 by Parliament, it was a statute that attempted to prevent fraud by requiring certain kinds of contracts to be in writing in order to be enforceable in a court of law (those involving real property, surety promises, etc.). The statute required certain sales contracts to be in writing, and §2-201 is its latest iteration.

At common law, when a contract fell within the Statute, *all* its terms and conditions had to be in writing or the contract was not enforceable. Under §2-201, a contract can be enforced even if a main term is omitted or misstated. The only term necessary for a sufficient memorandum under §2-201(1) is *quantity*.[1] Not only are the standards lessened by the Code, but also four exceptions are provided: merchant confirmation letters, special manufacture, part performance, and admission in legal proceedings.

Ellig v. Molina

United States District Court, Southern District of New York, 2014, 996 F. Supp. 2d 236

KATHERINE B. FORREST, District Judge:

Diamonds are not always a girl's best friend. Here, the particular diamond ring at issue — a 10-carat center stone in a platinum setting that included dozens of baguettes — drove friends apart.

The story starts with a cruise around the world, and ends in a courtroom in Manhattan. The cast of characters includes a jet-setting jeweler from Arizona; a financially conservative husband who is intent on investing wisely and who wants to (and does) buy his wife a special ring for a significant birthday, trusting in the ring's value; and a wife appreciative of the gesture, but concerned about the ring's cost and actual value. Buyer's and receiver's remorse set in; that might have been the end of the story, if it were not for the fact that the jeweler had promised that plaintiffs could return the ring within one year and that he would buy it back. In fact, plaintiffs claim that said jeweler, Alfred Molina himself, had also agreed to pay them 10% in addition to the purchase price — in effect, guaranteeing the price of the ring and a 10% return on the investment if returned within a year.

Unfortunately, this promise was not in writing. The parties generally agree that there was a promise of some sort; but, rather unsurprisingly, disagree as to important details. This lawsuit followed; a bench trial was held on January 10, 2014. At that trial, the now former friends testified as to their version of events. This Opinion & Order constitutes the Court's findings of fact and conclusions of law.

In summary, the Court finds that, in exchange for plaintiffs' purchase of the ring, defendants agreed to buy it back at full price plus 10% if tendered within one year. By failing to hold up their end of the bargain, defendants have breached the contract.

---

1. White and Summers note that one could (contrary to the weight of authority) interpret §2-201(1) *not* to require a quantity, but rather to say only that *if* a quantity is specified, the agreement cannot be enforced beyond that quantity. White & Summers §3-4, at 97 n.12.

I.   FINDINGS OF FACT

At trial, the Elligs and Mr. Molina provided direct testimony by written declaration and were subject to live cross-examination and re-direct. The Court found both of the Elligs very credible. Mrs. Ellig is an articulate and sophisticated businesswoman; her answers were consistent and direct. She was never evasive. The Court credits her testimony *in toto*. Mr. Ellig is also a sophisticated businessperson who is clearly very detail-oriented and careful. He was clear, consistent and articulate in Court. He was never evasive. The Court similarly credits his testimony *in toto*. In contrast, the Court found Mr. Molina lacking in credibility; he was evasive, argumentative and inconsistent. The Court does not believe his version of the agreement between the parties.

Plaintiffs and defendant Molina met on an around-the-world trip in 2007. (Decl. of Janice Ellig ("JE Decl.") ¶4, ECF No. 74.) He introduced himself as a world-renowned jeweler. (Decl. of Bruce R. Ellig ("BE Decl.") ¶5, ECF No. 75.) Mr. Molina is the sole shareholder in Molina, Inc., which operates two jewelry stores under the name Molina Fine Jewelers ("MFJ"). (Trial Decl. of Alfred Molina ("Molina Decl.") ¶3, ECF No. 77.) The Elligs and Mr. Molina became close friends and socialized together with Mr. Molina's then wife. (JE Decl. ¶¶5-6.) Mr. Molina was a regular guest in the Elligs' home when he came to New York for business. (Id. ¶8.) Mr. Molina would use the word "brother" when he contacted Mr. Ellig regarding a prospective visit — stating, for instance, "Hey, brother, I am coming to visit you and will arrive on _____." (BE Decl. ¶7.) The Elligs and Molinas also travelled together to Eastern Europe, Sicily and the Caribbean. (JE Decl. ¶9.)

During the time the Elligs and Molinas spent together, Mr. Molina spoke about diamonds as an investment. (BE Decl. ¶9.) Mr. Ellig considers himself fiscally conservative. (Id.) He has invested primarily in municipal bonds. (Id.) He conveyed this to Mr. Molina on a number of occasions. (Id.)

Mrs. Ellig's 65th birthday was in 2011. In December 2010, Mr. Ellig told Mr. Molina that Mrs. Ellig's 65th birthday was approaching, as was their 17th wedding anniversary, and that he wanted to do something special to mark those occasions. (BE Decl. ¶10.) Mr. Molina suggested that Mr. Ellig buy her a large diamond ring. (Id.) Mr. Molina stated that diamonds appreciate and therefore were a safe investment. (Id.) Mr. Ellig was initially skeptical; he was contemplating a gift in the range of a couple of hundred thousand dollars, and Mr. Molina told him that a large diamond befitting his wife would cost three times that amount. (BE Decl. ¶11.) Mr. Ellig told Mr. Molina that if he were even to consider spending that kind of money, the purchase would have to be not only a gift but also an investment. (Id.)

Mr. Ellig stated that, as much as he wanted to do something special for his wife, the appropriateness of the investment depended on his ability to get his money back. (BE Decl. ¶12.) In that very first conversation in December 2010, Mr. Molina stated that, if the Elligs purchased the ring and were unhappy with it for any reason at all, he would buy it back within a year for the full purchase price plus a guaranteed 10%. (Id. ¶13.) The agreement was not reduced to writing. Mr. Ellig and Mr. Molina had a number of conversations about the ring following this first one, and in each, Mr. Molina repeated the benefits of investing in diamonds and the guarantee he was providing. (Id. ¶¶15-16.) In each of these conversations, the terms of the guarantee remained the same. (Id. ¶16.)

At no time prior to the Elligs' purchase of the ring — and indeed not until July 2012 — did Mr. Molina mention a consignment arrangement or a waiting period before their money would be returned. (See BE Decl. ¶¶16-17.)

As her birthday approached, the Elligs discussed the possibility of Mr. Ellig buying his wife a diamond ring. (JE Decl. ¶15; BE Decl. ¶19.) The Elligs never discussed purchasing a loose diamond (that is, a diamond not yet set into a ring or other piece of jewelry); their discussions always related to a wearable diamond ring. (JE Decl. ¶21.)

Mrs. Ellig then spoke with Mr. Molina about acquiring a ring with a diamond in the 8-to-10 carat range. (JE Decl. ¶16.) Mrs. Ellig informed Mr. Molina that their budget was $300,000 to $350,000. (Id.) During April to June, the conversations became more serious. (Id. ¶17.)

Prior to receipt of the ring, Mrs. Ellig had a conversation with Mr. Molina in her kitchen in which she expressed to Mr. Molina her concern that, given the price of the ring, she had to be certain it was a good investment. (Trial Tr. 40, Jan. 10, 2014.) Molina told her in substance not to worry, that diamonds were an investment that did not lose value, and that he would repurchase the ring and guarantee another 10% if the Elligs were not happy with it. (Tr. 40-41.) Mrs. Ellig testified credibly at trial that Mr. Molina repeated his promise to buy the ring back (plus 10%) on multiple occasions. (JE Decl. ¶19.) The Elligs subsequently agreed to buy a ring for over $700,000. (Id. ¶¶25-26.) They both testified credibly that they did so in reliance on the specific and repeated representations by Mr. Molina regarding the buy-back promise. (Id. ¶¶21, 23.)

On June 21, 2011, Mr. Molina came to Manhattan with a ring with a more than 10-carat diamond center stone; he showed it to Mrs. Ellig. (JE Decl. ¶24; BE Decl. ¶¶21, 23.) The diamond was in a setting when Mr. Molina first showed it to her. (Tr. 64-65; JE Decl. ¶24.) Mrs. Ellig had some concerns about clarity and expressed them to Mr. Molina. (BE Decl. ¶20.) Mr. Molina stated that the ring was a good deal, and that what she was noticing was its blue fluorescence, which made it even more valuable. (Id.) At trial, Mr. Molina maintained that the blue fluorescence was an advantage and added value. (Molina Decl. ¶11.)

To address Mrs. Ellig's clarity concerns, Mr. Molina suggested boiling the ring; when Mrs. Ellig was still dissatisfied with the color of the ring, Mr. Molina suggested the addition of baguettes in the setting. (BE Decl. ¶¶21-22.)

Mr. Ellig paid for the diamond stone and the setting in two separate payments: he wired Mr. Molina $580,000 on June 21, 2011, and $71,188 on June 30, 2011. (BE Decl. ¶¶23-24.)

The Elligs' negotiations regarding purchase of the ring and the terms of return were solely with Mr. Molina; he made statements to them as an individual and not purporting to act through or on behalf of a corporate entity. However, the invoices for the ring were in the name of Molina Fine Jewelers, and the payments sent for the ring were to Molina Inc. (See PX1, PX2, PX12, DX1-DX4.) The Court finds that Mr. Molina made a personal promise that he and/or his wholly owned company — acting with regard to the ring indistinguishably — would buy back the ring within one year.

Mr. Molina did not leave the ring behind, but returned with it to Arizona, where a new setting was designed. (JE Decl. ¶29; BE Decl. ¶22.) The ring in the form in which it currently exists was finished and presented to Mrs. Ellig in late July or early August 2011; this was approximately two to three weeks after he showed the original ring to Mrs. Ellig. (Tr. 51-52; JE Decl. ¶¶28-29.) Mr. Molina provided the Elligs with a valuation by Mr. Molina himself, which they could use for insurance purposes, which valued the ring for $925,000. (BE Decl. ¶¶25-26.)

Shortly after receiving the ring, Mrs. Ellig began to have misgivings. She continued to be bothered by the center stone's strong blue fluorescence. (JE Decl. ¶30.) She expressed her concerns to Mr. Molina soon after she received it; he told her that the blue fluorescence made the ring whiter. (Id.)

Over the course of the next 10 months, Mrs. Ellig's concerns about the color of the ring continued. (Id. ¶33.) She had several people she believed were knowledgeable in the area provide her with their views as to the value of the ring; their valuations came in at a number far lower than the Elligs had paid. (JE Decl. ¶¶34, 37.) During the holiday season of 2011, Mrs. Ellig informed Mr. Molina of the third-party opinions regarding the ring's value; their relationship began to sour. (Id. ¶¶36-37.) In May 2012, Mrs. Ellig and Mr. Molina were both in attendance at a shareholders' conference in Omaha, Nebraska. (Id. ¶39.) Mrs. Ellig and Mr. Molina visited a jewelry store in town, and Mrs. Ellig was struck by how her ring compared to others at lower prices; she believed hers lacked the same sparkle. (Id.) Later that same month, the Elligs decided to return the ring. (Id. ¶41.) She called Mr. Molina at the end of May or beginning of June 2012 and informed him of that decision. (Tr. 61; JE Decl. ¶41; BE Decl. ¶¶29-30.)

On July 11, 2012, Mr. Molina sent the Elligs a letter, which was referred to throughout the trial as the "Dear Brother letter," (JE Decl. ¶42.) That letter confirms that the parties had an agreement with respect to the return of the ring. (See id.) The letter provided a chronology of the Elligs' purchase of the ring. It states that Mr. Molina presented the "diamond" to Mrs. Ellig in June and that she subsequently wanted changes to the setting. (Tr. 46-48; JE Decl. ¶42.) At trial, Mr. Molina testified that he had never presented Mrs. Ellig with a loose stone. (Tr. 116-17.) The letter reads in relevant part as follows:

> When we discussed the risk of you purchasing the diamond, I made several statements to both of you.
>   1. If you decide that you do not want the diamond a year from now, I would get your money back and a 10% return on your money. I understand that is your understanding that I committed to buy the stone and you are correct. The only gray area is that for me to do so I have to sell the stone. (I am prepared to provide you with a financial note that guarantees the funds and a return.)

(JE Decl. ¶42; BE Decl. ¶31; PX4.)

The "gray area" referred to in the letter (selling the diamond prior to giving the Elligs their money back) was not part of the original agreement between the parties. (BE Decl. ¶32.) Mr. Ellig testified credibly that a consignment arrangement emerged for the first time after the Elligs told Mr. Molina that they wanted to return the ring. Mr. Molina initially explained the need to sequence the events in this manner as due to a lack of immediate funds on his part. (Tr. 75.) The Court agrees that any consignment arrangement was an *ex post facto* attempt to avoid the terms of the guarantee that Mr. Molina had made to the Elligs.

Mr. Ellig declined to provide the ring — even with the financial guarantee offered — prior to receiving full payment. (Tr. 84-86.) At trial, he explained that he is a conservative investor, and that he did not want and had not bargained for the uncertainty that came with such an arrangement. (Tr. 86; BE Decl. ¶9.) In addition, Mrs. Ellig stated that she knew that Molina had debts and was concerned that if he sold the ring, the proceeds could be used to satisfy some other creditor. (JE Decl. ¶47.)

On July 12, 2012, Mr. Molina sent the Elligs a consignment agreement along with a guarantee of payment over time upon return of the ring. (JE Decl. ¶44; BE Decl. ¶33.) The Elligs did not enter into this agreement.

At trial, Mr. Molina testified that in his 45 years in the jewelry business, he has never promised or agreed to buy back any jewelry. (Molina Decl. ¶39.)

II.   Conclusions of Law

This is a straightforward breach of contract case: is there an enforceable buy-back guarantee between the parties and, if so, what are its terms?

Plainly, resolution of this dispute would have been far easier had the agreement between the parties been in writing at the outset. A clear writing would have provided certainty as to terms and therefore clarity as to breach. Neither party disputes that there was an oral agreement — but, as is clear from the above, they disagree as to certain provisions. Defendants argue that the lack of a writing at the outset dooms plaintiffs' claim: the statute of frauds requires, *inter alia*, contracts over a certain value or which cannot be completed within one year to be in writing. See N.Y. U.C.C. §2-201(1) (explaining that "a contract for the sale of goods for the price of $500 or more is not enforceable . . . unless there is some writing sufficient to indicate that a contract for sale has been made between the parties and signed by the party against whom enforcement is sought"); Dallas Aerospace, Inc. v. CIS Air Corp., 352 F.3d 775, 782 (2d Cir. 2003). The Elligs find themselves in the rather lucky position of having a confirming writing, with Mr. Molina's signature, that satisfies the statute of frauds: the "Dear Brother" letter is all that they need in this regard. Defendants also argue that the letter is not admissible under Federal Rule of Evidence 408 or that it cannot satisfy the statute of frauds, since the parties disagree as to whether the terms of the buy-back are accurately set forth in the letter. These arguments are both unavailing. . . .

Defendants' primary legal argument is that the statute of frauds requires a written contract, and that the lack of a written contract between the parties here therefore renders any promises unenforceable. Plaintiffs bear the burden of overcoming any statute of frauds requirement. See Trebor Sportswear Co., Inc. v. The Limited Stores, Inc., 865 F.2d 506, 509 (2d Cir. 1989). To carry this burden, plaintiffs must present sufficient admissible evidence of an agreement. Id. at 510. All that is required is that there is a writing that affords a basis for believing that the offered oral evidence of a contract and its terms refer to a real transaction. See Apex Oil Co. v. Vanguard Oil & Serv. Co., 760 F.2d 417, 423 (2d Cir. 1985). A sufficient writing in this regard (1) indicates that an agreement with obligations exists between the parties, (2) is signed, and (3) specifies a quantity of goods. See N.Y. U.C.C. §2-201(1). Several writings may be considered together. See Hawley Fuel Coalmart, Inc. v. Steag Handel GmbH, 796 F.2d 29, 30 (2d Cir. 1986).

THE CLASSIC PHRASE "HOISTED WITH HIS OWN PETARD" APPLIES HERE

Defendant Molina himself drafted and sent to plaintiffs the written instrument that lays out the chronology leading up to the agreement for the purchase and sale of one ring, concedes that a guarantee exists, and further concedes that Mrs. Ellig's version of events is "correct." (JE Decl. ¶42; BE Decl. ¶31; PX4.) This writing is sufficient to meet the requirements of the statute of frauds. See Great Destinations, Inc. v. Transportes Aereos Portugueses S.A.R.L., 460 F. Supp. 1160, 1163-64 (S.D.N.Y. 1978) (finding several letters setting forth the essential terms of contracts to satisfy the statute of frauds); Crabtree v. Elizabeth Arden Sales Corp., 305 N.Y. 48, 53-54, 110 N.E.2d 551 (1953) (finding payroll cards to constitute sufficient writings under the statute although they came into existence subsequent to the contract's execution, because they contained essential elements such as the parties to the contract, the compensation to be received, and the duration of the contract); Nausch v. AON Corp., 2 A.D.3d 101, 769 N.Y.S.2d 481, 483 (App. Div. 1st Dep't 2003) (finding that documents such as a letter agreement, internal memorandum, and handwritten notes satisfied the statute of frauds).

To the extent that the price paid itself is contained in separate writings (the invoices tendered by Mr. Molina and the wire transfers tendered by the Elligs), the fact that they are not signed in the classic sense of bearing a personal signature is not fatal. Under the circumstances here, neither party has contested the amount paid; the wires bear indicia of reliability, as do the invoices, though the date upon which the invoices were sent or whether they were sent was disputed. Under these circumstances, that the purchase price is contained in separate, not-classically signed documents is nonetheless sufficient. See Babdo Sales, Inc. v. Miller-Wohl Co., 440 F.2d 962, 966 (2d Cir. 1971) (explaining that only one writing "must bear the signature of the party to be charged," while the unsigned document must "refer to the same transaction"); Crabtree, 305 N.Y. at 54, 110 N.E.2d 551 (explaining that "separate writings, connected with one another either expressly or by the internal evidence of subject-matter and occasion," satisfy the statute of frauds). . . .

Defendants argue that the Dear Brother letter is inadmissible as an offer of settlement. They raised this before trial in a motion in limine. The Court denied that motion at that time, but specifically invited defendants to bring out any facts they desired at trial which would support their position that the letter was an offer of settlement. (Tr. 3-6.) Defendants failed to do so.

Defendants also argue that, even if admissible, the Dear Brother letter is insufficient to satisfy the statute of frauds because it lacks certain terms, including that the return needed to be exercised within a year, as well as the date from which that year would run. In addition, defendants assert that the Dear Brother letter does not specify that there was any agreement with regard to the "setting" for the ring, as opposed to only the center diamond stone. According to defendants, the absence of clarity (no pun intended) as to whether the guarantee is with respect to the stone or the entire ring, as well as the amount of time within which the return needed to be exercised, are material terms that must be in a writing. Put another way, while plaintiffs argue that the Dear Brother letter is a sufficient writing to constitute confirmation of a contract, they then disagree with the terms of the letter.

Under these circumstances, the issue becomes: if the letter satisfies the statute of frauds, must this Court take as true the additional terms of the contract as reflected in the letter? No. See, e.g., Nausch, 769 N.Y.S.2d at 483.

While the Dear Brother letter is sufficient to confirm the contract between the parties — because it contains the essential terms related to Mr. Molina's commitment to buy the stone within a year — the terms expressed in the letter relating to a "gray area" do not, and need not for purposes of the statute of frauds, form part of the contract. Rather, the oral contract, whose existence the letter confirms, obligated defendants to buy back the ring within one year for the purchase price plus 10%. . . .

III. Conclusion

For the reasons set forth above, the Court finds that defendants Alfred Molina and Molina, Inc. d/b/a Molina Fine Jewelers have breached their contract with plaintiffs Janice and Bruce Ellig. Plaintiffs shall submit a proposed judgment within seven days, or by Monday, February 17, 2014.

SO ORDERED.

PROBLEM 7

On December 10, James Ross, president of Ross Ice Cream Shoppes, Inc., phoned Robert Scott, president of Amundsen Ice Company, and negotiated the purchase of two tons of ice from Amundsen at $256/ton. As they talked on the phone, Scott picked up a memo pad inscribed "Amundsen Ice Company From the Desk of the President," wrote on it "2 tons Ross Co.," and then scribbled his initials on it. When the parties hung up the phones, Scott placed the memo on a spindle marked "Orders." Ross wrote Scott a letter beginning "Dear Bob: This is to confirm our ice purchase deal . . .," which described their transaction completely. Scott received the letter on December 14. On January 17, Scott phoned Ross and denied the existence of the contract detailed in the Ross letter. Answer these questions:

(a) Does the memo pad note satisfy §2-201(1)? See §1-201(b)(37) and Official Comment 37.

(b) What legal effect did the December 14 letter have? Same result if Ross's letter failed to mention the quantity? Even if the letter satisfies the Statute of Frauds, is it conclusive as to the existence and terms of the contract? See Hinson-Barr, Inc. v. Pinckard, 292 S.C. 267, 356 S.E.2d 115 (1987).

(c) Did Scott's denial of the terms contained in Ross's letter avoid the operation of §2-201(2)? Suppose Scott had immediately written Ross a letter stating, "You haven't stated the terms correctly. We only agreed to sell you 1 ton." Would that letter be a sufficient notice of objection? See Simmons Oil Corp. v. Bulk Sales Corp., 498 F. Supp. 457 (D.N.J. 1980); Annot., 82 A.L.R.4th 709.

(d) Would an unsigned receipt for artworks satisfy §2-201? Beard v. Chase, 2017 WL 2674494 (N.Y. Sup. Ct. 2017).

St. Ansgar Mills, Inc. v. Streit

Supreme Court of Iowa, 2000, 613 N.W.2d 289

CADY, Justice.

A grain dealer appeals from an order by the district court granting summary judgment in an action to enforce an oral contract for the sale of corn based on a written confirmation. The district court held the oral contract was unenforceable because the written confirmation was not delivered within a reasonable time after the oral contract as a matter of law. We reverse the decision of the district court and remand for further proceedings.

I.   BACKGROUND FACTS AND PROCEEDINGS

St. Ansgar Mills, Inc. is a family-owned agricultural business located in Mitchell County. As a part of its business, St. Ansgar Mills buys corn from local grain farmers and sells corn to livestock farmers for feed. The price of the corn sold to farmers is established by trades made on the Chicago Board of Trade for delivery with reference to five contract months. The sale of corn for future delivery is hedged by St. Ansgar Mills through an offsetting futures position on the Chicago Board of Trade.

A sale is typically made when a farmer calls St. Ansgar Mills and requests a quote for a cash price of grain for future delivery based on the Chicago Board of Trade price for the delivery. The farmer then accepts or rejects the price. If the price is accepted, St. Ansgar Mills protects the price through a licensed brokerage house by acquiring a hedge position on the Chicago Board of Trade. This hedge position, however, obligates St. Ansgar Mills to purchase the corn at the stated price at the time of delivery. Thus, St. Ansgar Mills relies on the farmer who purchased the grain to accept delivery at the agreed price.

Duane Streit formerly resided in Mitchell County and currently practices veterinarian medicine in Carroll County. He also raises hogs. He owns a large hog farrowing operation in Carroll County and a hog finishing operation in Mitchell County near Osage. Streit purchased the Osage farm from his father in 1993. Duane's father, John Streit, resides in Mitchell County and helps Duane operate the Osage finishing facility.

Duane and his father have been long-time customers of St. Ansgar Mills. Since 1989, Duane entered into numerous contracts with St. Ansgar Mills for the purchase of large quantities of corn and other grain products. Duane would generally initiate the purchase agreement by calling St. Ansgar Mills on the telephone to obtain a price quote. If an oral contract was made, an employee of St. Ansgar Mills would prepare a written confirmation of the sale and either mail it to Duane to sign and return, or wait for Duane or John to sign the confirmation when they would stop in to the business.

John would regularly stop by St. Ansgar Mills sometime during the first ten days of each month and pay the amount of the open account Duane maintained at St. Ansgar Mills for the purchase of supplies and other materials. On those occasions when St. Ansgar Mills sent the written confirmation to Duane, it was not unusual for Duane to fail to sign the confirmation for a long period of time. He also failed to return contracts sent to him. Nevertheless, Duane had never refused delivery of grain he purchased by telephone prior to the incident which gave rise to this case.

On July 1, 1996, John telephoned St. Ansgar Mills to place two orders for the purchase of 60,000 bushels of corn for delivery in December 1996 and May 1997. This order followed an earlier conversation between Duane and St. Ansgar Mills. After the order was placed, St. Ansgar Mills completed the written confirmation but set it aside for John to sign when he was expected to stop by the business to pay the open account. The agreed price of the December corn was $3.53 per bushel. The price of the May corn was $3.73 per bushel.

John failed to follow his monthly routine of stopping by the business during the month of July. St. Ansgar Mills then asked a local banker who was expected to see John to have John stop in to the business.

John did not stop by St. Ansgar Mills until August 10, 1996. On that date, St. Ansgar Mills delivered the written confirmation to him.

Duane later refused delivery of the corn orally purchased on July 1, 1996. The price of corn had started to decline shortly after July 1, and eventually plummeted well below the quoted price on July 1. After Duane refused delivery of the corn, he purchased corn for his hog operations on the open market at prices well below the contract prices of July 1. St. Ansgar Mills later told Duane it should have followed up earlier with the written confirmation and had no excuse for not doing so.

St. Ansgar Mills then brought this action for breach of contract. It sought damages of $152,100, which was the difference between the contract price of the corn and the market price at the time Duane refused delivery.

Duane filed a motion for summary judgment. He claimed the oral contract alleged by St. Ansgar Mills was governed by the provisions of the Uniform Commercial Code, and was unenforceable as a matter of law under the statute of frauds. He claimed the written confirmation delivered to John on August 10, 1996 did not satisfy the statute of frauds for two reasons. First, he was not a merchant. Second, the confirmation was not received within a reasonable time after the alleged oral agreement.

The district court determined a jury question was presented on whether Duane was a merchant under the Uniform Commercial Code. However, the district court found the written confirmation did not satisfy the writing requirements of the statute of frauds because the delivery of the confirmation to John, as Duane's agent, did not occur within a reasonable time after

the oral contract as a matter of law. The district court found the size of the
order, the volatility of the grain market, and the lack of an explanation by
St. Ansgar Mills for failing to send the confirmation to Duane after John
failed to stop by the business as expected made the delay between July 1 and
August 10 unreasonable as a matter of law.

St. Ansgar Mills appeals. It claims a jury question was presented on the
issue of whether a written confirmation was received within a reasonable
time. . . .

III. STATUTE OF FRAUDS

The statute of frauds is one of the most well-known and venerable rules
applicable to contract law. Generally, it establishes an exception to the proposition that oral contracts are enforceable in a lawsuit if sufficiently proven
by requiring certain types of contracts to be in writing and signed by the
party against whom enforcement is sought. See Iowa Code §554.2201(1).

The statute of frauds originated in 17th century England to combat
the use of fraud and perjury by litigants in court proceedings to establish
oral contracts. See 2 E. Allan Farnsworth, Contracts §6.1, at 82-83 (2d ed.
1990). At the time, court rules prohibited parties to a lawsuit from testifying
as witnesses in their case, and, consequently, an oral contract could only be
established with testimony of third parties. See Azevedo v. Minister, 86 Nev.
576, 471 P.2d 661, 663 (1970). This prohibition allowed witnesses to be persuaded to give false testimony on behalf of a party in an effort to establish an
oral contract, leaving the other party at a distinct disadvantage. See James
J. O'Connell, Jr., Boats Against a Current: The Courts and the Statute of
Frauds, 47 Emory L.J. 253, 257 (1998) [hereinafter O'Connell].

In 1677, in response to this unsavory practice of using perjury to establish oral contracts, Parliament enacted the statute of frauds to require certain contracts to be supported by written evidence to be enforceable. 29
Car. 2, ch. 3 (1677) (Eng.); see Hugh E. Willis, Statute of Frauds — A Legal
Anachronism, 3 Ind. L.J. 427, 427 (1928). The statute included contracts
which were not only particularly susceptible to fraud, but those which posed
serious consequences of fraud, including contracts for the sale of goods or
property. See O'Connell, 47 Emory L.J. at 258.

Despite a difference in the court rules which gave rise to this statute
of frauds, our American legal culture quickly adopted the principle. James
J. White & Robert S. Summers, Uniform Commercial Code §2-1, at 50 (2d ed.
1980) [hereinafter White & Summers]. Iowa adopted the statute of frauds in
1851. See Iowa Code §§2409-2410 (1851). The statute of frauds also became
a part of the Uniform Sales Act in 1906, which Iowa subsequently adopted
in 1924. See 1919 Iowa Acts ch. 396 (initially codified at Iowa Code §§9930-
10007 (1924)). This statute required all contracts for the sale of goods to be
in writing. Over time, the Uniform Sales Act was replaced by the Uniform

Commercial Code.[2] The Uniform Commercial Code continued to adhere to the statute of frauds, but was limited in its provisions to the sale of goods in excess of $500. Iowa enacted its version of the Uniform Commercial Code in 1966 including the statute of frauds. See 1965 Iowa Acts ch. 413. Iowa's statute of frauds for the sale of goods now provides:

> Except as otherwise provided in this section, a contract for the sale of goods for the price of $500 or more is not enforced by way of action or defense unless there is some writing sufficient to indicate that a contract for sale has been made between the parties and signed by the party against whom enforcement is sought or by that party's authorized agent or broker.

Iowa Code §554.2201(1) (1995).

Although the statute of frauds has been deeply engrained into our law, many of the forces which originally gave rise to the rule are no longer prevalent. White & Summers §2-1, at 51. This, in turn, has caused some of the rigid requirements of the rule to be modified.

One statutory exception or modification to the statute of frauds which has surfaced applies to merchants. Id. §554.2201(2). Under section 554.2201(2), the writing requirements of section 554.2201(1) are considered to be satisfied if, within a reasonable time, a writing in confirmation of the contract which is sufficient against the sender is received and the merchant receiving it has reason to know of its contents, unless written notice of objection of its contents is given within ten days after receipt. Id. Thus, a writing is still required, but it does not need to be signed by the party against whom the contract is sought to be enforced. The purpose of this exception was to put professional buyers and sellers on equal footing by changing the former law under which a party who received a written confirmation of an oral agreement of sale, but who had not signed anything, could hold the other party to a contract without being bound. See White & Summers §2-3, at 55; Kimball County Grain Coop. v. Yung, 200 Neb. 233, 263 N.W.2d 818, 820 (1978). It also encourages the common, prudent business practice of sending memoranda to confirm oral agreements. White & Summers §2-3, at 55.

---

2. After six years of deliberating, the National Conference of Commissioners on Uniform State Laws produced the 1952 Official Text of the Uniform Commercial Code. See William A. Schnader, A Short History of the Preparation and Enactment of the Uniform Commercial Code, 22 U. Miami L. Rev. 1, 1-2 (1967). In 1954, Pennsylvania was the first state to formally adopt the text. See 13 Pa. Const. Stat. §§1101 to 9507 (1953). By 1968, the Uniform Commercial Code was effective in 49 states, the District of Columbia, and the Virgin Islands. See Uniform Commercial Code Table, 1 U.L.A. 1-2 (Master ed. 1989). There have been three official revisions, the 1972, the 1978, and the 1987 Official Texts, offered by the Permanent Editorial Board, a board established in 1961 to keep the Code up to date. See William A. Schnader, The Permanent Editorial Board for the Uniform Commercial Code: Can it Accomplish its Object?, 3 Am. Bus. L.J. 137, 138 (1965).

While the written confirmation exception imposes a specific ten-day requirement for a merchant to object to a written confirmation, it employs a flexible standard of reasonableness to establish the time in which the confirmation must be received. Iowa Code §554.2201(2). The Uniform Commercial Code specifically defines a reasonable time for taking action in relationship to "the nature, purpose and circumstances" of the action. Id. §554.1204(2) [UCC §1-204[3]]. Additionally, the declared purpose of the Uniform Commercial Code is to permit the expansion of commercial practices through the custom and practice of the parties. See Iowa Code Ann. §554.1102 cmt. 2 (course of dealings, usage of trade or course of performance are material in determining a reasonable time). Furthermore, the Uniform Commercial Code relies upon course of dealings between the parties to help interpret their conduct. Iowa Code §554.1205(1). Thus, all relevant circumstances, including custom and practice of the parties, must be considered in determining what constitutes a reasonable time under section 554.2201(2).

Generally, the determination of the reasonableness of particular conduct is a jury question. See Pirelli-Armstrong Tire Co. v. Reynolds, 562 N.W.2d 433, 436 (Iowa 1997); see also Harvey v. Great Atl. & Pac. Tea Co., 388 F.2d 123, 125 (5th Cir. 1968) (passing judgment on the reasonableness of conduct of the parties must be accomplished in light of all the circumstances of the case and should rarely be disposed of by summary judgment). Thus, the reasonableness of time between an oral contract and a subsequent written confirmation is ordinarily a question of fact for the jury. Mortgageamerica Corp. v. American Nat'l Bank, 651 S.W.2d 851, 856 (Tex. Ct. App. 1983); Schiavi Mobile Homes, Inc. v. Gagne, 510 A.2d 236, 238 (Me. 1986) (reasonableness of parties' time for action is a question of fact). It is only in rare cases that a determination of the reasonableness of conduct should be decided by summary adjudication. Harvey, 388 F.2d at 125. Summary judgment is appropriate only when the evidence is so one-sided that a party must prevail at trial as a matter of law. Ridgeway v. Union County Comm'rs, 775 F. Supp. 1105, 1109 (S.D. Ohio 1991).

There are a host of cases from other jurisdictions which have considered the question of what constitutes a reasonable time under the written confirmation exception of the Uniform Commercial Code. See Gestetner Corp. v. Case Equip. Co., 815 F.2d 806, 810 (1st Cir. 1987) (roughly five-month delay reasonable in light of merchants 'relationship and parties' immediate action under contract following oral agreement); Serna, Inc. v. Harman, 742 F.2d 186, 189 (5th Cir. 1984) (three and one-half month delay reasonable in light of the parties' interaction in the interim, and non-fluctuating

---

3. Now §1-302(b). — Ed.

prices, thus no prejudice); Cargill, Inc. v. Stafford, 553 F.2d 1222, 1224 (10th Cir. 1977) (less than one-month delay unreasonable despite misdirection of confirmation due to mistaken addressing); Starry Constr. Co. v. Murphy Oil USA, Inc., 785 F. Supp. 1356, 1362-63 (D. Minn. 1992) (six-month delay for confirmation of modification order for additional oil unreasonable as a matter of law in light of Persian Gulf War, thus increased prices and demand); Rockland Indus., Inc. v. Frank Kasmir Assoc., 470 F. Supp. 1176, 1179 (N.D. Tex. 1979) (letter sent eight months after alleged oral agreement for two-year continuity agreement unreasonable in light of lack of evidence supporting reasonableness of delay); Yung, 263 N.W.2d at 820 (six-month delay in confirming oral agreement delivered one day prior to last possible day of delivery unreasonable); Azevedo, 471 P.2d at 666 (ten-week delay reasonable in light of immediate performance by both parties following oral agreement); Lish v. Compton, 547 P.2d 223, 226-27 (Utah 1976) (twelve-day delay "outside the ambit which fair-minded persons could conclude to be reasonable" in light of volatile price market and lack of excuse for delay other than casual delay). Most of these cases, however, were decided after a trial on the merits and cannot be used to establish a standard or time period as a matter of law. Only a few courts have decided the question as a matter of law under the facts of the case. Compare *Starry,* 785 F. Supp. at 1362-63 (granting summary judgment), and *Lish,* 547 P.2d at 226-27 (removing claim from jury's consideration), with Barron v. Edwards, 45 Mich. App. 210, 206 N.W.2d 508, 511 (1973) (remanding for further development of facts, summary judgment improper). However, these cases do not establish a strict principle to apply in this case. The resolution of each case depends upon the particular facts and circumstances.

In this case, the district court relied upon the large amount of the sale, volatile market conditions, and lack of an explanation by St. Ansgar Mills for failing to send the written confirmation to Duane in determining St. Ansgar Mills acted unreasonably as a matter of law in delaying delivery of the written confirmation until August 10, 1996. Volatile market conditions, combined with a large sale price, would normally narrow the window of reasonable time under section 554.2201(2). However, they are not the only factors to consider. Other relevant factors which must also be considered in this case reveal the parties had developed a custom or practice to delay delivery of the confirmation. The parties also maintained a long-time amicable business relationship and had engaged in many other similar business transactions without incident. There is also evidence to infer St. Ansgar Mills did not suspect John's failure to follow his customary practice in July of stopping by the business was a concern at the time. These factors reveal a genuine dispute over the reasonableness of the delay in delivering the written confirmation, and make the resolution of the issue appropriate for the jury. Moreover, conduct is not rendered unreasonable solely because the acting party had no particular explanation for not pursuing different conduct, or regretted not pursuing different conduct in retrospect. The reasonableness of conduct is determined by the facts and circumstances existing at the time.

Considering our principles governing summary adjudication and the need to resolve the legal issue by considering the particular facts and circumstances of each case, we conclude the trial court erred by granting summary judgment. We reverse and remand the case for further proceedings.

Article 2A (Leases) has a Statute of Frauds similar to §2-201, though the amount of the lease must be at least $1,000 before a writing is required, and the writing must describe the leased goods and the lease term in order to satisfy the Statute. See §2A-201. There is no "merchant's confirmation" subsection in this section because (according to the Official Comment) that situation does not often arise in lease transactions.

There is no Statute of Frauds for international sales under the CISG unless the country adopting the Convention stipulates that its own Statute of Frauds will apply. See Articles 11 and 96.

PROBLEM 8

The city manager of Thebes, Utah, which is world-famous for its beautiful desert golf course, orally ordered a huge water tank to be made in the shape of a golf ball on a tee from Tanks of America, Inc. The price was agreed to be $30,000, and the city sent Tanks a down payment check for $3,000, signed by the city comptroller and marked "Tank" on the memo line. Tanks of America built the tank and was in the process of painting "City of Thebes" on the side when a representative of a newly elected city administration called and said that the new administration considered the contract unenforceable. Answer these questions:

(a) Does the check satisfy §2-201(1)? Where is the *quantity?* See Beautiful Jewellers Private, Ltd. v. Tiffany & Co., 2007 WL 867202 (S.D.N.Y. 2007).

(b) What legal argument can Tanks of America make based on §§2-201(3)(a) and 2-201(3)(c)? Does the City of Thebes have a good response to the §2-201(3)(c) argument? See W.I. Snyder Corp. v. Caracciolo, 373 Pa. Super. 486, 541 A.2d 775 (1988).

(c) If the city had promised to sign a written contract but had never gotten around to doing so, can promissory estoppel or equitable estoppel be used to circumvent §2-201? Reread §1-103(b), and see Allen M. Campbell Co.

v. Virginia Metal Indus., Inc., 708 F.2d 930 (4th Cir. 1983); Amber Chemical, Inc. v. Reilly Industries, Inc., 2007 WL 512410 (E.D. Cal. 2007).

(d) Would it make a difference if the city had a Vender Buying Agreement posted on its website, which disclaimed the effectiveness of any oral agreements with the city? See Grandoe Corp. v. Gander Mt. Co., 761 F.3d 876 (8th Cir. 2014).

PROBLEM 9

Tomorrow, Inc. (a computer software company), and Systems Unlimited (a company specializing in advising other companies how to maximize their computer operations) entered into a written joint venture contract by which Tomorrow, Inc., promised to design and sell to Systems Unlimited software that would enable the latter's customers to receive engineering drawings by phone. The parties agreed that their arrangement was "non-exclusive" (meaning either was allowed to deal with other buyers and sellers of the same product). The contract described the obligations of the parties in some detail and stated that the contract would terminate after two years unless renewed. In fact, after working with Tomorrow, Inc., for only six months, Systems Unlimited decided it could develop its own software more cheaply than buying it from Tomorrow, Inc., so it faxed a letter to the latter stating that their contract was at an end. Systems Unlimited declined to purchase any further software. Tomorrow, Inc., which had incurred substantial startup costs in developing the software for this contract, was astounded and promptly filed suit. Systems Unlimited sought refuge in the Statute of Frauds, arguing that the contract signed by the parties stated no quantity. Does §2-201(1) always require a specific quantity? Look at the statutory language very carefully. Compare §2-306. See also Advent Sys. Ltd. v. Unisys Corp., 925 F.2d 670 (3d Cir. 1991); White & Summers §3-4, at 97 n.12.

PROBLEM 10

Sued by a trusting seller after refusing delivery, Renege Retail's president calmly testifies that he had agreed to buy the goods, but the parties never put anything in writing. Without a signed contract, memorandum, confirmation or any other writing, is Renege Retail off the hook? See §2-201(3)(b).

At both the federal and state level, statutes have been enacted to facilitate electronic commerce as civilization moves from the world of paper into cyberspace. The states acted first, with many of them adopting the Uniform

Electronic Transactions Act (UETA), and the federal government followed with the similar Electronic Signatures in Global and National Commerce Act, 15 U.S.C. §7001, commonly known as "E-Sign." The latter statute applies only in jurisdictions not adopting UETA. As of 2015, Illinois, New York, and Washington were the only states not to have enacted UETA. Both statutes should be in your statute book. White and Summers have a clear discussion of the statutes. See White & Summers §§1-3, 3-9.

The basic thrust of these statutes is to allow electronic records in most commercial transactions even if other statutes, such as the Statute of Frauds, require a writing or a written signature. With certain exceptions (utility cut-off notices, notices of default, repossession, foreclosure and eviction, insurance cancellations, etc.), almost all legal communications by the parties to a transaction can now be accomplished electronically. The statutes provide only that electronic communications may meet the requirements for a writing or signature. They do not provide substantive rules, such as how contracts are formed or what terms will be included in the contract. See Alliance Laundry Systems, LLC v. Thyssenkrupp Materials, NA, 570 F. Supp. 2d 1061 (E.D. Wis. 2008).

J.B.B. Investment Partners, Ltd. v. Fair

Court of Appeals of California, 2015
232 Cal. App. 4th 974, 182 Cal. Rptr. 3d 154

KLINE, P.J.

R. Thomas Fair (Fair), Bronco RE Corporation (Bronco), BRE Boulevard LLC (Boulevard) and BRE Cameron Creek LLC (Cameron; collectively, defendants) appeal from a judgment following the trial court's grant of a motion pursuant to Code of Civil Procedure section 664.6 by J.B.B. Investment Partners, Ltd. (JBB) and Silvester Rabic (collectively, plaintiffs) to enforce a settlement between plaintiffs and defendants. The trial court found that Fair's printed name at the end of his e-mail where he had agreed to settlement terms set forth in an e-mail from plaintiffs' counsel was an "electronic signature" within the meaning of California's Uniform Electronic Transactions Act (Civ. Code, §1633.1 et seq.) (UETA) and what the trial court referred to as the "common law of contract" or "contract case law."

Subsequently, plaintiffs requested attorney fees pursuant to a provision in an arbitration agreement between the parties. The trial court found plaintiffs to be the prevailing parties but denied the request for attorney fees because the matter never proceeded to arbitration and plaintiffs had failed to show that any contract authorized fees in the present litigation. Plaintiffs appeal from the order denying them attorney fees. . . .

BACKGROUND

Fair, an attorney and inactive member of the California State Bar, is the founder of Bronco, and Bronco is the managing member of Boulevard and Cameron. Boulevard and Cameron are Arizona limited liability companies formed in 2007, and they each own apartment units in Arizona.

Rabic is a non-attorney individual investor. JBB is a limited partnership based in Atherton, California, and Jonathan B. Buckheit is the general partner of JBB. In late 2007 and early 2008, JBB invested $150,000 and Rabic invested $100,000 in Boulevard and Cameron, and both became members of the limited liability companies.

Subsequently, plaintiffs asserted that they had discovered defendants had made various fraudulent representations and omissions; the parties attempted to negotiate a settlement of those disputes. One of plaintiffs' attorneys, Giacomo A. Russo, sent a settlement offer by e-mail on July 4, 2013 (the July 4 offer). The July 4 offer addressed to Fair stated, among other things, that Fair "must represent and warrant (and provide full disclosure that) no monies moved illegally from one entity to another[,]" that he must enter a stipulated judgment for $350,000, and that "[a]ll litigation would be stayed pending the payments" made by Fair.

The last section in the July 4 offer provided, in relevant part: "The Settlement paperwork would be drafted in parallel with your full disclosure of all documents and all information as required by the first paragraph hereof; it is a material inducement to this settlement that you demonstrate that there is, IN FACT, not a Ponzi or Ponzi-like scheme at work here and the misrepresentations and non-disclosures of which [plaintiffs] have complained are, in fact, simply at most a negligent mistake on your part — as was the failure to get signatures on the ACTUAL FULL-LENGTH LLC Operating Agreements AND at that time, you disclosed that 'priority' really has NO MEANING in the context of the 'priority payments' which they were promised." This section concluded with the following final paragraph: "WE require a YES or NO on this proposal; you need to say 'I accept.' . . . Anything less shifts all focus to the litigation and to the Court Orders we will seek now as well as in the future as well as the subpoenas we will serve. . . . It is now up to you to decide whether you would rather resolve this amicably or not. Let me know your decision." The July 4 offer and e-mail did not have a signature line or signature block, and the e-mail sent to Fair did not include any signature by Rabic and Buckheit.

Rabic and Buckheit both declared that they authorized Russo to make a final settlement offer to defendants and that they signed the July 4 offer on July 5, 2013. Fair declared that he did not receive the July 4 offer with the signatures of Rabic and Buckheit until August 6, 2013.

At 10:17 A.M., on July 5, Fair sent the following e-mail to Russo from his cell phone: "[Russo], the facts will not in any way support the theory in your e-mail. I believe in Cameron. So I agree. Tom [F]air[.]" Russo and another attorney for plaintiffs, Ansel J. Halliburton, responded that they did not understand Fair's e-mail and could not determine whether he was accepting or rejecting the settlement offer. Halliburton stated, "Please be unambiguous, because I am about to file the complaint and *ex parte* papers unless we hear an unambiguous acceptance."

Plaintiffs filed their lawsuit against defendants just before noon on July 5, 2013. Counsel for plaintiffs sent an e-mail at 12:25 P.M. to Fair, which attached the filed complaint and copies of an *ex parte* application for, among other things, expedited discovery.

At 1:02 P.M., on July 5, Fair sent Halliburton the following message from his cell phone: "I said I agree. Took wording right from [Russo's] e-mail. I agree[.]" At 1:04 P.M., Fair left the following voicemail message for Halliburton: "Hey Ansel, I just got your e-mail and your — and your voice-mail. I was playing golf on a course that doesn't allow cell phones. So anyway, I thought I was quite clear on my first response, I made another response by e-mail, I said I agree with [plaintiffs' counsel's] terms. You know? So, that's it."

Shortly thereafter, at 1:07 P.M., Fair sent a message from his cell phone to Halliburton and stated: "I do not believe you gave proper notice. Also I agreed with your terms. You should mot [*sic*] have filed. We clearly have an agreement. [T]om [F]air[.]" At 1:36 P.M., Fair sent by his cell phone the following message to Russo: "Filing does not obviate agreement/acceptance. Pls acknowledge[.]"

Russo responded to Fair at 1:53 P.M. with the following e-mail: "This confirms full agreement; I will work on the formal settlement paperwork which will conform to the settlement agreement made today based on the 10 numbered paragraphs below with no admission of liability or wrongdoing by anyone. I will seek to get that settlement paperwork to you for review by Monday with the goal of getting it all finalized and signed next week. The settlement is otherwise binding under [Code of Civil Procedure section] 664.6. . . ."

Two minutes later, at 1:55 P.M., Fair sent the following text message to Halliburton: "I have accepted by phone and [e-mail]. Stop proceeding. I said accept which is same as 'agreed.' You must stop and you must tell the court we have an agreement." Fair also left a voice message for Russo at some unknown time on July 5, 2013.

On July 11, 2103, Halliburton sent to Fair a draft of the final settlement (July 11 writing). This writing specified the names of plaintiffs and defendants and stated that the agreement was between them. It advised that the agreement could be "signed and delivered by facsimile" and that it could be "electronically signed" by each party. It also included signature blocks for each party.

On July 16, Halliburton sent an e-mail to Fair stating that he had not heard from Fair. In a separate e-mail, he indicated that he would get [Rabic's] signature once he received Fair's signature and a check for the initial payment. A few days later, on July 18, Fair responded that he expected to have comments for Halliburton by the following day and that his attorney had been out of town but was returning that day.

Fair sent an e-mail to Halliburton on July 19, and stated that he had spoken to his accounting firm and the firm suggested a call or a meeting to discuss "the unfounded suspicions and allegations of your clients." Halliburton, responding by e-mail on that same day, said, in relevant part: "It's a good thing we have a settlement, then; let's put pen to paper and close it." "We are not going to stay anything until we have a signed deal."

Fair did not sign the July 11 writing.

On August 6, 2013, plaintiffs filed a motion pursuant to Code of Civil Procedure section 664.6 to enforce the settlement. In support of the motion, plaintiffs submitted the various e-mail, voicemail, and text communications between Fair and their attorneys on July 5, 2013. They also submitted the videotaped deposition of Fair. At his deposition, Fair acknowledged that he deliberately typed his name when his name appeared at the end of an e-mail message and that his phone or software did not automatically place his name there. When asked whether he thought he had an agreement when he sent his e-mail on July 5, 2013, Fair replied: "I thought I had agreed to terms that were suggested in an e-mail during the morning, which had become moot, but I didn't know it until I reviewed all of this stuff later. I didn't read that long e-mail of the morning until maybe a couple of days later." When asked why he believed the agreement had become moot, he answered: "Because they did file, and I changed my mind."

In opposition to the motion, Fair filed, among other things, his declaration. He maintained that Russo's statements that he would contact other investors or go to newspapers to disclose "frivolous allegations" against defendants had made him fearful in July 2013. Additionally, he had not slept during the first week of July 2013 because he had to check repeatedly on his ailing mother. He noted that he was not represented by counsel when he sent the messages to plaintiffs and their counsel and his messages "were sent under severe duress, in particular because [p]laintiffs' counsel was barraging me with phone calls and e-mails, and demanding the names of the other investors in the [limited liability companies] — threatening to contact the other members of the [limited liability companies]." He insisted that his e-mail messages on July 5, 2013, simply signified his good faith and desire to work out a settlement. He asserted that there was no meeting of the minds and that he had not read more than the first paragraph of the July 5 offer. He declared that he did not consider his name on the e-mail to be a signature to a settlement agreement. He maintained that he did not sign important legal documents, such as settlement agreements, without the assistance of counsel.

The superior court held a hearing on plaintiffs' motion to enforce the settlement under Code of Civil Procedure section 664.6 on October 18, 2013. At its commencement the court advised counsel that it "had some real problems with Mr. Fair's declaration as far as credibility, I'll tell you that at the start," and the court felt entitled to take "the comparative credibility of the witnesses" into account. Indicating credibility was not the question, counsel for Fair answered that the central issue was whether there was an electronic signature that satisfied the requirements of UETA. Fair's printed name did not satisfy UETA, counsel insisted, because the July 7 offer did not authorize an electronic signature, nor did any other communication between the parties prior to the draft final settlement Halliburton sent Fair on July 11, which did state that it could be "electronically signed." Counsel for the plaintiffs agreed that whether Fair's printed name complied with UETA was the chief issue but maintained that it clearly complied, resting on the provision of UETA which states that "[i]f a law requires a signature, an electronic record satisfies the law." (§1633.7, subd. (d).)

As will be seen, although the court wondered how plaintiff's counsel can "be here asking me under [Code of Civil Procedure section] 664.6 to enforce a settlement that you didn't yourself think was binding" when counsel sent Fair a draft final settlement on July 11, the court adopted plaintiffs' contention.

It is clear from the court's explanation of its granting of plaintiffs' motion to enforce the settlement that it conceived the chief issue to be whether there was a meeting of the minds as to the terms of the settlement, which is a factual question. As the court stated, "I think that the preponderance of the evidence that's in front of me here is that there was an agreement struck on July 5th. It may not have been reduced to the more formal writing signed by both sides, but I think that there was more likely than not Mr. Fair's agreement that the matter had been settled according to what the e-mails and the voice mails said. The reason why I'm not stating that in more detail is that would have to go into things that are under seal, under the sealing order, but I think that is the case. And so that makes a commercial sense in my view because we have sophisticated parties on both sides."

The trial court continued: "You have at that point in time the equivalent of a situation of yesteryear that would have been not electronic where a lot of deals were done on backs of envelopes and maybe at that point down the road the parties would get lawyers to draft a more formal agreement. But there is older case law that recognizes that a preliminary scribbling like that, if it entailed out all of the materials [*sic*], it was good enough for a contract to warrant to be in place [*sic*]."

The trial court concluded that there was a settlement and that Fair was not under duress but "knew exactly what he was doing." The court emphasized that "[t]here is no coercion or duress here." The court said it was following the federal case law and finding that the e-mail coupled with the corroborating voicemail qualified as an "electronic signature" under UETA. The court added that, even if it should not follow the guidance of the federal case law, it found "that the communications that went back and forth electronically are tantamount to today's modern version of telegrams that used to go back and forth in the commercial world and follow the old cases." The court certified its ruling for interlocutory appeal under Code of Civil Procedure section 166.1.

On November 1, 2013, the trial court filed its judgment granting plaintiffs' motion to enforce the settlement. The court found that plaintiffs proved by a preponderance of the evidence that Fair, on behalf of all defendants, "did more likely than not agree to a settlement with counsel for [p]laintiffs by e-mail on July 5, 2013, confirmed by later e-mails and voicemails." The court found that the e-mails "include electronic signatures within the meaning of" UETA and "[p]laintiffs provided sufficient evidence that Mr. Fair deliberately typed his name at the end of those e-mails. Those e-mails were further corroborated with later e-mails and voicemails, as reflected in the record." The court added, "even without resort to the UETA and instead under contract common law, Mr. Fair's July 5 communications constitute acceptances of [p]laintiffs' offer to settle. The court follows the reasoning set out in Lamle v. Mattel [(Fed. Cir. 2005) 394 F.3d 1355 (*Lamle*)], as well as prior California cases finding typed names on telegrams sufficient to form a contract. . . ." The court concluded: "As stated on the record, the court is of the opinion that there are 'substantial grounds for difference of opinion' regarding the court's resolution of this motion" and "there is no California case law to guide the court's opinion, and the appellate court should look into this matter." The court retained jurisdiction to enforce the judgment.

On November 7, 2013, the trial court entered final judgment in favor of plaintiffs and ordered defendants to pay plaintiffs $362,810.96. Defendants filed a timely notice of appeal. . . .

C. FAIR'S PRINTED SIGNATURE WAS NOT AN "ELECTRONIC SIGNATURE" WITHIN THE MEANING OF UETA

At the hearing on the motion pursuant to Code of Civil Procedure section 664.6, counsel for the parties both stated that, in their view, the dispositive issue was whether Fair's printed signature on the e-mail responding to Russo's July 4 e-mail constituted an "electronic signature" within the meaning of UETA. According to counsel for Fair, Civil Code section 1633.7 is "really the meat of all of the issues that we are going to get to today, whether there was a signature or not, and I think that that is driving everything."

Section 1633.7 provides that "(a) A record or signature may not be denied legal effect of enforceability solely because it is in electronic form. (b) A contract may not be denied legal effect or enforceability solely because an electronic record was used in its formation. (c) If a law requires a record to be in writing, an electronic record satisfies the law. (d) *If a law requires a signature, an electronic signature satisfies the law.*" (Italics added.)

Counsel's argument that Fair's printed name was not an "electronic signature" within the meaning of the statute consisted of three points: First, that in subsequent e-mails to Fair, Russo, and Halliburton repeatedly indicated that there can be no genuine settlement until a formal agreement had been drafted "signed and delivered by facsimile" and thereafter "electronically signed." As Halliburton stated in one of his subsequent e-mails, "'Once we have your signature [on a final agreement] we will have the other plaintiff come in for his signature and we can be done.'" Counsel maintained, in other words, that there was no meeting of the minds as to a final agreement at the time Fair printed his name on the e-mail offer. Second, counsel argued the July 4 settlement offer indicated that, if the parties agreed, "there will be no litigation; everything would be stayed," so that, even if there was a settlement agreement, by filing the complaint on July 5 the plaintiffs either withdrew or breached it. Finally, counsel pointed out that, at the time Fair printed his name on the July 4 e-mail, none of the correspondence between the parties authorized the use of an electronic signature, such as that later included in the July 11 writing.

Counsel for plaintiffs agreed that section 1633.7 was controlling, but maintained that it definitively established that Fair's printed name was an "electronic signature" within the meaning of the UETA. Given the simplicity of the pertinent provision — "If the law requires a signature, an electronic signature satisfies the law" (§1633.7, subd. (d).) — counsel for plaintiffs felt there was no need to consult the case law or any other legal authority.

After the court pointed out that by proffering the July 11 draft settlement his clients did not act as if they had an executed final settlement after Fair printed his name on the July 4 offer, the court asked plaintiffs' counsel "how can you be here asking me under [Code of Civil Procedure] 664.6 to enforce the settlement that you didn't yourself think was binding." Counsel answered that plaintiffs "are not seeking to enforce that July 11th document; we are seeking to enforce the July 5th agreement which has ten clear, precise numbered paragraphs; that's what we are seeking to enforce. We are seeking to enforce against all of the defendants because doing anything else wouldn't make any sense," and "Mr. Fair controls all of those defendants. So when he says, 'I agree; I accept' he is speaking for all of them, clearly by context."

The trial court adopted plaintiffs' view. Finding that, a preponderance of the evidence showed that an agreement was struck on July 5th, the court reasoned that it was "more likely than not Mr. Fair's agreement that the matter had been settled according to what the e-mails and the voicemails said." Referring to section 1633.7, the court also found that "the e-mails in this case coupled with the corroborating voice mail can qualify as an electronic signature under the statute."

The views of counsel to the contrary notwithstanding, section 1633.7 is not the provision of UETA most applicable to the motion before the court, and the court's determination that Fair's printed name was an enforceable "electronic signature" was manifestly erroneous.

Under UETA (§1633.1 et seq.), which became effective January 1, 2000, an electronic record satisfies the requirement that a record be in writing (§1633.7, subd. (c)), and an electronic signature satisfies the requirement that the writing be signed (§1633.7, subd. (d)). "An electronic record or electronic signature is attributable to a person if it was the act of the person. The act of the person may be shown in any manner. . . ." (§1633.9, subd. (a); see also Ni v. Slocum (2011) 196 Cal. App. 4th 1636, 1647, 127 Cal. Rptr. 3d 620 ["the Legislature has, through these provisions, expressed general approval of the use of electronic signatures in commercial and governmental transactions"].)

Section 1633.2, subdivision (h) defines an "'[e]lectronic signature'" as "an electronic sound, symbol, or process attached to or logically associated with an electronic record and executed or adopted by a person with the intent to sign the electronic record." UETA applies, however, only when the parties consent to conduct the transaction by electronic means. (§1633.5, subd. (b).) "Whether the parties agree to conduct a transaction by electronic means is determined from the context and surrounding circumstances, including the parties' conduct. . . ." (Ibid.) "A party that agrees to conduct a transaction by electronic means may refuse to conduct other transactions by electronic means. . . ." (§1633.5, subd. (c).)

Nothing in the record indicates counsel or the court were aware of any of the provisions of UETA just cited, other than section 1633.7, or appreciated the complexity of the statutory scheme. Focusing only on section 1633.7, the court appears to have simplistically assumed, as did counsel for plaintiffs, that because Fair admitted at deposition that the signature was his, and the signature was indisputably electronic, the printed signature on the July 4 offer was therefore an "electronic signature" within the meaning of UETA.

We agree that a printed name or some other symbol might, under specific circumstances, be a signature under UETA and might satisfy the even more rigorous requirements under Code of Civil Procedure section 664.6. Courts in other jurisdictions that have adopted a version of UETA have concluded that names typed at the end of e-mails can be electronic signatures. (See, e.g., Preston Law Firm, L.L.C. v. Mariner Health Care Mgmt. Co. (5th

Cir. 2010) 622 F.3d 384, 391 [affirming that "[e]mails can qualify as the signed writings needed to form contracts" under Louisiana's UETA]; Cloud Corp. v. Hasbro, Inc. (7th Cir. 2002) 314 F.3d 289, 295-296 [holding that "the sender's name on an e-mail satisfies the signature requirement of the [Illinois] statute of frauds" and noting that it would be a valid signature under the federal Electronic Signatures in Global and National Commerce Act as well]; see also *Lamle,* supra, 394 F.3d at p. 1362 [e-mail was written prior to the enactment of California's UETA, but court opined that inclusion of individual's name on e-mail would be valid signature under California's UETA]; Gillis v. Wells Fargo Bank (E.D. Mich. 2012) 875 F. Supp. 2d 728, 734-735 [signed letter and e-mail messages that included the sender's salutation were sufficient to satisfy statute of frauds].)

The trial court's analysis was incomplete. Attributing the name on an e-mail to a particular person and determining that the printed name is "[t]he act of [this] person" is a necessary prerequisite but is insufficient, by itself, to establish that it is an "electronic signature." (§1633.9, subd. (a).) As counsel and the court seemed unaware, UETA defines the term "electronic signature." Subdivision (h) of section 1633.2 states that "'[e]lectronic signature' means an electronic sound, symbol, or process attached to or logically associated with an electronic record and *executed or adopted by a person with the intent to sign the electronic record.*" (Italics added. See also Cal. Civ. Jury Inst. No. 380 [party suing to enforce an agreement formalized by electronic means must prove "based on the context and surrounding circumstances, including the conduct of the parties, that the parties agreed to use (e.g., e-mail) to formalize their agreement"].)

We have independently reviewed the record and conclude, as a matter of law, that it does not show that Fair printed his name at the end of his e-mail with any intent to formalize an electronic transaction. Indeed, substantial evidence in the record refutes such a finding.

"Whether the parties agree to conduct a transaction by electronic means is determined from the context and surrounding circumstances, including the parties' conduct. . . ." (§1633.5, subd. (b).) The absence of an explicit agreement to conduct the transaction by electronic means is not determinative; however, it is a relevant factor to consider.

Plaintiffs argue that the July 4 offer expressly contemplated acceptance by electronic means as it specified that Fair needed to say, "I accept." They also cite Fair's testimony that he personally typed his name and that he refused to sign the July 11 writing because he had simply changed his mind. Plaintiffs' evidence is legally insufficient.

The exchange of e-mail messages shows that the parties clearly agreed to negotiate the terms of the settlement by e-mail, but plaintiffs did not demonstrate, as they must (§1633.5, subd. (b)), that the parties ever agreed to conduct transactions by electronic means or that Fair intended with his printed name at the end of his e-mail to sign electronically the July 4 offer. The July 4 offer did not contain any statement indicating that the parties agreed to enter into a final settlement by electronic means. The plain language of the July 4 offer made it clear that no signature was being requested as the offer included no signature line or signature block, contained no signature by any of the plaintiffs, and advised that future paperwork was forthcoming. The last section in the July 4 offer provided that "[t]he Settlement paperwork would be drafted. . . ." Additionally, this section advised that plaintiffs require "a YES or NO on this proposal; you need to say 'I accept[.]'" The last sentence in this section stated: "Let me know your decision." None of these sentences in the July 4 offer supports a conclusion that the parties agreed that Fair's agreement to the proposal was an agreement to sign a legally binding settlement. (See *Sully-Miller,* supra, 103 Cal. App. 4th at p. 37, 126 Cal. Rptr. 2d 400 [a party's signature added "to a document that does not call for it" is not a signed writing under Code of Civil Procedure section 664.6 because "[a] party's signature fails to convey" knowledge and express consent "unless it is contained in a document that was clearly intended by that party to be a binding settlement agreement"]; Powell v. City of Newton (2010) 364 N.C. 562, 703 S.E.2d 723, 727-728 [applying North Carolina's UETA and concluding that the parties did not agree to the use of electronic signatures "[i]n light of the express indication by [one party] that [the other party] should sign and forward the [agreements]"].) Moreover, Fair's subsequent voicemail and text messages from his cell phone did not indicate that he intended for his e-mail to be a signature to the electronic record as he simply stated that he "agree[d] with" or accepted Russo's terms.

Subsequently, the statements of plaintiffs' counsel provided further evidence that no party considered the July 4 offer attached to the July 5 e-mail as a final document requiring a signature. Russo stated that Fair's response "confirms full agreement" and he promised to work "on the formal settlement paperwork" and "get the settlement paperwork" for Fair's review "with the goal of getting it all finalized and signed next week." He added that the "settlement is otherwise binding under" Code of Civil Procedure section 664.6, but the settlement could not be binding without all of the parties' signatures. Halliburton sent Fair an e-mail on July 19, 2013, stating in relevant part: "It's a good thing we have a settlement, then; let's put pen to paper and close it." "We are not going to stay anything until we have a signed deal."

In contrast to the July 4 offer, the July 11 writing included a signature line at the end of the settlement agreement. Additionally, it specified that an electronic signature could be used. The July 11 writing provided: "This Settlement Agreement may be signed and delivered by facsimile and in counter-parts. It may also be electronically signed by each of the Parties through the use of EchoSign, DocuSign, or such other commercially available electronic signature software which results in confirmed signatures delivered electronically to each of the Parties, which shall be treated as an original as though in-signed by officers or other duly authorized represent-atives of each Party." No similar language was in the July 4 offer and, as already stressed, the July 4 offer did not indicate that a printed name at the bottom of an e-mail would be an electronic signature.

Accordingly, we conclude that the evidence in the record is as a matter of law insufficient to establish that Fair signed electronically a settlement agreement. Since Fair's printed name was not a signature under UETA, the trial court erred when it concluded that Fair's printed name at the bottom of the e-mail satisfied the strict signature requirements under Code of Civil Procedure section 664.6. . . .

DISPOSITION

The order enforcing the settlement pursuant to Code of Civil Procedure section 664.6 is reversed and the judgment is vacated. We affirm the order denying plaintiffs' attorney fees. Defendants are awarded costs in both appeals.

QUESTIONS

Is this case right in your opinion? Fair? What does the result suggest that you, as an attorney practicing in a jurisdiction adopting this result, should tell your clients to do when contracting through e-mails?

———————

There are a number of unsettled issues as to electronic signatures. Both of the statutes mentioned before the case require that if a consumer is involved, he or she must have *agreed* to electronic disclosures, but it is unclear exactly what this means. The federal statute is broader, requiring that there be *electronic agreement or confirmation of agreement,* and this agree-ment must be "affirmative"; 15 U.S.C. §7001(c)(1)(C)(ii). This means that the consumer must have agreed electronically to receive electronic records or have confirmed this consent electronically. UETA is less clear about this, though Comment 4 to §5 indicates that the consumer's agreement to receive electronic communications must be actual and not imposed unconscionably as part of the fine print in a written contract.

There is also no consensus on what electronic communication means. Is it sufficient for the required information to be posted on a website (the so-called "Come and Get It" notice) that the consumer must periodically access (which, of course, most won't do) to keep informed? In the 1990s, AOL posted rate changes only on its website, making customers agree that this was sufficient notice of any hike in the rate, only to back down when 19 attorneys general objected that the practice was unfair and deceptive. What about e-mail notification? Must it be highlighted in such a way that the consumer will recognize its importance and not delete it as "spam"? If the consumer has switched e-mail addresses, then what? Must the sender do something with bounced-back messages? These matters and others will have to await judicial determination. For a summary of the consumer issues and suggested resolutions, see Jean Braucher, Rent-Seeking and Risk-Fixing in the New Statutory Law of Electronic Commerce: Difficulties in Moving Consumer Protection Online, 2001 Wis. L. Rev. 527.

II.   THE PAROL EVIDENCE RULE

Read §2-202 and its Official Comment.

PROBLEM 11

Lawyers for Swinging Singles Magazine negotiated for an entire year with Space Age Aircraft Co. to obtain a contract for the construction of a special Swinging Singles airplane. (The plane was to be black and silver, with the Swinging Singles emblem painted on the tail; it was to contain a living room, bed chamber, swimming pool, hot tub, and a dance floor.) The resulting 30-page contract also contained a *merger* clause, stating that all prior negotiations were merged into the written contract that contained all the terms of the agreement. The contract was signed by both parties. Does §2-202 bar the introduction of evidence of the following?

(a) An alleged precontract agreement that Space Age would provide free flying lessons to Hi Handsome, president of Swinging Singles, Inc.? The contract says nothing about this. See the test found in Official Comment 3 to §2-202.

(b) An alleged precontract agreement that Swinging Singles could use the plane for two months, and if they did not like it, they could return it for a full refund?

To aid in the construction of agreements, the Code looks to the customs within the industry (called *usage of trade*), the parties' past contacts with one another (called *course of dealing*), and the parties' behavior during the existence of the contract in question (called *course of performance*) and presumes that these matters are relevant in fleshing out the express terms of the contract. See Nanakuli Paving & Rock Co. v. Shell Oil Co., 664 F.2d 772 (9th Cir. 1981) (good discussion of these terms). Read §1-303 carefully. Their relationship to §2-202 is explored in the case below.

Columbia Nitrogen Corp. v. Royster Co.
United States Court of Appeals, Fourth Circuit, 1971, 451 F.2d 3

BUTZNER, J. . . .

I

Royster manufactures and markets mixed fertilizers, the principal components of which are nitrogen, phosphate and potash. Columbia is primarily a producer of nitrogen, although it manufactures some mixed fertilizer. For several years Royster had been a major purchaser of Columbia's products, but Columbia had never been a significant customer of Royster. In the fall of 1966, Royster constructed a facility which enabled it to produce more phosphate than it needed in its own operations. After extensive negotiations, the companies executed a contract for Royster's sale of a minimum of 31,000 tons of phosphate each year for three years to Columbia, with an option to extend the term. The contract stated the price per ton, subject to an escalation clause dependent on production costs.

Phosphate prices soon plunged precipitously. Unable to resell the phosphate at a competitive price, Columbia ordered only part of the scheduled tonnage. At Columbia's request, Royster lowered its price for diammonium phosphate on shipments for three months in 1967, but specified that subsequent shipments would be at the original contract price. Even with this concession, Royster's price was still substantially above the market. As a result, Columbia ordered less than a tenth of the phosphate Royster was to ship in the first contract year. When pressed by Royster, Columbia offered to take the phosphate at the current market price and resell it without brokerage fee. Royster, however, insisted on the contract price. When Columbia refused delivery, Royster sold the unaccepted phosphate for Columbia's account at a price substantially below the contract price.

II

Columbia assigns error to the pretrial ruling of the district court excluding all evidence on usage of the trade and course of dealing between the parties. It offered the testimony of witnesses with long experience in the trade that because of uncertain crop and weather conditions, farming practices, and government agricultural programs, express price and quantity terms in contracts for materials in the mixed fertilizer industry are mere projections to be adjusted according to market forces.[4]

Columbia also offered proof of its business dealings with Royster over the six-year period preceding the phosphate contract. Since Columbia had not been a significant purchaser of Royster's products, these dealings were almost exclusively nitrogen sales to Royster or exchanges of stock carried in inventory. The pattern which emerges, Columbia claimed, is one of repeated and substantial deviation from the stated amount or price, including four instances where Royster took none of the goods for which it had contracted. Columbia offered proof that the total variance amounted to more than $500,000 in reduced sales. This experience, a Columbia officer offered to testify, formed the basis of an understanding on which he depended in conducting negotiations with Royster.

The district court held that the evidence should be excluded. It ruled that "custom and usage or course of dealing are not admissible to contradict

---

4. Typical of the proffered testimony are the following excerpts: "The contracts generally entered into between buyer and seller of materials has always been, in my opinion, construed to be the buyer's best estimate of his anticipated requirements for a given period of time. It is well known in our industry that weather conditions, farming practices, government farm control programs, change requirements from time to time. And therefore allowances were always made to meet these circumstances as they arose." "Tonnage requirements fluctuate greatly, and that is one reason that the contracts are not considered as binding as most contracts are, because the buyer normally would buy on historical basis, but his normal average use would be per annum of any given material. Now that can be affected very decidedly by adverse weather conditions such as a drought, or a flood, or maybe governmental programs which we have been faced with for many, many years, seed grain programs. They pay the farmer not to plant. If he doesn't plant, he doesn't use the fertilizer. When the contracts are made, we do not know of all these contingencies and what they are going to be. So the contract is made for what is considered a fair estimate of his requirements. And, the contract is considered binding to the extent, on him morally, that if he uses the tonnage that he will execute the contract in good faith as the buyer. . . ." "I have never heard of a contract of this type being enforced legally. . . ." Well, it undoubtedly sounds ridiculous to people from other industries, but there is a very definite, several very definite reasons why the fertilizer business is always operated under what we call gentlemen's agreements. . . . "The custom in the fertilizer industry is that the seller either meets the competitive situation or releases the buyer from it upon proof that he can buy it at that price. . . . [T]hey will either have the option of meeting it or releasing him from taking additional tonnage or holding him to that price. . . ." And this custom exists "regardless of the contractual provisions." "[T]he custom was that [these contracts] were not worth the cost of the paper they were printed on."

the express, plain, unambiguous language of a valid written contract, which by virtue of its detail negates the proposition that the contract is open to variances in its terms. . . ."

A number of Virginia cases have held that extrinsic evidence may not be received to explain or supplement a written contract unless the court finds the writing is ambiguous. E.g., Mathieson Alkali Works v. Virginia Banner Coal Corp., 147 Va. 125, 136 S.E. 673 (1927). This rule, however, has been changed by the Uniform Commercial Code which Virginia has adopted. The Code expressly states that it "shall be liberally construed and applied to promote its underlying purposes and policies," which include "the expansion of commercial practices through custom, usage and agreement of the parties. . . ." §1-102.[5] The importance of usage of trade and course of dealing between the parties is shown by §2-202, which authorizes their use to explain or supplement a contract. The official comment states this section rejects the old rule that evidence of course of dealing or usage of trade can be introduced only when the contract is ambiguous. And the Virginia commentators, noting that "[t]his section reflects a more liberal approach to the introduction of parol evidence . . . than has been followed in Virginia," express the opinion that *Mathieson,* supra, and similar Virginia cases no longer should be followed. §2-202, Va. Comment. See also Portsmouth Gas Co. v. Shebar, 209 Va. 250, 253 n.1, 163 S.E.2d 205, 208 n.1 (1968) (dictum). We hold, therefore, that a finding of ambiguity is not necessary for the admission of extrinsic evidence about the usage of the trade and the parties' course of dealing.

We turn next to Royster's claim that Columbia's evidence was properly excluded because it was inconsistent with the express terms of their agreement. There can be no doubt that the Uniform Commercial Code restates the well-established rule that evidence of usage of trade and course of dealing should be excluded whenever it cannot be reasonably construed as consistent with the terms of the contract. Division of Triple T Service, Inc. v. Mobil Oil Corp., 60 Misc. 2d 720, 304 N.Y.S.2d 191, 203 (1969), *aff'd mem.,* 311 N.Y.S.2d 961 (1970). Royster argues that the evidence should be excluded as inconsistent because the contract contains detailed provisions regarding the base price, escalation, minimum tonnage, and delivery schedules. The argument is based on the premise that because a contract appears on its face to be complete, evidence of course of dealing and usage of trade should be excluded. We believe, however, that neither the language nor the policy of the Code supports such a broad exclusionary rule. Section 2-202 expressly allows evidence of course of dealing or usage of trade to explain or supplement terms intended by the parties as a final expression of their agreement. When this section is read in light of §1-205(4),[6] it is clear that

5. Now §1-103(a)(2). — Ed.
6. Now §1-303(e). — Ed.

the test of admissibility is not whether the contract appears on its face to be complete in every detail, but whether the proffered evidence of course of dealing and trade usage reasonably can be construed as consistent with the express terms of the agreement.

The proffered testimony sought to establish that because of changing weather conditions, farming practices, and government agricultural programs, dealers adjusted prices, quantities, and delivery schedules to reflect declining market conditions. For the following reasons it is reasonable to construe this evidence as consistent with the express terms of the contract:

The contract does not expressly state that course of dealing and usage of trade cannot be used to explain or supplement the written contract.

The contract is silent about adjusting prices and quantities to reflect a declining market. It neither permits nor prohibits adjustment, and this neutrality provides a fitting occasion for recourse to usage of trade and prior dealing to supplement the contract and explain its terms.

Minimum tonnages and additional quantities are expressed in terms of "Products Supplied Under Contract." Significantly, they are not expressed as just "Products" or as "Products Purchased Under Contract." The description used by the parties is consistent with the proffered testimony.

Finally, the default clause of the contract refers only to the failure of the buyer to pay for delivered phosphate. During the contract negotiations, Columbia rejected a Royster proposal for liquidated damages of $10 for each ton Columbia declined to accept. On the other hand, Royster rejected a Columbia proposal for a clause that tied the price to the market by obligating Royster to conform its price to offers Columbia received from other phosphate producers. The parties, having rejected both proposals, failed to state any consequences of Columbia's refusal to take delivery — the kind of default Royster alleges in this case. Royster insists that we span this hiatus by applying the general law of contracts permitting recovery of damages upon the buyer's refusal to take delivery according to the written provisions of the contract. This solution is not what the Uniform Commercial Code prescribes. Before allowing damages, a court must first determine whether the buyer has in fact defaulted. It must do this by supplementing and explaining the agreement with evidence of trade usage and course of dealing that is consistent with the contract's express terms; §§1-205(4),[7] 2-202. Faithful adherence to this mandate reflects the reality of the marketplace and avoids the overly legalistic interpretations which the Code seeks to abolish.

Royster also contends that Columbia's proffered testimony was properly rejected because it dealt with mutual willingness of buyer and seller to adjust contract terms to the market. Columbia, Royster protests, seeks unilateral

7. Now §1-303(e). — Ed.

adjustment. This argument misses the point. What Columbia seeks to show is a practice of mutual adjustments so prevalent in the industry and in prior dealings between the parties that it formed a part of the agreement governing this transaction. It is not insisting on a unilateral right to modify the contract.

Nor can we accept Royster's contention that the testimony should be excluded under the contract clause:

> No verbal understanding will be recognized by either party hereto; this contract expresses all the terms and conditions of the agreement, shall be signed in duplicate, and shall not become operative until approved in writing by the Seller.

Course of dealing and trade usage are not synonymous with verbal understandings, terms and conditions. Section 2-202 draws a distinction between supplementing a written contract by consistent additional terms and supplementing it by course of dealing or usage of trade. Evidence of additional terms must be excluded when "the court finds the writing to have been intended also as a complete and exclusive statement of the terms of the agreement." Significantly, no similar limitation is placed on the introduction of evidence of course of dealing or usage of trade. Indeed the official comment notes that course of dealing and usage of trade, unless carefully negated, are admissible to supplement the terms of any writing, and that contracts are to be read on the assumption that these elements were taken for granted when the document was phrased. Since the Code assigns course of dealing and trade usage unique and important roles, they should not be conclusively rejected by reading them into stereotyped language that makes no specific reference to them. Cf. Provident Tradesmen's Bank & Trust Co. v. Pemberton, 196 Pa. Super. 180, 173 A.2d 780 (1961). Indeed, the Code's official commentators urge that overly simplistic and overly legalistic interpretation of a contract should be shunned.[8]

We conclude therefore that Columbia's evidence about course of dealing and usage of trade should have been admitted. Its exclusion requires that the judgment against Columbia must be set aside and the case retried. . . .

---

8. Referring to the general provisions about course of dealing and trade usage, §1-205, Comment 1 states:

> This Act rejects both the "lay dictionary" and the "conveyancer's" reading of a commercial agreement. Instead the meaning of the agreement of the parties is to be determined by the language used by them and by their action, read and interpreted in the light of commercial practices and other surrounding circumstances. The measure and background for interpretation are set by the commercial context, which may explain and supplement even the language of a formal or final writing.

QUESTION

If the merger clause in the contract between Columbia and Royster had stated that it barred all evidence of usage of trade and course of dealing, would the decision have been different? See Southern Concrete Servs., Inc. v. Mableton Contractors, Inc., 407 F. Supp. 581 (N.D. Ga. 1975).

III. OFFER AND ACCEPTANCE

A. General Rules

Common law rules of contract formation had too many technicalities and formalities to suit the drafters of the UCC. If, as often happens, people in business create contracts on a very informal basis, the Code does all it can to give legal meaning to the resulting deal.[9] Read §§2-204, 2-205, and 2-206 before doing the next Problems.

PROBLEM 12

Mastervoice TV ordered 20,000 fuses from the Generous Electric Company, the order stating "Reply by return mail." Instead of a formal reply, Generous immediately shipped the fuses. When the fuses arrived, they were found to be defective. Mastervoice, which had to procure substitute goods elsewhere to meet its production schedule, sued Generous Electric for breach of warranty. Answer these questions:

(a) At what moment was the contract formed? $2-204, shipment

(b) Can Generous make this defense: "There was never any contract since our alleged act of acceptance (the shipment of *defective* goods) did not comply with requirements of Mastervoice's offer (which contemplated only shipment of *good* fuses)"?   No $2-206(1)(b)

(c) Instead of the above, assume that when Generous received the order it discovered that it no longer manufactured the type of fuses Mastervoice

---

9. Article 2 specifically addresses the issue of when a binding contract to sell is formed at an *auction*. See §2-328; Callimanopulos v. Christie's Inc., 621 F. Supp. 2d 127 (S.D.N.Y. 2009) (holding that §2-328 authorized auctioneer to reopen bidding, after gavel had fallen on $3 million bid for painting, because auctioneer had not seen another bidder raise her paddle).

wanted, but that it did carry a very similar type of fuse that it believed would suit Mastervoice's needs. The shipping manager for Generous was unable to get through to the relevant people at Mastervoice, so in the end Generous shipped the slightly different fuses along with a cover note saying, "These are similar to the fuses you ordered, but may not be right for you. If they are not suitable, we will gladly take them back without charge." Is Generous now in breach because it shipped nonconforming goods? See §2-206(1)(b).

PROBLEM 13

For years P. Dreamer had wanted a Rolls Royce Silver Shadow with burgundy-colored trim (he had seen one in an ad and salivated). He saw one on the lot of Posh Motors. After Dreamer had dickered loud and long over the terms with Paula Posh, president of Posh Motors, they finally agreed on a price. Dreamer said he wanted to clear the deal with his wife before signing anything, so Posh promised she would hold the car for the Dreamers until the next day at noon. When Mr. and Mrs. Dreamer arrived at the dealership the next morning, the car was gone. Posh had made a better deal with another buyer. Do the Dreamers have a good cause of action? See §2-205.

make a deal with Posh.

B. The Battle of the Forms

As long as there are merchant buyers and sellers of goods, there will be forms with self-serving boilerplate. And as long as the transactions proceed without incident — which may be after a long while and many sales — their forms will pass like ships on a foggy sea. But when at last one of their transactions sinks, each retreats to the shelter of its favorable terms to claim victory.

Dependable Component Supply, Inc. v. Pace Electronics Inc., 772 So. 2d 582 (Fla. App. 2000).

The "battle of the forms" is a much litigated problem that arises from two sources: (1) the business practices of either negotiating deals orally and then exchanging printed forms that no one reads until a dispute arises, or dealing at arm's length with non-matching purchase orders and acknowledgments, and (2) the complexities of §2-207 and its Official Comment.

Subsection (1) to §2-207 is meant to reverse the common law rule that an *acceptance* that was not the *mirror image* of the offer was (impliedly) both a rejection and a counteroffer. Under §2-207(1), an acceptance adding new terms creates a contract based on the original offer, unless the *acceptance* very clearly states otherwise. As to what happens to the additional terms, see §2-207(2).

If, in spite of all logic and business judgment, the parties exchange documents that cannot be reconciled so as to produce a contract, no contract results, and either party may, on discovering this mishap, back out of the deal *if* that party acts prior to the beginning of performance. If performance has begun (with the parties wrongly believing a contract exists), subsection (3) of §2-207 regulates the ensuing mess.

Judges recognize that §2-207 is not a model of clarity: "Referred to as 'a murky bit of prose,' and 'like the amphibious tank that was originally designed to fight in the swamps, but was ultimately sent to fight in the desert,' §2-207 is a defiant, lurking demon patiently waiting to condemn its interpreters to the depths of despair. Nevertheless, §2-207 must and can be conquered." Reaction Molding Technologies, Inc. v. General Electric Co., 585 F. Supp. 1097, 1104 (E.D. Pa. 1984).

PROBLEM 14

The Magic Carpet Co. had a long and profitable business relationship with Alibaba Carpet Manufacturers of Bagdad, Illinois. Fifty-five times Alibaba had sold carpets to Magic Carpet. Each sale was carried out in the following manner. A partner of Magic Carpet telephoned Alibaba's order department and ordered a certain quantity of carpet at the price listed in Alibaba's catalog. After each oral order was placed, the credit department was consulted to determine if Magic Carpet was paid up. Then, if the credit was okay, the order department of Alibaba typed the information from the order on one of its printed acknowledgment forms, each of which had the following paragraph printed conspicuously on its face:

> The acceptance of your order is subject to all of the terms and conditions on the face and reverse side hereof, all of which are accepted by buyer; it supersedes buyer's order form, if any. It shall become a contract either (a) when signed and delivered by buyer to seller and accepted in writing by seller, or (b) at seller's option, when buyer shall have given to seller specification of assortments, delivery dates, shipping instructions, or instructions to bill and hold as to all or any part of the merchandise herein described, or when buyer has received delivery of the whole or any part thereof, or when buyer has otherwise assented to the terms and conditions hereof.

The provisions on the reverse side of the form provided, among other things, that the seller disclaimed all warranties, express or implied. Each acknowledgment form was signed by an employee in Alibaba's order department and mailed to the Magic Carpet Co. Shortly thereafter, the carpet was shipped. Magic Carpet always received the acknowledgment form before the carpet. They placed each form in a file, accepted delivery of the carpet, and paid for it promptly. On the 56th sale, the accepted and paid-for carpet proved to be nonconforming. Magic Carpet sued Alibaba for breach of warranty. Alibaba replied that its form disclaimed all warranties.

Answer these questions:

(a) Was a contract formed between Magic Carpet and Alibaba? See §2-207(1).

(b) Was the disclaimer of warranties part of that contract? See §2-207(2).

Problem 14 is based on Dorton v. Collins & Aikman Corp., 453 F.2d 1161 (6th Cir. 1972), where the court clearly and competently sorted through the complexities of §2-207. White and Summers discuss §2-207 exhaustively. See White & Summers §2-3.

Diamond Fruit Growers, Inc. v. Krack Corp.
United States Court of Appeals, Ninth Circuit, 1986, 794 F.2d 1440

WIGGINS, J.

Metal-Matic, Inc. (Metal-Matic) appeals from judgment entered after a jury verdict in favor of Krack Corporation (Krack) on Krack's third-party complaint against Metal-Matic. Metal-Matic also appeals from the district court's denial of its motion for judgment n.o.v. We have jurisdiction under 28 U.S.C. §1291 (1982) and affirm.

FACTS AND PROCEEDINGS BELOW

Krack is a manufacturer of cooling units that contain steel tubing it purchases from outside suppliers. Metal-Matic is one of Krack's tubing suppliers. At the time this dispute arose, Metal-Matic had been supplying tubing to Krack for about ten years. The parties followed the same course of dealing during the entire ten years. At the beginning of each year, Krack sent a blanket purchase order to Metal-Matic stating how much tubing Krack would need for the year. Then, throughout the year as Krack needed tubing, it sent release purchase orders to Metal-Matic requesting that tubing be shipped. Metal-Matic responded to Krack's release purchase orders by sending Krack an acknowledgment form and then shipping the tubing.

Metal-Matic's acknowledgment form disclaimed all liability for consequential damages and limited Metal-Matic's liability for defects in the tubing to refund of the purchase price or replacement or repair of the tubing. As one would expect, these terms were not contained in Krack's purchase order. The following statement was printed on Metal-Matic's form: "Metal-Matic, Inc.'s acceptance of purchaser's offer or its offer to purchaser is hereby expressly made conditional to purchaser's acceptance of the terms and provisions of the acknowledgment form." This statement and the disclaimer of liability were on the back of the acknowledgment form. However, printed at the bottom of the front of the form in boldface capitals was the following statement: "SEE REVERSE SIDE FOR TERMS AND CONDITIONS OF SALE."

On at least one occasion during the ten-year relationship between Metal-Matic and Krack, Allen Zver, Krack's purchasing manager, discussed the limitations of warranty and disclaimer of liability terms contained in Metal-Matic's acknowledgment form with Robert Van Krevelen, Executive Vice President of Metal-Matic. Zver told Van Krevelen that Krack objected to the terms and tried to convince him to change them, but Van Krevelen refused to do so. After the discussions, Krack continued to accept and pay for tubing from Metal-Matic.

In February 1981, Krack sold one of its cooling units to Diamond Fruit Growers, Inc. (Diamond) in Oregon, and in September 1981, Diamond installed the unit in a controlled-atmosphere warehouse. In January 1982, the unit began leaking ammonia from a cooling coil made of steel tubing.

After Diamond discovered that ammonia was leaking into the warehouse, Joseph Smith, the engineer who had been responsible for building Diamond's controlled-atmosphere warehouses, was called in to find the source of the leak. Smith testified that he found a pinhole leak in the cooling coil of the Krack cooling unit. Smith inspected the coil while it was still inside the unit. He last inspected the coil on April 23, 1982. The coil then sat in a hall at Diamond's warehouse until May 1984, when John Myers inspected the coil for Metal-Matic.

Myers cut the defective tubing out of the unit and took it to his office. At his office, he did more cutting on the tubing. After Myers inspected the tubing, it was also inspected by Bruce Wong for Diamond and Paul Irish for Krack.

Diamond sued Krack to recover the loss in value of fruit that it was forced to remove from the storage room as a result of the leak. Krack in turn brought a third-party complaint against Metal-Matic and Van Huffel Tube Corporation (Van Huffel), another of its tubing suppliers, seeking contribution or indemnity in the event it was held liable to Diamond. At the close of the evidence, both Metal-Matic and Van Huffel moved for a directed verdict on the third-party complaint. The court granted Van Huffel's motion based on evidence that the failed tubing was not manufactured by Van Huffel. The court denied Metal-Matic's motion.

The jury returned a verdict in favor of Diamond against Krack. It then found that Krack was entitled to contribution from Metal-Matic for thirty percent of Diamond's damages. Metal-Matic moved for judgment n.o.v. The court denied that motion and entered judgment on the jury verdict.

Metal-Matic raises two grounds for reversal. First, Metal-Matic contends that as part of its contract with Krack, it disclaimed all liability for consequential damages and specifically limited its liability for defects in the tubing to refund of the purchase price or replacement or repair of the tubing. Second, Metal-Matic asserts that the evidence does not support a finding that it manufactured the tubing in which the leak developed or that it caused the leak. We address each of these contentions in turn. . . .

DISCUSSION

A. METAL-MATIC'S DISCLAIMER OF LIABILITY FOR CONSEQUENTIAL DAMAGES

If the contract between Metal-Matic and Krack contains Metal-Matic's disclaimer of liability, Metal-Matic is not liable to indemnify Krack for part of Diamond's damages. Therefore, the principal issue before us on this appeal is whether Metal-Matic's disclaimer of liability became part of the contract between these parties.

Relying on Uniform Commercial Code (U.C.C.) §2-207, Or. Rev. Stat. §72.2070 (1985), Krack argues that Metal-Matic's disclaimer did not become part of the contract. Metal-Matic, on the other hand, argues that §2-207 is inapplicable to this case because the parties discussed the disclaimer, and Krack assented to it.

Krack is correct in its assertion that §2-207 applies to this case. One intended application of §2-207 is to commercial transactions in which the parties exchange printed purchase order and acknowledgment forms. See U.C.C. §2-207 comment 1. The drafters of the UCC recognized that "[b]ecause the [purchase order and acknowledgment] forms are oriented to the thinking of the respective drafting parties, the terms contained in them often do not correspond." Id. Section 2-207 is an attempt to provide rules of contract formation in such cases. In this case, Krack and Metal-Matic exchanged purchase order and acknowledgment forms that contained different or additional terms. This, then, is a typical §2-207 situation. The fact that the parties discussed the terms of their contract after they exchanged their forms does not put this case outside §2-207. See 3 R. Duesenburg & L. King, Sales and Bulk Transfers under the Uniform Commercial Code (Bender's U.C.C. Service) §3.05[2] (1986). Section 2-207 provides rules of contract formation in cases such as this one in which the parties exchange forms but do not agree on all the terms of their contract.

A brief summary of §2-207 is necessary to an understanding of its application to this case. Section 2-207 changes the common law's mirror-image rule for transactions that fall within article 2 of the U.C.C. At common law, an acceptance that varies the terms of the offer is a counteroffer and operates as a rejection of the original offer. See Idaho Power Co. v. Westinghouse Electric Corp., 596 F.2d 924, 926 (9th Cir. 1979). If the offeror goes ahead with the contract after receiving the counteroffer, his performance is an acceptance of the terms of the counteroffer. See C. Itoh & Co. v. Jordan International Co., 552 F.2d 1228, 1236 (7th Cir. 1977); J. White & R. Summers, Handbook of the Law Under the Uniform Commercial Code §1-2 at 34 (2d ed. 1980).

Generally §2-207(1) "converts a common law counteroffer into an acceptance even though it states additional or different terms." Idaho Power, 596 F.2d at 926; see U.C.C. §2-207(1). The only requirement under §2-207(1) is that the responding form contain a definite and seasonable expression of acceptance. The terms of the responding form that correspond to the offer constitute the contract. Under §2-207(2), the additional terms of the responding form become proposals for additions to the contract. Between merchants the additional terms become part of the contract unless the offer is specifically limited to its terms, the offeror objects to the additional terms, or the additional terms materially alter the terms of the offer. U.C.C. §2-207(2); see J. White & R. Summers, §1-2 at 32.

However, §2-207(1) is subject to a proviso. If a definite and seasonable expression of acceptance expressly conditions acceptance on the offeror's assent to additional or different terms contained therein, the parties' differing forms do not result in a contract unless the offeror assents to the additional terms. See J. White & R. Summers, §1-2 at 32-33. If the offeror assents, the parties have a contract and the additional terms are a part of that contract. If, however, the offeror does not assent, but the parties proceed with the transaction as if they have a contract, their performance results in formation of a contract. UCC §2-207(3). In that case, the terms of the contract are those on which the parties' forms agree plus any terms supplied by the UCC. Id.; see Boise Cascade Corp. v. Etsco, Ltd., 39 U.C.C. Rep. Serv. (Callaghan) 410, 414 (D. Or. 1984); J. White & R. Summers, §1-2 at 34.

In this case, Metal-Matic expressly conditioned its acceptance on Krack's assent to the additional terms contained in Metal-Matic's acknowledgment form. That form tracks the language of the §2-207(1) proviso, stating that "Metal-Matic, Inc.'s acceptance . . . is hereby *expressly made conditional* to purchaser's acceptance of the terms and provisions of the acknowledgment form" (emphasis added). See *C. Itoh & Co.,* 552 F.2d at 1235. Therefore, we must determine whether Krack assented to Metal-Matic's limitation of liability term.

Metal-Matic argues that Krack did assent to the limitation of liability term. This argument is based on the discussions between Zver for Krack and Van Krevelen for Metal-Matic. Some time during the ten-year relationship between the companies, these two men discussed Krack's objections to the warranty and liability limitation terms in Metal-Matic's acknowledgment form. Krack attempted to persuade Metal-Matic to change its forms, but Metal-Matic refused to do so. After the discussions, the companies continued to do business as in the past. Metal-Matic contends that Krack assented to the limitation of liability term when it continued to accept and pay for tubing after Metal-Matic insisted that the contract contain its terms.

To address Metal-Matic's argument, we must determine what constitutes assent to additional or different terms for purposes of §2-207(1). The parties have not directed us to any cases that analyze this question and our research has revealed none. We therefore look to the language and structure of §2-207 and to the purposes behind that section to determine the correct standard.

One of the principles underlying §2-207 is neutrality. If possible, the section should be interpreted so as to give neither party to a contract an advantage simply because it happened to send the first or in some cases the last form. See J. White & R. Summers, §1-2 at 26-27. Section 2-207 accomplishes this result in part by doing away with the common law's "last shot" rule. See 3 R. Duesenberg & L. King, §3.05[1][a][iii] at 3-73. At common law, the offeree/counterofferor gets all of its terms simply because it fired the last shot in the exchange of forms. Section 2-207(3) does away with this result by giving neither party the terms it attempted to impose unilaterally on the other. See id. at 3-71. Instead, all of the terms on which the parties' forms do not agree drop out, and the UCC supplies the missing terms.

Generally, this result is fair because both parties are responsible for the ambiguity in their contract. The parties could have negotiated a contract and agreed on its terms, but for whatever reason failed to do so. Therefore, neither party should get its terms. See 3 R. Duesenberg & L. King §3.05[2] at 3-88. However, as White and Summers point out, resort to §2-207(3) will often work to the disadvantage of the seller because he will "wish to undertake less responsibility for the quality of his goods than the Code imposes or else wish to limit his damages liability more narrowly than would the Code." J. White & R. Summers §1-2 at 34. Nevertheless, White and Summers recommend that §2-207(3) be applied in such cases. Id. We agree. Application of §2-207(3) is more equitable than giving one party its terms simply because it sent the last form. Further, the terms imposed by the code are presumably equitable and consistent with public policy because they are statutorily imposed. See 3 R. Duesenberg & L. King, §3.05 [2] at 3-88.

With these principles in mind, we turn now to Metal-Matic's argument that Krack assented to the disclaimer when it continued to accept and pay for tubing once Metal-Matic indicated that it was willing to sell tubing only if its warranty and liability terms were part of the contract. Metal-Matic's argument is appealing. Sound policy supports permitting a seller to control the terms on which it will sell its products, especially in a case in which the seller has indicated both in writing and orally that those terms are the only terms on which it is willing to sell the product. Nevertheless, we reject Metal-Matic's argument because we find that these considerations are outweighed by the public policy reflected by Oregon's enactment of the UCC.

If we were to accept Metal-Matic's argument, we would reinstate to some extent the common law's last shot rule. To illustrate, assume that the parties in this case had sent the same forms but in the reverse order and that Krack's form contained terms stating that Metal-Matic is liable for all consequential damages and conditioning acceptance on Metal-Matic's assent to Krack's terms. Assume also that Metal-Matic objected to Krack's terms but Krack refused to change them and that the parties continued with their transaction anyway. If we applied Metal-Matic's argument in that case, we would find that Krack's term was part of the contract because Metal-Matic continued to ship tubing to Krack after Krack reaffirmed that it would purchase tubing only if Metal-Matic were liable for consequential damages. Thus, the result would turn on which party sent the last form, and would therefore be inconsistent with §2-207's purpose of doing away with the last shot rule.

That result is avoided by requiring a specific and unequivocal expression of assent on the part of the offeror when the offeree conditions its acceptance on assent to additional or different terms. If the offeror does not give specific and unequivocal assent but the parties act as if they have a contract, the provisions of §2-207(3) apply to fill in the terms of the contract. Application of §2-207(3) is appropriate in that situation because by going ahead with the transaction without resolving their dispute, both parties are responsible for introducing ambiguity into the contract. Further, in a case such as this one, requiring the seller to assume more liability than it intends is not altogether inappropriate. The seller is most responsible for the ambiguity because it inserts a term in its form that requires assent to additional terms and then does not enforce that requirement. If the seller truly does not want to be bound unless the buyer assents to its terms, it can protect itself by not shipping until it obtains that assent. See *C. Itoh & Co.*, 552 F.2d at 1238.

We hold that because Krack's conduct did not indicate unequivocally that Krack intended to assent to Metal-Matic's terms, that conduct did not amount to the assent contemplated by §2-207(1). See 3 R. Duesenberg & L. King, §3.05[1][a][iii] at 3-74. . . .

The jury verdict is supported by the evidence and consistent with the UCC. Therefore, the district court did not err in denying Metal-Matic's motion for a judgment n.o.v.

PROBLEM 15

Would the following clause in the seller's acknowledgment to the buyer's order form be a material alteration under §2-207(2)(b): "Any disputes concerning this contract shall be subject to binding arbitration"? See ICC Chemical Corp. v. Vitol, Inc., 425 Fed. Appx. 57 (2d Cir. 2011) (arbitration clause not a material alteration where sometimes used in chemical industry sales); In re Cotton Yarn Antitrust Litigation, 505 F.3d 274 (4th Cir. 2007) (not a material alteration where arbitration was the usage of trade in the textile industry). How about a forum-selection clause providing that all disputes must be litigated in the seller's state? See Ridgelawn Cemetery Assn. v. Grantie Resources Corp., 2017 WL 3783401 (N.D. Ind. 2017).

If these clauses were in an acknowledgment of an international sale of goods to which CISG applies, would it be valid? See Article 19; Filanto, S.p.A. v. Chilewich Intl. Corp., 789 F. Supp. 1229 (S.D.N.Y. 1992), *appeal dismissed,* 984 F.2d 58 (2d Cir. 1993); Comment, The U.N. Convention on the International Sale of Goods and the "Battle of the Forms," 13 Fordham Intl. L.J. 649 (1990).

Bayway Refining Co. v. Oxygenated Marketing and Trading A.G.
United States Court of Appeals, Second Circuit, 2000, 215 F.3d 219

JACOBS, Circuit Judge.

Plaintiff-appellee Bayway Refining Company ("Bayway") paid federal excise tax on a petroleum transaction, as the Internal Revenue Code requires a petroleum dealer to do in a sale to a buyer who has not procured an exemption under the applicable tax provision. In this diversity suit against the buyer, Oxygenated Marketing and Trading A.G. ("OMT"), Bayway seeks to recover the amount of the tax it paid. One question in this "battle of the forms" contract case is whether, under N.Y. U.C.C. §2-207(2)(b) (McKinney 1993), a contract term allocating liability to the buyer for an excise tax is an additional term presumed to have been accepted (as the seller contends) or (as the buyer contends) a material alteration presumed to have been rejected. The United States District Court for the Southern District of New York (McKenna, J.) granted summary judgment in favor of the seller, Bayway.

We conclude that, in the circumstances presented: (i) the party opposing the inclusion of an additional term under §2-207(2)(b) bears the burden of proving that the term amounts to a material alteration; (ii) the district court properly granted summary judgment in favor of the seller, because the additional term here did not materially alter the contract; and (iii) the district court properly admitted evidence of custom and practice in the industry despite the fact that it was first proffered in the moving party's reply papers. Accordingly, we affirm.

BACKGROUND

Bayway and OMT are in the business of buying and selling petroleum products. Bayway contracted to sell to OMT 60,000 barrels of a gasoline blendstock called Methyl Tertiary Butyl Ether ("MTBE"). On February 12,

1998, OMT faxed Bayway a confirmation letter, which operated as the offer, and which stated in pertinent part:

> We are pleased to confirm the details of our purchase from you of MTBE as agreed between Mr. Ben Basil and Roger Ertle on [February 12, 1998.] . . .
>
> This confirmation constitutes the entire contract and represents our understanding of the terms and conditions of our agreement. . . . Any apparent discrepancies or omissions should be brought to our notice within the next two working days.

Bayway faxed its confirmation to OMT the next day. That document, which operated as the acceptance, stated in pertinent part: "We are pleased to confirm the following verbal agreement concluded on February 12, 1998 with your company. This document cancels and supersedes any correspondence in relation to this transaction." Bayway's acceptance then set forth the parties, price, amount and delivery terms, and undertook to incorporate the company's standard terms:

> Notwithstanding any other provision of this agreement, where not in conflict with the foregoing, the terms and conditions as set forth in Bayway Refining Company's General Terms and Conditions dated March 01, 1994 along with Bayway's Marine Provisions are hereby incorporated in full by reference in this contract.

The Bayway General Terms and Conditions were not transmitted with Bayway's fax, but Paragraph 10 of its General Terms and Conditions states:

> Buyer shall pay seller the amount of any federal, state and local excise, gross receipts, import, motor fuel, superfund and spill taxes and all other federal, state and local taxes however designated, other than taxes on income, paid or incurred by seller directly or indirectly with respect to the oil or product sold hereunder and/or on the value thereof.

This term is referenced as the "Tax Clause."

OMT did not object to Bayway's acceptance or to the incorporation of its General Terms and Conditions (which included the Tax Clause). OMT accepted delivery of the MTBE barrels on March 22, 1998.

The Internal Revenue Code imposes an excise tax, payable by the seller, on the sale of gasoline blendstocks such as MTBE "to any person who is not registered under [26 U.S.C. §4101]" for a tax exemption. 26 U.S.C.A. §4081(a)(1)(A)(iv) (West Supp. 1999). After delivery, Bayway learned that OMT was not registered with the Internal Revenue Service for the tax exemption. The transaction therefore created a tax liability of $464,035.12, which Bayway paid.

Invoking the Tax Clause, Bayway demanded payment of the $464,035.12 in taxes in addition to the purchase price of the MTBE. OMT denied that it had agreed to assume the tax liability and refused to pay that invoice item. In response, Bayway filed this diversity suit alleging breach of contract by OMT.

Upon Bayway's motion for summary judgment, the district court held that the Tax Clause was properly incorporated into the contract. See Tosco Corp. v. Oxygenated Mktg. & Trading A.G., No. 98 Civ. 4695, 1999 WL 328342, at *3-*6 (S.D.N.Y. May 24, 1999). The fact that Bayway had failed to attach a copy of the General Terms and Conditions was irrelevant because OMT could have obtained a copy if it had asked for one. See id. at *3. The court then analyzed the contract-forming documents, applied the "battle of the forms" framework set forth in N.Y. U.C.C. §2-207(2), and concluded that OMT failed to carry its burden of proving that the Tax Clause materially altered the contract. See id. at *3-*6. The court therefore granted summary judgment in favor of Bayway.

DISCUSSION

On appeal, OMT argues (i) that it succeeded in raising genuine issues of fact as to whether the Tax Clause materially altered the Bayway/OMT contract and (ii) that the evidence of custom and practice in the industry, upon which the grant of summary judgment turns, was improperly admitted. . . .

We affirm for substantially the reasons stated by the district court. We hold — on an issue of first impression in this Court — that in a "battle of the forms" case governed by N.Y. U.C.C. §2-207(2)(b), the party opposing the inclusion of an additional term bears the burden of proving that the term works a material alteration. Viewing the evidence in the light most favorable to OMT, we conclude that OMT failed to shoulder that burden. Finally, we hold that the district court properly admitted the evidence concerning industry custom and practice.

A.   BATTLE OF THE FORMS

Bayway argued its motion for summary judgment on the basis of New York law, presumably because one of the additional terms incorporated by its acceptance is a New York choice-of-law provision. OMT has accepted New York law as controlling for purposes of Bayway's summary judgment motion. [The court quoted §2-207(1) and (2).]

It was undisputed in the district court that Bayway's confirmation fax is effective to form a contract as an acceptance — even though it stated or referenced additional terms (including the Tax Clause) — because it was not made expressly conditional on OMT's assent to the additional terms. See id. §2-207(1). Therefore, under §2-207(2), the Tax Clause is a proposal for an addition to the contract. See id. §2-207(2). The parties are both merchants within the meaning of the U.C.C. See id. §2-104(1), (3). The Tax Clause therefore is presumed to become part of the contract unless one of the three enumerated exceptions applies. See id. §2-207(2). In its defense, OMT invokes the "material alteration" exception of §2-207(2)(b).

1. Burden of Proof (A) forum selection → material alteration → big change

The allocation of the burden of proof under this exception to §2-207(2) is a question of New York law, see United States v. McCombs, 30 F.3d 310, 323-24 (2d Cir. 1994) (holding that, under the Erie doctrine, federal courts sitting in diversity apply the forum state's law concerning burdens of proof), and is answered in the text of New York's U.C.C. §2-207(2). Section 2-207(2)(b) is an exception to the general rule of §2-207(2) that additional terms become part of a contract between merchants. That general rule is in the nature of a presumption concerning the intent of the contracting parties. Thus if neither party introduced any evidence, the Tax Clause would, by the plain language of §2-207(2), become part of the contract. To implement that presumption, the burden of proving the materiality of the alteration must fall on the party that opposes inclusion. Accordingly, we hold that under §2-207(2)(b) the party opposing the inclusion of additional terms shoulders the burden of proof. In so doing, we join almost every court to have considered this issue. [Citations omitted.]

2. Materiality and Per Se Materiality

A material alteration is one that would "result in surprise or *hardship* if incorporated without express awareness by the other party." N.Y. U.C.C. §2-207 cmt. 4 (emphasis added).

Certain additional terms are deemed material as a matter of law. For example, an arbitration clause is per se a material alteration in New York because New York law requires an express agreement to commit disputes to arbitration. See Marlene Indus. v. Carnac Textiles, Inc., 45 N.Y.2d 327, 408 N.Y.S.2d 410, 413, 380 N.E.2d 239 (1978); see also N.Y. U.C.C. §2-207 cmt. 4 (listing as examples of per se material alterations, inter alia, waivers of warranties of merchantability or fitness for a particular purpose and clauses granting the seller the power to cancel upon the buyer's failure to meet any invoice). OMT characterizes the Tax Clause as a broad-ranging indemnity clause, and analogizes it to these per se material alterations. We reject the analogy. The Tax Clause allocates responsibility for the tax payable on a specific sale of goods. See Union Carbide Corp. v. Oscar Mayer Foods Corp., 947 F.2d 1333, 1335, 1337 (7th Cir. 1991) (distinguishing between "open-ended" tax liability, which is a material alteration, from "responsibility for taxes shown on an individual invoice," which is not). And unlike an arbitration clause, which waives a range of rights that are solicitously protected, the Tax Clause is limited, discrete and the subject of no special protection. Unable to show that the Tax Clause is a material alteration per se, OMT must prove that in this case the Tax Clause resulted in surprise or hardship.[10]

3. Surprise

Surprise, within the meaning of the material alteration exception of §2-207(2)(b), has both the subjective element of what a party actually knew and the objective element of what a party should have known. See American Ins. Co. v. El Paso Pipe & Supply Co., 978 F.2d 1185, 1191 (10th Cir. 1992); In re Chateaugay, 162 B.R. at 956-57. A profession of surprise and raised eyebrows are not enough: "[C]onclusory statements, conjecture, or speculation by the party resisting the motion will not defeat summary judgment." Kulak v. City of New York, 88 F.3d 63, 71 (2d Cir. 1996). To carry the burden of showing surprise, a party must establish that, under the circumstances, it cannot be presumed that a reasonable merchant would have consented to the additional term. See Union Carbide, 947 F.2d at 1336.

OMT has adduced evidence that the Tax Clause came as an amazement to OMT's executives, who described the term's incorporation as "contract by ambush" and a "sl[e]ight-of-hand proposal." Thus OMT has sufficiently exhibited its subjective surprise. As to objective surprise, however, OMT has alleged no facts and introduced no evidence to show that a reasonable petroleum merchant would be surprised by the Tax Clause. See In re Chateaugay, 162 B.R. at 957 (including as types of evidence proving objective surprise "the parties' prior course of dealing and the number of written confirmations that they exchanged, industry custom and the conspicuousness of the term"). OMT had no prior contrary course of dealing with Bayway, and offered nothing concerning trade custom or practice.

Ordinarily, our inquiry into surprise would end here. However, in response to OMT's claim of surprise, Bayway introduced evidence that the Tax Clause reflects custom and practice in the petroleum industry, and on appeal OMT argues that Bayway's own evidence raises a genuine issue of material fact as to whether such a trade practice exists. Although the evidence was introduced by Bayway, we are "obligated to search the record and independently determine whether or not a genuine issue of fact exists." Jiminez v. Dreis & Krump Mfg. Co., 736 F.2d 51, 53 (2d Cir. 1984) (quoting

---

10. Even if an additional term that places the tax liability on the opposing party was a material alteration per se, New York law allows a party to rebut this conclusion in some limited circumstances with a sufficient showing that the additional term reflects the custom and practice in the particular industry. See Avedon Eng'g, 126 F.3d at 1285 & n.15 (discussing New York law); Schubtex, Inc. v. Allen Snyder, Inc., 49 N.Y.2d 1, 424 N.Y.S.2d 133, 135, 399 N.E.2d 1154 (1979). As discussed below, Bayway's evidence that the Tax Clause reflects the custom and practice in the petroleum industry is compelling and unrebutted.

Higgins v. Baker, 309 F. Supp. 635, 639 (S.D.N.Y. 1970)) (internal quotation marks omitted).

Upon our review of the evidence, we conclude that Bayway has adduced compelling proof that shifting tax liability to a buyer is the custom and practice in the petroleum industry. Two industry experts offered unchallenged testimony that it is customary for the buyer to pay all the taxes resulting from a petroleum transaction. One expert stated that "[t]his practice is so universally understood among traders in the industry, that I cannot recall an instance, in all my years of trading and overseeing trades, when the buyer refused to pay the seller for excise or sales taxes."

OMT cites the standard contracts of five major petroleum companies that Bayway introduced to illustrate contract terms similar to the Tax Clause. OMT argues that only three of the five place the tax liability on the buyer, and that there is therefore an issue of fact as to whether the Tax Clause would objectively surprise a merchant in this industry.

OMT misconstrues the evidence. Three of the contracts — those of CITGO Petroleum, Conoco, and Enron — mirror the Tax Clause. A fourth, Chevron's, differs from the others only in that the cost of the taxes is added into the contract price rather than separately itemized. Thus Chevron's standard contract affords OMT no support.

The fifth example, the Texaco contract, is silent as to the tax allocation issue in this case. But on this unrebutted record of universal trade custom and practice, silence supports no contrary inference.

Moreover, common sense supports Bayway's evidence of custom and practice. The federal excise tax is imposed when taxable fuels are sold "to any person who is not registered under [26 U.S.C. §4101]." 26 U.S.C. §4081(a)(1)(A)(iv). The buyer thereby controls whether any tax liability is incurred in a transaction. A trade practice that reflects a rational allocation of incentives (as trade practices usually do) would place the burden of the tax on the party that is in the position to obviate it — here, on OMT as the buyer.

Viewing Bayway's evidence in the light most favorable to OMT, we conclude that allocating the tax liability to the buyer is the custom and practice in the petroleum industry. OMT could not be objectively surprised by the incorporation of an additional term in the contract that reflects such a practice.

4. Hardship

To recapitulate: A material alteration is one that would "result in surprise *or* hardship if incorporated without express awareness by the other party." N.Y. U.C.C. §2-207 cmt. 4 (emphasis added). Although this Official Comment to the U.C.C. seemingly treats hardship as an independent ground for finding that an alteration is material, courts have expressed doubt: "You cannot walk away from a contract that you can fairly be deemed to have agreed to, merely because performance turns out to be a hardship for you, unless you can squeeze yourself into the impossibility defense or some related doctrine of excuse." *Union Carbide*, 947 F.2d at 1336 ("Hardship is a consequence [of material alteration], not a criterion. (Surprise can be either.)"); see also, e.g., Suzy Phillips Originals, Inc. v. Coville, Inc., 939 F. Supp. 1012, 1017-18 (E.D.N.Y. 1996) (citing *Union Carbide* with approval and limiting the test for material alteration to surprise); In re Chateaugay, 162 B.R. at 957 (same).

We need not decide whether hardship is an independent ground of material alteration, because even if it were, OMT failed to raise a genuine issue of material fact as to hardship. OMT's only evidence of hardship is (generally) that it is a small business dependent on precarious profit margins, and it would suffer a loss it cannot afford. That does not amount to hardship in the present circumstances.

Typically, courts that have relied on hardship to find that an additional term materially alters a contract have done so when the term is one that creates or allocates an open-ended and prolonged liability. See, e.g., St. Charles Cable TV, Inc. v. Eagle Comtronics, Inc., 687 F. Supp. 820, 827 (S.D.N.Y. 1988) (finding a hardship in "shift[ing] all risks for any dispute to the buyers"), *aff'd*, 895 F.2d 1410 (2d Cir. 1989) (unpublished table disposition); Charles J. King, Inc. v. Barge LM-10, 518 F. Supp. 1117, 1120 (S.D.N.Y. 1981).

The Tax Clause places on a buyer a contractual responsibility that bears on a specific sale of goods, that is (at least) not uncommon in the industry, and that the buyer could avoid by registration. The cry of hardship rings hollow, because any loss that the Tax Clause imposed on OMT is limited, routine and self-inflicted.

OMT failed to raise a factual issue as to hardship or surprise. Summary judgment was therefore appropriately granted in favor of Bayway. . . .

For the foregoing reasons, we affirm the judgment of the district court.

PROBLEM 16

The purchase order of the buyer ordered a tugboat, and the fine print demanded that the tugboat be warranted for a two-year period. The tugboat seller's acknowledgment form contained a statement that disclaimed all warranties. Neither party read the other's form, so the tugboat was shipped, accepted, and then had major problems remaining afloat. You are the attorney for the buyer. Advise your client whether the contract includes a warranty.

The last Problem raised the issue of how §2-207 resolves an exchange of forms containing *different* terms. While subsection (1) of the statute talks about both "additional" and "different" terms, subsection (2) mentions only "additional" ones. Official Comment 6, at first glance, appears to resolve the matter, but a careful reading of it shows that it is addressed only to written confirmations of an oral contract containing different terms, which the Official Comment says cancel each other out. The courts facing the different terms scenario of Problem 16 have divided into two major camps, as discussed in the following case.

Northrop Corporation v. Litronic Industries

United States Court of Appeals, Seventh Circuit, 1994, 29 F.3d 1173

POSNER, Chief Judge.

"Battle of the forms" refers to the not uncommon situation in which one business firm makes an offer in the form of a preprinted form contract and the offeree responds with its own form contract. At common law, any discrepancy between the forms would prevent the offeree's response from operating as an acceptance. See Poel v. Brunswick-Balke-Collender Co., 216 N.Y. 310, 110 N.E. 619, 621-22 (N.Y. 1915). So there would be no contract in such a case. This was the "mirror image" rule, which Article 2 of the Uniform Commercial Code jettisoned by providing that "a definite and seasonable expression of acceptance or a written confirmation which is sent within a reasonable time operates as an acceptance even though it states terms additional to or different from those offered or agreed upon, unless acceptance is made conditional on assent to the additional or different terms." UCC §2-207(1). See Union Carbide Corp. v. Oscar Mayer Foods Corp., 947 F.2d 1333, 1335-36 (7th Cir. 1991). Mischief lurks in the words "additional to or different from." The next subsection of 2-207 provides that if additional terms in the acceptance are not materially different from those in the offer, then, subject to certain other qualifications (id. at 1335-37), they become part of the contract, §2-207(2), while if the additional terms are materially different they operate as proposals and so have no effect unless the offeror agrees to them, UCC §2-207, comment 3; if the offeror does not agree to them, therefore, the terms of the contract are those in the offer. A clause providing for interest at normal rates on overdue invoices, or limiting the right to reject goods because of defects falling within customary trade tolerances for acceptance with adjustment, would be the sort of additional term that is not deemed material, and hence it would become a part of the contract even if the offeror never signified acceptance of it. Id., comment 5.

The Code does not explain, however, what happens if the offeree's response contains *different* terms (rather than additional ones) within the meaning of section 2-207(1). There is no consensus on that question. See James J. White & Robert S. Summers, Uniform Commercial Code 33-36 (3d ed. 1988); John E. Murray, Jr., "The Chaos of the 'Battle of the Forms': Solutions," 39 Vand. L. Rev. 1307, 1354-65 (1986). We know there is a contract because an acceptance is effective even though it contains different terms; but what are the terms of the contract that is brought into being by the offer and acceptance? One view is that the discrepant terms in both the nonidentical offer and the acceptance drop out, and default terms found elsewhere in the Code fill the resulting gap. Another view is that the offeree's discrepant terms drop out and the offeror's become part of the contract. A third view, possibly the most sensible, equates "different" with "additional" and makes the outcome turn on whether the new terms in the acceptance are materially different from the terms in the offer — in which event they operate as proposals, so that the offeror's terms prevail unless he agrees to the variant terms in the acceptance — or not materially different from the terms in the offer, in which event they become part of the contract. John L. Utz, "More on the Battle of the Forms: The Treatment of 'Different' Terms Under the Uniform Commercial Code," 16 U.C.C. L.J. 103 (1983). This interpretation equating "different" to "additional," bolstered by drafting history which shows that the omission of "or different" from section 2-207(2) was a drafting error, Utz, supra, 16 U.C.C. L.J. at 110-12; Murray, supra, 39 Vand. L. Rev. at 1355, substitutes a manageable inquiry into materiality, Union Carbide Corp. v. Oscar Mayer Foods Corp., supra, 947 F.2d at 1336-37; Schulze & Burch Biscuit Co. v. Tree Top, Inc., 831 F.2d 709, 715 (7th Cir. 1987); Douglas G. Baird & Robert Weisberg, "Rules, Standards, and the Battle of the Forms: A Reassessment of Section 2-207," 68 Va. L. Rev. 1217, 1246 (1982), for a hair-splitting inquiry into the difference between "different" and "additional." It is hair-splitting ("metaphysical," "casuistic," "semantic," in the pejorative senses of these words) because all different terms are additional and all additional terms are different.

Unfortunately, the Illinois courts — whose understanding of Article 2 of the UCC is binding on us because this is a diversity suit governed, all agree, by Illinois law — have had no occasion to choose among the different positions on the consequences of an acceptance that contains "different" terms from the offer. We shall have to choose.

The battle of the forms in this case takes the form of something very like a badminton game, but we can simplify it a bit without distorting the issues. The players are Northrop, the giant defense firm, and Litronic, which manufactures electronic components, including "printed wire boards" that are incorporated into defense weapon systems. In 1987 Northrop sent several manufacturers, including Litronic, a request to submit offers to sell Northrop a customized printed wire board designated by Northrop as a "1714 Board." The request stated that any purchase would be made by means of a purchase order that would set forth terms and conditions that would override any inconsistent terms in the offer. In response, Litronic mailed an offer to sell Northrop four boards for $19,000 apiece, to be delivered within six weeks. The offer contained a 90-day warranty stated to be in lieu of any other warranties, and provided that the terms of the offer would take precedence over any terms proposed by the buyer. Lynch, a purchasing officer of Northrop, responded to the offer in a phone conversation in which he told Litronic's man, Lair, that he was accepting the offer up to the limit of his authority, which was $24,999, and that a formal purchase order for all four boards would follow. Litronic was familiar with Northrop's purchase order form, having previously done business with Northrop, which had been using the same form for some time. Had Lair referred to any of the previous orders, he would have discovered that Northrop's order form provided for a warranty that contained no time limit.

Lynch followed up the phone conversation a month later with a "turn on" letter, authorizing Litronic to begin production of all four boards (it had done so already) and repeating that a purchase order would follow. The record is unclear when the actual purchase order was mailed; it may have been as much as four months after the phone conversation and three months after the turn-on letter. The purchase order required the seller to send a written acknowledgment to Northrop. Litronic never did so, however, and Northrop did not complain; it does not bother to follow up on its requirement of a signed acknowledgment.

Although Litronic had begun manufacturing the boards immediately after the telephone call from Lynch, for reasons that are unknown but that Northrop does not contend are culpable Litronic did not deliver the first three boards until more than a year later, in July of 1988. Northrop tested the boards for conformity to its specifications. The testing was protracted, either because the boards were highly complex or because Northrop's inspectors were busy, or perhaps for both reasons. At all events it was not until December and January, five or six months after delivery, that Northrop returned the three boards (the fourth had not been delivered), claiming that they were defective. Litronic refused to accept the return of the boards, on the ground that its 90-day warranty had lapsed. Northrop's position of course is that it had an unlimited warranty, as stated in the purchase order.

As an original matter one might suppose that this dispute is not over the terms of the warranty but over whether Northrop waited more than the "reasonable time" that the Uniform Commercial Code allows the buyer of nonconforming goods to reject them. UCC §2-602(1). That in fact is how the magistrate judge framed the issue, as we shall see. But the parties continue to treat it as a "warranty" case. Their implicit view is that Litronic's 90-day warranty, if a term of the contract, not only barred Northrop from complaining about defects that showed up more than 90 days after the delivery of the boards but also limited to 90 days the time within which Northrop was permitted to reject the boards because of defects that rendered them nonconforming. We accept this view for purposes of deciding these appeals.

Litronic's appeal concerns the breach of its warranty on the No. 1714 boards. It wins if the warranty really did expire after only 90 days. The parties agree that Litronic's offer to sell the No. 1714 boards to Northrop, the offer made in response to Northrop's request for bids, was — the offer. So far, so good. If Northrop's Mr. Lynch accepted the offer over the phone, the parties had a contract then and there, but the question would still be on what terms. Regarding the first question, whether there was a contract, we may assume to begin with that the acceptance was sufficiently "definite" to satisfy the requirement of definiteness in section 2-207(1); after all, it impelled Litronic to begin production immediately, and there is no suggestion that it acted precipitately in doing so. We do not know whether Lynch in his conversation with Lair made acceptance of the complete contract expressly conditional on approval by Lynch's superiors at Northrop. We know that he had authority to contract only up to $24,999, but we do not know whether he told Lair what the exact limitation on his authority was or whether Litronic knew it without being told. It does not matter. The condition, if it was a condition, was satisfied and so drops out.

We do not think that Northrop's acceptance, via Lynch, of Litronic's offer could be thought conditional on Litronic's yielding to Northrop's demand for an open-ended warranty. For while Lynch's reference to the purchase order might have alerted Litronic to Northrop's desire for a warranty not limited to 90 days, Lynch did not purport to make the more extensive warranty a condition of acceptance. So the condition, if there was one, was not an express condition, as the cases insist it be. See, e.g., McCarty v. Verson Allsteel Press Co., 89 Ill. App. 3d 498, 411 N.E.2d 936, 945, 44 Ill. Dec. 570 (Ill. App. 1980); Clifford-Jacobs Forging Co. v. Capital Engineering & Mfg. Co., 107 Ill. App. 3d 29, 437 N.E.2d 22, 24, 62 Ill. Dec. 785 (Ill. App. 1982); Dorton v. Collins & Aikman Corp., 453 F.2d 1161, 1168 (6th Cir. 1972); White & Summers, supra, at 39.

There was a contract, therefore; further, and, as we shall note, decisive, evidence being that the parties acted as if they had a contract — the boards were shipped and paid for. The question is then what the terms of the warranty in the contract were. Lynch's reference in the phone conversation to the forthcoming purchase order shows that Northrop's acceptance contained different terms from the offer, namely the discrepant terms in the purchase order, in particular the warranty — for it is plain that the Northrop warranty was intended to be indefinite in length, so that, at least in the absence of some industry custom setting a limit on warranties that do not specify a duration (cf. UCC §2-207, comments 4 and 5), a point not raised, any limitation on the length of the warranty in the offer would be a materially different term. Daitom, Inc. v. Pennwalt Corp., 741 F.2d 1569, 1577 (10th Cir. 1984); cf. Owens-Corning Fiberglas Corp. v. Sonic Development Corp., 546 F. Supp. 533, 538 (D. Kan. 1982). Of course the fact that Northrop preferred a longer warranty than Litronic was offering does not by itself establish that Northrop's acceptance contained different terms. But Lynch did not accept Litronic's offer and leave it at that. He said that he would issue a Northrop purchase order, and both he and Lair knew (or at least should have known) that the Northrop purchase order form contained a different warranty from Litronic's sale order form. And we have already said that Lynch did not, by his oral reference to the purchase order, condition Northrop's purchase on Litronic's agreeing to comply with all the terms in the purchase order form, given the courts' insistence that any such condition be explicit. (Judges are skeptical that even businesspeople read boilerplate, so they are reluctant, rightly or wrongly, to make a contract fail on the basis of a printed condition in a form contract.) But Lynch said enough to make clear to Lair that the acceptance contained different terms from the offer.

The Uniform Commercial Code, as we have said, does not say what the terms of the contract are if the offer and acceptance contain different terms, as distinct from cases in which the acceptance merely contains additional terms to those in the offer. The majority view is that the discrepant terms fall out and are replaced by a suitable UCC gap-filler. E.g., Daitom, Inc. v. Pennwalt Corp., supra, 741 F.2d at 1578-80; St. Paul Structural Steel Co. v. ABI Contracting, Inc., 364 N.W.2d 83 (N.D. 1985); Challenge Machinery Co. v. Mattison Machine Works, 138 Mich. App. 15, 359 N.W.2d 232, 236-38 (Mich. App. 1984) (per curiam). The magistrate judge followed this approach and proceeded to section 2-309, which provides that nonconforming goods may be rejected within a "reasonable" time (see also §2-601(1)), and she held that the six months that Northrop took to reject Litronic's boards was a reasonable time because of the complexity of the required testing. The leading minority view is that the discrepant terms *in the acceptance* are to be ignored, Valtrol, Inc. v. General Connectors Corp., 884 F.2d 149, 155 (4th Cir. 1989); Reaction Molding Technologies, Inc. v. General Electric Co., 588 F. Supp. 1280, 1289 (E.D. Pa. 1984), and that would give the palm to Litronic. Our own preferred view — the view that assimilates "different" to "additional," so that the terms in the offer prevail over the different terms in the acceptance only if the latter are not materially different, has as yet been adopted by only one state, California. Steiner v. Mobil Oil Corp., 20 Cal. 3d 90, 569 P.2d 751, 759 n.5, 141 Cal. Rptr. 157 (Cal. 1977). Under that view, as under what we are calling the "leading" minority view, the warranty in Litronic's offer, the 90-day warranty, was the contractual warranty, because the unlimited warranty contained in Northrop's acceptance was materially different.

Because Illinois in other UCC cases has tended to adopt majority rules, e.g., Rebaque v. Forsythe Racing, Inc., 134 Ill. App. 3d 778, 480 N.E.2d 1338, 1341, 89 Ill. Dec. 595 (Ill. App. 1985), and because the interest in the uniform nationwide application of the Code — an interest asserted in the Code itself (see §1-102) — argues for nudging majority views, even if imperfect (but not downright bad), toward unanimity, we start with a presumption that Illinois, whose position we are trying to predict, would adopt the majority view. We do not find the presumption rebutted. The idea behind the majority view is that the presence of different terms in the acceptance suggests that the offeree didn't *really* accede to the offeror's terms, yet both parties wanted to contract, so why not find a neutral term to govern the dispute that has arisen between them? Of course the offeree may not have had any serious objection to the terms *in the offer* at the time of contracting; he may have mailed a boilerplated form without giving any thought to its contents or to its suitability for the particular contract in question. But it is just as likely that the discrepant terms in the offer itself were the product of a thoughtless use of a boilerplate form rather than a considered condition of contracting. And if the offeror doesn't want to do business other than on the terms in the offer, he can protect himself by specifying that the offeree must accept all those terms for the parties to have a contract. UCC §2-207(2)(a); Tecumseh International Corp. v. City of Springfield, 70 Ill. App. 3d 101, 388 N.E.2d 460, 463, 26 Ill. Dec. 745 (Ill. App. 1979). Now as it happens Litronic did state in its offer that the terms in the offer "take precedence over terms and conditions of the buyer, unless specifically negotiated otherwise." But, for reasons that we do not and need not fathom, Litronic does not argue that this language conditioned the existence of the contract on Northrop's acceding to the 90-day warranty in the offer; any such argument is therefore waived.

It is true that the offeree likewise can protect himself by making his acceptance of the offer conditional on the offeror's acceding to any different terms in the acceptance. But so many acceptances are made over the phone by relatively junior employees, as in this case, that it may be unrealistic to expect offerees to protect themselves in this way. The offeror goes first and therefore has a little more time for careful specification of the terms on which he is willing to make a contract. What we are calling the leading minority view may tempt the offeror to spring a surprise on the offeree, hoping the latter won't read the fine print. Under the majority view, if the offeree tries to spring a surprise (the offeror can't, since his terms won't prevail if the acceptance contains different terms), the parties move to neutral ground; and the offeror can, we have suggested, more easily protect himself against being surprised than the offeree can protect *himself* against being surprised. The California rule dissolves all these problems, but has too little support to make it a plausible candidate for Illinois, or at least a plausible candidate for our guess as to Illinois's position.

There is a further wrinkle, however. The third subsection of section 2-207 provides that even if no contract is established under either of the first two subsections, it may be established by the "conduct of the parties," and in that event (as subsection (3) expressly provides) the discrepant terms vanish and are replaced by UCC gap fillers. This may seem to make it impossible for the offeror to protect himself from being contractually bound by specifying that the acceptance must mirror his offer. But subsection (3) comes into play only when the parties have by their conduct manifested the existence of a contract, as where the offeror, having specified that the acceptance must mirror the offer yet having received an acceptance that deviates from the offer, nonetheless goes ahead and performs as if there were a contract. That is one way to interpret what happened here but it leads to the same result as applying subsection (2) interpreted as the majority of states do, so we need not consider it separately.

Given the intricacy of the No. 1714 boards, it is unlikely that Northrop would have acceded to a 90-day limitation on its warranty protection. Litronic at argument stressed that it is a much smaller firm, hence presumably unwilling to assume burdensome warranty obligations; but it is a curious suggestion that little fellows are more likely than big ones to get their way in negotiations between firms of disparate size. And Northrop actually got only half its way, though enough for victory here; for by virtue of accepting Litronic's offer without expressly conditioning its acceptance on Litronic's acceding to Northrop's terms, Northrop got not a warranty unlimited in duration, as its purchase order provides, but (pursuant to the majority understanding of UCC §2-207(2)) a warranty of "reasonable" duration, courtesy the court. If special circumstances made a 90-day warranty reasonable, Litronic was free to argue for it in the district court.

On the view we take, the purchase order has no significance beyond showing that Northrop's acceptance contained (albeit by reference) different terms. The fact that Litronic never signed the order, and the fact that Northrop never called this omission to Litronic's attention, also drop out of the case, along with Northrop's argument that to enforce the 90-day limitation in Litronic's warranty would be unconscionable. But for future reference we remind Northrop and companies like it that the defense of unconscionability was not invented to protect multi-billion dollar corporations against mistakes committed by their employees, and indeed has rarely succeeded outside the area of consumer contracts. Original Great American Chocolate Chip Cookie Co. v. River Valley Cookies, Ltd., 970 F.2d 273, 281 (7th Cir. 1992); Salt River Project Agricultural Improvement & Power District v. Westinghouse Electric Corp., 143 Ariz. 368, 694 P.2d 198, 204 (Ariz. 1984); White & Summers, supra, §4-9.

AFFIRMED.

The interpretation of §2-207(2) adopted in *Northrup* is sometimes termed the *knockout* rule, on the theory that the respective parties' forms knock out each other's additional or different terms; see discussion in Reilly Foam Corp. v. Rubbermaid Corp, 206 F. Supp. 2d 643 (E.D. Pa. 2002).

Courts call the clause that ends subsection (1) of §2-207 ("unless acceptance is expressly made conditional on assent to the additional or different terms") the *proviso* clause. The proviso clause acts just like a railroad switch. If it is *not* used as part of the accepting form, then the purported acceptance does create a contract, and the parties are directed to subsection (2) to determine its terms. If the proviso is put into the accepting document, the exchange of forms does not create a contract, and the parties are directed to subsection (3) to see what results from their dealings. Our point is this: the presence or absence of the proviso shunts the parties into either subsection (2) or subsection (3), *but never both*.

PROBLEM 17   2-207(3)

On April 25, Plastic Furniture Mart sent a purchase order for 100 tables to the Ersatz Manufacturing Company. In addition to the usual boilerplate language, the purchase order also stated: "BUYER OBJECTS IN ADVANCE TO ANY TERMS PROPOSED BY SELLER THAT DIFFER IN ANY WAY FROM THE TERMS OF THIS PURCHASE ORDER." Ersatz received the order, and on May 3 it sent back its own acknowledgment form, which disclaimed all warranties and contained this clause: "THIS IS NOT AN ACCEPTANCE UNLESS BUYER ASSENTS TO ALL CHANGES MADE BY THIS ACKNOWLEDGMENT FORM." Neither party read the details of the other's form. On May 6, Ersatz shipped the tables. Is there a contract? See §§2-207(3), 2-206(1)(b); see Building Materials Corporation of America v. Henkel Corporation, 2016 WL 7666151 (M.D. Fla. 2016). Did Ersatz make a warranty as to the condition of the tables? See §2-314. On May 3 was there a contract?

QUESTION

Assume that you are an associate at a law firm that represents a seller who frequently receives purchase orders triggering §2-207's rules. Your client wants to disclaim warranties, and the senior partner asks you to come up with a way of doing this. What do you advise? How comfortable will be you be sleeping that night?

PROBLEM 18

Through a series of phone calls, the parties reached a complete oral agreement on the terms of a sales contract. Seller then sent buyer an e-mail saying "I'm delighted we've made this deal. The contract is attached." The attachment was seller's usual Acknowledgement Form, and it first disclaimed warranties (which had not been discussed in the oral communications), and then clearly tracked the language of §2-207(1)'s proviso, by stating that this was not an acceptance unless buyer expressly agreed to seller's new terms. Buyer responded by sending payment, and seller promptly shipped the goods. When the goods proved to be unmerchantable, buyer sued, and seller pointed to the disclaimer of warranties in its Acknowledgement Form. Can seller use the proviso in this situation? See Air Prods. & Chem., Inc. v. Fairbanks Morse, Inc., 58 Wis. 2d 193, 206 N.W.2d 414, 422-423 (1973). *acceptance is* [2-207 (2)]

Klocek v. Gateway, Inc.

transaction for the

United States District Court, Kansas, 2000, 104 F. Supp. 2d 1332

Subject article II
because gives movable

VRATIL, District Judge.

William S. Klocek brings suit against Gateway, Inc. and Hewlett-Packard, Inc. on claims arising from purchases of a Gateway computer and a Hewlett-Packard scanner. . . . For reasons stated below, the Court overrules Gateway's motion to dismiss, sustains Hewlett-Packard's motion to dismiss, and overrules the motions filed by plaintiff.

2-206 (1) (b)

I. GATEWAY'S MOTION TO DISMISS

Plaintiff brings individual and class action claims against Gateway, alleging that it induced him and other consumers to purchase computers and special support packages by making false promises of technical support. *Complaint,* ¶¶3 and 4. Individually, plaintiff also claims breach of contract and breach of warranty, in that Gateway breached certain warranties that its computer would be compatible with standard peripherals and standard internet services. *Complaint,* ¶¶2, 5, and 6.

Gateway asserts that plaintiff must arbitrate his claims under Gateway's Standard Terms and Conditions Agreement ("Standard Terms"). Whenever it sells a computer, Gateway includes a copy of the Standard Terms in the box which contains the computer battery power cables and instruction manuals. At the top of the first page, the Standard Terms include the following notice:

Note to the Customer:
This document contains Gateway 2000's Standard Terms and Conditions. By keeping your Gateway 2000 computer system beyond five (5) days after the date of delivery, you accept these Terms and Conditions.

The notice is in emphasized type and is located inside a printed box which sets it apart from other provisions of the document. The Standard Terms are four pages long and contain 16 numbered paragraphs. Paragraph 10 provides the following arbitration clause:

DISPUTE RESOLUTION. Any dispute or controversy arising out of or relating to this Agreement or its interpretation shall be settled exclusively and finally by arbitration. The arbitration shall be conducted in accordance with the Rules of Conciliation and Arbitration of the International Chamber of Commerce. The arbitration shall be conducted in Chicago, Illinois, U.S.A. before a sole arbitrator. Any award rendered in any such arbitration proceeding shall be final and binding on each of the parties, and judgment may be entered thereon in a court of competent jurisdiction.[11]

Gateway urges the Court to dismiss plaintiff's claims under the Federal Arbitration Act ("FAA"), 9 U.S.C. §1 et seq. The FAA ensures that written arbitration agreements in maritime transactions and transactions involving interstate commerce are "valid, irrevocable, and enforceable." 9 U.S.C. §2. Federal policy favors arbitration agreements and requires that we "rigorously enforce" them. Shearson/American Exp., Inc. v. McMahon, 482 U.S. 220, 226, 107 S. Ct. 2332, 96 L. Ed. 2d 185 (1987) (quoting Dean Witter Reynolds, Inc. v. Byrd, 470 U.S. 213, 105 S. Ct. 1238, 84 L. Ed. 2d 158 (1985)); *Moses,* 460 U.S. at 24, 103 S. Ct. 927. "[A]ny doubts concerning the scope of arbitrable issues should be resolved in favor of arbitration." *Moses,* 460 U.S. at 24-25, 103 S. Ct. 927.

FAA Section 3 states:

If any suit or proceeding be brought in any of the courts of the United States upon any issue referable to arbitration under an agreement in writing for such arbitration, the court in which such suit is pending, upon being satisfied that the issue involved in such suit or proceeding is referable to arbitration under

---

11. Gateway states that after it sold plaintiff's computer, it mailed all existing customers in the United States a copy of its quarterly magazine, which contained notice of a change in the arbitration policy set forth in the Standard Terms. The new arbitration policy afforded customers the option of arbitrating before the International Chamber of Commerce ("ICC"), the American Arbitration Association ("AAA"), or the National Arbitration Forum ("NAF") in Chicago, Illinois, or any other location agreed upon by the parties. Plaintiff denies receiving notice of the amended arbitration policy. Neither party explains why — if the arbitration agreement was an enforceable contract — Gateway was entitled to unilaterally amend it by sending a magazine to computer customers.

such agreement, shall on application of one of the parties stay the trial of the action until such arbitration has been had in accordance with the terms of the agreement, providing the applicant for the stay is not in default in proceeding with such arbitration.

9 U.S.C. §3. . . . [T]he Court concludes that dismissal is appropriate if plaintiff's claims are arbitrable.

Gateway bears an initial summary-judgment-like burden of establishing that it is entitled to arbitration. [Citations omitted.] Thus, Gateway must present evidence sufficient to demonstrate the existence of an enforceable agreement to arbitrate. See, e.g., Oppenheimer & Co. v. Neidhardt, 56 F.3d 352, 358 (2d Cir. 1995). If Gateway makes such a showing, the burden shifts to plaintiff to submit evidence demonstrating a genuine issue for trial. Id.; see also Naddy v. Piper Jaffray, Inc., 88 Wash. App. 1033, 1997 WL 749261, *2, Case Nos. 15431-9-III, 15681-8-III (Wash. App. Dec. 4, 1997). In this case, Gateway fails to present evidence establishing the most basic facts regarding the transaction. The gaping holes in the evidentiary record preclude the Court from determining what state law controls the formation of the contract in this case and, consequently, prevent the Court from agreeing that Gateway's motion is well taken.

Before granting a stay or dismissing a case pending arbitration, the Court must determine that the parties have a written agreement to arbitrate. See 9 U.S.C. §§3 and 4; Avedon Engineering, Inc. v. Seatex, 126 F.3d 1279, 1283 (10th Cir. 1997). When deciding whether the parties have agreed to arbitrate, the Court applies ordinary state law principles that govern the formation of contracts. First Options of Chicago, Inc. v. Kaplan, 514 U.S. 938, 944, 115 S. Ct. 1920, 131 L. Ed. 2d 985 (1995). The existence of an arbitration agreement "is simply a matter of contract between the parties; [arbitration] is a way to resolve those disputes — but only those disputes — that the parties have agreed to submit to arbitration." Avedon, 126 F.3d at 1283 (quoting Kaplan, 514 U.S. at 943-945, 115 S. Ct. 1920). If the parties dispute making an arbitration agreement, a jury trial on the existence of an agreement is warranted if the record reveals genuine issues of material fact regarding the parties' agreement. See Avedon, 126 F.3d at 1283. . . .

The Uniform Commercial Code ("UCC") governs the parties' transaction under both Kansas and Missouri law. See K.S.A. §84-2-102; V.A.M.S. §400.2-102 (UCC applies to "transactions in goods."); Kansas Comment 1 (main thrust of Article 2 is limited to sales); K.S.A. §84-2-105(1) V.A.M.S. §400.2-105(1) ("'Goods' means all things . . . which are movable at the time of identification to the contract for sale. . . ."). Regardless whether plaintiff purchased the computer in person or placed an order and received shipment of the computer, the parties agree that plaintiff paid for and received a computer from Gateway. This conduct clearly demonstrates a contract for the sale of a computer. See, e.g., Step-Saver Data Sys., Inc. v. Wyse Techn., 939 F.2d 91, 98 (3d Cir. 1991). Thus the issue is whether the contract of sale includes the Standard Terms as part of the agreement.

State courts in Kansas and Missouri apparently have not decided whether terms received with a product become part of the parties' agreement. Authority from other courts is split. Compare *Step-Saver*, 939 F.2d 91 (printed terms on computer software package not part of agreement); Arizona Retail Sys., Inc. v. Software Link, Inc., 831 F. Supp. 759 (D. Ariz. 1993) (license agreement shipped with computer software not part of agreement); and U.S. Surgical Corp. v. Orris, Inc., 5 F. Supp. 2d 1201 (D. Kan. 1998) (single use restriction on product package not binding agreement); with Hill v. Gateway 2000, Inc., 105 F.3d 1147 (7th Cir.), *cert. denied*, 522 U.S. 808, 118 S. Ct. 47, 139 L. Ed. 2d 13 (1997) (arbitration provision shipped with computer binding on buyer); ProCD, Inc. v. Zeidenberg, 86 F.3d 1447 (7th Cir. 1996) (shrinkwrap license binding on buyer)[12] and M.A. Mortenson Co., Inc. v. Timberline Software Corp., 140 Wash. 2d 568, 998 P.2d 305 (2000) (following *Hill* and *ProCD* on license agreement supplied with software).[13] It appears that at least in part, the cases turn on whether the court finds that the parties formed their contract *before* or *after* the vendor communicated its terms to the purchaser. Compare *Step-Saver*, 939 F.2d at 98 (parties' conduct in shipping, receiving and paying for product demonstrates existence of contract; box-top license constitutes proposal for additional terms under §2-207 which requires express agreement by purchaser); *Arizona Retail*, 831 F. Supp. at 765 (vendor entered into contract by agreeing to ship goods, or at latest by shipping goods to buyer; license agreement constitutes proposal to modify agreement under §2-209 which requires express assent by buyer); and *Orris*, 5 F. Supp. 2d at 1206 (sales contract concluded when vendor received consumer orders; single-use language on product's label was proposed modification under §2-209 which requires express assent by

---

12. The term "shrinkwrap license" gets its name from retail software packages that are covered in plastic or cellophane "shrinkwrap" and contain licenses that purport to become effective as soon as the customer tears the wrapping from the package. See *ProCD*, 86 F.3d at 1449.

13. The *Mortenson* court also found support for its holding in the proposed Uniform Computer Information Transactions Act ("UCITA") (formerly known as proposed UCC Article 2B), which the National Conference of Commissioners on Uniform State Laws approved and recommended for enactment by the states in July 1999. See *Mortenson*, 998 P.2d at 310 n.6, 313 n.10. The proposed UCITA, however, would not apply to the Court's analysis in this case. The UCITA applies to computer information transactions, which are defined as agreements "to create, modify, transfer, or license computer information or informational rights in computer information." UCITA, §§102(11), 103. In transactions involving the sale of computers, such as our case, the UCITA applies only to the computer programs and copies, not to the sale of the computer itself. See UCITA §103(c)(2).

purchaser); with *ProCD,* 86 F.3d at 1452 (under §2-204 vendor, as master of offer, may propose limitations on kind of conduct that constitutes acceptance; §2-207 does not apply in case with only one form); *Hill,* 105 F.3d at 1148-49 (same); and *Mortenson,* 998 P.2d at 311-314 (where vendor and purchaser utilized license agreement in prior course of dealing, shrinkwrap license agreement constituted issue of contract formation under §2-204, not contract alteration under §2-207).

Gateway urges the Court to follow the Seventh Circuit decision in *Hill.* That case involved the shipment of a Gateway computer with terms similar to the Standard Terms in this case, except that Gateway gave the customer 30 days — instead of 5 days — to return the computer. In enforcing the arbitration clause, the Seventh Circuit relied on its decision in *ProCD,* where it enforced a software license which was contained inside a product box. See *Hill,* 105 F.3d at 1148-50. In *ProCD,* the Seventh Circuit noted that the exchange of money frequently precedes the communication of detailed terms in a commercial transaction. See *ProCD,* 86 F.3d at 1451. Citing UCC §2-204, the court reasoned that by including the license with the software, the vendor proposed a contract that the buyer could accept by using the software after having an opportunity to read the license.[14] *ProCD,* 86 F.3d at 1452. Specifically, the court stated:

> A vendor, as master of the offer, may invite acceptance by conduct, and may propose limitations on the kind of conduct that constitutes acceptance. A buyer may accept by performing the acts the vendor proposes to treat as acceptance.

ProCD, 86 F.3d at 1452. The *Hill* court followed the *ProCD* analysis, noting that "[p]ractical considerations support allowing vendors to enclose the full legal terms with their products." *Hill,* 105 F.3d at 1149.[15]

---

14. Section 2-204 provides: "A contract for sale of goods may be made in any manner sufficient to show agreement, including conduct by both parties which recognizes the existence of such contract." K.S.A. §84-2-204; V.A.M.S. §400.2-204.

15. Legal commentators have criticized the reasoning of the Seventh Circuit in this regard. See, e.g., Jean R. Sternlight, *Gateway* Widens Doorway to Imposing Unfair Binding Arbitration on Consumers, Fla. Bar J., Nov. 1997, at 8, 10-12 (outcome in *Gateway* is questionable on federal statutory, common law and constitutional grounds and as a matter of contract law and is unwise as a matter of policy because it unreasonably shifts to consumers search cost of ascertaining existence of arbitration clause and return cost to avoid such clause); Thomas J. McCarthy et al., Survey: Uniform Commercial Code, 53 Bus. Law. 1461, 1465-66 (Seventh Circuit finding that UCC §2-207 did not apply is inconsistent with official comment); Batya Goodman, Honey, I Shrink-Wrapped the Consumer: the Shrinkwrap Agreement as an Adhesion Contract, 21 Cardozo L. Rev. 319, 344-352 (Seventh Circuit failed to consider principles of adhesion contracts); Jeremy Senderowicz, Consumer Arbitration and Freedom of Contract: A Proposal to Facilitate Consumers' Informed Consent to Arbitration Clauses in

The Court is not persuaded that Kansas or Missouri courts would follow the Seventh Circuit reasoning in *Hill* and *ProCD*. In each case the Seventh Circuit concluded without support that UCC §2-207 was irrelevant because the cases involved only one written form. See *ProCD*, 86 F.3d at 1452 (citing no authority); *Hill*, 105 F.3d at 1150 (citing *ProCD*). This conclusion is not supported by the statute or by Kansas or Missouri law. Disputes under §2-207 often arise in the context of a "battle of forms," see, e.g., Diatom, Inc. v. Pennwalt Corp., 741 F.2d 1569, 1574 (10th Cir. 1984), but nothing in its language precludes application in a case which involves only one form. The statute provides:

> Additional terms in acceptance or confirmation.
>
> (1) A definite and seasonable expression of acceptance or a written confirmation which is sent within a reasonable time operates as an acceptance even though it states terms additional to or different from those offered or agreed upon, unless acceptance is expressly made conditional on assent to the additional or different terms.
>
> (2) The additional terms are to be construed as proposals for addition to the contract [if the contract is not between merchants]. . . .

K.S.A. §84-2-207; V.A.M.S. §400.2-207. By its terms, §2-207 applies to an acceptance or written confirmation. It states nothing which requires another form before the provision becomes effective. In fact, the official comment to the section specifically provides that §2-207(1) and (2) apply "where an agreement has been reached orally . . . and is followed by one or both of the parties sending formal memoranda embodying the terms so far agreed and adding terms not discussed." Official Comment 1 of UCC §2-207. Kansas and Missouri courts have followed this analysis. See Southwest Engineering Co. v. Martin Tractor Co., 205 Kan. 684, 695, 473 P.2d 18, 26 (1970) (stating in dicta that §2-207 applies where open offer is accepted by expression of acceptance in writing or where oral agreement is later confirmed in writing); Central Bag Co. v. W. Scott and Co., 647 S.W.2d 828, 830 (Mo. App. 1983) (§2-207(1) and (2) govern cases where one or both parties send written confirmation after oral contract). Thus, the Court concludes

---

Form Contracts, 32 Colum. J.L. & Soc. Probs. 275, 296-299 (judiciary (in multiple decisions, including *Hill*) has ignored issue of consumer consent to an arbitration clause). Nonetheless, several courts have followed the Seventh Circuit decisions in *Hill* and *ProCD*. See, e.g., M.A. Mortenson Co., Inc. v. Timberline Software Corp., 140 Wash. 2d 568, 998 P.2d 305 (license agreement supplied with software); Rinaldi v. Iomega Corp., 1999 WL 1442014, Case No. 98C-09-064-RRC (Del. Super. Sept. 3, 1999) (warranty disclaimer included inside computer Zip drive packaging); Westendorf v. Gateway 2000, Inc., 2000 WL 307369, Case No. 16913 (Del. Ch. March 16, 2000) (arbitration provision shipped with computer); Brower v. Gateway 2000, Inc., 246 A.D.2d 246, 676 N.Y.S.2d 569 (N.Y. App. Div. 1998) (same); Levy v. Gateway 2000, Inc., 1997 WL 823611, 1060 (N.Y. Sup. Oct. 31, 1997) (same).

that Kansas and Missouri courts would apply §2-207 to the facts in this case. Accord *Avedon*, 126 F.3d at 1283 (parties agree that §2-207 controls whether arbitration clause in sales confirmation is part of contract).

In addition, the Seventh Circuit provided no explanation for its conclusion that "the vendor is the master of the offer." See *ProCD*, 86 F.3d at 1452 (citing nothing in support of proposition); *Hill*, 105 F.3d at 1149 (citing *ProCD*). In typical consumer transactions, the purchaser is the offeror, and the vendor is the offeree. See Brown Mach., Div. of John Brown, Inc. v. Hercules, Inc., 770 S.W.2d 416, 419 (Mo. App. 1989) (as general rule orders are considered offers to purchase); Rich Prods. Corp. v. Kemutec Inc., 66 F. Supp. 2d 937, 956 (E.D. Wis. 1999) (generally price quotation is invitation to make offer and purchase order is offer). While it is possible for the vendor to be the offeror, see *Brown Machine*, 770 S.W.2d at 419 (price quote can amount to offer if it reasonably appears from quote that assent to quote is all that is needed to ripen offer into contract), Gateway provides no factual evidence which would support such a finding in this case. The Court therefore assumes for purposes of the motion to dismiss that plaintiff offered to purchase the computer (either in person or through catalog order) and that Gateway accepted plaintiff's offer (either by completing the sales transaction in person or by agreeing to ship and/or shipping the computer to plaintiff).[16] Accord *Arizona Retail*, 831 F. Supp. at 765 (vendor entered into contract by agreeing to ship goods, or at latest, by shipping goods).

Under §2-207, the Standard Terms constitute either an expression of acceptance or written confirmation. As an expression of acceptance, the Standard Terms would constitute a counter-offer only if Gateway expressly made its acceptance conditional on plaintiff's assent to the additional or different terms. K.S.A. §84-2-207(1); V.A.M.S. §400.2-207(1). "[T]he conditional nature of the acceptance must be clearly expressed in a manner sufficient to notify the offeror that the offeree is unwilling to proceed with the transaction unless the additional or different terms are included in the contract." *Brown Machine*, 770 S.W.2d at 420. Gateway provides no evidence that at the time of the sales transaction, it informed plaintiff that the transaction was conditioned on plaintiff's acceptance of the Standard Terms. Moreover, the mere fact that Gateway shipped the goods with the terms attached did not communicate to plaintiff any unwillingness to proceed without plaintiff's agreement to the Standard Terms. See, e.g., *Arizona*

---

16. UCC §2-206(b) provides that "an order or other offer to buy goods for prompt or current shipment shall be construed as inviting acceptance either by a prompt promise to ship or by the prompt or current shipment. . . ." The official comment states that "[e]ither shipment or a prompt promise to ship is made a proper means of acceptance of an offer looking to current shipment." UCC §2-206, Official Comment 2.

Retail, 831 F. Supp. at 765 (conditional acceptance analysis rarely appropriate where contract formed by performance but goods arrive with conditions attached); Leighton Indus., Inc. v. Callier Steel Pipe & Tube, Inc., 1991 WL 18413, *6, Case No. 89-C-8235 (N.D. Ill. Feb. 6, 1991) (applying Missouri law) (preprinted forms insufficient to notify offeror of conditional nature of acceptance, particularly where form arrives after delivery of goods).

Because plaintiff is not a merchant, additional or different terms contained in the Standard Terms did not become part of the parties' agreement unless plaintiff expressly agreed to them. See K.S.A. §84-2-207, Kansas Comment 2 (if either party is not a merchant, additional terms are proposals for addition to the contract that do not become part of the contract unless the original offeror expressly agrees). Gateway argues that plaintiff demonstrated acceptance of the arbitration provision by keeping the computer more than five days after the date of delivery. Although the Standard Terms purport to work that result, Gateway has not presented evidence that plaintiff expressly agreed to those Standard Terms. Gateway states only that it enclosed the Standard Terms inside the computer box for plaintiff to read afterwards. It provides no evidence that it informed plaintiff of the five-day review-and-return period as a condition of the sales transaction, or that the parties contemplated additional terms to the agreement.[17] See *Step-Saver,* 939 F.2d at 99 (during negotiations leading to purchase, vendor never mentioned box-top license or obtained buyer's express assent thereto). The Court finds that the act of keeping the computer past five days was not sufficient to demonstrate that plaintiff expressly agreed to the Standard Terms. Accord *Brown Machine,* 770 S.W.2d at 421 (express assent cannot be presumed by silence or mere failure to object). Thus, because Gateway has not provided evidence sufficient to support a finding under Kansas or Missouri law that plaintiff agreed to the arbitration provision contained in Gateway's Standard Terms, the Court overrules Gateway's motion to dismiss. . . .

There are many cases disagreeing with the court's analysis and requiring arbitration or allowing warranty disclaimers in spite of §2-207's provisions. These courts typically find that an "approve or return" clause in the paperwork arriving with the goods prevents formation of the contract until the buyer assents to the new terms (usually by doing nothing more than retaining

17. The Court is mindful of the practical considerations which are involved in commercial transactions, but it is not unreasonable for a vendor to clearly communicate to a buyer — at the time of sale — either the complete terms of the sale or the fact that the vendor will propose additional terms as a condition of sale, if that be the case.

the goods); see Fiser v. Dell Computer Corp., 142 N.M. 331, 165 P.3d 328 (2007). These decisions are all of a piece with the *ProCD* and *Hill* opinions discussed in the last case, which create so-called rolling or layered contracts through the negotiations plus the shipment with new terms, followed by the buyer's failure to object to the changes first mentioned in documents that come with the shipment, while ignoring §2-207 as irrelevant. By contrast, the Ninth Circuit squarely rejected *Hill*, reasoning that "silence alone does not constitute assent" and so "Samsung's inclusion of a brochure in the Galaxy S4 box, and Norcia's failure to opt out, does not make the arbitration provision enforceable against Norcia." Norcia v. Samsung Telecommunications America, LLC, 845 F.3d 1279, 1289 (9th Cir. 2017).

Looking to the future, consumers may sometimes have little opportunity to review contract terms, in the coming era of the Internet of Things. Web-enabled devices from printers to washing machines to thermostats may order supplies and components without direct supervision of consumers. Such machine-to-machine transactions may raise many issues of contract formation and content. See Stacy-Ann Elvy, Contracting in the Age of the Internet of Things: Article 2 of the UCC and Beyond, 44 Hofstra L. Rev. 839 (2016). What contract formation and content issues do you see arising?

CHAPTER 3 REVIEW QUESTIONS

What are the exceptions to the UCC Article 2 Statute of Frauds?
What sorts of parol evidence are admissible and subject to what conditions?
What are the requirements for an effective electronic signature?
What different ways may an offer be accepted under UCC Article 2?
What is the structure of the Battle of the Forms rule?

ASSESSMENT: MULTIPLE CHOICE QUESTIONS

1. Avril and Mario had a long conversation, ending with them agreeing that Avril would build Mario a custom wheelchair for an agreed price. When the wheelchair was almost finished, Avril contacted Mario to arrange delivery and payment. Mario denied that they had an enforceable contract, because he had not signed a contract and she had not sent him a confirmation. Is there an enforceable contract?
   a. No, for lack of a signed writing.
   b. Yes, because an oral agreement for specially manufactured goods is enforceable where the seller has made a substantial beginning.

    c. Yes, because no writing is required where the parties are not both mer-
       chants.

    d. No, because a writing is required to enforce a contract against a non-
       merchant.

2. Steeply agreed over the phone with Orin to purchase a painting by Joelle
    for $7,000. Not long after, Joelle disappeared in a volcanic explosion,
    which drove the price of her artwork up. Orin refused to deliver the paint-
    ing. In court, Orin testified, "We had an agreement, but sorry to say that it
    cannot be enforced without a writing." Can Steeply enforce the contract?
    a. No, for lack of a signed writing.
    b. Yes, because the goods are unique.
    c. Yes, because Orin admitted they had a contract.
    d. No, because Steeply could have sent a confirmation.

3. Pemulis Auto signs a contract with Lyle for the sale of a 2007 Pluto auto-
    mobile. Which of the following could be introduced as evidence of terms
    that were not included in the writing?
    a. A common practice in the used car business that sellers would replace
       any parts that failed for the first year.
    b. A practice between Pemulis Auto and Lyle, in their previous trans-
       actions, that Lyle could return the car within 30 days and get his
       money back.
    c. An oral agreement between the two that Pemulis Auto would provide
       free service for the first two years.
    d. All of the above.

4. Gately Construction faxes an order to Van Dyne Apps for 50 tablet
    computers. Van Dyne faxes back an acceptance, with the following
    provision: "THERE ARE NO WARRANTIES EXPRESS OR IMPLIED,
    INCLUDING NO WARRANTY OF MERCHANTABILITY FOR THE
    TABLET COMPUTERS." The tablet computers are duly shipped,
    accepted, and paid for. Not long after, Gately Construction finds the
    performance of the computers to be sub-par. Did Van Dyne's provision
    excluding warranties become part of the parties' contract?
    a. Yes, because Gately Construction did not object to the provision.
    b. Yes, because Gately Construction's offer did not expressly limit accept-
       ance to the terms of the offer.
    c. No, because the provision would materially alter the contract.
    d. No, because an acceptance that is different from the offer is not effec-
       tive to form a contract.

5. Enfield Academy sent Microcenter an order for 25 Yushituyo Media
    Players. The order provided that "[a]n acceptance of this offer is not effec-
    tive if the acceptance changes any of the terms of the offer." Microcenter

quickly sent back an acceptance letter, which contained an arbitration provision. Enfield Academy paid for the media players on delivery, but was dissatisfied to learn they lack the capacity to show tennis videos shot with a special slow-motion feature. Will Enfield Academy be subject to the arbitration clause, if there is a dispute?

a. No, because the parties never formed a contract.

b. No, because the arbitration clause would not be part of the contract.

c. Yes. The arbitration clause would be part of the contract because it was not a material alteration.

d. Yes, the arbitration clause would be part of the contract because Enfield Academy did not object to the clause.

ANSWERS

1. *B* is the best answer. Section 2-201 provides that a signed contract is generally required, but, contrary to *A*, then provides several generous exceptions. One applies here. No writing is required if the goods are specially manufactured for the buyer, not suitable for sale to others, and seller has made a "substantial beginning of their manufacture." §2-201(3)(a). Merchant status is not a factor in the rule, contrary to *C* and *D*.

2. *C* is the best answer. One of the biggest exceptions to the writing requirement is that no writing is necessary if the defendant admits in court that there was a contract. This means that a defendant cannot rely on the mere formality of a writing requirement, unless the defendant can avoid admitting the truth in court. Answer *B*'s reference to unique goods is misdirected. There is an exception for specially manufactured goods, but not unique goods. No confirmation is required to be sent, contrary to *D*.

3. *D* is the best answer. This question reminds us that the written contract may be explained or supplemented by usage of trade (as in *A*), course of dealing (as in *B*), and consistent additional terms (as in *C*), where writing is not shown to be the complete and exclusive statement of the parties' terms.

4. *C* is the best answer. The acceptance is effective, under the Battle of the Forms provision, §2-207(1). Unlike a stricter view under some common law cases, the UCC allows an acceptance to be effective even if it does not match the offer, contrary to *D*. But the additional terms become part of the contract only if they are not excluded by §2-207(2). The exclusion of all warranties would be excluded by §2-207(2)(b), because it is a material alteration. This would be the case even though Gately Construction did not object (contrary to *A*) or limit its original offer to its terms (contrary to *B*).

5. *B* is the best answer. Microcenter's acceptance is not effective to form a contract. Under §2-207(1), if the offer limits acceptance to the terms of the offer, an acceptance on different terms is not effective. So even if the arbitration clause is not a material alteration, the parties' writings do not form a contract. But, contrary to *A*, their conduct may form a contract, under §2-207(3). The terms of that contract would be the agreed terms, which would not include the arbitration clause.

CHAPTER 4
WARRANTIES

There is sometimes confusion in the minds of the parties to a sales transaction as to what a warranty is and how it relates to other terms of the contract, such as "if not satisfied, return within 30 days for a full refund." If a customer receives such a promise and does not return the item within the specified period but then the product malfunctions, the expired 30-day period has nothing to do with the subsequent assertion that the seller is in breach of warranty. A warranty is a contractual obligation by the seller to remedy certain possible defects in the goods. It may be useful to think of it as a sort of insurance policy issued by the seller to the buyer at the time of sale that promises a remedy if the product does not work or meet some claimed level of performance. If the warranty is breached it's no defense that the seller was free of negligence or that the fault lies with some other party, such as the manufacturer. Just like an insurance policy, it is a promise to pay if something goes wrong, regardless of fault.

The UCC divides warranties into two basic types: warranties of *title* and warranties of *quality,* and we start with the former. Read §2-312.

I.   *THE WARRANTY OF TITLE*

PROBLEM 19

Fast Eddie stole Mabel Stanley's car from a shopping center in Phoenix. He drove it to Las Vegas, where he sold it for $500 to Sealed Lips Used Cars. This firm somehow obtained a Nevada certificate of title for the car, which showed clean title in Sealed Lips. The car was then sold for $2,000 to a bona fide purchaser, Frederick Duty. Duty drove it for a month until a bad run at the roulette wheel forced him to sell it in order to finance further recreational activity. Another bona fide purchaser, Samuel Pirate, bought the car from Duty for $1,900. He drove it for only one week before the Nevada State Police impounded it and returned it to Mabel in Phoenix. Pirate sued Duty for breach of the warranty of good title.

(a) Duty argues that he *thought* he had good title, and since he was not negligent or in any way at fault in so believing, the warranty was not breached. Does this defense succeed? See Brokke v. Williams, 766 P.2d 1311 (Mont. 1989).

(b) Duty argues that he *did* have good title, and hence the warranty was not breached. Did he? See §2-403(1); Inmi-Etti v. Aluisi, 63 Md. App. 293, 492 A.2d 917(1985) (*Nemo dat qui non habet* — "He who hath not cannot give.").

(c) Would your answer to (b) change if Fast Eddie had bought the car from Mabel with a bad check? See §2-403; Allan Nott Enters., Inc. v. Nicholas Starr Auto, L.L.C. 110 Ohio St. 3d 112, 851 N.E.2d 479 (2006).

(d) Does the law give any relief to Duty? See §2-607(5)(a) (describing a procedure known as *vouching in*).

PROBLEM 20

Before the Nevada State Police found Mabel's car, discussed in the last Problem, they accidentally impounded a very similar car owned by P.T. Boss. Boss had recently purchased the car from Croupier Motors. In order to convince the police that they had made a mistake and should release the car to him, Boss had to hire an attorney, Arnold Sunglasses. The latter did retrieve the car and then sent Boss a bill for $4,100. Boss forwarded the bill to Croupier Motors, along with a cover letter to the effect that title problems were the seller's headache per §2-312. Should the car dealership pay Sunglasses's bill? See Official Comment 1 to §2-312; White & Summers §10-15(b), at 501-502; Saber v. Dan Angelone Chevrolet, Inc., 811 A.2d 644 (R.I. 2002). See also §2-607(5).

PROBLEM 21

Sellers can sometimes evade or disclaim the warranty of title. Determine if the warranty is present in the following situations:

(a) The sales contract has this clause: "The product is sold 'As Is' and seller makes no warranties, express or implied, as part of this sale." See Official Comment 6 to §2-312.

(b) Repossession Motors sold a car on credit to a customer who returned it after failing to make the first payment. It then conducted an Article 9-type resale. (See §9-610(d).) Does the resale buyer get the benefit of a §2-312 warranty? See Official Comment 5.

(c) Ted Traveler walked into the men's room of the bus depot and, to his surprise, was offered an expensive watch at a bargain rate from a stranger. He bought the watch. Is there a warranty of title in this transaction? See §1-303(c).

Moore v. Pro Team Corvette Sales, Inc.

Court of Appeals of Ohio, 2002, 152 Ohio App. 3d 71, 786 N.E.2d 903

WALTERS, J.

Plaintiff-Appellant, Bryon Moore, brings this appeal from a Henry County Common Pleas Court decision which dismissed his action against Defendant-Appellee, Pro Team Corvette Sales, Inc., regarding a contract for the sale of a 1974 Chevrolet Corvette, which was subsequently discovered to be stolen. On appeal, Moore argues that terms within the agreement did not effectively disclaim the implied warranty of title under U.C.C. 2-312. Because U.C.C. 2-312 provides for a buyer's basic needs with respect to the type of title he in good faith expects to acquire by his purchase, namely, a good, clean title transferred to him in a rightful manner, we find that the provision lacks sufficient specificity to disclaim the implied warranty of title. Accordingly, we reverse the judgment of the trial court.

Facts and procedural history relevant to issues raised on appeal are as follows: In October 1994, Moore drove from his Gross Isle, Michigan, residence to Pro Team Corvette Sales, Inc. ("Pro Team"), located in Napoleon, Ohio, in order to purchase a Chevrolet Corvette. On October 17, 1994, he signed an agreement to purchase a 1974 Corvette, as well as a separate agreement to trade in his 1975 Corvette. When Moore attempted to register the car with the Michigan Bureau of Motor Vehicles, he learned that the car had been reported stolen in Texas, and therefore could not be registered. The Michigan State Police subsequently confiscated the car and returned it to Texas.

On October 15, 1996, Moore filed suit against Pro Team, arguing that its failure to provide good title to the vehicle was negligent. He also claimed unjust enrichment, breach of statutory warranties, and violations of Ohio's Consumer Sales Practices Act. Pro Team denied all liability, claiming that it had excluded all warranties, including the warranty of title, in the purchase agreement. Pro Team also filed a third-party complaint against the dealership that sold the car to Pro Team, as well as the person who sold the car to that dealer, the Michigan State Police, and the sheriff of San Patricio County, Texas.

In defending the suit, Pro Team relied upon language in its contract indicating that the Corvette was being sold "as is" and that the all warranties, including the warranty of title, were excluded from the agreement. Moore sought summary judgment, arguing that the language contained in the agreement was not sufficient to constitute a valid disclaimer of statutorily implied warranties of title. This motion was denied. Moore subsequently dismissed all counts unrelated to the warranty provisions. In February 2002, the trial court dismissed his remaining claims, concluding that the language contained in the agreement was sufficiently specific to permit exclusion of the warranty of title under U.C.C. 2-312.

Moore appeals the trial court's judgment, presenting the following single assignment of error for our review: "The Trial Court erred when it concluded that the dealer's contract properly excluded the warranty of title."

In Ohio, "a seller warrants that he will convey good title free from any security interest or other lien or encumbrance of which the buyer is without knowledge when the contract is made." This implied warranty of title is codified in U.C.C. 2-312 [which the court then quoted].

Accordingly, "[u]nless excluded or modified, U.C.C. 2-312(1) adds to a sales contract a warranty by the seller that the title conveyed shall be good and its transfer rightful." As provided by U.C.C. 2-312(2), a warranty of title may be excluded or modified by specific language giving the purchaser reasons to know that the vendor is only selling what title he possesses.

> [T]his code section provides for a buyer's basic needs in respect to the type of title he in good faith expects to acquire by his purchase, namely, a good, clean title transferred to him in a rightful manner so that he will not be exposed to a lawsuit in order to protect it. . . . In the usual case, the buyer expects to get a good title, and regards disclaimers as affecting only risks with regard to quality.[1]

The Michigan Court of Appeals, in Jones v. Linebaugh, held that "very precise and unambiguous language must be used to exclude a warranty so

---

1. 1 Hawkland UCC Series (2001) §2-312:5, Disclaimer of Warranty of Title-Contractual Terms.

basic to the sale of goods as is title." Specific language is necessary to relieve the buyer of the idea that any disclaimer of warranty relates only to quality.[2] In Sunseri v. RKO-Stanley Warner Theaters, Inc.,[3] the court found language stating that the seller "shall in nowise be . . . liable . . . upon or under guaranties [*sic*] or warranties . . . including, but not limited to, the implied warrant[y] of title" lacked sufficient specificity to disclaim the warranty of title. The court reasoned that the language used was ineffective because it was "couched in negative terminology," expressing what the seller will not be liable for rather than what the buyer is or is not receiving. The inadequacy of such a caveat is best illustrated by juxtaposing it with title disclaimer provisions suggested by authorities in the subject area. For example, 18 Am. Jur. Legal Forms 2d §253:825 (1974), provides:

> Seller makes no warranty as to the title to the goods, and buyer assumes all risks of nonownership of the goods by seller. . . . [W]here the language in a purported disclaimer expresses how the seller's liability will be limited rather than what title (or lack thereof) the seller purports to transfer, the purported disclaimer is ineffective.[4]

The relevant portion of the sale contract states: "All warranties pursuant to U.C.C. 2-312 are hereby excluded from this transaction." In light of the foregoing discussion, we find this language to be akin to that which expresses how the seller's liability will be limited, rather than what title the seller purports to transfer, and conclude that the provision lacks sufficient specificity to disclaim the implied warranty of title. Accordingly, Moore's assignment of error is sustained.

Having found error prejudicial to the appellant herein, in the particulars assigned and argued, the judgment of the trial court is hereby reversed and the matter is remanded for further proceedings in accordance with this opinion.

Judgment reversed and cause remanded.

QUESTION

Why is the court being so picky here? What policy is at work? Could this case have been better decided on the grounds that a disclaimer of

---

2. 1 Hawkland UCC Series (2001) §2-312:5, Disclaimer of Warranty of Title-Contractual Terms.

3. Sunseri v. RKO-Stanley Warner Theaters, Inc. (1977), 248 Pa. Super. 111, 374 A.2d 1342, 1344.

4. *Kel-Keef*, 738 N.E.2d at 536.

"UCC 2-312" is always insufficient because no one will know what that strange citation means? If you, future attorney, are going to draft a clause disclaiming liability for breach of the warranty of title, how should you phrase it?

Note that the warranty of title also includes:

(1) a warranty that there are no security interests (or other liens) on the goods other than those of which the buyer knows (§2-312(1)(b)), and

(2) a warranty given by merchant sellers against claims based on patent infringement or the like (§2-312(3)).

See Big Lots Stores, Inc. v. Luv N' Care, 2007 WL 1026448 (S.D. Ohio 2007) (breach of warranty of title to supply inventory bearing infringing trademark); Phoenix Solutions, Inc. v. Sony Electronics, Inc., 637 F. Supp. 2d 683 (N.D. Cal. 2009) (breach of warranty of title where buyer subject to patent infringement claim).

If the buyer furnishes specifications to the seller (which happens where the goods are to be specially manufactured to the buyer's order), the *buyer* automatically makes a warranty to the seller that protects the latter from infringement claims. Section 2-312(3). This is the *only* situation under the UCC where the buyer is the warrantor.

Entrustment. Closely related to the warranty of title is the doctrine of entrustment, under which a merchant may pass good title to goods someone has entrusted to the merchant, even though the merchant neither owns the goods nor has actual authority to sell them.

PROBLEM 22

Yankees fan Billy Slider bought a baseball at an auction that was supposedly signed by both Babe Ruth and Lou Gehrig. He was worried it wasn't authentic, so he took it to Sports Confidence, a company that specialized in examining the bona fides of sports memorabilia. He asked them to look into its history and authenticity. The owner of the company immediately recognized it as a major find and decided to steal it. He sold it a man named Alex Stewart and told Billy Slider that the baseball was a fake. On learning the truth, can Slider recover the baseball from Stewart? Do you need to know anything more about Stewart? See §2-403(2) and (3); Zaretsky v. William Goldberg Diamond Corp., 2014 WL 6469083 (S.D.N.Y. 2014); Galin v. Hamada, 2017 WL 4286309 (S.D.N.Y. 2017).

Lindholm v. Brant

Supreme Court of Connecticut, 2007, 283 Conn. 65, 925 A.2d 1048

SULLIVAN, J.

[Lindholm entrusted her painting, *Red Elvis* by Andy Warhol, to Malmberg, a respected art dealer, who arranged for it to be displayed at several leading museums in the United States and Europe — and then sold it for $2.9 million to Brant. Brant had ordered a lien search and a search of the Art Loss Register, neither of which disclosed any problems with title. Brant's presale efforts to get documents showing that the art dealer indeed owned the painting he was selling were unsuccessful.]

Section 42a-2-403 (2) provides that "[a]ny entrusting of possession of goods to a merchant who deals in goods of that kind gives him power to transfer all rights of the entruster to a buyer in ordinary course of business." "'Entrusting'" is defined as "any delivery and any acquiescence in retention of possession regardless of any condition expressed between the parties to the delivery or acquiescence and regardless of whether the procurement of the entrusting or the possessor's disposition of the goods have been such as to be larcenous under the criminal law." General Statutes §42a-2-403 (3).

There is no dispute in the present case that the plaintiff's March 20, 2000, letter authorizing the Guggenheim to release *Red Elvis* to Malmberg constituted an entrustment under §42a-2-403 (3), or that Malmberg, an art dealer, is a merchant dealing in "goods of that kind" — works of art — under §42a-2-403 (2). Under the plain language of §42a-2-403 (2) and (3), therefore, Malmberg, as a merchant dealing in art entrusted with the painting, had the power to transfer all the rights of the entruster to a buyer in the ordinary course of business.

A "'[b]uyer in [the] ordinary course of business'" is defined as "a person that buys goods in good faith, without knowledge that the sale violates the rights of another person in the goods, and in the ordinary course from a person . . . in the business of selling goods of that kind. A person buys goods in the ordinary course if the sale to the person comports with the usual or customary practices in the kind of business in which the seller is engaged or with the seller's own usual or customary practices. . . ." General Statutes §42a-1-201 (9). A person buys goods in good faith if there is "honesty in fact and the observance of reasonable commercial standards of fair dealing" in the conduct or transaction concerned. General Statutes §42a-1-201 (20).

We are required, therefore, to determine whether the defendant followed the usual or customary practices and observed reasonable commercial standards of fair dealing in the art industry in his dealings with Malmberg. As we have indicated, the defendant presented expert testimony that the vast majority of art transactions, in which the buyer has no reason for concern about the seller's ability to convey good title, are "completed on a handshake and an exchange of an invoice." It is not customary for sophisticated buyers and sellers to obtain a signed invoice from the original seller to the dealer prior to a transaction, nor is it an ordinary or customary practice to request the underlying invoice or corroborating information as to a dealer's authority to convey title. Moreover, it is not customary to approach the owner of an artwork if the owner regularly worked with a particular art dealer because any inquiries about an art transaction customarily are presented to the art dealer rather than directly to the principal. It is customary to rely upon representations made by respected dealers regarding their authority to sell works of art. A dealer customarily is not required to present an invoice establishing when and from whom he bought the artwork or the conditions of the purchase.

We are compelled to conclude, however, that the sale from Malmberg to the defendant was unlike the vast majority of art transactions. The defendant had good reason to be concerned that Lindholm might have claims to the painting. Several courts have held that, under such circumstances, a handshake and an exchange of invoice is not sufficient to confer status as a buyer in the ordinary course. In Porter v. Wertz, 416 N.Y.S.2d 254, 68 A.D.2d 141 (1979), aff'd, 53 N.Y.2d 696, 421 N.E.2d 500, 439 N.Y.S.2d 105 (1981), for example, the owner of a painting entrusted it to an individual with whom he previously had conducted art transactions for display in the individual's home. This individual then used the services of a delicatessen employee, posing as an art dealer, to sell the painting to a merchant art buyer. Id., 145-46. In discussing the good faith obligation of a merchant, the court stated that although the definition of good faith "by its terms embraces the reasonable commercial standards of fair dealing in the trade, it should not — and cannot — be interpreted to permit, countenance or condone commercial standards of sharp trade practice or indifference as to the provenance, i.e., history of ownership or the right to possess or sell an object d'art. . . ." (Internal quotation marks omitted.) Id., 146. The buyer made no inquiry as to whether the purported art dealer, who was in fact a delicatessen employee, was the owner of the painting or had been authorized by the owner to sell the painting. Id. Because a simple telephone call would have revealed the fact that the defendant was not an art merchant, thereby leading to doubt that would have required further verification, the court concluded that the buyer could not claim buyer in the ordinary course of business status. Id., 146-47.

In Howley v. Sotheby's, Inc., New York Law Journal, Vol. 195 (February 20, 1986) p. 6, col. 3B, the owner of a painting sought its recovery from the defendant art dealer. The defendant had purchased the painting from the caretaker of the owner's home, who had posed as the owner's nephew, even though the defendant was unsure whether the "owner's nephew" had authority to sell the painting. Id. The court concluded that, because the defendant was a professional art dealer, he should have been "scrupulously concerned with taking proper title in anything he purchases." Id. Because the defendant had not taken any steps to verify title, even after the "owner's nephew" informed him that the sale first needed the owner's approval, the defendant did not fulfill his obligation and was liable for conversion. Id.

In Cantor v. Anderson, 639 F. Supp. 364, 367-68 (S.D.N.Y.), *aff'd*, 833 F.2d 1002 (2d Cir. 1986), the court, citing *Howley*, imposed a duty upon a sophisticated buyer to inquire into a painting's ownership when circumstances dictate. In *Cantor*, the buyer and the seller had engaged in numerous previous art transactions. Id., 366. When the buyer sought the return of several of his artworks that were on consignment with the seller, the seller gave the buyer a painting, to which he claimed ownership, as security for the artworks on consignment. Id., 367. The buyer, who had been aware of the seller's financial difficulties and was familiar with the seller's practice of selling works on consignment, had reason to doubt the seller's ownership of the painting. Id., 368. This doubt led to a duty to obtain some verification that the seller had good title. Because the buyer had made no efforts to verify title to the painting, choosing to rely solely on the seller's assurances, the court concluded that the buyer had not fulfilled his duty and was liable for conversion. Id., 368-69.

Finally, in Morgold, Inc. v. Keeler, 891 F. Supp. 1361, 1369 (N.D. Cal. 1995), the court held that an art dealer buyer had obtained good title to a painting by satisfying "the reasonable commercial standards in the art industry. . . ." In that case, the buyer and the seller had engaged in previous art transactions for several years. Id., 1364. When the buyer purchased the painting from the seller, he was unaware that the seller had only a one-half interest in the painting. Id., 1363-65. The court imposed a duty on "dealers in art [to] take reasonable steps to inquire into the title to a painting, particularly if there are warnings that something is wrong with a transaction." Id., 1368. In *Morgold, Inc.*, the buyer had engaged in previous art transactions with the seller and had contacted an expert on the artist, who gave no indication of problems with the painting's title. Id., 1365. Because there were no other warning signs indicating problems with title, the court concluded that the buyer had fulfilled his duty to make a reasonable inquiry and had acquired good title and a right to possession of the painting. Id., 1369.

We agree with these courts that a merchant buyer has a heightened duty of inquiry when a reasonable merchant would have doubts or questions regarding the seller's authority to sell. We further conclude that the steps that a merchant must take to conform to reasonable commercial standards before consummating a deal depend on all of the facts and circumstances surrounding the sale. In the present case, the defendant had concerns about Malmberg's ability to convey good title to *Red Elvis* because he believed that

Lindholm might have had a claim to the painting. The defendant also was concerned that Malmberg had not yet acquired title to the painting or that the transaction might be a "flip."

Because of his concern that Lindholm might make a claim to *Red Elvis*, the defendant took the extraordinary step of hiring counsel to conduct an investigation and to negotiate a formal contract of sale on his behalf. He also insisted on and obtained a formal contract containing representations and warranties that Malmberg had title to the painting. In addition, during the course of the investigation, the defendant's counsel conducted both a lien search and an Art Loss Register search that revealed no competing claims to *Red Elvis*. Although the defendant was cautioned that the searches provided only minimal assurance that Malmberg had good title to the painting, such searches typically are not conducted during the course of a normal art transaction and, therefore, provided the defendant with at least some assurance that Lindholm had no claims to the painting.

Moreover, the evidence was sufficient for the trial court reasonably to conclude that at all times during the transaction, both Malmberg and Holm had reputations as honest, reliable, and trustworthy art dealers. This is not like the situation in Porter v. Wertz, supra, 68 A.D.2d 146, in which the court concluded that the buyer was not a buyer in the ordinary course of business because he did not know the dealer or his reputation. The defendant had little reason to doubt Malmberg's claim that he was the owner of *Red Elvis*, and any doubts that he did have reasonably were allayed by relying on Holm's assurances that Malmberg had bought the painting from the plaintiff because she needed money due to her divorce. The defendant established at trial that it is customary to rely on the assurances of respected art dealers when conducting a transaction, and the defendant had no reason to depart from this practice.

The defendant's concerns were further allayed when Malmberg delivered *Red Elvis* to a bonded warehouse in Denmark, the delivery location the parties had agreed to in the contract of sale. At the time of the sale, the painting was on loan to the Guggenheim, whose policy it was to release a painting on loan only to the true owner, or to someone the true owner had authorized to take possession. The defendant was not informed that the plaintiff had authorized release to Malmberg for the sole purpose of lending the painting to a museum in Denmark. Knowing that the Guggenheim would release the painting to an authorized party only, it was reasonable for the defendant to believe that Malmberg was the true owner of the painting. We conclude that these steps were sufficient to conform to reasonable commercial standards for the sale of artwork under the circumstances and, therefore, that the defendant had status as a buyer in the ordinary course of business.

We recognize that the customary practice in the art industry of not requiring a merchant buyer to obtain documentary proof that the seller owns the work of art whenever there are reasonable doubts or questions regarding the seller's authority to sell imposes risks on persons who entrust art to an art dealer. Section 42a-1-201(9) evinces a legislative desire, however, for courts to respect "the usual or customary practices in the kind of business in which the seller is engaged. . . ." We are not entitled to impose the type of business practices that we would prefer.

Moreover, the evidence presented at trial established that the reason that documentary proof of ownership customarily is not required is to protect the confidentiality of the owner and the buyer. Requiring a merchant buyer to obtain an invoice or other supporting documentation proving the seller's ownership would in every transaction destroy the privacy and confidentiality that buyers and sellers have come to desire and expect. Accordingly, only when circumstances surrounding the sale cast severe doubt on the ownership of the artwork are merchant buyers required to obtain documentary assurance that the seller has good title. In this instance, the Swedish-English letter was produced at Holm's suggestion to give the defendant assurance that the *plaintiff* had good title when she sold the painting to Malmberg. In light of the customary practices in the industry, the defendant reasonably could have concluded that Malmberg was unwilling to produce a signed copy of the letter because of his desire to protect the owner's expectation of confidentiality in their transaction. The purpose of the letter was not to give the defendant assurance that *Malmberg* had good title to the painting, and any concerns about Malmberg's title that could be inferred from the refusal to show the defendant a signed copy of the letter were quickly allayed by Malmberg's subsequent delivery of the painting to Denmark. Accordingly, we conclude, on the basis of all the circumstances surrounding this sale, that the defendant's failure to obtain an invoice from the plaintiff to Malmberg or a signed copy of the Swedish-English letter does not strip him of his status as a buyer in the ordinary course of business. For the same reasons, we conclude that the defendant was not required to contact directly the plaintiff or other parties who might have had knowledge concerning *Red Elvis*' title.

We conclude that the trial court properly determined that the defendant was a buyer in the ordinary course of business and, therefore, took all rights the plaintiff had to the painting pursuant to §42a-2-403(2).

The judgment is affirmed.

PROBLEM 23

Going on a family vacation, Kahr stowed sterling silver and credit cards in a bag in the attic. Not long after returning, Kahr took several bags of clothing to donate to Goodwill — and unknowingly brought along the bag of valuables. Kahr handed the bags over to Goodwill, and signed a form describing the donation as "used clothing." After sorting through the bags, a Goodwill employee set the credit cards aside, but put the silver out for sale. A bargain hunter soon snapped it up. Can Kahr recover the silver? See §2-403(2) and (3); Kahr v. Markland, 543 N.E.2d 579 (Ill. App. 1989).

II. WARRANTIES OF QUALITY

A. Express Warranties

An express warranty arises when the seller does something affirmative to create buyer expectations about the characteristics or performance of the goods. Typically this means that the seller will make oral or written representations about the product in advertisements, the verbal sales pitch, or the written contract. These representations must have some substance to them (more than mere "puffing") to rise to the dignity of an express warranty. In the Code's words, they must "relate to the goods" (an obvious requirement) and become part of the *basis of the bargain* (a not-so-obvious or explainable requirement). Under the now-replaced Uniform Sales Act (§12), the buyer had to prove *reliance* on the statement alleged to be an express warranty. Does *basis of bargain* mean this? Read Official Comment 3 to §2-313. Most courts (but not all) have not required a buyer to prove any specific reliance, but instead hold that a statement goes to the basis of the bargain if its natural tendency is to induce the buyer to purchase (even though that is not the sole reason). See In re General Motors Corp. Dex-Cool Products Liability Litigation, 241 F.R.D. 305 (S.D. Ill. 2007); White & Summers §10-5. This means that if the statement, however made, has any substance to it so that it *might* have played some part in the buyer's decision to buy, the burden is on the *seller* to prove that the buyer did *not* rely on the statement. If the seller cannot meet this burden, the buyer has the benefit of an express warranty. See Official Comment 8 to §2-313.

PROBLEM 24

(a) The salesman at the lot of Smiles Pre-Owned Vehicles told the woman buying the car that it was in "A-1 shape." She bought the car, but it broke down the next day, stranding her in the country. Was this oral statement mere puffing? See Wat Henry Pontiac Co. v. Bradley, 202 Okla. 82, 210 P.2d 348 (1949); White & Summers §10-4. Is it an easier case if the seller tells the buyer that the used car is in "mint condition"? See Taylor v. Alfama,

481 A.2d 1059 (Vt. 1984); Nigro v. Lee, 882 N.Y.S.2d 346 (App. Div. 2009) (no express warranty where eBay seller described Mercedes Benz automobile as "gorgeous" with "minor blemishes," but sold "as is").

(b) When the farmer looked over the young chickens he was contemplating purchasing from the poultry company, he complained that they looked pretty scruffy. The salesman explained that that was because they were on half-feed and that when they were placed on full-feed, they would "bloom out, straighten up, and fly right," and they would "do a good job in your chicken house." The farmer purchased the chickens, and two months later they started dying in droves. The farmer sued, claiming breach of an express warranty. Is he right? Is this a question of law or of fact for the jury? See Woodruff v. Clark County Farm Bureau Coop, 153 Ind. App. 31, 286 N.E.2d 188 (1972).

(c) Portia Moot, a third-year law student, had taken the course in Sales, so when she went to buy a used car, she listened very carefully to the sales pitch. The smarmy salesman was quite friendly, but he only made two statements about the car she bought: "This is a great car!" and "You're going to love it!" In fact, the car broke down a great deal, and Portia quickly grew to hate it. Does she have a cause of action here?

(d) Assume that the car salesman told Portia that the used car she was contemplating purchasing had been thoroughly inspected by the car dealership's crack repair department and was "mechanically in perfect condition." Is that an express warranty? See Bobholz v. Banaszak, 655 N.W.2d 547 (Wis. App. 2002). Portia was suspicious about the reliability of the car and before she bought it, she took it to her own favorite mechanic for an inspection. She didn't buy the car until her mechanic cleared it as fine. When the car broke down a few days later, she decided to bring suit on the express warranty. What defense will the car dealership raise?

(e) David Vargo purchased only very healthy foods. A vegetable oil he bought stated on the label that it was "All Natural" but then was found to contain genetically modified organisms. Has an express warranty been breached? See Ault v. J.M. Smucker Co., 2014 WL 1998235 (S.D.N.Y. 2014).

(f) Should a court accept the argument that a "Manufacturer's Suggested Retail Price" is an express warranty of product quality, because "status-conscious consumers tend to use a price cue also as a surrogate indicator of prestige"? Marino v. Coach, Inc., 2017 WL 3731954 (S.D.N.Y. 2017).

In re Toshiba America HD DVD Marketing and Sales Practices Litigation
United States District Court, District of New Jersey, 2009, WL 2940081

DEBEVOISE, Senior District Judge.

[Plaintiffs bought an HD DVD Player from Toshiba after the company had decided to discontinue future production of the product because it had lost the technological battle for its format's supremacy, but while Toshiba was still advertising the player as " 'For Today, Tomorrow and Beyond." When Plaintiffs discovered this deception, they sued for, among other things, breach of an express warranty.]

High Definition Digital Versatile Disc ("HD DVD") is an optical disc storage format for encoding audio-visual entertainment such as movies, and is available for playback on compatible HD DVD players, including Toshiba's HD DVD Player. (Id. ¶13.) Toshiba developed the HD DVD format to be a "next generation" format to succeed the standard DVD. (Id.) The HD DVD Player allows consumers to view movies in higher definition and fidelity than allowed by previous technologies. (Id.)

Toshiba introduced the HD DVD Player for sale to consumers in the United States in April 2006. (Id. ¶14.) At that time the list prices ranged from $499 to $799. (Id.) Plaintiffs allege that these prices were 200% to 500% of the cost of standard DVD players without high definition capabilities. (Id.)

The HD DVD Player faced competition from Blu-ray Disc, an optical disc format largely developed and supported by the Sony Corporation ("Sony"). (Id. ¶18.) Blu-ray Disc was also marketed as a "next generation" format for the encoding and playback of audio-visual entertainment. (Id.) Several major movie studios, which regularly release movies in the DVD format, chose to release movies in Blu-ray format rather than HD DVD. (Id. ¶25.) Disney (including Touchstone and Miramax), Sony Pictures (including MGM/Columbia Tristar) and 20th Century Fox all supported Blu-ray technology rather than HD DVD. (Id.) Plaintiffs allege that Toshiba "consistently failed to disclose to its customers" this information regarding the support of certain movie studios for Blu-ray rather than HD DVD technology. (Id.) In what the Plaintiffs characterize as "a desperate attempt by Toshiba to increase its market share and garner HD DVD movie studio support," on August 21, 2007, *The New York Times* reported that Paramount and Dream Works Animation would receive approximately $150 million in financial incentives for their commitment to HD DVD. (Id.)

The competition between Blu-ray and HD DVD was well reported in the media and was likened to the competition 30 years ago between the VHS and Betamax formats for home video recording. (Certification of David E. Sellinger, February 17, 2009 ("Sellinger Cert.") Ex. C at 2 and Ex. E at 1.) As *Business Week* reported in its December 6, 2007 edition,

> For two years now, rival camps have been battling over which new DVD format will prevail: Blu-ray, which is backed by Sony (SNE) and a consortium of 170 other companies, or HD DVD, which is being championed by Toshiba (TOSBF), Microsoft (MSFT), and others. Both technologies promise crisper video that looks better on the new generation of flat-panel, high definition

TVs. And the winner stands to control a lucrative new market worth billions. Each side has been competing to win the backing of the major movie studios. Only Warner Bros. (TWX), which currently uses both formats, is still playing hard to get.

(Sellinger Cert. Ex. D at 1.) That same article reported that there were rumors that "Warner [was] coming aboard-[Sony] soon," meaning that Warner Brothers was planning to discontinue production of movies in the HD DVD format and instead use the Blu-ray format. (Id.; CCAC ¶35.) *Business Week* also reported that the head of Toshiba's HD DVD business in Japan had made three trips since the summer to meet with Warner Brothers regarding its HD DVD business. (Sellinger Cert. Ex. D at 1; CCAC ¶35.) On December 10, 2007, *The New York Times* reported that Warner Brothers had signaled that it would choose one format — HD DVD or Blu-ray — after the 2007 holiday shopping season and that its choice would be determined by which format sold more DVDs during that season. (CCAC ¶35.)

Toshiba continued to market its HD DVD Players, with the slogan "For Today, Tomorrow and Beyond," throughout the 2007 holiday shopping seasons and thereafter. (Id. ¶27.) During that season, Plaintiffs allege that Toshiba lowered prices on its Players in order to induce additional sales. (Id.)

On January 4, 2008, Warner Brothers announced that it would no longer release movies in the HD DVD format. (Id. ¶26.) This announcement led to "a chain reaction in the industry," which included decisions by Best Buy, Wal-Mart and Circuit City to drop HD DVD from their stores. (Id.) Once Warner Brothers decided in favor of Blu-ray, that system's market share increased from 49% to 70%. (Id. ¶35.)

Toshiba continued marketing its HD DVD Players in January and the first weeks of February 2008. On January 14, 2008, Toshiba issued a press release stating "that it [was] stepping up its successful marketing campaign for HD DVD as it experienced record-breaking unit sales in the fourth quarter of 2007" (Id. ¶28.) That press release also stated that "HD DVD is proven to be the format of choice for consumers" and that Toshiba planned to execute an extended advertising campaign to further enhance consumer awareness of the benefits of HD DVD and drive sales. (Id.) On February 3, 2008, Toshiba ran an ad during the Super Bowl, "highlighting its HD-A3, HD-A30 and HD-A35 Players," which the Plaintiffs allege "thereby [characterized] the long-term viability of the Players." (Id. ¶29.)

Plaintiffs allege that "[m]arket insiders" predicted that Blu-ray would win the battle with the HD DVD format if for no other reason than the fact that Blu-ray was backed by Disney. (Id. ¶35.) Plaintiffs also allege that "Toshiba was aware of market trends and knew, despite its misleading marketing campaign, that it was only a matter of time before the company withdrew from the marketplace abandoning its customer base." (Id. ¶35.) Plaintiffs claim that, as a "direct result of Toshiba's abrupt exit from the HD DVD market," their investments in the HD DVD Players "lost significant value." (Id. ¶31.) . . . An express warranty by a seller is created by: "[a]ny affirmation of fact or promise made by the seller to the buyer which relates to the goods and becomes part of the basis of the bargain," or "[a]ny description of the goods which is made part of the basis of the bargain." N.J.S.A. § 12A:2-313(1)(a) & (b); Cal. Comm. Code §2313(1)(a) & (b); Fla. Stat. Ann. 672.313(1)(a) & (b); Idaho Code §28-2-313(1)(a) & (b); 810 Ill. Comp. Stat. 5/2-313(1)(a) & (b); Mich. Comp. Laws §440.2313(1)(a) & (b). The use of "formal words of promise or that the seller have a specific intention to warrant the good" is not necessary to create an express warranty. Liberty Lincoln-Mercury, Inc. v. Ford Motor Co., 171 F.3d 818, 824 (3d Cir. 1999) (citing N.J. Stat. Ann. §12A:2-313(2)). But "an affirmation merely of the value of the goods or a statement purporting to be merely the seller's opinion or commendation of the goods does not create a warranty." N.J. Stat. Ann §12A:2-313(2); Cal. Comm. Code §2313(2); Fla. Stat. Ann. 672.313(2); Idaho Code §28-2-313(2); 810 Ill. Comp. Stat. 5/2-313(2); Mich. Comp. Laws §440.2313(2).

Plaintiffs allege that Toshiba's "affirmations of fact and/or promises relating to the [HD DVD] Players created express warranties that Toshiba would continue to support the HD DVD format and continue to manufacture such players." (CCAC ¶117.) They allege that Toshiba breached these warranties when it announced in February 2008 that it would exit the HD DVD market. (Id. ¶118.) Specifically, Plaintiffs argue that "Toshiba warranted that its [HD DVD] Players could play HD DVDs 'Today, Tomorrow, and Beyond.'" (Plts.' Opp'n Br. 17.) Yet there is no allegation that the HD DVD Players cannot still play HD DVDs. Rather, the problem is that the availability of new HD DVDs has severely decreased. Plaintiffs further argue that the long-term viability of the HD DVD market "was a large part of the basis of the bargain between Toshiba and the putative Class, because consumers were concerned with choosing a high definition DVD player which would have long term viability." (Id. 17 & 18.) Toshiba's exit from the HD DVD market has, according to Plaintiffs, "substantially limited that viability." (Id. 18.)

Plaintiffs do not allege that their HD DVD Players no longer can play HD DVDs. Rather, they argue that Toshiba's tag line that its HD DVD Players were for "Today, Tomorrow, and Beyond" created an express warranty that, essentially, Toshiba would remain in the HD DVD market forever. As discussed with respect to the Plaintiffs' consumer fraud claims, the statement that HD DVD Players were for "Today, Tomorrow, and Beyond" is puffery and not specific enough to create an express warranty. Plaintiffs cite to L.S. Heath & Son, Inc. v. AT & T Information Systems, Inc., 9 F.3d 561, 570 (7th Cir. 1993), where the Court of Appeals for the Seventh Circuit, applying New Jersey law, noted that, "A statement can amount to a warranty, even if unintended to be such by the seller, 'if it could fairly be understood . . . to constitute an affirmation or representation that the [product] possesse[s] a certain quality or capacity relating to future performance.'" Id. (quoting *Gladden v. Cadillac Motor Car Div., Gen. Motors Corp.*, 83 N.J. 320, 416 A.2d 394, 396 (N.J. 1980)). While it is certainly true that a statement relating to future performance *may* create an express warranty, even if not intended by the seller, Toshiba's statement regarding its HD DVD Players does not rise to that level. In *L.S. Heath & Son*, the court found that AT & T's statement that its "complete intregated [sic] data processing and voice/data communications network [will] satisf[y] all of your aforementioned objectives," may have constituted an express warranty. Id. AT & T's statement was far more specific than Toshiba's statement that its HD DVD Players were for "Today, Tomorrow, and Beyond." Additionally, even if Toshiba created an express warranty of future *performance*, there is no allegation that the HD DVD Players do not perform as they are intended — i.e., to play HD DVDs.

The CCAC fails to state a claim for breach of express warranty. Count Five of the CCAC is therefore dismissed.

PROBLEM 25

Upon graduation from law school, Andrew Loner hung out his shingle and waited. Mr. and Mrs. Consumer were his first clients, and they told him the following story. Two weeks earlier they had visited a wallpaper store, Paper & Paste, Inc., and inquired about vinyl wallpaper for their dining room. The salesman told them that the "finest" wallpaper in the store was Expenso-Paper, a vinyl wallpaper selling at $75 a roll. When he learned that the Consumers had never before put up wallpaper, the salesman assured them that Expenso-Paper "goes up easily, can be put on with any paste, and dries immediately." He said that it "would look wonderful" and, moreover, that Expenso-Paper "was used by Mary Magic," the famous movie star, in her dining room. He showed them a sample book, and they picked out a pattern they liked and ordered ten rolls. When the paper arrived the next week, it proved to be very stiff and hard to work with. It tore easily and refused to stay flat on the wall (it either bubbled or, due to its heavy weight, fell down on drying). In addition, it was dyed a darker color than the version of the pattern in the sample book. The final result was that the Consumers' dining room looked terrible. To top it all off, the Consumers discovered that Mary Magic did not own a home (she lived exclusively in hotels).

Upon complaining to Paper & Paste, the Consumers were told by the manager that Expenso-Paper needs a special brand of paste, to wit, Expenso-Paste. They were also told that Expenso-Paper was an inferior brand and that next time they should buy Super Wall, a better product that the store carried.

The Consumers told Loner that they signed the contract without reading it and that the statement about Mary Magic's dining room was made *after* they signed the agreement. Loner (and you) have to answer these questions:

    (a) Which of the salesman's representations amount to express warranties?
      (1) finest?
      (2) goes up easily?
      (3) can be put on with any paste?
      (4) dries immediately?
      (5) would look wonderful?
      (6) was used by Mary Magic?
    Do you see any other express warranties?
    (b) Is the Mary Magic statement part of the *basis of the bargain,* arising as it did after the contract was signed? See §2-209(1); Official Comment 7 to §2-313.

PROBLEM 26

    Balding Paul bought a wig from Hair, Inc. He became annoyed when the wig changed colors slightly from season to season. He did not do anything about it until one day, while thumbing through a newspaper, he noticed an ad for Hair, Inc., that claimed that their wigs did not shrink or change color. On checking back, he discovered that Hair, Inc., had run an identical ad during the week prior to his purchase of the wig. He sues. On the witness stand Paul confesses that he never saw the ad until a year after his purchase of the wig. Is this admission fatal to his recovery on a theory of express warranty? See Winston Indus., Inc. v. Stuyvesant Ins. Co., 55 Ala. App. 525, 317 So. 2d 493 (1975) (buyer held protected by manufacturer's warranty on mobile home even though he never received a copy).

B. Implied Warranties

    In many ways implied warranties are the legal opposites of express warranties. An express warranty is created only where sellers do something *affirmative* (open their mouth and say something, take out a newspaper ad, display a sample). Implied warranties, on the other hand, are *automatically* part of the contract unless the seller (or the circumstance) does something affirmative to get rid of them. Implied warranties are implied as a matter of law; they are sometimes referred to as "children of the law." Like express warranties, the seller's intention to create any implied warranty is completely irrelevant.

1. Merchantability

The implied warranty of merchantability (which is easier to spell and pronounce if you think of it as two words — *merchant* and *ability* — tacked together) is not given a precise definition in the Code. The basic idea is that the item must be saleable and conform to the normal expectations of the parties. Notice that §2-314(2), which you should now read, sets minimum standards for its meaning. Clever lawyers can make much of the laundry list found in that subsection.

Shaffer v. Victoria Station, Inc.

Supreme Court of Washington, 1978, 91 Wash. 2d 295, 588 P.2d 233

DOLLIVER, J.

On March 26, 1974, plaintiff Shaffer ordered a glass of wine at the Victoria Station, a restaurant operated by defendant. In the course of taking his first or second sip, the wine glass broke in Mr. Shaffer's hand, resulting in alleged permanent injury.

Plaintiff brought this action based upon three theories: negligence, breach of implied warranty under the Uniform Commercial Code, and strict liability under the theory of Restatement (Second) of Torts §402A (1965). The manufacturer of the glass was named as a defendant, but was never served. Prior to trial, as counsel and the trial judge were discussing proposed instructions, plaintiff's attorney indicated that he could not prove negligence, and wished to submit the case to the jury on the grounds of breach of warranty and strict liability. Plaintiff then took a voluntary nonsuit on the negligence issue. At the same time, the court ruled the case sounded in negligence alone, and granted the defendant's motion for dismissal. The Court of Appeals affirmed. Shaffer v. Victoria Station, Inc., 18 Wash. App. 816, 572 P.2d 737 (1977). We reverse the Court of Appeals.

I

Defendant argues the Uniform Commercial Code does not apply since the restaurant was not a merchant with respect to wine glasses as defined in §2-104 and, since the glass itself was not sold, there was no passing of title as required under §2-106. Plaintiff, however, points to §2-314 as being decisive. We agree. Section 2-314 reads, inter alia:

(1) Unless excluded or modified (§2-316), a warranty that the goods shall be merchantable is implied in a contract for their sale if the seller is a

merchant with respect to goods of that kind. Under this section the serving for value of food or drink to be consumed either on the premises or elsewhere is a sale.

(2) Goods to be merchantable must be at least such as . . .

(c) are fit for the ordinary purposes for which such goods are used; and . . .

(e) are adequately contained, packaged, and labeled as the agreement may require; . . . .

It is our opinion that, when the Uniform Commercial Code states "the serving for value of food or drink to be consumed either on the premises or elsewhere is a sale" and that such food and drink must be "adequately contained, packaged, and labeled as the agreement may require," it covers entirely the situation before us. Plaintiff ordered a drink (a glass of wine) from defendant. Defendant sold and served the glass of wine to plaintiff to be consumed by plaintiff on the premises. The wine could not be served as a drink nor could it be consumed without an adequate container. The drink sold includes the wine and the container both of which must be fit for the ordinary purpose for which used. Plaintiff alleges the drink sold — wine in a glass — was unfit and has, therefore, stated a cause of action.

In addition to the language of §2-314, we believe the language of §1-103 is applicable. It states:

Unless displaced by the particular provisions of this Title, the principles of law and equity, including the law merchant and the law relative to capacity to contract, principal and agent, estoppel, fraud, misrepresentation, duress, coercion, mistake, bankruptcy, or other validating or invalidating cause shall supplement its provisions.

Plaintiff urges that cases which apply the Uniform Commercial Code where the goods are leased rather than sold (see, e.g., Baker v. Seattle, 79 Wash. 2d 198, 484 P.2d 405 (1971)), or are under a bailment for mutual benefit (see, e.g., Fulbright v. Klamath Gas Co., 271 Ore. 449, 533 P.2d 316 (1975)), be extended to the facts before us. We believe this is unnecessary. A more straightforward and less tortuous approach is that adopted in Hadley v. Hillcrest Dairy, Inc., 341 Mass. 624, 171 N.E.2d 293 (1961). In that case, a bottle of milk delivered to the plaintiff's home shattered and cut the plaintiff's hand. The Massachusetts Supreme Judicial Court, relying on the Massachusetts sales act (which was not, as argued by defendant, significantly different in its applicable part from the Uniform Commercial Code), held at 627, "In our view it is immaterial whether or not the property in the jug passed to the plaintiff." The court goes on to cite Geddling v. Marsh, (1920) 1 K.B. 668. In that case, a retailer received bottled mineral water from the manufacturer and was injured by an exploding bottle. The court found the bottles were not sold to the retailer but held the retailer could recover under a breach of an implied warranty of fitness. The court said at 671-672:

> In this case there was only one contract — namely, a contract between the plaintiff and the defendant that the plaintiff should be supplied with mineral waters. Mineral waters could not be supplied except in bottles, and therefore the plaintiff was asking to be supplied with mineral waters in bottles. That undoubtedly is a contract of sale, and I will assume that in that contract there might be a condition that the bottles should not be bought by the plaintiff but should be hired; but the question the county court judge had to consider was whether the bottles were not "supplied under a contract of sale." This was a contract of sale none the less because there was a special provision with regard to the bottles. The section, in my opinion, extends not only to the goods actually bought under the contract but to goods "supplied under the contract of sale." This particular bottle was thus "supplied under a contract of sale," and it follows that it should be reasonably fit for the purpose for which it was supplied. In fact it was not reasonably fit and in consequence of that unfitness the plaintiff was injured.

See also Sartin v. Blackwell, 200 Miss. 579, 28 So. 2d 222 (1946). Plaintiff has a cause of action both on the face of the statute and under the principles of case law elucidated above.

II

We also hold an action lies under the strict liability theory of Restatement (Second) of Torts §402A (1965). The policy questions of strict liability and their application to retailers have been previously determined. See Seattle-First Natl. Bank v. Tabert, 86 Wash. 2d 145, 542 P.2d 774 (1975); Ulmer v. Ford Motor Co., 75 Wash. 2d 522, 452 P.2d 729 (1969). The only question remaining is whether §402A applies to the transaction here. In addressing this issue, the Court of Appeals expressed concern over an uncontrollable broadening of the doctrine of strict liability:

> Were the wine glass in question held to be a mere facet of the sale of the "glass of wine" and thus a "product" for the purposes of section 402A, the theory of strict liability would be greatly and unnecessarily expanded. The reasonably clear standard of engagement "in the business of selling . . . a product" would be abandoned in deference to a less predictable question — whether the injury-producing aspect of the sale was necessary to the sale. If a wine glass renders a restaurateur strictly liable because he could not sell wine without it, what of other tableware, the waiters and the bus boys, the furnishings to effect an attractive atmosphere, or the building housing the establishment? The argument could be made that numerous aspects of a restaurant's operation,

or that of any other retailer, are integral to each sale. To ignore the fact that this allegedly defective glass was never sold would create great uncertainty as to the limits of strict liability.

Shaffer, at 820-821.

We do not agree with the gloomy view of the Court of Appeals of the consequences of allowing the plaintiff to proceed with this action. We hold the sale of a glass of wine is subject to the strict liability provisions of §402A. If their predictions as to future lawsuits come to pass, we will deal with the litigation at that time. Confirmation of the applicability of §402A to this case is given in comment h, which says:

> The defective condition may arise not only from harmful ingredients, not characteristic of the product itself either as to presence or quantity, but also from foreign objects contained in the product, from decay or deterioration before sale, or from the way in which the product is prepared or packed. No reason is apparent for distinguishing between the product itself and the container in which it is supplied; and the two are purchased by the user or consumer as an integrated whole. Where the container is itself dangerous, the product is sold in a defective condition. Thus a carbonated beverage in a bottle which is so weak, or cracked, or jagged at the edges, or bottled under such excessive pressure that it may explode or otherwise cause harm to the person who handles it, is in a defective and dangerous condition. The container cannot logically be separated from the contents when the two are sold as a unit, and the liability stated in this Section arises not only when the consumer drinks the beverage and is poisoned by it, but also when he is injured by the bottle while he is handling it preparatory to consumption.

Restatement (Second) of Torts §402A, comment h at 351-352 (1965).

Plaintiff has stated a cause of action under theories of implied warranty of fitness and strict liability. The Court of Appeals is reversed.

QUESTIONS

1 Would it be a defense to the restaurant that it was not negligent in any way in connection with its handling of the wine glass? See Official Comment 13 to §2-314; La Fountain v. Sears, Roebuck & Co., 680 F. Supp. 251 (E.D. Mich. 1988).
2 If a casino serves its patrons free drinks at the gaming tables and one of the drinks proves to contain chips of glass, would the Washington Supreme Court reach the same result it did in the last case? Phrased

another way: is there a "sale" going on? See Levondosky v. Marina Assocs., 731 F. Supp. 1210 (D.N.J. 1990).

By far the most important segment of §2-314(2) is found in subsection (2)(c): to be merchantable the goods must be "fit for the ordinary purposes for which such goods are used." (Or, as the South Carolina courts have put it since 1793, "a sound price warrants a sound commodity.") When you think about it, a warranty that the goods are fit for their *ordinary purpose* is a big warranty. It is the warranty that the goods will work, and it is typically the only warranty that the buyer needs. When sellers disclaim the implied warranty of merchantability (and they often do), why do buyers not routinely complain?

PROBLEM 27

Consider the following:

(a) Are cigarettes that cause lung cancer merchantable if used over a period of years? See Haglund v. Philip Morris, Inc., 446 Mass. 741, 847 N.E.2d 315 (2006); Franklin E. Crawford, Fit for Its Ordinary Purpose? Tobacco, Fast Food, and the Implied Warranty of Merchantability, 63 Ohio St. L.J. 1165 (2002); White & Summers §10-12; Annot. 80 A.L.R.2d 681. See also Hoyte v. Yum! Brands, Inc., 489 F. Supp. 2d 24 (D.D.C. 2007) (KFC did not breach implied warranty of merchantability, although its products contained trans fats); Bodie v. Purdue Pharma Co., 489 F. Supp. 2d 24 (D.D.C. 2007) (addictive nature of painkiller OxyContin did not breach warranty of merchantability). If the seller's advertisements stated that the cigarettes were "mild," would that create an express warranty?

(b) To treat menopausal symptoms, plaintiff took medicines manufactured by the defendant that combined the drug progestin and estrogen. As a consequence she developed breast cancer. Contending that the warranty of merchantability was breached when the defendant failed to warn her of this possibility, she sued. Does that warranty contain a "failure to warn" component? See Hines v. Wyeth, 2011 WL 1990496 (S.D. W.Va. 2011).

(c) Following a recipe in the Exotic Cookbook, Martha prepared pufferfish fillet for Thanksgiving. The book, however, neglected to advise chefs to remove the pufferfish's poisonous organs. After a lengthy recuperation, Martha sued the book store and publisher for breach of the implied warranty of merchantability. What result? See Cardozo v. True, 342 So. 2d 1053 (Fla. Dist. Ct. App. 1977). *Cardozo* emphasized one major consideration: "It is unthinkable that standards imposed on the quality of goods sold by a merchant would require that merchant, who is a book seller, to evaluate the thought processes of the many authors and publishers of the hundreds and often thousands of books which the merchant offers for sale. One can readily imagine the extent of potential litigation. Is the newsdealer, or for that matter the neighborhood news carrier, liable if the local paper's recipes call for inedible ingredients? We think not." Do you agree?

(d) Officer Krupke, a New York policeman by profession, sold his family car to his next-door neighbor, Maria, telling her it was a "good car." In fact, it was falling apart and blew up the first time she drove it. Has Krupke breached the implied warranty of merchantability? See §2-104(1); Official Comment 3 to §2-314; §1-304. Should §2-314 be extended so that the warranty is made by all sellers? See Ingrid Hillinger, The Merchant of §2-314: Who Needs Him?, 34 Hastings L.J. 747 (1983).

(e) If the dashboard touchscreen, which controlled the radio, climate control, and navigation systems, was defective, would that make the car in (d) unmerchantable? See Rasnic v. FCA US LLC, 2017 WL 6406880 (D. Kan. 2017).

Webster v. Blue Ship Tea Room, Inc.

Massachusetts Supreme Judicial Court, 1964, 347 Mass. 421, 198 N.E.2d 309

REARDON, J.

This is a case which by its nature evokes earnest study not only of the law but also of the culinary traditions of the Commonwealth which bear so heavily upon its outcome. It is an action to recover damages for personal injuries sustained by reason of a breach of implied warranty of food served by the defendant in its restaurant. An auditor, whose findings of fact were not to be final, found for the plaintiff. On a retrial in the Superior Court before a judge and jury, in which the plaintiff testified, the jury returned a verdict for her. The defendant is here on exceptions to the refusal of the judge (1) to strike certain portions of the auditor's report, (2) to direct a verdict for the defendant, and (3) to allow the defendant's motion for the entry of a verdict in its favor under leave reserved.

The jury could have found the following facts: On Saturday, April 25, 1959, about 1 p.m., the plaintiff, accompanied by her sister and her aunt, entered the Blue Ship Tea Room operated by the defendant. The group was seated at a table and supplied with menus.

This restaurant, which the plaintiff characterized as "quaint," was located in Boston "on the third floor of an old building in T Wharf which overlooks the ocean."

The plaintiff, who had been born and brought up in New England (a fact of some consequence), ordered clam chowder and crabmeat salad. Within a few minutes she received tidings to the effect that "there was no more clam chowder," whereupon she ordered a cup of fish chowder. Presently, there was set before her "a small bowl of fish chowder." She had previously enjoyed a breakfast about 9 a.m. which had given her no difficulty. "The fish chowder contained haddock, potatoes, milk, water and seasoning. The chowder was milky in color and not clear. The haddock and potatoes were in chunks" (also a fact of consequence). "She agitated it a little with the spoon and observed that it was a fairly full bowl. . . . It was hot when she got it, but she did not tip it with her spoon because it was hot . . . but stirred it in an up and under motion. She denied that she did this because she was looking for something, but it was rather because she wanted an even distribution of fish and potatoes." "She started to eat it, alternating between the chowder and crackers which were on the table with . . . [some] rolls. She ate about 3 or 4 spoonfuls then stopped. She looked at the spoonfuls as she was eating. She saw equal parts of liquid, potato and fish as she spooned it into her mouth. She did not see anything unusual about it. After 3 or 4 spoonfuls she was aware that something had lodged in her throat because she couldn't swallow and couldn't clear her throat by gulping and she could feel it." This misadventure led to two esophagoscopies at the Massachusetts General Hospital, in the second of which, on April 27, 1959, a fish bone was found and removed. The sequence of events produced injury to the plaintiff which was not insubstantial.

We must decide whether a fish bone lurking in a fish chowder, about the ingredients of which there is no other complaint, constitutes a breach of implied warranty under applicable provisions of the Uniform Commercial Code, the annotations to which are not helpful on this point. As the judge put it in his charge, "Was the fish chowder fit to be eaten and wholesome? . . . [N]obody is claiming that the fish itself wasn't wholesome. . . . But the bone of contention here — I don't mean that for a pun — but was this fish bone a foreign substance that made the fish chowder unwholesome or not fit to be eaten?"

The plaintiff has vigorously reminded us of the high standards imposed by this court where the sale of food is involved (see Flynn v. First Natl. Stores Inc., 296 Mass. 521, 523) and has made reference to cases involving stones in beans (Friend v. Childs Dining Hall Co., 231 Mass. 65), trichinae in pork (Holt v. Mann, 294 Mass. 21, 22), and to certain other cases, here and elsewhere, serving to bolster her contention of breach of warranty.

The defendant asserts that here was a native New Englander eating fish chowder in a "quaint" Boston dining place where she had been before; that "[f]ish chowder, as it is served and enjoyed by New Englanders, is a hearty dish, originally designed to satisfy the appetites of our seamen and fishermen"; that "[t]his court knows well that we are not talking of some insipid broth as is customarily served to convalescents." We are asked to rule in such fashion that no chef is forced "to reduce the pieces of fish in the chowder to minuscule size in an effort to ascertain if they contained any pieces of bone." "In so ruling," we are told (in the defendant's brief), "the court will not only uphold its reputation for legal knowledge and acumen, but will, as loyal sons of Massachusetts, save our world-renowned fish chowder from degenerating into an insipid broth containing the mere essence of its former stature as a culinary masterpiece." Notwithstanding these passionate entreaties we are bound to examine with detachment the nature of fish chowder and what might happen to it under varying interpretations of the Uniform Commercial Code.

Chowder is an ancient dish preexisting even "the appetites of our seamen and fishermen." It was perhaps the common ancestor of the "more refined cream soups, purees, and bisques." Berolzheimer, The American Woman's Cook Book (Publisher's Guild Inc., New York, 1941) p. 176. The word "chowder" comes from the French "chaudiere," meaning a "cauldron" or "pot." "In the fishing villages of Brittany . . . 'faire la chaudiere' means to supply a cauldron in which is cooked a mess of fish and biscuit with some savoury condiments, a hodgepodge contributed by the fishermen themselves, each of whom in return receives his share of the prepared dish. The Breton fishermen probably carried the custom to Newfoundland, long famous for its chowder, whence it has spread to Nova Scotia, New Brunswick, and New England." A New England Dictionary (MacMillan and Co., 1893) p. 386. Our literature over the years abounds in references not only to the delights of chowder but also to its manufacture. A namesake of the plaintiff, Daniel Webster, had a recipe for fish chowder which has survived into a number of modern cookbooks[5] and in which the removal of fish bones is not mentioned at all. One old-time recipe recited in the New English Dictionary study defines chowder as "A dish made of fresh fish (esp. cod) or clams, stewed with slices of pork or bacon, onions, and biscuit. Cider and champagne are sometimes added." Hawthorne, in The House of the Seven Gables (Allyn and Bacon, Boston, 1957) p. 8, speaks of

5. "Take a cod of ten pounds, well cleaned, leaving on the skin. Cut into pieces one and a half pounds thick, preserving the head whole. Take one and a half pounds of clear, fat salt pork, cut in thin slices. Do the same with twelve potatoes. Take the largest pot you have. Try out the pork first, then take out the pieces of pork, leaving in the drippings. Add to that three parts of water, a layer of fish, so as to cover the bottom of the pot; next a layer of potatoes, then two tablespoons of salt, 1 teaspoon of pepper, then the pork, another layer of fish, and the remainder of the potatoes. Fill the pot with water to cover the ingredients. Put over a good fire. Let the chowder boil twenty-five minutes. When this is done have a quart of boiling milk ready, and ten hard crackers split and dipped in cold water. Add milk and crackers. Let the whole boil five minutes. The chowder is then ready to be first-rate if you have followed the directions. An onion may be added if you like the flavor." "This chowder," he adds, "is suitable for a large fishing party." Wolcott, The Yankee Cook Book (Coward-McCann, Inc., New York City, 1939) p. 9.

"[a] codfish of sixty pounds, caught in the bay [which] had been dissolved into the rich liquid of a chowder." A chowder variant, cod "Muddle," was made in Plymouth in the 1890s by taking "a three or four pound codfish, head added. Season with salt and pepper and boil in just enough water to keep from burning. When cooked, add milk and a piece of butter." The recitation of these ancient formulae suffices to indicate that in the construction of chowders in these parts in other years, worries about fish bones played no role whatsoever. This broad outlook on chowders has persisted in more modern cookbooks. "The chowder of today is much the same as the old chowder. . . ." The American Women's Cook Book, supra, p. 176. The all embracing Fannie Farmer states in a portion of her recipe, fish chowder is made with a "fish skinned, but head and tail left on. Cut fish in 2-inch pieces and set aside. Put head, tail, and backbone broken in pieces, in stew-pan; add 2 cups cold water and bring slowly to boiling point. . . ." The liquor thus produced from the bones is added to the balance of the chowder. Farmer, The Boston Cooking School Cook Book (Little Brown Co., 1937) p. 166.

Thus, we consider a dish which for many long years, if well made, has been made generally as outlined above. It is not too much to say that a person sitting down in New England to consume a good New England fish chowder embarks on gustatory adventure which may entail the removal of some fish bones from his bowl as he proceeds. We are not inclined to tamper with age-old recipes by any amendment reflecting the plaintiff's view of the effect of the Uniform Commercial Code upon them. We are aware of the heavy body of case law involving foreign substances in food, but we sense a strong distinction between them and those relative to unwholesomeness of the food itself, e.g., tainted mackerel (Smith v. Gerrish, 256 Mass. 183), and a fish bone in a fish chowder. Certain Massachusetts cooks might cavil at the ingredients contained in the chowder in this case in that it lacked the heartening lift of salt pork. In any event, we consider that the joys of life in New England include the ready availability of fresh fish chowder. We should be prepared to cope with the hazards of fish bones, the occasional presence of which in chowders is, it seems to us, to be anticipated, and which, in the light of a hallowed tradition, do not impair their fitness or merchantability. While we are buoyed up in this conclusion by Shapiro v. Hotel Statler Corp., 132 F. Supp. 891 (S.D. Cal.), in which the bone which afflicted the plaintiff appeared in "Hot Barquette of Seafood Mornay," we know that the United States District Court of Southern California, situated as are we upon a coast, might be expected to share our views. We are most impressed, however, by Allen v. Grafton, 170 Ohio St. 249, where in Ohio, the Midwest, in a case where the plaintiff was injured by a piece of oyster shell in an order of fried oysters, Mr. Justice Taft (now Chief Justice) in a majority opinion held that "the possible presence of a

piece of oyster shell in or attached to an oyster is so well known to anyone who eats oysters that we can say as a matter of law that one who eats
oysters can reasonably anticipate and guard against eating such a piece of
shell. . . ." (p. 259)

Thus, while we sympathize with the plaintiff who has suffered a peculiarly New England injury, the order must be

Exceptions sustained.

Judgment for the defendant.

QUESTIONS

1. Is the court saying that a natural substance does not breach the warranty or that the plaintiff's reasonable expectation should have included the
bone? See Phillips v. Town of West Springfield, 405 Mass. 411, 540 N.E.2d
1331 (1989).

2. Would the plaintiff have recovered if she had been born and reared
in South Dakota and was on her first visit to New England?

3. Would the result be the same if the plaintiff had purchased a *can* of
fish chowder and encountered the bone?

PROBLEM 28

Natty Bumpo was driving through upstate New York when a deer ran in
front of his car. He swerved to avoid it and ran into a tree. His major injuries
came from his sudden contact with the steering wheel and the inside of the
driver's door, where he smashed up against sharp points on the dashboard's
GPS system. Natty sued the car manufacturer, the Mohican Motor Company,
for breach of the warranty of merchantability. His theory was that the manufacturer should have designed a much safer dashboard. The manufacturer's defense was that the car was fit for its ordinary purpose and that Natty
had misused it. How should this come out? See Larsen v. General Motors
Corp., 391 F.2d 495 (8th Cir. 1968); Comment, Intended Use and the Unsafe
Automobile: Manufacturers' Liability for Negligent Design, 28 Md. L. Rev.
386 (1968); Annot., 76 A.L.R.2d 91.

PROBLEM 29

Carry Nation, on the advice of her beautician, Parker Pillsbury,
bought a hair dye named "Intoxicating Fragrance" and proceeded to use
it in accordance with the instructions on the package. Unfortunately the

product contained alcohol, to which Ms. Nation was allergic, and she suffered considerable burn damage to her scalp and ears. When she sued the manufacturer, Harper's Hair Products, Inc., the basic defense was that only 0.5 percent of the population had this allergic reaction. Is this a good defense?

In re Carrier IQ, Inc.

United States District Court, Northern District of California, 2015, 2015 WL 274054

EDWARD M. CHEN, United States District Judge

I. INTRODUCTION

Plaintiffs in this multidistrict litigation — eighteen (18) individuals from thirteen different states — have filed a second consolidated amended complaint ("SCAC" or "Complaint") against Defendant Carrier IQ, Inc. and a number of manufacturers of mobile devices. The Complaint alleges that Defendants have violated the Federal Wiretap Act as well as a number of state's privacy and consumer protection statutes through the creation and use of Carrier IQ's software on Plaintiffs' mobile devices. Plaintiffs allege that Carrier IQ designed, and the Device Manufacturers Defendants embedded, the Carrier IQ Software on their mobile devices and, once embedded, this software surreptitiously intercepted personal data and communications and transmitted this data to Carrier IQ and its customers. Pending before the Court is Defendants' joint motion to dismiss the SCAC in its entirety. For the reasons that follow, the Court **GRANTS** in part and **DENIES** in part Defendants' joint motion, and will afford Plaintiffs leave to file a third consolidated amended complaint.

II. FACTUAL AND PROCEDURAL BACKGROUND

A. PLAINTIFFS

There are 18 plaintiffs in this action, from 13 different states. . . . In describing each Plaintiff, the SCAC provides that "[u]pon information and belief, [the Plaintiff's] mobile device came with the Carrier IQ Software and implementing or porting software pre-installed. In addition to using his devices to make phone calls, [the Plaintiff] has used it for web browsing and text messaging, including accessing, inputting, and transmitting personal, private, confidential, and sensitive information. [The Plaintiff] would not have purchased his mobile device had he known that the Carrier IQ Software and related implementing or porting software was installed and operating on his device, and taxing his device's battery, processor, and memory, as alleged herein." See SCAC ¶¶8-25.

B. DEFENDANTS

The remaining defendants in this action are a number of mobile device manufacturers. Plaintiffs allege that Carrier IQ is the "designer, author, programmer, and vendor" of the IQ Agent software and provided the mobile device manufacturers the "guide or template" needed for the "related implementing or porting software known as the CIQ Interface." Id. ¶26. The IQ Agent and CIQ Interface software forms the basis of Plaintiffs' claims, as described *infra*.

The remaining Defendants are: (1) HTC America, Inc. and HTC Corporation (collectively "HTC"); (2) Huawei Device USA, Inc. ("Huawei"), (3) LG Electronics MobileComm U.S.A., Inc. and LG Electronics, Inc. (collectively "LG"); (4) Motorola Mobility LLC ("Motorola"); (5) Pantech Wireless, Inc. ("Pantech"); (6) Samsung Telecommunications America, Inc. and Samsung Electronics Co., Ltd. (collectively "Samsung"). Each Defendant is alleged to have installed the Carrier IQ Software and CIQ Interface software on at least some of their mobile device models.

C. ASSERTED CAUSES OF ACTION

The SCAC alleges five causes of action:

- **Count 1: Violation of the Federal Wiretap Act (18 U.S.C. §2551)**
- **Count 2: Violation of State Privacy Laws:** Plaintiffs assert their claims on behalf of all residents of the United States under Cal. Penal Code §502 and on behalf of citizens of the following 35 states under those states' respective privacy laws: Arizona, California, Connecticut, Delaware, Florida, Hawaii, Idaho, Illinois, Indiana, Iowa, Louisiana, Maine, Maryland, Massachusetts, Michigan, Minnesota, Nebraska, Nevada, New Hampshire, New Jersey, New Mexico, North Carolina, Ohio, Oregon, Pennsylvania, Rhode Island, South Carolina, Tennessee, Texas, Utah, Virginia, Washington, West Virginia, Wisconsin, and Wyoming.
- **Count 3: Violation of State Consumer Protection Acts:** Asserted on behalf of residents of the following 21 states under those states' respective consumer protection statutes: Arkansas, California, Connecticut, Delaware, Florida, Hawaii, Kansas, Maryland, Michigan, Missouri, Nevada, New Hampshire, New Jersey, Oklahoma, Rhode Island, South Carolina, South Dakota, Texas, Vermont, Washington, and West Virginia.
- **Count 4: Violation of the Magnuson-Moss Warranty Act (15 U.S.C. §2301-2312):** Asserted on behalf of the residents of the following 34

states (and the District of Columbia): Alaska, Arkansas, California, Colorado, Delaware, District of Columbia, Hawaii, Indiana, Kansas, Louisiana, Maine, Maryland, Massachusetts, Michigan, Minnesota, Mississippi, Missouri, Montana, Nebraska, Nevada, New Hampshire, New Jersey, New Mexico, North Dakota, Oklahoma, Pennsylvania, Rhode Island, South Carolina, South Dakota, Texas, Utah, Virginia, Washington, West Virginia, and Wyoming.

- **Count 5: Violation of the Implied Warranty of Merchantability:** asserted on behalf of residents of the states enumerated under Count 4.

D.   CARRIER IQ SOFTWARE BACKGROUND

Carrier IQ "designed, authored, programmed, and caused the installation and activation of the Carrier IQ Software, including the so-called IQ Agent, on the devices at issue in this case." Id. ¶62. It also "designed, authored, and provided guides to the Device Manufacturers for designing, authoring, programming, installing, and activating the CIQ Interface in deployments" through the "embedded" method of installation. Id.

Carrier IQ represents that its software is a "network diagnostics tool" for cell phone service providers. Id. ¶40. It is alleged that in reality, the software collects, and transfers, sensitive personal data off of a user's mobile device. See id. ¶¶1-2. Specifically, the CIQ Interface software is alleged to be a "wrapping or porting layer of code designed to see, recognize, and intercept a host of data and content, including SMS text message content and URLs containing search terms, user names, and passwords . . . and to send that material down to the IQ Agent for further processing and possible transmittals." Id. ¶63. The SCAC alleges that the Device Manufacturers "design and program" the CIQ Interface (with Carrier IQ's aid) and then install the CIQ Interface and IQ Agent software on their mobile devices. Id. Once installed, the software "operates in the background," such that the typical user has no idea that it is running and cannot turn it off. Id. ¶64. Users are never given the choice of opting into or out of the Carrier IQ Software's functionality. Id. Because it is always running, the Plaintiffs allege that it "taxes the device's battery power, processor functions, and system memory." Id.

Plaintiffs allege that the data intercepted by the Carrier IQ Software includes the following: (1) URLs (including those which contain query strings with embedded information such as search terms, user names, passwords, and GPS-based geo-location information); (2) GPS-location information; (3) SMS text messages; (4) telephone numbers dialed and received; (5) the user's keypad presses/keystrokes; and (6) application purchases and uses. Id. ¶65. This information is intercepted as part of the Carrier IQ Software's "calls" on the device operating system for "metrics." Id. It then stores the information in the mobile device's RAM memory on a rolling basis. Id.

The Carrier IQ Software also has a feature referred to as "Profiles." Via Profiles, Carrier IQ customers (who are typically wireless carriers, but can also include device manufacturers) will specify which data they want from the above described "metrics." Id. ¶68. At designated times (or as requested), the Profile-specified data would then be transmitted from the mobile device to the requesting customer (the wireless carriers or device manufacturers). Id.

The SCAC quotes from a number of letters which the various Device Manufacturers sent to Senator Al Franken in response to his inquiries regarding the Carrier IQ Software. These letters provide a glimpse into the potential scope of the Carrier IQ Software deployment. AT & T stated that Carrier IQ's Software was installed on approximately "900,000 devices, with about 575,000 of those collecting and reporting wireless and service performance information to AT & T." Id. ¶53. Sprint indicated that there were "26 million active Sprint devices that have Carrier IQ Software Installed" and stated that Sprint queried information from a fraction of those (c. 1.3 million) at any given time for diagnostic needs and that a 30,000 device subset of this 1.3 million were used for "research specific problems." Id. ¶54. T-Mobile stated that there were "approximately 450,000 T-Mobile customers [that] use devices that contain Carrier IQ's diagnostic software." Id. ¶56.

The SCAC recounts two ways where deployment of the Carrier IQ Software has resulted in "grave breaches of privacy." Id. ¶69. First, due to a "programming error," the SCAC alleges that AT & T has admitted that the "Carrier IQ Software transmitted text message content to it." Id. Plaintiffs use this as evidence that the Carrier IQ Software does, in fact, intercept and capture text message content. Id. Second, Plaintiffs state that "with some deployments, including those on HTC mobile devices and possibly on certain other devices," the data and content intercepted by the Carrier IQ Software was sent in unencrypted, human-readable form into the system logs of the affected devices. Id. ¶71. Accordingly, this information was vulnerable to anyone with access to the system logs, including to individuals with malicious intent. Id. ¶72. Further, because this information was contained in system logs, the private information improperly intercepted and stored was transmitted to Google (who is the author of the Android Operating System) as part of crash reports. Id. ¶73. Similarly, HTC has acknowledged that they have also received this private information through its "Tell HTC" tool which "draws on content stored in the device logs." Id. Accordingly, Plaintiffs contend that this information "may have gone to application developers who draw on device logs as a means of diagnosing application crashes (or for other purposes), including via widely available software tools." Id.

Plaintiffs allege that the Carrier IQ Software continues to operate even if the consumer is using the device solely on a Wi-Fi network (as opposed to a cellular network). Id. ¶74.

E.   FTC INVESTIGATION OF AND ACTION AGAINST HTC RE: CARRIER IQ SOFTWARE

Since the filing of the First Consolidated Amended Complaint in this action, the FTC commenced an investigation into HTC regarding the Carrier IQ Software and a "related privacy and security flaw" in HTC mobile devices. Id. ¶75. This investigation culminated in a Consent Order agreement in February 2013. Id. ¶76.

The FTC found that HTC had "failed to take reasonable steps to secure the software it developed for its smartphones and tablet computers, introducing security flaws that placed sensitive information about millions of consumers at risk." Id. One of the failures cited, was HTC's failure to use "documented secure communications mechanisms in implementing logging applications," thus placing sensitive information at risk. Id. ¶77. Because of HTC's failure to implement security measures, "any third-party application that could connect to the internet could communicate with the logging applications on HTC devices and access a variety of sensitive information." Id. One of the "logging" applications noted by the FTC was the Carrier IQ Software. Relevant to this case, the Consent Order noted: The information collected by the Carrier IQ software was supposed to have been accessible only by network operators, but because HTC used an insecure communications mechanism, any third-party application on the user's device that could connect to the internet could exploit the vulnerability to communicate with the CIQ Interface." Id. This permitted interception of "the sensitive information being collected by the Carrier IQ software" and potentially allowed individuals to perform "malicious actions" such as "sending text messages without permission." Id.

The FTC Consent Order explained how this security flaw occurred. During the development of its CIQ Interface, HTC activated "debug code" in the operating system to test whether the CIQ Interface was operating properly. "The debug code accomplished this by writing the information to a particular device log known as the Android system log, which could then be reviewed. However, HTC failed to deactivate the debug code before its devices shipped for sale to consumers." Id. Thus, "all information that the CIQ Interface sent to the Carrier IQ software . . . was also written to the Android system log on the device." Id. Once in the system log, the sensitive information was then "[a]ccessible to any third-party application with permission to read the system log" and was sent to HTC through its "Tell HTC" error reporting tool." Id. The FTC noted the consumers had "little, if any, reason to know their information was at risk because of the vulnerabilities introduced by HTC." Id. ¶78. Ultimately, the FTC found that HTC had engaged in unfair or deceptive acts or practices in violation of the Federal Trade Commission Act given deceptive statements in its user manuals and user interface. Id. ¶79. . . .

F. Plaintiffs' Implied Warranty of Merchantability Claims

Plaintiffs' fifth cause of action alleges a breach of the implied warranty of merchantability under the laws of over thirty states and the District of Columbia against the Device Manufacturers. The Device Manufacturers have moved to dismiss these claims on a variety of grounds. First, Defendants argue that the implied warranty claims under California, Maryland, Michigan, New Hampshire, Texas, and Washington law should be dismissed as Plaintiffs failed to afford them pre-suit notice of any alleged breach. Second, Defendants argue that Plaintiffs California-based implied warranty claims fail because Plaintiffs were not in privity with the Device Manufacturer and have failed to allege that they purchased their mobile devices in California. Finally, Defendants contend that Plaintiffs have failed to allege that their mobile devices were not "merchantable."

4. Plaintiffs Have Sufficiently Alleged That Their Mobile Devices Were Unmerchantable for Purposes of Their Implied Warranty Claims

Defendants substantively attack Plaintiffs' implied warranty of merchantability claims alleging that Plaintiffs have not — and cannot — allege that the presence and operation of the Carrier IQ Software rendered their mobile devices unmerchantable. Docket No. 304, at 72. Defendants accordingly seek dismissal of Plaintiffs' implied warranty claims arising under the laws of California, Maryland, Michigan, Mississippi, New Hampshire, Texas, and Washington.

Under the laws of each of these states, the implied warranty of merchantability warrants that a purchased good is "fit for the ordinary purposes for which such goods are used." See, e.g., Cal. Comm. Code §2314(2)(c); Md. Code, Comm. Law §2-314(2)(c); Miss. Code Ann. §75-2-314(2)(c); N.H. Rev. Stat. §382-A:2-314(2)(c); Tex. Bus. & Com. Code §2.314(b)(3); Wash. Rev. Code §62A.2-314(2)(c). Courts across various jurisdictions have recognized that the concept of whether a product is "fit for ordinary purposes" necessarily "incorporates . . . the consumer's reasonable expectations into the concept of merchantability." Robinson v. American Honda Motor Co., Inc., 551 F.3d 218 (4th Cir. 2009); see also Venezia v. Miller Brewing Co., 626 F.2d 188, 190 (1st Cir. 1980) ("Under Massachusetts law the question of fitness for ordinary purposes is largely one centering around reasonable consumer expectations."); Denny v. Ford Motor Co., 87 N.Y.2d 248, 639 N.Y.S.2d 250, 662 N.E.2d 730, 736 (1995) (noting that the "fit for the ordinary purposes for which such goods are used" inquiry "focuses on the expectations for the performance of the product when used in the customary, usual and reasonably foreseeable manners").

At the same time, the implied warranty of merchantability merely guarantees that the product will perform at a "minimum level of quality." Birdsong v. Apple, Inc., 590 F.3d 955, 958 (9th Cir. 2009). As such, the implied warranty "does not impose a general requirement that goods precisely fulfill the expectation of the buyer," Am. Suzuki Motor Corp. v. Superior Court, 37 Cal. App. 4th 1291, 1296, 44 Cal. Rptr. 2d 526 (1995). Therefore, a product which "performs its ordinary function adequately does not breach the implied warranty of merchantability merely because it does not function as well as the buyer would like, or even as well as it could." Gen. Motors Corp. v. Brewer, 966 S.W.2d 56, 57 (Tex. 1998). Rather, the alleged defect in the product must be so fundamental as to render the product unfit for its ordinary purpose. See Tietsworth v. Sears, Roebuck & Co., 720 F. Supp. 2d 1123, 1142 (N.D. Cal. 2010) ("The mere manifestation of a defect by itself does not constitute a breach of the implied warranty of merchantability. Instead, there must be a fundamental defect that renders the product unfit for its ordinary purpose.").

Defendants contend that the "ordinary purpose" of mobile devices is communication — making and receiving phone calls, text messages, facilitating internet usage, and allowing usage of apps. Because of this, Defendants argue, Plaintiffs cannot establish that the Carrier IQ Software renders their mobile devices unfit for this ordinary purpose because there are no allegations that the software rendered the devices unable to make and receive phone calls, text messages, and the like. See Docket No. 304, at 73.

Defendants' definition of mobile devices' "ordinary purpose" finds some support in case law from courts in this District. Specifically, in In re iPhone 4S Consumer Litig., No. C12-1227 CW, 2013 WL 3829653 (N.D. Cal. July 23, 2013), the court stated that the "iPhone 4S's intended and ordinary use is as a smartphone, 'which the court safely presumes includes functions like making and receiving calls, sending and receiving text messages, or allowing for use of mobile applications.'" Id. at *16 (quoting Williamson v. Apple, Inc., No. 5:11-cv-0377 EJD, 2012 WL 3835104, at *8-9 (N.D. Cal. Sept. 4, 2012)). Notably, as this quote demonstrates, the court merely found that a mobile device's ordinary and intended use "includes" making and receiving calls, text messages, and the like, suggesting that the courts were not intending to provide an exhaustive definition of a mobile device's ordinary and intended use. Cf. Dairy v. Bonham, No. C-13-1519 EMC, 2013 WL 3829268, at *3 (N.D. Cal. July 23, 2013) ("[U]se of the word 'including' indicates the enumerated ways . . . is not exhaustive.").

Nonetheless, these courts have found that alleged defects which did not affect this core functionality did not render the mobile devices unfit for their ordinary purposes. For example, in *In re iPhone,* plaintiffs alleged that the iPhone was rendered unfit because Apple's "Siri" feature did not perform as advertised. 2013 WL 3829653, at *16. The court, however, found that this allegation failed to state a claim for breach of the implied warranty because plaintiffs had "not alleged that the iPhone 4S is deficient" in "making and receiving calls, sending and receiving text messages, or allowing the use of mobile applications." Rather, plaintiffs had alleged that the iPhone was deficient "in providing the Siri feature to access these functions." Id. Similarly, in *Williamson,* plaintiffs alleged that the glass on their iPhone was defective as it was easily scarred and broken, despite Apple's representations to the contrary. See *Williamson,* 2012 WL 3835104, at *1. The court rejected plaintiff's implied warranty claim, finding that the glass defect did not render deficient the iPhone's ability to make calls, send or receive text messages, or use mobile applications. Id. at *8. Finally, in In re Google Phone Litig., No. 10-CV-0117-EJD, 2012 WL 3155571 (N.D. Cal. Aug. 2, 2012), plaintiffs did allege defects which touched on the core functionality of the Google phone — specifically, they alleged, *inter alia,* that the phone's 3G data connectivity was inconsistent and the phone occasionally dropped or missed phone calls. The court found, however, that plaintiffs had failed to "demonstrate that this alleged defect is more than inconvenience" such that the phone was unfit for its ordinary purpose. Id. at *5.

This Court finds that Defendants' argument that the Carrier IQ Software does not render Plaintiffs' mobile devices unfit for the devices' ordinary purpose simply because the devices could make and receive phone calls, text messages, use mobile apps, and access the internet is overly simplistic and underinclusive. While a defect must be "fundamental" to implicate the implied warranty, "this does not mean the alleged defect must preclude any use of the product at all." Stearns v. Select Comfort Retail Corp., No. 08-2746 JF, 2009 WL 1635931, at *8 (N.D. Cal. June 5, 2009). There are a number of examples of courts which have held that a defect can render a product unfit notwithstanding the fact the product at issue could, in a technical sense, perform its base function. These courts have found that the implied warranty can be breached when, although capable of performing its ordinary function, the product nonetheless fails in a significant way to perform as a reasonable consumer would expect.

Thus, in *Stearns,* plaintiffs alleged an implied warranty claim against a bed manufacturer on the basis of mold growing on its beds. The court determined that the plaintiffs had adequately alleged that the beds at issue "did not conform to expectations regarding ordinary use," and simply because "a person still may sleep on a moldy bed does not bar as a matter of law a claim for breach of the implied warranty of merchantability." Id. at *8. Similarly, in Long v. Graco Children's Products Inc., No. 13-cv-01257-WHO, 2013 WL 4655763 (N.D. Cal. Aug. 26, 2013), plaintiff alleged that defendants' car seats contained a defective buckle that was "unreasonably difficult or impossible to unlatch." Id. at *1. Even though it was not disputed that the car seat provided "adequate protective restraint" for the child, the court found plaintiffs adequately alleged the car seat was unfit. Id. at *12. It held that "[c]onsumers do not merely expect a car seat to serve its bare-minimum purpose" but rather would expect that they "would be able to quickly unlatch the harness or buckle in case of an emergency." Id. Finally, in Isip v. Mercedes-Benz USA, 155 Cal. App. 4th 19, 65 Cal. Rptr. 3d 695 (2007), a car manufacturer argued that so long as a vehicle provided transportation from point A to point B, it necessarily was fit for its ordinary purpose. The court rejected this argument, finding it to be an "unjustified dilution" of the implied warranty. Rather, it held that a vehicle that "smells, lurches, clanks, and emits smoke over an extended period of time is not fit for its intended purpose. Id. at 27, 65 Cal. Rptr. 3d 695; see also Fleisher v. Fiber Composites, LLC, No. 12-1326, 2012 WL 5381381 (E.D. Pa. Nov. 2, 2012) (plaintiffs adequately alleged outdoor deck that became discolored by mold as a result of a defect was unfit for ordinary purpose as consumers expect outdoor decks to not only provide structural support, but to also to meet "a certain aesthetic expectation").

The Court concludes that in determining if a defect rises to the level of rendering a product unfit for its ordinary purpose, the Court must ask two questions. First, the defect in question must be "fundamental" in that it affects the core functionality of the product. See, e.g., *Stearns*, 2009 WL 1635931, at *7 (requiring a "fundamental defect'). Thus defects which only affect functionality that is peripheral or tangential to the core function of the product — for example the strength of glass used in a mobile device or the effectiveness of Apple's Siri function, see, e.g., *In re iPhone*, 2013 WL 3829653, at *16 — would be insufficient. In defining a product's core functionality, a court should not seek to reduce a product to its most basic, bare minimum purpose, but rather should take a common sense view informed by reasonable consumers' expectations about the function of the type of product in a general sense. See *Long*, 2013 WL 4655763, at *12 (rejecting "bare-minimum" view of a car seat's purpose in light of consumer expectations); see also *Robinson*, 551 F.3d at 224 ("This definition of merchantability incorporates trade quality standards and the consumer's reasonable expectations into the concept of merchantability."). Thus, the core function of a vehicle is not to provide transportation, it is to provide safe and reliable transportation, see *Isip*, 155 Cal. App. 4th at 27, 65 Cal. Rptr. 3d 695, and the core function of a bed is not simply to provide a place on which an individual can sleep, but rather to provide a place where an individual can sleep that is free from mold, see *Stearns*, 2009 WL 1635931, at *7. Second, just because a defect affects the core functionality of a product does not automatically mean that the product is unfit for its ordinary purposes. Rather, as discussed, the implied warranty only ensures that a product will meet a "minimum level of quality." *Birdsong*, 590 F.3d at 958. The impairment of the core functionality must be significant enough to prevent the product from reaching a reasonably expected minimum level of quality.

On this basis, the Court finds, for purposes of the motion to dismiss, that Plaintiffs have adequately alleged that the Carrier IQ Software rendered their mobile devices unmerchantable. While there is no dispute that the Carrier IQ Software did not make it impossible for Plaintiffs to make and receive phone calls, text messages, and the like on their devices, that alone is not dispositive. Consumers have a reasonable expectation that mobile devices, in general, will allow them to communicate with others without having a third party surreptitiously intercept and transmit those communications to third parties. Stated another way, it is beyond controversy that individuals have a reasonable expectation of privacy as to the contents of communications made with their mobile devices. Cf. Riley v. California, __ U.S. __, 134 S. Ct. 2473, 2489-91, 189 L. Ed. 2d 430 (2014) (discussing the privacy interests at stake in searches of cell phones by law enforcement and recognizing the user's expectation of privacy). Just as a consumer would likely choose not to sleep on a bed contaminated with mold, a consumer would likely choose to not use a mobile device that actively intercepted his or her private communication data and potentially share that data with third parties.

Plaintiffs have, in the SCAC, provided sufficient factual allegations for the Court to conclude, at this stage, that the Carrier IQ Software intercepts and/or transmits personal communication data to third parties. See, e.g., SCAC ¶65, 68 (alleging that the Carrier IQ Software intercepts and transmits to Carrier IQ and its customers data that can include URLS which contain internet search terms, user names and passwords; text messages; app purchases and uses; a user's keystrokes; numbers dialed and received; etc.). Taking all inferences in favor of the Plaintiffs, these allegations are sufficient for the Court to conclude that the Carrier IQ Software undermines consumers' reasonable expectations in privacy to such a degree so as to render their mobile devices unfit to perform their core functions. During discovery, the parties will have the opportunity to flesh out the precise way the Carrier IQ Software operates, including the degree to which Plaintiffs' personal data or communications were in fact compromised by the Carrier IQ Software. Based on development of a factual record, Carrier IQ Software may renew their argument via motion for summary judgment.

Accordingly, for the foregoing reasons, Plaintiffs have adequately alleged that their mobile devices were unmerchantable and Defendants motion to dismiss the implied warranty claims on this ground is **DENIED**. . . .

2. Fitness for a Particular Purpose

Where the buyer wants to use the goods for something beyond their *ordinary* purpose, a warranty of merchantability is not enough. But the buyer may be able to sue for breach of the implied warranty of fitness for a particular purpose if the buyer can satisfy all of the elements of §2-315. Read the section and its Official Comment.

PROBLEM 30

When Christopher Wren finished building a recreation room in his basement, he wanted a heater for it. He saw an ad for the A-1 Hotblast Heater, which seemed to be what he needed. A good friend of Wren's named Inigo Jones ran a nearby appliance store. Wren went there and told Jones that he wanted the A-1 Hotblast Heater for the new room. Jones knew the room well; he had helped build it. When the heater arrived, it worked perfectly, but it simply did not have the capacity to heat the room. May Wren sue Jones for breach of either §2-314 or §2-315? See Comment 5 to §2-315; Englebreacht v. W.D. Brannan & Sons, Inc., 501 S.W.2d 707 (Tex. Civ. App. 1973).

PROBLEM 31

Lee Matheson went to the Easy Paint Store and bought a can of green paint, which the store mixed on the premises from various pigments. Lee used the paint on his dining room walls, but due to a miscalculation on his part, he ran out when he was half finished. He took the empty paint can back to the store. He told the clerk that he was only half done with the job and needed another can, which the clerk promptly mixed and sold him. Lee finished the painting and then noticed two things: (1) the dried paint gave off an offensive odor, and (2) the paint from the second can did not match the first. What cause(s) of action does he have?

PROBLEM 32

Donald Souse ordered a martini at the Tired Executives Club. When he bit into the olive, he cracked his new $2,000 dentures on a pit. Is there a cause of action under either §2-314 or §2-315? See Hochberg v. O'Donnell's Restaurant, Inc., 272 A.2d 846 (D.C. 1971).

Courts faced with this last Problem (harmful substances in food) have split into two camps: those that deny liability if the object is a *natural substance,* as opposed to a *foreign object,* and those that permit recovery even where the consumer is injured by a natural substance as long as the biter's "reasonable expectation" is that it would have been removed. The problem reoccurs in the cases as gourmands encounter stones in cherry pies, pits in olives, or, as in the *Webster* case above, bones in fish. See Annot., 7 A.L.R.2d 1027.

C. *Warranty Disclaimers and Limitations*

1. Disclaiming Express Warranties

The drafters of the Uniform Commercial Code thought that it was basically unfair for a seller to create an express warranty and then try to disclaim it, so they drafted §2-316(1) in such a way as to make disclaimer of an express warranty virtually impossible. Read it. The proper way to avoid liability for an express warranty is *to not make it in the first place.* Note that express warranties are created by *affirmative* seller conduct. The seller must take out an ad, publish a booklet, say something orally about the product, or point to a sample or model, or the warranty will never arise. Having done one of these things and created buyer expectations that the product will comply with the representations made, the seller must live with the liability assumed. See Official Comment 4 to §2-313; Travis v. Washington Horse Breeders Assn., 111 Wash. 2d 396, 759 P.2d 418 (1988).

Bell Sports, Inc. v. Yarusso

Supreme Court of Delaware, 2000, 759 A.2d 582

WALSH, Justice:

This is an appeal from a Superior Court denial of judgment as a matter of law, or alternatively, for a new trial following an award of damages in a product liability action. The defendant-appellant claims error on the part of the trial judge in ruling on the qualifications of plaintiff's expert witnesses and in permitting the substance of that testimony to establish a jury question on claims for breach of warranty. The appellant further asserts that the jury verdict was internally inconsistent and that the Superior Court should have declared a mistrial after discharging a juror for cause during trial. Upon careful review of the record, we conclude that the Superior Court did not abuse its discretion in permitting the testimony of plaintiff's experts nor in submitting the issues of breach of warranty to the jury. We further conclude that the jury's verdict did not lack consistency and that the refusal to grant a mistrial was not error.

I

On October 20, 1991, Brian J. Yarusso ("Yarusso"), then 22 years of age, was riding his off-road motorcycle[6] at a dirt motocross track located off Church Road in Newark, Delaware. Yarusso was wearing a full complement of safety equipment in addition to the helmet that is the subject of this dispute. While traveling over a series of dirt moguls, or bumps, Yarusso hit one of the moguls in such a way that he was catapulted over the handlebars of the motorcycle. He landed on his head, flipped over and came to rest face down in the dirt. As a result of his fall, Yarusso sustained a burst fracture of the C5 vertebral body and was rendered a quadriplegic.[7]

Yarusso filed suit in the Superior Court against Bell Sports, Inc. ("Bell"), the manufacturer of the Bell Moto-5 helmet he was wearing at the time of the accident. Yarusso's suit against Bell was predicated on a claim that the enhanced injuries he suffered were the proximate result of a defect in the helmet's design. The Bell Moto-5 is a full-face motocross helmet that was designed for off-road use. It complies with federal Department of Transportation ("DOT") standards and is also certified by the Snell Foundation, a leading worldwide helmet research and testing laboratory. The helmet is constructed of a fiberglass outer shell, an inner crushable liner, and a retention system consisting of a chinstrap and D-ring pull-tab. While all three of these components are designed to interact, the inner liner is considered the most important safety feature of the helmet. The expanded polystyrene material of which this liner is primarily constructed is designed to compress upon contact with a solid object.

Yarusso's complaint contained alternative grounds for recovery. He alleged negligence in the design and construction of the helmet, breach of express warranties and breach of an implied warranty of merchantability. Yarusso's express warranty claim arose from specific textual representations in the helmet's accompanying owner's manual (the "manual"), the relevant portions of which are as follows (emphasis printed in manual also reproduced below):

Five Year Limited Warranty: Any Bell helmet found by the factory to be defective in materials or workmanship within five years from the date of purchase

---

6. "Off-road" motorcycles are equipped with motors, tires, seats and suspension components specifically designed to function effectively under adverse riding conditions typical of motocross tracks, woods and fields. They are generally much lighter in weight than motorcycles designed for street use, have a higher degree of suspension clearance/compliance and are usually not equipped with horns, lights and other features required for legal street operation.

7. Dr. Joseph Cusick, a neurosurgeon, described Yarusso's specific injuries. He testified that Yarusso's C5 vertebral body sustained major damage due to a "severe axiocompression load, usually . . . without much extension or flexion." The magnitude of the load was sufficient to crack the bone, push the spinal disk into the soft bone, and "explode" the disc into the spinal cord and some of the other disks.

will be repaired or replaced at the option of the manufacturer, free of charge, when received at the factory, freight pre-paid. . . . This warranty is expressly in lieu of all other warranties, and any implied warranties of merchantability or fitness for a particular purpose created hereby, are limited in duration to the same duration as the express warranty herein. Bell shall not be liable for any incidental or consequential damages. . . .

Introduction: Your new Moto-5 helmet is another in the long line of innovative off-road helmets from Bell. . . . (T)he primary function of a helmet is to reduce the harmful effects of a blow to the head. However, it is important to recognize that the wearing of a helmet is not an assurance of absolute protection. NO HELMET CAN PROTECT THE WEARER AGAINST ALL FORESEEABLE IMPACTS.

Helmet Performance: The Moto-5 is designed to absorb the force of a blow first by spreading it over as wide an area of the outer shell as possible, and second by the crushing of the non-resilient inner liner. Damage to the helmet after an impact is not a sign of any defect in the helmet design or construction. It is exactly what the helmet is designed to do.

NOTICE: No helmet can protect the user from all foreseeable impacts. To obtain the maximum protection offered by any helmet, it must fit firmly on the head and the chinstrap must be securely fastened.

Yarusso testified at trial that he purchased this particular helmet based on the specific assertions, quoted above, that "(t)he primary function of a helmet is to reduce the harmful effects of a blow to the head."

Yarusso's implied warranty of merchantability claim arose out of his contention that the helmet was not merchantable because it was sold as an off-road helmet but was designed to function for "on-road" use. Because the helmet met DOT street helmet standards, Yarusso claimed that it was actually designed with a very stiff liner that would effectively function for on-road use but would not protect a rider against foreseeable off-road falls, where the impact surface could conceivably be softer.

A pivotal factual issue at trial was whether the helmet liner properly crushed, as designed, at the time Yarusso's head impacted the ground after his fall. Yarusso claimed that the injuries to his neck were caused by the stiffness or density of the liner material at the helmet crown. At trial, he offered expert testimony by Maurice Fox ("Fox"), a safety consultant who had been employed by a helmet manufacturer during the 1970s. Fox opined that Yarusso's helmet sustained the majority of the fall's impact at its crown where the liner was too dense to crush sufficiently, thereby transmitting excessive force to Yarusso's neck, resulting in his paralysis. Fox's testimony however, was directed primarily at Yarusso's negligence claim against Bell, which the jury subsequently rejected.

Joseph Cusick, M.D. ("Cusick"), a neurological expert, similarly testified that the neck injuries sustained by Yarusso were consistent with impact at the top, or crown, of the helmet. Cusick further testified that a 20-30% reduction of force to Yarusso's body would have been sufficient to avoid injury because his body would have been able to withstand this lower level of force.

Richard Stalnaker, Ph.D. ("Stalnaker"), a biomechanical engineer, also testified on behalf of Yarusso and largely affirmed Fox's opinion. His testimony was crucial in the jury's determination that Bell had breached express and implied warranties. Stalnaker determined that the force of Yarusso's impact with the ground was equivalent to 60 foot pounds, and that adequate crush of the helmet liner would have reduced it significantly to avert injury. Although Stalnaker modified the analytical process used to reconstruct the accident to coincide with that presented by Bell's expert reconstruction witness at trial, Bell's counsel rejected an opportunity to delay the trial and requested only a mistrial. Because the trial judge determined that the factual foundation for Stalnaker's testimony was unchanged despite his use of an alternative analytical, she denied the motion for mistrial leaving the matter for attack through cross-examination.

Bell offered its own expert testimony at trial disputing the helmet's point of impact from the accident and asserting the inability of any helmet to protect its user from severe neck injuries. The principal designer of the helmet, James Sundahl ("Sundahl"), testified that any helmet must be designed to protect its user from a multitude of accident types. He further opined that in circumstances involving a helmet's impact with a soft surface, the surface itself, rather than the helmet, absorbs a greater portion of the energy. When questioned about the representation in the helmet's manual, Sundahl testified that it was "wrong."

James McElhaney, Ph.D. ("McElhaney"), a professor of biomechanics at Duke University, testified for Bell and disputed Yarusso's contention that the helmet was impacted at its crown. McElhaney testified that the front of Yarusso's helmet liner was crushed in a fashion indicating a substantial blow to that area. Both Sundahl and McElhaney presented evidence of industry-wide research to the effect that no helmet can offer "any significant protection of the neck because the mass of the torso is so much more than the energy levels that a helmet can manage." Bell's experts claimed that this helmet and helmets in general are designed to protect users from head and brain injuries and the helmet in this case did precisely that.

Upon the conclusion of Yarusso's case, he abandoned his failure to warn claim. At the close of all the evidence, Bell moved for judgment as a matter of law as to liability. The trial court granted judgment as a matter of law on Yarusso's breach of implied warranty for a particular purpose claim, but denied Bell's motion on the remaining counts. The jury was then charged on the remaining claims of negligence, breach of implied warranty of merchantability and breach of express warranty.

On the second day of jury deliberations, one juror notified the trial court that he had reviewed outside information regarding motorcycle helmets in connection with securing a motorcycle licensing examiner's certificate. The jury also notified the court that they were deadlocked. The trial judge subsequently interrogated the juror who had disclosed his outside knowledge out of the presence of the remaining jurors. The trial judge determined that while the juror had not yet shared this extraneous information with other jurors, he had violated the direct instruction to decide the case solely from the evidence presented. The trial judge dismissed the juror prompting a motion from Bell for a mistrial, which was denied. Because both parties had agreed at the outset of the trial to accept a jury of eleven members, the remaining jurors were permitted to deliberate.

Through specific answers to interrogatories, the jury ultimately found that Bell was not negligent, but had breached an express or implied warranty, which proximately caused Yarusso's enhanced injury. Yarusso was awarded $1,812,000 in damages. Bell objected that the verdict was inconsistent and renewed its motions for judgment as a matter of law or alternatively for a new trial on liability only, all of which were denied by the Superior Court. This appeal followed. . . .

II

By its verdict, the jury specifically determined that Bell had not negligently designed the Moto-5 helmet but that Bell had breached "an express or implied warranty" when it sold the helmet and that "conduct proximately caused Brian Yarusso to suffer enhanced injuries." Bell argues on appeal that Yarusso failed, as a matter of law, to establish an evidentiary basis for recovery under either express or implied warranty and the trial court should have granted judgment in its favor as to those claims.

Preliminarily, we note that the jury was permitted to find liability under alternative forms of breach of warranty, express or implied, without differentiating between the two. Bell did not object to the warranty claims being submitted in that format and, thus, the verdict may be sustained if there is record and legal support for recovery under either theory.

A.

The statutory basis for a claim for damages based on breach of an express warranty arising out of a sale of goods under Delaware law is found in this State's counterpart of the Uniform Commercial Code. Title 6, section 2-313 [which the court quotes — Ed.].

The official commentary to that section under the U.C.C. indicates that the drafters intended its warranty provisions to be construed and applied liberally in favor of a buyer of goods. See U.C.C. §2-313 cmt. 1 (1977) ("Express warranties rest on 'dickered' aspects of the individual bargain, and go so clearly to the essence of that bargain that words of a disclaimer in a form are repugnant to the basic dickered terms."); U.C.C. §2-313 cmt. 3 ("In actual practice affirmations of fact made by a seller about the goods during a bargain are regarded as part of the description of those goods; hence no particular reliance on such statements need be shown in order to weave them into the fabric of the agreement."); U.C.C. §2-313 cmt. 4 ("[A] contract is normally a contract for a sale of something describable and described. A clause generally disclaiming 'all warranties, express or implied' cannot reduce the seller's obligation with respect to such description. . . ."). The language of the U.C.C.'s official commentary may be applied by analogy to the sale of goods governed by 6 Del. C. §2-313 in the reconciliation of any ensuing express warranty disputes. Thus, Bell's argument in this case that the express warranty terms in the manual are strictly limited to the "Five Year Limited Warranty" section, which also contained a purportedly effective disclaimer of those terms, is unfounded.

Formal wording is not necessary to create a warranty and a seller does not have to express any specific intention to create one. See Pack & Process, Inc. v. Celotex Corp., Del. Super., 503 A.2d 646, 658-59 (1985). Here the additional terms found in the manual's "Introduction" and "Helmet Performance" sections (stating that "the primary function of a helmet is to reduce the harmful effects of a blow to the head . . ." and ". . . the [helmet] is designed to absorb the force of a blow by spreading it over as wide an area of the outer shell as possible . . .") are textual representations constituting affirmations of fact upon which a buyer is entitled to rely. While this Court does not appear to have specifically addressed the issue, other courts have held that express warranties can arise from similar textual representations found in owners' manuals even where not specifically labeled as such. See e.g., Kinlaw v. Long Mfg. N.C., Inc., 298 N.C. 494, 259 S.E.2d 552, 557 (1979); Hawkins Constr. Co. v. Matthews Co., 190 Neb. 546, 209 N.W.2d 643, 654-55 (1973).

The restrictive provision of 6 Del. C. §2-316(1), renders Bell's effort to disclaim any express warranties in the manual's "Five Year Limited Warranty" ineffective as a matter of law. See U.C.C. §2-316(1) cmt. 1 (stating that "this section . . . seeks to protect a buyer from unexpected and unbargained language of disclaimer by denying effect to such language when inconsistent with language of express warranty. . . ."). While the manual contains disclaimers warning potential users that the helmet cannot prevent all injuries, other representations were made to assure a potential buyer that the helmet's liner was designed to reduce the harmful effects of a blow to the head. Those representations constituted essential elements of a valid express warranty that may not be effectively disclaimed as a matter of law. See Jensen v. Seigel Mobile Homes Group, 105 Idaho 189, 668 P.2d 65, 71-72 (1983) (holding that one principle of the law of warranty is to hold a seller responsible for its representations and assuring that a buyer receives that which he bargained for).

Bell argues that even if an express warranty was created and not effectively disclaimed here, the manual's textual representations promise only to prevent injuries to the head, not to a user's neck. Furthermore, Bell argues, the helmet's liner did crush as designed, thereby precluding a finding that the warranty was breached. Yarusso counters this argument by pointing out that injuries to the neck may logically follow a blow to the head, the helmet's liner did not sufficiently crush to prevent his injury and, as a result, he did not get what he bargained for. Upon review of the evidence, much of which was admittedly supplied by testimony of Yarusso's experts, the jury came to a logical conclusion that an express warranty was made in the helmet's manual. Upon consideration of this representation in relation to the specific facts of this case, they also concluded that the warranty was breached. In view of the evidence presented by the experts for both parties on the relationship between the helmet's design and the risk of neck injury, a factual predicate existed for the jury to determine whether there was a basis for recovery under the express warranty claim. The Superior Court did not err in submitting that issue to the jury.

B.

Our holding sustaining the jury's verdict on the claim of breach of express warranty renders an in-depth consideration of Bell's implied warranty arguments unnecessary, since the jury was permitted to find a breach of warranty on alternative grounds. The Superior Court in rejecting Bell's post-trial motions also declined to rule on the merits of Bell's attack on the implied warranty finding in view of the jury's finding of liability on the express warranty claim. We also are not required to address Bell's contention that Yarusso was obligated, as a matter of law, to present evidence of a safer alternative design. See Mazda Motor Corp. v. Lindahl, Del. Supr., 706 A.2d 526, 530 (1998). We note, however, that Yarusso's experts never claimed that a helmet can reduce the probability of a user's neck injury in all circumstances, and they were not required to present evidence that a helmet could be designed to achieve this. Expert evidence was presented, however, that a helmet could be designed with a softer liner that would, in theory, limit the amount of force placed on the user's neck, thereby reducing the probability of partial-load direct downward neck injuries, particularly upon impact with harder surfaces. There was, thus, a sufficient factual predicate for submission of the implied warranty claim to the jury.

III

In a related vein, Bell next argues that the jury's finding for Yarusso on breach of express and implied warranties is inconsistent with its finding that Bell was not negligent. Because the jury found no product defect leading to negligent conduct on Bell's part, it could not have properly found, the argument runs, that a defect existed in the helmet upon which any warranty claims relied. See Ruffin v. Shaw Indus., Inc., 4th Cir., 149 F.3d 294, 301 (1998) (holding that the requirements of both actions are nearly alike and that a finding on one claim often "applies equally" to the other); Prentis v. Yale Mfg. Co., 421 Mich. 670, 365 N.W.2d 176, 186 (1984) (both actions "involve identical evidence and require proof of exactly the same elements"). In essence, Bell contends that because its product was not defective, a verdict in favor of Yarusso on warranty and negligence claims was precluded.

A claim for breach of warranty, express or implied, is conceptually distinct from a negligence claim because the latter focuses on the manufacturer's conduct, whereas a breach of warranty claim evaluates the product itself. See Cline v. Prowler Indus. of Md., Inc., Del. Supr., 418 A.2d 968, 978, n.19 (1980) (the focus of a negligence claim is the manufacturer's conduct and the breach of an accepted standard of conduct); Borel v. Fibreboard Paper Prod. Corp., 5th Cir., 493 F.2d 1076, 1094 (1973) (in a products liability case with inconsistent verdicts, it is within the jury's prerogative so long as evidence supports the finding); Community Television Serv. v. Dresser Indus., Inc., D.S.D., 435 F. Supp. 214, 216 (1977) (jury could find defendant neither negligent nor strictly liable while finding as a matter of law that representations in a brochure created an express warranty that defendant breached). Based on the foregoing authorities, we find no fatal inconsistency between the jury's verdict negating negligence but finding breach of warranty. . . .

The judgment of the Superior Court is AFFIRMED.

PROBLEM 33

When Portia Moot went to buy a new car, she asked the salesman how many miles to the gallon it would get. He replied that it would get "between 30 and 35 MPG in the city and 40 to 45 on the highway." Delighted, she bought the car. The very best the car ever did, even in highway driving, was 27 MPG, and Portia was upset. When she threatened a lawsuit, the dealership pointed out the following three clauses in the contract she had signed that it relied on to avoid liability. This contract said nothing about miles per gallon of gas. In your opinion is there any way around these clauses?

(1) "This is the entire contract, and there are no other matters agreed to by the parties that are not contained herein." Would this clause be more

effective in a business contract to exclude oral statements made during negotiations on the theory that the written disclaimer keeps such oral matters
from being part of the "basis of the bargain"? See Lincoln Sav. Bank v. Open
Solutions, Inc., 2013 WL 997894 (N.D. Iowa 2013).

(2) "There are no other express or implied warranties except those contained herein."

(3) "No salesperson has the authority to give express warranties other
than those contained herein." (As to this last clause, see White & Summers
§13-4, and the brief reference to the matter in Official Comment 2 to §2-316.)

2.   Disclaiming Implied Warranties

In contrast to express warranties, implied warranties are much more
easily disclaimed. Since they are created by the legislature of the enacting
state and not by seller conduct, there is less unfairness in their destruction
as long as the seller or the circumstances alert the buyer to the disclaimer.
Read §2-316(2) and (3) carefully.

Cate v. Dover Corp.

Supreme Court of Texas, 1990, 790 S.W.2d 559

DOGGETT, J.
We consider the enforceability of a disclaimer of implied warranties.
The trial court upheld the disclaimer and granted summary judgment in
favor of Dover Corporation. The court of appeals affirmed. 776 S.W.2d 680.
We reverse the judgment of the court of appeals and remand this cause to
the trial court for further proceedings consistent with this opinion.

In September 1984, Edward Cate, doing business as Cate's Transmission
Service, purchased from Beech Tire Mart three lifts manufactured and
designed by Dover Corporation to elevate vehicles for maintenance. Despite
repairs made by Beech and Dover, the lifts never functioned properly. Dover
contends that Cate's subsequent claim against it for breach of the implied
warranty of merchantability is barred by a disclaimer contained within a written, express warranty.

This warranty is set forth on a separate page headed in blue half inch
block print, with the heading: "YOU CAN TAKE ROTARY'S NEW 5-YEAR
WARRANTY AND TEAR IT APART." The statement is followed by bold
black type stating, "And, when you are through, it'll be just as solid as the
No. 1 lift company in America, Rotary." The text of the warranty itself is
in black type, contained within double blue lines, and appears under the

blue three-eighths inch block print heading "WARRANTY." The disclaimer of implied warranties, although contained in a separate paragraph within the warranty text, is in the same typeface, size, and color as the remainder of the text.

WARRANTY

All Rotary Surface Mounted Lifts are guaranteed to the original owner for five years from invoice date. Rotary Lift Division here after is known as "The Company". The Company shall replace for the full five years those parts returned to the factory which prove upon inspection by the Company to be defective. The Company shall pay for reasonable costs of transportation and labor for replacement of said parts for the first 12 months only. Purchaser will bear costs of transportation and labor for parts returned after the first year and the remainder of this warranty. This warranty shall not apply unless the product is installed, used and maintained in accordance with the Company's specifications as set forth in the Company's installation, operation and maintenance instructions.

This warranty does not cover normal maintenance or adjustments, damage or malfunction caused by improper handling, installation, abuse, misuse, negligence or carelessness of operation.

This warranty is exclusive and is in lieu of all other warranties expressed or implied including any implied warranty of merchantability or any implied warranty of fitness for a particular purpose, which implied warranties are hereby expressly excluded.

The remedies described are exclusive and in no event shall the Company be liable for special, consequential or incidental damages for the breach of or delay in performance of the warranty.

This warranty shall be governed by the State of Indiana, and shall be subject to the exclusive jurisdiction of the Court of the State of Indiana in the County of Jefferson.

American made

Rotary®

Exhibit A

An implied warranty of merchantability arises in a contract for the sale of goods unless expressly excluded or modified by conspicuous language. Tex. Bus. & Com. Code Ann. §§2.314(a), 2.316(b) (Vernon 1968). Whether a particular disclaimer is conspicuous is a question of law to be determined by the following definition:

> A term or clause is conspicuous when it is so written that a reasonable person against whom it is to operate ought to have noticed it. A printed heading in capitals (as: NON-NEGOTIABLE BILL OF LADING) is conspicuous. Language in a body of a form is conspicuous if it is larger or of other contrasting type or color. But in a telegram, any stated term is conspicuous.

Id. §1.201(10). Further explanation is provided by comment 10 thereto:

> This [section] is intended to indicate some of the methods of making a term attention-calling. But the test is whether attention can reasonably be expected to be called to it.

In interpreting this language, Dover argues that a lesser standard of conspicuousness should apply to a disclaimer made to a merchant, such as Cate. Admittedly, an ambiguity is created by the requirement that disclaimer language be conspicuous to "a reasonable person *against whom it is to operate.*" Comment 10, however, clearly contemplated an objective standard, stating the test as "whether attention can reasonably be expected to be called to it."

We then turn to an application of an objective standard of conspicuousness to Dover's warranty. The top forty percent of the written warranty is devoted to extolling its virtues. The warranty itself, contained within double blue lines, is then set out in five paragraphs in normal black type under the heading "WARRANTY." Nothing distinguishes the third paragraph, which contains the exclusionary language. It is printed in the same typeface, size and color as the rest of the warranty text. Although the warranty in its entirety may be considered conspicuous, the disclaimer is hidden among attention-getting language purporting to grant the best warranty available. . . .

Although this is a case of first impression in Texas, the facts here parallel those reviewed in other states. In Massey-Ferguson, Inc. v. Utley, 439 S.W.2d 57, 59 (Ky. Ct. App. 1969), a disclaimer hidden under the heading "WARRANTY and AGREEMENT" was found not to be conspicuous:

> It is true that the *heading was* in large, bold-face type, but there was nothing to suggest that an exclusion was being made; on the contrary, the words of the headings indicated a *making* of warranties rather than a *disclaimer.*

(Emphasis in original.) Similarly, in Hartman v. Jensen's, Inc., 289 S.E.2d 648 (S.C. 1982), the court found that placing a disclaimer under the bold heading "Terms of Warranty" failed to alert the consumer to the fact that an exclusion was intended. Dover's disclaimer similarly fails to attract the attention of a reasonable person and is not conspicuous. . . .

Dover argues that even an inconspicuous disclaimer should be given effect because Cate had actual knowledge of it at the time of the purchase. Because the object of the conspicuousness requirement is to protect the buyer from surprise and an unknowing waiver of his or her rights, inconspicuous language is immaterial when the buyer has actual knowledge of the disclaimer. This knowledge can result from the buyer's prior dealings with the seller, or by the seller specifically bringing the inconspicuous waiver to the buyer's attention. The Code appears to recognize that actual knowledge of the disclaimer overrides the question of conspicuousness. For example, §2.316(b) does not mandate a written disclaimer of the implied warranty of merchantability but clearly provides that an oral disclaimer may be effective.[8] Similarly, §2.316(c)(3) allows an implied warranty to be excluded or modified by methods other than a conspicuous writing: course of dealing, course of performance, or usage of trade. When the buyer is not surprised by the disclaimer, insisting on compliance with the conspicuousness requirement serves no purpose. See R. Anderson, Uniform Commercial Code §2-316:49-50 (1983). The extent of a buyer's knowledge of a disclaimer of the implied warranty of merchantability is thus clearly relevant to a determination of its enforceability. See Singleton v. LaCoure, 712 S.W.2d 757, 759 (Tex. App. Houston [14th Dist.] 1986, writ ref'd n.r.e.) (relying in part on buyer's acknowledgement to enforce disclaimer). The seller has the burden of proving the buyer's actual knowledge of the disclaimer.

As this is a summary judgment case, the issue on appeal is whether Dover met its burden by establishing that there exists no genuine issue of material fact thereby entitling it to judgment as a matter of law. City of Houston v. Clear Creek Basin Authority, 589 S.W.2d 671, 678 (Tex. 1979). All doubts as to the existence of a genuine issue of material fact are resolved against the movant, and we must view the evidence in the light most favorable to the Petitioner. Great American Reserve Ins. Co. v. San Antonio Plumbing Supply Co., 391 S.W.2d 41, 47 (Tex. 1965). In support of its claim that Cate

---

8. Tex. Bus. & Com. Code §2.136, comment 1 (section seeks to protect buyer from unexpected and unbargained language of disclaimer by permitting exclusion of implied warranties only by conspicuous language or other circumstances which protect buyer from surprise); see also Weintraub, Disclaimer of Warranties and Limitation of Damages for Breach of Warranty Under the UCC, 53 Tex. L. Rev. 60, 66 (1974); J. White & R. Summers, Uniform Commercial Code §12-5, n.76 (2d ed. 1980) (seller may effectively disclaim by orally explaining inconspicuous written disclaimer, provided word "merchantability" used).

had actual knowledge of the disclaimer, Dover relies on Cate's deposition testimony, as follows:

> *Q:* Do you know, or do you remember what kinds of warranties you received when you bought the lifts?
> *A:* I may be wrong, but I think it was a five-year warranty.
> *Q:* What was your understanding of that warranty?
> *A:* Any problems would be taken care of within the five year period.
> *Q:* Do you know if that warranty was from Beech Equipment, or from Dover?
> *A:* I believe it was from Dover.
> *Q:* Did you receive any written documentation in regard to that warranty?
> *A:* Yes, ma'am.

Although it is clear that Cate understood the warranty to extend for only five years, it is not clear that he understood any other limitations or exclusions. Merely providing a buyer a copy of documents containing an inconspicuous disclaimer does not establish actual knowledge. Dover has failed to establish that as a matter of law Cate had actual knowledge of the disclaimer.

We hold that, to be enforceable, a written disclaimer of the implied warranty of merchantability made in connection with a sale of goods must be conspicuous to a reasonable person. We further hold that such a disclaimer contained in text undistinguished in typeface, size or color within a form purporting to grant a warranty is not conspicuous, and is unenforceable unless the buyer has actual knowledge of the disclaimer. For the reasons stated herein, we reverse the judgment of the court of appeals and remand to the trial court for further proceedings consistent with this opinion.

SPEARS, J. concurs and files a separate opinion (in which MAUZY, J. joins).

RAY, J. files a concurring and dissenting opinion.

SPEARS, J. Although I concur in the court's opinion, I write separately to declare that the time has come for the legislature to consider the realities of the marketplace and prohibit all disclaimers of the implied warranties of merchantability and fitness.

These implied warranties, created by common-law courts long before the adoption of the UCC, developed to protect purchasers from losses suffered because of "the frustration of their expectations about the worth, efficacy, or desirability" of a product. W. Keeton, Prosser and Keeton on the Law of Torts §95A (5th ed. 1984). Implication of these warranties into every goods contract, without regard to the parties' actual assent to their terms, served "to police, to prevent, and to remedy" unfair consumer transactions. Llewellyn, On Warranty of Quality, and Society, 39 Colum. L. Rev. 699, 699 (1936); Humber v. Morton, 426 S.W.2d 554, 557-558 (Tex. 1968). These implied warranties also serve other important purposes: they create incentives to produce and market higher quality products; they discourage shoddy workmanship and unethical trade practices; and they place responsibility on those who profit from the sale of goods, have the greatest control over the products, and are better able to bear the risk of loss. See *Humber,* 426 S.W.2d at 562; Decker & Sons v. Capp, 139 Tex. 609, 610, 164 S.W.2d 828, 829 (1942). Section 2-316 of the U.C.C., however, subverts all of these purposes by giving sellers almost unlimited license to disclaim implied warranties.

We live in an age when sellers of goods "saturate the marketplace and all of our senses" with the most extraordinary claims about the worth of their products. Anderson, The Supreme Court of Texas and the Duty to Read the Contracts You Sign, 15 Tex. Tech L. Rev. 517, 544 (1984); Henningsen v. BloomField Motors, Inc., 161 A.2d 69, 84 (N.J. 1960). Yet, the same sellers under the carte blanche granted them by §2-316 of the U.C.C. refuse to guarantee and indeed expressly disclaim that their products are merchantable or even fit for their intended purposes. Under §2-316, not much is actually required for an effective disclaimer. To disclaim the implied warranty of merchantability the seller need only include the word "merchantability" in a conspicuous fashion. Tex. Bus. & Com. Code Ann. §2-316(b) (Vernon 1968). To disclaim the implied warranty of fitness the seller must use a writing and must make the disclaimer conspicuous. Id. at §2-316(2). No particular form of words is needed to disclaim an implied warranty of fitness, nor does §2-316 require the buyer to be actually aware of the disclaimer before it will be enforced. All implied warranties can be disclaimed by the mere inclusion of expressions like "as is" or "with all faults." Id. at §2-316, comment 1. Finally, as today's majority makes clear, §2-316 does not even require the disclaimer to be conspicuous if the buyer's actual knowledge of the disclaimer can be shown.

By establishing specific "requirements" for disclaimers §2-316 ostensibly "seeks to protect a buyer from unexpected and unbargained language of disclaimer." Tex. Bus. & Com. Code §2-316, comment 1 (Vernon 1968). In reality, however, §2-316 completely undermines implied warranties. Implicitly, §2-316 adopts the position that disclaimers should be enforced because society benefits when parties to a contract are allowed to set *all* the terms of their agreement. The problem with this position, and with §2-316 generally, is two-fold: it ignores the fact that governmental implication of protective terms into private contracts is commonplace (e.g., the *implied* warranties of merchantability and fitness); and, more importantly, it rests on the faulty premise that contractual disclaimers are generally freely bargained for elements of a contract.

Freedom of contract arguments generally, and §2-316 specifically, presuppose and are based on "the image of individuals meeting in the marketplace" on equal ground to negotiate the terms of a contract. Rakoff, Contracts of Adhesion: An Essay in Reconstruction, 96 Harv. L. Rev. 1174, 1216 (1983). At one time, this image may have accurately reflected marketplace realities. However, the last half of the twentieth century has witnessed "the rise of the corporation" and, increasingly, the displacement of physical persons as sellers in consumer and commercial contracts. Phillips, Unconscionability and Article 2 Implied Warranty Disclaimers, 62 Chi.-Kent L. Rev. 199, 239 (1985). This development has led to innumerable situations in which consumers deal from an unequal bargaining position, the most prominent example being the ubiquitous standard form contract which is now used by most sellers of goods and which invariably contains an implied warranty disclaimer. See Melody Home Mfg. Co. v. Barnes, 741 S.W.2d 349, 355 (Tex. 1987); *Henningsen,* 161 A.2d at 86-89; Slawson, Standard Form Contracts and Democratic Control of Lawmaking Power, 84 Harv. L. Rev. 529, 529 (1971) ("standard form contracts probably account for more than ninety-nine percent of all the contracts now made"); L. Vold, Handbook of the Law of Sales 447 (2d ed. 1959) (dramatic rise in corporate power has yielded the standard form contract whose terms are drafted by the seller and usually contain implied warranty disclaimers).

The great majority of buyers never read an implied warranty disclaimer found in a standard form contract.[9] Even when implied warranty disclaimers are read, their legal significance is not generally understood. Such disclaimers include unfamiliar terminology (e.g., "implied warranty of merchantability"), and comprehending their legal effect requires one not only to understand what substantive rights are involved, but also to grasp that

---

9. See Restatement (Second) of Contracts §211, Comment b (1981):

> A party who makes regular use of a standardized form of agreement does not ordinarily expect his customers to understand or even to read the standard terms. One purpose of standardization is to eliminate bargaining over details of individual transactions, and that purpose would not be served if a substantial number of customers retained counsel and reviewed the standard terms. . . . Customers do not in fact ordinarily understand or even read the standard terms.

Id.; see also Rakoff, Contracts of Adhesion: An Essay in Reconstruction, 96 Harv. L. Rev. 1174, 1179 n.21 (1983) (citing numerous commentators who declare that standard terms not read or understood, and some empirical studies asserting same proposition); Phillips, Unconscionability and Article 2 Implied Warranty Disclaimers, 62 Chi.-Kent L. Rev. 199, 243 (1985) (many sales do not involve a written sales contract that is presented before the goods change hands; usually, the disclaimer is inside the package and is not seen until after the sale is completed).

these rights have been lost via the disclaimer. Phillips, Unconscionability and Article 2 Implied Warranty Disclaimers, 62 Chi.-Kent L. Rev. 199, 243 (1985); see also Federal Trade Commission, Facts for Consumers (Mar. 23, 1979) (more than 35% of those surveyed mistakenly believed that an "as is" disclaimer meant the dealer would have to pay some, if not all, costs if a car broke down within 25 days of a sale). Finally, even if a buyer reads and understands an implied warranty disclaimer, chances are he will be without power to either strike these terms or "shop around" for better ones. If the buyer attempts the former, he will likely run into an employee who is unauthorized to alter the form contract; if he attempts the latter, he will likely confront a competitor who offers substantially the same form terms. *Henningsen,* 161 A.2d at 87. In short, the "marketplace reality" suggests that freedom of contract in the sale of goods is actually nonexistent; a buyer today can either take the contract with the disclaimer attached or leave it and go without the good. . . .

The realities of the modern marketplace demand that the legislature prohibit implied warranty disclaimers by repealing §2-316 of the U.C.C. Without such action, Texas courts will be forced to rely on "covert tools," such as the unconscionability provision in §2-302 or the "conspicuous" requirement in §2-316, to reach a just and fair result in disclaimer suits. When these tools are used, guidance, predictability and consistency in the law is sacrificed, while limited judicial resources are spent policing unjust bargains that could have been avoided. Were it up to the judicial branch, the courts could declare such disclaimers void as against public policy. If the legislature has the interests of Texas citizens at heart, it will repeal §2-316 because, no matter how conspicuous, such disclaimers are abusive of consumers.

MAUZY, J. joins in this concurring opinion.

RAY, J. I concur in that portion of the court's opinion requiring that a written disclaimer of the implied warranty of merchantability must be conspicuous to a reasonable person. I write separately, however, to take issue with the court's immediate erosion of that standard by permitting a showing of actual knowledge of the disclaimer to override a lack of conspicuousness.

The statute, on its face, provides for no actual knowledge exception. There is no room for judicial crafting of those omitted by the legislature. I would hold that the extent of a buyer's knowledge of a disclaimer is irrelevant to a determination of its enforceability under §2-316(b) of the U.C.C.

The effect of actual knowledge is subject to debate among leading commentators on commercial law. The purpose of the objective standard of conspicuousness adopted by the court today reflects the view that "the drafters intended a rigid adherence to the conspicuousness requirement in order to avoid arguments concerning what the parties said about the warranties at the time of the sale." J. White and R. Summers, Uniform Commercial Code §12-5 (2d ed. 1980). An absolute rule that an inconspicuous disclaimer is invalid, despite the buyer's actual knowledge, encourages sellers to make their disclaimers conspicuous, thereby reducing the need for courts to evaluate swearing matches as to actual awareness in particular cases. See W. Powers, Texas Products Liability Law §2.0723 (1989). Today's decision condemns our court to a parade of such cases.

PROBLEM 34

(a) A statement buried in the fine print of a used car purchase agreement states that "There are no express or implied warranties that are part of this sale." See §§2-316(2), 1-201(b)(10).

(1) Are the implied warranties effectively disclaimed?

(2) If the car dealership asks you to redraft this clause so as to comply with the Code, what changes would you make in the language? See the extended discussion, particularly in the dissent, in Hicks v. Superior Court, 8 Cal. Rptr. 3d 703 (Cal. App. 2004).

(3) What changes would you make in the physical appearance of the clause in the contract? Is it all right to put the disclaimer in a clause labeled *WARRANTY*? See Benedict v. Hankook Tire Co. Ltd., 295 F. Supp. 3d 632 (E.D. Va. 2018); Agropur, Inc. v. Scoular Company, 2017 WL 3411944 (D. Minn. 2017) (disclaimer in contract section titled "CONTAMINATION & GUARANTEE").

(4) Can the car dealer win the legal dispute by arguing that usage of trade (§1-303(c)) permits the burial of warranty disclaimers in the fine print? (For an annotation collecting the automobile warranty disclaimer cases, see Annot., 54 A.L.R.3d 1217.)

(b) The words *AS IS* are written with soap in large letters across the front windshield of the used car. See §2-316(3)(a). Is this effective to disclaim implied warranties? Express warranties? See Woodard v. Labrada, 2017 WL 3309765 (C.D. Cal. 2017); Annot., 24 A.L.R.3d 465. Must the "as is" language be conspicuous? See §2-316(3)(a); Lumber Mut. Ins. Co. v. Clarklift of Detroit, Inc., 224 Mich. App. 737, 569 N.W.2d 681 (1997); R.J. Robertson, Jr., A Modest Proposal Regarding the Enforceability of "As Is" Disclaimers of Implied Warranties: What the Buyer Doesn't Know Shouldn't Hurt Him, 99 Com. L.J. 1 (1994). Would a conspicuous statement of AS IS on a *new* recreational vehicle exclude the implied warranty of merchantability? See Chaudoin v. Thor Motor Coach, Inc., 2017 WL 3485803 (E.D. Mich. 2017). Certainly it is clear that "As Is" will not protect a seller from tort theories such as fraud. Sorchaga v. Ride Auto, LLC, 893 N.W.2d 360 (Wis. App. 2017).

(c) The car salesman asks the buyer, "Would you like to examine the car?" and the buyer, who is in a hurry, says, "No." Effective disclaimer? See §2-316(3)(b); see also Official Comment 8.

(d) Remember Ted Traveler (Problem 21), who walked into the men's room of the bus depot and bought an expensive watch? We decided there was no warranty of title in that transaction. However, a warranty of quality is a separate question. Are there implied warranties in this sale? See §2-316(3)(c).

PROBLEM 35

If your client is the manufacturer of products and asks you to draft up contracts for the sale of the company's products, should you recommend disclaiming warranties? You could do this by making no express warranties except vague puffs — "This product is outstanding!" — and carefully disclaim all implied warranties, mentioning "merchantability" conspicuously. Is this a good idea either from a business or legal standpoint? Be prepared to discuss this in class.

PROBLEM 36

Joe College bought a new car from Flash Motors, relying on the seller's extravagant claims about the car's superior qualities. He signed a purchase order on August 1, and the car was delivered two weeks later. In the glove compartment he found the warranty booklet and on reading it was dismayed to learn that the actual written warranty was very limited in coverage. Is he bound by the written warranty's terms? What argument can he make? See Comment 7 to §2-313; §2-209; White & Summers §13-5, at 582-583.

Bowdoin v. Showell Growers, Inc.

United States Court of Appeals, Eleventh Circuit, 1987, 817 F.2d 1543

WISDOM, J.

This appeal raises a single question: whether the defendants effectively disclaimed the implied warranties of fitness and merchantability with respect to a high pressure spray rig that caused injuries to the plaintiffs. The district court concluded that a disclaimer found in the instruction manual that accompanied the spray rig when it was delivered to the purchaser was conspicuous and therefore effective. We disagree. Even assuming that the disclaimer was otherwise conspicuous, it was delivered to the purchaser *after* the sale. Such a post-sale disclaimer is not effective because it did not form a part of the basis of the bargain between the parties to the sale. The decision of the district court is therefore reversed.

FACTS

At the time this controversy arose, the plaintiffs in this action, Rachel and Billy Bowdoin, raised chickens in Sampson, Alabama, for Showell Growers, Inc., a Maryland corporation. Under their contract with Showell Growers, the Bowdoins were required once a year to give a thorough cleaning to their chicken house and the chicken coop pallets. To aid them in this annual task, Showell Growers lent the Bowdoins a high pressure spray rig. In December 1980, Mrs. Bowdoin was using the spray rig to clean the pallets when an article of her clothing caught in the safety shield covering the spray rig's power take-off shaft. Mrs. Bowdoin was pulled into the shaft and suffered severe injuries.

The spray rig in question was manufactured by FMC Corporation, an Illinois corporation. The safety shield and drive shaft component was manufactured for FMC by NEAPCO, Inc., a Pennsylvania corporation. Showell purchased the spray rig from FMC through an FMC dealer, Brushy Mountain Co-op of Moravian Falls, North Carolina. Two weeks after the sale, the spray rig was shipped to Brushy Mountain and then delivered to Showell Growers. An instruction manual was included with the spray rig when it was delivered to Showell Growers. The last page of the instruction manual included a purported warranty disclaimer, which stated: *"The foregoing warranty is expressly in lieu of any and all other warranties, express, implied, statutory or otherwise (including, but without limitation, the implied warranties of merchantability and fitness for a particular purpose). . . ."*

Usually, FMC required its dealer and the purchaser to complete an "agriculture delivery report" before a sale. The report contains a disclaimer of the implied warranties of fitness and merchantability. The purchaser is required to read the report and sign it acknowledging that he has read the warranty information. The report is then returned to FMC. The record shows that no agriculture delivery report was completed in connection with the purchase by Showell Growers.

In 1982, the Bowdoins filed a diversity action against Showell Growers and FMC in the United States District Court for the Northern District of Florida. The Bowdoins later added NEAPCO as a defendant. The Bowdoins sought to recover on a number of counts including one count alleging breach by FMC and NEAPCO of the implied warranties of fitness and merchantability. FMC and NEAPCO moved for summary judgment on this count. The district court concluded that the law of Alabama applied to the warranty claims and that under Alabama law, FMC and NEAPCO had effectively disclaimed the implied warranties with the disclaimer in the instruction manual. The district court therefore granted summary judgment in favor of FMC and NEAPCO, and dismissed with prejudice the Bowdoins' implied warranties claims.

The Bowdoins now appeal that ruling. The sole issue on appeal is whether the district court correctly determined that FMC and NEAPCO had effectively disclaimed the implied warranties. The Bowdoins contend that the district court's ruling in favor of FMC and NEAPCO is erroneous for several reasons: the disclaimer was not part of the bargain and is therefore ineffective; the disclaimer is not conspicuous as required under Alabama law; the spray rig comes within the classification of "consumer goods" and therefore a manufacturer cannot disclaim implied warranties; the disclaimer is unconscionable; and finally, even if the disclaimer is effective as to FMC, it is ineffective as to NEAPCO, which manufactured the drive shaft and safety shield component. We conclude that the disclaimer is ineffective as to both FMC and NEAPCO because it did not form a part of the basis of the bargain. We therefore do not reach the Bowdoins' other arguments.

Discussion

Under the Uniform Commercial Code as adopted by Alabama and virtually every other state, a manufacturer may disclaim the implied warranties of merchantability and fitness provided that the disclaimer is in writing and conspicuous, and provided that the disclaimer is part of the parties' bargain. If a disclaimer was conspicuous to the purchaser *before the sale,* a court will generally hold the disclaimer effective based on the assumption that the disclaimer formed a part of the basis of the bargain. If, however, the disclaimer was not presented to the purchaser before the sale, the court will hold such a disclaimer ineffective because it did not form a part of the basis of the bargain. This "basis of the bargain" rule protects purchasers from unexpected and coercive disclaimers.

We turn now to determine whether the FMC disclaimer was a part of the basis of the bargain. The parties agree that for purposes of this analysis, the Bowdoins stand in the shoes of Showell Growers. The question therefore is whether the disclaimer is effective as to Showell Growers. We conclude that it is not.

Showell Growers purchased the spray rig at least two weeks before it was delivered. When the rig was delivered, an instruction manual was enclosed, and in that instruction manual is the disclaimer upon which FMC and NEAPCO rely. The disclaimer was never brought to Showell's attention.

Such a post-sale disclaimer is ineffective. "By definition, a disclaimer that appears for the first time after the sale in something supplied by the seller is not a part of the basis of the bargain and therefore is not binding on the buyer. Thus, the buyer is not bound by the disclaimer to which he had never agreed at the time of the sale and which first appears in the manufacturer's manual delivered to the buyer with the goods [or] the manufacturer's printed material brochure, or warranty booklet that accompanies the goods. . . ."[10]

The leading Alabama decision on disclaimers of implied warranties is in harmony with this position. In Tiger Motor Co. v. McMurtry, the Alabama Supreme Court addressed the validity of a disclaimer of implied warranties with respect to an automobile. The evidence showed that the day after the sale took place, the automobile was delivered to the purchaser along with the disclaimer. The evidence also showed that the disclaimer was never called to the purchaser's attention before the sale. The court concluded that the disclaimer was ineffective. Decisions of other courts construing the same provisions of the Uniform Commercial Code have also concluded that a post-sale disclaimer is not effective. [Citations omitted.]

FMC attempts to distinguish these cases on three grounds. First, FMC argues that unlike the purchasers involved in most of the cases, who were, for the most part, individual consumers, Showell Growers is a sophisticated commercial enterprise. But FMC has not offered and we have not found a post-sale disclaimer case in which such a distinction was material. Indeed, several of the cases in other states did involve commercial transactions between sophisticated commercial enterprises or businessmen, and the results reached were not affected: Courts consistently held that post-sale disclaimers were ineffective.

FMC next argues that here the post-sale disclaimer was effective because it was conspicuous. Specifically, FMC asserts that the cases which have held post-sale disclaimers ineffective involved "egregious facts involving the combination of the failure of a disclaimer to be conspicuous and its appearance subsequent to the parties' transaction."

FMC's argument is, however, wrong on both the facts and the law. Several of the cases holding post-sale disclaimers ineffective did not even mention whether the disclaimer was otherwise conspicuous. And the cases to which FMC is apparently referring typically involved not one disclaimer but two: one in the sales contract and the other in a document delivered after the sale, such as an instruction manual or a warranty. In those cases,

---

10. R. Anderson, 3 Uniform Commercial Code §2-316:32, p. 345 (footnotes omitted).

the courts held both disclaimers ineffective: the disclaimer in the sales contract because it was in small print and therefore not conspicuous, and the post-sale disclaimer because it was not a part of the basis of the bargain. In these cases, as in the cases involving only a post-sale disclaimer, the courts generally did not discuss whether the disclaimer was otherwise conspicuous. The absence of such a discussion is not surprising, because as a general rule the conspicuousness of a post-sale disclaimer is immaterial. By definition, a post-sale disclaimer is not conspicuous in the full sense of that term because the reasonable person against whom it is intended to operate could not have noticed it before the consummation of the transaction. A post-sale disclaimer is therefore not effective merely because it was otherwise conspicuous.

Finally, FMC argues that its post-sale disclaimer is effective because of prior dealings with Showell Growers that put Showell on notice that FMC's practice was to disclaim implied warranties with respect to high pressure spray rigs. Showell Growers had previously purchased an FMC spray rig similar to the one that caused Mrs. Bowdoin's injuries. The instruction manual accompanying the first spray rig contained a disclaimer of implied warranties, and according to one Showell employee, that instruction manual appeared to be identical to the one accompanying the spray rig in question. From this, FMC argues that Showell was on notice that FMC was disclaiming the implied warranties with respect to the second spray rig.

This argument misses the point. Even assuming that the mere similar appearance of two instruction manuals could put a purchaser on notice that a disclaimer in the first would also be found in the second, FMC's argument fails for the same reason its argument that a post-sale disclaimer can be effective if it was otherwise conspicuous failed. A disclaimer must be conspicuous before the sale, for only then will the law presume that the disclaimer was part of the bargain. In this case, Showell Growers did not receive the second instruction manual until after the second sale was consummated. The disclaimer in that instruction manual was therefore without significance. This is not less true merely because earlier Showell had received a similar instruction manual. Until it received the second instruction manual, it could not know what it would look like or what it would contain.

Conclusion

We conclude that the post-sale disclaimer of implied warranties found in the instruction manual that accompanied the FMC spray rig is ineffective because it did not form a part of the basis of the bargain. The decision of the district court is therefore reversed, and the district court is instructed to reinstate the Bowdoins' breach of implied warranties of fitness and merchantability claims against FMC and NEAPCO.

Rinaldi v. Iomega Corp.

Delaware Superior Court, 1999, WL 1442014

Cooch, J.

I. Introduction: Factual and Procedural History

This proposed class action was commenced in September 1998 on behalf of all persons who have purchased purportedly defective "Zip drives" from January 1, 1995, to the present. The Zip drives are manufactured by defendant Iomega Corporation, a computer storage device maker incorporated in Delaware and based in Utah. A Zip drive is a large capacity personal computer data storage drive. The complaint alleges inter alia that the alleged defect, said by Plaintiffs to be commonly known as the "Click of Death," causes irreparable damage to the removable magnetic media storage disks on which the drives store data. Plaintiffs also allege that the defect renders the data on the disks unreadable and that when another drive attempts to read the data from a disk that has been infected, the defect transfers to the second drive, causing further damage.

Plaintiffs' complaint has four counts. Count I alleges that Defendant breached the implied warranty of merchantability by manufacturing a product that was not fit for the ordinary purpose for which such products are used and that Defendant's disclaimer of the implied warranty of merchantability contained in the packaging of the product was ineffective because it was not sufficiently "conspicuous" as required by 6 Del. C. §2-316(2). Count II alleges that Defendant was negligent in manufacturing and designing the Zip drive without using the reasonable care, skill, and diligence required when placing such a product into the stream of commerce. Count III alleges that Defendant committed consumer fraud in violation of the Delaware Consumer Fraud Act by falsely misrepresenting through advertising to the consuming public that the Zip drives were suitable for their intended purpose. Count IV alleges that Defendant was negligent in failing to warn the consuming public about the risks of its product when it knew or should have known that the product could cause damage when used for its intended purpose. . . .

Defendant's Motion to Dismiss Count I on the grounds that Plaintiffs have failed to state a claim for breach of the implied warranty of merchantability is GRANTED since the Court finds that the disclaimer is "conspicuous." . . .

Defendant contends that Plaintiffs' claim for breach of the implied warranty of merchantability has failed to state a claim because Defendant's disclaimer of the implied warranty of merchantability, contained within the packaging of the Zip drive, effectively disclaimed all liability. The sole issue to be resolved here is whether Count I of the complaint should be dismissed because Defendant's disclaimer of the implied warranty of merchantability was not "conspicuous," as required by 6 Del. C. §2-316, because the disclaimer was contained within the packaging of the Zip drive product itself and therefore not "discovered" by the purchaser prior to the purchaser's purchase of the product.

Defendant's disclaimer inside the Zip drive package provides:

> EXCEPT AS STATED ABOVE IN THIS PARAGRAPH, THE FOREGOING WARRANTIES ARE IN LIEU OF ALL OTHER CONDITIONS OR WARRANTIES, EXPRESS, IMPLIED, OR STATUTORY, INCLUDING, WITHOUT LIMITATION, ANY IMPLIED CONDITION OR WARRANTY OF MERCHANTABILITY OR FITNESS FOR A PARTICULAR PURPOSE AND OF ANY OTHER WARRANTY OBLIGATION ON THE PART OF IOMEGA (capitals in original).

The above disclaimer appears near the bottom of a document labeled "IOMEGA LIMITED WARRANTY" located inside the packaging.

6 Del. C. §2-316(2) provides, in pertinent part, ". . . to exclude or modify the implied warranty of merchantability or any part of it the language must mention merchantability and in the case of a writing must be conspicuous. . . ." 6 Del. C. §2-316(2) is identical to §2-316(2) of the Uniform Commercial Code.

The usual arguments concerning the conspicuousness requirement of U.C.C. §2-316(2) have been based on issues such as the size of the type set and the location of the disclaimer in the warranty itself. Defendant contends that the conspicuousness requirement has been met regardless of the location of the disclaimer inside the Zip drive package so long as the disclaimer is "noticeable and easily readable." Defendant asserts that "modern commercial realities of how contracts are formed with consumers of prepackaged products necessitates that the terms of [its] warranty disclaimer be given effect."

Plaintiffs do not claim that the disclaimer was improperly worded, that the text of the disclaimer was improperly placed in the rest of the warranty or that the typeface of the disclaimer was too small, but instead argue that the disclaimer, located in the packaging of the product, could not realistically be called to the attention of the consumer until after the sale had been consummated, thus rendering the disclaimer not "conspicuous" as a matter or law and therefore ineffective. Although similar issues of additional terms to a contract such as a shrinkwrap license,[11] an arbitration clause[12]

---

11. ProCd, Inc. v. Zeidenberg, 7th Cir., 86 F.3d 1447 (1996).
12. Hill v. Gateway 2000, Inc., 7th Cir., 105 F.3d 1147 (1997), *cert. denied*, 118 S. Ct. 47 (1997).

and a license agreement,[13] each physically located within the packaging of the product, has been litigated in other jurisdictions, the parties have cited no case directly addressing the effectiveness, under U.C.C. §2-316(2), of a disclaimer of the implied warranty of merchantability by virtue of its location within the packaging of a product itself, nor has the Court found any such case.

The issue of conspicuousness, generally, under §2-316 has been the topic of various law review articles, periodicals and texts,[14] and has been the subject of much litigation. As stated, however, no authorities have been located that squarely addressed the issue in this case. The traditional focus has been on the "mention"[15] of merchantability and the visible characteristics of the disclaimer, such as type set and location within the warranty document itself. In determining if a disclaimer of the implied warranty of merchantability is effective as being "conspicuous," the secondary authorities and courts have often looked to the purpose of §2-316.[16] The purpose of that section is to "protect a buyer from unexpected and unbargained for language of disclaimer."[17] That purpose is the real backbone in determining if a disclaimer is conspicuous when looking at factors beyond the mentioning of merchantability and type set.

Analogous support for this Court's conclusion that the physical location of the disclaimer of the implied warranty of merchantability inside the Zip drive packaging does not make the disclaimer inconspicuous can be found in some cases from other jurisdictions. In ProCD, Inc. v. Zeidenberg,[18] the Seventh Circuit held that a shrinkwrap license located inside the packaging of the computer program was enforceable as an additional term of the contract, and stated that the commercial practicalities of modern retail purchasing dictate where terms such as a shrinkwrap license should be located. The *ProCD* court held that it would be otherwise impractical for these additional terms to be located on the outside of the box in "microscopic" type. The *ProCD* court stated, "[t]ransactions in which the exchange of money precedes the communication of detailed

---

13. M.A. Mortenson Co. v. Timberline Software Corp., Wash. App., 970 P.2d 803 (1999).

14. See, e.g., Bernard F. Kistler, Jr., U.C.C. Article Two Warranty Disclaimers and the "Conspicuousness" Requirement of Section 2-316, 43 Mercer L. Rev. 943, 945-953 (1992); Jeffrey C. Selman and Christopher S. Chen, Steering the Titanic Clear of the Iceberg: Saving the Sale of Software from the Perils of Warranties, 31 U.S.F. L. Rev. 531, 533-536 (1997); William H. Danne, Jr., Construction and Effect of UCC §2-316(2) Providing That Implied Warranty Disclaimer Must Be "Conspicuous," 73 A.L.R.3d 248, Vol. 73 (1976).

15. 6 Del. C. §2-316(2).

16. Ronald A. Anderson, Anderson on the Uniform Commercial Code, §2-316:144-153 (3d ed. 1983); Debra L. Goetz, Special Project: Article Two Warranties in Commercial Transactions, An Update, 72 Cornell L. Rev. 1159, 1264-1275 (1978).

17. U.C.C. §2-316 cmt. 1 (1962).

18. 7th Cir., 86 F.3d at 1447.

terms are common." The *ProCD* court then looked to other sections of the U.C.C. that dealt with the issue in terms of acceptance and rejection of goods: "A buyer accepts goods under §2-606(1)(b) when, after an opportunity to inspect, [the buyer] fails to make an effective rejection under §2-602(1). [The seller] extended an opportunity to reject if a buyer should find the license unsatisfactory." The *ProCD* court continued its analysis and observed that

> [c]onsumer goods work the same way. Someone who wants to buy a radio set visits a store, pays and walks out with a box. Inside the box is a leaflet containing some terms, the most important of which usually is the warranty, read for the first time in the comfort of home. By [the buyer's] lights, the warranty in the box is irrelevant; every consumer gets the standard warranty implied by the UCC in the event the contract is silent; yet so far as we are aware no state disregards warranties furnished with consumer products.[19]

Plaintiffs argue that *ProCD* is inapposite because it specifically concerned the validity of a shrinkwrap license which is not governed by U.C.C. §2-316(2). Although that is correct, *ProCD* stressed that "the U.C.C. . . . permits parties to structure their relations so that the buyer has a chance to make a final decision after a detailed review" of the contract terms.[20] All of the additional terms, which included the shrinkwrap license, became part of the contract in *ProCD*.

In Hill v. Gateway 2000, Inc.,[21] the Seventh Circuit relied on *ProCD* in holding that an arbitration clause located inside the packaging of a computer was enforceable as an additional term to the contract, and stated, "[p]ractical considerations support allowing vendors to enclose the full legal terms with their products. . . . [C]ustomers as a group are better off when vendors skip costly and ineffectual steps such as telephonic recitation, and use instead a simple approve-or-return device."[22] In holding that the arbitration clause was effective, the Hill court concluded that an additional term physically located outside of the contract was nevertheless an enforceable term of the contract.

In M.A. Mortenson Co. v. Timberline Software Corp.,[23] the Washington Court of Appeals relied on *ProCD* and *Hill* and held that a licensing agreement located inside the packaging of a software program was enforceable as an additional term to the contract. In *Mortenson* the court stated, " . . . the terms of the present license agreement are part of the contract as formed

19. Id. at 152.
20. Id. at 1453.
21. 7th Cir., 105 F.3d at 1147.
22. Id. at 1149.
23. 970 P.2d at 803.

between parties. We find that [the purchaser's] installation and use of the software manifested its assent to the terms of the license. . . ."[24] As in *ProCD* and *Hill,* the *Mortenson* court held that a licensing agreement located within the packaging of the product, not in the contract itself, was an enforceable additional term of the contract.

Other courts have also addressed the issue of the physical location of the disclaimer of the implied warranty of merchantability from different perspectives. Thus in Step-Saver Data Systems, Inc. v. Wyse Technology,[25] the United States District Court for the Eastern District of Pennsylvania discussed the location of a disclaimer of the implied warranty of merchantability inside computer software packaging and held the location of an additional term (in *Step-Saver,* a disclaimer) is to be considered independently of conspicuousness. The *Step-Saver* court held that "[t]here is no question that pursuant to the U.C.C., limitation of warranty and remedies are valid when packaged with the product so long as the limitation is clear, conspicuous and one that a reasonable person would have noticed and understood."[26] The holding in *Step-Saver* that conspicuousness and location are to be considered independently is not directly on point with the issue at bar. However, the *Step-Saver* court relied on the purpose behind §2-316 in finding that so long as a disclaimer of the implied warranty of merchantability is one that could be noticed and understood, the disclaimer is conspicuous.

This Court has addressed the issue of conspicuousness under §2-316(2) in Lecates v. Hertrick Pontiac Buick Co.[27] In *Lecates,* a case on which Plaintiffs rely, the issue was whether the implied warranties were effectively disclaimed by an automobile dealer when the car that was sold malfunctioned, causing physical injuries. The court held that the seller's disclaimer of the implied warranty of merchantability located in a sales invoice satisfied the conspicuous requirement of §2-316(2). In *Lecates,* the specific question was whether or not the disclaimer had been delivered by the seller to the buyer only after the sale had already been consummated. The *Lecates* court addressed this narrow issue in light of the specific facts in that case and observed that disclaimer clauses have been held ineffective "if it appeared that the documents in which such clauses appeared were given to the buyer after the sale had been consummated."[28] *Lecates* addressed the issue of what terms and conditions were a part of the contract at the point of contract consummation, but here, Defendant's disclaimer of the implied warranty

---

24. Id. at 831.
25. E.D. Pa., C.A. No. 89-7203, 1990 WL 87334, Broderick, J. (June 21, 1990).
26. Id. at *7.
27. Del. Super., 515 A.2d 163 (1986).
28. Id. at 170.

of merchantability was an additional term of each contract between each plaintiff and Defendant to purchase the Zip drives. Defendant's sales of the Zip drives to the six plaintiffs were each not "consummated" until after each plaintiff had had an opportunity to inspect and then to reject or to accept the product with the additional terms that were enclosed within the packaging of the Zip drive.

The commercial practicalities of modern retail purchasing make it eminently reasonable for a seller of a product such as a Zip drive to place a disclaimer of the implied warranty of merchantability within the plastic packaging. The buyer can read the disclaimer after payment for the Zip drive and then later have the opportunity to reject the contract terms (i.e., the disclaimer) if the buyer so chooses. This Court concludes that Defendant's disclaimer of the implied warranty of merchantability was effective despite its physical placement inside the packaging of the Zip drive and has satisfied the conspicuousness requirement of 6 Del. C. §2-316(2).

Defendant's Motion to Dismiss Count I on the grounds that Plaintiffs have failed to state a claim for breach of the implied warranty of merchantability is granted. . . .

QUESTION

Do these last two cases conflict? If so, which is right and which wrong? The second case, of course, is part of the "rolling contracts" theory of offer and acceptance advanced in cases such as the Seventh Circuit's famous *ProCD* opinion, discussed both in this case and in another case earlier in this book at page 115-117.

We will return to the issue of whether the buyer can return a defective item directly to the manufacturer later in the book. Note that even if a seller disclaimed all express and implied warranties, there might still be liability in some states for breach of the obligation of good faith, such as where the goods sold were virtually unusable. See Accessdata Corporation v. Alste Technologies Gmbh, 2009 WL 2338172 (D. Utah 2009).

3. Limitations on the Warranty

Sometimes a seller is willing to give a warranty to the buyer, but wants in some way to limit the scope of the liability that a breach creates. The Code permits such a limitation, but puts various restrictions on its use. Read §§2-316(4) and 2-719.

Wilson Trading Corp. v. David Ferguson, Ltd.

Court of Appeals of New York, 1968, 23 N.Y.2d 398, 244 N.E.2d 685, 297 N.Y.S.2d 108

JASEN, J.

The plaintiff, the Wilson Trading Corporation, entered into a contract of sale with the defendant, David Ferguson, Ltd., for the sale of a specified quantity of yarn. After the yarn was delivered, cut and knitted into sweaters, the finished product was washed. It was during this washing that it was discovered that the color of the yarn had "shaded" — that is, "there was a variation of color from piece to piece and within the pieces." This defect, the defendant claims, rendered the sweaters "unmarketable."

This action for the contract price of the yarn was commenced after the defendant refused payment. As a defense to the action and as a counterclaim for damages, the defendant alleges that "[p]laintiff has failed to perform all of the conditions of the contract on its part required to be performed, and has delivered . . . defective and unworkmanlike goods."

The sales contract provides in pertinent part:

> 2. No claims relating to excessive moisture content, short weight, count variations, twist, quality or shade shall be allowed *if made after weaving, knitting, or processing*, or more than 10 days after receipt of shipment. . . . The buyer shall within 10 days of the receipt of the merchandise by himself or agent examine the merchandise for any and all defects. [Emphasis supplied.]

> 4. This instrument constitutes the entire agreement between the parties, superseding all previous communications, oral or written, and no changes, amendments or additions hereto will be recognized unless in writing signed by both seller and buyer or buyer's agent. It is expressly agreed that no representations or warranties, express or implied, have been or are made by the seller except as stated herein, and the seller makes no warranty, express or implied, as to the fitness for buyer's purposes of yarn purchased hereunder, seller's obligations, except as expressly stated herein, being limited to the *delivery of good merchantable yarn of the description stated herein*. [Emphasis supplied.]

Special Term granted plaintiff summary judgment for the contract price of the yarn sold on the ground that "notice of the alleged breach of warranty for defect in shading was not given within the time expressly limited and is not now available by way of defense or counterclaim." The Appellate Division affirmed, without opinion.

The defendant on this appeal urges that the time limitation provision on claims in the contract was unreasonable since the defect in the color of the yarn was latent and could not be discovered until after the yarn was processed and the finished product washed.

Defendant's affidavits allege that its sweaters were rendered unsaleable because of latent defects in the yarn which caused "variation in color from piece to piece and within the pieces." This allegation is sufficient to create a question of fact concerning the merchantability of the yarn (Uniform Commercial Code, §2-314, subd. [2]). Indeed, the plaintiff does not seriously dispute the fact that its yarn was unmerchantable, but instead, like Special Term, relies upon the failure of defendant to give notice of the breach of warranty within the time limits prescribed by paragraph two of the contract.

Subdivision (3) (par. [a]) of section 2-607 of the Uniform Commercial Code expressly provides that a buyer who accepts goods has a reasonable time after he discovers or should have discovered a breach to notify the seller of such breach. (Cf. 5 Williston, Contracts [3d ed.] §173.) Defendant's affidavits allege that a claim was made immediately upon discovery of the breach of warranty after the yarn was knitted and washed, and that this was the earliest possible moment that the defects could reasonably be discovered in the normal manufacturing process. Defendant's affidavits are, therefore, sufficient to create a question of fact concerning whether notice of the latent defects alleged was given within a reasonable time. (Cf. Ann., 17 A.L.R.3d 1010, 1112-1115 [1968]).

However, the Uniform Commercial Code allows the parties, within limits established by the code, to modify or exclude warranties and to limit remedies for breach of warranty. The courts below have found that the sales contract bars all claims not made before knitting and processing. Concededly, defendant discovered and gave notice of the alleged breach of warranty after knitting and washing.

We are, therefore, confronted with the effect to be given the time limitation provision in paragraph two of the contract. Analytically, paragraph two presents separate and distinct issues concerning its effect as a valid limitation on remedies for breach of warranty (Uniform Commercial Code, §§2-316, subd. [4]; 2-719) and its effect as a modification of the express warranty of merchantability (Uniform Commercial Code, §2-316, subd. [1]) established by paragraph four of the contract.

Parties to a contract are given broad latitude within which to fashion their own remedies for breach of contract (Uniform Commercial Code, §2-316, subd. [4]; §§2-718; 2-719). Nevertheless, it is clear from the official section 2-719 of the Uniform Commercial Code that it is the very essence of a sale contract that at least minimum adequate remedies be available for its breach. "If the parties intend to conclude a contract for sale within this Article they must accept the legal consequence that there be at least a fair quantum of remedy for breach of the obligations or duties outlined in the contract. Thus any clause purporting to modify or limit the remedial provisions of this Article in an *unconscionable manner* is subject to deletion and in that event the remedies made available by this Article are applicable as if the stricken clause had never existed." (Uniform Commercial Code, §2-719, official comment 1; emphasis supplied.)

It follows that contractual limitations upon remedies are generally to be enforced unless unconscionable. This analysis is buttressed by the fact that the official comments to section 2-302 of the Uniform Commercial Code, the code provision pertaining to unconscionable contracts or clauses, cites Kansas City Wholesale Grocery Co. v. Weber Packing Corp. (93 Utah 414 [1937]), a case invalidating a time limitation provision as applied to latent defects, as illustrating the underlying basis for section 2-302. . . .

However, it is unnecessary to decide the issue of whether the time limitation is unconscionable on this appeal for section 2-719, subd. (2) of the Uniform Commercial Code provides that the general remedy provisions of the code apply when "circumstances cause an exclusive or limited remedy to fail of its essential purpose." As explained by the official comments to this section: "where an apparently fair and reasonable clause because of circumstances fails in its purpose or operates to deprive either party of the substantial value of the bargain, it must give way to the general remedy provisions of this Article." (Uniform Commercial Code, §2-719, official comment 1.) Here, paragraph 2 of the contract bars all claims for shade and other specified defects made after knitting and processing. Its effect is to eliminate any remedy for shade defects not reasonably discoverable within the time limitation period. It is true that parties may set by agreement any time not manifestly unreasonable whenever the code "requires any action to be taken within a reasonable time" (Uniform Commercial Code, §1-204, subd. [1][29]), but here the time provision eliminates all remedy for defects not discoverable before knitting and processing and section 2-719, subd. (2) of the Uniform Commercial Code therefore applies.

Defendant's affidavits allege that sweaters manufactured from the yarn were rendered unmarketable because of latent shading defects not reasonably discoverable before knitting and processing of the yarn into sweaters. If these factual allegations are established at trial, the limited remedy established by paragraph two has failed its "essential purpose" and the buyer is, in effect, without remedy. The time limitation clause of the contract must give way to the general code rule that a buyer has a reasonable time to notify the seller of breach of contract after he discovers or should have discovered the defect. (Uniform Commercial Code, §2-207, subd. [3], par. [a].) As indicated above, defendant's affidavits are sufficient to create a question of fact concerning whether notice was given within a reasonable time after the shading defect should have been discovered.

It can be argued that paragraph two of the contract, insofar as it bars all claims for enumerated defects not reasonably discoverable within

---

29. Now §1-302(b) — Ed.

the time period established, purports to exclude these defects from the coverage of the express warranty of merchantability. By this analysis, the contract not only limits its remedies for its breach, but also purports to modify the warranty of merchantability. An attempt to both warrant and refuse to warrant goods creates an ambiguity which can only be resolved by making one term yield to the other (cf. Hawkland, Limitation of Warranty under the Uniform Commercial Code, 11 How. L.J. 28 [1965]). Section 2-316 (subd. [1]) of the Uniform Commercial Code provides that warranty language prevails over the disclaimer if the two cannot be reasonably reconciled.

Here, the contract expressly creates an unlimited express warranty of merchantability while in a separate clause purports to indirectly modify the warranty without expressly mentioning the word merchantability. Under these circumstances, the language creating the unlimited express warranty must prevail over the time limitation insofar as the latter modifies the warranty. It follows that the express warranty of merchantability includes latent shading defects and defendant may claim for such defects not reasonably discoverable within the time limits established by the contract if plaintiff was notified of these defects within a reasonable time after they should have been discovered. . . .

In sum, there are factual issues for trial concerning whether the shading defects alleged were discoverable before knitting and processing, and if not, whether notice of the defects was given within a reasonable time after the defects were or should have been discovered. If the shading defects were not reasonably discoverable before knitting and processing and notice was given within a reasonable time after the defects were or should have been discovered, a further factual issue of whether the sweaters were rendered unsaleable because of the defect is presented for trial.

The order of the Appellate Division should be reversed, with costs, and plaintiff's motion for summary judgment should be denied.

Chief Judge FULD (concurring). I agree that there should be a reversal but on the sole ground that a substantial question of fact has been raised as to whether the clause limiting the time in which to make a claim is "manifestly unreasonable" (Uniform Commercial Code, §1-204[30]) as applied to the type of defect here complained of. In this view, it is not necessary to consider the relevancy, if any, of other provisions of the Uniform Commercial Code (e.g., §§2-302, 2-316, 2-719), dealing with "unconscionable" contracts or clauses, exclusion of implied warranties or limitations on damages.

---

30. Now §1-302(b). — Ed.

PROBLEM 37

On November 1, Jack Frost of Portland, Maine, bought a snowmobile from King Cold Recreationland. Jack used the snowmobile to get to work during the week in the winter and for fun on the weekends. The contract that he signed stated that the seller warranted that the vehicle was merchantable, but that, in the event of breach, "the buyer's remedy was limited solely to repair or replacement of defective parts." Moreover, the contract conspicuously stated that the seller was not responsible for "any consequential damages."

One week after he received the snowmobile, Jack noticed a strange rumble in the engine. He took the machine back to the King Cold service department. The machine was returned to him in three days allegedly repaired. These events repeated themselves three times over the next three weeks. Four weeks after he bought the snowmobile, Frost was seriously injured when it blew up while he was riding it. The machine, which cost $1,200, was destroyed. Frost temporarily lost the use of his left arm, incurred hospital expenses of $2,500, and lost pay of $1,600. Moreover, when he did return to work, he had to rent a snowmobile for $40 a week until spring (16 weeks — spring is very late in Maine). In addition, a $350 camera he was carrying was also destroyed. Frost brought suit against King Cold. King Cold defended on the ground that its liability was limited to the cost of repair or replacement. Frost argued that the remedy limitation was "unconscionable" and failed of its "essential purpose." All the parties pointed to §§2-316(4), 2-302, 2-719, and 2-715. How should this suit come out? See Beal v. General Motors Corp., 354 F. Supp. 423 (D. Del. 1973); Earl M. Jorgensen Co. v. Mark Constr., Inc., 56 Haw. 466, 540 P.2d 978 (1975).

The New Jersey Supreme Court has produced two leading opinions on the validity of a disclaimer of liability for consequential damages in automobile tire blowout cases. In Collins v. Uniroyal, Inc., 64 N.J. 260, 315 A.2d 16 (1974), a consumer was killed in an automobile accident when his right rear tire failed. The tire manufacturer tried to avoid §2-719(3) by saying that its disclaimer of liability for personal injury damages overcame the prima facie presumption of unconscionability because its warranty made a conspicuous statement limiting the remedy for blowout to repair or replacement. The court held that this argument was not "consonant with the commercial and human realities," and added:

> A tire manufacturer warrants against blowouts in order to increase tire sales. Public advertising by defendant relative to these tires stated: "If it only saves your life once, it's a bargain." The seller should be held to realize that the purchaser of a tire buying it because so warranted is far more likely to have made the purchase decision in order to protect himself and the passengers in his car from death or personal injury in a blowout accident than to assure himself of a

refund of the price of the tire in such an event. That being the natural reliance and the reasonable expectation of the purchaser flowing from the warranty, it appears to us patently unconscionable for the manufacturer to be permitted to limit his damages for a breach of warranty proximately resulting in the purchaser's death to a price refund or replacement of the tire.

In a later case, no personal injury occurred, but the car was destroyed when the tire blew. The tire manufacturer argued that since §2-719(3)'s "prima facie unconscionable" language applies only to "injury to the person," the consumer was limited in her recovery to a replacement of the defective tire. The New Jersey Supreme Court, however, still applied §2-719(3) because it found the warranty limitation to be "seriously lacking in clarity." The court stated:

> [T]he booklet presents the owner with a linguistic maze. Throughout the document there is an admixture of terms relating to quality, capacity, and performance, together with disclaimers and exclusions of coverage, as well as limitations and restrictions upon liability and remedies. There are fulsome and repeated references to the term "guarantee," seemingly relating to quality and performance followed by the rather sudden, isolated use of the term "promise," purportedly limiting the entire contractual undertaking to tire replacement. What is thus given to a purchaser is not a simple and straight-forward document defining on the one hand that which constitutes an affirmation of quality or performance and, on the other, the liability which flows from a breach thereof. Rather what is presented is a melange of overlapping, variant, misleading, and contradictory provisions.

Gladden v. Cadillac Motor Car Div., 83 N.J. 320, 333, 416 A.2d 394, 401 (1980). For a similar result in a commercial setting, see Andover Air Ltd. Partnership v. Piper Aircraft Corp., 7 U.C.C. Rep. Serv. 2d 1494 (D. Mass. 1989) (remedy limitation to repair or replacement held unconscionable where defective and inexpensive bracket caused $100,000 in damages in an airplane crash). Not all courts are this sympathetic to buyers. In NEC Technologies, Inc. v. Nelson, 267 Ga. 390, 478 S.E.2d 769 (1996), the Georgia Supreme Court held that a disclaimer of liability for consequential damages was not unconscionable where a TV malfunctioned, and the resulting fire caused extensive damage to the consumer's home but no personal injuries.

PROBLEM 38

Since you are in charge of drafting the warranty provisions for your manufacturing client's sales contracts, you have decided to make some express warranties and disclaim all implied ones. For the express warranties you are thinking about limiting the buyer's remedies to just repair and replacement so that (as in the Georgia case just cited) your client at most will have to return the purchase price but never pay consequential damages, which could be huge, particularly if there is personal injury involved. Is this a good idea? Are there moral questions here? Who should bear these types of damages? See Hennings v. Camping Time RV Centers, LLC, 2017 WL 4552896 (N.D. Ga. 2017).

One other point: although §2-719 does not say so, most courts have required that any remedy limitation be *conspicuous* in order to be effective. See, e.g., Stauffer Chem. Co. v. Curry, 778 P.2d 1083 (Wyo. 1989) (any other result "absurd"); but see Apex Supply Co. v. Benbow Indus., 189 Ga. App. 598, 376 S.E.2d 694 (1988) (conspicuousness not required because a limitation of remedy is not as serious a matter as a disclaimer of warranty).

Pierce v. Catalina Yachts, Inc.

Supreme Court of Alaska, 1999, 2 P.3d 618

BRYNER, Justice.

I. INTRODUCTION

After finding that Catalina Yachts, a sailboat manufacturer, breached its limited warranty to repair a defect in a boat that it sold to Jim and Karen Pierce, a jury awarded the Pierces monetary damages for the reasonable cost of repair. Before submitting the case to the jury, the trial court dismissed the Pierces' claim for consequential damages, finding it barred by an express provision in the warranty. On appeal, the Pierces contend that they were entitled to consequential damages despite this provision. We agree, holding that because Catalina acted in bad faith when it breached the warranty, the company cannot conscionably enforce the warranty's provision barring consequential damages. Accordingly, we remand for a trial to determine consequential damages.

II. FACTS AND PROCEEDINGS

In June 1992 Jim and Karen Pierce purchased a forty-two-foot sailboat newly built by Catalina Yachts. Catalina gave the Pierces a limited warranty, promising to repair or pay for repair of any below-waterline blisters that might appear in the gel coat — a smooth outer layer of resin on the boat's hull.[31] The warranty expressly disclaimed Catalina's responsibility for consequential damages.

---

31. This limited warranty provided, in relevant part: "Catalina will repair or, at its option, pay for 100% of the labor and material costs necessary to repair any below-the-waterline gel coat blisters that occur within the first year after the boat is placed in the water."

In June 1994 the Pierces hauled the boat out of the water to perform maintenance and discovered gel-coat blisters on its hull and rudder. They promptly notified Catalina of the problem and submitted a repair estimate of $10,645, which included the cost of removing and replacing the gel coat below the waterline. Catalina refused to accept this estimate, insisting that the hull only needed minor patching. Six months later, after their repeated efforts failed to convince Catalina that the gel coat needed to be replaced, the Pierces sued the company, claiming tort and contract damages. They later amended their complaint to allege a separate claim for unfair trade practices. Before trial, the superior court ruled that the limited warranty's provision barring consequential damages was not unconscionable. Based on this ruling, the court later precluded the Pierces from submitting their consequential damages claim to the jury, restricting the Pierces' recovery on their claim of breach of contract to their cost of repair, as specified in the limited warranty. The jury awarded the Pierces $12,445 as the reasonable cost of repair, specifically finding that the Pierces had given Catalina timely notice of the blister problem, that Catalina breached its gel-coat warranty, that it acted in bad faith in failing to honor its warranty obligations, and that the Pierces could not have avoided any of their losses.

The Pierces appeal, contending that the trial court erred in striking their claim for consequential damages, in excluding evidence supporting their unfair trade practices claim, and in calculating the attorney's fee award. Catalina cross-appeals, also contesting the attorney's fee order.

III. DISCUSSION

A. THE PIERCES ARE ENTITLED TO CONSEQUENTIAL DAMAGES

The Pierces' consequential damages argument requires us to consider a question of first impression concerning how a warranty provision that creates a limited remedy interacts with another provision that excludes consequential damages: if the limited remedy fails, should the exclusion of consequential damages survive?

Alaska's commercial code addresses these issues in AS 45.02.719. The first paragraph of this provision, subsection .719(a), authorizes limited warranties, allowing parties entering into commercial transactions to "limit or alter the measure of damages recoverable under [chapter 7 of the U.C.C.], as by limiting the buyer's remedies to . . . repair and replacement of nonconforming goods or parts" and to agree that the limited remedy is "exclusive, in which case it is the sole remedy." But when a limited remedy fails, the second paragraph of AS 45.02.719, subsection .719(b), nullifies the warranty's limitation, restoring the buyer's right to rely on any authorized remedy: "If circumstances cause an exclusive or limited remedy to fail of its essential purpose, remedy may be had as provided in the code."

Courts construing U.C.C. subsection 719(b) agree that a limited warranty to repair "fails of its essential purpose," "when the seller is either unwilling or unable to conform the goods to the contract."[32]

The policy behind the failure of essential purpose rule is to insure that the buyer has "at least minimum adequate remedies." Typically, a limited repair/replacement remedy fails of its essential purpose where (1) the "[s]eller is unsuccessful in repairing or replacing the defective part, regardless of good or bad faith; or (2) [t]here is unreasonable delay in repairing or replacing defective components.[33]

Here, by specifically finding that the Pierces' boat experienced gel-coat blisters, that the Pierces gave Catalina timely notice of the problem, that Catalina thereafter breached its obligations under the limited gel-coat warranty, and that the Pierces could not have avoided their damages, the jury effectively determined that the gel-coat warranty had failed of its essential purpose. Under subsection .719(b), then, the Pierces seemingly can pursue any remedy available under the commercial code, including consequential damages.

But the Pierces' right to consequential damages under subsection .719(b) is not as certain as it seems. The last paragraph of AS 45.02.719, subsection .719(c), separately provides that consequential damages may be limited or excluded "unless the limitation or exclusion is unconscionable." By validating consequential damages exclusions subject only to unconscionability, subsection .719(c) casts doubt upon subsection .719(b)'s implied promise that, when a limited remedy fails, the buyer may claim consequential damages because they are a "remedy . . . provided in the code."

The commercial code does not directly resolve this tension between subsections .719(b) and .719(c).[34] When, as here, a limited repair remedy fails, and a separate provision of the warranty bars consequential damages, the code fails to say whether a court should apply subsection .719(b) by restoring the buyer's right to seek consequential damages, or whether it

---

32. Chatlos Sys., Inc. v. National Cash Register Corp., 635 F.2d 1081, 1085 (3d Cir. 1980).

33. McDermott, Inc. v. Clyde Iron, 979 F.2d 1068, 1073 (5th Cir. 1993) (internal citations omitted), *rev'd on other grounds,* McDermott, Inc. v. AmClyde, 511 U.S. 202, 114 S. Ct. 1461, 128 L. Ed. 2d 148 (1994). See also S.M. Wilson & Co. v. Smith Int'l, Inc., 587 F.2d 1363, 1375 (9th Cir. 1978); Liberty Truck Sales, Inc. v. Kimbrel, 548 So. 2d 1379, 1384 (Ala. 1989). See generally Daniel C. Hagen, Sections 2-719(2) & 2-719(3) of the Uniform Commercial Code: The Limited Warranty Package & Consequential Damages, 31 Val. U. L. Rev. 111, 115 (1996).

34. See *S.M. Wilson & Co.*, 587 F.2d at 1375 ("The failure of the limited repair warranty to achieve its essential purpose makes available . . . the remedies 'as may be had as provided in this code.' This does not mean, however, that the bar to recovery of consequential damages should be eliminated.").

should instead apply subsection .719(c) by enforcing the bar against consequential damages "unless . . . unconscionable."

Courts addressing this dilemma in other jurisdictions have come to differing conclusions. Some have found the two subsections to be dependent, ruling that when a warranty fails, subsection .719(b)'s command to restore all available remedies trumps subsection .719(c)'s approval of a specific clause that bars consequential damages, regardless of whether that clause might itself be unconscionable. [Citations omitted.] Other courts have applied a case-by-case analysis. [Citations omitted.] But the majority of jurisdictions view these subsections to be independent, ruling that when a warranty fails, a separate provision barring consequential damages will survive under subsection .719(c) as long as the bar itself is not unconscionable. [Citations omitted.]

We believe that the majority approach best serves the Uniform Commercial Code's underlying purposes "to simplify, clarify and modernize the law governing commercial transactions; to permit the continued expansion of commercial practices through custom, usage and agreement of the parties; [and] to make uniform the law among the various jurisdictions."[35] Moreover, this approach balances the purposes of subsections .719(b) and (c) by allowing parties latitude to contract around consequential damages, while protecting buyers from unconscionable results.[36] We therefore adopt the independent approach as the most sensible rule in light of precedent, reason, and policy.

Courts applying this approach recognize that contractual provisions limiting remedies and excluding consequential damages shift the risk of a limited remedy's failure from the seller to the buyer; they examine the totality of the circumstances at issue — including those surrounding the limited remedy's failure — to determine whether there is anything "in the formation of the contract or the circumstances resulting in failure of performance that makes it unconscionable to enforce the parties' allocation of risk."[37]

In determining whether an exclusion is unconscionable, courts examine the circumstances existing when the contract was signed, asking whether "there was . . . reason to conclude that the parties could not competently agree upon the allocation of risk."[38] Courts are more likely to find

---

35. U.C.C. §1-102(2) (1996).

36. See McKernan v. United Tech. Corp., 717 F. Supp. 60, 71 (D. Conn. 1989). The comments to U.C.C. §2-719 provide that, while "minimum adequate remedies must be available" to the buyer when a contract fails, "parties are left free to shape their remedies to their particular requirements and reasonable agreements limiting or modifying remedies are to be given effect." U.C.C. §2-719 cmt. 1. In discussing subsection 2-719(3), the U.C.C. comments also recognize that clauses limiting consequential damages are "merely an allocation of unknown or undeterminable risks." U.C.C. §2-719 cmt. 3.

37. *Chatlos*, 635 F.2d at 1087.

38. Id. at 1087.

unconscionability when a consumer is involved, when there is a disparity in bargaining power, and when the consequential damages clause is on a pre-printed form; conversely, they are unlikely to find unconscionability when "such a limitation is freely negotiated between sophisticated parties, which will most likely occur in a commercial setting. . . ."[39]

In addition to inquiring into the circumstances at the time of the sale, courts examine the case "[f]rom the perspective of later events," inquiring whether "it appears that the type of damage claimed . . . came within the realm of expectable losses."[40] The reason for the limited warranty's failure affects this analysis:

> Whether the preclusion of consequential damages should be effective in this case depends upon the circumstances involved. The repair remedy's failure of essential purpose, while a discrete question, is not completely irrelevant to the issue of the conscionability of enforcing the consequential damages exclusion. The latter term is "merely an allocation of unknown or undeterminable risks." Recognizing this, *the question . . . narrows to the unconscionability of the buyer retaining the risk of consequential damages upon the failure of the essential purpose of the exclusive repair remedy.*[41]

And in examining why a limited remedy failed of its essential purpose, courts consider it significant if the seller acted unreasonably or in bad faith.

In the present case, the nature of the Pierces' warranty and the circumstances surrounding Catalina's breach weigh heavily against enforcing the consequential damages bar. The contract at issue was a consumer sale, not a commercial transaction between sophisticated businesses with equivalent bargaining power. Catalina unilaterally drafted the damages bar and evidently included it in a preprinted standard limited warranty. Moreover, the jury's sizable award for the reasonable cost of repairing the boat's gel coat establishes that Catalina's breach deprived the Pierces of a substantial benefit of their bargain. Though some gel-coat blistering might have been foreseeable, a defect of this magnitude does not fit neatly "within the realm of expectable losses."

But the decisive factor in this case is the nature of Catalina's breach, which caused the limited remedy to fail of its essential purpose. The jury specifically found that Catalina acted in bad faith in failing to honor its warranty. This finding virtually establishes a "circumstance[] resulting in failure of performance that makes it unconscionable to enforce the parties'

---

39. *Schurtz,* 814 P.2d at 1114; see also Associated Press v. Southern Ark. Radio Co., 34 Ark. App. 211, 809 S.W.2d 695, 697 (1991); Construction Assocs. v. Fargo Water Equip. Co., 446 N.W.2d 237, 242 (N.D. 1989).
40. *Chatlos,* 635 F.2d at 1087.
41. Id. at 1086-87 (internal citation omitted; emphasis added).

allocation of risk." Because the jury found that Catalina consciously deprived the Pierces of their rights under the warranty, the company cannot conscionably demand to enforce its own warranty rights against the Pierces:

> This Court would be in an untenable position if it allowed the defendant to shelter itself behind one segment of the warranty when it has allegedly repudiated and ignored its very limited obligations under another segment of the same warranty, which alleged repudiation has caused the very need for relief which the defendant is attempting to avoid.[42]

Moreover, in light of Catalina's bad faith, allowing the company to enforce the consequential damages bar would conflict with the commercial code's imperative that "[e]very contract or duty in the code imposes an obligation of good faith in its performance or enforcement."[43] Finally, because it is self-evident that the Pierces did not bargain to assume the risk of a bad faith breach by Catalina, enforcing the bar against consequential damages would thwart AS 45.02.719's basic goal of implementing the parties' agreement.

For these reasons, we hold the superior court erred in ruling that it would be conscionable to enforce the warranty's bar against consequential damages and in declining to allow the Pierces to present their consequential damages claim to the jury. We further hold that this error requires us to remand the case for a trial to determine the extent of these damages. . . .

IV. CONCLUSION

For these reasons, we VACATE the judgment and REMAND for a trial to determine the amount of the Pierces' consequential damages.

NOTE

As this decision notes, there was once sharp judicial disagreement on the issue presented in this last case, but the trend in recent years is to read §2-719(2) and (3) as *independent* of one another, so that an essential failure of the remedy limitation's purpose does not automatically create a claim for disclaimed consequential damages; see Razor v. Hyundai Motor America, 222 Ill. 2d 75, 854 N.E.2d 607 (2006). Predictably, as the court notes, consumers have had an easier time recovering disclaimed consequential damages than have commercial buyers.

---

42. Jones and McKnight Corp. v. Birdsboro Corp., 320 F. Supp. 39, 43-44 (N.D. Ill. 1970).
43. See AS 47.01.203; U.C.C. §1-304.

Helena Chemical Co. v. Williamson

United States District Court, Western District of Louisiana, 2015, WL 1298435

ROBERT G. JAMES, District Judge.

This action was brought by Plaintiff Helena Chemical Co. ("Helena") against Defendant Lavelle Williamson ("Williamson") to recover amounts due for goods and services provided to Williamson under a Credit Sales and Services Agreement. Williamson filed a counterclaim asserting that Helena was negligent for selling him wet corn seed, which resulted in his decreased production, loss of higher contract price, and increased farming expenses.

Pending before the Court is Helena's Motion for Summary Judgment on Consequential Damages. . . . For the following reasons, Helena's motion is DENIED.

I. FACTS AND BACKGROUND

Williamson began farming in 2010. Prior to that time, he had worked in the oilfield industry, marked timber, and as a painter. He has a tenth-grade education.

Until 2010, Williamson had never purchased seeds or chemicals for farming purposes. During his first year of farming, he sought to purchase goods and services from Helena on credit. Helena presented him with a Credit Sales and Services Agreement ("the Agreement"), which he signed. [Doc. No. 1-2, Exh. A]. The terms were not discussed or explained to him.

Between 2010 and 2013, Williamson purchased seed, fertilizer, and chemicals from Helena under the Agreement. The Agreement was not superseded or cancelled at any time.

For the 2013 crop year, Helena provided certain goods and services to Williamson, including corn seed and soybeans and related products, for a total price of $79,188.50. After Helena's delivery, Williamson had difficulty getting the corn seed out of Helena's tender. He contacted Helena's sales representative, Paul McKinley, to complain about this issue, but proceeded with planting the corn seed.

Williamson's corn seed failed to germinate, and a sufficient stand of corn was not realized for the 2013 crop year. He avers that "it was determined" that Helena's corn seed was wet when it was delivered in Helena's tender. [Doc. No. 16, Williamson Aff., ¶4]. According to Williamson, the wet corn seed absorbed more chemicals than it would normally, resulting in a loss of "at least eighty (80) bushels of corn per acre." [Doc. No. 16, Williamson Aff., ¶3]. Helena contends, however, that Williamson's corn crop failure was a result of his own improper application of fertilizer.

Williamson made one payment to Helena, but has not made any further payments on his account, arguing that Helena is liable to him in negligence.

Helena has filed the instant motion seeking a ruling by the Court that Williamson cannot recover consequential damages based on the exclusion/limitations of remedies provision of the Agreement. Williamson opposes the motion.

The Court is now prepared to rule.

II. LAW AND ANALYSIS

* * *

B. CONSEQUENTIAL DAMAGES

In his counterclaim, Williamson seeks to recover damages from Helena based on its alleged negligence, claiming that he suffered damages in the amount of $148,964.15 for decreased corn production, $64,439.16 for loss of a higher contract price, and $13,491.50 for increased farming expenses for the 2013 crop year.

Helena moves the Court for judgment as a matter of law that Williamson cannot recover on his counterclaim, arguing that the clear and unambiguous language of the Agreement prevents him from recovering consequential damages.

Williamson opposes Helena's motion and argues that the exclusion/limitations of remedy provision in the Agreement is unenforceable under Tennessee law.

The Agreement contains the following pertinent provisions:

> THE EXCLUSIVE REMEDY FOR ANY CAUSE OF ACTION BY OR ON BEHALF OF PURCHASER UNDER THIS STATEMENT AND RELATED TRANSACTION(S) IS A CLAIM FOR DAMAGES AND IN NO EVENT SHALL DAMAGES OR ANY OTHER RECOVERY OF ANY KIND AGAINST HELENA . . . EXCEED THE PRICE OF THE SPECIFIC GOODS OR SERVICES WHICH CAUSE THE ALLEGED LOSS, DAMAGE, INJURY OR OTHER CLAIM. NEITHER HELENA . . . SHALL BE LIABLE AND ANY AND ALL CLAIMS AGAINST HELENA . . . ARE WAIVED FOR SPECIAL, DIRECT OR CONSEQUENTIAL DAMAGES, OR EXPENSES, OF ANY NATURE INCLUDING, BUT NOT LIMITED TO, LOSS OF PROFITS OR INCOME, CROP OR PROPERTY LOSS OR DAMAGE, LABOR CHARGES AND FREIGHT CHARGES, WHETHER OR NOT BASED ON HELENA'S, ITS OFFICERS', DIRECTORS', EMPLOYEES' AND/OR AFFILIATES' NEGLIGENCE, BREACH OF WARRANTY, STRICT LIABILITY IN TORT OR ANY OTHER CAUSE OF ACTION. . . .

The Agreement's choice of law clause provides that Tennessee law governs, which the parties do not dispute. Under Tennessee law, "[t]he interpretation of a contract is a matter of law." Guiliano v. Cleo, Inc., 995 S.W.2d 88, 95 (Tenn. 1999). Consequently, "[q]uestions of contract interpretation . . . are especially well-suited for resolution by summary judgment." Ross Prods. Div. Abbott Labs. v. Tennessee, No. M2006-01113-COA-R3-CV, 2007 Tenn. App. LEXIS 752, at *7 (Tenn. Ct. App. Dec. 5, 2007). "If the language [of a contract] is clear and unambiguous, the literal meaning controls the outcome of the dispute." Allstate Ins. Co. v. Watson, 195 S.W.3d 609, 611 (Tenn. 2006). . . . [The court then quoted §2-719 of the UCC.]

The comments following the statute explain:

> 1. Under this section parties are left free to shape their remedies to their particular requirements and reasonable agreements limiting or modifying remedies are to be given effect.
>
> However, it is of the very essence of a sales contract that at least minimum adequate remedies be available. If the parties intend to conclude a contract for sale within this Article they must accept the legal consequence that there be at least a fair quantum of remedy for breach of the obligations or duties outlined in the contract. Thus any clause purporting to modify or limit the remedial provisions of this Article in an unconscionable manner is subject to deletion and in that event the remedies made available by this Article are applicable as if the stricken clause had never existed. Similarly, under subsection (2), where an apparently fair and reasonable clause because of circumstances fails in its purpose or operates to deprive either party of the substantial value of the bargain, it must give way to the general remedy provisions of this Article.
>
> . . .
>
> 3. Subsection (3) recognizes the validity of clauses limiting or excluding consequential damages but makes it clear that they may not operate in an unconscionable manner. Actually such terms are merely an allocation of unknown or undeterminable risks. The seller in all cases is free to disclaim warranties in the manner provided in Section 2-316.

Tenn. Code Ann. 47-2-719 cmts. 1, 3. Thus, Tennessee permits the limitation of remedies unless circumstances causes the remedy to fail of its essential purpose. Specifically, commercial parties may limit or exclude consequential damages unless the limitation or exclusion is unconscionable.

The Court considers, first, whether the Agreement's clause excluding consequential damages is unconscionable. Whether a contract term is unconscionable is a question of law, and a presumption of permissible dealings exists between commercial parties. [Citations omitted.] "In contrast with failure of essential purpose, the determination of unconscionability focuses on the circumstances as they existed when the parties entered into the contract." Baptist Memorial Hosp. v. Argo Const. Corp., 308 S.W.3d 337, 346 (Tenn. Ct. App. 2009).

The Tennessee Court of Appeals has discussed unconscionability in the commercial context:

Is the limitation on consequential damages unconscionable? This is a question of law for the court in light of the commercial setting, purpose and effect of the provision. (Citation omitted.) Unconscionability may arise from a lack of meaningful choice on the part of one party (procedural unconscionability) or from contract terms that are unreasonably harsh (substantive unconscionability). (Citation omitted.) In Tennessee we have tended to lump the two together and speak of unconscionability resulting when the inequality of the bargain is so manifest as to shock the judgment of a person of common sense, and where the terms are so oppressive that no reasonable person would make them on one hand, and no honest and fair person would accept them on the other. (Citation omitted.) Where the parties possess equal bargaining power the courts are unlikely to find that their negotiations resulted in an unconscionable bargain, and terms that are common in the industry are generally not unconscionable. (Citation omitted.)

Trinity Industries, Inc. v. McKinnon Bridge Company, Inc., 77 S.W.3d 159 (Tenn. Ct. App. 2001).

Although there are no Tennessee cases directly on point, Williamson has cited to the Court nine cases in other state and federal jurisdictions which have addressed this issue and found that the exclusion or limitations of remedies provision was unconscionable. In many of those cases, the seller or manufacturer held such a strong bargaining position that it could impose a provision on the farmer which deprived him of "virtually all protection." Martin v. Joseph Harris Co., 767 F.2d 296, 301 (6th Cir. 1985) (internal quotation marks omitted) (quoting J. White & R. Summers, the Handbook of the Law Under the Uniform Commercial Code, §12-11, at 477 (2d ed. 1980)). In Hanson v. Funk Seeds, Int'l, 373 N.W.2d 30 (S.D. Sup. Ct. 1985), the Supreme Court of South Dakota reviewed and upheld a trial court's determination that a corn seed supplier could not enforce a remedy provision limiting the farmer/buyer to a refund of the corn seed price because the provision was unconscionable. The *Hanson* Court explained:

> Appellee Hanson, like most farmers, was not in a position to bargain for more favorable contract terms, nor was he able to test the seed before the purchase. A crop failure is inevitable if the corn seed is ineffective and to enforce the provisions here in question, which would only allow the return of the purchase price, would leave appellee without any substantial recourse for his loss. In essence, appellee would be left without a remedy for another's breach. Cf. Rozeboom v. Northwestern Bell Telephone Co., 358 N.W.2d 241, 242 (S.D. 1984). The trial court's determination that these provisions were unconscionable is therefore not in error and we uphold its decision in this regard.

Id. at 35; cf. Jones v. Asgrow Seed Co., 749 F. Supp. 836 (N.D. Ohio 1990) (limitation of liability not unconscionable where limitation was conspicuous, buyer was experienced commercial tomato seed buyer, and seed contained undiscoverable latent defect); Nunes Turfgrass v. Vaughan-Jacklin Seed Co., 200 Cal. App. 3d 1518, 246 Cal. Rptr. 823 (1988) (seller's limitation of consequential damages clause in sales confirmation for sale of commercial sod seed mix was not unconscionable where buyer and seller were large commercial entities familiar with sod seed business and had done business together for 20 years).

In this case, at the time the Agreement was entered, Williamson was a first-time farmer with a tenth-grade education and no apparent experience in the agricultural industry. He needed the goods and services Helena provided to begin his farming career. Helena then presented him with an agreement which had to be signed if he wished to purchase from Helena. Although the Agreement was not *prima facie* unconscionable under Tennessee law and commercial parties are presumed to have engaged in permissible dealings, this simply was not a commercial transaction between two parties on equal footing. See *Aquascene,* 831 F. Supp. at 604 (The state legislature "intended to allow merchants to allocate risks when making business contracts," but a provision may be invalidated "where one party is overwhelmed."). Williamson was in no position to bargain and thus signed an Agreement which left him without recourse, even if Helena's action resulted in substantial damages to him. Under these circumstances and finding the decisions of every other court to consider this issue persuasive, the Court finds that the exclusion/limitations of remedies provision is unconscionable and unenforceable. . . .

III.   CONCLUSION

For the foregoing reasons, Helena's Motion for Summary Judgment on Consequential Damages [Doc. No. 10] is DENIED. If Williamson prevails on his counterclaim, he may seek to recover consequential damages from Helena.

D.   *Defenses in Warranty Actions*

1. Notice

In all warranty actions a buyer loses all UCC rights if there is a failure to give the seller *notice* of the breach within a reasonable period of time after the breach should have been discovered. Read §2-607(3)(a) and Official Comment 4 to that section. The reason for this technical requirement is to preserve for the seller the right to inspect the goods (§2-515) and the right to *cure* (§2-508) and, of course, to facilitate an early settlement of the dispute.

PROBLEM 39

Pearl, a farmer, exhibited to Dave samples of her apples, but said that the bulk of the apples had less color and were one-fifth smaller in size than the samples. Dave said, "Bring your apples to my warehouse; such size apples are worth $3 a bushel, and I will pay you that for them." Pearl agreed to do so.

The next day Pearl delivered 150 bushels of apples to Dave's warehouse. These apples were not as good, on an average, as the samples and were one-third smaller in size than the samples were. Dave, without inspecting the apples, delivered them ten days later to his commission merchant, who the same day sold them on the market, bringing only $1.50 per bushel.

The commission merchant, immediately upon making the sale, called Dave and informed him of the price brought by the apples. Dave was disgusted and decided to wait until Pearl billed him for the apples, at which time he would give her a piece of his mind. Sixty days later Pearl billed Dave in the amount of $450 for the 150 bushels of apples. Dave refused to pay, telling Pearl that the apples had not measured up to the contract. Pearl sued Dave. Dave contended that Pearl breached an express warranty under the Uniform Commercial Code since a contract of sale by sample was involved. What result? Review §2-313.

Fitl v. Strek

Supreme Court of Nebraska, 2005, 269 Neb. 51, 690 N.W.2d 605

WRIGHT, J.

NATURE OF CASE

James G. Fitl purchased a baseball card from Mark Strek, doing business as Star Cards of San Francisco. When Fitl discovered that the baseball card had been altered and was of no value, he sued Strek for what he argued was the current fair market value of an unaltered version of the same card. Following a bench trial, judgment was entered against Strek in the amount of $17,750 plus costs. Strek appeals. . . .

FACTS

In September 1995, Fitl attended a sports card show in San Francisco, California, where Strek was an exhibitor. Fitl subsequently purchased from Strek a 1952 Mickey Mantle Topps baseball card for $17,750. According to Fitl, Strek represented that the card was in near mint condition. After

Strek delivered the card to Fitl in Omaha, Nebraska, Fitl placed it in a safe-deposit box.

In May 1997, Fitl sent the baseball card to Professional Sports Authenticators (PSA), a grading service for sports cards that is located in Newport Beach, California. PSA reported to Fitl that the baseball card was ungradable because it had been discolored and doctored.

On May 29, 1997, Fitl wrote to Strek and indicated that he planned to pursue "legal methods" to resolve the matter. Strek replied that Fitl should have initiated a return of the baseball card in a timely fashion so that Strek could have confronted his source and remedied the situation. Strek asserted that a typical grace period for the unconditional return of a card was from 7 days to 1 month.

In August 1997, Fitl sent the baseball card to ASA Accugrade, Inc. (ASA), in Longwood, Florida, for a second opinion. ASA also concluded that the baseball card had been refinished and trimmed.

On September 8, 1997, Fitl sued Strek, alleging that Strek knew the baseball card had been recolored or otherwise altered and had concealed this fact from him. Fitl claimed he had reasonably relied upon Strek's status as a reputable sports card dealer. Strek's answer generally denied Fitl's allegations.

In a trial to the court, Fitl appeared with counsel and offered evidence. Strek was represented by counsel but did not appear or offer any evidence. Fitl testified that he was in San Francisco over the Labor Day weekend of 1995, where he met Strek at a sports card show. Fitl subsequently purchased from Strek a 1952 Mickey Mantle Topps baseball card and placed it in a safe-deposit box. In 1997, Fitl retrieved the baseball card and sent it to PSA, a sports card grading service.

Steve Orand testified that he had been a sports card collector for 27 years and that he bought, sold, and traded cards. He testified that PSA originated in 1996 or 1997 and was a leader in the sports card grading industry. He stated that PSA would not grade an altered card because alteration would totally devalue the card. He opined that any touchup or trimming of a card would render the card valueless and that an altered card is worth no more than the paper on which it is printed.

Orand examined the baseball card in question the week before trial and said that the edges of the card had been trimmed and reglued. One spot on the front of the baseball card and a larger spot on the back had been repainted, which left the card with no value. He testified that the standard for sports memorabilia was a lifetime guarantee and that a reputable collector would stand behind what he sold and refund the money if an item were fake or had been altered.

The district court entered judgment for Fitl in the amount of $17,750 and costs. The court found that Fitl had notified Strek as soon as he realized the baseball card was altered and worthless and that Fitl had notified Strek of the defect within a reasonable time after its discovery. The court rejected Strek's theory that Fitl should have determined the authenticity of the baseball card immediately after it had been purchased.

ASSIGNMENT OF ERROR

Strek claims that the district court erred in determining that notification of the defective condition of the baseball card 2 years after the date of purchase was timely pursuant to Neb. U.C.C. §2-607(3)(a) (Reissue 2001).

ANALYSIS

In a bench trial of a law action, a trial court's factual findings have the effect of a jury verdict and will not be set aside on appeal unless clearly erroneous. Webb v. American Employers Group, 268 Neb. 473, 684 N.W.2d 33 (2004). The district court found that Fitl had notified Strek within a reasonable time after discovery of the breach. Therefore, our review is whether the district court's finding as to the reasonableness of the notice was clearly erroneous.

Section 2-607(3)(a) states: "Where a tender has been accepted . . . the buyer must within a reasonable time after he discovers or should have discovered any breach notify the seller of breach or be barred from any remedy[.]" "What is a reasonable time for taking any action depends on the nature, purpose and circumstances of such action." Neb. U.C.C. §1-204(2) (Reissue 2001).

The notice requirement set forth in §2-607(3)(a) serves three purposes. It provides the seller with an opportunity to correct any defect, to prepare for negotiation and litigation, and to protect itself against stale claims asserted after it is too late for the seller to investigate them. See Cheyenne Mountain Bank v. Whetstone Corp., 787 P.2d 210 (Colo. App. 1990). "Whether the notice given is satisfactory and whether it is given within a reasonable time are generally questions of fact to be measured by all the circumstances of the case." Id. at 213.

In Maybank v. Kresge Co., 302 N.C. 129, 273 S.E.2d 681 (1981), the court reviewed the policies behind the notice requirement. The most important one is to enable the seller "to make efforts to cure the breach by making adjustments or replacements in order to minimize the buyer's damages and the seller's liability." Id. at 134, 273 S.E.2d at 684. A second policy is to provide the seller "a reasonable opportunity to learn the facts so that he may adequately prepare for negotiation and defend himself in a suit." Id. A third policy, designated the "least compelling" by the court, is the same as the policy behind statutes of limitation: "to provide a seller with a terminal point in time for liability." Id. at 135, 273 S.E.2d at 684.

Fitl purchased the baseball card in 1995 and immediately placed it in a safe-deposit box. Two years later, he retrieved the baseball card, had it appraised, and learned that it was of no value. Fitl testified that he had relied on Strek's position as a dealer of sports cards and on his representations that the baseball card was authentic. In Cao v. Nguyen, 258 Neb. 1027, 607 N.W.2d 528 (2000), we stated that a party is justified in relying upon a representation made to the party as a positive statement of fact when an investigation would be required to ascertain its falsity. In order for Fitl to have determined that the baseball card had been altered, he would have been required to conduct an investigation. We find that he was not required to do so. Once Fitl learned that the baseball card had been altered, he gave notice to Strek.

As the court noted in Maybank v. Kresge Co., supra, one of the most important policies behind the notice requirement of North Carolina's equivalent to §2-607(3)(a) is to allow the seller to cure the breach by making adjustments or replacements to minimize the buyer's damages and the seller's liability. However, even if Fitl had learned immediately upon taking possession of the baseball card that it was not authentic and had notified Strek at that time, there is no evidence that Strek could have made any adjustment or taken any action that would have minimized his liability. In its altered condition, the baseball card was worthless.

Strek claimed via his correspondence to Fitl that if Strek had received notice earlier, he could have contacted the person who sold him the baseball card to determine the source of the alteration, but there is no evidence to support this allegation. In fact, Strek offered no evidence at trial. His letter is merely an assertion that is unsupported. Earlier notification would not have helped Strek prepare for negotiation or defend himself in a suit because the damage to Fitl could not be repaired. Thus, the policies behind the notice requirement, to allow the seller to correct a defect, to prepare for negotiation and litigation, and to protect against stale claims at a time beyond which an investigation can be completed, were not unfairly prejudiced by the lack of an earlier notice to Strek. Any problem Strek may have had with the party from whom he obtained the baseball card was a separate matter from his transaction with Fitl, and an investigation into the source of the altered card would not have minimized Fitl's damages.

Strek represented himself as a sports card dealer at a card show in San Francisco. After Fitl expressed interest in a specific baseball card, Strek contacted Fitl to sell him just such a card. Orand stated that a reputable dealer will stand behind what he sells and refund the money if an item is fake or has been altered. In the context of whether a rejection of goods was made in a reasonable amount of time, we have stated that "when there is no precise rule of law which governs, the question of what, under the circumstances of a particular case, is a reasonable amount of time is usually a question for the jury." See Smith v. Paoli Popcorn Co., 255 Neb. 910, 917, 587 N.W.2d 660, 664 (1999).

The district court found that it was reasonable to give Strek notice of a defect 2 years after the purchase. This finding was not clearly erroneous. Pursuant to §2-607(4), the burden is on the buyer to show a breach with respect to the goods accepted. Fitl presented evidence that the baseball card was not authentic, as he had been led to believe by Strek's representations. Strek did not refute Fitl's evidence.

CONCLUSION

The judgment of the district court is affirmed.

PROBLEM 40

Icarus Airlines ordered 40 new airplanes from the Daedalus Aircraft Company. Twenty were to be delivered on May 8 and the rest on November 10. The first shipment actually came on September 11, but Icarus did not complain. The second came on January 12 of the next year. On January 30 the president of Icarus wrote Daedalus that "[w]e are very disappointed by your late shipment, which has caused us much expense and inconvenience." Three months later Icarus sued, claiming some $24 million in damages caused by the delayed deliveries. In its answer Daedalus responded by stating that it had received no notice of the breach as to the first shipment and that the notice concerning the second shipment was defective because it did not announce Icarus's intention to claim a breach as a result of the late delivery. At trial, Icarus countered by stating that no notice is required where, as here, the breach is obvious to the seller. As to the lack of formal notice of breach in the January letter, Icarus pointed to Official Comment 4 to §2-607.

As the trial court judge, how would you rule on the notice issues? See Aqualon Co. v. MAC Equipment, Inc., 149 F.3d 262 (4th Cir. 1998); Peavey Electronics Corp. v. Baan U.S.A., Inc., 10 So. 3d 945 (Miss. App. 2009) (noting split among courts and holding that merchant did not give notice by merely giving notice of problems, because notice requirement "exists to prevent commercial bad faith, promote mitigation and cure, enable the seller to collect evidence while still fresh, and promote settlement"). What if on January 30 Icarus had filed suit against Daedalus rather than waiting three months? Would the notice requirement have been satisfied? See Armco Steel Co. v. Isaacson Structure Steel Co., 611 P.2d 507 (Alaska 1980). In *Armco*, the court held that filing suit was not sufficient notice. However, the dissenting judge said: "[F]iling suit without prior notice may be impolite but it is not deceptive or dishonest and it certainly is no hindrance to 'normal settlement through negotiation.' Often, in fact, serious settlement negotiations do not take place until a lawsuit is filed." See also In re Bridgestone/Firestone, Inc. Tires Products Liability Litigation, 155 F. Supp. 2d 1069 (S.D. Ind. 2001). Some courts have held that consumers can give adequate notice by filing suit, particularly in personal injury actions (see Buzadzhi v. Bexco Enter., Inc., 2011 WL 43086 (N.D. Wis. 2011)), but others have not relaxed the law for consumers with complaints alleging only financial losses (see In re Carrier IQ, Inc., 2015 WL 274054 (N.D. Cal. 2015)). Is notice required if the seller is already aware of the nonconformity on the delivery date? See Muir v. Nature's Bounty, Inc., 2017 WL 4310650 (N.D. Ill. 2017).

PROBLEM 41

Alonso Quijano invited his good friend Sancho to dinner and served him a pheasant for the meal. The wine specially uncorked for the meal had been bottled by La Mancha Vineyards. It proved to be laced with a poisonous chemical, but only Sancho drank enough to have a serious reaction: it put him in the hospital for eight months. When he was discharged, he hired an attorney and filed suit against La Mancha Vineyards, which defended on the lack of notice required by §2-607(3)(a). How should this come out? Read §2-318 and Official Comment 5 to §2-607. If the person who had been injured had been Alonso Quijano and if he had given notice of breach to the retail seller, Carrasco Liquors, would that preserve his rights against the manufacturer, La Mancha Vineyards? See Felice v. Invicta Watch Co. of America, 2017 WL 3336715 (S.D. Fla. 2017).

2. Burden of Proof

In a warranty suit the plaintiff has the burden of proving (1) the creation of the warranty, (2) its breach, (3) its causal connection to the plaintiff's injury ("proximate cause," your old friend from the Torts course, being the usual measure), and (4) the fact and the extent of the injury. See Martineau v. Walker, 542 P.2d 1165 (Idaho 1975). Proof can be an overwhelming obstacle in many situations.

PROBLEM 42

Richard Sharpe loved to eat the hamburgers at Wendy's and routinely dined at the same franchise three times a week, never going to a different

Wendy's in the two months before he was rushed to a hospital with trouble breathing. A small piece of a Wendy's fork was found in his lungs. He sued the local Wendy's franchise owner for breach of the warranty of merchantability. Is he going to have causation problems? See Manley v. Doe, 849 F. Supp. 2d 594 (E.D.N.C. 2012).

Flippo v. Mode O'Day Frock Shops of Hollywood
Supreme Court of Arkansas, 1970, 248 Ark. 1, 449 S.W.2d 692

HARRIS, Chief Justice.

This litigation is occasioned by a spider bite. Gladys Flippo, appellant herein, went into a ladies clothing store in Batesville, operated by Rosie Goforth, and known as Mode O'Day Frock Shops of Hollywood. Mrs. Flippo tried on two pairs of pants, of slacks, which were shown to her by Mrs. Goforth. The first pair proved to be too small, and according to appellant's evidence, when Mrs. Flippo put on the second pair, she suddenly felt a burning sensation on her thigh; she immediately removed the pants, shook them, and a spider fell to the floor which was then stepped upon. An examination of her thigh revealed a reddened area, which progressively grew worse. Mrs. Flippo was subsequently hospitalized for approximately 30 days. According to her physician, the injury was caused by the bite of a brown recluse spider.[1] Suit for damages was instituted against Mode O'Day Frock Shops and Rosie Goforth, the complaint asserting three grounds for recovery, first that a pair of slacks in a defective condition (by reason of the presence of a poisonous spider), and unreasonably dangerous was sold to appellant; second, that both appellees were guilty of several acts of negligence, and third, that there was an implied warranty that the slacks were fit for the purpose for which they were purchased, though actually not fit, because of the poisonous spider concealed therein. On trial, the court refused requested instructions offered by appellant on theories of implied warranty, and strict tort liability, and instructed the jury only on the issue of appellees' alleged negligence as the proximate cause of the injury. The jury returned a verdict for both appellees, and judgment was entered accordingly. From the judgment so entered, appellant brings this appeal, not however, appellant from the finding of no negligence; instead, the appeal is based entirely upon the court's refusal to submit the case upon implied warranty and strict tort liability theories. Accordingly, for reversal, it is first urged that "there was sufficient

---

1. In "Changing Times, the Kiplinger Magazine," issue of April, 1969, Page 45, there is an interesting article with reference to this spider, entitled "Beware the Brown Recluse." The views of several Arkansas physicians are set out, this state being one with a large infestation of this particular species of spider.

evidence to justify a finding that Mrs. Flippo was injured by goods unfit for their intended use, supplied by a merchant with respect to goods of that kind, and therefore the trial court erred in refusing to instruct upon the law of implied warranty of merchantability."

It might be said at the outset that appellant has filed a very thorough and comprehensive brief in support of the positions taken; however, we are unable to agree with the views presented under the circumstances of this case. As pointed out by appellant, there was ample evidence to support a finding that Mrs. Flippo suffered a bite by a brown recluse spider concealed on the slacks furnished her by Mrs. Goforth (it is not conceded by appellees that the bite occurred in this manner). Appellant says:

> . . . If that be true, then appellant submits that such an article of clothing is not reasonably fit for use as an article of clothing and is thus not merchantable.

It is contended that appellees were bound by the implied warranty of merchantability imposed by Ark. Stat. Ann. §85-2-314 (Add. 1961), this statute providing that, in order to be merchantable, the goods must, *inter alia*, be fit for the ordinary purposes for which such goods are used. Appellant argues that an article of clothing which conceals a venomous creature is certainly unfit for use, and therefore at the time the slacks were handed to Mrs. Flippo, the garment was unfit for the use for which it was intended, and there was accordingly a breach of the implied warranty of merchantability under either the statute or common law.

We cannot agree that the law of implied warranty of merchantability is applicable to a case of this nature. The pair of pants itself was fit for the ordinary purposes for which stretch pants are used; there was nothing wrong from a manufacturing standpoint. In fact, the evidence reflects that Mrs. Flippo bought this particular pair after being bitten, and she has worn and laundered them since the accident. There is absolutely no evidence that the goods were defective in any manner. It is, of course, readily apparent that the spider was not a part of the product, and there is no evidence that either the manufacturer or retailer had any control of the spider, or caused it to be in the pants. Mrs. Goforth said she receives the shipments once a week in pasteboard cartons sealed with tape, and that upon receiving the cartons, she immediately opens them, places the garments on plastic hangers, and hangs them out. The cartons are delivered by truck line, and the witness stated that the slacks in question had been in the store for some time in excess of 20 days.

Irrespective of whether the spider attached itself to the garment in Kansas City, or in Batesville,[2] it was not a part of the garment. The three

---

2. The evidence reflected that Mrs. Flippo had, at some previous time, been in the business of raising chickens, and owned a chicken house. She said that she had seen spiders in this chicken house, though not at the time chickens were being raised. It is suggested by appellees that she could have brought the spider into the store with her.

cases cited by appellant as authority for the common law implied warranty of merchantability, all deal with a defective product, which is not the situation in the present litigation. Perhaps our position can best be made clear by simply stating that the spider was not a part of the manufactured article, and the injury to Mrs. Flippo was caused by the spider — and not the product. We find no cause of action under either the statute or the common law.

Nor can we agree that the trial court erred in refusing to instruct the jury upon the principles of strict tort liability. In Restatement (Second), Torts §402A, which deals with products that are defective, and thus made unreasonably dangerous to the user or consumer, we find:

> (1) One who sells any product in a defective condition unreasonably dangerous to the user or consumer or to his property is subject to liability for physical harm thereby caused to the ultimate user or consumer, or to his property, if
> (a) the seller is engaged in the business of selling such a product, and
> (b) it is expected to and does reach the user or consumer without substantial change in the condition in which it is sold. . . .

It is at once obvious that the product sold in the instant case was a pair of slacks, and the slacks were not in a defective condition; nor were they unreasonably dangerous; in fact, they were not dangerous at all; still further, the slacks did not cause any physical harm to Mrs. Flippo. Without elaboration, it is at once apparent that subheadings (a) and (b) are not applicable to this litigation, for no one can really contend that the spider was a part of the product, nor can anyone do more than guess at when the spider attached itself to the slacks. . . .

Affirmed.

3. Privity

Because suits on warranties are contract actions, the buyer must establish that there was in fact and in law a contract between the two parties. This "legal connection" is called *privity*. Where a buyer has purchased the goods directly from the retailer who gave the warranty, there is obviously privity between the two parties. Suppose, however, the warranty was made by the manufacturer, who sold to a wholesaler, who sold to a retailer, who sold to the buyer. If the buyer wishes to sue the manufacturer, the issue of lack of privity arises. At common law the manufacturer could successfully maintain a defense based on lack of privity, because the manufacturer did not deal directly with the buyer. The problem of how far back up the distribution chain the buyer can go is said to be an issue of *vertical privity*.

To complicate matters, there is a second type of privity called *horizontal privity*. Horizontal privity deals with identifying to whom the retail seller is liable other than the immediate purchaser. The next Problem illustrates the difference.

PROBLEM 43

The Girard Instruments Corporation manufactured a pocket calculator called the Descartes 1000. It bought the paint used on the machine from the Hamilton Paint Company. Girard sold the calculators to the retailer, Leibnitz Department Store, which sold a calculator to Sylvester Cayley. He in turn gave it to his wife as a birthday gift. The Descartes 1000 was a popular gift. Joan Cayley used it all the time, as did the Cayley children (for homework) and even Mr. Gauss, the mailman, who borrowed it one day to compute the distance he walked on his route. After this last use, Mr. Gauss went home, where his dog, Diophantus, eagerly licked his hand and promptly dropped dead of lead poisoning. It turned out that the paint used on the Descartes 1000 had an extraordinarily high lead content. All the Cayleys and Mr. Gauss became very ill and, on recovery, brought suit for their pain and suffering, lost wages, medical expenses, and, in Mr. Gauss's case, the value of his dog. Whom should they sue?

The privity problem looks like the following diagram.

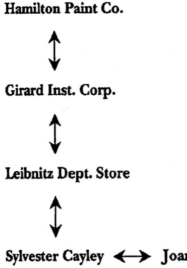

Hamilton Paint Co.

↕

Girard Inst. Corp.

↕

Leibnitz Dept. Store

↕

Sylvester Cayley ←→ **Joan Cayley** ←→ **Children** ←→ **Mr. Gauss**

The question "Can Mr. Gauss sue the Leibnitz Department Store?" is a question of horizontal privity. The question "Can Mr. Cayley sue the Hamilton Paint Company?" is a question of vertical privity. The question "Can Mr. Gauss sue the Hamilton Paint Company?" is a question involving both horizontal and vertical privity.

If the Hamilton Paint Company had made express warranties (either in ads or in writings contained in the calculator box), most courts would have had no problem finding a cause of action in contract on the warranty in favor of anyone relying thereon. And if negligence could be proved (the doctrine of *res ipsa loquitur* helps here), a tort action was possible. Another theory Mr. Cayley (the retail buyer) could have tried, where no express warranty was involved, was that he was a third-party beneficiary of the implied warranties made in the sales between Hamilton and Girard and between Girard and Leibnitz. The other potential plaintiffs might also try the third-party beneficiary argument.

However, all these theories have technical, practical, or historical problems. Even with the doctrine of *res ipsa loquitur*, negligence can be hard to prove. Contract/warranty actions are bound by centuries of "no privity—no lawsuit" decisions. And, as we have seen, warranty suits have upheld requirements like that in §2-607(3)(a), *notice* within a reasonable amount of time (a requirement the mailman is not likely to meet even if his attorney remembers it).

The original 1962 version of the UCC had §2-318, which spoke in a limited fashion to the question of how much horizontal privity was excused under the Code. That version (now called Alternative A) protected the retail buyer's family and house guests from personal injury. Official Comment 3 to §2-318 invited the courts to extend warranty protection. But this version did not help the buyer's employees or casual bystanders, nor did it protect property losses (for example, the loss of the dog by Mr. Gauss). In 1966, the UCC's Permanent Editorial Board proposed two more versions of §2-318: Alternative B, which spoke to privity in terms of a foreseeable personal injury test, and Alternative C, which protected even property damage and nonnatural persons (for example, corporations). Read these versions and the Official Comments (especially Official Comment 3).

Does §2-318 restrict the limits of *vertical* privity so as to answer the question "Can Sylvester Cayley sue the Hamilton Paint Company?" See Official Comment 3 to §2-318, second sentence, and consider the following Problem.

PROBLEM 44

When Alan Turing needed a new computer he went to Big Sale Department Store and bought the Enigma 1000, the best selling computer on the market, made by Code Manufacturing Company. The computer worked well for a few months, but then had a spectacular electrical event that turned it into a useless piece of machinery and caused a fire, burning up much of Turing's office. Turing sued both Big Sale and Code Manufacturing, but the latter filed a motion for dismissal for lack of privity since it had no direct dealings with Alan Turing. Code Manufacturing had made an express warranty that the computer would be defect free, but this was only on a paper contained in the box that the computer came in. Code Manufacturing also argued that any implied warranty of merchantability was only made to the retailer, Big Sale, with which it had direct dealings, and not to Turing, with whom it did not. The trial court bought these arguments and dismissed Code Manufacturing from the lawsuit. Is this right? Compare Hyundai Motor America, Inc. v. Goodin, 822 N.E.2d 947 (Ind. 2005) (no privity needed to sue manufacturer) with Curl v. Volkswagen of America, Inc., 114 Ohio St. 3d 266, 871 N.E.2d 1141 (2007) (manufacturer's implied warranty to retailer did not create necessary privity with buyer). Suppose you are the attorney for Big Sale. You are annoyed that your client really did nothing wrong except pass on a defective product from the manufacturer, but is nonetheless liable (due to a technicality — lack of privity — that this state stupidly adopts) to the consumer. Is there anything you can do to make Code Manufacturing interested in defending this lawsuit even if privity would otherwise protect it? See §2-607(5)(a).

Reed v. City of Chicago

United States District Court, Northern District of Illinois, 2003, 263 F. Supp. 2d 1123

MORAN, Senior District Judge.

Plaintiff Ruby Reed brought this action against defendants City of Chicago (City), police officers Timothy Gould, Bruce Young, Brian Pemberton, and Susan Madison (officers), and Edwards Medical Supply, Inc. (Edwards), Cypress Medical Products, Ltd. and Cypress Medical Products, Inc. (together, Cypress), and Medline Industries (Medline) arising from her son's death in a Chicago jail cell. Defendant Cypress filed a motion to dismiss count VI of the complaint — breach of warranty — pursuant to Federal Rule of Civil Procedure 12 (b)(6). For the following reasons, Cypress' motion is denied.

BACKGROUND

Plaintiff Ruby Reed filed this suit as the special administrator of her son J.C. Reed's estate. On November 12, 2000, J.C. Reed (Reed) was allegedly arrested and brought to the City's Fifth District Police Station, where he was placed in a detention cell controlled and managed by the officers. The officers allegedly knew that Reed was mentally unstable, had witnessed him attempting suicide by slitting his wrists, and failed to adequately monitor the cell. The officers removed his clothing and provided him with a paper isolation gown. Plaintiff claims that Reed used this gown to hang himself, and that officers found him in the cell and failed to give him proper medical care, resulting in his death.

Plaintiff further alleges that the gown was manufactured and designed by defendants Edwards, Cypress and Medline, and that these defendants breached implied and express warranties when the gown failed to tear away when used by Reed in an attempt to hang himself.

DISCUSSION

The single issue we must decide is whether plaintiff, as a non-purchaser, can recover from the manufacturer and designer of the gown for breach of warranty. Historically, Illinois law has required plaintiffs suing for breach of warranty to establish both horizontal and vertical privity.[44] [The court quotes Alternative A to §2-318, the version adopted in Illinois. — Ed.]

The Illinois Supreme Court has determined that the privity is no longer an absolute requirement for breach of warranty actions. Berry v. G.D. Searle & Co., 56 Ill. 2d 548, 309 N.E.2d 550 (Ill. 1974) (stating "privity is of no consequence when a buyer who purportedly has sustained personal injuries predicates recovery against a remote manufacturer for breach of an implied warranty under the code"); see also Suvada v. White Motor Co., 32 Ill. 2d 612, 210 N.E.2d 182 (Ill. 1965), *overruled on other grounds* (holding, prior to the enactment of the UCC in Illinois, that the privity requirement should be abolished in food and drug cases). While section 2-318 lists specific exceptions to the privity requirement, Illinois courts have noted that this list is not necessarily exhaustive. See Wheeler v. Sunbelt Tool Co., Inc., 181 Ill. App. 3d 1088, 1099, 537 N.E.2d 1332, 1340, 130 Ill. Dec. 863, 871 (1989); see also UCC §2-318, comment 3 (stating that "the section in this form is neutral and is not intended to enlarge or restrict the developing case law on whether the seller's warranties, given to his buyer who resells, extend to other persons in the distributive chain").

The vast majority of cases examining the limits of section 2-318 in Illinois have dealt with the employment context, expanding the class of potential breach of warranty plaintiffs to employees of the ultimate purchaser. [Citing

---

44. Lack of vertical privity occurs when a consumer seeks to sue a remote manufacturer who was not involved in the sale to the consumer. Lack of horizontal privity occurs when a user of the product, beside the consumer, is injured. See Thomas v. Bombardier-Rotax Motorenfabrik, 869 F. Supp. 551, 557 n.7 (N.D. Ill. 1994).

cases.] In these cases courts have allowed employees to sue for breach of warranty despite a lack of horizontal privity.

In [Whitaker v. Lian Feng Mach. Co., 156 Ill. App. 3d 316, 509 N.E.2d 591 (1987)] plaintiff was injured while using a band-saw that had been purchased by his employer. . . . The court determined that section 2-318 does not state any limitation on the rights of persons to recover for breach of warranty, nor does it differentiate between horizontal and vertical privity (id. at 593-94). It reasoned that the purpose of warranties is to determine what the seller has agreed to sell . . ., quoting UCC §2-313, comment 4. The employee was essentially a third-party beneficiary to the sale in that the employee's safety while using the bandsaw was "either explicitly or implicitly part of the basis of the bargain when the employer purchased the goods" (id. at 595). . . .

While no Illinois courts have expanded the plaintiff class for breach of warranty actions beyond employees, we believe that the law requires us to do so here. The beneficiary of any warranty made by the manufacturer and designer of the gown is necessarily a potentially suicidal detainee like Reed. If protection is not provided to plaintiffs like Reed, any warranty as to the safety of the gown would have little, if any, effect. In designing and manufacturing the gown, defendants contemplated that the users of the gown would be detainees. Moreover, the safety of these detainees was necessarily a part of the bargain, whether explicitly or implicitly, between the seller and buyer. For these reasons, a detainee of the City like Reed must be able to enforce the protections of any warranties made by the manufacturer and designer of the gown.

CONCLUSION

For the foregoing reasons, defendants' motion to dismiss count VI of the complaint is denied.

4.   A Note on Strict Products Liability

About the same time that the UCC drafters were wrestling with §2-318, another legal revolution was occurring: the development of *strict products liability*. See W. Prosser, Torts 692 (5th ed. 1984). This concept has been described by Professor William Prosser as "a freak hybrid born of the illicit intercourse of tort and contract." Prosser, The Fall of the Citadel (Strict Liability to the Consumer), 50 Minn. L. Rev. 791, 800 (1966). Basically, strict products liability permits recovery by an injured consumer in a suit against the manufacturer as long as the consumer can prove that the manufacturer distributed into commerce a product that contained a dangerous defect. There is no necessity of proving either negligence or privity.

The primary source of the doctrine is §402A of the Restatement (Second) of Torts:

§402A *Special Liability of Seller of Product for Physical Harm to User or Consumer*

(1) One who sells any product in a defective condition unreasonably dangerous to the user or consumer or to his property is subject to liability for physical harm thereby caused to the ultimate user or consumer, or to his property, if

(a) the seller is engaged in the business of selling such a product, and

(b) it is expected to and does reach the user or consumer without substantial change in the condition in which it is sold.

(2) The rule stated in Subsection (1) applies although

(a) the seller has exercised all possible care in the preparation and sale of his product, and

(b) the user or consumer has not bought the product from or entered into any contractual relation with the seller.

Strict products liability as a separate cause of action has been adopted by most (but not all) courts. Starting with Henningsen v. Bloomfield Motors, Inc., 32 N.J. 358, 161 A.2d 69 (1960), and proceeding through landmark opinions such as Greenman v. Yuba Power Prods., Inc., 59 Cal. 2d 57, 377 P.2d 897, 27 Cal. Rptr. 697 (1962); Seely v. White Motor Co., 63 Cal. 2d 9, 403 P.2d 145, 45 Cal. Rptr. 17 (1965); State ex rel. Western Seed Prod. Corp. v. Campbell, 250 Or. 262, 442 P.2d 215 (1968); and Kassab v. Central Soya, 432 Pa. 217, 246 A.2d 848 (1968), the courts have worked one by one what Prosser has called "the most rapid and altogether spectacular overturn of an established rule in the entire history of the law of torts." W. Prosser, Torts 690 (5th ed. 1984). A cause of action based on strict products liability is very similar to the UCC implied warranty of merchantability ("fitness for ordinary purpose" is only slight degrees away from freedom from "unreasonably dangerous" defects, the §402A test), and some courts have held the two doctrines are to be measured by the same rules as to privity and defenses. See, e.g., Gregory v. White Truck & Equip. Co., 163 Ind. App. 240, 323 N.E.2d 280 (1975) (held contributory negligence is not a defense in a §2-315 suit nor in a §402A suit unless it amounts to an assumption of the risk so that plaintiff proceeded to encounter a known danger); see also Annot., 4 A.L.R.3d 501, and Annot., 46 A.L.R.3d 240, on the defense of contributory negligence in warranty/products liability suits.

In 1997, the American Law Institute published a new Restatement, the Restatement (Third) of Torts: Products Liability, designed to update the law in this field. The new promulgation answers a host of questions that had been raised under old Restatement §402A, and is a lot more complicated than its predecessor. The primary change made by Restatement Third is that while it retains strict liability for manufacturing defects, it shifts to a negligence standard for design defects and injuries caused by failure to give a proper warning. See Restatement (Third) of Torts: Products Liability §2. For a summary of the new Restatement, see David G. Owen & Mary J. Davis, 1 Madden & Owen on Products Liability chs. 5-8 (2014). Courts have been split on whether to adopt the new Restatement. See, e.g., Bifolck v. Philip Morris, Inc., 324 Conn. 402, 152 A.3d 1183 (2016) (declining to adopt the Restatement Third and noting broad disagreement among jurisdictions on whether to follow the Restatement Third).

Lincoln Company v. Detroit Diesel Corporation General Insurance

Supreme Court of Tennessee, 2009, 293 S.W.3d 487

JANICE M. HOLDER, C.J.

* * *

FACTS AND PROCEDURAL HISTORY

Senators Rental, Inc. ("Senators Rental"), an insured of Lincoln General Insurance Company ("Lincoln General"), purchased a bus manufactured by Prevost Car (US) Inc. ("Prevost"). The engine in the bus was produced by Detroit Diesel Corporation ("Detroit Diesel"). On May 8, 2006, the bus was traveling south on Interstate 65 near Goodlettsville, Tennessee, when it caught fire due to an alleged engine defect. The fire did not cause personal injury or damage to any property other than the bus itself. Lincoln General paid Senators Rental $405,250 for the fire damage pursuant to its insurance policy.

Lincoln General filed a complaint against Prevost and Detroit Diesel. The complaint included counts of breach of express and implied warranties, negligence, and strict products liability. Prevost and Detroit Diesel removed the case to the United States District Court for the Middle District of Tennessee. Prevost filed a motion to dismiss for failure to state a claim pursuant to Federal Rule of Civil Procedure 12(b)(6), arguing that Lincoln General's tort claims are barred by the economic loss doctrine.

On July 1, 2008, the United States District Court certified one question of law to this Court, which we accepted pursuant to Tennessee Supreme Court Rule 23. . . .

ANALYSIS

The United States District Court certified the following question of law: Does Tennessee law recognize an exception to the economic loss doctrine under which recovery in tort is possible for damage to the defective product itself when the defect renders the product unreasonably dangerous and causes the damage by means of a sudden, calamitous event?

This certified question presupposes that Tennessee recognizes the economic loss doctrine, a judicially created principle that reflects an attempt to maintain separation between contract law and tort law by barring recovery in tort for purely economic loss. See generally, Vincent R. Johnson, The Boundary-Line Function of the Economic Loss Rule, 66 Wash. & Lee L. Rev. 523 (2009). Although this Court has never expressly adopted the economic loss doctrine, we expressed agreement with the policies underlying the doctrine in Ritter v. Custom Chemicides, Inc., 912 S.W.2d 128 (Tenn. 1995). In Ritter, this Court stated that "Tennessee has joined those jurisdictions which hold that product liability claims resulting in pure economic loss can be better resolved on theories other than negligence. . . . In Tennessee, the consumer does not have an action in tort for economic damages under strict liability." Id. at 133 (footnote omitted); see also First Nat'l Bank of Louisville v. Brooks Farms, 821 S.W.2d 925, 930-31 (Tenn. 1991) (finding that actions under the Tennessee Products Liability Act are limited to those brought on account of personal injury, death, or property damage and do not include actions brought for pecuniary loss).

The economic loss doctrine is implicated in products liability cases when a defective product damages itself without causing personal injury or damage to other property. In this context, "economic loss" is defined generally as "the diminution in the value of the product because it is inferior in quality and does not work for the general purposes for which it was manufactured and sold." Comment, Manufacturers' Liability to Remote Purchasers for "Economic Loss" Damages — Tort or Contract?, 114 U. Pa. L. Rev. 539, 541 (1966). Two types of economic loss, direct and consequential, occur when a defective product is damaged. See, e.g., Restatement (Third) of Torts: Products Liability §21, cmt. d (1998). Direct economic loss may be measured by the defective product's cost of repair or replacement. Id. Consequential economic losses, such as lost profits, result from the product owner's inability to use the product. Id.

The question certified presents us with our first opportunity to examine the proper application of the economic loss doctrine when only the defective product is damaged. In the seminal case of East River Steamship Corp. v. Transamerica Delaval, Inc., 476 U.S. 858, 868-71, 106 S. Ct. 2295, 90 L. Ed. 2d 865 (1986), the United States Supreme Court examined three approaches to the economic loss doctrine used by various state and federal courts, which it described as the "majority," "minority," and "intermediate" positions, and adopted the majority approach. In *East River*, a shipbuilder contracted with a manufacturer for the production of turbines to propel four oil-transporting super tankers. While at sea, the turbines malfunctioned due to design and manufacturing defects. Only the turbines themselves were damaged. In a unanimous decision, the Supreme Court held that the economic loss doctrine barred the shipbuilder's products liability suit in admiralty against the manufacturer.

In adopting the "majority approach" to the economic loss doctrine, the Supreme Court chose a bright-line rule that precludes recovery in tort when a product damages itself without causing personal injury or damage to other property. In reaching this conclusion, the Supreme Court observed that "[w]hen a product injures only itself the reasons for imposing a tort duty are weak and those for leaving the party to its contractual remedies are strong." Id. at 871, 106 S. Ct. 2295. Specifically, the Supreme Court reasoned that damage to a defective product is merely a failure of the product to meet the purchaser's expectations, a risk that the parties had the opportunity to allocate by negotiating contract terms and acquiring insurance. Id. at 871-72, 106 S. Ct. 2295. In contrast, the "'cost of an injury and the loss of time or health may be an overwhelming misfortune,' and one the person is not prepared to meet." Id. at 871, 106 S. Ct. 2295 (quoting Escola v. Coca Cola Bottling Co., 24 Cal. 2d 453, 150 P.2d 436, 441 (1944)). Finally, the Supreme Court expressed concern that permitting recovery in tort for purely economic loss could subject the manufacturer to an indefinite amount of damages. Id. at 874, 106 S. Ct. 2295. A warranty action, on the other hand, has a "built-in limitation on liability." Id.

In contrast, the "minority approach" to the economic loss doctrine permits tort recovery for purely economic loss. The Supreme Court explained that jurisdictions following the minority approach do not distinguish between economic loss and personal injury or property damage because in either circumstance, the damage was caused by the defendant's conduct. Id. at 869, 106 S. Ct. 2295; see *Farm Bureau Ins. Co.*, 878 S.W.2d at 743. In the minority view, the manufacturer's duty to produce non-defective products and tort law's corresponding concern with safety apply equally when the harm is purely economic. *E. River S.S. Corp.*, 476 U.S. at 868-69, 106 S. Ct. 2295; see *Thompson*, 647 P.2d at 337. Ultimately, the Supreme Court rejected the minority approach because it "fails to account for the need to keep products liability and contract law in separate spheres and to maintain a realistic limitation on damages." *E. River S.S. Corp.*, 476 U.S. at 870-71, 106 S. Ct. 2295.

Lincoln General urges us to recognize a variation of the third approach to the economic loss doctrine, the "intermediate approach." States that follow the intermediate approach permit tort recovery for damage to the defective product alone under limited exceptions that "turn on the nature of the defect, the type of risk, and the manner in which the injury arose." Id. at 870, 106 S. Ct. 2295. The exception advanced by Lincoln General would permit recovery for unreasonably dangerous products that cause damage to themselves during sudden, calamitous events. This exception would require courts to distinguish between those products that expose a product owner to an unreasonable risk of injury during an abrupt and disastrous occurrence and those products that merely disappoint a product owner's expectations. See id. at 869-70, 106 S. Ct. 2295.

The *East River* Court rejected the dichotomy between disappointed and endangered product owners as "too indeterminate to enable manufacturers easily to structure their business behavior." Id. at 870, 106 S. Ct. 2295. The Court also found unpersuasive an exception that focuses on the manner in which the harm occurred:

> We realize that the damage may be qualitative, occurring through gradual deterioration or internal breakage. Or it may be calamitous. But either way, since by definition no person or other property is damaged, the resulting loss is purely economic. Even when the harm to the product itself occurs through an abrupt, accident — like event, the resulting loss due to repair costs, decreased value, and lost profits is essentially the failure of the purchaser to receive the benefit of its bargain — traditionally the core concern of contract law.

Id. (citations omitted).

We agree with the United States Supreme Court that the owner of a defective product that creates a risk of injury and was damaged during a fire, a crash, or other similar occurrence is in the same position as the owner of a defective product that malfunctions and simply does not work. It follows that the remedies available to these similarly situated product owners should derive from the parties' agreements, not from the law of torts, lest we disrupt the parties' allocation of risk. See Prosser & Keeton on the Law of Torts §101(3), at 709 (5th ed. 1984) ("[R]isk of harm to the product itself due to the condition of the product would seem to be a type of risk that the parties to a purchase and sale contract should be allowed to allocate pursuant to the terms of the contract."). To hold otherwise would make it more difficult for parties to predict the consequences of their business transactions, the cost of which ultimately falls on consumers in the form of increased prices. See *E. River S.S. Corp.*, 476 U.S. at 872, 106 S. Ct. 2295 ("The increased cost to the public that would result from holding a manufacturer liable in tort for injury to the product itself is not justified."); Bocre Leasing Corp. v. Gen. Motors Corp. (Allison Gas Turbine Div.), 84 N.Y.2d 685, 692, 621 N.Y.S.2d 497, 645 N.E.2d 1195 (1995) ("In essence, all consumers would subsidize or 'pay premiums' for purchasers of assertedly 'unduly dangerous' products.").

It is difficult, moreover, for parties and courts to apply a rule that focuses on the degree of risk and the manner in which the product was damaged as opposed to a rule that hinges on harm the plaintiff actually sustains. Lincoln General suggests, nonetheless, that adopting the bright-line rule espoused in *East River* would come at too great a price — the decreased safety of Tennessee citizens. We believe, however, that deterrence is adequately promoted by existing law that permits tort recovery for personal injury and damage to property other than the product itself. As explained by the Illinois Supreme Court, "[b]ecause no manufacturer can predict with any certainty that the damage his unsafe product causes will be confined to the product itself, tort liability will continue to loom as a possibility." Trans States Airlines v. Pratt & Whitney Can., Inc., 177 Ill. 2d 21, 224 Ill. Dec. 484, 682 N.E.2d 45, 53 (1997).

Finally, Lincoln General argues that adopting the *East River* approach is inconsistent with the General Assembly's intentions under the Tennessee Products Liability Act of 1978, Tenn. Code Ann. §§29-28-101 to 108 (2000). We disagree. Application of the Tennessee Products Liability Act is limited to "actions brought for or on account of personal injury, death or property damage." Tenn. Code Ann. §29-28-102(6) (emphasis added). We interpret "property damage" to mean damage to property other than the defective product. See Progressive Ins. Co. v. Gen. Motors Corp., 749 N.E.2d 484, 487-89 (Ind. 2001). A product's self-destruction is naturally understood as "economic loss" because it "is indistinguishable in consequence from the product's simple failure to function." *Progressive Ins. Co.*, 749 N.E.2d at 488. This Court previously held in *Ritter* that the Tennessee Products Liability Act does not afford the right to recover purely economic losses. 912 S.W.2d at 132-33; see also *First Nat'l Bank*, 821 S.W.2d at 931 ("[T]he rights and liabilities of parties to actions based on diminished economic expectations can be better adjudicated on other legal theories."); Olin Corp. v. Lambda Elecs., Inc., 39 F. Supp. 2d 912, 914 (E.D. Tenn. 1998). In the almost fourteen years since our decision in *Ritter*, the General Assembly has not amended the Tennessee Products Liability Act to permit claims for purely economic loss.

In our view, the *East River* approach fairly balances the competing policy interests and clearly delineates between the law of contract and the law of tort. We therefore hold that Tennessee law does not recognize an exception to the economic loss doctrine under which recovery in tort is possible for damage to the defective product itself when the defect renders the product unreasonably dangerous and causes damage by means of a sudden, calamitous event.

In so holding, we join the majority of state appellate courts that have considered the adoption of an exception to the economic loss doctrine based on unreasonably dangerous products; sudden, calamitous events; or both. [Citations omitted.]

Finally, our holding is consistent with the Restatement (Third) of Torts: Products Liability (1998). Section 21 specifically excludes harm to "the defective product itself" from the definition of "harm to persons or property" for which economic loss is recoverable. Comment (d) to section 21 further explains:

> A plausible argument can be made that products that are dangerous, rather than merely ineffectual, should be governed by the rules governing products liability law. However, a majority of courts have concluded that the remedies provided under the Uniform Commercial Code — repair and replacement costs and, in appropriate circumstances, consequential economic loss — are sufficient. Thus, the rules of this Restatement do not apply in such situations.

Conclusion

In addressing the United States District Court's certified question, we are persuaded that the rationale proffered by the United States Supreme Court in *East River* is sound. We therefore hold that Tennessee does not recognize an exception to the economic loss doctrine under which recovery in tort is possible for damage to the defective product itself when the defect renders the product unreasonably dangerous and causes the damage by means of a sudden, calamitous event. The costs of this appeal are taxed to the respondent, Lincoln General Insurance Company, for which execution may issue if necessary.

Strict products liability suits are largely similar to implied warranty suits, though some courts struggle mightily to draw distinctions between the two causes of action; see Denny v. Ford Motor Co., 87 N.Y.2d 248, 662 N.E.2d 730 (N.Y. 1995). Typically, either a suit under §402A or a suit for breach of the implied warranty of merchantability can be a viable legal alternative under the same facts. There are some differences that are immediately visible:

(1) A §402A cause of action does not require notice; a UCC cause of action does. See §2-607(3)(a).

(2) In a §402A cause of action, damages are limited to those for physical injury; the damages in a UCC cause of action are not. See §2-715.

(3) A §402A cause of action has the statute of limitations imposed by state law for tort actions; the UCC action is governed by §2-725. The time periods may differ significantly.

(4) A §402A cause of action is not affected by disclaimers or remedy limitations; a UCC action may be so limited. See §§2-316, 2-719.

(5) Privity is not an issue in §402A suits; privity may be an issue in UCC suits.

(6) Section 402A requires that the product contain a "defect," but a UCC warranty may be breached even if the product is not defective. For example, a perfectly good product may neither fulfill the express warranty nor be fit for the particular purpose for which the buyer needs the goods. See Malawy v. Richards Mfg. Co., 150 Ill. App. 3d 549, 501 N.E.2d 376 (1986).

PROBLEM 45

The axle on Monty Python's new car snapped in two while he was driving at a high rate of speed on the interstate. Python's car skidded across the median and ran into a hitchhiker, Thumbs Bystander, killing him instantly. As Bystander's attorney, decide which is the best cause of action: negligence, §402A, or §2-314. Whom should you sue? See Martin v. Ryder Truck Rental, Inc., 353 A.2d 581 (Del. 1976).

E.   UCC Warranties and the Magnuson-Moss Act

In 1975, Congress passed the Magnuson-Moss Warranty Act,[45] which applies to all consumer products manufactured after July 4, 1975, that are covered by a written warranty. Magnuson-Moss was enacted in response to many years of consumer complaints about warranties — in particular about manufacturers' statements that were labeled warranties, but that upon testing in the courts took away more rights than they gave. The stated purposes of the statute are to improve the adequacy of information available to consumers, to prevent deception, and to improve competition in the marketing of consumer products.[46] For a comprehensive study, see C. Reitz, Consumer Protection Under the Magnuson-Moss Warranty Act (1978).

---

45. The full name of the statute is the Magnuson-Moss Warranty — Federal Trade Commission Improvement Act, 15 U.S.C. §§2301-2312 (1975). Title I deals with consumer product warranties. Title II deals with Federal Trade Commission powers. Only Title I will be discussed in this text.

46. Title I, 15 U.S.C. §2302(a).

To apply Magnuson-Moss, the warranty given must fall within its scope. Read Mag.-Moss §101,[47] and answer the following Problems.

PROBLEM 46

Attorney Sam Ambulance formed a professional corporation, Ambulance, LPC, under which he practices law. When the corporation buys a company car, is it entitled to the protection of the Magnuson-Moss Warranty Act? See §101(1) and (3).

PROBLEM 47

(a) When Tom Jeffire bought his car from Sharp Sam's Used Car lot, Sam said, "I refuse to warrant my cars in any way." Is there a possible Magnuson-Moss action? See Mag.-Moss §102(b)(2). Is there a UCC warranty?

(b) When Michele Bean bought her car from Sharp Sam, she demanded that he warrant the car. Sam said, "I promise that this car has a sound engine that will last five years." Is there a possible Magnuson-Moss action? See Mag.-Moss §102(a). Is there a UCC warranty?

(c) When Norman Anderson bought his car from Sharp Sam, he demanded that Sam write down his warranty. Sam wrote the following: "I guarantee that the only person to ever own this car was a little old lady who only drove it to church every Sunday." If it turns out that in fact the car was owned by Hotdog Harry, a speedway racer, is there a possible Magnuson-Moss action? See Mag.-Moss §101(6). Is there a UCC warranty? See Skelton v. General Motors Corp., 500 F. Supp. 1181 (N.D. Ill. 1981).

(d) When Ann Leonard bought her car from Sharp Sam, she, too, demanded a written warranty. Before the sale Sam took her into his salesroom and pointed out two loose-leaf binders. Inside one of the binders under the model name of the car that Ann desired, Super Z, there was written the following statement:

The Super Z Has a Full Life-Time Guarantee.

Has Sam subjected himself to Magnuson-Moss? See Mag.-Moss §104. Is there a UCC warranty?

---

47. Citations styled Mag.-Moss § _____ refer to 15 U.S.C. §2301 et seq., Magnuson-Moss Warranty — Federal Trade Commission Improvement Act (1975). Note: section enumeration in textbooks is not always consistent with the enumeration in the U.S.C. In some texts, §2301 of the U.S.C. is labeled as §101, §2302 is labeled as §102, etc.

(e) Mammoth Motors phones you, its corporate counsel, and says that it has heard that two types of written warranties are possible under Magnuson-Moss: a *Full* (statement of duration, e.g., 1 year or 90 days) *Warranty* and a *Limited Warranty*. It is very proud of the performance of its vehicles and is considering giving the full warranty. What differences are there between the two types? See Mag.-Moss §§103, 104, 105, 108. What do you advise?

The most important intersection between the UCC and the Magnuson-Moss Act lies in the area of implied warranties. Read Mag.-Moss §108.

PROBLEM 48

Fenton Hardy bought a new car from Dixon Motors. The car carried a full three-month warranty, which guaranteed all the parts except the tires as defect-free. The warranty conspicuously stated that "this warranty is in lieu of all other warranties, express or implied, particularly the warranty of merchantability." One day after the three-month period expired, every part in the car (except the tires) malfunctioned. Hardy sued in state court using UCC §2-314 as his theory. Was the warranty disclaimer effective? See Mag.-Moss §108. Would it have been effective had Dixon offered only a "limited warranty"? See Mag.-Moss §108 again. In an action based on §2-314, may Hardy recover his attorney fees? See Mag.-Moss §110(d); Champion Ford Sales, Inc. v. Levine, 49 Md. App. 547, 433 A.2d 1218 (1981).

Pursuant to the Act's command, the Federal Trade Commission has promulgated rules to supplement the statute; see 16 C.F.R. §701 et seq. These regulations have delineated the precise information required for the §102 warranties, provided for presale availability of the warranty through signs or warranty binders to be kept at the place of sale, and specified the makeup and procedure to be followed by entities (called *mechanisms*) engaging in §110's informal settlement of disputes. The rules also call for mandatory language about protection of implied warranties, quoted in the second footnote of the next case, which must be included in warranty disclosures.

Ventura v. Ford Motor Corp.

New Jersey Superior Court, Appellate Division, 1981, 180 N.J. Super. 45, 433 A.2d 801

BOTTER, J.

Ford Motor Company (Ford) appeals from the final judgment in this action in which plaintiff, the purchaser of a new 1978 Mercury Marquis Brougham, sued Ford's authorized dealer, Marino Auto Sales, Inc. (Marino Auto), and Ford, as manufacturer, for damages due to defects in the vehicle. Marino Auto cross-claimed against Ford for indemnification. The final judgment (a) granted plaintiff rescission of the purchase and damages of $6,745.59 against Marino Auto Sales (representing the purchase price of $7,847.49 less an allowance for plaintiff's use of the car and the sales tax), (b) awarded damages in favor of Marino Auto against Ford on the cross-claim in the sum of $2,910.59 (representing $6,745.59 less the resale value of the car), and (c) awarded counsel fees to plaintiff against Ford in the sum of $5,165. Plaintiff's demands for interest, punitive damages in excess of $2,000,000 and treble damages were denied. The trial court's published opinion was limited to the issue of counsel fees awarded under the Magnuson-Moss Warranty — Federal Trade Commission Improvement Act, 15 U.S.C. §2301 et seq., 173 N.J. Super. 501 (Ch. Div. 1980).

Plaintiff took delivery of the automobile on April 12, 1978. According to the testimony of plaintiff and his wife they experienced engine hesitation and stalling problems early in their use of the car which continued without interruption despite repeated attempts by Marino Auto to cure the problem. Stanley Bednarz, Ford's zone service manager and mechanical specialist who assists dealers in satisfying customers, inspected the vehicle on July 13, 1978 and recommended replacing the exhaust regulator valve. Plaintiff testified that he was told by Bednarz that there was nothing wrong with the car and he would "have to live with this one." Plaintiff also testified that later in July 1978 he returned to Marino Auto intending to ask Mr. Marino to take the car back if it could not be fixed but that he was prevented from doing so and was forcibly removed from the premises. . . .

At the conclusion of plaintiff's case against Ford the trial judge announced his findings and conclusions that Ford had breached its warranty, that the car was substantially impaired because of persistent and continual stalling and hesitation, but that plaintiff had not proven damages against Ford. He held that the only remedy to which plaintiff was entitled was rescission or revocation of acceptance against Marino Auto, see §2-608; Herbstman v. Eastman Kodak Co., 68 N.J. 1, 9-10 (1975), except that plaintiff would also have a claim for attorney's fees against Ford under the Magnuson-Moss Warranty Act, supra, 15 U.S.C. §2310(d)(2). Various reasons were given for affording plaintiff the right to rescind the purchase and receive a refund of the purchase price from Marino Auto. At one point in his oral decision the trial judge alternatively relied upon the theory of strict liability in tort and breach of an implied warranty of merchantability and fitness. In his written opinion he stated that this result "pierced through the dealership system, granting rescission against the selling dealer Marino, based upon defects in breach of the manufacturer Ford's express warranty." 173 N.J. Super. At 504. He also said: "The only remedy under the Magnuson-Moss Warranty Act for Ford's violation of the act was rescission against the selling dealer Marino"; and he viewed Marino Auto as Ford's "authorized agent to remedy defects. . . ." Id. Punitive damages against Ford were denied because of the absence of "deliberate, willful, malicious fraud or wanton and gross negligence or unconscionable commercial practice. . . ." Thus, the case was continued to permit plaintiff to claim a refund of the purchase price, less an allowance for the use of the car, on a rescission basis against Marino Auto, and to permit Marino Auto to claim indemnification against Ford. Ford was to be afforded the opportunity to defend by establishing Marino Auto's fault in failing properly to repair the auto.

On the next trial date Marino Auto stipulated the sale of the car to plaintiff and seemingly conceded at one point that plaintiff would be entitled to a judgment against Marino Auto based on the finding of Ford's breach of warranty on the proofs offered by plaintiff against Ford. The issues to be tried, then, were declared to be damages on rescission or revocation of acceptance, §2-608, i.e., the purchase price less the value of the car to be returned to the dealer, minus an allowance for the limited use of the car. (There was evidence that plaintiff was financially compelled to continue to use the vehicle in its imperfect state. Upon the seller's breach the buyer has the right to "cover" by acquiring substituted goods but is not barred from any other remedy if he fails to effect "cover." Sections 2-711 and 712. See also §2-711(3) which gives the buyer a security interest in and the right to retain or resell goods after revocation of acceptance.) The case proceeded on the cross-claim although Ford contended that no claim ever could arise until plaintiff recovered a judgment against Marino Auto. On the assumption that proof of Ford's breach of an express warranty established plaintiff's right to recover against Marino Auto, 173 N.J. Super. at 503-504, the trial judge ordered the trial to proceed on Marino Auto's indemnification claim. Proof of plaintiff's damage claim was also anticipated before a final judgment was to be entered on the complaint and cross-claim.

Proofs were presented by Ford to show that the car was not defective and that there could be other causes for engine hesitation or stalling, such as contaminated fuel. Although Ford contends that Marino Auto was negligent in not checking the fuel system, there was no proof that contaminated fuel was the actual cause of the problem. Thus, there was no proof that the defect in the vehicle would have been discovered but for Marino Auto's lack of reasonable care in attempting to repair the car. Marino Auto cannot be denied indemnification because it failed to successfully diagnose the cause of the problem. Ford's expert could find nothing wrong with the car, and, on the facts of this case the trial judge could properly have rejected Ford's contention that Marino Auto was at fault for not correcting it, regardless of where the burden of proving Marino Auto's negligence was placed.

At the conclusion of this testimony Marino Auto contended that there was no proof of any wrongdoing by Marino Auto and no basis for rescission.

However, Marino Auto also claimed indemnification from Ford for any damage award granted to plaintiff against Marino Auto. Ford contended that no judgment should be entered against Marino Auto, that there was no basis for rescission and therefore no need for indemnification. Ford also protested the lack of sufficient notice of plaintiff's complaints about the car's performance.

We have considered the merits of this appeal on the assumption that, although Marino Auto has not appealed the judgment against it, Ford can contend that no judgment should have been entered against Marino Auto. Ford has an interest in the judgment against Marino Auto since it was the basis for Ford's indemnification obligation. In fact, the trial judge did consider Ford's arguments against Marino Auto's liability to plaintiff.

Our reasoning through the body of law applicable to this commonplace contractual skein, which binds consumers, car dealers and manufacturers together, differs from that of the trial judge. But we affirm plaintiff's recovery. We conclude that, despite Marino Auto's attempted disclaimer of all warranties, plaintiff can recover from Marino Auto for the breach of implied warranty of merchantability. We also uphold the award of counsel fees against Ford pursuant to the Magnuson-Moss Warranty Act.

The contract of sale between Marino Auto and plaintiff conspicuously contained the following legend on its face:

> The seller, MARINO AUTO SALES, Inc., hereby expressly disclaims all warranties, either expressed or implied, including any implied warranty of merchantability or fitness for a particular purpose, and MARINO AUTO SALES, Inc., neither assumes nor authorizes another person to assume for it any liability in connection with the sale of the vehicle.

On the back of this sales order-contract were the following terms which were made part of the contract:

> 7. It is expressly agreed that there are no warranties, express or implied, made by either the selling dealer or the manufacturer on the motor vehicle, chassis or parts furnished hereunder except, in the case of a new motor vehicle the warranty expressly given to the purchaser upon the delivery of such motor vehicle or chassis.
>
> The selling dealer also agrees to promptly perform and fulfill all terms and conditions of the owner service policy.

For the purpose of this opinion we will assume that the disclaimer of implied warranties of merchantability and fitness was effective under the Uniform Commercial Code §2-316. Since the dealer passed on to the purchaser a warranty from the manufacturer, we will not consider whether the attempted disclaimer by Marino Auto should be voided as unconscionable and contrary to public policy under §2-302 even though such disclaimer could foreclose rescission or other remedies against the dealer and, without privity between buyer and manufacturer, rescission has been held ordinarily unavailable under the Code against the manufacturer. Edelstein v. Toyota Motors Distributors, 176 N.J. Super. 57, 64 (App. Div. 1980); see Henningsen v. Bloomfield Motors, Inc., 32 N.J. 358, 372-373, 406-408 (1960); Gladden v. Cadillac Motor Car Div., 83 N.J. 320, 330-331 (1980); Herbstman v. Eastman Kodak Co., supra, 68 N.J. at 9-10; cf. Santor v. A. & M. Karagheusian, Inc., 44 N.J. 52 (1965). Section 2-316(1) provides that "words or conduct tending to negate or limit warranty shall be construed wherever reasonable as consistent with each other; but subject to the provisions of this Chapter on parol or extrinsic evidence (§2-202) negation or limitation is inoperative to the extent that such construction is unreasonable." It may be argued that the dealer's conduct in transmitting Ford's warranty to plaintiff, the reference to such warranty in paragraph 7 on the back of the purchase order-contract, and the undertaking "to promptly perform and fulfill all terms and conditions of the owner service policy," are inconsistent with a disclaimer of all warranties and that such a disclaimer is an unreasonable construction. See Gladden v. Cadillac Motor Car Div., supra, 83 N.J. at 330; Henningsen v. Bloomfield Motors, Inc., supra, 32 N.J. at 407-408; cf. Murray v. Holiday Rambler, Inc., 83 Wis. 2d 406, ___, 265 N.W.2d 513, 519 (Sup. Ct. 1978). The contract in the *Henningsen* case contained the identical obligation to perform all terms and conditions of the owner service policy. Id. The combination of the dealer's undertaking and the automobile manufacturer's warranty was interpreted in *Henningsen* to rebut the disclaimer of implied warranty of merchantability by the dealer. The court held that the attempt to limit liability to the replacement of defective parts was contrary to public policy and void with respect to a claim for personal injuries resulting from an accident caused by defects in an automobile. However, we need not explore these issues further because the Magnuson-Moss Warranty Act has solved many of the problems posed by the intricacies confronting consumers under the preexisting law of sales.

The Magnuson-Moss Warranty — Federal Trade Commission Improvement Act, supra, was adopted on January 4, 1975, 88 Stat. 2183. Its purpose was to make "warranties on consumer products more readily understandable and enforceable." Note, 7 Rutgers-Camden L.J. 379 (1976). The act enhances the consumer's position by allowing recovery under a warranty without regard to privity of contract between the consumer and warrantor, by prohibiting the disclaimer of implied warranties in a written warranty, and by enlarging the remedies available to a consumer for breach of warranty, including the award of attorneys' fees. Id. The requirement of privity of contract between the consumer and the warrantor has been removed by assuring consumers a remedy against all warrantors of the product.[48] A consumer is defined in 15 U.S.C. §2301(3) as follows:

> (3) The term "consumer" means a buyer (other than for purposes of resale) of any consumer product, any person to whom such product is transferred during the duration of an implied or written warranty (or service contract) applicable to the product, and any other person who is entitled by the terms of such warranty (or service contract) or under applicable State law to enforce against the warrantor (or service contractor) the obligations of the warranty (or service contract).

A "supplier" is defined as any person engaged in the business of making a consumer product directly or indirectly available to consumers, §2301(4), and a "warrantor" includes any supplier or other person who gives or offers to give a written warranty or who is obligated under an implied warranty. §2301(5). The term "written warranty" is defined in §2301(6) to include:

> (A) any written affirmation of fact or written promise made in connection with the sale of a consumer product by a supplier to a buyer which relates to the nature of the material or workmanship and affirms or promises that such material or workmanship is defect free or will meet a specified level of performance over a specified period of time, or
> (B) any undertaking in writing in connection with the sale by a supplier of a consumer product to refund, repair, replace or take other remedial action with respect to such product in the event that such product fails to meet the specifications set forth in the undertaking.

The Magnuson-Moss Warranty Act provides for two types of written warranties on consumer products, those described as "full" warranties and those described as "limited" warranties. 15 U.S.C. §2303. The nature of the "full" warranty is prescribed by §2304. It expressly provides in subsection (a)(4) that a consumer must be given the election to receive a refund or replacement without charge of a product or part which is defective or malfunctions after a reasonable number of attempts by the warrantor to correct such condition. For the breach of any warranty, express or implied, or of a service contract (defined in 15 U.S.C. §2301(8)), consumers are given the right to sue for damages and "other legal and equitable relief afforded under state or federal law, 15 U.S.C.A. §2310(d); 15 U.S.C. §2311(b)(1).

Appellant Ford contends that the trial judge improperly invoked section 2304 of the act as a basis for allowing "rescission" in the case since the warranty given by Ford was a limited warranty and not a full warranty.

---

48. In Miller and Kanter, "Litigation Under Magnuson-Moss: New Opportunities in Private Actions," 13 U.C.C. L.J. 10, 21-22 (1980), the authors discuss the broad definition of a *consumer* and state that "an assumption is now created that no privity restriction exists."

15 U.S.C. §2303(a)(2) provides that all warranties that do not meet federal minimum standards for warranty contained in §2304 shall be conspicuously designated a "limited warranty." "Limited warranties" protect consumers by prohibiting disclaimers of implied warranties, §2308, but are otherwise not described in the act. Note, supra 7, Rutgers-Camden L.J. at 381. Clearly, Ford's warranty, which is quoted later in this opinion, was a limited warranty.

15 U.S.C. §2308 provides as follows:

(a) No supplier may disclaim or modify (except as provided in subsection (b) of this section) any implied warranty to a consumer with respect to such consumer product if (1) such supplier makes any written warranty to the consumer with respect to such consumer product, or (2) at the time of sale, or within 90 days thereafter, such supplier enters into a service contract with the consumer which applies to such consumer product.

(b) For purposes of this chapter (other than section 2304(a)(2) of this title), implied warranties may be limited in duration to the duration of a written warranty of reasonable duration, if such limitation is conscionable and is set forth in clear and unmistakable language and prominently displayed on the face of the warranty.

(c) A disclaimer, modification, or limitation made in violation of this section shall be ineffective for purposes of this chapter and State law.

We will first consider the application of this act to the dealer, Marino Auto. As quoted above, paragraph 7 of the purchase order-contract provides that there are no warranties, express or implied, made by the selling dealer or manufacturer except, in the case of a new motor vehicle, "the warranty expressly given to the purchaser upon delivery of such motor vehicle. . . ." This section also provides: "The selling dealer also agrees to promptly perform and fulfill all terms and conditions of the owner service policy." Ford contended in the trial court that Marino Auto had "a duty" to properly diagnose and make repairs, that such duty was "fixed both by the express warranty . . . which they passed on . . . and by the terms of [paragraph 7 of the contract with plaintiff]" by which Marino Auto expressly undertook "to perform its obligations under the owner service policy." See 15 U.S.C. §2310(f); 16 C.F.R. §700.4 (1980). The provision in paragraph 7 in these circumstances is a "written warranty" within the meaning of §2301(6)(B) since it constitutes an undertaking in connection with the sale to take "remedial action with respect to such product in the event that such product fails to meet the specifications set forth in the undertaking. . . ." In our view the specifications of the undertaking include, at the least, the provisions of the limited warranty furnished by Ford, namely:

LIMITED   WARRANTY   (12   MONTHS   OR   12,000   MILES/19,312 KILOMETRES) 1978 NEW CAR AND LIGHT TRUCK

Ford warrants for its 1978 model cars and light trucks that the Selling Dealer will repair or replace free any parts, except tires, found under normal use in the U.S. or Canada to be defective in factory materials or workmanship within the earlier of 12 months or 12,000 miles/19,312 km from either first use or retail delivery.

All we require is that you properly operate and maintain your vehicle and that you return for warranty service to your Selling Dealer or any Ford or Lincoln-Mercury Dealer if you are traveling, have moved a long distance or need emergency repairs. Warranty repairs will be made with Ford Authorized Service or Remanufactured Parts.

THERE IS NO OTHER EXPRESS WARRANTY ON THIS VEHICLE.[49]

The record does not contain a written description of the "owner service policy" which the dealer agreed to perform. Nevertheless, since Ford is the appellant here, we take its contentions at trial and documents in the record to establish the dealer's obligation to Ford and to plaintiff to make the warranty repairs on behalf of Ford (subject to the right of reimbursement or other terms that may be contained in their agreement). For the purpose of this appeal we are satisfied that the dealer's undertaking in paragraph 7 constitutes a written warranty within the meaning of 15 U.S.C. §2301(6)(B). Accordingly, having furnished a written warranty to the consumer, the dealer as a supplier may not "disclaim or modify [except to limit in duration] any implied warranty to a consumer. . . ." The result of this analysis is to invalidate the attempted disclaimer by the dealer of the implied warranties of merchantability and fitness. Being bound by those implied warranties arising under state law, §§2-314 and 315, Marino Auto was liable to plaintiff for the breach thereof as found by the trial judge, and plaintiff could timely revoke his acceptance of the automobile and claim a refund of his purchase price. §§2-608, 2-711. Zabriskie Chevrolet, Inc. v. Smith, 99 N.J. Super. 441 (L. Div. 1968). In this connection we note that the trial judge found that plaintiff's attempted revocation of acceptance was made in timely fashion, and that finding has adequate support in the evidence.

---

49. The warranty also provided:

TO THE EXTENT ALLOWED BY LAW:

1. ANY IMPLIED WARRANTY OF MERCHANTABILITY OR FITNESS IS LIMITED TO THE 12 MONTH OR 12,000-MILE/19,312-KM DURATION OF THIS WRITTEN WARRANTY.

2. NEITHER FORD NOR THE SELLING DEALER SHALL HAVE ANY RESPONSIBILITY FOR LOSS OF USE OF THE VEHICLE, LOSS OF TIME, INCONVENIENCE, COMMERCIAL LOSS OR CONSEQUENTIAL DAMAGES.

Some states do not allow limitations on how long an implied warranty lasts or the exclusion or limitation of incidental or consequential damages, so the above limitations may not apply to you.

This warranty gives you specific legal rights, and you also may have other rights which vary from state to state.

As the trial judge noted, 15 U.S.C. §2310(d)(1) provides that a consumer who is damaged by the failure of a warrantor to comply with any obligation under the act, or under a written warranty or implied warranty or service contract, may bring suit "for damages and other legal and equitable relief. . . ." Although the remedy of refund of the purchase price is expressly provided by the Magnuson-Moss Warranty Act for breach of a full warranty, granting this remedy under state law for breach of a limited warranty is not barred by or inconsistent with the act. 15 U.S.C. §2311(b)(1) provides that nothing in the act restricts "any right or remedy of any consumer under State law or other Federal law." See also 15 U.S.C. §2311(c)(2). Thus, for breach of the implied warranty of merchantability, plaintiff was entitled to revoke acceptance against Marino Auto, and a judgment for the purchase price less an allowance for the use of the vehicle was properly entered against Marino Auto. Sections 2-608 and 711. Cf. 15 U.S.C. §2301(12) which defines "refund" as the return of the purchase price "less reasonable depreciation based on actual use where permitted" by regulations.

Plaintiff also could have recovered damages against Ford for Ford's breach of its written limited warranty. Marino Auto was Ford's representative for the purpose of making repairs to plaintiff's vehicle under the warranty. See Henningsen v. Bloomfield Motors, Inc., supra, 32 N.J. at 374; cf. Conte v. Dwan Lincoln-Mercury, Inc., 172 Conn. 112, ___, 374 A.2d 144, 149-150 (Sup. Ct. 1976). The limited warranty expressly required the purchaser to return the vehicle "for warranty service" to the dealer or to any Ford or Lincoln-Mercury dealer if the purchaser is traveling or has moved a long distance or needs emergency repairs. Ford contends that it put purchasers on notice that they should advise Ford's district office if they have problems with their cars that a dealer is unable to fix. The record contains a document listing "frequently asked warranty questions" which states:

> The Dealership where you purchased your vehicle has the responsibility for performing warranty repairs; therefore, take your vehicle to that Dealership. . . .
> If you encounter a service problem, refer to the service assistance section of your Owner's Guide for suggested action.

We do not read these provisions as requiring notice to Ford as a condition of relief against Ford when Ford's dealer has failed after numerous attempts to correct defects under warranty. . . .

One question posed by this case is whether recovery of the purchase price from the manufacturer was available to plaintiff for breach of the manufacturer's warranty. If the warranty were a full warranty plaintiff would have been entitled to a refund of the purchase price under the Magnuson-Moss Warranty Act. Since Ford's warranty was a limited warranty we must look to state law to determine plaintiff's right to damages or other legal and equitable relief. 15 U.S.C. §2310(d)(1). Once privity is removed as an obstacle to relief we see no reason why a purchaser cannot also elect the equitable remedy of returning the goods to the manufacturer who is a warrantor and claiming a refund of the purchase price less an allowance for use of the product. See Seely v. White Motor Co., 45 Cal. Rptr. 17, ___, 403 P.2d 145, 148 (Sup. Ct. 1965); Durfee v. Rod Baxter Imports, Inc., supra, 262 N.W.2d at 357-358, where the Minnesota Supreme Court held as a matter of state law that lack of privity does not bar a purchaser of a foreign car from revoking acceptance and recovering the purchase price from the distributor of such cars as distinguished from the local dealer. The decision was made without regard to the Magnuson-Moss Warranty Act.

We are dealing with the breach of an express contractual obligation. Nothing prevents us from granting an adequate remedy under state law for that breach of contract, including rescission when appropriate. Under state law the right to revoke acceptance for defects substantially impairing the value of the product (§2-608) and to receive a refund of the purchase price (§2-711) are rights available to a buyer against a seller in privity. Where the manufacturer gives a warranty to induce the sale it is consistent to allow the same type of remedy as against that manufacturer. See Durfee v. Rod Baxter Imports, Inc., supra; cf. Seely v. White Motor Co., supra. Only the privity concept, which is frequently viewed as a relic these days, Koperski v. Husker Dodge, Inc., 208 Neb. 29, ___, 302 N.W.2d 655, 664 (Sup. Ct. 1981); see Kinlaw v. Long Mfg. N.C., Inc., 298 N.C. 494, 259 S.E.2d 552 (Sup. Ct. 1979), has interfered with a rescission-type remedy against the manufacturer of goods not purchased directly from the manufacturer. If we focus on the fact that the warranty creates a direct contractual obligation to the buyer, the reason for allowing the same remedy that is available against a direct seller becomes clear. Although the manufacturer intended to limit the remedy to the repair and replacement of defective parts, the failure of that remedy, see §2-719(2); Goddard v. General Motors Corp., 60 Ohio St. 2d 41, 396 N.E.2d 761 (Sup. Ct. 1979); Seely v. White Motor Co., supra, and the consequent breach of the implied warranty of merchantability which accompanied the limited warranty by virtue of the Magnuson-Moss Warranty Act, make a rescission-type remedy appropriate when revocation of acceptance is justified. Durfee v. Rod Baxter Imports, Inc., supra, 262 N.W.2d at 357.

Lastly, we consider Ford's contention that a counsel fee was improperly granted to plaintiff since no judgment was entered in favor of plaintiff against Ford and Ford contends it was not given adequate notice of the defects in the car. 15 U.S.C. §2310(d)(2) provides that a consumer who "prevails in any action brought [in any court] under paragraph (1) of this subsection . . . may be allowed by the court to recover as part of the judgment . . . expenses (including attorneys' fees based on the actual time expended). . . ." This section is subject to the provisions contained in §2310(e). Subsection

(e) provides that, with certain exceptions, no action based upon breach of a written or implied warranty or service contract may be prosecuted unless a person obligated under the warranty or service contract "is afforded a reasonable opportunity to cure such failure to comply." Here that opportunity was given to Ford's designated representative to whom the purchaser was required to bring the car. A direct employee of Ford, Bednarz, also met with plaintiff or his wife and was made aware of some difficulty with the car. We are not certain of the extent of Ford's knowledge of those difficulties. However, in our view the opportunities given to Marino Auto to repair the vehicle satisfied the requirements of 15 U.S.C. §2310(e) in this case.

As noted, Ford also contends that a counsel fee could not be awarded against Ford because plaintiff did not recover a judgment against Ford. The Magnuson-Moss Warranty Act permits a prevailing consumer to recover attorney's fees "as part of the judgment." The trial judge found that Ford had breached its warranty and that the car's value was substantially impaired. He entered no damage judgment against Ford. However, in the absence of proof of actual damages, plaintiff was entitled to a judgment against Ford for nominal damages. Ruane Dev. Corp. v. Cullere, 134 N.J. Super. 245, 252 (App. Div. 1975); Ench v. Bluestein, 52 N.J. Super. 169, 173-174 (App. Div. 1958); Winkler v. Hartford Accident and Indem. Co., 66 N.J. Super. 22, 29 (App. Div.), *cert. den.*, 34 N.J. 581 (1961); Packard Englewood Motors, Inc. v. Packard Motor Car Co., 215 F.2d 503, 510 (3d Cir. 1954). Ford was not prejudiced by the failure of the trial judge to enter a judgment for nominal damages to which the award of attorney's fees could be attached. See Nobility Homes, Inc. v. Ballentine, 386 So. 2d 727, 730-731 (Sup. Ct. Ala. 1980). The award of counsel fees fulfills the intent of the Magnuson-Moss Warranty Act. Without such an award consumers frequently would be unable to vindicate warranty rights accorded by law.

As to the amount of counsel fees allowed by the trial judge, we find no abuse of discretion. The allowance was for actual time spent at an hourly rate of $75.00. Consideration could properly be given to the fact that plaintiff's attorney undertook this claim on a contingency basis with a relatively small retainer. D.R. 2-106(A)(8). The normal breach of warranty case ought not require four separate appearances before the trial court. To some extent this was not in the control of plaintiff's attorney; and plaintiff might have obtained all the relief required against Ford on the first day of trial. But it did not work out that way. In other cases it may be possible to stipulate damages and simplify the issues, thus limiting the cost of this type of litigation for consumers and suppliers alike. But the issues raised in this case were novel in this state, and no one can be faulted for the difficulty and time consumed in this litigation. . . .

Affirmed.

At one point in its opinion the court says that the Magnuson-Moss Act does away with the requirement of privity. That was certainly the intention of the drafters, who wanted a broad statute that would give consumers an effective remedy against any entity warranting a product sold to them that breached the warranties provided either by the law or the contract.

PROBLEM 49

When consumer Alan Turing learned of a new computer called "The Quantum" manufactured by Bletchley Corporation, he bought one from Morcom Electronics, a local store in his city. The Quantum worked well for a while but then exploded one day when Turing was sitting at it, putting him in the hospital and burning down a portion of his house. Bletchley Corporation had issued a written Limited Warranty for the Quantum promising that it would be defect free for one year, and limiting the implied warranty of merchantability to the same period. When Turing comes to your office for legal advice he has done some research and has a number of questions.

(a) May he use the Magnuson-Moss Act to sue Morcom Electronics? The retail contract conspicuously disclaimed all warranties, mentioning merchantability especially. Morcom made no express warranties when it sold him the product, but merely passed on the one given by Bletchley. Study the language of §110(d)(1) carefully. He wants to use the federal statute because it provides him with attorney fees. See McNamara v. Nomero, 26 F. Supp. 2d 1168 (D. Minn. 1998) (no, since that section applies only to the entity that gave an express warranty).

(b) In the jurisdiction that Turing lives in, the state courts have always said that privity is required before a consumer can sue the manufacturer, though Magnuson-Moss had not been enacted when those decisions were decided. Does the statute now mandate that the state courts must allow the direct suit against Enigma Corporation?

It was clear that Congress thought it was abolishing privity when it passed the Magnuson-Moss Act, but the courts have divided on that question. A splendid law review article written by Professor Janet Stevenson, The Unfulfilled Promise of the Magnuson-Moss Warranty Act, 18 Lewis & Clark L. Rev. 155 (2014), lists the decisions going each way and explains that those finding that lack of privity can still block suits against the manufacturer are wrong. However, until the United States Supreme Court takes up the question (which it has never done) and holds that the states can't circumvent the clear intention of Congress by this route, those decisions cause many consumers with defective products to have no remedy at all if the retailer either made no warranties or is judgment-proof. In some states the manufacturer is liable for express warranties made on the product on the theory that this creates sufficient privity with the eventual purchaser, but even in those jurisdictions some courts will not extend this same logic to create privity for breach of implied warranties. Does this make sense? Is it good policy for these juris-dictions to protect manufacturers but not retailers from implied warranties? In warranties suits who should bear the ultimate responsibility for a product that won't work?

F. Warranties and Article 2A

The warranty rules for the lease of goods found in Article 2A are, with minor variations, mere carbon copies of the Article 2 rules. There is one major difference, however, which arises in what Article 2A calls a "finance lease."

PROBLEM 50

Chemicals of Tomorrow Corp. decided that the safest way to work with hazardous materials was through the use of an advanced robot. It persuaded Aurora Robotics, Inc., to design a robot that would meet its needs. To finance the purchase of the robot, Chemicals of Tomorrow went to Octopus National Bank, which bought the robot from Aurora Robotics and then leased it to Chemicals of Tomorrow. The robot was subject to both express and implied warranties, which became important when the robot ran amok in one of Chemicals of Tomorrow's laboratories and caused extensive damage. Answer these questions:

(a) Is this a "finance lease"? What factors do and do not influence this decision? See §2A-103(1)(g) and its Official Comment (g); Information Leasing Corp. v. King, 155 Ohio App. 3d 201, 800 N.E.2d 73 (2003). As the leas-ing officer for the bank, what steps would you have recommended to make sure that a court would hold that this lease so qualified? See Construction Resources Group, LLC v. Element Fin. Corp., 2017 WL 2266894 (W.D. Okla. 2017).

(b) What name does Article 2A give to Aurora Robotics in this situation? See §2A-103(1)(x).

(c) Does Chemicals of Tomorrow Corp. have the benefit of whatever warranties Aurora gave to Octopus National? See §2A-209 and its Official Comment.

(d) Is Octopus National Bank responsible for breach of the implied war-ranty of merchantability? See §2A-212.

(e) If Octopus National's leasing officer had told Chemicals of Tomorrow's president, "We have investigated this robot, and I guarantee you it will cause you no trouble," must the lessor then respond in a warranty lawsuit to a claim for damages? See §2A-210 and Official Comment (g), third paragraph, to §2A-103.

(f) The lease between Octopus National Bank and Chemicals of Tomorrow contained a clause stating that the lessee had to pay the lessor even if the goods did not work, a "hell or high water" clause, so called because the lessee binds itself to pay the lessor no matter what happens in connection with the performance of the leased goods. After the robot ruins the laboratory, must Chemicals of Tomorrow nonetheless pay Octopus National Bank? See §2A-407 and its Official Comment. Would we reach the same result if the lessee were a consumer?

Information Leasing Corporation v. GDR Investments, Inc., d/b/a/ Pinnacle Exxon

Court of Appeals of Ohio, First District, Hamilton County, 2003
152 Ohio App. 3d 260, 787 N.E.2d 652

GORMAN, Judge.

[¶1] The plaintiff-appellant, Information Leasing Corporation ("ILC"), appeals from the order of the trial court rendering judgment in favor of the defendants-appellees, GDR Investments, d.b.a. Pinnacle Exxon, and Avtar S. Arora, in an action to recover $15,877.37 on a five-year commercial lease of an Automated Teller Machine ("ATM"). In its sole assignment of error, ILC argues that the trial court's judgment constituted "an abuse of discretion" because it failed to address the effect of [§2A-103(A)(7)] on the issue of GDR's liability under the lease. For the following reasons, we reverse and remand this cause to the trial court.

[¶2] This is one of many cases involving ILC that have been recently before this court. ILC is an Ohio corporation wholly owned by the Provident Bank. ILC is in the business of leasing ATMs through a third party, or vendor. In all of these cases, the vendor has been a third-party corporation, JRA 222, Inc., d.b.a. Credit Card Center ("CCC"). CCC was in the business of finding lessees for the machines and then providing the services necessary to operate them, offering the lessees attractive commissions. Essentially, CCC would find a customer, usually a small business interested in having an ATM available on its premises, arrange for its customer to sign a lease with ILC, and then agree to service the machine, keeping it stocked with cash and paying the customer a certain monthly commission. Usually, as in the case of GDR, the owner of the business was required to sign as a personal guarantor of the lease. The twist in this story is that CCC soon went bankrupt, leaving its customers stuck with ATMs under the terms of leases with ILC but with no service provider. Rather than seeking to find another company to service the ATMs, many of CCC's former customers, like GDR, simply decided that they no longer wanted the ATMs and were no longer going to make lease payments to ILC.

[¶3] The terms of each lease, however, prohibited cancellation. The pertinent section read, "LEASE NON-CANCELABLE AND NO WARRANTY. THIS LEASE CANNOT BE CANCELED BY YOU FOR ANY REASON, INCLUDING EQUIPMENT FAILURE, LOSS OR DAMAGE. YOU MAY NOT REVOKE ACCEPTANCE OF THE EQUIPMENT. YOU, NOT WE, SELECTED THE EQUIPMENT AND THE VENDOR. WE ARE NOT RESPONSIBLE FOR EQUIPMENT FAILURE OR THE VENDOR'S ACTS. YOU ARE LEASING THE EQUIPMENT 'AS IS', [sic] AND WE DISCLAIM ALL WARRANTIES, EXPRESS OR IMPLIED. WE ARE NOT RESPONSIBLE FOR SERVICE OR REPAIRS."

[¶4] Either out of a sense of fair play or a further desire to make enforcement of the lease ironclad, ILC put a notice on the top of the lease that stated, "NOTICE: THIS IS A NON-CANCELABLE, BINDING CONTRACT. THIS CONTRACT WAS WRITTEN IN PLAIN LANGUAGE FOR YOUR BENEFIT. IT CONTAINS IMPORTANT TERMS AND CONDITIONS AND HAS LEGAL AND FINANCIAL CONSEQUENCES TO YOU. PLEASE READ IT CAREFULLY; FEEL FREE TO ASK QUESTIONS BEFORE SIGNING BY CALLING THE LEASING COMPANY AT 1-513-421-9191."

[¶5] Arora, the owner of GDR, was a resident alien with degrees in commerce and economics from the University of Delhi, India. Arora wished to have an ATM on the premises of his Exxon station in the hope of increasing business. He made the mistake of arranging acquisition of the ATM through CCC. According to his testimony, a representative of CCC showed up at the station one day and gave him "formality papers" to sign before the ATM could be delivered. Arora stated that he was busy with other customers when the CCC representative asked him to sign the papers. He testified that when he informed the CCC representative that he needed time to read the documents before signing them, he was told not to worry and, in effect, given the CCC representative's word that the papers did not need his attention and that his signature was a mere formality. Arora signed the ILC lease, having never read it.

[¶6] Within days, CCC went into bankruptcy. Arora found himself with an ATM that he no longer wanted. Although the testimony was spotty, it appears that he never attempted to look for another service provider. According to his testimony, he tried unsuccessfully to contact ILC to take back the ATM. Soon Arora suffered a mild heart attack, the gas station went out of business, and the ATM, which had been in place for approximately eighteen days, was left sitting in the garage, no longer in use until ILC came and removed it several months later.

[¶7] Unfortunately for Arora, the lease also had an acceleration clause that read, "DEFAULT. If you fail to pay us or perform as agreed, we will have the right to (i) terminate this lease, (ii) sue you for all past due payment AND ALL FUTURE PAYMENTS UNDER THIS LEASE, plus the Residual Value we have placed on the equipment and other charges you owe us, (iii) repossess the equipment at your expense and (iv) exercise any other right or remedy which may be available under applicable law or proceed by court act."

[¶8] The trial court listened to the evidence in this case, which was awkwardly presented due in large part to Arora's decision to act as his own trial counsel. Obviously impressed with Arora's honesty and sympathetic to his situation, the trial court found that Arora owed ILC nothing. In so ruling, the court stated that ILC "ha[d] not complied with any of its contractual obligations and that [Arora] appropriately canceled any obligations by him, if there really were any." The court also found that ILC, "if they did have a contract, failed to mitigate any damages by timely picking up the machine after [Arora] gave them notice to pick up the machine."

[¶9] In its assignment of error, ILC asserts that the trial court "abused its discretion" by not applying [§2A-103(A)(7)]. Initially we note that the assignment is miscast, as it actually challenges the judgment as being contrary to law, not an abuse of discretion. The decision whether to apply the correct law to the case is, thankfully, not a matter of judicial discretion. This aside, we turn our attention to the Uniform Commercial Code and the world of lease financing.

[¶10] ILC contends, and we do not disagree, that the lease in question satisfied the definition of a "finance lease" under the UCC. See [§2A-103(A) (7)]. A finance lease is considerably different from an ordinary lease in that it adds a third party, the equipment supplier or manufacturer (in this case, the now defunct CCC). As noted by White and Summers, "In effect, the finance lessee * * * is relying upon the manufacturer * * * to provide the promised goods and stand by its promises and warranties; the [lessee] does not look to the [lessor] for these. The [lessor] is only a finance lessor and deals largely in paper, rather than goods." 1 White & Summers, Uniform Commercial Code (3d Ed. 1988) 20.

[¶11] One notorious feature of a finance lease is its typically noncancelable nature, which is specifically authorized by statute. [§2A-407(A)] provides in the case of a finance lease that is not a consumer lease, "[T]he lessee's promises under the lease contract become irrevocable and independent upon the lessee's acceptance of the goods." The same statutory section also makes clear that the finance lease is "not subject to cancellation, termination, modification, repudiation, excuse, or substitution without the consent of the party to whom it runs." [§2A-407(B)(2)].

[¶12] Because of their noncancelable nature, finance leases enjoy somewhat of a reputation. The titles of law review articles written about them reveal more than a little cynicism regarding their fairness: Strauss, Equipment

Leases Under U.C.C. Article 2A—Analysis and Practice Suggestions. U.C.C. Revisions: Promises and Pitfalls (1992), 43 Mercer L. Rev. 853; King, Major Problems with Article 2A: Unfairness, Cutting Off Consumer Defenses, Unfiled Interest and Uneven Adoption (1992), 43 Mercer L. Rev. 869; Breslauer, Finance Lease, Hell or High Water Clause and Third Party Beneficiary Theory in Article 2A of the Uniform Commercial Code (1992), 77 Cornell L. Rev. 318; Heckman, Article 2A of the Uniform Commercial Code: Government of the Lessor, by the Lessor, and for the Lessor (1992), 36 S. & L.U.L.J. 303.

[¶13] The "hell or high water clause" referred to in one of these titles makes the lessee's obligations to the lessor survive no matter what—come hell or high water. As described by Professors White and Summers, "The parties can draft a lease agreement that carefully excludes warranty and promissory liability of the finance lessor to the lessee, and that sets out what is known in the trade as a 'hell or high water clause,' namely, a clause that requires the lessee to continue to make rent payments to the finance lessor even though the [equipment] is unsuitable, defective, or destroyed." 1 White & Summers, supra, at 20. To offset this one-sidedness, the lessee is generally considered a third-party beneficiary of any warranties between the manufacturer and the lessor. Id. In short, the lessor is merely a disinterested provider of financing. As White and Summers describe the relationship, "The lessor's responsibility is merely to provide the money, not to instruct the lessee like a wayward child concerning a suitable purchase * * *. Absent contrary agreement, even if[, for example, a finance-leased] Boeing 747 explodes into small pieces in flight and is completely uninsured, lessee's obligation to pay continues." Id. at 25.

[¶14] Although fortunately not finding himself in the same situation as the hypothetical, Arora did find himself with an ATM that he did not want, and for which he felt he had no use after CCC dropped out of the picture. Some people complain about being stuck with the bill; Arora's complaint was that he was stuck with the ATM.

[¶15] Initially, we reject the trial court's analysis, which was that ILC did not satisfy its contractual obligations. This was an obvious error. ILC's only contractual obligation was to provide the ATM, which it did. Clearly ILC had an expectancy interest of $15,877.73 that it would lose if the lease were not enforced. We must reject also the trial court's doubts about whether Arora had any obligations under the lease—clearly he did—as well as the court's assertion that he "appropriately cancelled any obligations by him"—a statement that seems to willingly ignore the noncancelable nature of the lease.

[¶16] To begin the proper legal analysis, we note first that this was not a "consumer lease" expressly excepted from [§2A-407(A)]. A "consumer lease" is defined in [§2A-103(A)(5)] as one in which the lessee is "an individual and who takes under the lease primarily for a personal, family, or household purpose." This would definitely not apply here, where the ATM was placed on the business premises of the Exxon station, and where the lessee was GDR Investments and not Arora individually. (Arora was liable individually as the personal guarantor of GDR's obligations under the lease.)

[¶17] Even commercial finance leases, however, are subject to certain defenses, including lack of acceptance and unconscionability. It is noteworthy that ILC argues that Arora irrevocably accepted the ATM by merely signing a certificate of acceptance. (ILC also indicates in its brief that five payments were made on the lease, but it is unclear from the record who made these payments and when.) According to the UCC, however, in the case of finance leases, acceptance occurs only after the lessee has been given a reasonable time to inspect the goods and either (1) signifies acceptance, (2) fails to make an effective rejection, or (3) does any act that signifies acceptance. [§2A-515(A)]. The requirement that the lessee be given a reasonable time cannot be circumvented. "Taking possession of the goods is not determinative of acceptance, nor is the signing of a form of acceptance before receipt of the goods, nor the making of a lease payment." Colonial Pacific Leasing Corp. v. J.W.C.J.R. Corp. (Utah App. 1999), 977 P.2d 541, 545. "A 'reasonable time to inspect' under the UCC must allow an opportunity to put the product to its intended use, or for testing to verify its capability to perform as intended." Capitol Dodge Sales v. Northern Concrete Pipe (1983), 131 Mich. App. 149, 158, 346 N.W.2d 535. See also, Tri-Continental Leasing Corp. v. Law Office of Richard W. Burns (Tex. App. 1985), 710 S.W.2d 604, and Horrocks v. Westfalia Systemat (Utah App. 1995), 892 P.2d 14.

[¶18] Although it was available as a defense, it does not appear that Arora was entitled to claim a valid rejection of the goods in this case. [§2A-509(A)] applies the UCC's "perfect tender" rule to finance leases, allowing the lessee to reject any goods that "fail in any respect to conform to the lease contract." Nothing in the record, however, indicates that Arora rejected the ATM because of its nonconformity, i.e., its failure to work mechanically as intended. Rather, the record demonstrates quite clearly that he rejected it only because he no longer wanted an ATM after CCC went bankrupt. Although the UCC adopts the "perfect tender" rule, it does not adopt the "perfectly happy tenderee" rule.

[¶19] Certain defenses do remain, however. First, the UCC expressly allows for the application of the doctrine of unconscionability to finance leases, both consumer and commercial. [1310.06(A)] authorizes the trial court to find "any clause of a lease contract to have been unconscionable at the time it was made * * *." If it so finds, the court is given the power to "refuse to enforce the lease contract, * * * enforce the remainder of the lease contract without the unconscionable clause, or * * * limit the application of the unconscionable clause as to avoid any unconscionable result." Id.

[¶20] In this case, the trial court made no findings as to whether the finance lease was unconscionable. The primary purpose of the doctrine of unconscionability is to prevent oppression and unfair surprise. Calamari & Perillo, Contracts (3d Ed. 1982), Section 9-40. "Oppression" refers to substantive unconscionability and arises from overly burdensome or punitive terms of a contract, whereas "unfair surprise" refers to procedural unconscionability and is implicated in the formation of a contract, when one of the parties is either overborne by a lack of equal bargaining power or otherwise unfairly or unjustly drawn into a contract. Id. at Sections 9-37 and 9-38.

[¶21] It should be pointed that, although harsh, many characteristics of a finance lease are not inherently unconscionable and, as we have discussed, are specifically authorized by statute. Simply because a finance lease has a "hell or high water clause" does not make it unconscionable. As noted, a finance lease is a separate animal—it is supposed to secure minimal risk to the lessor. At least one court has rejected the argument that an acceleration clause in a commercial finance lease is punitive and unconscionable in the context of parties of relatively equal bargaining power. See Emlee Equip. Leasing Corp. v. Waterbury Transmission, Inc. (1993), 31 Conn. App. 455, 468, 626 A.2d 307.

[¶22] At the heart of Arora's defense in this case was his claim that he was misled into signing the finance lease by the CCC representative and was unfairly surprised to find himself the unwitting signatory of an oppressive lease. This is clearly an argument that implicated procedural unconscionability. His claim of being an unwitting signatory, however, must be carefully balanced against the law in Ohio that places upon a person a duty to read any contract before signing it, a duty that is not excused simply because a person willingly gives into the encouragement to "just go ahead and sign." See Whelan v. E.F. Hutton Credit Corp. (1983), 8th Dist. No. 46724, 1983 WL 2923.

[¶23] Moreover, we note that courts have also recognized that the lessor may give, through word or conduct, the lessee consent to cancel an otherwise noncancelable lease. [§2A-407(B)(2)] makes a finance lease "not subject to cancellation, termination, modification, repudiation, excuse, or substitution *without the consent of the party to whom it runs*." (Emphasis supplied.) As noted by the court in *Colonial Pacific Leasing,* supra, the UCC does not say anything with respect to the form or content of the consent. 977 P.2d at 548. The *Colonial Pacific* court concluded, therefore, "that the consent may be oral and may be established by conduct that reasonably manifests an intent. * * * Any manifestations that the obligation of the lessee will not be enforced independently of the obligation that runs to the consenting party is sufficient." Id. The question whether consent has been given to a cancellation is a question of fact for the trier of fact. Id.

[¶24] We raise this point because the evidence indicates that there was some communication between Arora and ILC before ILC retrieved the

ATM. It is unclear whether ILC removed the ATM at Arora's request, or whether the company was forcibly repossessing the equipment pursuant to the default provision of the lease. In view of the murkiness of the testimony, it is unclear when the ATM was taken back and when the final lease payment was made. One interesting question that arises from ILC's retrieval of the ATM, not addressed in the record, is what ILC did with the equipment afterward. Did ILC warehouse the equipment for the next four and one-half years (conduct that would appear unprofitable and therefore unlikely) or did the company then turn around and lease the ATM to someone else? If there was another lease, was ILC actually seeking a double recovery on the ATM's rental value? In this regard, we note that the trial court ruled that ILC had failed to mitigate its damages, a finding that is not supported by the current record, but may well prove to be true upon further trial of the matter.

[¶25] In sum, this is a case that requires a much more elaborate presentation of evidence by the parties, and much more detailed findings of fact and conclusions of law than those actually made by the trial court. We sustain ILC's assignment of error upon the basis that the trial court did not apply the correct legal analysis, and that the evidence of record did not mandate a judgment in Arora's favor. Because of the number of outstanding issues and unresolved factual questions, we reverse the trial court's judgment and remand this case for a new trial consistent with the law set forth in this opinion.

Judgment reversed and cause remanded.

G. *Warranties in International Sales*

The warranty provisions of the CISG for the international sale of goods are very similar to the UCC rules. The major difference is not one of substance, but one of terminology: the treaty drafters, wanting to write on a clean slate, eschewed use of the term *warranty* and all the historical baggage that comes with it. Read Articles 35 to 44 of the Convention, and see whether you can nevertheless find within them counterparts to the following:

(a) a warranty of title;
(b) express warranty liability; and
(c) implied warranties of merchantability and/or fitness for a particular purpose.

How are warranties disclaimed under the treaty? See Articles 6 and 35.

———————————

CHAPTER 4 REVIEW QUESTIONS

How does a seller's status as merchant affect warranties?
When are express and implied warranties created?
How can a seller disclaim implied warranties? Express warranties?
What is the difference between basis of the bargain and reliance?
What is the consequence of failing to give notice of breach of warranty?
How does the Magnuson-Moss Act affect warranty law?

ASSESSMENT: MULTIPLE CHOICE QUESTIONS

1. Barnet burglarized Alban's home and stole a painting, *Blue Memphis*. Finchley Gallery innocently bought the painting from Barnet and sold it to Totteridge. Alban managed to track the painting down and demanded it back. Is Alban entitled to the painting?
   a. No, because Totteridge bought the painting in good faith with no notice that it was stolen.
   b. No, because Alban and Totteridge had no contract with each other to rescind.
   c. Yes. The entrustment doctrine does not protect Totteridge, because Alban did not entrust the painting to Finchley Gallery.
   d. Yes. "Buyer Beware" governs sales law.

2. Is Totteridge entitled to recover from Finchley Gallery?
   a. No. Totteridge has not been harmed, because Totteridge is entitled to keep the painting.
   b. No. "Buyer Beware" governs sales law.
   c. Yes. Finchley Gallery breached the warranty of title.
   d. Yes. Finchley Gallery defrauded Totteridge.

3. Euston visited Pemulis Auto looking for a sports car. The sales person showed Euston a 2001 Hal Roadster, telling Euston that the Roadster had a top speed of 120 m.p.h. The manager, however, advised Euston that the car was not that speedy and that the sales person was misguided. Euston purchased the car, signing a contract with a merger clause and clause conspicuously stating that the car was sold "AS IS, with no warranties whatsoever." The car disappointed Euston, who found it was capable of 120 m.p.h. only when going steeply downhill. Was there a breach of warranty?
   a. No, due to the exclusion of warranties.
   b. No, because the top speed of the car was not an express warranty.
   c. No, because warranties must be in writing.
   d. Yes, because express warranties are not excluded by language to the contrary.

4. When Pemulis Auto decided to close one of its sales locations, it got a visit from the manager of a competitor, Stice Auto. The manager purchased Pemulis Auto's computer system. Within a week, the system burned up due to a faulty microchip. Did Pemulis Auto breach any warranty?
   a. Pemulis Auto breached the implied warranty of merchantability, because Pemulis Auto is a merchant and the computer system was defective.
   b. Pemulis Auto breached an express warranty, because the system had a latent defect.
   c. Pemulis Auto breached the warranty of fitness for a particular purpose, because Pemulis Auto knew that Stice Auto desired a functional computer system.
   d. Pemulis Auto did not breach any warranty.

5. Joelle's stay at the Ennet Hotel is marred by bedbugs. When the hotel refused to refund her payment, she sued for breach of the implied warranty of merchantability under §2-314. Will she succeed?
   a. Yes, because a hotel room with bed bugs is not merchantable.
   b. No. As long as someone could stay overnight in the room, it was merchantable.
   c. No, because there was no express warranty about bed bugs.
   d. No, because the Ennet Hotel did not make a warranty under §2-314.

ANSWERS

1. *C* is the best answer. The entrustment doctrine does not apply, because Alban did not entrust the painting to a merchant. Rather, Barnet stole the painting from Alban. So Barnet did not have title to the painting or the power to give title to Finchley Gallery. Likewise, when Finchley Gallery sold the painting, Totteridge received only Finchley Gallery's interest in the painting, which was nothing. *A* is wrong, because a good faith buyer does not take priority over the interest of the owner, unless something like the entrustment doctrine applies. *B* is wrong, because Alban is not trying to rescind a contract, Alban is simply seeking return of Alban's property.

2. *C* is the best answer. Although Totteridge must return the painting to Alban, Totteridge is entitled to recover from Finchley Gallery for breach of the warranty of title. Under §2-312, a seller warrants that the seller that rightful title will be conveyed. Finchley Gallery breached the warranty, because it did not have title to the goods or power to transfer title. Contrary to *B*, "Buyer Beware" no longer governs sales law. Rather, sellers make the warranties created by Article 2, unless excluded. Finchley Gallery did not intend to deceive, so it did not defraud Totteridge. But warranty is breached even if the seller does not know of the defect.

3. *B* is the best answer. The question illustrates the basic practical rule for express warranties: the only way to exclude an express warranty is not to make it. An exclusion of warranty will not exclude express warranties, because any inconsistent language is inoperative to exclude the express warranty. Nor need warranties be in writing, contrary to *C.* But here Pemulis Auto took steps to avoid any representation about the top speed of the car becoming an express warranty. An express warranty is an affirmation of fact that is part of the basis of the bargain of the parties. Pemulis Auto advised Euston that the car was not capable of 120 m.p.h. The contract also included a merger clause, indicating the oral statements were not part of the agreement.

4. *D* is the best answer. Pemulis Auto did not make an implied warranty of merchantability, because Pemulis Auto was not a merchant with respect to computer systems. Pemulis Auto did not make any express warranties, because it made no representations about the computer system. Pemulis Auto did not make a warranty of fitness for a particular purpose, because Stice Auto was not relying on Pemulis Auto's skill or judgment to select suitable goods.

5. *D* is the best answer. The question reminds us that UCC Article 2 applies only to sales of goods. This was a contract for services, lodging at a hotel. Article 2 does not apply, so §2-314 does not apply.

TERMS OF THE CONTRACT

Most law students do not come to the study of law with experience in dealing with commercial matters. This chapter will in part rectify that by exposing you to legal terminology used in trade and to practices that the Uniform Commercial Code deals with by specific rules. We begin with how the law fills in missing terms in contracts, then move on to the regulation of unfair bargaining practices, and finally to how the law determines which goods are meant for the contract at issue and how it distributes unexpected losses (such as destruction of the goods).

I. FILLING IN THE GAPS

In the nineteenth and early twentieth centuries, if the parties left a major term out of the contract, the courts typically found no legally enforceable agreement. Judges declared themselves powerless to "make a contract for the parties." As the twentieth century progressed, the courts became more willing to save the contract by implying reasonable terms where possible. The drafters of the Code fueled this practice by giving the courts statutory guidance in their gap-filling role. Glance through §§2-305 to 2-311.

PROBLEM 51

Edwin Drake wrote to the Watsons Flat Motor Oil Company and said that he wanted to buy 100 cases of its motor oil, some cases to be Type A (the expensive oil) and some to be Type B (a cheaper kind). He said he would let the company know later how much he wanted of each type. The company told him that Type B was selling for $30 a case, but that since the price of Type A was fluctuating, the sale price would have to be set by the company at the time of delivery. Drake agreed. The parties signed a written contract for the delivery of 100 cases, types to be specified by Drake one week prior to the delivery date, which was set for April 8. On April 1, the agent of the oil company called Drake to ask how much he would take of each type. Drake said, "April Fool! I'm not taking any," and hung up the phone. The company calls you, its attorney, for advice. In the past dealings that it has had with Drake, he always has ordered 100 cases and has taken 50 to 65 percent in Type A and the rest in Type B. The usual price for Type A has been $50 a case, but due to a Middle East oil situation, the price has now jumped to $125 a case. What should the company do? See §§2-305, 2-311, 1-205; Citgo Petroleum Corporation v. US Lubes, LLC, 2014 WL 3887773 (E.D. Pa. 2014). If this were an international sale of goods under the CISG, what result? See Article 65. What if Drake had simply said, "April Fool!" and hung up? Is this a definite repudiation? See §§2-610, 2-611. What action can the oil company take to clear up Drake's ambiguous statement? Read §2-609 and its Official Comment; see Pittsburgh-Des Moines Steel Co. v. Brookhaven Manor Water Co., 532 F.2d 572 (7th Cir. 1976). Would a seller have the right to adequate assurance of performance, if shortly before making the goods seller learned that buyer had a poor history of paying sellers? Starchem Laboratories, LLC v. Kabco Pharmaceuticals, Inc., 988 N.Y.S.2d 525 (2014).

Section 1-304 provides that every contract or duty within the Uniform Commercial Code "imposes an obligation of good faith in its performance and enforcement." Many of the UCC provisions specifically require good faith. Good faith is defined in §1-201(b)(20) to include a subjective component ("honesty in fact") and an objective component ("observance of reasonable commercial standards of fair dealing."). Courts often struggle to determine whether good faith limits a party's ability to enforce the literal terms of the contract and the relevant provisions of the UCC.

Casserlie v. Shell Oil Company

Supreme Court of Ohio, 2009, 121 Ohio St. 3d 25, 902 N.E.2d 1

MOYER, C.J.

I

Appellants' proposition of law proposes that "[t]he definition of Good Faith under the [Uniform Commercial Code] incorporating an 'honesty in fact' component requires a subjective inquiry." We disagree and affirm the judgment of the court of appeals.

II

Appellants, Donald Casserlie and others, are a group of independent Shell lessee-dealers in the greater Cleveland area (collectively, "the dealers"). The appellees in this case are Shell Oil Company, its partners, and its successors (collectively, "Shell"), who at various times between 1995 and the time the complaint was filed sold Shell-branded gasoline to the dealers in the greater Cleveland area. The dealers leased gas stations, including equipment and land, from Shell and operated them as franchisees. The parties' contracts obligated the dealers to buy gasoline only from Shell at a wholesale price set by Shell at the time of delivery. This type of term in a contract is known as an open-price term.

The price paid by the dealers is referred to as the dealer-tank-wagon ("DTW") price because it includes the cost of delivery to the stations. Shell charged the dealers a DTW price that was based on market factors including the prices offered by its major competitor, British Petroleum ("BP"), and the street price within areas of Cleveland. In each area of the city, called a price administration district ("PAD"), Shell charged all dealers the same DTW price.

In 1998, Shell, Texaco, and Saudi Aramco formed Equilon Enterprises L.L.C.; Shell's agreements with service stations in Cleveland were assigned to Equilon. In November 1999, Equilon and appellee Lyden Company entered into a joint venture called True North Energy, L.L.C. True North became the distributor of Shell-branded gasoline in the Cleveland area, including to the stations operated by the dealers. True North set the DTW price as the wholesale price it had paid Equilon for gasoline plus six or seven cents per gallon.

Shell also sold gasoline to "jobbers," which were independent companies operating non-Shell-owned gas stations. Jobbers purchased gasoline directly at the oil company's terminal and paid the "rack" price, which was the cost of purchasing gasoline at the oil company's terminal and thus did not include delivery costs.

In 1999, the dealers filed suit against Shell, alleging, among other claims, that Shell had engaged in bad faith when it set the DTW price. The dealers alleged that the rack price was often substantially lower than the DTW price. This allowed jobbers, including Lyden Company, to offer wholesale DTW prices that were substantially lower than the DTW price charged to the dealers. The dealers contend that this pricing is unreasonable and is part of a marketing plan proposed by Shell that was designed to drive them out of business. The dealers assert that Shell's goal was to eliminate them so that Shell could take over operation of the gas stations, thus profiting from all of the sales, including nonfuel sales, at the stations, and not just from wholesale gasoline sales to and rental income from the dealers.

The parties agreed to bifurcate the proceedings and move forward only on the bad-faith claim. On April 13, 2005, the trial court granted summary judgment for Shell. The court found that Shell did not violate R.C. 1302.18, which codifies Uniform Commercial Code ("UCC") section 2-305 and requires a price to be fixed in good faith, when it set the DTW price and that the dealers had not proven that the price had been set in a commercially unreasonable manner.

The dealers appealed, arguing that bad faith may be shown either by evidence of a party's intent, a subjective standard, or by evidence of its commercial unreasonableness, which is an objective standard. The court of appeals affirmed the trial court's ruling and adopted an objective standard based on Tom-Lin Ents. v. Sunoco, Inc. (R&M) (C.A.6, 2003), 349 F.3d 277. The court determined that the dealers failed to show that Shell's prices were not commercially reasonable. The cause is before this court upon our acceptance of a discretionary appeal.

III

As a preliminary matter, we review de novo the granting of summary judgment. Comer v. Risko, 106 Ohio St. 3d 185, 2005 Ohio 4559, 833 N.E.2d 712, ¶8.

The parties agree that Shell has authority pursuant to the dealer agreements to set the price of gasoline at the time of delivery. They agree that the price must be set subject to R.C. 1302.18, which requires the price to be "reasonable." R.C. 1302.18(A). Pursuant to R.C. 1302.18(B) (UCC section 2-305(2)), the price must be set "in good faith." "Good faith" is defined generally as "honesty in fact in the conduct or transaction concerned," R.C. 1301.01(S), but in the case of a merchant, "'good faith' . . . means honesty in fact and the observance of reasonable commercial standards of fair dealing in the trade." R.C. 1302.01(A)(2). It is undisputed that Shell is a "merchant," as defined in R.C. 1302.01(A)(5).

Shell argues that good faith requires an objective inquiry and is demonstrated when a seller's price is within the range of its competitors and the seller has not discriminated between similarly situated buyers. Shell also contends that "an inquiry into the seller's subjective intent is neither permitted nor required." The dealers argue that good faith requires a subjective inquiry and ask, "[H]ow can an open price, specifically calculated to drive a contractual partner out of business, be a 'good faith' price."

The trial court and court of appeals agreed with Shell, relying on *Tom-Lin Enters.*, 349 F.3d 277. In *Tom-Lin*, the court confronted an agreement nearly identical to the one between the dealers and Shell and concluded, applying Ohio law, that an inquiry into good faith required "an objective analysis of the merchant-seller's conduct." (Emphasis sic and footnote omitted.) Id. at 281-282. Thus, neither the trial court nor the court of appeals considered whether an examination into "good faith" required a subjective inquiry, and neither court engaged in a subjective inquiry.

It is not disputed that the latter half of the definition of good faith, "the observance of reasonable commercial standards of fair dealing in the trade," requires only an objective analysis. The issue before us is whether there is room for a subjective inquiry within the honesty-in-fact analysis in these circumstances.

The UCC does not define the term "honesty in fact." It should also be noted that "[c]ourts and commentators have recognized that the meaning of 'good faith' is not uniform throughout the [UCC]." Mathis v. Exxon Corp. (C.A. 5, 2002), 302 F.3d 448, 456. See also Martin Marietta Corp. v. New Jersey Nat'l Bank (C.A.3, 1979), 612 F.2d 745, 751 (noting that good faith is considered subjective in Article 1 but objective in Article 2). Thus, case law defining good faith in other areas of the UCC, such as the Article 1 covenant of good faith and fair dealing, is of somewhat limited value here. Non-UCC cases defining good faith are of even less relevance.

Official Comment 3 to UCC section 2-305 does provide some guidance. That comment provides, in full:

"[UCC section 2-305(2)], dealing with the situation where the price is to be fixed by one party rejects the uncommercial idea that an agreement that the seller may fix the price means that he may fix any price he may wish by the express qualification that the price so fixed must be fixed in good faith. Good faith includes observance of reasonable commercial standards of fair dealing in the trade if the party is a merchant. (Section 2-103 [R.C. 1302.01]). But in the normal case a 'posted price' or a future seller's or buyer's 'given price,' 'price in effect,' 'market price,' or the like satisfies the good faith requirement."

Comment 3 explains that the purpose of R.C. 1302.18(B) is to restrict the price a seller or buyer may set when the contract price has been left open, by requiring the price to be fixed in good faith. The second sentence of the comment does not remove honesty in fact from the definition of good faith in this context, because it uses the nonexclusive term "includes." The last sentence, however, is not limited to part of the good-faith definition but rather provides a safe harbor where a "posted price" satisfies good faith in its entirety.

A number of cases from other jurisdictions considering open price terms have relied on the posted-price comment. This court has noted in the past that "it is desirable to conform our interpretations of the Uniform Commercial Code to those of our sister states." Edward A. Kemmler Mem. Found. v. 691/733 E. Dublin-Granville Rd. Co. (1992), 62 Ohio St. 3d 494, 499, 584 N.E.2d 695. Relying on the Official Comments to the UCC helps to achieve this uniformity, as does reviewing case law that has previously interpreted particular provisions.

The Supreme Court of Texas addressed the very issue before us here in an essentially identical fact pattern in Shell Oil Co. v. HRN, Inc. (Tex. 2004), 144 S.W.3d 429. Independent gasoline dealers brought suit against Shell, alleging that the prices were not set in good faith under UCC section 2-305(2) because Shell had set the prices intending to put them out of business. 144 S.W.3d 429, 431-432. The court held that Shell did not violate its duty of good faith, because the posted price was both commercially reasonable and nondiscriminatory. Id. at 435-436. It noted that "'[i]t is abundantly clear . . . that the chief concern of the UCC Drafting Committee in adopting § 2-305(2) was to prevent discriminatory pricing.'" Id. at 434, quoting *Wayman*, 923 F. Supp. at 1346-1347. A subjective good-faith inquiry "injects uncertainty into the law of contracts and undermines one of the UCC's primary goals—to 'promot[e] certainty and predictability in commercial transactions.'" Id. at 435, quoting Am. Airlines Emps. Fed. Credit Union v. Martin (Tex. 2000), 29 S.W.3d 86, 92, quoting Putnam Rolling Ladder Co., Inc. v. Mfrs. Hanover Trust Co. (1989), 74 N.Y.2d 340, 349, 547 N.Y.S.2d 611, 546 N.E.2d 904. The drafters of the UCC, therefore, incorporated the posted-price safe harbor to prevent extensive litigation involving any open-price term, "while seeking 'to avoid discriminatory prices.'" Id., quoting Malcolm, The Proposed Commercial Code: A Report on Developments from May 1950 Through February 1951 (1951), 6 Bus. Law. 113, 186. The court concluded that subjective intent was not intended to stand alone as a basis for liability: "[A]llegations of dishonesty under this section must also have some basis in objective fact which at a minimum requires some connection to the commercial realities of the case." Id. at 435-436.

A few cases note the posted-price comment but conclude that it does not provide a safe harbor where there is subjective bad faith. See Marcoux v. Shell Oil Prods. Co. L.L.C. (C.A.1, 2008), 524 F.3d 33, 50; *Mathis*, 302 F.3d at 455-456; Bob's Shell, Inc. v. O'Connell Oil Assoc., Inc. (Aug. 31, 2005), D. Mass. No. 03-30169, 2005 U.S. Dist. LEXIS 21318, 2005 WL 2365324; see also Allapattah Servs., Inc. v. Exxon Corp. (S.D. Fla. 1999), 61 F. Supp. 2d

1308, 1322 (finding that when the seller double charged for credit-card processing, the action was not a "normal case," because the dispute was not over the actual price charged but over the manner in which the price was calculated; thus, the safe-harbor provision did not apply). Those cases contend that the comment is limited to the "normal case," which does not include a situation where the seller is purposefully trying to drive the buyer out of business.

This interpretation would eviscerate the safe harbor in any action in which the plaintiff alleges circumstantial evidence of an improper motive, leading to drawn-out litigation "even if the prices ultimately charged were undisputedly within the range of those charged throughout the industry." *HRN*, 144 S.W.3d at 435. See Berry, Byers, & Oates, Open Price Agreements: Good Faith Pricing in the Franchise Relationship (2007), 27 Franchise L.J. 45, 49. If a subjective inquiry could determine bad faith, a seller charging a fair price, even exactly the same price as another, good-faith seller, could be deemed to be acting in bad faith. . . .

All of this is not to say that intent is necessarily irrelevant to an analysis of good faith under UCC section 2-305(2), but only that a subjective inquiry is not permitted when the posted-price safe harbor applies. By its language, the safe harbor does not apply when it is not the "normal case" or when the price setter is not imposing a "posted price," "given price," "price in effect," "market price," or the like. As long as a price is commercially reasonable, it qualifies as the "normal case." The touchstone of prices set through open-price term contracts under UCC section 2-305 is reasonableness. A price that is nondiscriminatory among similarly situated buyers correspondingly qualifies as a "posted price" or the like. A discriminatory price could not be considered a "posted" or "market" price, because, in effect, the seller is not being "honest in fact" about the price that it is charging as a posted price, since it is charging a different price to other buyers.

Therefore, a price that is both commercially reasonable and nondiscriminatory fits within the limits of the safe harbor and complies with the statute's good-faith requirement. Given our conclusion below that the safe harbor applies to the facts of this case, we are not required to precisely define good faith as it is used in section 2-305(2). We offer no opinion, in particular, on the role of subjective intent within the good-faith analysis beyond the safe harbor.

IV

The facts of this case demonstrate that the prices set by Shell were both commercially reasonable and nondiscriminatory. Aside from claiming that Shell's goal in setting prices was to drive the dealers out of business, the only evidence of bad faith was that the prices set were too high for dealers to remain profitable and compete with jobbers in the Cleveland area. However,

Shell is not required to sell gasoline at a price that is profitable for buyers. "A good-faith price under section [2-305] is not synonymous with a fair market price or the lowest price available." HRN, 144 S.W.3d at 437. As noted by the court of appeals: "The trial court . . . found that Shell submitted expert testimony which established that the DTW prices set by the company were within the range set by its competitors." Casserlie v. Shell Oil Co., 2007 Ohio 2633, at P 31. The dealers failed to rebut this evidence. Id.

The dealers also point out that Shell's prices varied throughout the area because of PAD pricing. But the fact that Shell's DTW prices varied by PADs does not itself demonstrate unreasonable or discriminatory pricing. It is reasonable for Shell to adjust according to competition, and there is no evidence that Shell discriminated among similarly situated buyers, such as dealers within a given PAD or dealers in similar PADs.

Finally, the only other argument of discrimination put forth by the dealers is that jobbers were charged significantly less, specifically, the rack price rather than the DTW price. Jobbers and dealers are not, however, similarly situated buyers. The price difference is partially explained by the fact that the DTW price includes a delivery charge, while the rack price does not. We further find the Sixth Circuit Court of Appeals analysis comparing jobbers and dealers in *Tom-Lin* instructive, just as the lower courts did. See *Tom-Lin Ents.*, 349 F.3d at 285-286. *Tom-Lin* noted that jobbers perform additional functions compared to dealers, such as maintaining the properties they own and bearing the risk of environmental liability. Id. at 285. Because jobbers relieve Shell of these obligations, they are charged a lower price. The dealers have not challenged these differences. The disparate pricing between jobbers and dealers is not evidence of discrimination.

V

When a price that has been left open in a contract is fixed at a price posted by a seller or buyer, and the posted price is both commercially reasonable and nondiscriminatory, the price setter has acted in good faith as required by R.C. 1302.18(B), and a subjective inquiry into the motives of the price setter is not permitted. In this case, the dealers have not provided any evidence that the prices set by Shell were commercially unreasonable or discriminatory. The posted-price safe harbor therefore applies, and we affirm the judgment of the court of appeals.

Judgment affirmed.

[A dissenting judge argued that good faith for open-price terms should, as in other contexts, have both subjective and objective components. The Official Comment, in the dissent's view, should not be given such authority, because it was not enacted as law by the Ohio legislature.]

II. *UNCONSCIONABILITY*

The opposite of the incomplete contract is the one that contains too much. In the name of *freedom of contract, caveat emptor,* and the *duty to read,* courts have permitted some rapacious merchants to insulate themselves in legally formidable contracts that have bordered on fraud and were filled with "I win — you lose" provisions. Early attacks on these *adhesion contracts* (so called because the lesser party had to adhere to the will of the stronger) were made in well-known articles like Friedrich Kessler's famous article: Contracts of Adhesion — Some Thoughts About Freedom of Contract, 43 Colum. L. Rev. 629 (1943). Later, the chief reporter for the UCC, Karl Llewellyn, proposed this famous "true answer" to the problem:

> The answer, I suggest, is this: Instead of thinking about "assent" to boiler-plate clauses, we can recognize that so far as concerns the specific, there is no assent at all. What has in fact been assented to, specifically, are the few dickered terms, and the broad type of the transaction, and but one thing more. That one thing more is a blanket assent (not a specific assent) to any not unreasonable or indecent terms the seller may have on his form, which do not alter or eviscerate the reasonable meaning of the dickered terms. The fine print which has not been read has no business to cut under the reasonable meaning of those dickered terms which constitute the dominant and only real expression of agreement, but much of it commonly belongs in.

K. Llewellyn, The Common Law Tradition: Deciding Appeals 370 (1960).

The UCC tackled the problem in §2-302. This provision caused whole forests to be stripped to supply the paper for scholarly analysis on a grand scale. The redoubtable Professor Arthur Leff set the tone in a celebrated article attacking §2-302 and its unconscionability principle as "an emotionally satisfying incantation" having "no reality referent"; see Leff, Unconscionability and the Code — The Emperor's New Clause, 115 U. Pa. L. Rev. 485 (1967). Professor Leff's chief contribution to the analysis of §2-302 was his division of "unconscionability" into two types: unfair conduct in the formation of the contract (called *procedural unconscionability*), and unfairness in the terms of the resulting bargain (called *substantive unconscionability*). It was Leff's idea that both are required before a court can make a finding of §2-302 unconscionability.

Read §2-302 and its Official Comment, and then answer the following questions.

QUESTIONS

1. Is *unconscionability* defined in the Code? If asked, how would you define the meaning to a judge? Are the example cases in the Official Comment helpful?

2. Is the unconscionability issue one for the judge or the jury? What is the policy reason for the Code drafters' decision on this matter?

3. Is the §2-302(2) hearing mandatory as a technical step prior to a finding of unconscionability? See Haugen v. Ford Motor Co., 219 N.W.2d 462 (N.D. 1974), holding that the hearing *is* mandatory and that summary judgment is inappropriate without such a hearing.

4. Would the answers to these questions change if this were a lease of goods to a consumer? See §2A-108.

Sacramento E.D.M., Inc. v. Hynes Aviation Industries

United States District Court, Eastern District of California, 2017, WL 1383289

KENDALL J. NEWMAN, United States Magistrate Judge.

Order

. . . In addition to concluding that Hynes both breached his fiduciary duty of loyalty and committed constructive fraud with regard to his misrepresentations concerning the interest and duration terms of the equipment leases, the court also concludes that those terms are unconscionable as a matter of law at the time they were made. See Langemeier v. Nat'l Oats Co., 775 F.2d 975, 977 (8th Cir. 1985) (holding that U.C.C. §2-302, which Missouri has adopted verbatim via Missouri Revised Statute §400.2-302, permits a court to raise the issue of unconscionability of a contract *sua sponte*).

Under applicable Missouri law, a contract's term may be deemed invalid when there is both procedural and substantive unconscionability. Funding Sys. Leasing Corp. v. King Louie Int'l, Inc., 597 S.W.2d 624, 634-35 (Mo. App. 1979). Procedural unconscionability arises during the contracting process when there is fine print in the contract, there has been some misrepresentation, or there is unequal bargaining power. World Enterprises, Inc. v. Midcoast Aviation Servs., Inc., 713 S.W.2d 606 (Mo. App. 1986). Substantive unconscionability, on the other hand, occurs when the contractual terms are unduly harsh. Id.; Lyster v. Ryan's Family Steak Houses, Inc., 239 F.3d 943 (8th Cir. 2001). Provisions that an objective reasonable person would find unexpected and unconscionably unfair are unenforceable. Hartland Computer Leasing Corp., Inc. v. Insurance Man, Inc., 770 S.W.2d 525, 527-28 (Mo. App. 1989). Procedural and substantive unconscionability are considered on a sliding scale, so that when more substantive unconscionability is present less procedural unconscionability is necessary to invalidate a contract and vice versa. *Funding Sys. Leasing Corp.*, 597 S.W.2d at 634-45.

Here, procedural unconscionability arose when Hynes misrepresented the lease contracts' terms regarding the rate of interest being charged and the lease period. Furthermore, the leases' terms with regard to interest and duration are also substantively unconscionable as they are unduly harsh. As discussed above, the 30 percent interest added on to each month's payment is usurious under the applicable Missouri law, which allows for only 10 percent interest under the circumstances. Similarly, the actual duration of each lease is nearly twice as long as Hynes represented they would be, and would result in Sac EDM paying more than double what defendants paid for each piece of equipment, including the equipment that Sac EDM had owned outright prior to the sale, before it could finally buyout that equipment and conclude the lease term if it were to follow the payment schedule contemplated in the terms of each lease agreement. Such a lease term was both contrary to the parties' intentions and goals set forth in their business plan, which was to obtain more favorable lease terms for Sac EDM, and was structured in such a fashion as to clearly benefit defendants to the long-term detriment of Sac EDM. Finally, Sac EDM could apply only 50 percent of its lease payments towards its purchase of the equipment, a substantial portion of which was equipment that it had previously owned outright. This fact not only substantially increased the overall duration of each lease, but also ensured that Sac EDM would have paid more than double defendants' purchase cost for that equipment by the time it could exercise its purchase option. Such a term is entirely contrary to the provisions of the parties' agreement and business plan regarding the operation of the OK EDM joint venture that stated that defendants were to obtain more favorable purchase options with regard to any equipment Sac EDM leased. Accordingly, the court concludes that the interest, duration, and purchase terms of the leases are unconscionable.

[The court ordered that Sac EDM recover interest payments made beyond the rate of 10 percent interest.]

Green Tree Servicing, LLC v. Duncan

Navajo Nation Supreme Court, 2008, 7 Am. Tribal Law 633, 2008 WL 5435566

Judges: Before YAZZIE, Chief Justice, and FERGUSON and BLACK, Associate Justices.

. . . The final issue is whether the arbitration clause in the contract bars Duncan's claims. The lengthy arbitration clause in the contract states "[a]ll claims and controversies arising from or relating to this [c]ontract . . . shall be resolved by binding arbitration by one arbitrator selected by Assignee

[Green Tree] with consent of the Buyer(s) [Duncan]." It further states that "[t]he parties agree and understand that they choose arbitration instead of litigation to resolve disputes." In all capital letters, it further states that "THE PARTIES VOLUNTARILY AND KNOWINGLY WAIVE ANY RIGHT THEY HAVE TO A JURY TRIAL EITHER PURSUANT TO ARBITRATION UNDER THIS CLAUSE OR PURSUANT TO A COURT ACTION BY ASSIGNEE (AS PROVIDED HEREIN)." The court action referenced at the end of the last sentence is authorized later in the clause, stating that "Assignee [Green Tree] retains an option to use judicial or non-judicial relief to enforce a security agreement relating to the [mobile home] secured by a transaction underlying this arbitration agreement, to enforce the monetary obligation to be secured by the [mobile home] or to foreclose on the [mobile home]." In other words, Duncan agreed to waive her right to file any court action and to instead arbitrate any dispute with Green Tree, and waived her right to a jury completely, but agreed to allow Green Tree to file a court action to repossess the mobile home.

The question is whether such an agreement is enforceable under Navajo law. Green Tree submits that under Navajo law words are sacred. This Court has upheld contracts if the language is clear and the parties voluntarily entered into the agreement. See, e.g., Smith v. Navajo Nation Dept. of Headstart, No. SC-CV-50-04, slip op. at 4-6, 2005 Navajo Sup. LEXIS 8 (Nav. Sup. Ct. September 21, 2005). However, despite the clarity of language, the Court has also stricken agreements if they violate Navajo public policy expressed in our statutory law or in *Diné bi beenahaz'áanii*. See Allstate Indemnity Co. v. Blackgoat, No. SC-CV-15-01, slip op. at 8, 2005 Navajo Sup. LEXIS 5 (Nav. Sup. Ct. May 20, 2005) (striking liability cap in insurance contract for purposes of prejudgment interest as violative of Navajo principle of *nályééh*); see also *Smith*, No. SC-CV-50-04, 2005 Navajo Sup. LEXIS 8, slip op. at 5 (stating test).

To discern Navajo public policy, the Court turns first to several provisions of the Navajo Nation Code. One important principle is that contracts are not enforceable if they are "unconscionable." The clearest articulation of this principle is in Section 2-302(A) of the Navajo Uniform Commercial Code. That provision states that if a court determines whether a contract, or any part of it, is "unconscionable," it is empowered (1) to refuse enforcement of the entire contract, (2) to enforce the remainder of the contract without the unconscionable clause or clauses, or (3) limit the application of any clause to avoid an unjust result. Id. The basic test is whether, "in the light of the general commercial background and the commercial needs of the particular trade or case, the clauses involved are so one-sided as to be unconscionable under the circumstances existing at the time of the making of the contract." Official Comment, 5A N.N.C. §2-302 (2005). The concept of unconscionability "recognizes that in some cases the lack of bargaining power of one party compared to that of the other party will result in an oppressive contract." Special Plain Language Comment, 5A N.N.C. §2-302 (2005). Similarly, the Navajo Nation Unfair Consumer Practices Act discusses the concept of "unconscionable trade practice," which also considers the difference in understanding and bargaining power, and prohibits acts that result in unfair transactions. See 5 N.N.C. §1103(E) (2005).

The Navajo Nation Code also includes provisions encouraging arbitration. The recently enacted Navajo Nation Arbitration Act authorizes the use of arbitration clauses, but lacks a definition of "arbitration." See 7 N.N.C. §§1001, et seq. Black's Law Dictionary defines "Arbitration" as, "a method of dispute resolution involving one or more neutral third parties and whose decision is binding." Black's Law Dictionary, Seventh Edition, at 100 (1999). The Arbitration Act's provisions are consistent with this general concept, and through the Act the Council appears to encourage the use of non-judicial dispute resolution as a matter of contract.[1] However, the Act does not recognize all arbitration agreements, as it states that "[a] written agreement to submit any existing or future controversy to arbitration is valid, enforceable and irrevocable, save upon such grounds as exist at law or in equity for the revocation of the contract." 7 N.N.C. §1103 (2005) (emphasis added). The Act then balances the value of arbitration agreements with the value of fairness, and states that not all agreements to arbitrate are enforceable in the Navajo Nation.

There are also Fundamental Law principles that inform Navajo public policy on arbitration agreements in mobile home contracts. The Navajo maxim of *házhó'ógó* mandates "more than the mere provision of an English form stating certain rights . . . and requires a patient, respectful discussion ... before a waiver is effective." Eriacho v. Ramah District Court, No. SC-CV-61-04, slip op. at 7, 2005 Navajo Sup. LEXIS 1 (Nav. Sup. Ct. January 5, 2005). *Házhó'ógó* requires a meaningful notice and explanation of a right before a waiver of that right is effective. Id. *Házhó'ógó* is not man-made law, but rather a fundamental tenet informing us how we must approach each other as individuals. Navajo Nation v. Rodriguez, No. SC-CR-03-04, slip op. at 10, 2004 Navajo Sup. LEXIS 13 (Nav. Sup. Ct. December 16, 2004). It is "an underlying principle in everyday dealings with relatives and other individuals." Id. Though primarily discussed previously in the criminal context, *házhó'ógó* equally applies in civil situations. See Kesoli v. Anderson Security Agency, No. SC-CV-01-05, slip op. at 6, 2005 Navajo Sup. LEXIS 4 (Nav. Sup. Ct. October 12, 2005).

Several other principles are relevant. In a recent case, the Court discussed the Navajo concept of *nábináheezlágo be t'áá lahjį algha' deet'ą,*

---

1. Of course, Peacemaking is another type of non-judicial dispute resolution. However, Peacemaking, unlike arbitration, is based on Navajo principles of non-adversarial decision making that emphasize bringing the parties back into harmony.

which is, finality is established when all participants agree that all of the concerns or issues have been comprehensively resolved in the agreement. Casaus v. Dine College, No. SC-CV-48-05, slip op. at 7, 2007 Navajo Sup. LEXIS 18 (Nav. Sup. Ct. March 8, 2007). It is also said that in the process of "talking things out," or meeting the Navajo common law procedural requirement that everything must be talked over, see Navajo Nation v. Crockett, 7 Nav. R. 237, 241, 1996 Navajo Sup. LEXIS 14 (Nav. Sup. Ct. 1996), there is a requirement of *íishjání ádooniíl*, that is, making something clear or obvious. See Phillips v. Navajo Housing Authority, No. SC-CV-13-05, slip op. at 7, 2005 Navajo Sup. LEXIS 15 (Nav. Sup. Ct. December 8, 2005) (applying Navajo concept of iishjani & Iowa to require clear intent to retroactively grant sovereign immunity to Navajo Housing Authority); Yazzie v. Thompson, No. SC-CV-69-04, slip op. at 4, 2005 Navajo Sup. LEXIS 7 (Nav. Sup. Ct. July 21, 2005) (same for Court rules on fees in domestic violence cases); Rough Rock Community School v. Navajo Nation, 7 Nav. R. 168, 174, 1995 Navajo Sup. LEXIS 4 (Nav. Sup. Ct. 1995) (same for qualifications of school board candidates). Navajo decision-making is practical and pragmatic, and the result of "talking things out" is a clear plan. Rough Rock Community School v. Navajo Nation, 7 Nav. R. 168, 174, 1995 Navajo Sup. LEXIS 4 (Nav. Sup. Ct. 1995). When faced with important matters, it is inappropriate to rush to conclusion or to push a decision without explanation and consideration to those involved. *Áádóó na'nile'dii éi dooda*, that is, delicate matters and things of importance must not be approached recklessly, carelessly, or with indifference to consequences. *Rodriguez*, No. SC-CR-03-04, 2004 Navajo Sup. LEXIS 13, slip op. at 10. This is *házhó'ógó*. Id. If things are not done *házhó'ógó*, it is said that it is done *t'aa bizaka*.

An arbitration clause must be set in the manner of *házhó'ogó* (standard of care), so as to make a clause *íishjání ádooniíl* (clear and obvious), therefore it will not be made *t'aa na'nile'dii* (not recklessly, carelessly or with indifference to consequences) resulting in making the arbitration clause *nábináheezlágo be t'áá lahjį algha' deet'ą* (comprehensive agreement). This was shown in *Eriacho*, wherein the Navajo Nation argued that the explanation of right to a jury trial was not necessary due to Ms. Eriacho's apparent education level. See No. SC-CV-61-04, 2005 Navajo Sup. LEXIS 1, slip op. at 7 n. 2. In response, this Court rejected "any rule that conditions the respectful explanation of rights under Navajo due process on subjective assumption concerning the defendant. This right exists for all defendants in our system." Id.

Finally, these principles must be applied in the context of the importance of a home in Navajo thought. This Court has noted that a home is not just a dwelling, but a place at the center of Navajo life. Fort Defiance Housing Corp. v. Lowe, No. SC-CV-32-03, slip op. at 4, 2004 Navajo Sup. LEXIS 11 (Nav. Sup. Ct. April 12, 2004). Based on this principle, the Court scrutinizes procedures to make sure they protect a home owner's ability to maintain a healthy home and family. See id.; *Phillips*, No. SC-CV-13-05, 2005 Navajo Sup. LEXIS 15, slip op. at 7.

Considering all of these principles together, the Court holds that the specific arbitration clause in the financing contract is unenforceable. Though arbitration generally is encouraged, clauses that mandate arbitration are not immune from scrutiny for unconscionability or consistency with Fundamental Law. This case ultimately concerns the repossession of a mobile home, and the ability to keep the home may depend on the availability of a home owner's counterclaims against a finance company seeking to take the home. The requirement that Duncan engage in arbitration instead of filing counterclaims in an action brought by Green Tree in a Navajo district court greatly burdens her ability to defend herself. She must figure out the arbitration process, spend potentially significant amounts of money and travel off the Nation to participate. Importantly, Green Tree is under no similar obligation; under the agreement it may file a Navajo court action to assert its rights, and is protected from defending counterclaims. The burden is then only one way. The effect of this grossly unequal position is not clearly explained in the clause. An arbitration clause in a mobile home finance contract cannot be enforced if the contract does not contain clear and specific language explaining that the Navajo consumer understands that he or she is surrendering his or her rights to bring claims in a Navajo court, but nonetheless is allowing claims against him or her to compel surrender of the home.

Let the parties be clear on the effect of this holding. The Court does not say that all arbitration clauses are unenforceable. Arbitration serves important purposes, and is one of the possible methods of dispute resolution approved by the Navajo Nation Council. The holding of this case only applies to the specific clause under the circumstances of this case.

VIII

Based on the above, the Court VACATES the District Court's dismissal of Duncan's counterclaims. The case is REMANDED for further proceedings consistent with this opinion.

––––––––––––––––

In a major book entitled Boilerplate: The Fine Print, Vanishing Rights, and the Rule of Law (2012), Professor Margaret Jane Radin discusses boilerplate from many angles. She begins by comparing two worlds: "World A," where parties actually negotiate the terms of their contract, and "World B," where one party dictates all the terms and refuses to negotiate at all. In World

B she states that the so-called contracts are in reality "contracts *not* to contract." Rather, the contracts are dictated by the superior party and filled with what she calls "boilerplate rights deletion schemes." Professor Radin has a raft of solutions: legislative action to forbid such clauses, private rating systems of contracts according to how odious they are, etc., but when it comes to judicial treatment of offending boilerplate she urges the courts to look beyond existing doctrines like unconscionability and treat the use of harmful boilerplate as an intentional tort resulting in both punitive damages and attorney fees.

PROBLEM 52

Professor Chalk went into the Swank Boating Company and inquired about the possibility of buying a sailboat. He told the salesman that he knew nothing about sailboats, but had always wanted to get into sailing. The salesman showed him a boat, a handsome catamaran, costing $3,150. Chalk, delighted, signed a contract. On his way home from the store, he passed another boat showplace and saw the same type of sailboat advertised at a price of $1,000. Subsequent investigation proved that the highest price any other store was asking for the boat was $1,200. Chalk, who had done no comparison shopping, had not known this. Does §2-302 permit Chalk to avoid the sale? See Morris v. Capitol Furniture & Appliance Co., 280 A.2d 775 (D.C. 1971); Jones v. Star Credit Corp., 59 Misc. 2d 189, 298 N.Y.S.2d 264 (Sup. Ct. 1969); Annot., 38 A.L.R.4th 25. For a historical viewpoint, see Hamilton, The Ancient Maxim *Caveat Emptor*, 40 Yale L.J. 1133 (1931). See also Ellinghaus, In Defense of Unconscionability, 78 Yale L.J. 757 (1969).

III. IDENTIFICATION OF THE GOODS

The Code's provisions on risk of loss, casualty to goods, damages, and other matters frequently draw distinctions based on whether the goods have been *identified* as the specific goods to which the contract refers. Read §2-501, and note the general policy favoring early identification found in Official Comment 2.

PROBLEM 53

Decide if *identification* per §2-501 has occurred in the following situations.

(a) Seller, a fisherman, contracts to sell his entire catch for the coming season. Does identification occur on the making of the contract, on the catching of the fish, or on their packaging with a label indicating they belong to this particular buyer? See Official Comment 6.

(b) Three Ring Circus contracted to sell the unborn calf of the circus's elephant Nancy as soon as the calf was born; the contract was made when Nancy was two months pregnant. Does the identification occur on the date of contracting, on the calf's birth, or when the calf is marked for shipment?

(c) Farmer Carl agreed to sell to Breakfast Cereals, Inc. one-half of the grain he had stored in Rural Silo, where Farmer Carl's grain was mixed with that of other farmers. Does identification occur on contracting or on segregation of the grain? Read Official Comment 5. See §§2-105(3), 2-105(4).

(d) Wonder Widgets contracted to sell 5,000 widgets to a buyer. Its warehouse contained 2 million widgets, all alike. Does identification occur on contracting or when the goods are picked out and marked as pertaining to this contract?

(e) Laputa agreed to sell its wrecked helicopter to Sheeta, and agreed to repair it extensively before delivery. After Sheeta paid the contract price but before Laputa did any repairs, Laputa filed bankruptcy. When would the helicopter be identified to the contract: at the time of contracting (meaning title would pass to Sheeta) or not until the helicopter was repaired (meaning that it would stay in the bankruptcy estate)? See In re Phoenix Heliparts Inc., 2018 WL 2107796 (B.A.P. 9th Cir. 2018).

IV.   RISK OF LOSS: NO BREACH

A.   General Rules

Under the old Uniform Sales Act, risk of loss stayed with the person having technical title to the goods and passed to the buyer only when *title* to the goods switched to the buyer. The UCC expressly states that its rules as to who bears the risk of loss have nothing to do with who has technical title (§2-401(1)). This astounded Samuel Williston, the original drafter of the Uniform Sales Act, who called this abandonment of title the "most iconoclastic" idea in the Code; in a famous and rather sad article, he vainly argued against the adoption of the UCC. See Williston, The Law of Sales in the Proposed Uniform Commercial Code, 63 Harv. L. Rev. 561 (1950). Compare Corbin, The Uniform Commercial Code — Sales; Should It Be Enacted?, 59 Yale L.J. 821 (1950), in which Professor Arthur Corbin announced his enthusiastic indorsement of the Code. The general Code rule on the transfer of the risk of loss is that, absent contrary agreement, (1) where the seller is a *merchant*, the risk of loss passes to the buyer on the buyer's actual *receipt* of the goods; and (2) where the seller is not a merchant, risk of loss passes to the buyer when the seller tenders delivery. See §2-509(3).

PROBLEM 54

William College bought a car from Honest John, the friendly car dealer. He paid the price in full, and Honest John promised delivery on the next Monday. On Monday the car was ready, and Honest John phoned College and said, "Take it away." College said he was busy and that he would pick it up the next day, to which Honest John agreed. That night the car was stolen from the lot due to no fault of Honest John, who had taken reasonable precautions against such a thing. Who had the risk of loss? See §2-509(3) and Official Comment 3. Ramos v. Wheel Sports Center, 96 Misc. 2d 646, 409 N.Y.S.2d 505 (Civ. Ct. 1978). Might Honest John claim he was a *bailee* so that §2-509(2) applies? See White & Summers §6-3; Galbraith v. American Motor Home Corp., 14 Wash. App. 754, 545 P.2d 561 (1976).

PROBLEM 55

Janice Junk decided to hold a garage sale to clean up her home and get some extra cash. In the course of the sale, which was a huge success, her neighbor, Barbara Bargain, offered Junk $200 for her piano, and the two women shook hands. Junk said to Bargain, "Take it away. It's yours." Bargain replied that she would come to get it the next day with four strong friends and a truck. That night Junk's home burned to the ground, and the piano was destroyed. Did the risk of loss pass from Junk to Bargain? See §2-503. If Bargain never picked up the piano and if it was destroyed in a fire *six months* after the sale, what result? See §2-709(1)(a).

Section 2-509(3) applies only when §2-509(1) or §2-509(2) does not.

In many contracts where the goods are in an independent warehouse, the seller must arrange for the warehouse company (bailee) to change its records to show the buyer as the new owner. Subsection (2) of §2-509 sets out the rules as to when the risk of loss passes to the buyer in such a situation. In essence, the risk of loss rests on whoever has control over the bailee. Read §2-509(2).

Since understanding Subsection (2) of §2-509 depends in large part on understanding the nature of warehouse receipts and delivery orders, both negotiable and nonnegotiable, risk of loss under §2-509(2) will be covered in greater depth later in the book, in the Article 7 chapter.

In some contracts, the seller is required to ship the goods by independent carrier to the buyer. Such transportation contracts are governed by §2-509(1). Read that section. Note that in transportation contracts the test as to when the risk passes depends on whether the contract requires the seller to "deliver [the goods] at a particular destination." How do you know whether the contract requires the seller to deliver the goods to the buyer or merely to see that they are delivered to the carrier? The next section deals with that issue.

B. Delivery Terms

In sales contracts, the parties often agree that the seller need only get the goods to the carrier and then the buyer will take the risk of loss. This type of contract is called a *shipment contract*. On the other hand, the parties may agree that the goods must be delivered by the carrier before the risk passes from seller to buyer. Such a contract is called a *destination contract*. According to Official Comment 5 to §2-503, the presumption made by Article 2 is in favor of a shipment contract. Read that Comment. Where the contract is silent on risk of loss, the courts have enforced this presumption that a shipment contract was intended; Deiter v. Coons, 162 Idaho 44, 394 P.3d 87 (2017). Through the years, merchants have developed a set of *delivery terms* like F.O.B. (free on board), F.A.S. (free alongside), C.I.F. (cost, insurance, freight), C. & F. (cost and freight), and ex-ship (off the ship), which are shorthand methods of stating whether the sale calls for a shipment or a destination contract. These terms (and similar ones) are defined and their legal implications stated clearly in §§2-319 through 2-324. Not only are these terms *delivery* terms, defining the passage of the risk of loss, but also they are *price* terms that inform the buyer that the price quoted includes freight paid to the point indicated. Thus, if the seller is in New York and the buyer is in Chicago, a *$2,000 F.O.B. New York* term means that the risk of loss passes on delivery to the carrier and that the price quoted includes only delivery to the carrier (the buyer must pay the freight charges to get the goods to Chicago). Remember:

(1) C.I.F. and C. & F. always indicate a *shipment* contract. C.I.F. means that the price stated includes the *cost* of the item, the *insurance* premium, and the *freight* charge. The law merchant concluded the C.I.F. was obviously a shipment contract (where the buyer takes the risk of loss during shipment) because the buyer agreed to pay insurance as part of the price. If the buyer did not have the risk of loss, why would insurance be needed?

C. & F. is the same as C.I.F. without the buyer's agreeing to pay the insurance. One might think therefore that C. & F. would indicate a destination contract. It does not for two reasons. First, the buyer frequently asks for a C. & F. price because a blanket insurance policy already covers goods the buyer owns. Second, the law merchant regarded C. & F. as a shipment term, and businesses have arranged their affairs accordingly ever since. Read §2-320.

(2) F.A.S. and ex-ship are delivery terms used in connection with ships. Read §§2-319(2) and 2-322, and use them in answering Problem 56.

(3) F.O.B. can indicate *either* a shipment or a destination contract. In a contract it is always followed by a named place (like F.O.B. Pittsburgh). The risk of loss passes *at the named place.* Thus, if the named place is the seller's warehouse, the F.O.B. term calls for a shipment contract; if it is the buyer's store, a destination contract results. Read §2-319.

PROBLEM 56

Seller in New York City contracted to sell 80 boxes of clothing to buyer in Savannah, Georgia. The delivery term was "$1,800 F.A.S. S.S. Seaworthy, N.Y.C." Seller delivered the 80 boxes to the dock alongside the *S.S. Seaworthy* and received a bill of lading from the ship as a receipt. Before the boxes could be loaded, the dock collapsed, and everything thereon disappeared into the water. Under §2-319(2) must buyer pay the $1,800 anyway? What if the delivery term had been "Ex-ship S.S. Seaworthy, Savannah," and the boxes had been properly unloaded just before the dock collapsed? Would §2-322 make the buyer pay?

PROBLEM 57

Seller in Detroit, Michigan, contracted to sell and ship 50 automobiles to buyer in Birmingham, Alabama. Assume lightning strikes, destroying the vehicles *after* the carrier has received them but before they are loaded on board the railroad car that was to take them to Birmingham. Who had the risk of loss if (a) the contract said, "F.O.B. Detroit"? (see §2-319(1)(a)); (b) the contract said, "F.O.B. railroad cars Detroit"? (see §2-319(1)(c) and Pagano v. Occidental Chem. Corp., 629 N.E.2d 569 (Ill. App. 1994)); or (c) the contract said, "C.I.F. Birmingham"? (see §2-320). If the buyer had inspected the automobiles and accepted them at the factory, would the risk shift to buyer or remain on seller until the automobiles reached the railroad cars? See Southern Recycling, LLC v. Gibbs International, Inc., 2016 WL 1258402 (D.S.C. 2016).

PROBLEM 58

The dispatcher for Perfect Pineapples, Inc., had just finished loading five boxcars of the company's product on board the cars of an independent railroad carrier when he received a notice from PPI's sales department that the company had agreed to sell one boxcar load to Grocery King Food Stores "F.O.B. seller's processing plant." The dispatcher agreed to divert one of the boxcars to Grocery King, but before he could do so, a hurricane destroyed all five boxcars and their contents. Who bears the risk of loss? See Official Comment 2 to §2-509 and §2-501.

Cook Specialty Co. v. Schrlock

United States District Court, Eastern District of Pennsylvania, 1991, 772 F. Supp. 1532

WALDMAN, J.

Defendant Machinery Systems, Inc. ("MSI") contracted to sell plaintiff a machine known as a Dries & Krump Hydraulic Press Brake. When the machine was lost in transit, plaintiff sued defendants to recover for the loss. Presently before the court is plaintiff's motion for summary judgment and defendant MSI's cross-motion for summary judgment. . . .

II. FACTS

The pertinent facts are not contested and are as follow.

Plaintiff entered into a sales contract with defendant MSI for the purchase of a Dries & Krump Press Brake in August of 1989 for $28,000. The terms of the contract were F.O.B. MSI's warehouse in Schaumburg, Illinois. Defendant R.T.L., also known as Randy's Truck Lines, ("the carrier") was used to deliver the press brake from the defendant's warehouse to the plaintiff in Pennsylvania. MSI obtained a certificate of insurance from the carrier with a face amount of $100,000 and showing a $2,500 deductible. (See dfdt. ex. D.)

On October 20, 1989, the carrier took possession of the press brake at MSI's warehouse. While still in transit, the press brake fell from the carrier's truck. The carrier was cited by the Illinois State Police for not properly securing the load. Plaintiff has recovered damages of $5,000 from the carrier's insurer, the applicable policy limit for this particular incident. The machine was worth $28,000.[2]

---

2. Plaintiff, who also sued for certain consequential damages, asserts a claim for a total of $81,000.

III. Discussion

This dispute is governed by the Uniform Commercial Code ("U.C.C.") provisions regarding risk of loss. The parties agree that there is no meaningful distinction between the pertinent law of Pennsylvania and Illinois, both of which have adopted the UCC.

The term "F.O.B., place of shipment," means that "the seller must at that place ship the goods in the manner provided in this Article (§2-504) and bear the expense and risk of putting them into the possession of the carrier." 13 Pa. C.S.A. §2319. Thus, MSI bore the expense and risk of putting the machine into the carrier's possession for delivery. At the time the carrier takes possession, the risk of loss shifts to the buyer. The UCC provides:

> Where the contract requires or authorizes the seller to ship the goods by carrier
>
> a) if it does not require him to deliver them at a particular destination, the risk of loss passes to the buyer when the goods are duly delivered to the carrier. . . .

13 Pa. C.S.A. §2509.

Goods are not "duly delivered" under §2-509, however, unless a contract is entered which satisfies the provisions of §2-504. See 13 Pa. C.S.A. §2509, Official Comment 2. Section 2-504, entitled "Shipment by Seller" provides that:

> Where the seller is required or authorized to send the goods to the buyer and the contract does not require him to deliver them at a particular destination, then unless otherwise agreed he must a) put the goods in the possession of such a carrier and make such a contract for their transportation *as may be reasonable having regard to the nature of the goods* and other circumstances of the case.

13 Pa. C.S.A. §2504 (emphasis added).

Plaintiff argues that the contract MSI made for the delivery of the press brake was not reasonable because defendant failed to ensure that the carrier had sufficient insurance coverage to compensate plaintiff for a loss in transit. Plaintiff thus argues that the press brake was never duly delivered to a carrier within the meaning of §2-509 and accordingly the risk of loss never passed to plaintiff.

Plaintiff relies on two cases. In the first, La Casse v. Blaustein, 93 Misc. 2d 572, 403 N.Y.S.2d 440 (Civ. Ct. 1978), the defendant seller shipped calculators to the plaintiff buyer, a college student, in two cartons by fourth class mail. The buyer authorized the seller to spend up to $50 for shipping and insurance. The seller spent only $9.98 and insured each carton, valued at $1,663, for $200. The seller wrongly addressed one of the cartons, and inscribed a theft-tempting notation on it. The New York County Civil Court held that the defendant had improperly arranged for transportation of the calculators.

La Casse is the only reported case which suggests that a seller's failure to obtain adequate insurance may breach his duty to make a reasonable contract for shipment under §2-504. The dearth of support for plaintiff's position is instructive. A leading UCC authority has remarked: "Under this subsection [§2-504], what constitutes an 'unreasonable' contract of transportation? *Egregious* cases do arise." See J. White and R. Summers, Uniform Commercial Code §5-2 (1988). The only such "egregious case" identified by White and Summers is *La Casse,* where "the package was underinsured, misaddressed, shipped by fourth class mail, and bore a 'theft-tempting' inscription." White and Summers, supra, at §5-2.

The actions taken by the defendant in *La Casse* were utterly reckless. Moreover, unlike the defendant in that case, MSI did not undertake the responsibility to insure the shipment, and did not ship the press brake at a lower cost than the plaintiff expressly authorized it to pay.

Plaintiff also relies on Miller v. Harvey, 221 N.Y. 57, 116 N.E. 781 (1917). This pre-Code case is inapplicable. In *Miller,* by failing to declare the actual value of goods shipped on a form provided for that purpose, the seller effectively contracted away the buyer's rights against the carrier. Official Comment 3 to §2-504 states:

> [i]t is an improper contract under paragraph (a) for the seller to agree with the carrier to a limited valuation below the true value and thus cut off the buyer's opportunity to recover from the carrier in the event of loss, when the risk of shipment is placed on the buyer.

Thus, a contract is improper if the seller agrees to an inadequate valuation of the shipment and thereby extinguishes the buyer's opportunity to recover from the carrier. That is quite different from a seller's failure to ensure that a carrier has sufficient insurance to cover a particular potential loss, in which case the carrier is still liable to the buyer.

Plaintiff's focus on a single sentence of Official Comment 3 ignores the explicit language of the statute which defines reasonable in the context of "having regard to the nature of the goods," 3 Pa. C.S.A. §2504, and the portion of the Comment which states:

> Whether or not the shipment is at the buyer's expense the seller must see to any arrangements, *reasonable in the circumstances,* such as refrigeration, watering of live stock, protection against cold . . . and the like. . . .

Id., Official Comment 3.

The clear implication is that the reasonableness of a shipper's conduct under §2-504 is determined with regard to the mode of transport selected. It would be unreasonable, for example, to send perishables without refrigeration. See Larsen v. A.C. Carpenter, Inc., 620 F. Supp. 1084, 1119 (E.D.N.Y. 1985). No inference fairly can be drawn from the section that a seller has an obligation to investigate the amount and terms of insurance held by the carrier.

The court finds as a matter of law that MSI's conduct was not unreasonable under §2-504. MSI obtained from the carrier a certificate of insurance and did nothing to impair plaintiff's right to recover for any loss from the carrier.[3] Accidents occur in transit. For this reason, the UCC has specifically established mercantile symbols which delineate the risk of loss in a transaction so that the appropriate party might obtain insurance on the shipment. The contract in this case was "F.O.B." seller's warehouse. Plaintiff clearly bears the risk of loss in transit.

There are no material facts in dispute and MSI is entitled to judgment as a matter of law.

Rheinberg-Kellerei GmbH v. Vineyard Wine Co.
Court of Appeals of North Carolina, 1981, 53 N.C. App. 560, 281 S.E.2d 425

Plaintiff, a West German wine producer and exporter, instituted this action to recover the purchase price of a shipment of wine sold to defendant and lost at sea en route between Germany and the United States. Subsequent to a hearing, the court, sitting without a jury, made the following findings of fact.

Plaintiff is a West German corporation engaged in the business of producing, selling, and exporting wine. Defendant, a North Carolina corporation, is a distributor of wine, buying and selling foreign and domestic wines at wholesale. Frank Sutton, d/b/a Frank Sutton & Company and d/b/a The Empress Importing Company, and other names, of Miami Beach, Florida, is a licensed importer and seller of wines. During 1978-1979 Sutton served as an agent for plaintiff and was authorized to sell and solicit orders for plaintiff's wine in the United States. During 1978 and early 1979, Randall F. Switzer, then of Raleigh, North Carolina, was a broker soliciting orders

---

3. Plaintiff's argument that because the carrier used an allegedly unprofessional sounding name, Randy's Truck Line, and inelegant stationery, MSI was on notice that the carrier was unreliable is untenable. The Philadelphia telephone directory alone lists dozens of moving companies bearing the name, often just the first name, of an individual. Moreover, plaintiff has made no showing that the carrier, which is a party defendant, does not in fact have the means to satisfy a judgment in the amount sought.

of wine on behalf of several producers and brokers, including Sutton, on a commission basis.

During the summer of 1978, Switzer, on behalf of Frank Sutton, began to solicit orders from prospective customers in North Carolina for wines produced by plaintiff. He contacted Bennett Distributing Company in Salisbury, North Carolina and the defendant in Charlotte, North Carolina, soliciting orders for sale through Sutton of wine produced by plaintiff to be shipped from West Germany consolidated in one container. Switzer, in late August 1978, called the office of Sutton in Miami Beach, Florida, reporting that he had secured orders from Bennett Distributing Company and defendant for 625 cases and 620 cases, respectively, of plaintiff's wines. Switzer then mailed to Sutton a copy of the proposed orders. Switzer also left a copy of the proposed order by defendant with the defendant's sales manager.

On 25 August 1978, the office of Sutton prepared a written confirmation of the orders and mailed them to defendant. Defendant received the written confirmation of orders, but never gave written notice of objection to the contents thereof to plaintiff or plaintiff's agent, Sutton. Written confirmation of the orders together with "Special Instructions" which reflected the instructions to plaintiff regarding the proposed consolidated shipment, were mailed to the plaintiff in West Germany on or about 25 August 1978.

According to the stated prices for the wine, the purchase price of the 620 cases of wine ordered by the defendant was 15.125,00 German marks. On 15 September 1980, the rate of exchange of German marks to United States dollars was such that one German mark equals $.57. Therefore, the purchase price of the 620 cases of wine, 15.125,00 German marks, equals $8,621.25.

Between August and December 1978, defendant's president, Cremilde D. Blank, and Switzer made telephone inquiries to Sutton concerning the status of the wine orders, but were not furnished any information concerning when and how the wine would be shipped or when and where it would arrive. On or about 8 November 1978, Mrs. Blank telephoned Sutton's office and obtained certain details concerning the consolidated order and then wrote to Bennett Distributing Company. Thereafter, in November 1978, Bennett Distributing Company informed Mrs. Blank that it had cancelled its order with the plaintiff, and Switzer thereafter attempted to resell Bennett's share of the order.

On or about 27 November 1978, plaintiff issued notice to Sutton giving the date of the shipment, port of origin, vessel, estimated date of arrival and port of arrival. Sutton did not give any of such information to defendant or to Switzer and did not notify defendant of anything. There was never any communication of any kind between plaintiff and defendant, and defendant was not aware of the details of the shipment.

Plaintiff delivered the wine ordered by defendant, consolidated in a container with the other wine, to a shipping line on 29 November 1978, for shipment from Rotterdam to Wilmington, North Carolina, on board the *M.S. Munchen*. Defendant did not request the plaintiff to deliver the wine ordered to any particular destination, and plaintiff and its agent, Sutton, selected the port of Wilmington for the port of entry into the United States. The entire container of wine was consigned by plaintiff to defendant, with freight payable at destination by defendant.

After delivering the wine to the ocean vessel for shipment, plaintiff forwarded the invoice for the entire container, certificate of origin and bill of lading, to its bank in West Germany, which forwarded the documents to Wachovia Bank and Trust Company, N.A., in Charlotte, North Carolina. The documents were received by Wachovia on 27 December 1978. The method of payment for the sale was for plaintiff's bank in West Germany to send the invoice, certificate of origin and bill of lading, to Wachovia whereupon defendant was to pay the purchase price to Wachovia and obtain the shipping documents. Wachovia then would forward payment to plaintiff's bank, and defendant could present the shipping documents to the carrier to obtain possession.

Wachovia mailed to defendant on 29 December 1978, a notice requesting payment for the entire consolidated shipment, by sight draft in exchange for documents. The notice was not returned by the Post Office to the sender.

On or about 24 January 1979, defendant first learned that the container of wine had left Germany in early December 1978 aboard the *M.S. Munchen*, which was lost in the North Atlantic with all hands and cargo aboard between 12 December and 22 December 1978.

Defendant did not receive any wine from plaintiff and did not pay Wachovia for the lost shipment. Plaintiff released the sight draft documents to Frank Sutton. Defendant was not furnished with any copy of said documents until receiving some in March and April 1979 and the others through discovery after this action was filed.

The order and "Special Instructions," mailed by Sutton to plaintiff, but not to defendant, provided inter alia: (1) "Insurance to be covered by purchaser"; (2) "Send a 'Notice of Arrival' to both the customer and to Frank Sutton & Company"; and (3) "Payment may be deferred until the merchandise has arrived at the port of entry."

Based upon the foregoing findings of fact, the trial court made the following pertinent conclusions of law:

> 2. The defendant agreed to purchase 620 cases of wine from the plaintiff through its agent or broker, Frank Sutton, in late August 1978.
> 3. Plaintiff failed to comply with §2-504, which provides:

Where the seller is required or authorized to send the goods to the buyer and the contract does not require him to deliver them at a particular destination, then unless otherwise agreed he must . . .

"(c) promptly notify the buyer of the shipment.

4. The purpose of such notification requirement is so the buyer (as defendant in this instance would have been) may make necessary arrangements for cargo insurance and otherwise to protect itself against any ensuing loss.

5. The plaintiff failed to deliver any such notice to defendant herein prior to the sailing of the ship and the ensuing loss. While plaintiff gave such notice to its agent, Frank Sutton did not pass such information on to defendant, so defendant was unaware of details vital to securing cargo insurance or otherwise protecting itself against loss in transit. The mailing of documents after shipment to Wachovia Bank & Trust Company, N.A. to collect the invoice amount plus freight and charges from defendant by sight draft, of which defendant was unaware until some weeks after the loss of the ship was not prompt notice to the defendant as required by the above statute.

6. Risk of loss of the wine therefore did not pass from the plaintiff to defendant upon delivery of the container of wine to the carrier, as provided in §2-509(1)(a).

7. Plaintiff is not entitled to recover any amount from the defendant due to such lack of notice.

From judgment in favor of the defendant, dismissing plaintiff's action, both plaintiff and defendant have appealed. . . .

Wells, J.

The first question presented by plaintiff's appeal is whether the trial court was correct in its conclusion that the risk of loss for the wine never passed from plaintiff to defendant due to the failure of plaintiff to give prompt notice of the shipment to defendant. Plaintiff made no exceptions to the findings of fact contained in the judgment and does not contend that the facts found were unsupported by the evidence. Our review on appeal is limited to a determination of whether the facts found support the court's conclusions and the judgment entered. Rule 10(a), N.C. Rules of Appellate Procedure; Swygert v. Swygert, 46 N.C. App. 173, 180-81, 264 S.E.2d 902, 907 (1980).

All parties agree that the contract in question was a "shipment" contract, i.e., one not requiring delivery of the wine at any particular destination. See J. White & R. Summers, Uniform Commercial Code §5-2, at 140-42 (1972). The Uniform Commercial Code, as adopted in North Carolina, dictates when the transfer of risk of loss occurs in this situation. Section 2-509(1)(a) provides, in pertinent part:

Risk of loss in the absence of breach. — (1) Where the contract requires or authorizes the seller to ship the goods by carrier (a) if it does not require him to deliver them at a particular destination, the risk of loss passes to the buyer when the goods are duly delivered to the carrier even though the shipment is under reservation (§2-505)....

Before a seller will be deemed to have "duly delivered" the goods to the carrier, however, he must fulfill certain duties owed to the buyer. In the absence of any agreement to the contrary, these responsibilities, set out in §2-504, are as follows: [the court quotes §2-504 — Ed.].

The trial court concluded that the plaintiff's failure to notify the defendant of the shipment until after the sailing of the ship and the ensuing loss, was not "prompt notice" within the meaning of §2-504, and therefore, the risk of loss did not pass to defendant upon the delivery of the wine to the carrier pursuant to the provisions of §2-509(1)(a). We hold that the conclusions of the trial court were correct. The seller is burdened with special responsibilities under a shipment contract because of the nature of the risk of loss being transferred. See W. Hawkland, 1 A Transactional Guide to the UCC §1.2104, at 102-107 (1964). Where the buyer, upon shipment by seller, assumes the perils involved in carriage, he must have a reasonable opportunity to guard against these risks by independent arrangements with the carrier. The requirement of prompt notification by the seller, as used in §2-504(c), must be construed as taking into consideration the need of a buyer to be informed of the shipment in sufficient time for him to take action to protect himself from the risk of damage to or loss of the goods while in transit. But see J. White & R. Summers, Uniform Commercial Code §5-2, fn.12 (1972). It would not be practical or desirable, however, for the courts to attempt to engraft onto §2-504 of the U.C.C. a rigid definition of prompt notice. Given the myriad factual situations which arise in business dealings, and keeping in mind the commercial realities, whether notification has been "prompt" within the meaning of UCC will have to be determined on a case-by-case basis, under all the circumstances. See W. Hawkland, 1 A Transactional Guide to the U.C.C. §1.2104, at 106 (1964).

In the case at hand, the shipment of wine was lost at sea sometime between 12 December and 22 December 1978. Although plaintiff did notify its agent, Frank Sutton, regarding pertinent details of the shipment on or about 27 November 1978, this information was not passed along to defendant. The shipping documents were not received by defendant's bank for forwarding to defendant until 27 December 1978, days after the loss had already been incurred. Since the defendant was never notified directly or by the forwarding of shipping documents within the time in which its interest could have been protected by insurance or otherwise, defendant was entitled to reject the shipment pursuant to the term of §2-504(c)....

In the plaintiff's appeal, the judgment is affirmed.

In the defendant's appeal, the appeal is dismissed.

PROBLEM 59

The University of Beijing in China ordered video equipment to be shipped from Applied Technology, Inc., in San Jose, California. If nothing is said about the subject, as a matter of international law, will this create a shipment or a destination contract? See CISG Articles 67 and 69. If the parties had been negotiating for the purchase of this equipment but had not gotten around to signing the contract until the goods were already on board an airplane crossing the Pacific Ocean, does the buyer have the risk of loss only from the moment of the signing of the contract or from the delivery of the equipment to the air carrier? See Article 68.

PROBLEM 60

Dime-A-Minute Rent-A-Car rented a new sports car to Joseph Armstrong. Due to a snafu at the rental office, Armstrong did not sign a rental agreement. As he was leaving the rental car lot, the car was struck by a city bus due to no fault of Armstrong (who was unhurt). The sports car was totaled. Dime-A-Minute demanded that Armstrong look to his insurance to replace the car. Did he have the risk of loss here? See §2A-219. If he had signed a rental agreement making him responsible for the car, would that agreement be valid? See §§1-302, 2A-108.

The above discussion of risk of loss, both under the UCC and under the CISG, presupposes that neither of the parties is in breach of their agreement at the moment when the risk would normally pass. If this is not true (for instance, when the seller is in breach because the goods do not conform to the warranties made in the contract), §2-509 does not apply (and neither does Article 67 of the CISG); the relevant risk of loss section is §2-510 (§2A-220 for leases and Articles 66 and 70 in the CISG). Before considering §2-510, we need to explore the UCC's definition of *breach*, and that brings us to the standards of performance set by the Code.

CHAPTER 5 REVIEW QUESTIONS

When does a party have a right to adequate assurance of performance?
Are unfair contract terms necessarily unconscionable?
What is the effect of this provision in Amazon's Terms of Use: "All purchases of physical items from Amazon are made pursuant to a shipment contract. This means that the risk of loss and title for such items pass to you upon our delivery to the carrier"?

What are the meanings of F.O.B., C.I.F., C. & F., F.A.S., and ex-ship?

Does risk of loss depend on ownership of the goods or whether they have been accepted by buyer?

ASSESSMENT: MULTIPLE CHOICE QUESTIONS

1. Curious Liquids signed a contract to sell Pemulis Auto its requirements of motor oil for the year, in monthly shipments at a price of $5 per quart. Pemulis Auto usually needed about 3,000 quarts per month. After fracking-related earthquakes shut down production of many wells, motor oil prices spiked. Pemulis Auto signed another contract to sell Josephson Jobber 100,000 quarts at $10 per quart. Pemulis Auto then informed Curious Liquids that the requirement for the next month would be 103,000 quarts. Is Curious Liquids obliged to deliver 103,000 quarts next month, which would be ruinous for it?
   a. Yes. Curious Liquids made a bad deal, but is bound by the contract.
   b. No. The parties have no sales contract, because they did not agree about the most basic term, the quantity of goods.
   c. No. Pemulis Auto is entitled only to its good faith, actual requirement. Its demand is not good faith or its actual requirement.
   d. Yes. Pemulis Auto has an actual requirement for 103,000 gallons, because it is obliged to deliver 100,000 quarts to Josephson Jobber and needs 3,000 quarts for its own operations.

2. On June 1, Pemulis Auto signed a contract to sell Redford a "2016 Model Excalibur Hardtop" automobile. A week later, Pemulis Auto received three 2016 Model Excalibur Hardtops from the manufacturer. Two days after that, Pemulis Auto placed a sticker on one of the three cars, designating it for delivery to Redford. On July 1, Redford tendered payment, Pemulis Auto signed the certificate of title and handed over the keys, and Redford drove away. When were goods identified to the contract?
   a. On June 1, when the parties signed a contract specifically identifying the car to be sold.
   b. When Pemulis Auto received three cars, meaning it could now deliver one to Redford.
   c. When Pemulis Auto put a sticker on one of the cars.
   d. When the car was paid for and driven away.

3. Word got around that Pemulis Auto had some 2016 Model Excalibur Hardtops in stock. Pompeia soon made a contract with Pemulis Auto to buy one as her retirement present to herself. Pompeia wired the full payment, and Pemulis Auto parked one of the cars to deliver to her the next

day. It was stolen overnight. Is Pompeia entitled to either get her payment back or a different car delivered?

   a. No. She had bought and paid for the car, so it was her car that was stolen.
   b. No. She would be reasonably required to obtain insurance for the car.
   c. Yes. The risk of loss would not pass to her until delivery, which did not occur.
   d. Yes. A merchant is required to insure the goods.

4. Blackhorse Goods signed a contract to sell 100 washing machines to Otto Automats. The washing machines were stored in a warehouse. Blackhorse Goods negotiated the warehouse receipt to Otto Automats, who promised to pay the contract price in 30 days. Before that time, the warehouse was destroyed by a fire, through no fault of the warehouse operator. Is Otto Automats obliged to pay for washing machines that are now scrap?

   a. No. Blackhorse Goods has not delivered the goods.
   b. No. The machines still belonged to Blackhorse Goods.
   c. Yes. The risk of loss of the goods passed to Otto Automats with the warehouse receipt.
   d. Yes. The risk of loss passed to Otto Automats upon signing the contract.

5. Obergefell Furniture, in Boston, MA, entered into a contract with Unterwasser Healthcare, in Charleston, S.C., for the sale of medical devices, to be delivered by a trucking company. In which case would the risk of loss pass from the seller to the buyer when the goods were tendered to the carrier?

   a. If the parties did not specifically address the issue in the contract.
   b. If they used the shipping term "C.I.F. Charleston."
   c. If the used the shipping term "F.O.B. Boston."
   d. All of the above.

ANSWERS

1. *C* is the best answer. Article 2 does allow the parties flexibility in forming a contract, without specifying all terms. Section 2-306 permits quantity to be measured by the seller's output or buyer's requirements, contrary to *B*. But it means the "actual output or requirements as may occur in good faith." §2-306(1). Here, Pemulis Auto asked for more than its actual requirements, as contemplated at the time of the agreement. Nor did Pemulis Auto act in good faith, where it misrepresented its actual requirements to take advantage of changing market conditions.

2. *C* is the best answer. Identification of goods to the contract is not the same as specifying what the seller is obliged to deliver, so *A* is not correct. Nor does it require the goods to be paid for and delivered, contrary to *D*. Rather, §2-501 states how the seller, in effect, marks specific goods as the ones to be delivered to the buyer. If the contract is for goods already existing and identified, identification occurs when the contract was made. §2-501(1)(a). When the contract was made, Pemulis Auto was obliged to deliver *a* 2016 Model Excalibur Hardtop, but no particular car had been designated to deliver to Redford. Even when three Hardtops were delivered, no particular one was designated for Redford. Rather, when Pemulis Auto put a sticker on one, that identified that particular car to the contract.

3. *C* is the best answer. The general rule, for nonmerchant buyers, is that risk of loss passes when the goods are delivered. §2-509(3). There are other rules where the goods are being transported, §2-509(1), or held by a bailee, §2-509(2), but neither is the case here. The parties can agree that one should provide insurance, but did not do so, so *B* and *D* are incorrect. Likewise, the parties can agree about when the risk of loss will pass, but did not do so here, so the general rule will apply. The risk of loss does not depend on whether payment has been made, contrary to *A*.

4. *C* is the best answer. When goods are held by a bailee, the risk of loss passes when a negotiable document covering the goods is delivered to the buyer. §2-509(2)(a). The provision also addresses the issue when there is no document covering the goods or when the document is not negotiable.

5. *D* is the best answer. This question illustrates the role of shipping terms. In a transportation contract, if the parties do not address the issue, the contract is a "shipment" contract, meaning risk of loss shifts upon shipment. The parties may decide when the risk of loss shifts. The term *C.I.F.* designates a shipment contract, so the risk of loss would also shift upon shipment in *B*. *F.O.B.* means the risk of loss shifts at the place designated. *F.O.B. Boston* means risk of loss shifts in Boston, where the seller is, so this is also a shipment contract. So "all of the above" is correct.

PERFORMANCE OF
THE CONTRACT

Most contracts are performed without incident, but life, with all its complexities, snares many a deal, and the parties can end up in litigation arguing about who did what to whom. Sometimes the difficulty is with the product, sometimes with the delivery schedule, sometimes with an unwillingness to perform, and sometimes completion of the contract is outright impossible. In this chapter we explore what levels of performance are required for compliance with contractual duties, the choices available for nonperformance by the other side, and the duties of each party when things go south.

Section 2-301 states that the seller's basic obligation is "to transfer and deliver" and the buyer's is "to pay in accordance with the contract." Thus, the seller must tender (offer to deliver) conforming goods, and the buyer must pay for them. Read and compare §2-507(1) with §2-511(1). They appear to be conflicting, don't they? The conflict disappears when the sections are considered in light of the technical/procedural snarl that they are designed to unravel. It is this: in any contract action, the plaintiff loses unless it can be shown that the other party is in breach. Where a sale of goods is involved, it is frequently true that the parties contemplated a contemporaneous swap of money for the goods. If at the appointed time neither party shows up, the buyer is not in breach because the seller did not tender, and vice versa. If the parties did not intend a contemporaneous swap, but instead

Perfect tender Rule

contracted so that one or the other's performance was to come first, then either §2-507(1) or §2-511(1) will not apply, since the parties will have "otherwise agreed." When, for example, the parties agree that buyer is to be given six months after delivery in which to pay, failure of the seller to deliver on time is a breach, and the seller may be sued without the buyer's having to allege a §2-511(1) tender of payment. Knowing that the seller's basic duty is to tender conforming goods, and that the buyer's duty is to pay for them, leaves unanswered a host of legal questions. What does the seller's *tender* entail? (Answer: §§2-503, 2-504.) What does *conforming* mean? (Answer: §2-106(2).) What means of payment can the buyer use? (Answer: §2-511(2), (3).) These and other questions are the subject of this portion of the book.

I.   INSTALLMENT SALES

At common law, successful plaintiffs in contract actions were generally required to prove *substantial performance* (as opposed to a technically perfect performance) of the terms of the contract. From your Contracts course you may remember Judge Cardozo's opinion in Jacob & Youngs Inc. v. Kent, 230 N.Y. 239, 129 N.E. 889 (1921), the so-called *Reading Pipe* case. The court held that the construction contract was substantially performed even though the contractor installed a different but similar brand of pipe instead of the Reading brand called for under the explicit terms of the contract.

In installment contracts, defined in §2-612(1), substantial performance is still the law. The seller is entitled to payment even where the tender of the goods fails to conform exactly to the contract as long as it "substantially" conforms. Read §2-612. For a good discussion of this section (and many others), see Ellen A. Peters, Remedies for Breach of Contracts Relating to the Sale of Goods Under the Uniform Commercial Code: A Roadmap for Article Two, 73 Yale L.J. 199, 223-229 (1963).

PROBLEM 61

Travis Galleries developed a market in copies of famous statues. It ordered monthly shipments of the statues from Ersatz Imports, agreeing to take 12 shipments of 20 statues each over the coming year. The first month all of the statues arrived upside down in their cartons. The manager of Travis Galleries was amazed that most had survived the trip in this condition. Only one was broken, and a phone call to Ersatz Imports resulted in a promise to ship a replacement at once. The next month the statues were again packaged upside down, and half of them were broken. Does §2-612 permit rejection for this reason? Assume that Ersatz replaced the broken statues within a week, but that the next month the shipment contained no statues at all. Instead, Ersatz had mistakenly shipped Travis poor copies of 20 French Impressionist paintings. Travis Galleries called you, its attorney. May it reject this shipment? Under what theory? May it now cancel the remainder of the Ersatz contract? In any rejection situation, is it wise for attorneys to ask their clients what really underlies their own actions?

Cherwell-Ralli, Inc. v. Rytman Grain Co.

Supreme Court of Connecticut, 1980, 433 A.2d 984

PETERS, J.

This case involves a dispute about which of the parties to an oral installment contract was the first to be in breach. The plaintiff, Cherwell-Ralli, Inc., sued the defendant, Rytman Grain Co., Inc., for the nonpayment of moneys due and owing for accepted deliveries of products known as Cherco Meal and C-R-T Meal. The defendant, conceding its indebtedness, counterclaimed for damages arising out of the plaintiff's refusal to deliver remaining installments under the contract. The trial court, Bordon, J., trial referee, having found all issues for the plaintiff, rendered judgment accordingly, and the defendant appealed.

The trial court's unchallenged finding of fact establishes the following: The parties, on July 26, 1974, entered into an installment contract for the sale of Cherco Meal and C-R-T Meal on the basis of a memorandum executed by the Getkin Brokerage House. As modified, the contract called for shipments according to weekly instructions from the buyer, with payments to be made within ten days after delivery. Almost immediately the buyer was behind in its payments, and these arrearages were often quite substantial. The seller repeatedly called these arrearages to the buyer's attention but continued to make all shipments as requested by the buyer from July 29, 1974 to April 23, 1975.

By April 15, 1975, the buyer had become concerned that the seller might not complete performance of the contract, because the seller's plant might close and because the market price of the goods had come significantly to exceed the contract price. In a telephonic conversation between the buyer's president and the seller's president on that day, the buyer was assured by the seller that deliveries would continue if the buyer would make the payments for which it was obligated. Thereupon, the buyer sent the seller a check in the amount of $9,825.60 to cover shipments through March 31, 1975.

Several days later, on April 23, 1975, the buyer stopped payment on this check because he was told by a truck driver, not employed by the seller, that this shipment would be his last load. The trial court found that this was not a valid reason for stoppage of payment. Upon inquiry by the seller, the buyer restated his earlier concerns about future deliveries. Two letters, both dated April 28, 1975, describe the impasse between the parties: the seller again demanded payment, and the buyer, for the first time in writing, demanded adequate assurance of further deliveries. The buyer's demand for assurance was reiterated in its direct reply to the seller's demand for payment. The buyer, however, made no further payments, either to replace the stopped check or otherwise to pay for the nineteen accepted shipments for which balances were outstanding. The seller made no further deliveries after April 23, 1975, when it heard about the stopped check; the buyer never made specific requests for shipments after that date. Inability to deliver the goods forced the seller to close its plant, on May 2, 1975, because of stockpiling of excess material.

The trial court concluded, on the basis of these facts, that the party in breach was the buyer and not the seller. The court concluded that the seller was entitled to recover the final balance of $21,013.60, which both parties agreed to be due and owing. It concluded that the buyer could not prevail on its counterclaim because it had no reasonable grounds to doubt performance from the seller and had in fact received reasonable assurances. Further, the buyer had presented no reasonably accurate evidence to establish the damages it might have sustained because of the seller's failure to deliver.

The buyer on this appeal challenges first the conclusion that the buyer's failure to pay "substantially impaired the value of the whole contract" so as to constitute "a breach of the whole contract," as is required by the applicable law governing installment contracts. U.C.C. §2-612(3). What constitutes impairment of the value of the whole contract is a question of fact; Graulich Caterer, Inc. v. Holterbosch, Inc., 101 N.J. Super. 61, 75, 243 A.2d 253 (1968); Holiday Mfg. Co. v. B.A.S.F. Systems, Inc., 380 F. Supp. 1096, 1102 (D. Neb. 1974). The record below amply sustains the trial court's conclusion in this regard, particularly in light of the undenied and uncured stoppage of a check given to comply with the buyer's promise to reduce significantly the amount of its outstanding arrearages. See Frigiking, Inc. v. Century Tire & Sales Co., 452 F. Supp. 935, 938 (N.D. Tex. 1978).

The buyer argues that the seller in an installment contract may never terminate a contract, despite repeated default in payment by the buyer, without first invoking the insecurity methodology of §2-609. That is not the law. If there is reasonable doubt about whether the buyer's default is substantial, the seller may be well advised to temporize by suspending further performance until it can ascertain whether the buyer is able to offer adequate assurance of future payments. Kunian v. Development Corporation of America, 165 Conn. 300, 312, 334 A.2d 427 (1973); Dangerfield v. Markel, 252 N.W.2d 184, 192-93 (N.D. 1977). But if the buyer's conduct is sufficiently egregious, such conduct will, in and of itself, constitute substantial impairment of the value of the whole contract and a present breach of the contract as a whole. An aggrieved seller is expressly permitted, by §2-703(f), upon breach of a contract as a whole, to cancel the remainder of the contract "with respect to the whole undelivered balance." See Frigiking, Inc. v. Century Tire & Sales Co., supra. Nor is the seller's remedy to cancel waived, as the buyer argues, by a lawsuit seeking recovery for payments due. While §2-612(3) states that a contract is reinstated if the seller "brings an action with respect *only* to past installments" (emphasis added), it is clear in this case that the seller intended, as the buyer well knew, to bring this contract to an end because of the buyer's breach.

The buyer's attack on the court's conclusions with respect to its counterclaim is equally unavailing. The buyer's principal argument is that the seller was obligated, on pain of default, to provide assurance of its further performance. The right to such assurance is premised on reasonable grounds for insecurity. Whether a buyer has reasonable grounds to be insecure is a question of fact. AMF, Inc. v. McDonald's Corp., 536 F.2d 1167, 1170 (7th Cir. 1976). The trial court concluded that in this case the buyer's insecurity was not reasonable and we agree. A party to a sales contract may not suspend performance of its own for which it has "already received the agreed return." At all times, the buyer had received all the goods which it had ordered. The buyer could not rely on its own nonpayments as a basis for its own insecurity. The presidents of the parties had exchanged adequate verbal assurances only eight days before the buyer itself again delayed its own performance on the basis of information that was facially unreliable. Contrary to the buyer's argument, subsequent events proved the buyer's fears to be incorrect, since the seller's plant closed due to a surplus rather than due to a shortage of materials. Finally, it is fatal to the buyer's appeal that neither its oral argument nor its brief addressed its failure to substantiate, with probative evidence, the damages it alleged to be attributable to the seller's nondeliveries.

There is no error.

In this opinion the other judges concurred.

II. THE PERFECT TENDER RULE

The substantial performance rule has never (at least in theory) applied to single-delivery contracts between merchants. Learned Hand once stated that "[t]here is no room in commercial contracts for the doctrine of substantial performance." Mitsubishi Goshi Kaisha v. J. Aron & Co., 16 F.2d 185, 186 (2d Cir. 1926). To prevail in a single-delivery sale, the seller must make a *perfect tender,* one that complied with all of the terms of the contract, and then show that the buyer refused to take the goods. The reason for this higher standard in single-delivery sales is that in such cases the buyer does not have the same bargaining position a buyer would have in installment sales (where the seller needs to keep dealing with the buyer on repeated occasions and therefore must, as a business matter, keep the buyer happy).

The Code's perfect tender rule is found in §2-601. Read it. (*Commercial unit* is defined in §2-105(6).)

PROBLEM 62

Stella Speculator, a wealthy investor, signed a contract with Swank Motors to buy five new cars. All five were to be delivered on October 1. When the cars arrived, she test drove each of them and then returned two of them, saying she would keep the other three. She rejected the two cars because the audio system did not work in one of them (she was a great music lover) and the carpeting in the trunk of the other was ripping. Swank Motors offered to repair both defects. When Speculator refused to permit repair, Swank sued. Answer these questions:

(a) Does the common law doctrine *de minimis non curat lex* ("the law does not notice small defects") survive §2-601? If so, in spite of the tiny defects, the cars would be conforming. See Official Comment 2 to §2-106; see D.P. Technology Corp. v. Sherwood Tool, Inc., 751 F. Supp. 1038 (D. Conn. 1990) (where goods specially manufactured, buyer not in good faith in rejecting because of insubstantial delay in delivery).

(b) A seller has a right to *cure* in some circumstances; see §2-508. Is this section of use to Swank Motors? See Wilson v. Scampoli, 228 A.2d 848 (D.C. 1967), reprinted below.

(c) Suppose Swank can demonstrate that it is common for car sellers to correct small defects. Will Swank succeed if it argues that such correction is a *usage of trade* (§1-303(c)) and thus either that the goods are *conforming* or that because of this usage of trade, the parties have impliedly agreed that a §2-601 perfect tender is not required? See §§1-302, 1-201(b)(3).

III. CURE

If the seller has not made a *perfect* tender, and as a result the buyer has rejected the goods, the seller has the right in some circumstances to *cure* the defective performance. The key section is §2-508. Read it and its Official Comments. For an annotation on the subject, see Annot., 36 A.L.R.4th 544.

PROBLEM 63

On August 8, Francis and Sophie Ferdinand ordered a new car from Princip Motors for $22,000. The car was scheduled for delivery "no later than September 1" (it had special accessories that had to be installed at the factory). On August 15, Princip Motors told the Ferdinands that the car was ready, so they picked it up. Halfway home (three miles from the car dealer), the engine blew up without warning. The Ferdinands were not hurt, but the engine was destroyed. On being informed that the Ferdinands wanted their money back, Princip made the following responses:

(a) Princip offered to take an engine out of a car of the same model and install it in the original automobile (which was otherwise undamaged).

(b) Princip refused to refund the money; instead, it claimed a right to give the Ferdinands a new car to be delivered fresh from the factory on August 20.

Does §2-508 require the Ferdinands to accept either of these cure offers?

In resolving this Problem it may help you to know about the *Shaken Faith Doctrine*, developed in a similar situation by the court in a leading case (worth reading):

> For a majority of people the purchase of a new car is a major investment, rationalized by the peace of mind that flows from its dependability and safety. Once their faith is shaken, the vehicle loses not only its real value in their eyes, but becomes an instrument whose integrity is substantially impaired and whose operation is fraught with apprehension. The attempted cure in the present case was ineffective.

Zabriskie Chevrolet, Inc. v. Smith, 99 N.J. Super. 441, 458, 240 A.2d 195, 205 (1968).

And, in the words of one pedant, "The court should be willing to take judicial notice of what all modern day consumers 'know': things that do not work well at the start are not likely to work well in the future unless the original defect is minor in nature." Douglas Whaley, Tender, Acceptance, Rejection and Revocation — The UCC's "TARR-Baby," 24 Drake L. Rev. 52, 58 (1974).

Wilson v. Scampoli

Court of Appeals of the District of Columbia, 1967, 228 A.2d 848

MYERS, J.

This is an appeal from an order of the trial court granting rescission of a sales contract for a color television set and directing the return of the purchase price plus interest and costs.

Appellee purchased the set in question on November 4, 1965, paying the total purchase price in cash. The transaction was evidenced by a sales ticket showing the price paid and guaranteeing ninety days' free service and replacement of any defective tube and parts for a period of one year. Two days after purchase the set was delivered and uncrated, the antennae adjusted and the set plugged into an electrical outlet to "cook out."[1] When the set was turned on, however, it did not function properly, the picture having a reddish tinge. Appellant's delivery man advised the buyer's daughter, Mrs. Kolley, that it was not his duty to tune in or adjust the color but that a service representative would shortly call at her house for that purpose. After the departure of the delivery men, Mrs. Kolley unplugged the set and did not use it.[2]

On November 8, 1965, a service representative arrived, and after spending an hour in an effort to eliminate the red cast from the picture advised Mrs. Kolley that he would have to remove the chassis from the cabinet and take it to the shop as he could not determine the cause of the difficulty from his examination at the house. He also made a written memorandum of his service call, noting that the television "Needs Shop Work (Red Screen)." Mrs. Kolley refused to allow the chassis to be removed, asserting she did not want a "repaired" set but another "brand new" set. Later she demanded the return of the purchase price, although retaining the set. Appellant refused to refund the purchase price, but renewed his offer to adjust, repair, or, if the set could not be made to function properly, to replace it. Ultimately, appellee instituted this suit against appellant seeking a refund of the purchase price. After a trial, the court ruled that "under the facts and circumstances the complaint is justified. Under the equity powers of the court I will order the parties put back in their original status, let the $675 be returned, and the set returned to the defendant."

Appellant does not contest the jurisdiction of the trial court to order rescission in a proper case, but contends the trial judge erred in holding that rescission here was appropriate. He argues that he was always willing to comply with the terms of the sale either by correcting the malfunction by minor repairs or, in the event the set could not be made thereby properly operative, by replacement; that as he was denied the opportunity to try to correct the difficulty, he did not breach the contract of sale or any warranty thereunder, expressed or implied. [The court quotes §2-508. — Ed.] A retail dealer would certainly expect and have reasonable grounds to believe that merchandise like color television sets, new and delivered as crated at the factory, would be

1. Such a "cook out," usually over several days, allows the set to magnetize itself and to heat up the circuit in order to indicate faulty wiring.

2. Appellee, who made his home with Mrs. Kolley, had been hospitalized shortly before delivery of the set. The remaining negotiations were carried on by Mrs. Kolley, acting on behalf of her father.

acceptable as delivered and that, if defective in some way, he would have the right to substitute a conforming tender. The question then resolves itself to whether the dealer may conform his tender by adjustment or minor repair or whether he must conform by substituting brand new merchandise. The problem seems to be one of first impression in other jurisdictions adopting the Uniform Commercial Code as well as in the District of Columbia.

Although the Official Code Comments do not reach this precise issue, there are cases and comments under other provisions of the Code which indicate that under certain circumstances repairs and adjustments are contemplated as remedies under implied warranties. In L & N Sales Co. v. Little Brown Jug, Inc., 12 Pa. D. & C. 2d 469 (Phila. County Ct. 1957), where the language of a disclaimer was found insufficient to defeat warranties under §§2-314 and 2-315, the court noted that the buyer had notified the seller of defects in the merchandise, and as the seller was unable to remedy them and later refused to accept return of the articles, it was held to be a breach of warranty. In Hall v. Everett Motors, Inc., 340 Mass. 430, 165 N.E.2d 107 (1960), decided shortly before the effective date of the Code in Massachusetts, the court reluctantly found that a disclaimer of warranties was sufficient to insulate the seller. Several references were made in the ruling to the seller's unsuccessful attempts at repairs, the court indicating the result would have been different under the Code.

While these cases provide no mandate to require the buyer to accept patchwork goods or substantially repaired articles in lieu of flawless merchandise, they do indicate that minor repairs or reasonable adjustments are frequently the means by which an imperfect tender may be cured. In discussing the analogous question of defective title, it has been stated that:

> The seller, then, should be able to cure [the defect] under subsection 2-508(2) in those cases in which he can do so without subjecting the buyer to any great inconvenience, risk or loss. [Hawkland, Curing an Improper Tender of Title to Chattels: Past, Present and Commercial Code, 46 Minn. L. Rev. 697, 724 (1962).]

See also Willer & Hart, Forms and Procedures under the U.C.C., §24.07[4]; D.C. Code §28:2-608(1)(a) (Supp. V, 1966).

Removal of a television chassis for a short period of time in order to determine the cause of color malfunction and ascertain the extent of adjustment or correction needed to effect full operational efficiency presents no great inconvenience to the buyer. In the instant case, appellant's expert witness testified that this was not infrequently necessary with new televisions. Should the set be defective in workmanship or parts, the loss would be upon the manufacturer who warranted it free from mechanical defect. Here the adamant refusal of Mrs. Kolley, acting on behalf of appellee, to allow inspection essential to the determination of the cause of the excessive red tinge to the picture defeated any effort by the seller to provide timely repair or even replacement of the set if the difficulty could not be corrected. The cause of the defect might have been minor and easily adjusted or it may have been substantial and required replacement by another new set but the seller was never given an adequate opportunity to make a determination.

We do not hold that appellant has no liability to appellee,[3] but as he was denied access and a reasonable opportunity to repair, appellee has not shown a breach of warranty entitling him either to a brand new set or to rescission. We therefore reverse the judgment of the trial court granting rescission and directing the return of the purchase price of the set.

Reversed.

QUESTIONS

1. Is the court following the perfect tender rule here? See §2-601.

2. What portion of §2-508 is relevant to this case?

3. The court says that a "retail dealer would certainly expect . . . that merchandise like color television sets, new and delivered as crated at the factory, would be acceptable as delivered and that, if defective in some way, he would have the right to substitute a conforming tender." How does the court know this? Is this a matter of judicial notice (which means that judges can assume something everyone knows—for example, that we are living on the planet Earth)? Color televisions were very new in 1967 and frequently did need adjustments to work properly. Would the same thing be presumed in the twenty-first century?

4. In this case, the buyer rejected the goods but refused to return them to the seller. Is this permissible? See §2-711(3).

IV. REJECTION AND ACCEPTANCE

When the seller makes a tender of the goods, the buyer must choose between two possible legal responses: rejection (§2-602) and acceptance (§§2-606, 2-607). A buyer cannot do both since rejection and acceptance are mutually exclusive actions. Failure to act results in a technical *acceptance,*

---

3. Appellant on appeal has renewed his willingness to remedy any defect in the tender, and thus there is no problem of expiration of his warranties. He should be afforded the right to inspect and correct any malfunction. If appellee refuses to allow appellant an opportunity to do so, then no cause of action can lie for breach of warranty, express or implied, and the loss must be borne by appellee.

since rejection must come within a reasonable period of time after delivery of the goods. Read §2-602. The definition of *acceptance* is found in §2-606, and its legal consequences are spelled out in §2-607. Note two important things about these sections as you read them: (1) a buyer is entitled to a reasonable *trial-use* period to see if the goods conform (this is phrased in the Code as a "reasonable opportunity to inspect"; see §2-513), and (2) on acceptance, the burden of proof as to defects shifts to the buyer (§2-607(4)). Prior to acceptance, the seller must prove that a perfect tender was made under §2-601.

Koviack Irrigation and Farm Services, Inc. v. Maple Row Farms, LLC
Court of Appeals of Michigan, 2017, WL 4182409

PER CURIAM.

Plaintiff appeals by right the trial court's judgment in favor of defendant, following a bench trial. The court determined that defendant was not liable to plaintiff for the cost of equipment that plaintiff supplied for defendant's irrigation system because defendant properly rejected the equipment under the Uniform Commercial Code (UCC), MCL 440.1101 *et seq.* The court ordered defendant to return the equipment to plaintiff at defendant's own expense. Plaintiff also appeals the trial court's award of case evaluation sanctions of $11,362.50. We affirm in both appeals.

Plaintiff sold defendant component parts for an irrigation system for defendant's farm, which included a pump for distributing water from a retention pond. Plaintiff also helped design and install the system. Because the pump was delivered late in the harvest season, defendant waited until the following spring to install it. At that time, plaintiff was unwilling to assist in installing the pump because defendant had not paid for it or its operating panel. Defendant was unwilling to pay for the pump and panel until they were installed, and defendant could confirm that they would work as intended with the irrigation system. Defendant therefore hired another irrigation specialist to install the pump; he was then advised that the pump would not work with defendant's retention pond. Defendant then purchased another type of pump that was compatible with its retention pond and irrigation system. Plaintiff sued defendant for breach of contract, account stated, and unjust enrichment. Defendant filed a counterclaim, alleging that plaintiff had not provided a proper pump for the irrigation system, and that plaintiff refused to correct the problem. Following a two-day bench trial, the trial court found that defendant properly rejected the pump and its panel; consequently, plaintiff was not entitled to recover the costs of those items under the parties' agreement. The court ordered defendant to return the goods at its own expense.

I.   REJECTION OF GOODS

The trial court ruled that defendant properly rejected the pump and its operating panel in the spring of 2014 and, therefore, was not liable for the cost of that equipment under the parties' contract. [UCC §2-602(1)] provides, in relevant part:

> (1) Rejection of goods must be within a reasonable time after their delivery or tender. It is ineffective unless the buyer seasonably notifies the seller.
> (2) Subject to the provisions of the two following sections on rejected goods (sections 2-603 and 2-604),
>> (a) after rejection any exercise of ownership by the buyer with respect to any commercial unit is wrongful as against the seller; and
>> (b) if the buyer has before rejection taken physical possession of goods in which he does not have a security interest under the provisions of this article (subsection (3) of section 2-711), he is under a duty after rejection to hold them with reasonable care at the seller's disposition for a time sufficient to permit the seller to remove them; but
>> (c) the buyer has no further obligations with regard to goods rightfully rejected.

Plaintiff first argues that defendant did not timely reject the pump. Where goods are rejected, what constitutes a reasonable time to act depends on the nature, purpose, and circumstances of the case. See [UCC §1-205]; Kelynack v. Yamaha Motor Corp., USA, 152 Mich. App. 105, 113; 394 N.W.2d 17 (1986). Where the product at issue involves goods of a complex nature and the buyer depends on the seller's expertise that the goods will perform properly for the intended use, a buyer has an opportunity to put those goods to use or to test the goods before determining whether the goods conform to the contract. See Capitol Dodge Sales, Inc. v. Northern Concrete Pipe, Inc., 131 Mich. App. 149, 157-158; 346 N.W.2d 535 (1983).

In this case, the pump was delivered late in the harvest season, so it could not be put to use right away. Also, some installation work still needed to be performed, such as hooking it up to the electrical system to see if it would work. Under the circumstances, it was reasonable for defendant to wait until the pump was actually installed to see if it would work before deciding whether to reject it, particularly considering that defendant relied on plaintiff's expertise in selecting a pump appropriate for its intended use. The trial court did not clearly err in finding that defendant rejected the goods within a reasonable time when it determined the following spring that the pump was not appropriate for defendant's irrigation system. During the interim period, the pump sat in its original packaging until it could be installed to determine if it would work as intended for defendant's purposes.

Plaintiff also argues that defendant did not actually reject the pump because it did not formally give notice that it was rejecting the pump. We disagree. Again, the reasonableness of defendant's action depends on the nature, purpose, and circumstances of the case. See UCC [§1-205(a).]

Plaintiff's salesman, Anthony Belcher, met with defendant's owner, Dean McClenathen, in April 2014 to inquire about defendant's intention to pay for the pump. Belcher agreed that McClenathen told him that he did not intend to pay for anything more until he saw that the irrigation system would work as planned. Belcher admitted that the pump and panel were still in their original packaging at that time; however, plaintiff's owner, Terry Koviack, refused to do any more work on the project until defendant paid for the equipment. At that point, plaintiff was on notice that defendant intended to reject the pump if it would not work as planned. When Koviack refused to do any further work to assist in installing the pump, defendant reasonably took steps to follow through with the parties' agreement by hiring another irrigation specialist, Mark Ackerman, to install the pump. Ackerman informed defendant that because the pump was not appropriate for defendant's retention pond and irrigation system, it would not work as intended. At that time, defendant had grounds to reject the pump and panel. According to the evidence, however, plaintiff had ceased communications with defendant. While defendant could have more effectively conveyed to plaintiff its reasons for rejecting the pump, such as send a letter or email, given that plaintiff had refused to further communicate with defendant or perform any more work on the project, defendant's failure to take more formal steps to communicate its rejection was not unreasonable. See, e.g., Fargo Machine & Tool Co. v. Kearney & Trecker Corp., 428 F. Supp. 364, 375 (E.D. Mich. 1977). It is apparent that plaintiff had notice that defendant would not accept the pump until it was determined that it would work as intended, and defendant had agreed to pay for it when it was installed and properly working. This evidence supports that plaintiff had notice of defendant's intent to reject the pump if it were to not work as intended, and Ackerman's testimony supports that the pump was not suitable for defendant's intended purposes.

Accordingly, the trial court did not err in finding that under these circumstances defendant properly rejected the pump and panel in a reasonably timely manner. . . .

We affirm. As the prevailing party, defendant may tax costs pursuant to MCR 7.219.

PROBLEM 64

Midwestern Seafoods, headquartered in Iowa, ordered 50 live lobsters from Maine Exports, "F.O.B. Portland." On September 1, Maine Exports loaded the lobsters on board an airplane in Portland, from where they were flown to Boston and then to Des Moines. Maine Exports failed to notify Midwestern Seafoods of the date of the flight until two days later, when Midwestern's purchasing agent called to inquire. He then made a few calls and located the lobsters in Des Moines, where they had been sitting for a day. Midwestern signed a receipt and picked the lobsters up. Twenty of them were clearly dying (15 due to bad handling by Maine Exports before they were handed over to the airline and 5 due to damage in transit); the other 30 were fine. Midwestern decided, for reasons that are unclear, that it wanted none of the lobsters.

(a) Is the seller's failure to notify Midwestern of the shipment a ground for rejection? See §2-504.

(b) May Midwestern reject because of the 20 defective lobsters? See §§2-601, 2-503, 2-509(1), 2-510(1).

(c) How quickly must Midwestern act if it wishes to reject? What technical steps is it required to take? See §§2-602, 1-205.

(d) Must Midwestern reship the goods to Maine Exports if the latter offers to pay the freight? See §2-602(2) with its Official Comment 2; §§2-603, 2-604.

(e) If Midwestern decides to keep 30 of the lobsters for resale, is this allowed? See §§2-602(2)(a), 2-606; cf. §§2-601, 2-105(6); Annot., 67 A.L.R.3d 363.

(f) If Midwestern rejects the goods, must it give its reasons in the notice of rejection? What penalty is there for not doing so? See §2-605 and its Official Comment 2.

(g) If Midwestern gives a valid notice of rejection within a reasonable period of time after the lobsters are delivered, what should it then do with the lobsters? See §2-602(2).

Ramirez v. Autosport

Supreme Court of New Jersey, 1982, 88 N.J. 277, 440 A.2d 1345

POLLOCK, J.

This case raises several issues under the Uniform Commercial Code ("the Code" and "UCC") concerning whether a buyer may reject a tender of goods with minor defects and whether a seller may cure the defects. We consider also the remedies available to the buyer, including cancellation of the contract. The main issue is whether plaintiffs, Mr. and Mrs. Ramirez, could reject the tender by defendant, Autosport, of a camper van with minor defects and cancel the contract for the purchase of the van.

The trial court ruled that Mr. and Mrs. Ramirez rightfully rejected the van and awarded them the fair market value of their trade-in van. The Appellate Division affirmed in a brief per curiam decision which, like the trial court opinion, was unreported. We affirm the judgment of the Appellate Division.

I

Following a mobile home show at the Meadowlands Sports Complex, Mr. and Mrs. Ramirez visited Autosport's showroom in Somerville. On July 20, 1978, the Ramirezes and Donald Graff, a salesman for Autosport, agreed on the sale of a new camper and the trade-in of the van owned by Mr. and Mrs. Ramirez. Autosport and the Ramirezes signed a simple contract reflecting a $14,100 purchase price for the new van with a $4,700 trade-in allowance for the Ramirez van, which Mr. and Mrs. Ramirez left with Autosport. After further allowance for taxes, title and documentary fees, the net price was $9,902. Because Autosport needed two weeks to prepare the new van, the contract provided for delivery on or about August 3, 1978.

On that date, Mr. and Mrs. Ramirez returned with their checks to Autosport to pick up the new van. Graff was not there so Mr. White, another salesman, met them. Inspection disclosed several defects in the van. The paint was scratched, both the electric and sewer hookups were missing, and the hubcaps were not installed. White advised the Ramirezes not to accept the camper because it was not ready.

Mr. and Mrs. Ramirez wanted the van for a summer vacation and called Graff several times. Each time Graff told them it was not ready for delivery. Finally, Graff called to notify them that the camper was ready. On August 14, Mr. and Mrs. Ramirez went to Autosport to accept delivery, but workers were still touching up the outside paint. Also, the camper windows were open, and the dining area cushions were soaking wet. Mr. and Mrs. Ramirez could not use the camper in that condition, but Mr. Leis, Autosport's manager, suggested that they take the van and that Autosport would replace the cushions later. Mrs. Ramirez counteroffered to accept the van if they could withhold $2,000, but Leis agreed to no more than $250, which she refused. Leis then agreed to replace the cushions and to call them when the van was ready.

On August 15, 1978, Autosport transferred title to the van to Mr. and Mrs. Ramirez, a fact unknown to them until the summer of 1979. Between August 15 and September 1, 1978, Mrs. Ramirez called Graff several times urging him to complete the preparation of the van, but Graff constantly advised her that the van was not ready. He finally informed her that they could pick it up on September 1.

When Mr. and Mrs. Ramirez went to the showroom on September 1, Graff asked them to wait. And wait they did — for one and a half hours. No one from Autosport came forward to talk with them, and the Ramirezes left in disgust.

On October 5, 1978, Mr. and Mrs. Ramirez went to Autosport with an attorney friend. Although the parties disagreed on what occurred, the general topic was whether they should proceed with the deal or Autosport should return to the Ramirezes their trade-in van. Mrs. Ramirez claimed they rejected the new van and requested the return of their trade-in. Mr. Lustig, the owner of Autosport, thought, however, that the deal could be salvaged if the parties could agree on the dollar amount of a credit for the Ramirezes. Mr. and Mrs. Ramirez never took possession of the new van and repeated their request for the return of their trade-in. Later in October, however, Autosport sold the trade-in to an innocent third party for $4,995. Autosport claimed that the Ramirezes' van had a book value of $3,200 and claimed further that it spent $1,159.62 to repair their van. By subtracting the total of those two figures, $4,159.62, from the $4,995.00 sale price, Autosport claimed a $600-700 profit on the sale.

On November 20, 1978, the Ramirezes sued Autosport seeking, among other things, rescission of the contract. Autosport counterclaimed for breach of contract.

II

Our initial inquiry is whether a consumer may reject defective goods that do not conform to the contract of sale. The basic issue is whether under the UCC, adopted in New Jersey as N.J.S.A. 12A:1-101 et seq., a seller has the duty to deliver goods that conform precisely to the contract. We conclude that the seller is under such a duty to make a "perfect tender" and that a buyer has the right to reject goods that do not conform to the contract. That conclusion, however, does not resolve the entire dispute between buyer and seller. A more complete answer requires a brief statement of the history of the mutual obligations of buyers and sellers of commercial goods.

In the nineteenth century, sellers were required to deliver goods that complied exactly with the sales agreement. See Filley v. Polk, 115 U.S. 213, 29 L. Ed. 372, 373 (1885) (buyer not obliged to accept otherwise conforming scrap iron shipped to New Orleans from Leith, rather than Glasgow, Scotland, as required by contract); Columbian Iron Works & Dry-Dock Co. v. Douglas, 84 Md. 44, 34 A. 1118, 1120-1121 (1896) (buyer who agreed to purchase steel scrap from United States cruisers not obliged to take any other kind of scrap). That rule, known as the "perfect tender" rule, remained part of the law of sales well into the twentieth century. By the 1920's the doctrine was so entrenched in the law that Judge Learned Hand declared "[t]here is no room in commercial contracts for the doctrine of substantial performance." Mitsubishi Goshi Kaisha v. J. Aron & Co., Inc., 16 F.2d 185, 186 (2d Cir. 1926).

The harshness of the rule led courts to seek to ameliorate its effect and to bring the law of sales in closer harmony with the law of contracts, which allows rescission only for material breaches. LeRoy Dyal Co. v. Allen, 161 F.2d 152, 155 (4th Cir. 1947). See 5 Corbin, Contracts §1104 at 464 (1951); 12 Williston, Contracts §1455 at 14 (3d ed. 1970). Nevertheless, a variation of the perfect tender rule appeared in the Uniform Sales Act. N.J.S.A. 46:30-75 (purchasers permitted to reject goods or rescind contracts for any breach of warranty); N.J.S.A. 46:30-18 to -21 (warranties extended to include all the seller's obligations to the goods). See Honnold, "Buyer's Right of Rejection, A Study in the Impact of Codification Upon a Commercial Problem," 97 U. Pa. L. Rev. 457, 460 (1949). The chief objection to the continuation of the perfect tender rule was that buyers in a declining market would reject goods for minor nonconformities and force the loss on surprised sellers. See Hawkland, Sales and Bulk Sales Under the Uniform Commercial Code, 120-122 (1958), cited in N.J.S.A. 12A:2-508, New Jersey Study Comment 3.

To the extent that a buyer can reject goods for any nonconformity, the UCC retains the perfect tender rule. Section 2-106 states that goods conform to a contract "when they are in accordance with the obligations under the contract." Section 2-601 authorizes a buyer to reject goods if they "or the tender of delivery fail in any respect to conform to the contract." The Code, however, mitigates the harshness of the perfect tender rule and balances the interests of buyer and seller. See Restatement (Second), Contracts, §241 comment (b) (1981). The Code achieves that result through its provisions for revocation of acceptance and cure. N.J.S.A. 2-608, 2-508.

Initially, the rights of the parties vary depending on whether the rejection occurs before or after acceptance of the goods. Before acceptance, the buyer may reject goods for any nonconformity. N.J.S.A. 2-601. Because of the seller's right to cure, however, the buyer's rejection does not necessarily discharge the contract. N.J.S.A. 2-508. Within the time set for performance in the contract, the seller's right to cure is unconditional. Id., subsec. (1); see id., Official Comment 1. Some authorities recommend granting a breaching party a right to cure in all contracts, not merely those for the sale of goods. Restatement (Second), Contracts, ch. 10, especially §§237 and 241. Underlying the right to cure in both kinds of contracts is the recognition that parties should be encouraged to communicate with each other and to resolve their own problems. Id., Introduction p. 193.

The rights of the parties also vary if rejection occurs after the time set for performance. After expiration of that time, the seller has a further reasonable time to cure if he believed reasonably that the goods would be acceptable with or without a money allowance. N.J.S.A. 2-508(2). The determination of what constitutes a further reasonable time depends on the surrounding circumstances, which include the change of position by and the amount of inconvenience to the buyer. N.J.S.A. 2-508, Official Comment 3. Those circumstances also include the length of time needed by the seller to correct the nonconformity and his ability to salvage the goods by resale to others. See Restatement (Second), Contracts, §241 comment (d). Thus, the Code balances the buyer's right to reject nonconforming goods with a "second chance" for the seller to conform the goods to the contract under certain limited circumstances. N.J.S.A. 2-508, New Jersey Study Comment 1.

After acceptance, the Code strikes a different balance: the buyer may revoke acceptance only if the nonconformity substantially impairs the value of the goods to him. N.J.S.A. 2-608. See Herbstman v. Eastman Kodak Co., 68 N.J. 1, 9 (1975). See generally, Priest, "Breach and Remedy for the Tender of Non-Conforming Goods Under the Uniform Commercial Code: An Economic Approach," 92 Harv. L. Rev. 960, 971-973 (1978). This provision protects the seller from revocation for trivial defects. *Herbstman*, supra, 68 N.J. at 9. It also prevents the buyer from taking undue advantage of the seller by allowing goods to depreciate and then returning them because of asserted minor defects. See White & Summers, Uniform Commercial Code, §8-3 at 391 (2d ed. 1980). Because this case involves rejection of goods, we need not decide whether a seller has a right to cure substantial defects that justify revocation of acceptance. See Pavesi v. Ford Motor Co., 155 N.J. Super. 373, 378 (App. Div. 1978) (right to cure after acceptance limited to trivial defects) and White & Summers, supra, §8-4 at 319 n.76 (open question as to the relationship between §§2-608 and 2-508).

Other courts agree that the buyer has a right of rejection for any non-conformity, but that the seller has a countervailing right to cure within a reasonable time. Marine Mart Inc. v. Pearce, 480 S.W.2d 133, 137 (Ark. 1972). See Intermeat, Inc. v. American Poultry, Inc., 575 F.2d 1017, 1024 (2d Cir. 1978); Moulton Cavity & Mold, Inc. v. Lyn-Flex Industries, 396 A.2d 1024, 1027 n.6 (Me. 1979); Uchitel v. F.R. Tripler & Co., 434 N.Y.S.2d 77, 81, 107 Misc. 2d 310 (App. Term 1980); Rutland Music Services, Inc. v. Ford Motor Co., 422 A.2d 248, 249 (Vt. 1980). But see McKenzie v. Alla-Ohio Coals, Inc., 29 U.C.C. Rep. 852, 856-857 (D. D.C. 1979).

One New Jersey case, Gindy Mfg. Corp. v. Cardinale Trucking Corp., suggests that, because some defects can be cured, they do not justify rejection. 111 N.J. Super. 383, 387 n.1 (Law Div. 1970). Accord, Adams v. Tremontin, 42 N.J. Super. 313, 325 (App. Div. 1956) (Uniform Sales Act). But see Sudol v. Rudy Papa Motors, 175 N.J. Super. 238, 240-241 (D. Ct. 1980) (§2-601 contains perfect tender rule). Nonetheless we conclude that the perfect tender rule is preserved to the extent of permitting a buyer to reject goods for any defects. Because of the seller's right to cure, rejection does not terminate the contract. Accordingly, we disapprove the suggestion in *Gindy* that curable defects do not justify rejection.

A further problem, however, is identifying the remedy available to a buyer who rejects goods with insubstantial defects that the seller fails to cure within a reasonable time. The Code provides expressly that when "the buyer rightfully rejects, then with respect to the goods involved, the buyer may cancel." N.J.S.A. 2-711. "Cancellation" occurs when either party puts an end to the contract for breach by the other. N.J.S.A. 2-106(4). Nonetheless, some confusion exists whether the equitable remedy of rescission survives under the Code. Compare Ventura v. Ford Motor Corp., 173 N.J. Super. 501, 503 (Ch. Div. 1980) (rescission under UCC) and Pavesi v. Ford Motor Corp., supra, 155 N.J. Super. at 377 (equitable remedies still available since not specifically superseded, §1-103) with Edelstein v. Toyota Motors Dist., 176 N.J. Super. 57, 63-64 (App. Div. 1980) (under UCC rescission is revocation of acceptance) and Sudol v. Rudy Papa Motors, supra, 175 N.J. Super. at 241-242 (under UCC, rescission no longer exists as such).

The Code eschews the word "rescission" and substitutes the terms "cancellation," "revocation of acceptance," and "rightful rejection." N.J.S.A. 2-106(4); 2-608; and 2-711 & Official Comment 1. Although neither "rejection" nor "revocation of acceptance" is defined in the Code, rejection includes both the buyer's refusal to accept or keep delivered goods and his notification to the seller that he will not keep them. White & Summers, supra, §8-1 at 293. Revocation of acceptance is like rejection, but occurs after the buyer has accepted the goods. Nonetheless, revocation of acceptance is intended to provide the same relief as rescission of a contract of sale of goods. N.J.S.A. 2-608 Official Comment 1; N.J. Study Comment 2. In brief, revocation is tantamount to rescission. See Herbstman v. Eastman Kodak Co., supra, 68 N.J. at 9; accord, Peckham v. Larsen Chevrolet-Buick-Oldsmobile, Inc., 99 Idaho 675, ___, 587 P.2d 816, 818 (1978) (rescission and revocation of acceptance amount to the same thing). Similarly, subject to the seller's right to cure, a buyer who rightfully rejects goods, like one who revokes his acceptance, may cancel the contract. N.J.S.A. 2-711 & Official Comment 1. We need not resolve the extent to which rescission for reasons other than rejection or revocation of acceptance, e.g., fraud and mistake, survives as a remedy outside the Code. Compare N.J.S.A. 1-103 and White & Summers, supra, §8-1, p. 295, with N.J.S.A. 2-721. Accordingly, we approve *Edelstein* and *Sudol*, which recognize that explicit Code remedies replace rescission, and disapprove *Ventura* and *Pavesi* to the extent they suggest the UCC expressly recognizes rescission as a remedy.

Although the complaint requested rescission of the contract, plaintiffs actually sought not only the end of their contractual obligations, but also restoration to their pre-contractual position. That request incorporated the equitable doctrine of restitution, the purpose of which is to restore plaintiff to as good a position as he occupied before the contract. Corbin, supra, §1102 at 455. In UCC parlance, plaintiffs' request was for the cancellation of the contract and recovery of the price paid. N.J.S.A. 2-106(4), 2-711.

General contract law permits rescission only for material breaches, and the Code restates "materiality" in terms of "substantial impairment." See Herbstman v. Eastman Kodak Co., supra, 68 N.J. at 9; id. at 15 (Conford, J., concurring). The Code permits a buyer who rightfully rejects goods to cancel a contract of sale. N.J.S.A. 2-711. Because a buyer may reject goods with insubstantial defects, he also may cancel the contract if those defects remain uncured. Otherwise, a seller's failure to cure minor defects would compel a buyer to accept imperfect goods and collect for any loss caused by the non-conformity. N.J.S.A. 2-714.

Although the Code permits cancellation by rejection for minor defects, it permits revocation of acceptance only for substantial impairments. That distinction is consistent with other Code provisions that depend on whether the buyer has accepted the goods. Acceptance creates liability in the buyer for the price, N.J.S.A. 2-709 (1), and precludes rejection. N.J.S.A. 2-607(2); N.J.S.A. 2-606, New Jersey Study Comment 1. Also, once a buyer accepts goods, he has the burden to prove any defect. N.J.S.A. 2-607(4); White & Summers, supra, §8-2 at 297. By contrast, where goods are rejected for not conforming to the contract, the burden is on the seller to prove that the nonconformity was corrected. Miron v. Yonkers Raceway, Inc., 400 F.2d 112, 119 (2d Cir. 1968).

Underlying the Code provisions is the recognition of the revolutionary change in business practices in this century. The purchase of goods is no longer a simple transaction in which a buyer purchases individually made goods from a seller in a face-to-face transaction. Our economy depends on a complex system for the manufacture, distribution, and sale of goods, a system in which manufacturers and consumers rarely meet. Faceless manu-facturers mass-produce goods for unknown consumers who purchase those goods from merchants exercising little or no control over the quality of their production. In an age of assembly lines, we are accustomed to cars with scratches, television sets without knobs and other goods with all kinds of defects. Buyers no longer expect a "perfect tender." If a merchant sells defective goods, the reasonable expectation of the parties is that the buyer will return those goods and that the seller will repair or replace them.

Recognizing this commercial reality, the Code permits a seller to cure imperfect tenders. Should the seller fail to cure the defects, whether substantial or not, the balance shifts again in favor of the buyer, who has the right to cancel or seek damages. N.J.S.A. 2-711. In general, economic considerations would induce sellers to cure minor defects. See generally Priest, supra, 92 Harv. L. Rev. 973-974. Assuming the seller does not cure, however, the buyer should be permitted to exercise his remedies under N.J.S.A. 2-711. The Code remedies for consumers are to be liberally con-strued, and the buyer should have the option of cancelling if the seller does not provide conforming goods. See N.J.S.A. 1-106.

To summarize, the UCC preserves the perfect tender rule to the extent of permitting a buyer to reject goods for any nonconformity. Nonetheless, that rejection does not automatically terminate the contract. A seller may still effect a cure and preclude unfair rejection and cancellation by the buyer. N.J.S.A. 2-508, Official Comment 2; N.J.S.A. 2-711, Official Comment 1.

III

The trial court found that Mr. and Mrs. Ramirez had rejected the van within a reasonable time under N.J.S.A. 12A:2-602. The court found that on August 3, 1978, Autosport's salesman advised the Ramirezes not to accept the van and that on August 14, they rejected delivery and Autosport agreed to replace the cushions. Those findings are supported by substantial credible evidence, and we sustain them. See Rova Farms Resort v. Investors Ins. Co., 65 N.J. 474, 483-484 (1974). Although the trial court did not find whether Autosport cured the defects within a reasonable time, we find that Autosport did not effect a cure. Clearly the van was not ready for delivery during August, 1978, when Mr. and Mrs. Ramirez rejected it, and Autosport had the burden of proving that it had corrected the defects. Although the Ramirezes gave Autosport ample time to correct the defects, Autosport did not demonstrate that the van conformed to the contract on September 1. In fact, on that date, when Mr. and Mrs. Ramirez returned at Autosport's invitation, all they received was discourtesy.

On the assumption that substantial impairment is necessary only when a purchaser seeks to revoke acceptance under N.J.S.A. 2-608, the trial court correctly refrained from deciding whether the defects substantially impaired the van. The court properly concluded that plaintiffs were entitled to "rescind" — i.e., to "cancel" — the contract.

Because Autosport had sold the trade-in to an innocent third party, the trial court determined that the Ramirezes were entitled not to the return of the trade-in, but to its fair market value, which the court set at the contract price of $4,700. A buyer who rightfully rejects goods and cancels the contract may, among other possible remedies, recover so much of the purchase price as has been paid. N.J.S.A. 2-711. The Code, however, does not define "pay" and does not require payment to be made in cash. . . .

For the preceding reasons, we affirm the judgment of the Appellate Division.

QUESTIONS

1. Did the defendant's grounds for cure fit within §2-508?
2. Is the court creating a right to cure outside of §2-508?

PROBLEM 65

Ulysses Sinon ran a dude ranch in Troy, Colorado. He decided to erect a statue of a giant horse near the entrance to the ranch as a tourist attraction. The horse was specially manufactured by Epeius of Paris and arrived in six boxes to be assembled by Sinon. When the horse was put together, Sinon was displeased with the appearance of the tail. The horse had been designed by Epeius, and the scale model Sinon had seen when he decided to buy the horse had had a different tail. Sinon removed the tail and substituted one of his own design. He returned the original to Epeius along with a letter of rejection. In the meantime, Sinon painted the rest of the horse black (in the delivered state it was white) and used it extensively in advertising for the ranch. The horse failed to attract new business to the ranch. After three months of display, Sinon took it down and shipped it back to Epeius with a letter of rejection that stated that the problem with the tail made the horse unattractive and unusable. Epeius sues. Did Sinon make a rejection or an acceptance? See Technology and Supply Management, LLC v. Johnson Controls Building Automation Systems, LLC, 2017 WL 3219281 (E.D. Va. 2017). If the tail did not conform to the model, is that a ground for rejection? See §2-601. If Sinon had made a technical acceptance, does that fact preclude a suit for breach of warranty? See §2-607(2). What steps should Sinon take to preserve his legal rights? See §2-607(3)(a). What reasons lie behind the notice requirement? See §§2-508, 2-515.

Plateq Corp. of North Haven v. Machlett Laboratories, Inc.
Supreme Court of Connecticut, 1983, 189 Conn. 433, 456 A.2d 786

PETERS, J.

In this action by a seller of specially manufactured goods to recover their purchase price from a commercial buyer, the principal issue is whether the buyer accepted the goods before it attempted to cancel the contract of sale. The plaintiff, Plateq Corporation of North Haven, sued the defendant, The Machlett Laboratories, Inc., to recover damages, measured by the contract price and incidental damages, arising out of the defendant's allegedly wrongful cancellation of a written contract for the manufacture and sale of two lead-covered steel tanks and appurtenant stands. The defendant denied liability and counterclaimed for damages. After a full hearing, the trial court found for the plaintiff both on its complaint and on the defendant's counterclaim. The defendant has appealed.

The trial court, in its memorandum of decision, found the following facts. On July 9, 1976, the defendant ordered from the plaintiff two lead-covered steel tanks to be constructed by the plaintiff according to specifications supplied by the defendant. The parties understood that the tanks were designed for the special purpose of testing x-ray tubes and were required to be radiation-proof within certain federal standards. Accordingly, the contract provided that the tanks would be tested for radiation leaks after their installation on the defendant's premises. The plaintiff undertook to correct, at its own cost, any deficiencies that this post-installation test might uncover. The plaintiff had not previously constructed such tanks, nor had the defendant previously designed tanks for this purpose. The contract was amended on August 9, 1976, to add construction of two metal stands to hold the tanks. All the goods were to be delivered to the defendant at the plaintiff's place of business.

Although the plaintiff encountered difficulties both in performing according to the contract specifications and in completing performance within the time required, the defendant did no more than call these deficiencies to the plaintiff's attention during various inspections in September and early October, 1976. By October 11, 1976, performance was belatedly but substantially completed. On that date, Albert Yannello, the defendant's engineer, noted some remaining deficiencies which the plaintiff promised to remedy by the next day, so that the goods would then be ready for delivery. Yannello gave no indication to the plaintiff that this arrangement was in any way unsatisfactory to the defendant. Not only did Yannello communicate general acquiescence in the plaintiff's proposed tender but he specifically led the plaintiff to believe that the defendant's truck would pick up the tanks and the stands within a day or two. Instead of sending its truck, the defendant sent a notice of total cancellation which the plaintiff received on October 14, 1976. That notice failed to particularize the grounds upon which cancellation was based.

On this factual basis, the trial court, having concluded that the transaction was a contract for the sale of goods falling within the Uniform Commercial Code, General Statutes §§2-101 et seq., considered whether the defendant had accepted the goods. The court determined that the defendant had accepted the tanks, primarily by signifying its willingness to take them despite their nonconformities, in accordance with General Statutes §2-606(1)(a), and secondarily by failing to make an effective rejection, in accordance with General Statutes §2-606(1)(b). Once the tanks had been accepted, the defendant could rightfully revoke its acceptance under General Statutes §2-608 only by showing substantial impairment of their value to the defendant. In part because the defendant's conduct had foreclosed any post-installation inspection, the court concluded that such impairment had not been proved. Since the tanks were not readily resalable on the open market, the plaintiff was entitled, upon the defendant's wrongful revocation of acceptance, to recover their contract price, minus salvage value, plus interest. General Statutes §§2-703; 2-709(1)(b). Accordingly, the trial court awarded the plaintiff damages in the amount of $14,837.92.

In its appeal, the defendant raises four principal claims of error. It maintains that the trial court erred: (1) in invoking the "cure" section, General Statutes §2-508, when there had been no tender by the plaintiff seller; (2) in concluding, in accordance with the acceptance section, General Statutes

§2-606(1), that the defendant had "signified" to the plaintiff its willingness to take the contract goods; (3) in misconstruing the defendant's statutory and contractual rights of inspection; and (4) in refusing to find that the defendant's letter of cancellation was occasioned by the plaintiff's breach. We find no error.

Upon analysis, all of the defendant's claims of error are variations upon one central theme. The defendant claims that on October 11, when its engineer Yannello conducted the last examination on the plaintiff's premises, the tanks were so incomplete and unsatisfactory that the defendant was rightfully entitled to conclude that the plaintiff would never make a conforming tender. From this scenario, the defendant argues that it was justified in cancelling the contract of sale. It denies that the seller's conduct was sufficient to warrant a finding of tender, or its own conduct sufficient to warrant a finding of acceptance. The difficulty with this argument is that it is inconsistent with the underlying facts found by the trial court. Although the testimony was in dispute, there was evidence of record to support the trial court's findings to the contrary. The defendant cannot sustain its burden of establishing that a trial court's findings of fact are clearly erroneous; Practice Book §3060D; Pandolphe's Auto Parts, Inc. v. Manchester, 181 Conn. 217, 221-22, 435 A.2d 24 (1980); by the mere recitation in its brief of conflicting testimony entirely unsupported by reference to pages of the transcript. Practice Book §3060F(b). There is simply no fit between the defendant's claims and the trial court's finding that, by October 11, 1976, performance was in substantial compliance with the terms of the contract. The trial court further found that on that day the defendant was notified that the goods would be ready for tender the following day and that the defendant responded to this notification by promising to send its truck to pick up the tanks in accordance with the contract.

On the trial court's finding of facts, it was warranted in concluding, on two independent grounds, that the defendant had accepted the goods it had ordered from the plaintiff. Under the provisions of the Uniform Commercial Code, General Statutes §32a-2-606(1) "[a]cceptance of goods occurs when the buyer (a) after a reasonable opportunity to inspect the goods signifies to the seller . . . that he will take . . . them in spite of their nonconformity; or (b) fails to make an effective rejection."

In concluding that the defendant had "signified" to the plaintiff its willingness to "take" the tanks despite possible remaining minor defects, the trial court necessarily found that the defendant had had a reasonable opportunity to inspect the goods. The defendant does not maintain that its engineer, or the other inspectors on previous visits, had inadequate access to the tanks, or inadequate experience to conduct a reasonable examination. It recognizes that inspection of goods when the buyer undertakes to pick up the goods is ordinarily at the seller's place of tender. See General Statutes

§§42a-2-503, 42a-2-507, 42a-2-513; see also White & Summers, Uniform Commercial Code §3-5 (2d ed. 1980). The defendant argues, however, that its contract, in providing for inspection for radiation leaks after installation of the tanks at its premises, necessarily postponed its inspection rights to that time. The trial court considered this argument and rejected it, and so do we. It was reasonable, in the context of this contract for the special manufacture of goods with which neither party had had prior experience, to limit this clause to adjustments to take place after tender and acceptance. After acceptance, a buyer may still, in appropriate cases, revoke its acceptance, General Statutes §42a-2-608, or recover damages for breach of warranty, General Statutes §42a-2-714. The trial court reasonably concluded that a post-installation test was intended to safeguard these rights of the defendant as well as to afford the plaintiff a final opportunity to make needed adjustments. The court was therefore justified in concluding that there had been an acceptance within §42a-2-606(1)(a). A buyer may be found to have accepted goods despite their known nonconformity; [citations omitted].

The trial court's alternate ground for concluding that the tanks had been accepted was the defendant's failure to make an effective rejection. Pursuant to General Statutes §42a-2-606(1)(b), an acceptance occurs when, after a reasonable opportunity to inspect, a buyer has failed to make "an effective rejection as provided by subsection (1) of section 42a-2-602." The latter subsection, in turn, makes a rejection "ineffective unless the buyer reasonably notifies the seller." General Statutes §42a-2-605(1)(a) goes on to provide that a buyer is precluded from relying, as a basis for rejection, upon unparticularized defects in his notice of rejection, if the defects were such that, with reasonable notice, the seller could have cured by making a substituted, conforming tender. The defendant does not question the trial court's determination that its telegram of cancellation failed to comply with the requirement of particularization contained in §2-605(1). Instead, the defendant argues that the plaintiff was not entitled to an opportunity to cure, under General Statutes §2-508, because the plaintiff had never made a tender of the tanks. That argument founders, however, on the trial court's finding that the seller was ready to make a tender on the day following the last inspection by the defendant's engineer and would have done so but for its receipt of the defendant's telegram of cancellation. The trial court furthermore found that the defendant's unparticularized telegram of cancellation wrongfully interfered with the plaintiff's contractual right to cure any remaining post-installation defects. In these circumstances, the telegram of cancellation constituted both a wrongful and an ineffective rejection on the part of the defendant. See Uchitel v. F.R. Tripler & Co., 107 Misc. 2d 310, 434 N.Y.S.2d 77, 81-82 (Supreme Court 1980); White & Summers, supra, §8-3, p. 315.

Once the conclusion is reached that the defendant accepted the tanks, its further rights of cancellation under the contract are limited by the governing provisions of the Uniform Commercial Code. "The buyer's acceptance of goods, despite their alleged non-conformity, is a watershed. After acceptance, the buyer must pay for the goods at the contract rate; General Statutes §2-607(1); and bears the burden of establishing their nonconformity. General Statutes §2-607(4)." Stelco Industries, Inc. v. Cohen, 182 Conn. 561, 563-64, 438 A.2d 759 (1980). After acceptance, the buyer may only avoid liability for the contract price by invoking the provision which permits revocation of acceptance. That provision, General Statutes §2-608(1), requires proof that the "nonconformity [of the goods] substantially impairs [their] value to him." See Superior Wire & Paper Products, Ltd. v. Talcott Tool & Machine, Inc., 184 Conn. 10 (42 C.L.J. 44, pp. 4, 6), 441 A.2d 43 (1981); Conte v. Dwan Lincoln-Mercury, Inc., 172 Conn. 112, 120-21, 374 A.2d 144 (1976). On this question, which is an issue of fact; Superior Wire & Paper Products, Ltd. v. Talcott Tool & Machine, Inc., supra, 6-7; Conte v. Dwan Lincoln-Mercury, Inc., supra, 121; the trial court again found against the defendant. Since the defendant has provided no basis for any argument that the trial court was clearly erroneous in finding that the defendant had not met its burden of proof to show that the goods were substantially nonconforming, we can find no error in the conclusion that the defendant's cancellation constituted an unauthorized and hence wrongful revocation of acceptance.

Finally, the defendant in its brief, although not in its statement of the issues presented, challenges the trial court's conclusion about the remedial consequences of its earlier determinations. Although the trial court might have found the plaintiff entitled to recover the contract price because of the defendant's acceptance of the goods; General Statutes §§2-703(e) and 2-709(1)(a); the court chose instead to rely on General Statutes §2-709(1)(b), which permits a price action for contract goods that cannot, after reasonable effort, be resold at a reasonable price. Since the contract goods in this case were concededly specially manufactured for the defendant, the defendant cannot and does not contest the trial court's finding that any effort to resell them on the open market would have been unavailing. In the light of this finding, the defendant can only reiterate its argument, which we have already rejected, that the primary default was that of the plaintiff rather than that of the defendant. The trial court's conclusion to the contrary supports both its award to the plaintiff and its denial of the defendant's counterclaim.

There is no error.

NOTE

If the parties specifically provide that the buyer will have the right to inspect and test the goods, that will extend the reasonable time to accept or reject the goods. See Virginia Elec. and Power Co. v. Bransen Energy, Inc., 2015 WL 2061983 (E.D. Va. 2015) (time for rejection extended where contract provided for buyer to send coal samples for independent laboratory analysis).

V. *REVOCATION OF ACCEPTANCE*

Having made a technical acceptance, a buyer may still bring a breach of warranty action provided that a proper §2-607(3)(a) notice has been given. If the buyer wins, damages based on §§2-714 and 2-715 will be awarded, and the buyer will still have the goods. If the buyer does not want the goods, but wants the return of the price, the proper UCC method is called *revocation of acceptance*. Read §2-608. At common law this action was called *rescission*. However, revocation of acceptance differs from common law rescission because the buyer not only recovers the price, but may recover consequential damages as well. See Official Comment 1 to §2-608; cf. §§2-711(1), 2-715 (also note Official Comment 1 to §2-715).

In both rejection and revocation of acceptance, the buyer in essence disclaims the goods. The standards under which a buyer can revoke acceptance are more difficult to meet than are the standards for rejection. In rejection, a buyer can in theory reject if the goods "fail in any respect"; however, to revoke an acceptance, the buyer must show that the defect "substantially impairs the value" of the goods. See Annot., 98 A.L.R.3d 1183.

Waddell v. L.V.R.V. Inc.
Supreme Court of Nevada, 2006, 122 Nev. 15, 125 P.3d 1160

GIBBONS, J.

This is an appeal and cross-appeal from a district court judgment allowing revocation of acceptance of a contract and an order awarding attorney fees and costs.

Respondent/cross-appellant L.V.R.V. Inc., D/B/A Wheeler's Las Vegas RV (Wheeler's) sold a 1996 Coachmen Santara motor home (the RV) to appellants/cross-respondents Arthur R. Waddell and Roswitha M. Waddell (the Waddells). The Waddells noticed numerous problems with the RV and "continually" had to return it to Wheeler's service department for repairs. Eventually, the Waddells stopped attempting to have Wheeler's make repairs and filed a complaint seeking to revoke their acceptance of the RV or, in the alternative, money damages. Wheeler's answered the complaint and filed a third-party complaint seeking indemnification from respondent

Coachmen Recreational Vehicle Company, Inc. (Coachmen). After a bench trial, the district court granted judgment in favor of the Waddells and Coachmen.

On appeal, Wheeler's argues that (1) the district court erred in allowing the Waddells to revoke their acceptance, (2) the district court abused its discretion by admitting two documents into evidence, (3) the district court erred in denying Wheeler's motion for attorney fees, and (4) the district court erred in denying indemnification from Coachmen. The Waddells argue on cross-appeal that the district court erred in denying them (1) computerized research costs and (2) post-judgment interest on their attorney fees award.

FACTS

In 1996, the Waddells served jointly as president of the Las Vegas area Coachmen Association Camping Club. During the course of that group's meetings, the Waddells spoke with Tom Pender, Wheeler's sales manager, about upgrading from the motor home they then owned to a "diesel pusher" motor coach. As a result of that conversation, Pender took the Waddells to the Wheeler's lot and showed them a 1996 Coachmen Santara model diesel pusher coach.

The Waddells test-drove and eventually agreed to purchase the RV and an extended warranty. Before they took possession of the RV, the Waddells requested that Wheeler's perform various repairs. The Waddells' request included a service on the RV's engine cooling system, new batteries, and alignment of the door frames. Wheeler's told Arthur Waddell that the repairs had been performed as requested. The Waddells took delivery of the RV on September 1, 1997.

The Waddells first noticed a problem with the RV's engine shortly after they took possession of it. They drove the RV from Las Vegas to Hemet, California. On the return trip, the entry door popped open and the RV's engine overheated while ascending a moderate grade to such a degree that Mr. Waddell had to pull over to the side of the road and wait for the engine to cool down.

When the Waddells returned from California, they took the RV back to Wheeler's for repairs. Despite Wheeler's attempts to repair the RV, the Waddells continually experienced more problems with the RV, including further episodes of engine overheating. Between September 1997 and March 1999, Wheeler's service department spent a total of seven months during different periods of time attempting to repair the RV.

On June 9, 2000, the Waddells filed a complaint in district court seeking both equitable relief and money damages. Wheeler's answered the complaint and ultimately filed a third-party complaint against Coachmen seeking equitable indemnification and contribution.

Following a three-day bench trial, the district court issued its findings of fact, conclusions of law, and judgment. The district court concluded that the RV's nonconformities substantially impaired its value to the Waddells. The district court allowed the Waddells to revoke their acceptance of the RV and ordered Wheeler's to return all of the Waddells' out-of-pocket expenses, but further concluded that Wheeler's was not entitled to indemnification from Coachmen. Following entry of judgment, the district court awarded the Waddells $15,000 in attorney fees, entered supplemental findings of fact and conclusions of law, issued an amended judgment, entered a separate order denying post-judgment interest on the attorney fee award, and denied the Waddells' motion to retax their costs to include computerized research fees. This timely appeal and cross-appeal followed.

DISCUSSION

Wheeler's argues that the district court erred in allowing the Waddells to revoke their acceptance of the RV because the Waddells failed to prove that the RV suffered nonconformities that substantially impaired its value. We disagree.

The district court found that despite Wheeler's good-faith attempts to repair the RV, the nonconformities persisted and rendered the RV unfit for its intended use. Some of those nonconformities identified by the district court included: the bedroom air conditioning does not cool, the front air conditioning does not cool, the dash heater does not blow hot air, RV batteries do not stay charged, and chronic engine overheating. The district court concluded that these nonconformities and others substantially impaired the RV's value to the Waddells and that the Waddells had revoked their acceptance of the RV within a reasonable time.

SUBSTANTIAL IMPAIRMENT

NRS 104.2608(1) provides that a buyer may revoke his acceptance if the item suffers from a "nonconformity [that] substantially impairs its value *to him*" and (a) the buyer accepted the goods on the understanding that the seller would cure the nonconformity or (b) the buyer was unaware of the nonconformity and the nonconformity was concealed by the difficulty of discovery or by the seller's assurances that the good was conforming. (Emphasis added.)

We have never before determined when a nonconformity substantially impairs the value of a good to the buyer. Other jurisdictions treat this determination as an issue of fact,[4] which "is made in light of the 'totality of the circumstances' of each particular case, including the number of deficiencies and type of nonconformity and the time and inconvenience spent in downtime and attempts at repair."[5]

The Supreme Court of Oregon has established a two-part test to determine whether a nonconformity, under the totality of the circumstances, substantially impairs the value of the goods to the buyer. The test has both an objective and a subjective prong:

> Since [the statute] provides that the buyer may revoke acceptance of goods "whose nonconformity substantially impairs its value to him," the value of conforming goods to the plaintiff must first be determined. This is a subjective question in the sense that it calls for a consideration of the needs and circumstances of the plaintiff who seeks to revoke; not the needs and circumstances of an average buyer. The second inquiry is whether the nonconformity in fact substantially impairs the value of the goods to the buyer, having in mind his particular needs. This is an objective question in the sense that it calls for evidence of something more than plaintiff's assertion that the nonconformity impaired the value to him; it requires evidence from which it can be inferred that plaintiff's needs were not met because of the nonconformity.[6]

Since Nevada, like Oregon, adopted Uniform Commercial Code §2-608 verbatim, we conclude that this test applies to NRS 104.2608. Accordingly, we adopt the Supreme Court of Oregon's two-part test for determining whether a nonconformity substantially affects the good's value to the buyer under NRS 104.2608(1).

SUBJECTIVE VALUE TO THE WADDELLS

Arthur Waddell testified that he purchased the RV to enjoy the RV lifestyle. Before purchasing the RV, the Waddells owned similar vehicles that they used both as a residence and for camping trips. In fact, Mr. Waddell testified that he and his wife intended to sell their house and spend two to three years traveling around the country.

4. See, e.g., Frontier Mobile Home Sales, Inc. v. Trigleth, 256 Ark. 101, 505 S.W.2d 516, 517 (1974); Rester v. Morrow, 491 So. 2d 204, 209 (Miss. 1986); McCullough v. Bill Swad Chrysler-Plymouth, 5 Ohio St. 3d 181, 449 N.E.2d 1289, 1294 (1983).
5. Fortin v. Ox-Bow Marina, Inc., 408 Mass. 310, 557 N.E.2d 1157, 1162 (1990) (quoting *Rester*, 491 So. 2d at 210).
6. Jorgensen v. Pressnall, 274 Or. 285, 545 P.2d 1382, 1384-85 (1976) (footnote omitted), quoted with approval in McGilbray v. Scholfield Winnebago, Inc., 221 Kan. 605, 561 P.2d 832, 836 (1977); see also Milicevic v. Mercedes-Benz USA, LLC, 256 F. Supp. 2d 1168, 1176 (D. Nev. 2003) (applying a two-part test that addressed both objective and subjective considerations); Haight v. Dales Used Cars, Inc., 139 Idaho 853, 87 P.3d 962, 966 (App. 2003) (applying a similar two-part test).

Mr. Waddell further testified that he shopped at Wheeler's based on Wheeler's advertisements. Marlene Wheeler, president and chief operating officer, testified that Wheeler's advertising encouraged the purchase of an RV to find unlimited freedom. When Mr. Waddell spoke with Tom Pender, sales manager at Wheeler's, about upgrading to an RV for those purposes, Pender told him that he had an RV on the lot that would meet his needs.

Mr. Waddell's testimony demonstrates that the RV's subjective value to the Waddells was based on their ability to spend two or three years driving the RV around the country. Thus, we must consider whether the RV's nonconformities substantially impaired the value of the RV based on the Waddells' particular needs.

OBJECTIVE IMPAIRMENT

Mr. Waddell testified that as a result of the RV's defects, he and his wife were unable to enjoy the RV as they had intended. Mr. Waddell further testified that the RV's engine would overheat within ten miles of embarking if the travel included any climbing. As a result of the overheating, the Waddells were forced to park on the side of the road and wait for the engine to cool down before continuing. Consequently, the RV spent a total of 213 days, or seven months and one day, at Wheeler's service department during the eighteen months immediately following the purchase. This testimony is sufficient to demonstrate an objective, substantial impairment of value.

The Supreme Court of Ohio has stated that a nonconformity effects a substantial impairment of value if it "shakes the buyer's faith or undermines his confidence in the reliability and integrity of the purchased item."[7] The Supreme Judicial Court of Massachusetts has recognized that "even cosmetic or minor defects that go unrepaired . . . or defects which do not totally prevent the buyer from using the goods, but circumscribe that use . . . can substantially impair the goods' value to the buyer."[8] The United States District Court for the District of Nevada recently reiterated that "'the [seller's] inability to correct defects in [motor] vehicles creates a major hardship and an unacceptable economic burden on the consumer.'"[9]

In this case, the chronic engine overheating shook the Waddells' faith in the RV and undermined their confidence in the RV's reliability and integrity. Not only did this problem make travel in the RV unreliable and stressful to the Waddells, the overheating made travel in the vehicle objectively unsafe.

---

7. *McCullough*, 449 N.E.2d at 1294; see also *Rester*, 491 So. 2d at 210-211.

8. *Fortin*, 557 N.E.2d at 1162.

9. *Milicevic*, 256 F. Supp. 2d at 1176 (quoting Berrie v. Toyota Motor Sales, USA, Inc., 267 N.J. Super. 152, 630 A.2d 1180, 1181 (1993)).

Accordingly, we conclude that substantial evidence exists to support revocation of acceptance under NRS 104.2608(1).

REASONABLE TIME FOR REVOKING ACCEPTANCE

Wheeler's argues that the Waddells should not have been allowed to revoke their acceptance because they did not attempt to revoke within a reasonable time after purchasing the RV. We disagree.

Under NRS 104.2608(2), "[r]evocation of acceptance must occur within a reasonable time after the buyer discovers or should have discovered the ground for it and before any substantial change in condition of the goods which is not caused by their own defects." The statute further provides that revocation "is not effective until the buyer notifies the seller of it." We have never before determined a reasonable timeline for revocation of acceptance. However, other jurisdictions have held that the reasonable time determination "depends upon the nature, purpose and circumstances of the transaction."[10] The reasonable time determination is generally considered to be an issue of fact for the trial court.

Here, the district court found that the Waddells were entitled to revoke their acceptance since they notified Wheeler's of their intent to revoke within a reasonable time. Mr. Waddell testified that he first noticed the RV's defects immediately after his purchase. Mr. Waddell took the RV to Wheeler's service department whenever he noticed a defect and Wheeler's always attempted, often unsuccessfully, to repair the RV. In September 1998, Mr. Waddell took the RV to Wheeler's after continued engine overheating. As a result of these defects, Wheeler's service department kept the RV for approximately seven months of the eighteen months that the Waddells owned the RV. Roger Beauchemin, a former employee of Wheeler's service department, testified that Wheeler's was unable to repair some of the defects, including the engine's chronic overheating problems. In January 1999, the Waddells again brought the RV to Wheeler's complaining of persistent engine overheating. The Waddells demanded a full refund of the purchase price in March 1999 and sought legal counsel. Through counsel, the Waddells wrote to Wheeler's during the summer of 1999 to resolve the matter. Wheeler's did not respond to these inquiries until early 2000. Unable to resolve the dispute with Wheeler's, the Waddells revoked their acceptance of the RV in June 2000.

The seller of nonconforming goods must generally receive an opportunity to cure the nonconformity before the buyer may revoke his acceptance.

---

10. DeVoe Chevrolet-Cadillac v. Cartwright, 526 N.E.2d 1237, 1240 (Ind. Ct. App. 1988); see also Golembieski v. O'Rielly R.V. Center, Inc., 147 Ariz. 134, 708 P.2d 1325, 1328 (Ariz. Ct. App. 1985) (noting that "[r]easonableness of the time for revocation is a question of fact unique to the circumstances of each case").

However, as the Supreme Court of Mississippi has recognized, the seller may not "postpone revocation in perpetuity by fixing everything that goes wrong."[11] Rather, "[t]here comes a time when . . . [the buyer] is entitled to say, 'That's all,' and revoke, notwithstanding the seller's repeated good faith efforts to [cure]."

Furthermore, the seller's attempts to cure do not count against the buyer regarding timely revocation. The United States District Court for the District of Nevada has held that the "time for revocation of acceptance will be tolled while the seller attempts repairs."[12] Tolling the reasonable time for revocation of acceptance is appropriate given "the buyer's obligation to act in good faith, and to afford the seller a reasonable opportunity to cure any defect in the goods."

The Waddells gave Wheeler's several opportunities to repair the defects before revoking their acceptance. Because Wheeler's was unable to repair the defects after a total of seven months, the Waddells were entitled to say "that's all" and revoke their acceptance, notwithstanding Wheeler's good-faith attempts to repair the RV. Also, the reasonable time for revocation was tolled during the seven months that Wheeler's kept the RV and attempted to repair the defects. Accordingly, the district court's determination is supported by substantial evidence and is not clearly erroneous. . . .

CONCLUSION

The district court did not err in allowing the Waddells to revoke their acceptance of the RV within a reasonable time because chronic engine overheating problems substantially impaired the RV's value to the Waddells. . . .

QUESTIONS

1. Sometimes the buyer will return the car to the seller when giving a notice of revocation. Need the buyer do this? Read carefully §§2-711(3); cf. §2-706. See Mobile Home Sales Management, Inc. v. Brown, 562 P.2d 1378 (Ariz. App. 1977) ("when the buyer has a security interest in the goods and the seller makes no request for their return, the buyer should not be penalized by making tender back a prerequisite to revocation of acceptance"). See also Deaton, Inc. v. Aeroglide Corp., 99 N.M. 253, 657 P.2d 109 (1982). What if the buyer did not have a security interest in the car? See §§2-608(3), 2-602.

---

11. See *Rester,* 491 So. 2d at 210.
12. Sierra Diesel Injection Service v. Burroughs Corp., 651 F. Supp. 1371, 1378 (D. Nev. 1987).

2. Should the court, when allowing revocation, make an allowance for the use the buyer got from the car? Is the seller entitled to a setoff for the amount of benefits the purchaser received? See §1-103; compare Barco Auto Leasing Corp. v. House, 202 Conn. 106, 520 A.2d 162 (1987) with Moore v. Howard Pontiac-American, Inc., 492 S.W.2d 227 (Tenn. App. 1973).

3. If the buyer keeps the car after revoking acceptance, may the buyer keep driving it without negating the effectiveness of the revocation of acceptance? See §§2-606(1)(c), 2-602(2)(a), (b). Compare Computerized Radiological Serv. v. Syntex Corp., 786 F.2d 72 (2d Cir. 1986) (use of CAT scanner for 22 months after sending letter of revocation constituted acceptance), Wadsworth Plumbing & Heating Co., Inc. v. Tallycraft Corp., 277 Or. 433, 560 P.2d 1080 (1977) ("such use would appear to be an 'act inconsistent with the seller's ownership'"), and Fecik v. Capindale, 54 Pa. D. & C.2d 701 (1971) (post-revocation use destroys buyer's §2-608 suit), with Deere & Co. v. Johnson, 271 F.3d 613 (5th Cir. 2001) (farmer's continued use of combine excused where replacement cost high); Pittman v. Henry Moncure Motors, Inc., 243 N.C. App. 207 (2015) (reasonable for buyers to continue to reside in manufactured home for 11 years, pending resolution of dispute); Star of the West Milling Company v. Hartwick Sales and Service Limited, 2016 WL 3753530 (E.D. Mich. 2016) ("Following Hartwick's refusal to honor Star's revocation, it appears from the evidence that continued use of the System is the only reasonable way for Star to mitigate damages while it awaits a new system"), and Keller v. Inland Metals All Weather Conditioning, Inc., 76 P.3d 977 (Idaho 2003) (use of rejected dehumidifier excused where unavoidable). In a leading case involving vehicles, the Kansas Supreme Court permitted post-revocation use (with a setoff to seller for the benefit buyer received thereby); Johnson v. General Motors Corp., 233 Kan. 1044, 668 P.2d 139 (1983) ("Here buyers were placed in a position where if they stored the truck . . . they would not have had a vehicle for transportation. . . . With little or no low-cost public transportation available to the public, private transportation has changed from a luxury to a necessity."). The Massachusetts Supreme Judicial Court has agreed with this, stating that a jury should be instructed to consider a number of circumstances in deciding the reasonableness of the buyer's actions: the seller's instructions to the buyer after revocation of acceptance; the degree of economic and other hardship that the buyer would suffer if he or she discontinued using the defective goods; the reasonableness of the buyer's use after revocation as a method of mitigating damages; the degree of prejudice to the seller; and whether the seller acted in bad faith; Liarikos v. Mello, 418 Mass. 669, 639 N.E.2d 716 (1994).

Given this, if your client tells you, the attorney, that it is necessary to continue to use the goods following rejection/revocation, what do you advise? Cf. §2-714.

4. Is the seller entitled to more than one opportunity to cure? See Car Transportation Brokerage Company, Inc. v. Blue Bird Body, 322 Fed. Appx. 891 (11th Cir. 2009) (holding that because the electrical system for a motor coach is a complex piece of equipment, buyer must give seller more than one chance to cure before revoking acceptance).

5. Could a buyer revoke acceptance after buyer has already resold nonconforming goods at a loss? See §§2-706(1), 2-711(3); Summit Auto Sales, Inc. v. Draco, Inc., 2017 WL 3896691 (N.D. Ala. 2017).

NOTE: LEMON LAWS

A number of states have enacted so-called Lemon Laws that resolve some of the disputes we have been exploring when they arise in connection with a consumer's purchase of an automobile. For example, the issue addressed in the last question is specifically covered by many of these statutes. New York General Business Law §198a says that a refund from the defendant may be reduced by "a reasonable allowance for the consumer's use of the vehicle in excess of the first 12,000 miles of operation and a reasonable allowance for any damage not attributable to normal wear or improvements." For an exploration of what the various states have done, see Annot., 51 A.L.R.4th 872.

PROBLEM 66

The day after Alice Bluegown bought her new car, the right rear fender fell off. May she use §2-608 or must she give the car dealer a right to cure? Pretend she is sitting in your office expecting an immediate answer; glance at §2-608 and decide. The next day she took the car back to have the fender repaired; this made her late for work. The dealer fixed it, and the fender gave her no more trouble. However, the first time it rained all the paint washed off the car. May she revoke now? She took the car back to the dealer when the rain stopped and rode the bus to work (late again). The car dealer did a nice job repainting the car. Two weeks later the engine quit on her when she was in the middle lane of a superhighway at rush hour. The car had to be towed to the car dealer, and Alice missed an important sales meeting. The car dealer fixed the engine. Now Alice is back in your office. The car's trunk will not open. Must she permit them to fix it, or can she revoke? See Foss, The Seller's Right to Cure When the Buyer Revokes Acceptance: Erase the Line in the Sand, 16 S. Ill. U. L.J. 1 (1991). She has missed enough work to worry about hurting her career. She's also concerned that the car is going to keep breaking down right through and past the warranty period. What do you advise? Is §2-609 of use to her? If she decides to revoke acceptance and if the court agrees that this is allowed, would it also permit her to recover for the cost of a rental car used as substitute transportation while she was attempting to purchase a new car? See McGinnis v. Wentworth Chevrolet Co., 295 Or. 494, 668 P.2d 365 (1983). If she goes out and buys a *new* car, can she make the first car dealer pay for it? See §2-712.

PROBLEM 67

Suppose in the last Problem the contract between the dealer and Bluegown explicitly limits the remedy for breach to repair or replacement of defective parts. The dealer argues that all defects have been promptly and successfully repaired and that the remedy of revocation of acceptance is therefore unavailable to Bluegown. See §2-719(2); Durfee v. Rod Baxter Imports, Inc., 262 N.W.2d 349 (Minn. 1977); see also Andover Air Ltd. Partnership v. Piper Aircraft Corp., 1989 WL 110453 (D. Mass. 1989).

PROBLEM 68

Arthur Author ordered an expensive computer (the ION #740) from ION Business Machines. ION sent him model #745, a newer and better version of the machine he had ordered, at the same price. When he saw the computer, he liked it and wrote them a letter of acceptance, enclosing a check in payment. However, when he began to use it, he was horrified to learn that the computer was turned on by a hidden switch under the front panel. Arthur Author's father had lost a finger when he reached under a machine to activate it. Arthur had witnessed the accident as a child. Arthur sent a notice of revocation of acceptance to ION, stating that the #740 had a visible switch and explaining that the hidden switch on the #745 brought back childhood memories that kept him from wanting the computer. Does §2-608 permit him to revoke for this reason? See Official Comment 2. Is §2-508(2) relevant? How would you advise ION to respond to Arthur Author's letter? See Annot., 98 A.L.R.3d 1183.

PROBLEM 69

After his car had broken down with the same defect six times, Zack Taylor decided to revoke acceptance and return the car to Fillmore Motors, the dealership that had sold him the vehicle but that had been unable to repair it. To Zack's dismay, he discovered that Fillmore Motors had gone bankrupt and was out of business. Zack is now in your office with this issue: may he revoke acceptance against the *manufacturer* of the car (which had covered its product with a limited warranty)? Compare Newmar Corp. v. McCrary, 309 P.3d 1021 (Nev. 2013), with Gasque v. Mooers Motor Car Co., Inc., 227 Va. 154, 313 S.E.2d 384 (1984); Gregory J. Krabacher, Revocation of Tripartite Rolling Contracts: Finding a Remedy in the Twenty-First Century Usage of Trade, 66 Ohio St. L.J. 397 (2005).

Note that the Magnuson-Moss Warranty Act might help consumers win this battle. Section 110(d) of the Act allows a civil action against the warrantor that includes both legal and *equitable* relief (and, revocation of acceptance, being a form of rescission, qualifies as an equitable remedy). Revocation of acceptance, being a form of rescission, arguably qualifies as an equitable remedy, but the courts have split on whether it can be used in Magnuson-Moss actions against a manufacturer not in privity with the consumer; see Mydlach v. DaimlerChrysler Corp., 226 Ill. 2d 307, 314 Ill. Dec. 760, 875 N.E.2d 1047, 1062-1065 (2007) (discussing split among courts on the issue).

Just as the United Nations CISG treaty does not use the value-loaded word *warranty*, it substitutes the word *avoidance* for concepts such as rescission, rejection, and revocation of acceptance, while keeping much of the substance. The concept of avoidance under the treaty is the subject of the next Problem.

PROBLEM 70

Jeans of the World, a retail clothing outlet in Helsinki, Finland, ordered 20 boxes of jeans from Grey Goods of Manhattan in New York, to be delivered September 1. Use the CISG to answer these questions:

(a) If the goods arrive on July 20, must Jeans of the World take them? See Article 52(1).

(b) If the goods arrive on the appointed date, but there are only 18 boxes, must Jeans of the World accept them? See Articles 35, 49, 51, and 25. Can the buyer get the other two boxes? See Article 46. If the buyer avoids the contract, can the seller reinstate it by delivering the missing two boxes? See Articles 48 and 49.

(c) If a flood causes water damage to the boxes before Jeans of the World tries to avoid the contract, does this affect its ability to do so? See Article 82.

PROBLEM 71

Ambiance Hotel decided to acquire ten horse-carriages to be specially designed to carry its guests around the tourist areas of the scenic city in which it is located. It had the plans for the carriages transmitted to Buggies, Inc., a carriage manufacturer, which assured Ambiance that there would be no problem with the creation of the carriages. Ambiance financed this transaction by having Octopus National Bank purchase the carriages from Buggies, Inc., and then lease them to Ambiance for a ten-year period. Assume that this transaction qualifies as a finance lease; see §2A-103(1)(g).

(a) If the carriages are delivered to the hotel and Ambiance rejects them because they are the wrong color, must Ambiance pay the lease amounts to Octopus National Bank? (You may assume that the finance lease contained a "hell or high water" clause.) See §§2A-407(1), 2A-515.

(b) If the hotel accepts the carriages, but becomes upset when they constantly break down, can it revoke its acceptance and refuse to pay the lessor? See §§2A-407, 2A-516 and its Official Comment, 2A. See GreatAmerica Fin. Serv. Corp. v. Meisels, 2016 WL 5480718 (Iowa App. 2016).

VI. RISK OF LOSS: BREACH

The Code's general rules on risk of loss are found in §2-509, but that section applies only where neither party has breached the sales contract. If a breach has occurred, §2-510 is the relevant section. Read it.

Jakowski v. Carole Chevrolet, Inc.

New Jersey Superior Court, 1981, 180 N.J. Super. 122, 433 A.2d 841

NEWMAN, J.

Plaintiff seeks summary judgment on Count I alleging breach of a new car sales contract by the defendant, Carole Chevrolet.

The essential facts are not in dispute. On March 8, 1980, plaintiff, Jakowski, (hereinafter referred to as buyer), entered into a contract of sale with defendant, Carole Chevrolet, (hereinafter referred to as seller), calling for the purchase by plaintiff of one brand new 1980 Chevrolet Camaro. The parties also agreed that the car would be both undercoated and that its finish would have a polymer coating. While there is some disagreement as to exactly when the buyer ordered the coatings, it is undisputed that prior to delivery the seller agreed to deliver the car with the coatings applied. Likewise, it is undisputed that the car in question was delivered to the buyer without the required coatings on May 19, 1980.

The next day, May 20, 1980, the seller contacted the buyer and informed him that the car delivered to him lacked the coatings in question and seller instructed buyer to return the car to seller so that the coatings could be applied. On May 22, 1980, the buyer returned the auto to the seller for application of the coatings. Sometime during the evening of the 22nd or the morning of the 23rd the car was stolen from seller's premises and it was never recovered. Seller has refused to either provide a replacement auto to buyer or to refund the purchase price. Buyer remains accountable on the loan, provided through GMAC, for the purchase of the car.

The narrow question thus presented is upon whom, as between buyer and seller, this loss should fall. In UCC terminology, on May 22, 1980, which party bore the risk of the car's loss.

Seller argues that the risk of loss passed to the buyer upon his receipt of the auto. This is consistent with U.C.C. §2-509(3) pursuant to which the risk of loss passes to the buyer upon his receipt of the goods. Section 2-509(4), however, expressly provides that the general rules of §2-509 are subject to the more specific provisions of §2-510 which deals with the effect of breach upon risk of loss.

Buyer relies upon §2-510(1) which provides:

> Where a tender or delivery of goods so fails to conform to the contract as to give a right of rejection the risk of their loss remains on the seller until cure or acceptance.

Application of this section to the instant facts requires that three questions be answered. First, did the car "so fail to conform" as to give this buyer a right to reject it? If so, did the buyer "accept" the car despite the non-conformity? Finally, did the seller cure the defect prior to the theft of the auto?

The first question must be answered in the affirmative. The contract provided that the car would be delivered with undercoating and a polymer finish and it is undisputed that it was delivered without these coatings. The goods were thus clearly non-conforming and despite seller's assertion to the contrary, the degree of their non-conformity is irrelevant in assessing the buyer's concomitant right to reject them. Section 2-106 is clear in its intent to preserve the rule of strict compliance; that is, the "perfect tender" rule:

> Goods . . . are "conforming" or conform to the contract *when they are in accordance with* the obligations under the contract. [Section 2-106(2). (Emphasis supplied.) See also Comment 2 to §2-106.]

The language of §2-510(1), "so fails to conform," is misleading in this respect: no particular quantum of non-conformity is required where a single delivery is contemplated. The allusion is to §2-612 which substitutes a rule of substantial compliance where, *and only where,* an installment deal is contemplated. White & Summers, Uniform Commercial Code (2d ed. 1980), §5.5 at 187-188.

Secondly, did buyer "accept" the auto by taking possession of it? This question was presented in Zabriskie Chevrolet, Inc. v. Smith, 99 N.J. Super. 441 (Law Div. 1968). In *Zabriskie* it was held that the mere taking of possession by the purchaser is not equivalent to acceptance. Before he can be held to have accepted, a buyer must be afforded a "reasonable opportunity to inspect" the goods. *Zabriskie,* supra, at 452-453; §2-606.

Seller's actions in this matter preclude analysis in conventional "acceptance" terms. Buyer had no opportunity, indeed, no reason, to reject given seller's own communication to buyer shortly after delivery, to the effect that the goods did not conform and that the seller was exercising its right to cure said non-conformity. See §2-508 (seller's right to cure). This communication, in effect an acknowledgment of non-conformity, obviated the need for a formal rejection on buyer's part, if, indeed, §2-510(1) imposes such an obligation. Put another way, it precluded the buyer from rejecting the car. Consistent with this analysis, I find as a matter of law that there was no acceptance by buyer of this non-conforming auto.

As to the final question of whether the seller effected a cure, there is no evidence, in fact defendant does not even contend, that cure was ever effected.

Given the undisputed facts the operation of §2-510(1) is inescapable. The goods failed to conform, the buyer never accepted them and the defect was never cured. Accordingly, the risk of loss remained on the seller and judgment is granted for plaintiff.

A further note on the law is in order. It is possible to conjure up a host of hypotheticals leading to seemingly perverse results under §2-510. The section has been the subject of some scholarly criticism. See, e.g., White & Summers, supra, §5.5 at 187. Williston, "The Law of Sales in the Proposed Uniform Commercial Code," 63 Harv. L. Rev. 561, 583 (1950).

The fact is, however, that those courts considering it have had little difficulty in applying it as written. See, e.g., United Airlines, Inc. v. Conductron Corp., 69 Ill. App. 3d 847, 26 Ill. Dec. 344, 387 N.E.2d 1272 (Ill. App. 1979) (Flight trainer destroyed in fire after delivery to buyer); Southland Mobile Home v. Chyrchol, 255 Ark. 366, 500 S.W.2d 778 (Ark. Sup. 1973) (Mobile home destroyed in fire after delivery to buyer); Graybar Elec. Co. v. Shook, 283 N.C. 213, 195 S.E.2d 514 (N.C. Sup. 1973) (Non-conforming cable stolen while in buyer's possession); Wilkie v. Cummins Diesel Eng. Inc.,

252 Md. 611, 250 A.2d 886 (Md. Ct. App. 1969) (Engine block frozen while in buyer's possession).

The rule is simple enough: under §2-510(1) where goods fail to conform to the contract of sale, the risk of loss remains on the seller until the buyer accepts the goods or until the seller cures the defect. In the aforecited cases, such was the result even though in all of them the goods were still in the *buyer's* possession at the time of their destruction.

For present purposes it is adequate to hold simply that where a seller obtains possession of the goods in an effort to cure defects in them so as to comply with his end of the bargain, he is under a contractual duty to redeliver them to the buyer. In failing to do so, he has breached the contract.

Pursuant to §2-711 buyer is entitled to a refund of so much of the purchase price as has been paid to seller. Included in the cost of the automobile are the finance charges incurred by the buyer who secured financing from GMAC pursuant to a retail installment sales contract entered into with the seller. There is no dispute about including these charges in the purchase cost and the buyer, as of March 30, 1981, indicated the total amount due on any judgment to be $9,398.75. However, since this case was first heard some additional time has passed and a current pay off figure should be obtained for inclusion in this judgment. Plaintiff is directed to submit an appropriate order.

PROBLEM 72

The Lamia Museum's director, Mandrake Griffin, ordered three new pieces for the museum: an Egyptian sphinx, an Old World gargoyle, and an Etruscan statue of a centaur. These objets d'art were purchased under separate contracts from Empusa Exports of London, England. All were to be shipped "F.A.S. S.S. Titanic" on or about April 9, on their way to the museum, which was located in New Jersey. The parties agreed that New Jersey law would apply. Prior to April 9, Empusa Exports received a call from Griffin cancelling the purchase of the centaur statue. Empusa protested the cancellation, but agreed to ship the other two pieces. Empusa's manager discovered that the sphinx was a phony, but kept her mouth shut and shipped it anyway. She also discovered that the gargoyle's condition was such that it could not survive the exposure to sea air, so she decided to send it by air in spite of the contract's F.A.S. *Titanic* term. This decision proved wise since the *Titanic* encountered an obstacle on its sea voyage and foundered, taking the sphinx with it. The gargoyle arrived in good condition, and Griffin wrote a letter to Empusa accepting the gargoyle and enclosing the museum's check. A week later Griffin learned that the gargoyle was not from the "Old World," but instead had been cast in Hoboken many years ago, had somehow found its way to Europe, and now was home again. He sent Empusa a letter demanding that the museum's money be returned and stating that he canceled the sale. Before Empusa could respond, two things happened: the museum burned to the ground, and the centaur statue was stolen from Empusa's warehouse (through no fault of Empusa, which was not negligent in guarding it). Both the museum and Empusa were fully insured. Answer these questions:

(a) By shipping the other two objects after the museum refused to take the centaur statue, did Empusa waive its right to sue for the repudiation? See §§2-209(1), 2-106(3), 2-106(4). Would §1-308 have helped Empusa? What should it have done to use this section?

(b) Which party took the risk of loss on
   (1) the centaur?
   (2) the sphinx?
   (3) the gargoyle?

(c) When Empusa shipped the gargoyle by air instead of by sea, could Lamia have treated this as an imperfect tender and rejected the gargoyle for that reason? See §§2-503(1), 2-503(2), 2-504, 2-614.

(d) The Lamia Museum's insurance policy with the Pegasus Insurance Company contains two clauses relevant to §2-510. One provided that on payment of a claim the insurance company was subrogated to any claim its insured had against any other person. The other stated that the policy should not be deemed to provide protection for any claim where the risk of loss rested with another person. What is the effect of these provisions? See Official Comment 3 to §2-510; White & Summers §6-7.

VII. IMPOSSIBILITY OF PERFORMANCE

The Code has four provisions designed to straighten out the legal tangles created by those unexpected events of life that make the performance of a contract impossible or (the UCC equivalent) *commercially impracticable.* By creating a new standard of commercial impracticability, the Code drafters intended to broaden the common law concept of *impossibility.* Many commentators believe that the courts have essentially ignored the drafters' intentions and treated commercial impracticability as synonymous with common law impossibility. See Annot., 93 A.L.R.3d 584.

Read §§2-613 to 2-616, and work through the following Problems.

PROBLEM 73

Virgil Escapement had always wanted a sundial for his garden, and he ordered one for $250 from Horology Timepieces, Inc. The latter had 12 sundials of the type Escapement ordered in its storage room when an earthquake shook the building. All 12 fell over, and all but 3 were smashed. The remaining three were slightly damaged. Escapement, on being informed of the problem, insisted on the right to look over the three remaining sundials and to select one for his purchase, possibly at a reduced price due to the damage. Horology comes to you. Is §2-613 or §2-615 relevant? Must it let Escapement pick out a sundial, and must it offer to let him purchase at a reduced price, or can it simply cancel without fear of legal liability? For the test for impossibility of performance in international sales, see CISG Article 79; cf. Articles 71 and 72.

If the agreed-upon delivery or payment means become unavailable, §2-614 may require use of a substitute. See Macromex v. Globex International, 330 Fed. Appx. 241 (2d Cir. 2009) (under §2-614 Romanian importation ban triggered obligation to change delivery location where original facilities unavailable).

PROBLEM 74

Suppose the following, using the basic facts of the last Problem. When Horology received Virgil's order, one of their salespersons immediately put a red tag on one of the sundials. It said, "Hold for Virgil Escapement." Then the earthquake occurred, and miraculously only Virgil's sundial was destroyed. The other 11 sundials, all exactly like Virgil's, were undamaged. When Virgil demanded his sundial, Horology pleaded §2-613. Will that section excuse them? See Valley Forge Flag Co. v. New York Dowel & Molding Import Co., 90 Misc. 2d 414, 395 N.Y.S.2d 138 (Civ. Ct. 1977).

Arabian Score v. Lasma Arabian Ltd.

United States Court of Appeals, Eighth Circuit, 1987, 814 F.2d 529

WOLLMAN, J.

Beating dead horses is the sport of appellate judges, a generally harmless pastime painful only to the readers of appellate opinions. Paying for the promotion of dead horses can be an expensive proposition, however, as the facts of this case make abundantly clear.

Arabian Score (Arabian), a Minnesota limited partnership, appeals from the district court's orders granting summary judgment in favor of

Lasma Arabian Ltd. (Limited), a Florida limited partnership, and Lasma Corporation (Lasma), an Arizona corporation. We affirm.

On October 27, 1983, Arabian entered into an agreement to purchase from Limited an Arabian colt named Score. The agreement, which the parties agreed would be governed by and construed in accordance with the laws of Arizona, provided that Arabian would pay Limited $1 million "for the purchase of Score and the performance by Lasma of various services in the promotion of Score." The contract required Lasma to spend $250,000 for the performance of those services which consisted of advertising and promoting Score as a 2 Star Stallion under a license agreement with Lasma Star Stallion, Inc., a separate corporation that is not a party to this lawsuit.

Paragraph 4 of the agreement provided that for a period of five years after the date of his purchase, Score would be a 2 Star Stallion, as defined by the Star Stallion license agreement, with the result that Score's foals would be eligible for nomination to all Lasma-sponsored sales open to the get of Lasma stallions.[13] If Lasma Star Stallion, Inc., in its sole discretion, determined that Score was not eligible to participate in the Star Stallion Program, Lasma would, at Arabian's option, replace Score with an eligible stallion or refund to Arabian the unused portion of the money Lasma would otherwise be required to spend promoting Score pursuant to the terms of the paragraph 5 of the agreement.

Paragraph 5 of the agreement provided that for five consecutive calendar years commencing with 1984, Lasma would implement a complete annual program for the promotion of Score as a 2 Star Stallion. Lasma was to pay $70,000 for the 1984 program and $45,000 for each of the remaining four annual programs. The annual programs were to "include advertising in various trade publications, direct mail programs and the training, boarding, conditioning and showing of SCORE by Lasma."

Pursuant to paragraph 6 of the agreement, Lasma guaranteed that Score was not infertile.

Paragraph 9 of the agreement provided: "Except as provided by paragraphs 4 and 6 above, the Partnership accepts SCORE *AS IS,* all implied warranties being excluded. Risk of loss passes upon closing. All incidental and consequential damages are excluded."

On February 8, 1984, Arabian obtained a mortality insurance policy from Transit Casualty Company insuring Score for his actual cash value. Alas — memento mori — Score went to his reward within the year, dying on September 11, 1984, having sired two foals during his brief life. Misfortune

---

13. As near as we can tell from the materials presented to the trial court, the Star Stallion program is to the ranking of Arabian horses what the Mobil Guide is to the ranking of restaurants. This may not be a totally accurate description, but it will do for the purposes of this case.

compounding, Transit Casualty Company (its name bespeaks its character?) went broke. Lasma having expended only $52,891.14 for the promotion of Score, Arabian brought suit against Lasma and Limited, seeking recovery of the $197,108.86 not expended from the $250,000 that the purchase agreement allocated for the promotion of Score.

Count I of Arabian's complaint (later dismissed by stipulation) alleged that Lasma and Limited had breached the contract by not promoting Score. Count II sought recovery of the unspent portion of the $250,000 on the ground of impossibility of performance. Count III sought recovery under paragraph 4 of the purchase agreement.

The district court ruled that because Score's death was a foreseeable risk that was assumed by Arabian by the terms of the purchase agreement, neither the doctrine of impossibility nor of commercial frustration was applicable. Likewise, because the unrebutted evidence established that it is not unusual for Lasma Star Stallions, Inc. and Lasma to promote deceased horses, it was not an arbitrary, capricious, or irrational exercise of discretion by Lasma to determine that Score was still eligible postmortem to participate in the Star Stallion Program.

As provided by the agreement, we look to Arizona law to resolve the issues presented by Arabian's complaint.

In Garner v. Ellingson, 18 Ariz. App. 181, 501 P.2d 22 (1972), the Arizona Court of Appeals defined commercial frustration as circumstances beyond the control of the parties which render performance of the contract impossible and exonerate the party failing to perform. The court did not limit the doctrine to strict impossibility but included impracticability caused by extreme or unreasonable difficulty or expense. Id. at 23. The court did require, however, proof that the supervening frustrating event was not reasonably foreseeable. Id. at 24.

In Mohave County v. Mohave-Kingman Estates, 120 Ariz. 417, 586 P.2d 978, 983 (1978), the Arizona Supreme Court stated that "while Arizona recognizes the doctrine of commercial frustration . . . we do not see fit to interpret it as general absolution whenever performance under the contract becomes difficult or expensive. Proper application of this doctrine requires us to examine whether the allegedly frustrating event was reasonably foreseeable." In that case, the court refused to apply the doctrine where a zoning change had affected the economic feasibility of a contract to buy and develop land. The court reasoned that "the doctrine of commercial frustration does not apply to the instant case because the risk of change in the zoning ordinances was an event properly foreseeable by the defendants, and one which they would have contracted against." Id. at 984.

Arizona rejects the application of the commercial frustration doctrine when a party assumes the risk of the frustrating event. Kintner v. Wolfe, 102 Ariz. 164, 426 P.2d 798 (1967). In *Kintner,* the Arizona Supreme Court rejected a commercial frustration claim by a guarantor who had agreed to remain liable for the rent due on a liquor license lease "without respect to future changes in conditions." A change in law made renting liquor licenses illegal, but the court required the guarantor to pay, stating: "If the parties to a contract have agreed in express or implied terms that the risk of loss shall fall upon one or the other of the parties, full effect is given to such provision." Id. at 803.

We conclude that the trial court was correct in holding that the commercial frustration doctrine is inapplicable in this case, both because Score's death was foreseeable, as evidenced by Arabian's purchase of insurance, and because Arabian assumed the risk that Score might die prematurely. Moreover, the doctrine of impossibility/commercial frustration is not applicable because the party obligated to perform — Lasma — does not contend that it is unable or unwilling to complete its duty to promote Score.

Arabian further contends that by virtue of his death Score is no longer eligible to participate in the Star Stallion Program; consequently, paragraph 4 of the agreement obligates Lasma to return any unspent portion of the funds earmarked for promotional purposes.

As indicated earlier, Lasma Star Stallion, Inc. is not a party to this lawsuit, and there are no findings by the district court that Lasma or Limited controls Lasma Star Stallion, Inc. in the exercise of its discretion. Because Lasma Star Stallion, Inc. has not declared Score to be ineligible for the Star Stallion Program, the condition precedent to Lasma's obligation under paragraph 4 of the agreement has not been satisfied.

Even if it were within Lasma's discretion to declare Score ineligible to participate in the Star Stallion Program, we could not say that the decision that Score is still eligible for the program was an arbitrary or capricious abuse of discretion.

Arabian argues that the decision to promote a dead horse is per se arbitrary.[14] As indicated above, however, Lasma's unrebutted evidence shows that Lasma Star Stallion, Inc. and Lasma regularly promote deceased horses. This is done to enhance the owning entity's reputation and to increase the value of the stallion's progeny. Further, the language of paragraph 4 was not intended to cover the risk of death but of ineligibility for other reasons, such as infertility or substandard offspring.

It is with some reluctance that we affirm the district court's grant of summary judgment. That reluctance stems from the thought that spending $197,108.86 to promote a dead horse borders on the bizarre. The parties to

14. At oral argument, counsel for Arabian asked, rhetorically we assume, "How are you going to show a dead horse?" Considerations of judicial decorum and a due regard for the financial loss suffered by Arabian dissuaded us from suggesting the construction of a mausoleum — an equestrian Lenin's Tomb, if you will.

this agreement were sophisticated and, we assume, well-heeled businesspersons, however, and that which we find to be somewhat unusual may be commonplace to those who inhabit the wealthy world of the horsey set.

The judgment dismissing Arabian's complaint is affirmed.

PROBLEM 75

In the mid-1960s, in an effort to boost sales of its nuclear reactors, Westinghouse Corporation agreed to sell 27 utility companies 80 million pounds of uranium over the next 20 years. The average sale price per pound was $10. When Westinghouse made the sale, it actually owned only 15 million pounds of uranium. By the mid-1970s, the price of uranium had risen to $40 a pound. In late 1975, Westinghouse announced that it would not honor its contract. The utilities sued. Westinghouse argued that the best evidence in the late 1960s and early 1970s indicated uranium prices would be stable over the long term. The Corporation claimed that the price rise was unforeseeable and that the contracts were excused under §2-615 as "commercially impracticable." In particular, Westinghouse blamed the 1973 oil embargo and worldwide price fixing for the "unpredictable" price rises. See Official Comments 4 and 5 to §2-615. How should the dispute be resolved? See Publicker Indus. v. Union Carbide Corp., 1975 WL 22890 (E.D. Pa. 1975); Ecology Services, Inc. v. Granturk Equipment, Inc., 443 F. Supp. 2d 756 (D. Md. 2006); Eagan, The Westinghouse Uranium Contracts: Commercial Impracticability and Related Matters, 18 Am. Bus. L.J. 281 (1980); Rochester Gas and Electric Corporation v. Delta Star, Inc., 2009 WL 368508 (W.D.N.Y. 2009) (seller of goods at a fixed price was not relieved of obligation where price of component increased due to Hurricane Katrina). If you could advise Westinghouse on how to avoid this problem in the future, what would you suggest? See §2-305.

Louisiana Power & Light Co. v. Allegheny Ludlum Industries, Inc.
United States District Court, Eastern District of Louisiana, 1981, 517 F. Supp. 1319

Gordon, J.

This breach of contract case is before the court on plaintiff's motion for summary judgment. The material facts which are not in dispute are as follows:

Plaintiff, Louisiana Power & Light Company (hereinafter referred to as "LP & L"), entered into a contract with defendants, Allegheny Ludlum Industries, Inc. and Allegheny Ludlum Steel Corporation (hereinafter referred to collectively as "Allegheny,") in which Allegheny agreed to supply condenser tubing to LP & L for use at LP & L's Waterford 3 nuclear power plant. The contract was awarded to Allegheny Ludlum Steel Corporation, then a division of Allegheny Ludlum Industries, Inc., after the solicitation of bids by LP & L's agent, Ebasco Services, Incorporated. The contract, dated February 8, 1974, was accepted by Allegheny in mid-March of 1974.

Pursuant to the terms of the contract Allegheny undertook to furnish, fabricate and deliver to LP & L stainless steel condenser tubing in accordance with the specifications of LP & L's agent, Ebasco. Equal shipments of the tubing were to be made on June 1, 1976, June 15, 1976, and July 1, 1976, for a total price of $1,127,387.82. The contract also provided that if LP & L delayed shipment beyond August 31, 1976, but not later than January 31, 1977, the contract price would be increased by three percent (3%). A further adjustment at the rate of ten percent (10%) would take place if LP & L delayed shipment beyond January 31, 1977, but not later than January 31, 1978. No other escalation clauses were included in the contract.

On May 19, 1975, Allegheny sent a letter to LP & L seeking "additional compensation" for performance under the contract. Allegheny informed LP & L that subsequent to the formulation of the contract its "costs [had] risen at such a high rate that escalators built into our contracts have in no way adequately compensated for them. For example, since March of 1974 the price of electrolytic nickel has increased 24%, low carbon ferrochrome 185% and labor 21%." Allegheny sought the opportunity to meet with representatives of LP & L in order to discuss Allegheny's price increases and possible solutions to Allegheny's problem. Allegheny suggested a renegotiation of the contract price, but LP & L chose not to meet with Allegheny to discuss the matter.

In October of 1975, LP & L, through Ebasco, advised Allegheny that it considered Allegheny's price increases to be business risks which must be absorbed by Allegheny. On November 4, 1975, Allegheny informed LP & L, by letter from C.R. Hastings, General Manager of Allegheny's Wallingford Tubular Products Division, that a "[c]urrent review of this matter suggests that Allegheny Ludlum might be well advised not to perform under the contract." On November 19, 1975, Ebasco wrote to Allegheny's Wallingford Tubular Products Division, and demanded written assurances within thirty days, pursuant to §2-609 of the New York Commercial Code,[15] that Allegheny would fully and properly perform under the contract.

As of January 19, 1976, LP & L had not received any such written assurance of performance from Allegheny and on January 30, 1976, LP & L notified Allegheny by letter that it considered the contract repudiated by

15. The contract between LP & L and Allegheny stated that the contract was to be governed by the laws of the State of New York, hence the invocation of §2-609 of the New York Commercial Code.

Allegheny. Thereafter, on February 17, 1976, C.R. Hastings at Allegheny wrote to LP & L informing it that Allegheny was willing to "make delivery under the subject purchase order at $1.80 per lb . . . [Allegheny's] full cost of producing the material. . . ."

LP & L rejected Allegheny's offer to supply the tubing at Allegheny's cost and through its agent, Ebasco, LP & L solicited bids from other vendors for supply of the requisite condenser tubing. LP & L steadfastly rejected the offer of Allegheny to supply the tubing at Allegheny's cost, a price higher than that specified in the LP & L/Allegheny contract. On June 16, 1976, LP & L, through Ebasco, entered into a contract with Trent Tube Division of Crucible, Inc. for the purchase of condenser tubing at a price of $1,729,278.

Allegheny intended that the condenser tubing which was the subject of its contract with LP & L would be supplied by its Wallingford Tubular Products Division at Wallingford, Connecticut. C. R. Hastings, General Manager of the Wallingford Tubular Division, stated in his deposition that performance under the terms of the LP & L/Allegheny contract would have caused Allegheny to sustain a projected loss of $428,500 on the contract. Hastings indicated that such a loss would have reduced the planned profit for 1976 at the Wallingford plant from $1,018,000 to $589,500.

Plaintiff seeks by way of its lawsuit to recover from Allegheny the costs of its "cover," the monetary difference between the LP & L/Allegheny contract and the LP & L/Trent Tube contract, plus the expenses which it incurred in the re-solicitation of bids for the tubing. Allegheny has defended this action on four principal bases: commercial impracticability, mutual mistake, unconscionability and alleged bad faith conduct by LP & L. Plaintiff's claim and Allegheny's defenses will be considered in accord with the appropriate standards for summary judgment motions.

LP & L claims that Allegheny breached its contract to supply condenser tubing to LP & L. The first evidence which LP & L received that indicated that Allegheny would not perform under the contract as written was Allegheny's letter of May 19, 1975, to LP & L in which Allegheny sought "additional compensation" for supplying the condenser tubing. In response to that submission, LP & L sent a letter to Allegheny, invoking the provisions of §2-609 of the New York Uniform Commercial Code and requesting assurance from Allegheny that it would perform under the contract.

The pertinent provisions of §2-609 of the UCC, invoked by LP & L, provide:

2-609 Right to Adequate Assurance of Performance
     (1) A contract for sale imposes an obligation on each party that the other's expectation of receiving due performance will not be impaired. When reasonable grounds for insecurity arise with respect to the performance of either party the other may in writing demand adequate assurance of due performance. . . .

(4) After receipt of a justified demand failure to provide within a reasonable time not exceeding thirty days such assurance of due performance as is adequate under the circumstances of the particular case is a repudiation of the contract.

The letter which LP & L received from Allegheny requesting "additional compensation" provided LP & L with a reasonable basis for insecurity as to Allegheny's performance under the contract. LP & L's letter of November 19, 1975, to Allegheny constituted an adequate demand on Allegheny for an assurance of performance. When LP & L failed to receive such an assurance by January 19, 1976, it was justified in characterizing the contract as repudiated. LP & L notified Allegheny of that fact on January 30, 1976. Subsequently, Allegheny indicated to plaintiff that it would perform under the contract for added compensation. Such a belated and qualified offer of performance cannot, however, be viewed as an assurance of performance under §2-609 of the U.C.C. Allegheny's failure to supply an assurance of performance within the allotted time period operated as a repudiation of the contract.

The UCC provides that:

> When either party repudiates the contract with respect to a performance not yet due the loss of which will substantially impair the value of the contract to the other, the aggrieved party may . . . (b) resort to any remedy for breach (Section 2-703 or Section 2-711). . . . [Uniform Commercial Code §2-610.]

One available remedy in the event of a breach is for the buyer to obtain a "cover" by purchasing goods in substitution for the goods due from the seller. A buyer and non-breaching party may then seek to recover from the seller and breaching party the price of such substituted goods plus incidental and consequential damages. See U.C.C. §2-711 and §2-712. It is just such a claim that plaintiff is making in the instant case. Based on the undisputed facts in this case, plaintiff is entitled to recover on that claim, unless Allegheny prevails on one of its defenses.

COMMERCIAL IMPRACTICABILITY

The first of Allegheny's defenses to be considered is that of commercial impracticability. The Uniform Commercial Code provides that performance under a contract may be excused if performance under the contract is commercially impracticable. Section 2-615 of the UCC, upon which Allegheny relies in its defense of commercial impracticability, states in pertinent part:

2-615 Excuse by Failure of Presupposed Conditions
    Except so far as a seller may have assumed a greater obligation and subject to the preceding section on substituted performance:

(a) Delay in delivery or non-delivery in whole or in parts by a seller who complies with paragraphs (b) and (c) is not a breach of his duty under a contract for sale if performance as agreed has been made impracticable by the occurrence of a contingency the non-occurrence of which was a basic assumption on which the contract was made. . . .

In reliance upon that rule of law Allegheny argues that its performance under the contract with LP & L was rendered commercially impracticable because of a "severe shortage of critical raw materials and an increase in the cost of labor, an unexpected contingency which caused a dramatic increase in the price of those raw materials and the condenser tubing. The non-occurrence of such was a basic assumption on which the contract was founded and altered the essential nature of performance."

There are three conditions which must be met pursuant to §2-615 before performance under a contract can be excused because of commercial impracticability: "(1) a contingency must occur, (2) performance must thereby be made 'impracticable' and (3) the non-occurrence of the contingency must have been a basic assumption on which the contract was made." Neal-Cooper Grain Co. v. Texas Gulf Sulphur Co., 508 F.2d 283, 293 (7th Cir. 1974).

The rule has also been stated as "excus[ing] delay or nondelivery when the agreed upon performance has been rendered 'commercially impracticable' by an unforeseen supervening event not within the contemplation of the parties at the time the contract was entered into." Eastern Air Lines, Inc. v. McDonnell Douglas Corp., 532 F.2d 957, 988 (5th Cir. 1976). The rationale behind the doctrine of commercial impracticability is that when an event occurs which renders performance so "vitally different" from that which is anticipated, the contract cannot be reasonably considered to govern and performance under that contract is excused. Eastern Air Lines, Inc., supra, at 991.

The burden of proof on a claim of commercial impracticability rests with the party making the claim, in this case the defendants. Allegheny must meet its burden as to each of the requisite three elements in order to be successful in this defense. See Eastern Air Lines, Inc. v. Gulf Oil Corp., 415 F. Supp. 429, 438 (S.D. Fla. 1975), citing Ocean Air Tradeways, Inc. v. Arkay Realty Corp., 480 F.2d 1112, 1117 (9th Cir. 1973).

The undisputed facts in this case show that Allegheny has not and cannot meet its burden of proof as to this defense because it is unable to show that performance under the contract was commercially impracticable. Allegheny contacted LP & L in May of 1975 and informed LP & L that between March of 1974 and May of 1975, its costs for electrolytic nickel had risen by 24%, for low carbon ferrochrome had risen by 185%, and that its labor costs had risen by 21%. C.R. Hastings, General Manager of

Allegheny's Wallingford Tubular Division stated in his deposition that had Allegheny performed under the contract as written, it would have sustained a loss of $428,500 on the contract and that the planned profitability of the Wallingford plant would have been reduced to an overall profit of $589,500 for the year of performance.

There are no facts which indicate that Allegheny's costs increased by more than the amount indicated to LP & L in the Allegheny letter of May 19, 1975. Moreover, there are no facts which indicate that Allegheny would have sustained a greater loss than that attested to by C.R. Hastings had it performed under the contract. There are also no facts which indicate that Allegheny would have been unprofitable during 1976 in either its overall corporate structure or in its Wallingford Tubular Division had it performed under the contract as written. Hastings testified in his deposition that a profit was anticipated for the Wallingford plant even had Allegheny been required to perform under the contract's terms. The material facts in this regard are clear, simple and undisputed. When viewed in the context of a claim of commercial impracticability, as that term has been interpreted in the case law, it must be said that performance under the contract was not commercially impracticable.

The mere fact that performance under the contract would have deprived Allegheny of its anticipated profit and resulted in a loss on the contract is not sufficient to show commercial impracticability. Rather, ". . . [t]he party seeking to excuse his performance must not only show that he can perform only at a loss but also that the loss will be especially severe and unreasonable." Gulf Oil Corp. v. Federal Power Commission, 563 F.2d 588, 600 (3d Cir. 1977), *cert. denied,* 434 U.S. 1062 (1978), *petition for cert. dismissed,* 435 U.S. 911 (1978).

Allegheny's loss by performance would not have been especially severe and unreasonable in this case. On the contrary, by Allegheny's own estimate its costs of performance under the contract increased only 38% over the original contract price of $1,127,387.82. While no seller desires to be called upon to perform under a contract when performance will result in a financial loss, such are the realities of commercial life. Whereas the law quite properly provides relief for situations in which performance can only be had at an excessive and unreasonable cost, see Transatlantic Financing Corp. v. United States, 363 F.2d 312 (D.C. Cir. 1960), Allegheny's cost of performance did not increase to the extent necessary to excuse its performance under the doctrine of commercial impracticability.[16]

---

16. When consideration is given to Allegheny's anticipated profitability in 1976, it becomes more apparent that this was not a situation wherein performance under the contract would have been especially severe and unreasonable.

Eastern Air Lines, Inc. v. Gulf Oil Corp., 415 F. Supp. 429, 438 (S.D. Fla. 1975) is instructive:

> The modern U.C.C. §2-615 doctrine of commercial impracticability has its roots in the common law doctrine of frustration or impossibility and finds its most recognized illustrations in the so-called "Suez Cases," arising out of the various closings of the Suez Canal and the consequent increases in shipping costs around the Cape of Good Hope. Those cases offered little encouragement to those who would wield the sword of commercial impracticability. As a leading British case arising out of the 1957 Suez closure declared, the unforeseen cost increase that would excuse performance "must be more than merely onerous or expensive. It must be positively unjust to hold the parties bound." Ocean Tramp Tankers v. V/O Sovfracht (The Eugenia), 2 Q.B. 226, 239 (1964). To the same effect are Tsakiroglou and Co. Ltd. v. Noblee Thorl G.m.b.H., 2 Q.B. 348, (1960), *aff'd*, A.C. 93 (1962), and Caparanoyoti & Co., Ltd. v. E.T. Green, Ltd., 1 Q.B. 131, 148 (1959). These British precedents were followed by the District of Columbia Circuit, which gave specific consideration to UCC §2-615, Comment 4, in Transatlantic Financing Corp. v. United States, 124 U.S. App. D.C. 183, 363 F.2d 312, 319 (1966).

In *Transatlantic Financing Corp.*, supra, Judge J. Skelly Wright considered a claim of commercial impracticability and impossibility in connection with a suit seeking additional compensation for transport of a cargo of wheat around the Cape of Good Hope. The plaintiff was forced to abandon its customary route through the Suez Canal when Egypt obstructed the canal and closed it to traffic. Plaintiff argued that it was subjected to an additional expense of $43,972.00 above the contract price of $305,842.92 because of the longer journey necessitated by the closing of the canal. The court stated:

> . . . While it may be an overstatement to say that increased cost and difficulty of performance never constitute impracticability, to justify relief there must be more of a variation between expected cost and the cost of performing by an available alternative than is present in this case, where the promisor can legitimately be presumed to have accepted some degree of abnormal risk, and where impracticability is urged on the basis of added expense alone. [363 F.2d at 319.] The court affirmed the dismissal of the plaintiff's action because performance under the contract had not been rendered legally impossible.

In a similar case resulting from the closure of the Suez Canal, it was held that extra expense of 31.6% of the contract price, incurred in bringing the vessel around the Cape of Good Hope, was not sufficient to constitute commercial impracticability. American Trading and Production Corp. v. Shell International Marine, Ltd., 453 F.2d 939 (2d Cir. 1972). In discussing the degree of increase in costs that would constitute impossibility or commercial impracticability, it was stated that:

> Mere increase in cost alone is not a sufficient excuse for non-performance (Restatement of Contracts §467 (1932)). It must be an "extreme and unreasonable" expense (Restatement of Contracts §454 (1932)). While in the *Transatlantic* case supra, the increased cost amounted to an increase of about 14% over the contract price, the court did cite with approval the two leading English cases Ocean Tramp Tankers Corp. v. V/O Sovfracht (The Eugenia), [1964] 2 Q.B. 226, 233 (C.A. 1963) (which expressly overruled Societe Franco Tunisienne D'Armement v. Sidemar S.P.A. (The Messalia), [1961] 2 Q.B. 278 (1960), where the court had found frustration because the Cape route was highly circuitous and involved an increase in cost of approximately 50%), and Tsakiroglou & Co. Ltd. v. Noblee Thorl G.m.b.H., [1960] 2 Q.B. 318, 348, *aff'd*, [1962] A.C., 93 (1961) where the House of Lords found no frustration though the freight costs were exactly doubled due to the Canal closure. [453 F.2d at 942.]

In Iowa Electric Light and Power Company v. Atlas Corp., 467 F. Supp. 129 (N.D. Iowa, 1978) the court held that an increase in seller's costs by 52.2%, resulting in the seller's loss of approximately $2,673,125.00, failed to constitute commercial impracticability thereby precluding judicial adjustment or discharge of the contract for supply of uranium concentrate. In making such a determination, the court noted that cost increases of 50-58 percent had generally not been considered of sufficient magnitude to excuse performance under a contractual agreement.

As the jurisprudence indicates, Allegheny's performance under the contract was not commercially impracticable. Even if Allegheny were to show that its increased costs constituted a contingency, the non-occurrence of which was a basic assumption on which the contract was made, it still could not show that performance had been rendered commercially impracticable as a result. Allegheny bears the burden of proof as to each of the requisite three elements on its claim of commercial impracticability. Being unable to prove all three elements, its defense must fall.

Allegheny has suggested that claims of commercial impracticability are inherently insusceptible of resolution by summary judgment. That position is incorrect. While great care should be exercised in granting summary judgment motions in cases of this sort, the mere invocation of the term "commercial impracticability" is not a talisman behind which a defaulting seller may hide and be guaranteed a trial in the absence of a dispute as to the material facts in the matter. Were that the case, every seller or buyer caught in a burdensome position under a contract would find it hard to resist the natural temptation to compel renegotiation of unprofitable contracts by threatening to invoke a claim of commercial impracticability, knowing that it would be assured of a trial on the merits and knowing that even if it lost at trial, it would be required to do no more than fulfill its obligation under the contract. Such a rule of law would constitute a misuse of the protections afforded by the doctrine of commercial impracticability, particularly in cases of this sort where the facts are clear and undisputed and in which the seller in breach has been unable to cite a case wherein a claim of commercial impracticability has been upheld under similar factual circumstances.[17]

The clear undisputed facts require resolution of the commercial impracticability defense in plaintiff's favor. Allegheny is unable to meet its burden of proof. . . .

UNCONSCIONABILITY

Section 4 of the Supplementary Terms and Conditions of the LP & L/ Allegheny contract provides that:

4. Provision for Cancellation

At any time after the acceptance of this Order the Purchaser shall have the absolute right to cancel the entire Order upon the payment to the Seller for all disbursements and expenses which the Seller has incurred or become obligated for prior to date of notice of cancellation, less the reasonable resale value of equipment which shall have been obtained or ordered to become an integral part of the Equipment plus a sum as profit bearing the same ratio to the profit that the Seller would have received upon completing the Work as that portion of Work done bears to the entire amount of Work to be done by the Seller under this Order.

Allegheny argues that the aforementioned cancellation provision is unconscionable, that it taints the contract in its entirety and that as a result the contract is unenforceable. Accordingly, Allegheny urges that LP & L be barred from any recovery for damages.

The unconscionability which Allegheny suggests is rooted in the alleged one-sidedness of the provision which provides a right of cancellation to LP & L with no concomitant right given to Allegheny. The defendants submit that until production commenced, LP & L could cancel its order with impunity

17. In Aluminum Company of America v. Essex Group, Inc., 499 F. Supp. 53 (W.D. Pa. 1980), a claim of commercial impracticability was upheld. The facts surrounding the claim of commercial impracticability in *Alcoa* are, however, distinguishable from those in the instant case. Plaintiff stood to lose $60,000,000.00 in *Alcoa* if its performance under the contract was compelled while the defendant stood to gain a concomitant "windfall profit." There are no comparable facts in the instant case. Allegheny stood to lose $428,500 on a $1,127,387.82 contract. It cannot be said that LP & L would be the beneficiary of a "windfall profit" like that in *Alcoa*.

and would only be required to pay a penalty for cancellation "if Allegheny would be making a profit on the order, which LP & L now knew it would not. . . ."

Section 2-302 of the U.C.C., which is the basis for Allegheny's claim of unconscionability states: [the court quotes §2-302 — Ed.].

Comment 1 to U.C.C. §2-302 sets forth the standards to be used in making a determination on an unconscionability claim. "The basic test is whether in the light of the general commercial background and the commercial needs of the particular trade or case, the clauses involved are so one-sided as to be unconscionable under the circumstances existing at the time of the making of the contract. . . . The principle is one of prevention of oppression and unfair surprise . . . and not of disturbance of allocation of risks because of superior bargaining power."

Allegheny's allegation of unconscionability presents a question of law to be decided by the court. It is not a jury issue. U.C.C. §2-302. W.L. May Co., Inc. v. Philco-Ford Corp., 543 P.2d 283 (Or. 1975). However, plaintiff's claim that the cancellation clause and the contract were unconscionable entitles the parties to "a reasonable opportunity to present evidence as to . . . commercial setting, purpose and effect to aid the court in making . . . [its] determination." U.C.C. §2-302(2). The unconscionability claim is not susceptible of resolution by summary judgment. The court's determination of the issue cannot be made without a hearing. Zicari v. Joseph Harris Co., 304 N.Y.S.2d 918 (N.Y. 1969). Accordingly, plaintiff's motion for summary judgment must be denied in this regard.

BAD FAITH

Allegheny also asserts that bad faith conduct by LP & L serves as a defense to LP & L's claim for breach of contract. The basis of Allegheny's allegation of bad faith is that LP & L refused to meet with it in a timely fashion to discuss renegotiation of the contract. Allegheny argues that its bad faith allegation must be resolved at trial by the finder of fact.

The Uniform Commercial Code imposes an obligation of good faith on the performance or enforcement of contracts under the Code. U.C.C. §1-203.[18] "Good faith" is defined as "honesty in fact and the observance of reasonable commercial standards of fair dealing in the trade." U.C.C. §2-103(1)(b).

Allegheny's defense of bad faith based on LP & L's failure to engage in timely renegotiation of the contract is without merit. There is no obligation imposed under law which would have required LP & L to engage in renegotiation or even discuss renegotiation of its contract with Allegheny. See

18. Now §1-304. — Ed.

Missouri Public Service Company v. Peabody Coal Co., 583 S.W.2d 721, 725 (Mo. App. 1979), *cert. denied,* 444 U.S. 865. Allegheny has not attempted to show any requirement for renegotiation. Allegheny's claim that LP & L was in bad faith for failure to do what it had no obligation to do cannot withstand scrutiny. It cannot survive the test of plaintiff's summary judgment motion.

Insofar, however, as Allegheny makes a claim of bad faith conduct in connection with LP & L's purchase of goods in substitution for those due from Allegheny, the "cover" under U.C.C. §2-712(1), that defense relates to the damages portion of LP & L's lawsuit. The issue awaits resolution with LP & L's claim for damages.

In that regard, this court cannot now say that there are no genuine issues of material fact surrounding LP & L's claim for damages. The facts surrounding the obtaining of a "cover," timeliness, mitigation of damages, good faith and costs cannot be decided at this time. Unlike the liability portion of plaintiff's claim and consideration of certain of Allegheny's defenses, the issue of LP & L's damages awaits resolution at trial.

CONCLUSION

Based on the foregoing authorities and analysis, the court hereby grants the motion of Louisiana Power & Light Co. for summary judgment on the issue of liability and Allegheny's defenses of commercial impracticability, mistakes of fact and bad faith. The motion for summary judgment must be denied insofar as Allegheny's defense of unconscionability and the issue of LP & L's damages are concerned.

———————————

CHAPTER 6 REVIEW QUESTIONS

Is a buyer obliged to accept the goods if the seller has substantially performed?

What are the exceptions to the perfect tender rule?

How can a buyer avoid accepting the goods?

What is an ineffective rejection?

Can a buyer make an effective rejection that breaches the contract?

Is a buyer bound by an acceptance of the goods if seller has breached?

What is the difference between rejection and revocation of acceptance?

What is the effect of breach, by seller or buyer, on risk of loss?

When will a party be excused from performance by failure of presupposed conditions?

ASSESSMENT: MULTIPLE CHOICE QUESTIONS

1. Wambach Retail ordered 10,000 folding chairs from Lloyd Furniture, to be delivered in 5 shipments of 2,000 chairs, on the first days of July, August, and September. The first shipment arrived on July 1, missing a chair. On July 2, may Wambach Retail rightfully reject the shipment?
   a. Yes. In sales law, buyer may reject a seller's tender unless it is a perfect tender.
   b. Yes. The missing chair can never be delivered on time, because July 1 is in the past, so the defect cannot be cured.
   c. No. The non-conformity is not substantial enough to reject.
   d. No. Buyers must always accept a good faith attempt by sellers to meet the contract requirements.

2. A question with a slight but important difference: *can* Wambach Retail reject the shipment?
   a. No. The non-conformity is not substantial enough to reject.
   b. Yes. A buyer can reject a shipment, even if the rejection is wrongful, although buyer would then be in breach.
   c. No. If seller makes a tender that may not be rejected, then buyer cannot reject the tender.
   d. Yes. Buyer always has complete discretion about whether to accept a tender.

3. Lloyd Furniture carefully counted the chairs for a different contract, a single delivery of 1,000 chairs to Rapinoe Raptures, made on the agreed delivery date. Finding the shipment 1 chair short, Lloyd made the delivery as scheduled, arranging for another chair to be delivered the following day. But Rapinoe Raptures rejected the tender of 999 chairs and refused to allow Lloyd Furniture to cure the defect, because the delivery date was now past. Does Lloyd Furniture have a right to cure the defect?
   a. No. The delivery date is past and so the defect cannot be cured.
   b. No. The shaken faith doctrine would apply to prevent cure.
   c. Yes. Lloyd Furniture may cure the defect, where it reasonably believed the tender was conforming.
   d. Yes. A seller always has a right to cure.

4. Pemulis Auto signed yet another contract, to sell a 2016 Model Excalibur Hardtop to Hamlet. As agreed, Hamlet showed up Monday morning at Pemulis Auto to pick up the car. But after Hamlet paid and the papers were signed, Hamlet abruptly decided to wait a couple of days before driving away. That delay breached the contract, which required Hamlet to take delivery upon payment. The next day, the car was struck by lightning

and destroyed. Pemulis Auto did not have insurance covering the car. Is Hamlet entitled to return of the price paid?

a. No. Once the car was paid for and the papers signed, the car belonged to Hamlet.

b. No. Hamlet was in breach, so the risk of loss was on Hamlet.

c. Yes. Hamlet had not taken delivery, so the risk of loss was still on the seller.

d. Yes. Pemulis Auto was at fault for failure to obtain insurance.

5. Pemulis Auto sold a used Hekla sedan to Rapinoe, assuring her that the engine had been thoroughly tested for reliability and safety. Rapinoe agreed to take the car, signed the papers to get title transferred, and set off for home in the car. The engine burst into flames after a mile. Pemulis Auto offers to set off the price of a new engine, but refuses to take the car back. Is Rapinoe obliged to pay for the car, minus the cost of a new engine?

a. Yes. Rapinoe accepted the car, so is obliged to pay for it, minus damages for the breach.

b. Yes. Rapinoe should have tested the car herself.

c. No. Rapinoe may revoke her acceptance.

d. No. A buyer is never obliged to pay for defective goods.

e. Yes. Rapinoe cannot revoke acceptance, because the car is damaged and cannot be returned intact.

ANSWERS

1. *C* is the best answer. In sales contract generally, a buyer may reject a tender "if the goods or the tender of delivery fail in any respect to conform to the contract." §2-601. This requirement of perfect tender protects buyers from being required to accept and pay unless the seller delivers exactly as promised. But a lower standard exists for installment contracts, where the parties have repeated dealings and so the buyer is at less of a bargaining disadvantage. In installment contracts, a buyer may reject only "an installment which is non-conforming if the non-conformity substantially impairs the value of that installment and cannot be cured or if non-conformity is a defect in the required documents." One missing chair of 2,000 is not substantial (unless there were special circumstances, not present here). Even if it were, it could be quickly cured. We are not told of any problems with the documents. Grounds for rejecting an installment delivery are lacking.

2. *B* is the best answer. Wambach Retail does not have grounds to reject the shipment. But Wambach Retail can still reject the shipment. That would be an effective, but wrongful rejection. As the next chapter discusses, Wambach Retail would not be liable for the price, because it did not

accept the goods, but would be liable for any damages, such as Lloyd Furniture reselling the chairs at a loss.

3. *C* is the best answer. A seller does not always have a right to cure. Under §2-508, a seller has a right to cure if the time for performance has not expired (not applicable here) or the seller had reasonable grounds to believe the tender would be accepted. Here, the seller could reasonably believe that one missing chair of one thousand would not result in rejection of the delivery.

4. *B* is the best answer. Normally, when the buyer is not a merchant, the risk of loss does not pass until the goods have been delivered. §2-509(3). But when one party breaches, a different set of rules may apply under §2-510. Where the buyer is in breach, the seller may treat the risk of loss as resting on the buyer for a commercially reasonable time. §2-510(3). The parties may agree on different rules for risk of loss or for one party to obtain insurance, but they did not do so here. So, contrary to *D*, Pemulis Auto was not required to obtain insurance.

5. *C* is the best answer. Rapinoe accepted the car. She agreed to take the car, and had ownership transferred, either of which would be acceptance. §2-606. Normally a buyer that accepts the goods must pay the price, with a counterclaim for any breach by seller. §2-607. But sometimes a buyer may revoke acceptance. §2-608. Rapinoe meets the requirements for revocation of acceptance. She accepted the goods with assurances from the seller that the engine was not defective. §2-608(1)(b). The nonconformity substantially impairs the value of the car to Rapinoe. §2-608. There has been a substantial change in the condition of the goods, but that does not prevent revocation where that change was caused by the defect in the goods. §2-608(2).

CHAPTER 7
REMEDIES

When the deal has collapsed and the parties have turned to their lawyers with questions such as what steps can be taken to minimize damages and then what should be done to recover those that cannot be avoided, of particular interest are any mandatory actions imposed by the law and what choices the law gives to the aggrieved party. Sometimes the attorney will be asked by the client, "What is the smart thing to do"? At this point the lawyer should be careful to draw a distinction between what the law mandates while being careful not to make business decisions that the lawyer is typically unqualified to assess. The Uniform Commercial Code tends to reward conduct that is "reasonable" and taken "in good faith" and with "ordinary care." Those terms call for a business judgment the lawyer doesn't usually have. Instead, go for the practical: ask the client what steps would be taken if there were no possible legal relief, and that will often give surprising guidance by which to frame the legal battle that follows. Often this leads to a settlement, which is almost always a better result than a lawsuit.

I. SPECIAL REMEDIES

The 2-700s of the UCC are the basic remedy provisions (though some remedies, such as rejection and revocation of acceptance, which we covered earlier, found in other parts of Article 2). The 2-700s may be further divided into two parts: the seller's remedies when the buyer is in breach (§§2-703 to 2-710) and the buyer's remedies when the seller is in breach (§§2-711 to 2-717). These two areas will be discussed below; but before getting to them, pedagogical tidiness calls for a quick look at some special situations.

A. Remedies on Insolvency

When one contracting party becomes insolvent while in possession of goods that have been identified to the contract, the other may, in some circumstances, elect to forgo damages and try to get the goods themselves. This action is called *reclamation*. The key Code sections are §§2-502 and 2-702; read them. Both refer to the *insolvency* of the seller as a triggering event, but what does that term mean? In the Bankruptcy Code, it is defined as having more liabilities than assets, a bookkeeping test that is hard to determine without much investigation. The equitable definition of *insolvency*, however, defined the term as being unable to pay one's debts as they matured, a much easier thing to prove. Which of these does the UCC adopt? See §1-201(b)(23).

PROBLEM 76

Ratchett Tools delivered a truckload of inventory to Madoff Hardware. The next day, Ratchett Tools read that Madoff Hardware had shut its doors, failed to pay its many creditors, and has few assets to go after. Can Ratchett get the inventory back? See §2-702(2). Would it help sellers to include a clause in their sales contract forms making buyers promise they had the wherewithal to pay for goods ordered? See §2-702(2). What if Ratchett learned of the financial distress before delivery? §2-702(1). What if Madoff Hardware files for bankruptcy? See 11 U.S.C. §546(c).

Quite often a battle develops between a party (buyer or seller) seeking to reclaim goods and either a trustee in bankruptcy or a secured creditor of the party with the goods. If the battle is between the reclaiming seller and the trustee in bankruptcy, a section of the Bankruptcy Reform Act, revised in 2005, protects a seller's reclamation right from the trustee's avoiding powers even more broadly than §2-702; see 11 U.S.C.A. §546(c) (allowing seller to reclaim goods that were delivered to insolvent buyer within 45 days before buyer's bankruptcy). The battle between the secured creditor and the reclaiming party is governed by meshing Article 2 with Article 9, not always an easy task. The leading case is In re Samuels & Co., 510 F.2d 139 (5th Cir. 1975), *rev'd on other grounds,* 526 F.2d 1238 (5th Cir. 1976), *cert. denied,* 429 U.S. 834 (1976), where the secured creditor won over an unpaid cash seller. See also White & Summers §24-7 (suggesting that courts are likely to continue to favor secured creditors, under Bankruptcy Code §546(c)).

B. Liquidated Damages

At common law, if the parties put a liquidated damages clause in their contract, it was upheld by the courts only if the parties truly intended the figure named to be compensatory and had made in good faith an attempt to pre-estimate the damages. The courts struck the clause and made the aggrieved party prove actual damages if the courts decided that the parties had intended the liquidated figure to be a penalty amount to be forfeited in the event of breach. See Equitable Lumber Co. v. IPA Land Dev. Corp., 38 N.Y.2d 516, 344 N.E.2d 391, 381 N.Y.S.2d 459 (1976); J. Perillo, Contracts §§14-31, 14-32 (7th ed. 2014).

The Code's liquidated damages provision is §2-718(1). It makes little change from the common law rules except that it provides that the validity of the liquidated damages clause is to be tested, in part, against the *actual* harm caused by the breach (a criterion of no importance at common law). See Note, A New Standard for Liquidated Damage Provisions Under the Uniform Commercial Code?, 38 Ohio St. L.J. 437 (1977). For a case exploring the relationship between the liquidated damages clause and the actual damages incurred in the particular breach at issue, see Garden Ridge, L.P. v. Advance Intl., Inc., 2013 WL 1410145 (Tex. App. 2013).

Interestingly enough, the liquidated damages provision in Article 2A for the leasing of goods no longer refers to actual damages, specifically allows a *formula* to be used to compute damages, and drops all reference to the effect of an unreasonably large liquidated damages clause. Read §2A-504 and its Official Comment. Would this section permit the parties to contract for an outrageous amount (obviously a penalty) in the event of lessee default? See Benfield, Lessor's Damages Under Article 2A After Default by the Lessee as to Accepted Goods, 39 Ala. L. Rev. 915, 953 (1988).

C.   *The Breaching Buyer's Restitution*

PROBLEM 77

The zoo officials for the Minerun (West Virginia) Zoo contracted to buy an elephant from the zoo in White Cliffs, Delaware. The terms of the deal were that the West Virginia zoo would deliver a black bear worth $300 as a down payment and pay $100 a month for 20 months, at the end of which time the Delaware zoo would deliver the elephant. The bear was tendered and accepted. The West Virginia zoo duly made its $100 payments for 15 months before it ran out of money and could pay no more. The West Virginia zoo comes to you. Can it recover the $1,500 it has paid? The bear? Look at §§2-718(2), 2-718(3), and 2-718(4). Assuming the bear was and is still worth $300, calculate the amount that the West Virginia zoo is likely to recover in a restitution action.

II.   *SELLER'S REMEDIES*

The plan of the 2-700s is to describe briefly the seller's remedies in §2-703 and the buyer's in §2-711 and then to flesh out these brief descriptions in the sections immediately following. All of these remedies sections are to be read in light of the Code's guiding remedial principle, §1-305(a):

> The remedies provided by this Act shall be liberally administered to the end that the aggrieved party may be put in as good a position as if the other party had fully performed but neither consequential or special nor penal damages may be had except as specifically provided in this Act or by other rule of law.[1]

Now read §2-703 and its Official Comment.

A.   *Accepted Goods*

The seller's recovery of damages is measured by §2-709 (Action for the Price) if the buyer has made a technical *acceptance* of the goods or if the

---

1. The Wyoming Supreme Court has read this section as prohibiting punitive damages awards in suits alleging fraud; Waters v. Trenckmann, 503 P.2d 1187 (Wyo. 1972). Other courts have disagreed; see the discussion in Seaton v. Lawson Chevrolet-Mazda, Inc., 821 S.W.2d 137 (Tenn. 1991).

goods are destroyed within a commercially reasonable period of time after the risk of loss shifts to the buyer. In effect, §2-709 is the equivalent of a specific performance remedy for the seller. As discussed below, if the seller still has possession of the goods (or had the risk of loss at the time of their destruction), damages are measured by other sections in the 2-700s. For now, read §2-709. This section is annotated in 90 A.L.R.3d 1141.

PROBLEM 78

Backslappers Auto Sales sold a new blue sports car to Dwane Diletante on credit. He accepted the car and drove it for a month. He then sent Backslappers a notice of revocation of acceptance and gave as his reason the recent repainting of his garage in a color that clashed with the blue car. The notice stated that Diletante had parked the car down the block from his home (away from the clashing garage) and that Backslappers should come and get it. Dwane also refused to make any more car payments. Three days after Backslappers received the notice, the car disappeared and has never been found. May the seller recover the price under §2-709? Who had the risk of loss? See §§2-608(1) and (3), 2-606(1), 2-510; note Official Comment 5 to §2-709. There is a good discussion of this problem in White & Summers §8-3. Would it make a difference if Diletante had *rejected* the goods for the same reason? Would a seller be entitled to recover the price if the market price for the goods had declined considerably after the delivery date? See Brewer v. J-Six Farms, 350 P.3d 420 (Okla. App. 2015).

B.   Unaccepted Goods

When the buyer repudiates before delivery or rejects the goods, the relevant Code section is §2-706 if the seller resells the goods to someone else. If no resale occurs, damages are measured under §2-708. Other relevant sections are cited in the following Problems.

PROBLEM 79

Lannie Light was the sole proprietor of Light's Bulbs, a lighting fixtures business in Austin, Texas. She contracted to sell 80 neon light fixtures to Signs, Inc., a firm in San Antonio. The price was $1,500 "F.O.B. Austin," and the shipment date was to be March 15. On March 5, Signs, Inc., phoned Light and told her that the deal was off, but Lannie refused to agree to a cancellation. She went to her warehouse and picked 80 of the fixtures from her large stock. Then she posted a notice on the bulletin board near the cash register in her store, stating that 80 of the fixtures would be sold to the person making the best offer. Carl Customer (who was always buying these types of items) saw the sign and offered Light $1,000 for the fixtures. Light sold Customer the goods and took payment. Now Light comes to you. She tells you that on March 5 the fixtures were selling on the open market at $800 for 80 and that on March 15 the price for 80 such fixtures was $900 in Austin and $800 in San Antonio. Answer these questions:

(a) Does the UCC permit Light to select goods from the warehouse *after* the buyer repudiates? See §2-704.

(b) Was the resale proper? See §2-706 and Official Comment 2.

(c) Suppose Signs, Inc. had no cash for the purchase price, but offered to take the light fixtures on credit, even offering to provide a motorcycle as collateral. Could Light sell the light fixtures to someone else at a lower price and recover damages? Star Funding, Inc. v. Vault Minerals, LLC, 2018 WL 1581685 (S.D.N.Y. 2018).

(d) If Light's damages are measured under §2-708(1), what amount may she collect? What amount under §2-706?

(e) Does Light have the choice between the §2-706 (Resale) computation and the §2-708 (Repudiation) computation? See Official Comment 1 to §2-703; White & Summers §8-7.

Peace River Seed Co-Operative, Ltd. v. Proseeds Marketing, Inc.
Supreme Court of Oregon, 2014, 355 Or. 44, 322 P.3d 531

BALMER, C.J.

In this breach of contract case, we examine the availability of different remedies under the Uniform Commercial Code (UCC) for an aggrieved seller of goods after a buyer breaches a contract to purchase those goods. Specifically, we consider the relationship between ORS 72.7080(1), which measures a seller's damages as the difference between the unpaid contract price and the *market* price at the time and place for tender, and ORS 72.7060, which measures a seller's damages as the difference between the contract price and the *resale* price. We examine those provisions to determine whether an aggrieved seller who has resold goods can recover a greater amount of damages using the market price measure of damages than the seller would recover using the resale price measure of damages.

Plaintiff, a seller seeking damages from a buyer that breached contracts to purchase goods, argued at trial that it was entitled to recover its market price damages. The trial court determined that plaintiff was entitled to the lesser of its market price damages or its resale price damages, and the court ultimately awarded plaintiff its resale price damages. The Court of

Appeals reversed and remanded, because the court determined that plaintiff could recover its market price damages, even though it had resold some of the goods at issue. Peace River Seed Co-Op. v. Proseeds Marketing, 253 Or. App. 704, 717, 293 P.3d 1058 (2012). The Court of Appeals also reversed the trial court's decision not to award plaintiff its attorney fees under the parties' contracts, and remanded for the trial court to determine whether the parties intended the ambiguous contract term "charges for collection" to include attorney fees. Id. at 724-25, 293 P.3d 1058. For the reasons that follow, we agree that plaintiff was entitled to recover its market price damages, even if those damages exceeded plaintiff's resale price damages. We conclude, however, that plaintiff is not entitled to recover its attorney fees under the parties' contracts.

FACTS AND PROCEEDINGS BELOW

The facts material to our discussion are mostly undisputed. Peace River Seed Co-Operative ("plaintiff") is a Canadian company that buys grass seed from and sells grass seed for grass seed producers. Proseeds Marketing ("defendant") is an Oregon corporation that purchases grass seed from various sources to resell to end users. A broker prepared and the parties agreed to multiple contracts for defendant to purchase from plaintiff the total production of grass seed from a certain number of acres for a fixed price over a period of two years. The contracts incorporated the NORAMSEED Rules for the Trade of Seeds for Planting, which have been adopted by the American and Canadian Seed Trade Associations to govern the trade of seed. The NORAMSEED Rules provide that the UCC applies to transactions within the United States, and both parties have litigated this case under the UCC.

Under the contracts, defendant was to provide shipping and delivery instructions to plaintiff. During the contract period, however, the price of grass seed fell dramatically. Although defendant initially provided shipping instructions and plaintiff shipped conforming seed, defendant eventually refused to provide shipping instructions for delivery of additional seed under the contracts. After multiple requests for shipping instructions, and defendant's continued refusal to provide them, plaintiff cancelled the contracts. Over the next three years, plaintiff was able to sell at least some of the seed that defendant had agreed to purchase to other buyers.

The parties submitted their contract dispute to arbitration. Following an arbitrator's award in plaintiff's favor, plaintiff sought to enforce the award in court, and the trial court entered judgment over defendant's objection. Defendant appealed, and the Court of Appeals remanded for trial after concluding that the arbitration was not binding. Peace River Seed Co-Op v. Proseeds Marketing, 204 Or. App. 523, 526, 534, 132 P.3d 31, *rev. den.*, 341 Or. 216, 140 P.3d 1133 (2006). In the subsequent bench trial, the court concluded that defendant had breached the contracts and that plaintiff had been entitled to cancel the contracts and seek damages. When the trial court awarded plaintiff its damages, the court noted that the parties had entered into fixed price contracts, "regardless of the market price at the time of harvest and shipment," and the court explained that "[e]ach party takes certain risks and hopes for certain benefits in this type of a contract." Nonetheless, the court concluded that plaintiff had an "obligation to mitigate damages" and was "not entitled to recover damages in an amount greater than actually incurred." Accordingly, the trial court awarded plaintiff the lesser of two measures of damages: the difference between the unpaid contract price and the market price (the measure under ORS 72.7080(1)) or the difference between the contract price and the resale price (the measure under ORS 72.7060). The trial court directed plaintiff to submit calculations of each measure of damages.

Both parties sought reconsideration. At a hearing on those motions, the trial court stated that it would not be "absolutely one-hundred percent convinced" about the appropriate measure of damages until it could see how each party calculated market price damages and resale price damages. The trial court acknowledged that plaintiff previously had submitted its calculation of market price damages and had proven those damages, but the court also directed the parties to calculate damages to account for any seed that had been resold. Subsequently, defendant submitted its analysis of damages based on the prices that plaintiff had received when it resold. Plaintiff criticized defendant's analysis and stuck by its calculation of market price damages, without submitting an analysis of damages based on resale prices.

Each party's calculation of damages for one of the breached contracts, contract 1874, illustrates the implications of using the market price or the resale price to calculate damages. The evidence at trial showed that the contract price for contract 1874 was $0.72 per pound. Plaintiff sought damages of $3,736.00 for that contract, apparently based on a market price of $0.64 per pound, resulting in a contract price minus market price differential of $0.08 per pound for 46,700 pounds of seed not accepted by defendant. Defendant argued, however, that plaintiff had resold at least some of that seed for $0.75 per pound, $0.03 per pound above the contract price and $0.11 per pound above plaintiff's market price calculation. Thus, according to defendant, plaintiff did not have any damages for that resold seed because plaintiff had resold for more than the contract price. If plaintiff recovered $0.08 per pound in market price damages, in addition to the $0.75 per pound that plaintiff allegedly had received on the resale, plaintiff ultimately would recover $0.83 per pound, which was $0.11 more than the contract price.

For that same contract, however, where the contract price was $0.72 per pound, defendant noted that some of the seed had been resold for $0.60

per pound. That meant that the resale price damages would be $0.12 per pound. That is, for at least some of the resold seed from contract 1874, plaintiff's resale price damages of $0.12 per pound would exceed plaintiff's claimed market price damages of $0.08 per pound. In sum, the parties' calculations of damages for contract 1874 showed that, with regard to some seed, the market price damage calculation would lead to a larger award, but that, with regard to other seed, the resale price damage calculation would lead to a larger award. On the whole, however, defendant calculated that plaintiff would receive a smaller amount of damages using the resale price measure of damages than plaintiff calculated that it would receive using the market price measure of damages.

The trial court awarded plaintiff damages using the resale price measure of damages as calculated by defendant. The trial court reasoned that plaintiff had not calculated damages as ordered by the court. The court stated that "even if Plaintiff [was] correct that Defendant's calculations [were] somehow flawed or incorrect, no alternative calculation ha[d] been offered." Thus, the trial court concluded that it was "left with no option but to accept Defendant's calculation." . . .

The Court of Appeals reversed and remanded. On the first issue, the court noted that, at least on its face, the UCC allows a seller to recover damages as calculated under either ORS 72.7060 (contract price less resale price) or ORS 72.7080(1) (contract price less market price). Id. at 713, 293 P.3d 1058. After reviewing the relevant statutory provisions, the court went on to conclude that, "[i]n the absence of a restriction within the UCC that precludes an aggrieved seller from seeking its remedy pursuant to ORS 72.7080 if the seller has resold, we would decline to impose such a restriction." Id. at 715, 293 P.3d 1058. In support of that conclusion, the court explained that, once the buyer breaches, the buyer loses any right to control the goods or to "insist upon a different measure of damages." Id. at 716-17, 293 P.3d 1058. Moreover, the court noted, market price damages require the buyer to fulfill only the bargain to which it agreed. Id. at 717, 293 P.3d 1058. Although the court acknowledged that the UCC policy is that remedies should put an aggrieved party "in as good a position as if the other party had fully performed," ORS 71.3050(1), the court concluded that the intent of the UCC is to allow an aggrieved seller to recover market price damages, even if the seller has resold the goods. Id. at 715-16 n.7, 293 P.3d 1058. The court remanded the case for a proper calculation of plaintiff's market price damages. Id. at 717, 293 P.3d 1058. . . .

AN AGGRIEVED SELLER'S REMEDIES UNDER THE UCC

The UCC provides a variety of remedies to an aggrieved seller. See ORS 72.7030 (providing an index of a seller's remedies). As noted, the issue in this case is whether an aggrieved seller who has resold goods can recover the difference between the unpaid contract price and the market price under ORS 72.7080(1), even when market price damages would exceed resale price damages under ORS 72.7060.

Commentators and courts have taken two different approaches to this issue. Relying on the text and context of the sellers' remedies provisions, some commentators have argued that the drafters of the UCC intended for sellers to be able to recover either market price damages or resale price damages, even if the seller resold the goods for more than the market price. See, e.g., Henry Gabriel, The Seller's Election of Remedies Under the Uniform Commercial Code: An Expectation Theory, 23 Wake Forest L. Rev. 429, 429 (1988) (arguing that an aggrieved seller "should be allowed to elect between the two remedies regardless of the seller's good faith post-breach activities concerning the non-accepted goods"); Ellen A. Peters, Remedies for Breach of Contracts Relating to the Sale of Goods Under the Uniform Commercial Code: A Roadmap for Article Two, 73 Yale L.J. 199, 260 (1963) (arguing for a "non-restrictive reading of the various remedies sections to preserve full options to use or to ignore substitute transactions as a measure of damages"). On the other hand, Professors White and Summers, whose view has been adopted by a number of courts, have argued that the UCC's general policy is that damages should put a seller only in "as good a position as if the other party had fully performed," ORS 71.3050(1), meaning a seller who has resold should not be allowed to recover more in market price damages than it could recover in resale price damages. James J. White, Robert S. Summers and Robert A. Hillman, 1 Uniform Commercial Code §8:13, 689 (6th ed. 2012) (so stating). We agree with those commentators who have observed that the drafters did not clearly resolve this issue. See, e.g., id. at 691 (noting that the UCC and the comments are "equivocal" about whether a seller can recover more under section 2-708(1) than it could recover under section 2-706); Gabriel, 23 Wake Forest L. Rev. at 430 (noting "the failure of the drafters to clearly resolve the problem of election between sections 2-706 and 2-708(1)"). Nonetheless, we conclude that the text, context, and legislative history of the sellers' remedies provisions support a seller's right to recover either market price damages or resale price damages, even if market price damages lead to a larger recovery.

We analyze the relevant statutory provisions using the framework described in State v. Gaines, 346 Or. 160, 171-72, 206 P.3d 1042 (2009). We begin by examining the statute's text and context to determine the legislature's intent regarding a seller's remedies under the UCC. Because the relevant statutes are part of the UCC, we also consider the official UCC comments as an indication of the legislature's intent. Security Bank v. Chiapuzio, 304 Or. 438, 445 n.6, 747 P.2d 335 (1987) (noting that the Oregon legislature took note of the official comments of the UCC, which are "statements of the purpose of each section"). In addition, "the legislative intent to make the UCC a uniform code makes relevant the decisions of other courts that have examined these questions and the discussions of the questions by scholars in the field, especially those scholars who participated in drafting the UCC." Id. We also examine legislative history. The Oregon legislature enacted the UCC in 1961 "with little debate or discussion of the legislative intent," but the UCC was proposed so that Oregon could "obtain the same advantages that other states had gained from the adoption of a uniform and comprehensive set of commercial statutes." Id. Given "the legislative intent to make the UCC a uniform code," id., we consider prior drafts of the UCC, as drafted by the National Conference of Commissioners on Uniform State Laws (NCCUSL), as part of the legislative history. Cf. Datt v. Hill, 347 Or. 672, 680, 227 P.3d 714 (2010) (examining history of uniform act in interpreting Oregon statute taken from that act).

Before examining the statutory scheme, however, we briefly review the law as it existed prior to the enactment of the UCC in Oregon. At common law, an aggrieved seller

> ha[d] the election of three remedies: (1) To hold the property for the purchaser, and to recover of him the entire purchase money; (2) to sell it, after notice to the purchaser, as his agent for that purpose, and recover the difference between the contract price and that realized on the sale; (3) to retain it as his own, and recover the difference between the contract and market prices at the time and place of delivery[.]"

Krebs Hop Co. v. Livesley, 59 Or. 574, 588, 118 P. 165 (1911). *Krebs Hop Co.* suggests that, before Oregon adopted the UCC, an aggrieved seller had to elect between remedies, and if the seller resold the goods, it had elected its remedy and could recover only resale price damages, but not market price damages. See Gabriel, 23 Wake Forest L. Rev. at 446 (explaining that, under pre-UCC law, an aggrieved seller who resold the goods was assumed to have elected the resale remedy and was barred from using an inconsistent remedy, such as market price damages). Although the UCC retained some aspect of each of the remedies available at common law, as explained below, it specifically rejected the doctrine of election of remedies. See Legislative Comment 1 to ORS 72.7030, reprinted in Legislative Counsel Committee, Oregon's Uniform Commercial Code with Comments and Index and Tables 101 (1962) (noting that the UCC chapter on sales "reject[s] any doctrine of election of remedy as a fundamental policy"); Peters, 73 Yale L.J. at 204 n.16 (noting that many sections of the UCC were "designed to mitigate the effect of prior law insofar as it forced a choice of remedy on the party aggrieved without regard to the adequacy of compensation").

[The court quoted §2-703 on Seller's Remedies.] That section lists the seller's remedies, which, as relevant here, include resale price damages,

ORS 72.7060, and market price damages, ORS 72.7080. Moreover, it lists those remedies without any limiting conjunction, such as "or," that might suggest that the remedies are mutually exclusive. In contrast, a similar index of a buyer's remedies after a seller's breach provides that the buyer may "(a) 'Cover' and have damages . . . *or* (b) Recover damages for nondelivery." ORS 72.7110(1) (emphasis added.) Thus, although the buyer's index of remedies suggests that a buyer who covers may be precluded from seeking market price damages, the seller's index of remedies does not contain a similar limitation if the seller chooses to resell. It follows that the text of ORS 72.7030 supports plaintiff's argument that a seller who has resold is not necessarily limited to its resale price damages under ORS 72.7060, but has the option of seeking to recover market price damages under ORS 72.7080.

The UCC comments to the statute describing a seller's remedies confirm that interpretation. Although the comments acknowledge that, in a particular case, the pursuit of one remedy may prevent a seller from obtaining certain damages, the comments also state that the UCC chapter on sales "reject[s] any doctrine of election of remedy as a fundamental policy and thus the remedies are essentially cumulative in nature and include all of the available remedies for breach." Legislative Comment 1 to ORS 72.7030 at 101; id. ("Whether the pursuit of one remedy bars another depends entirely on the facts of the individual case."). In contrast, the comments to the statute describing a buyer's market price remedy explain that that remedy "is completely alternative to 'cover' under ORS 72.7120 and applies *only when and to the extent that the buyer has not covered*." Legislative Comment 5 to ORS 72.7130 at 110 (emphasis added). Thus, while the comments to the statute describing a seller's remedies expressly reject the doctrine of election of remedies, the comments to the statute describing a buyer's market price remedy appear to adopt that doctrine. Those comments further indicate that a seller who resells goods after a buyer's breach would not be considered to have "elected" the resale remedy and thus would not be precluded from seeking a larger damage recovery using the market price measure of damages.

The text of ORS 72.7060, which sets forth the seller's resale remedy, similarly suggests that a seller who resells goods is not necessarily precluded from using the market price measure of damages, even if it leads to a larger recovery. ORS 72.7060(1) states that "the seller *may* resell the goods concerned or the undelivered balance thereof," which suggests that an aggrieved seller is not required to resell. (Emphasis added.) See White, Summers and Hillman, 1 Uniform Commercial Code §8:6 at 671 ("Resale is not mandatory."). Similarly, the text of ORS 72.7060 indicates that a seller who resells is not required to seek damages using the resale remedy. See ORS 72.7060(1) ("Where the resale is made in good faith and in a commercially reasonable manner the seller *may* recover the difference between the resale price and the contract price. . . ." (Emphasis added.)). In fact, the unqualified text of ORS 72.7080(1) seems to suggest that market price is in fact the default measure of damages. See ORS 72.7080(1) ("Subject to . . . the provisions of ORS 72.7230 with respect to proof of market price, *the* measure of damages for nonacceptance or repudiation by the buyer is the difference between the market price at the time and place for tender and the unpaid contract price. . . ." (Emphasis added.)). Thus, the text of the remedy provisions does not limit a seller who resells to its resale price damages.

As defendant notes, however, one of the comments to ORS 72.7060 does indicate that the drafters intended ORS 72.7060 to be a seller's primary remedy, and did not intend to allow a seller to recover more under the market price remedy. Comment 2 to ORS 72.7060 explains that "[f]ailure to act properly under ORS 72.7060 *deprives* the seller of the measure of damages there provided and *relegates* him to that provided in ORS 72.7080 [market price damages]." Legislative Comment 2 to ORS 72.7060 at 104 (emphasis added). That language suggests that the comment drafters viewed market price damages as less favorable, but it does not indicate *why* they viewed them that way. The pejorative language used in the comments does not necessarily lead to the conclusion that a seller who resells cannot use the market price remedy or must use the resale price remedy if it would yield the same or a smaller amount of damages than the market price remedy. That language instead could indicate that market price damages are considered less favorable because market price is often hard to prove, as many commentators have noted. See, e.g., Henry J. Bailey III, 1 The Oregon Uniform Commercial Code §2.140, 279 (2d ed. 1990) (noting that the remedy under ORS 72.7080(1) "is often a less advantageous remedy for the seller because of difficulty of proof of market price"). As a result, that comment language is not dispositive, particularly in light of the text of the remedy provisions.

Turning to legislative history, prior drafts of the UCC provide additional insight into the drafters' intent to allow a seller to recover its market price damages, even if the seller has resold. In particular, in an earlier draft of the section describing the resale price remedy, section 2-706, one of the comments stated that that section provided

> "the *exclusive* measure of the seller's damages where the resale has been made in accordance with the requirements of this section. Evidence of market or current prices at any particular time or place is relevant *only* on the question of whether the seller acted with commercially reasonable care and judgment in making the resale."

See Gabriel, 23 Wake Forest L. Rev. at 436 (quoting UCC §2-706 cmt. 3 (May 1949 Draft) (emphasis added)). Under that version of the UCC, a seller who had met the resale requirements would be required to use the resale price measure of damages. That comment later was revised, however, and when Oregon adopted the UCC, the comment included language that also had been in the 1949 draft comment, but the mandatory language had been removed, leaving only the permissive wording: "If the seller complies with the prescribed standard of duty in making the resale, he *may* recover from the buyer the damages provided for in subsection (1)." Legislative Comment 3 to ORS 72.7060 at 104 (emphasis added). That shift, from resale as the exclusive remedy to resale as a permissible remedy, indicates that the drafters intended for a seller to be able to choose to recover market price damages, even after reselling under ORS 72.7060.

Defendant argues, however, that even if a seller who resells can recover market price damages under ORS 72.7080(1), those damages cannot exceed the seller's resale price damages. Defendant primarily relies on the general policy statement set forth in ORS 71.3050 to support its argument. ORS 71.3050(1) provides,

> The remedies provided by the Uniform Commercial Code must be liberally administered to the end that the aggrieved party may be put *in as good a position as if the other party had fully performed* but consequential damages, special damages or penal damages may not be had except as specifically provided in the Uniform Commercial Code or by other rule of law.

(Emphasis added.) Defendant reasons that the reference in ORS 71.3050(1) to putting an aggrieved party "in as good a position as if the other party had fully performed" acts as a limit on the damages that a party can receive. Commentators and courts likewise have relied on that provision in concluding that a seller's market price damages should be limited to the actual loss suffered, by taking into account any goods that have been resold. See, e.g., White, Summers and Hillman, 1 Uniform Commercial Code §8:13 at 689 ("We conclude that a seller should not be permitted to recover more under 2-708(1) [market price damages] than under 2-706 [resale price damages]. . . . Section 1-305 indicates that a seller who has resold may not invoke 2-708(1)."); Coast Trading Co. v. Cudahy Co., 592 F.2d 1074, 1081-83 (9th Cir. 1979) (adopting approach of White and Summers and reducing section 2-708(1) market price damages of seller who conducted commercially unreasonable resale to what seller could have recovered under section 2-706 if resale had been commercially reasonable); Tesoro Petroleum Corp. v. Holborn Oil Co., 145 Misc. 2d 715, 547 N.Y.S.2d 1012, 1016-17 (N.Y. Sup. Ct. 1989) (adopting approach of White and Summers and limiting seller to resale price damages because higher market price damages would create a "windfall" inconsistent with the general policy of the UCC).

The text of ORS 71.3050(1) indicates that the drafters of the UCC intended a seller's remedies to be compensatory. See Legislative Comment 1 to *former* ORS 71.1060 at 6 (1963), amended and renumbered as ORS 71.3050 (2009) (noting that statute is intended to "make it clear that compensatory damages are limited to compensation"). The text of that section, however, also provides that the remedies in the UCC are to be "liberally administered." ORS 71.3050(1); see also Legislative Comment 4 to ORS 72.7030 at 101 ("It should also be noted that the Uniform Commercial Code requires its remedies to be liberally administered. . . ."). Nonetheless, we agree with defendant that the general policy of compensation provided in ORS 71.3050(1) must be taken into account.

We do not agree, however, that that policy necessarily limits an aggrieved seller who has resold to its resale price damages. Defendant argues that if it had fully performed, plaintiff could expect to recover only the contract price, and that limiting plaintiff to the difference between the contract price and the resale price therefore gives it the benefit of its bargain. As Professor Gabriel notes, however, limiting a seller to its resale price damages does not account fully for either party's expectations upon entering into the contract. He explains that a seller expects to be able to recover the difference between the contract price and the market price because it is the "logical and expected measure of damages," and because the ability to recover market price damages "is the natural assumption the seller makes in return for the risk inherent in the contract that the sale may not turn out to be economically beneficial to the seller. That the seller then resells the goods in no way diminishes this expectancy regarding the first contract." Gabriel, 23 Wake Forest L. Rev. at 449, 453. From the buyer's perspective, he argues that "the [buyer] has specific obligations and will suffer the consequences of the failure to perform these obligations because this is the [buyer's] expectation." Id. at 450. In other words, contrary to defendant's argument, an aggrieved seller expects to be able to recover market price damages under the contract, and a breaching buyer expects to have to fulfill its obligation to the seller — even if a seller resells and recovers market price damages, "the buyer's obligation is no more than the right the buyer originally conferred upon the seller." Id. at 449.

Moreover, limiting an aggrieved seller to its resale price damages ignores the risk for which the parties bargained. When parties bargain for fixed price contracts, each party assumes the risk of market price fluctuations. The parties are willing to take that risk because of the benefits that they might receive: if the market price decreases, the seller benefits, and if the market price increases, the buyer benefits. In a fixed price contract, therefore, market price damages represent the risk for which both parties bargained. Cf. id. ("The logical and expected measure of damages is the contract price-market price differential. *This measure of damages is the risk the buyer assumed by entering into the contract;* it is the right conferred upon the seller by the buyer." (Emphasis added.)).[2] For those reasons, we conclude that a seller can recover market price damages, even if the seller resells some of the goods at above the market price at the time and place for tender.

Defendant argues, however, that that conclusion does not account for an aggrieved party's duty to mitigate, which is consistent with the UCC's policy of minimizing damages. See Legislative Comment 1 to *former* ORS 71.1060 at 6 (1963) ("[T]he Code elsewhere makes it clear that damages must be minimized."); Roy Ryden Anderson, 1 Damages Under the Uniform Commercial Code §1:6, 11-12 (2012) (noting that the duty to mitigate is "implicit in every damage remedy" and typically is justified under section 1-305). We do not understand the duty to mitigate to be a limit on a seller's market price damages because, as noted, the text demonstrates and commentators agree that a seller is not required to resell goods after a buyer's breach. If the duty to mitigate does not require the aggrieved seller to resell its goods, we do not think that the duty to mitigate can require the seller to use the resale price measure of damages. See Gabriel, 23 Wake Forest L. Rev. at 445 ("The seller has no obligation to resell, and the failure to resell the goods does not affect the right to proceed under section 2-708(1). If non-action by the seller does not impact on the statutory right under section 2-708(1), common sense dictates that an affirmative act by the seller to resell should not have any impact on that right." (Footnote omitted.)). The comments to the resale remedy provision also acknowledge that the seller who resells does so for its own benefit, and not for the benefit of the breaching party as mitigation. See Legislative Comment 2 to ORS 72.7060 at 104 (noting that the seller resells "in his own behalf, for his own benefit and for the purpose of fixing his damages"); *cf.* ORS 72.7060(6) ("The seller is not accountable to the buyer for any profit made on any resale."). Therefore, the principle of mitigation does not appear to limit an aggrieved seller's recovery to resale price damages under ORS 72.7060; the seller may instead seek market price damages under ORS 72.7080(1).

---

2. Professor Gabriel's explanation also responds to the argument that to permit a seller to recover market price damages when it has resold some or all of the goods confers an improper "windfall" on the seller. If a seller is limited to its resale price damages, it is just as accurate to say that the breaching buyer has received a "windfall," because the seller's success in reselling reduces the damages that the buyer must pay — and not because of anything the buyer did, but only because of the seller's successful efforts. As discussed in the text, the UCC imposes no obligation on the seller to resell, and the buyer's expectation, at the time the buyer entered into the contract, was that it might have to pay market price damages if it breached the contract. The point is not that one party or the other gets an undeserved "windfall," but rather that the provisions of the UCC, as we have interpreted them here, determine the rights and obligations of each party and therefore what is expected of each party and what each may expect of the other, as well as the consequences of either party's breach. The result we reach here is consistent with those expectations. *See generally* Gabriel, 23 Wake Forest L. Rev. at 453.

In sum, when viewed in light of the bargained-for market risks and the UCC's rejection of the doctrine of election of remedies, the text, context, and legislative history of the sellers' remedy provisions demonstrate that an aggrieved seller can seek damages under either ORS 72.7080(1) or ORS 72.7060. That means that an aggrieved seller can seek damages under ORS 72.7080(1) even if the seller has resold the goods and market price damages exceed resale price damages. . . .

CONCLUSION

For the reasons explained above, we conclude that plaintiff can recover its market price damages under ORS 72.7080(1). Because the trial court determined that plaintiff had proven its market price damages at trial, but later declined to award those damages for reasons that we have concluded were legally erroneous, plaintiff is entitled to recover market price damages in the amount calculated in plaintiff's Exhibit 409, together with pre-judgment interest on that amount. However, we agree with the trial court, although for different reasons, that plaintiff is not entitled to recover its attorney fees under the NORAMSEED Rule that allows a seller to recover "charges for collection."

The decision of the Court of Appeals is affirmed in part and reversed in part. The judgment of the circuit court is affirmed in part and reversed in part, and the case is remanded to the circuit court.

PROBLEM 80

Fun in the Sun, Inc., sells swimming pools. Its president comes to your law office with this problem. A customer named Esther Swimmer ordered one of the standard above-ground pools, retailing for $2,000. The pool's components are purchased by Fun in the Sun at a wholesale price of $800 and are assembled into the finished product. The assembly process costs the seller $400. Swimmer has now repudiated the contract, and Fun in the Sun wants to sue. The current market price is $2,000 for such a pool. Fun in the Sun is sure it can find another buyer at that price if it resells the pool. Does it have damages? How are they measured? See §2-708(2), along with Official Comment 2. See also White & Summers §§8-8 to 8-13.

The problem with sellers in Fun in the Sun's position (sellers having an unlimited supply of goods) is that if the law forces them to measure damages under §2-706 or §2-708(1), they lose the profit they would have made from the sale to the second customer. A seller in such a position is called a *lost volume seller*. The drafters meant for §2-708(2) to rescue such a seller from this dilemma, but the actual mechanics of the operation of the section are not clear. The problem arises in part from the undefined phrase "profit (including reasonable overhead)," which contains accounting terms having no fixed legal meaning. For an analysis of their import, see Speidel & Clay, Seller's Recovery of Overhead Under U.C.C. Section 2-708(2): Economic Cost Theory and Contract Remedial Policy, 57 Cornell L. Rev. 681 (1972). See also Scott, The Case for Market Damages: Revisiting the Lost Profits Puzzle, 57 U. Chi. L. Rev. 1155 (1990).

Teradyne, Inc. v. Teledyne Industries, Inc.
United States Court of Appeals, First Circuit, 1982, 676 F.2d 865

WYZANSKI, J.

In this diversity action, Teradyne, Inc. sued Teledyne Industries, Inc. and its subsidiary for damages pursuant to §2-708(2) of the U.C.C. Teledyne does not dispute the facts that it is bound as a buyer under a sales contract with Teradyne, that it broke the contract, and that Teradyne's right to damages is governed by §2-708(2). The principal dispute concerns the calculation of damages.

The district court referred the case to a master whose report the district court approved and made the basis of the judgment here on appeal.

The following facts, derived from the master's report, are undisputed.

On July 30, 1976 Teradyne, Inc. ["the seller"], a Massachusetts corporation, entered into a Quantity Purchase Contract ["the contract"] which, though made with a subsidiary, binds Teledyne Industries, Inc., a California corporation ["the buyer"]. That contract governed an earlier contract resulting from the seller's acceptance of the buyer's July 23, 1976 purchase order to buy at the list price of $98,400 (which was also its fair market value) a T-347A transistor test system ["the T-347A"]. One consequence of such governance was that the buyer was entitled to a $984 discount from the $98,400 price.

The buyer canceled its order for the T-347A when it was packed ready for shipment scheduled to occur two days later. The seller refused to accept the cancellation.

The buyer offered to purchase instead of the T-347A a $65,000 Field Effects Transistor System ["the FET"] which would also have been governed by "the contract." The seller refused the offer.

After dismantling, testing, and reassembling at an estimated cost of $614 the T-347A, the seller, pursuant to an order that was on hand prior to the cancellation, sold it for $98,400 to another purchaser [hereafter "resale purchaser"].

Teradyne would have made the sale to the resale purchaser even if Teledyne had not broken its contract. Thus if there had been no breach, Teradyne would have made two sales and earned two profits rather than one.

The seller was a volume seller of the equipment covered by the July 23, 1976, purchase order. The equipment represented standard products of the seller and the seller had the means and capacity to duplicate the equipment for a second sale had the buyer honored its purchase order.

Teradyne being of the view that the measure of damages under §2-708(2) was the contract price less ascertainable costs saved as a result of the breach — see Jericho Sash and Door Company, Inc. v. Building Erectors, Inc., 362 Mass. 871, 872, 286 N.E.2d 343 (1972) [hereafter *"Jericho"*] — offered as evidence of its cost prices its Inventory Standards Catalog ["the Catalog"] — a document which was prepared for tax purposes not claimed to have been illegitimate, but which admittedly disclosed "low inventory valuations." Relying on that Catalog, Teradyne's Controller, McCabe, testified that the *only* costs which the seller saved as a result of the breach were:

direct labor costs associated with production	$3,301
material charges	17,045
sales commission on one T-347A	492
expense	1,800
Total	$22,638

McCabe admitted that he had not included as costs saved the labor costs of employees associated with testing, shipping, installing, servicing, or fulfilling 10-year warranties on the T-347A (although he acknowledged that in forms of accounting for purposes other than damage suits the costs of those employees would not be regarded as "overhead"). His reason was that those costs would not have been affected by the production of one machine more or less. McCabe also admitted that he had not included fringe benefits which amounted to 12% in the case of both included and excluded labor costs.

During McCabe's direct examination, he referred to the 10-K report which Teradyne had filed with the SEC. On cross-examination McCabe admitted that the 10-K form showed that on average the seller's revenues were distributed as follows:

profit	9%
"selling and administrative" expense	26%
interest	1%
"costs of sales and engineering" (including substantial research and development costs incidental to a high technology business)	64%

He also admitted that the average figures applied to the T-347a.

Teledyne contended that the 10-K report was a better index of lost profits than was the Catalog. The master disagreed and concluded that the more appropriate formula for calculating Teradyne's damages under §2-708(2) was the one approved in *Jericho,* supra — " 'gross' profit including fixed costs but not costs saved as a result of the breach." He then stated:

> In accordance with the statutory mandate that the remedy "be liberally administered to the end that the aggrieved party may be put in as good a position as if the other party had fully performed," MGL c106 §1-106(1),[3] I find that the Plaintiff has met its burden of proof of damages, and has established the accuracy of its direct costs and the ascertainability of its variable costs with reasonable certainty and "whatever definiteness and accuracy the facts permit." Comment 1 to §1-106(1) of the U.C.C.

In effect, this was a finding that Teradyne had saved only $22,638 as a result of the breach. Subtracting that amount and also the $984 quantity discount from the original contract price of $98,400, the master found that the lost "profit (including reasonable overhead)" was $74,778. To that amount the master added $614 for "incidental damages" which Teradyne incurred in preparing the T-347A for its new customer. Thus he found that Teradyne's total §2-708(2) damages amounted to $75,392.

The master declined to make a deduction from the $75,392 on account of the refusal of the seller to accept the buyer's offer to purchase an FET tester in partial substitution for the repudiated T-347A.

At the time of the reference to the master, the court, without securing the agreement of the parties, had ordered that the master's costs should be paid by them in equal parts.

Teradyne filed a motion praying that the district court (1) should adopt the master's report allowing it to recover $75,392, and (2) should require Teledyne to pay all the master's costs. The district court, without opinion, entered a judgment which grants the first prayer and denies the second. Teledyne appealed from the first part of the judgment; Teradyne appealed from the second part.

1. The parties are agreed that §2-708(2) applies to the case at bar. Inasmuch as this conclusion is not plain from the text, we explain the reasons why we concur in that agreement.

Section 2-708(2) applies only if the damages provided by §2-708(1) are inadequate to put the seller in as good a position as performance would have done. Under §2-708(1) the measure of damages is the difference between unpaid contract price and market price. Here the unpaid contract price was $97,416 and the market price was $98,400. Hence no damages would be recoverable under §2-708(1). On the other hand, if the buyer had performed, the seller (1) would have had the proceeds of two contracts, one

---

3. Now §1-305(a). — Ed.

with the buyer Teledyne and the other with the "resale purchaser" and (2) *it seems* would have had in 1976-7 one more T-347A sale.

A literal reading of the last sentence of §2-708(2) — providing for "due credit for payments or proceeds of resale" — would indicate that Teradyne recovers nothing because the proceeds of the resale exceeded the price set in the Teledyne-Teradyne contract. However, in light of the statutory history of the subsection, it is universally agreed that in a case where after the buyer's default a seller resells the goods, the proceeds of the resale are not to be credited to the buyer if the seller is a lost volume seller[4] — that is, one who had there been no breach by the buyer, could and would have had the benefit of both the original contract and the resale contract.[5]

Thus, despite the resale of the T-347A, Teradyne is entitled to recover from Teledyne what §2-708(2) calls its expected "profit (including reasonable overhead)" on the broken Teledyne contract.[6]

2. Teledyne not only "does not dispute that damages are to be calculated pursuant to §2-708(2)" but concedes that the formula used in Jericho Sash & Door Co. v. Building Erectors Inc., 362 Mass. 871 (1972), for determining lost profit including overhead — that is, the formula under which direct costs of producing and selling manufactured goods are deducted from the contract price in order to arrive at "profit (including reasonable overhead)" as that term is used in §2-708(2) — "is permissible provided all variable expenses are identified."

What Teledyne contends is that all variable costs were not identified because the cost figures came from a catalog, prepared for tax purposes, which did not fully reflect all direct costs. The master found that the statement of costs based on the catalog was reliable and that Teledyne's method

---

4. The term "lost volume seller" was apparently coined by Professor Robert J. Harris in his article A Radical Restatement of the Law of Seller's Damages: Sales Act and Commercial Code Results Compared, 18 Stan. L. Rev. 66 (1965). The terminology has been widely adopted. See Famous Knitwear Corp. v. Drug Fair Inc., 493 F.2d 251, 254 n.5 (4th Cir. 1974); Snyder v. Herbert Greenbaum & Assoc. Inc., 38 Md. App. 144, 157, 380 A.2d 618, 624 (1977); Publicker Industries, Inc. v. Roman Ceramics Corp., 652 F.2d 340, 346 (3d Cir. 1981). See Restatement (Second) Contracts §347 Comment f; J. White and R. Summers, Uniform Commercial Code, 2d ed. (1980) [hereinafter "White and Summers"] §7-9, particularly p. 276 first full paragraph.

5. Famous Knitwear Corp. v. Drug Fair Inc., supra, 493 F.2d 254 n.7; Snyder v. Herbert Greenbaum & Assoc. Inc., supra, 380 A.2d 625-626; Neri v. Retail Marine Corp., 30 N.Y.2d 393, 399, 285 N.E.2d 311, 314 (1972). See White and Summers, §7-13, particularly 284-285.

6. Ibid. White and Summers at pp. 284-285 give the following suppositious case which parallels the instant case. Boeing is able to make and sell in one year 100 airplanes. TWA contracts to buy the third plane off the assembly line, but it breaks the contract and Boeing resells the plane to Pan Am which had already agreed to buy the fourth plane. Because of the breach Boeing sells only 99 aircraft during the year. White and Summers say that the right result, despite the words of §2-708(2), is that Boeing recovers from TWA both the net profit and the overhead components of the TWA contract price, no credit being given for any part of the proceeds Boeing received from its sale to Pan Am.

of calculating costs based on the 10-K statements was not more accurate. Those findings are not clearly erroneous and therefore we may not reverse the judgment on the ground that allegedly the items of cost which were deducted are unreliable. Fed. R. Civ. P. 52(a); Merrill Trust Co. v. Bradford, 507 F.2d 467, 468 (1st Cir. 1974); Van Alen v. Dominick & Dominick, Inc., 560 F.2d 547, 551 (2d Cir. 1977).

Teledyne's more significant objection to Teradyne's and the master's application of the *Jericho* formula in the case at bar is that neither of them made deductions on account of the wages paid to testers, shippers, installers, and other Teradyne employees who directly handled the T-347A, or on account of the fringe benefits amounting in the case of those and other employees to 12 per cent of wages. Teradyne gave as the reason for the omission of the wages of the testers, etc. that those wages would not have been affected if each of the testers, etc. handled one product more or less. However, the work of those employees entered as directly into producing and supplying the T-347A as did the work of a fabricator of a T-347A. Surely no one would regard as "reasonable overhead" within §2-708(2) the wages of a fabricator of a T-347A even if his wages were the same whether he made one product more or less. We conclude that the wages of the testers, etc., likewise are not part of overhead and as a "direct cost" should have been deducted from the contract price. A fortiori fringe benefits amounting to 12 per cent of wages should also have been deducted as direct costs. Taken together we cannot view these omitted items as what *Jericho* called "relatively insignificant items." We, therefore, must vacate the district court's judgment. In accordance with the procedure followed in Publicker Industries, Inc. v. Roman Ceramics Corp., 603 F.2d 1065, 1072-3 (3d Cir. 1979) and Famous Knitwear Corp. v. Drug Fair, Inc., 493 F.2d 251, 255-256 (4th Cir. 1974), we remand this case so that with respect to the omitted direct labor costs specified above the parties may offer further evidence and the court may make findings "with whatever definiteness and accuracy the facts permit, but no more." *Jericho*, p. 872.

There are two other matters which may properly be dealt with before the case is remanded to the district court.

3. Teledyne contends that Teradyne was required to mitigate damages by acceptance of Teledyne's offer to purchase instead of the T-347A the FET system.

That point is without merit.

The meaning of Teledyne's offer was that if Teradyne would forego its profit-loss claim arising out of Teledyne's breach of the T-347A contract, Teledyne would purchase another type of machine which it was under no obligation to buy. The seller's failure to accept such an offer does not preclude it from recovering the full damages to which it would otherwise be entitled. As Restatement (Second) Contracts, §350 Comment c indicates, there is no right to so-called mitigation of damages where the offer of a substitute contract "is conditioned on surrender by the injured party of his claim for breach." "One is not required to mitigate his losses by accepting an arrangement with the repudiator if that is made conditional on his surrender of his rights under the repudiated contract." 5 Corbin, Contracts 2d (1964) §1043 at 274. Acc. Campfield v. Sauer, 189 F. 576 (6th Cir. 1911); Stanspec Corp. v. Jelco, Inc., 464 F.2d 1184, 1187 (10th Cir. 1972). Teradyne acted in a commercially reasonable manner in refusing to accept Teledyne's offer. . . .

The district court's judgment is vacated and the case is remanded to the district court to proceed in accordance with this opinion.

QUESTIONS

1. Exactly who qualifies as a "lost volume seller"? If a college student advertises his guitar for sale in the campus newspaper, he contracts to sell it to a caller, the caller then backs out, and the student sells the guitar to someone else, can the student qualify as a lost volume seller?

2. Why does the court draw a distinction between overhead costs and variable expenses (which the court calls "direct costs")? Which was which here?

3. Section 2-708(2) specifically requires a subtraction of the "proceeds of resale." Doesn't this language always defeat the lost volume seller, who will typically have resold the unaccepted goods? See R.E. Davis Chem. Corp. v. Diasonics, Inc., 826 F.2d 678 (7th Cir. 1987).

4. For a case requiring the seller to measure damages at no more than the lost profit amount where the market price/contract price differential under §2-708(1) would overcompensate the seller, see Purina Mills, L.L.C. v. Less, 295 F. Supp. 2d 1017 (N.D. Iowa 2003).

5. The lost volume concept also applies to lessors of goods. See §2A-529's Official Comment 2 and C.I.C. Corp. v. Ragtime, Inc., 319 N.J. Super. 662, 726 A.2d 316 (N.J. App. 1999).

PROBLEM 81

Milo Veep, sales agent for the Complex Computer Corporation (CCC), negotiated a contract whereby his company was to design and manufacture a special computer that would regulate the timing of subway trains for the City of Plantation, Mississippi. The price was $20,000 F.O.B. CCC's plant in Atlanta, Georgia. When the computer was half completed, the City of Plantation underwent a change of administration, and the new city leaders decided to dump the subway renovations. They phoned CCC and canceled the computer order. Now Veep phones your law office for advice. To help in your decision, Veep states that as scrap the computer and its components are now worth $5,000. Veep has heard that three other cities have subway systems similar to Plantation's, and if the computer is finished, they might be enticed to buy it at a price between $15,000 and $20,000. On the other hand, it will cost CCC $9,000 to complete the computer.

(a) Should CCC stop the manufacture of the computer and sell it for scrap or complete manufacture and then try to resell it? See §2-704(2) and its Official Comment 2.

(b) If CCC completes manufacture and then, after a good faith effort, is unable to find a new buyer for the computer, can it make Plantation pay for the finished product? See §2-709(1)(b); Official Comment 1 to §2-704.

PROBLEM 82

Stern Oil entered into a ten-year Motor Fuel Supply Agreement with James Brown, which required Brown each year to purchase a certain amount of ExxonMobil branded fuel from Stern Oil for Brown's two convenience stores. Brown breached the agreement and stopped purchasing fuel from Stern. As a result, Stern Oil did not receive profits from a 1.5 cent markup per gallon or a 1.25 percent discount from ExxonMobil. Brown conceded the 1.5 cent markup per gallon was duly awarded as lost profits, but argued that the lost discount was not recoverable as damages. Should it be? See §§1-305(a), 2-715(2), 1-103, 2-708(2); Stern Oil Co. v. Brown, 2018 S.D. 15, 908 N.W.2d 144 (2018).

Courts routinely hold that sellers are not entitled to consequential damages. For example, a seller was not entitled to recover where lost sales due to buyer's breach caused seller to fail to qualify for quantity discounts on other contracts with its own seller. Nobs Chemical, U.S.A., Inc. v. Koppers Co., Inc., 616 F.2d 212 (5th Cir. 1980). Section 1-305(a) provides that consequential damages may only be had "as specifically provided in [the Uniform Commercial Code] or by other rule of law." In Article 2, §2-715(2) provides that *buyers* may receive consequential damages, but does not say so for sellers. White & Summers question cases like *Nobs*, arguing that consequential damages could be permitted on the theory that §1-103 incorporates general rules of contract law, which could qualify as a permissible "other rule of law" under §1-305(a).

The *Stern Oil* court did not reach the question. Rather, it distinguished cases like *Nobs*, holding the lost discount in the case before it (on which the Problem above is based) was recoverable because it was not consequential damages but direct damages:

> Thus, while it is true that lost profits may fall within the larger category of consequential damages, lost profits that flow directly from the contract itself are

properly characterized as direct damages. They are damages that reflect a party's loss of the benefit of the bargain from the agreement between the parties, not other economic harm caused by agreements collateral to the contract.

Stern Oil Co. v. Brown, 2018 S.D. 15, 908 N.W.2d 144, 153 (2018).

The remedies provided for the parties in a lease of goods by Article 2A have been slavishly copied from the corresponding provisions in Article 2. For the most part this does no harm, but the Article 2A equivalent to §2-709's "Action for the Price" has generated a lot of discord. Read §2A-529, "Lessor's Action for the Rent."

PROBLEM 83

Lawyer Portia Moot decided to rent a computer from Machines Unlimited and use it in her office. The computer arrived, and Portia found it most satisfactory, but her struggling practice made it difficult for her to make the lease payments on time. After she had missed two payments in a row, Machines Unlimited sent a goon to her office to repossess the computer. Portia was not there at the time, but her loyal administrative assistant protested mightily when the goon grabbed the machine, at one point blocking the door with her body, but she was shoved aside and the computer was taken. The lease still had a year to run, with payments of $100 due each month. Machines Unlimited sued Portia for $1,200.

(a) Was Machines Unlimited's repossession valid? See §2A-525. What remedy does Portia have if it was not?

(b) Assuming there was no problem with the repossession, is the lessor required to try to mitigate damages by re-leasing the machine? See §2A-529 and its Official Comment.

(c) Could the lessor avoid any possible duty to mitigate by so stipulating in the lease agreement? See §§1-302, 2A-503; Homer Kripke, Some Dissonant Notes About Article 2A, 39 Ala. L. Rev. 792, 795-796 (1988).

III. BUYER'S REMEDIES

The general list of the buyer's remedies is found in §2-711. This section also gives the buyer a right to cancel and recover the price if the buyer has already paid. In most circumstances, the buyer has further recoverable damages, as identified in other sections. All the sections are designed to follow §1-305's admonition that the Code's goal is to put the aggrieved party in as good a position as performance would have. As for which sections are appropriate in a given case as far as monetary damages are concerned, the answer depends on whether the buyer has *accepted* the goods or not.

A.   Accepted Goods

If a technical §2-606 acceptance of the goods has been made and is not later revoked, the buyer may still sue for breach of warranty (or other breach of contract) if a notice of the defect has been given to the seller within a reasonable time after the defect should have been discovered; §2-607(3)(a). Damages are then measured by §§2-714 and 2-715. Read those sections. See Annot., 96 A.L.R.3d 299.

PROBLEM 84

The world-famous pianist Bart Cristofori made $50,000 a year giving concerts. Recently he decided to experiment with some new sounds. He purchased an electric piano for $3,000 from the Silbermann Electronic Music Company. The purchase was negotiated orally; there was no written contract. Cristofori practiced day and night to master the new instrument. After three months of arduous practice, he noticed a strange ringing in his ears. Subsequent medical examination revealed that Cristofori was going deaf. The cause was a high-pitched whine (above the level of human perception) emanating from the electric piano. On learning that the piano had done this to him, Cristofori took an axe and chopped the piano into unrecognizable bits. (This action ended his ability to revoke his acceptance; §§2-608(3), 2-602(2)(b).) When he calmed down, he brought suit against the piano company for breach of warranty. His damages were claimed as $1,755,505, based on the following elements: $3,000 was the cost of the piano, $2,000 was doctor's fees, $500 was paid to experts to examine the piano and determine if it was the cause of the ear problem, $750,000 was lost income for the next 15 years, $1,000,000 was the value of Cristofori's hearing, and $5 was for the axe. Silbermann Electronic Music defended by (1) denying that it had warranted the piano in any way, and (2) proving that the whine was harmless to everybody in the world except Cristofori. (The company proved that the accident occurred to him only because of the bone structure of his skull coupled with the fact that he had a metal plate installed in his head as a result of an auto accident in his youth.) Answer these questions:

(a) What warranty, if any, did the Silbermann Company breach? Does the company's care in manufacturing the piano or the freakishness of the injury keep the warranty from being breached?

(b) Which, if any, of Cristofori's damages are recoverable under §2-714?

(c) Which, if any, of the items claimed are *incidental damages* under §2-715(1)?

(d) The §2-715(2)(a) test of consequential damages with its "reason to know" language is a restatement of our old friend Hadley v. Baxendale. Is it relevant here?

(e) If you were the judge of both the facts and the law, what amount would you award Cristofori, and why?

PROBLEM 85

Sheila Spin made it to the finals of the USA Yo-Yo Championship, where she was widely thought to be a cinch to win the $10,000 first prize. The day of the competition she went into the Smalltime Drug Store owned by her Uncle Mort and told him that she wanted to buy a four-foot nylon yo-yo cord to use in the competition. Mort sold her one for $1.50 (he put it on her bill) and wished her luck. That she did not have. The cord was defective and broke during her first trick, thus eliminating her from the competition. When the bill came from the drug store, Sheila refused to pay it. In fact, she filed suit against Mort, asking for $50,000 consequential damages. Every expert witness who testified stated that Sheila's ability with the yo-yo was the greatest in the world. Mort defended on two grounds: (1) merely knowing about the intended use of the yo-yo in the competition was not enough to impose liability on him unless the parties had agreed to put this risk on him, and (2) her damages were too speculative. Answer these questions:

(a) Does the UCC permit Sheila to refuse to pay the bill? See §2-717. If a buyer feels obligated to pay only part of the bill, what procedure should be followed? See §3-311 (dealing with payment-in-full checks).

(b) Are the consequential damages for which Sheila asked too speculative? See Official Comment 4 to §2-715; White & Summers §11-4. Cf. Wachtel v. National Alfalfa Journal, 190 Iowa 1293, 176 N.W. 801 (1920) (leading contender in canceled contest entitled to value of the chance of winning).

(c) Is knowledge of the possible consequential damages alone sufficient to impose liability on a seller? Or is Mort right in saying that the liability for consequential damages attaches only if the seller has agreed (expressly or impliedly) to assume the risk? See Official Comment 2 to §2-715; White & Summers §11-4; Beal v. General Motors Corp., 354 F. Supp. 423 (D. Del. 1973).

(d) May Sheila recover her attorney fees as consequential damages? See Equitable Lumber Corp. v. IPA Land Dev. Corp., 38 N.Y.2d 516, 344 N.E.2d 391, 381 N.Y.S.2d 459 (1976) (may be recovered if the contract so provides, but any specified amount must be valid as a liquidated damages provision); Too Marker Products, Inc. v. Creation Supply, Inc., 2014 WL 3818675 (D. Or. 2014) (no fees awarded under Illinois law without statutory or contractual provision). Cady v. Dick Loehr's, Inc., 100 Mich. App. 543, 299 N.W.2d 69 (1980) (trial court has discretion to award attorney fees as consequential damages); Modine Mfg. Co. v. North East Indep. Sch. Dist., 503 S.W.2d 833 (Tex. Civ. App. 1974) (no, because such fees are penal in nature and the Code does not authorize punitive damages).

PROBLEM 86

Rambo Trucks, Inc., sold Hercules Moving Company a large moving van. The contract of sale limited the buyer's remedy for breach of warranty to replacement or repair only and clearly disclaimed liability for consequential damages. The first day on the job, the truck proved incapable of climbing even small hills, so Hercules Moving Company revoked its acceptance of the truck. It claimed a security interest in the truck pursuant to §2-711(3) and pending sale stored it at a truck depot, which charged it $50 a day for storage.

Must Rambo Trucks pay the storage charges, or is the company protected by the disclaimer of consequential damages? See §§2-719(3), 2-715(1); Commonwealth Edison Co. v. Allied Chem. Nuclear Prods., Inc., 684 F. Supp. 1429 (N.D. Ill. 1988) (storage charges of $293 million!); Dietec Co., Ltd. v. Osirius Group, LLC, 2017 WL 6039557 (E.D. Mich. 2017) (seller's costs caused by buyer's breach, in securing additional raw materials and financing, held to be incidental damages).

Suppose Rambo Trucks had delivered the van without a bill of sale or proper title, but delivered the title months later. What would be the damages for breach of the warranty of title? See McCoolidge v. Oyvetsky, 2016 WL 852059 (Neb. 2016).

B. Unaccepted Goods

Where the seller never delivers the goods or where the buyer rejects or revokes acceptance, §2-711 states that the buyer may recover the price and other damages. These generally include incidental and consequential damages under §2-715. See Official Comment 1 to that section. In addition, the buyer may seek specific performance or replevin under §2-716. Read §2-716 and its Official Comment.

As Comment 1 indicates, the drafters intended to "liberalize" the application of the doctrine of specific performance. Thus, §2-716 provides for the use of specific performance not only when goods are unique, but also "in other proper circumstances." What are "proper circumstances"? See Laclede Gas Co. v. Amoco Oil Co., 522 F.2d 33 (8th Cir. 1975), *rev'd on other grounds*, 531 F.2d 942 (8th Cir. 1975) (the court gave the buyer, a distributor of propane gas, a mandatory injunction against the seller, who had promised to supply gas over a long term); Eastern Airlines Inc. v. Gulf Oil Corp., 415 F. Supp. 429 (S.D. Fla. 1975) (Gulf Oil was enjoined from breaching its contract with Eastern for jet fuel); Sedmak v. Charlie's Chevrolet, Inc., 622 S.W.2d 694 (Mo. App. 1981) (holding buyers entitled to specific performance of contract to buy one of a limited edition of Corvette automobiles); Almetals, Inc. v. Wickeder Westfalenstahl, GmbH, 2008 WL 4791377 (E.D. Mich. 2008) (specific performance awarded where the varieties of clad metal supplied by the seller were unique, with no known alternative source); Annot., 26 A.L.R.4th 294.

Mirion Technologies (Canberra), Inc. v. Sunpower, Inc.

United States District Court, Southern District of Ohio, 2017, WL 5090436

JAMES L. GRAHAM, United States District Judge

This contract dispute is before the court on the motion of plaintiff Mirion Technologies (Canberra), Inc. for a preliminary injunction. Mirion alleges that it entered into a supply agreement with defendant Sunpower, Inc., whereby Sunpower would produce and supply cryocoolers, a device used in nuclear radiation detectors. Mirion asserts that it placed a valid purchase order for 250 cryocoolers but Sunpower breached the agreement by refusing to fill the purchase order.

Mirion seeks a preliminary injunction requiring specific performance of the supply agreement, such that Sunpower would be ordered to manufacture 250 cryocoolers and supply them to Mirion. The court conducted an evidentiary hearing on September 25, 2017. For the reasons that follow, the motion for a preliminary injunction is denied.

I. BACKGROUND

A. THE PARTIES AND THEIR PRODUCTS

Mirion is a Delaware corporation based in Connecticut which offers products and support services for the nuclear energy industry. Among other things, Mirion manufactures radiation detection instruments and offers radiation monitoring systems. The president of Mirion's Spectroscopy Division is Sheila Webb, who formerly served as vice president of engineering at Canberra Industries, Inc.

Mirion acquired Canberra in July 2016. Canberra manufactures high-purity germanium detectors, an instrument described by Webb as the most sensitive type of sensor available for detecting radioisotopes. Canberra also manufactures cryostats, which is a device that can be used on radiation detectors in order to maintain extremely low temperatures.

Webb testified that a germanium crystal inside a high-purity germanium detector needs to be kept at a temperature of about negative 296 degrees Fahrenheit. This is accomplished in one of three ways: (1) a dewar, or open-mouth container, filled with liquid nitrogen and having a lead shield at the mouth; (2) an electrically-cooled system; or (3) a hybrid cooler having a closed system with a container of liquid nitrogen, which, as it evaporates, is condensed by a cryocooler. The drawback of the dewar method is that the liquid nitrogen supply needs to be replenished. The drawback of the electrically-cooled method is the need for a constant power supply. Webb testified that the hybrid method is viewed as the best solution because it recirculates liquid nitrogen and can operate without a power supply for a period of several days.

Mirion and Canberra produce and sell a hybrid cooler called the Canberra Cryo-Cycle II. The Cryo-Cycle II is a cryostat and is comprised three basic parts: a cryocooler, a container holding about 22 liters of liquid nitrogen and electrical components which connect the cryostat to a germanium detector. The Cryo-Cycle II keeps the detector at the temperature required for it to operate. According to Webb, there are several other manufactures of hybrid coolers, but Sunpower is not one of them.

Sunpower is an Ohio corporation based in Athens, Ohio. It manufactures CryoTel GT cryocoolers. A cryocooler is a small electrical device that performs a cooling function in certain kinds of radiation detectors, including in high-purity germanium detectors. Sunpower is owned by AMETEK, Inc., which is a global manufacturer of electronic instruments and electromechanical devices.

Webb testified that there are only a handful of manufacturers in the world who produce high-purity germanium detectors. One of those entities is ORTEC, Inc., which is owned by AMETEK. Germanium detectors are sold to various interests associated with the nuclear energy industry, including nuclear power plants and laboratories, research facilities and other entities in the governmental, military, energy and educational sectors. Webb testified that Mirion/Canberra and AMETEK/ORTEC each have nearly a 50% share of the market for high-purity germanium detectors that use hybrid coolers. . . .

F. THE SUPPLY AGREEMENT AND ENSUING PURCHASE ORDER

On June 16, 2017, Mirion and Sunpower entered into a Supply Agreement, under which Sunpower agreed to supply CryoTel GT cryocoolers to Mirion for a three-year period whenever Mirion submitted a purchase order. The parties agreed that the per-unit cost of the cryocoolers would be $9,835. For orders of 1 to 10 cryocoolers, Sunpower agreed to make delivery in 6 weeks. For quantities greater than 10 cryocoolers, the parties would determine a mutually agreeable delivery schedule. The cryocoolers came with a two-year warranty.

Alec Bounds, Mirion's chief procurement officer, negotiated the Supply Agreement on behalf of Mirion. Bounds testified that he and Jim Wade, his point of contact at Sunpower, discussed and agreed to a "ramp-up schedule" on June 7, 2017, prior to the signing of the Supply Agreement. The ramp-up schedule provided a forecast of the number of cryocoolers that Mirion would want supplied each month. The schedule accommodated Mirion's transition away from Lihan and provided Sunpower with time to increase production in order to meet Mirion's supply demand. Under this schedule, Sunpower would supply a smaller number of units in the first few months of the Agreement and then increase production, such that Sunpower would supply 110 units in the first six months of the Agreement and 20 units per month for several additional months.

On or about June 23, 2017, Wade called Bounds and communicated that Mirion should place a "large" purchase order soon. On that same day, individuals at AMETEK/Sunpower emailed the ramp-up schedule amongst themselves. (Hearing Ex. 18).

On June 29, 2017, Mirion submitted a purchase order for 250 CryoTel GT units. (Hearing Ex. 7). When combined with miscellaneous costs, the total purchase order was for $2.65 million. The purchase order was based upon Canberra's forecast that it would need 250 units over the next 18 months.

On June 29, the President of Sunpower, who was not involved in negotiating or signing the Supply Agreement, emailed a letter to Mirion in which he purported to "elect[] not to enter into the proposed Supply Agreement." (Hearing Ex. 6). On June 30, a Sunpower representative sent Mirion an email purporting to reject the Agreement and the June 29 purchase order. (Hearing Ex. 8).

After legal counsel for Mirion objected to the purported rejection, legal counsel for Sunpower responded with a July 7, 2017 letter in which it withdrew the purported notice of rejection. (Hearing Ex. 32). In the same letter, Sunpower exercised its contractual right to terminate the Supply Agreement with six months' notice. Under the Agreement, Sunpower was obligated to fill purchase orders placed prior to the effective date of termination, January 7, 2018.

On July 10, 2017, Mirion delivered a revised purchase order for 250 cryocoolers. Sunpower refused to fill the order and this litigation followed.

G. MIRION'S ABILITY TO OBTAIN AN ALTERNATIVE SUPPLY OF CRYOCOOLERS

Following Sunpower's refusal to fill the purchase order, Mirion continues to obtain cryocoolers from Lihan. James Colaresi, Mirion's director of detector engineering and manufacturing, testified that Mirion is able to obtain an adequate supply of cryocoolers from Lihan to produce the Cryo-Cycle II and to replace defective cryocoolers returned under warranty. According to Webb and Colaresi, Lihan's cryocoolers still suffer from a reliability problem, and Mirion and Lihan continue to work together to address that problem. Bounds testified that Mirion has increased its efforts with Lihan and meets with Lihan on a weekly basis and has implemented a quality improvement plan.

Mirion also has continued to have discussions with Thales. However, it will take at least 18 months to have a product ready from Thales because of the research and development that must be done. Bounds testified that cost and the per-unit price point continues to be an obstacle with Thales.

. . .

C. ENTITLEMENT TO SPECIFIC PERFORMANCE

Specific performance is a remedy that is available only when "there is no adequate remedy at law, i.e., damages." Sashti, Inc. v. Glunt Industries, Inc., 140 F. Supp. 2d 813, 817 (N.D. Ohio 2001) (citing Gleason v. Gleason, 64 Ohio App. 3d 667, 672, 582 N.E.2d 657, 661 (Ohio Ct. App. 1991)). This principle is reflected in the Uniform Commercial Code with the concept of the "commercial feasibility of replacement." U.C.C. §2-716, Off. Cmt. 2. Ohio Revised Code §1302.90(A) states, "Specific performance may be decreed where the goods are unique or in other proper circumstances." The Official Comment to the statute provides that the "inability to cover is strong evidence of 'other proper circumstances.'" O.R.C. §1302.90, Off. Cmt. 2. See also Triple-A Baseball Club Assocs. v. Northeastern Baseball, Inc., 832 F.2d 214, 224 (1st Cir. 1987) (noting in the case law an "emphasis on ability to 'cover' as a major criterion in deciding the appropriateness of specific performance").

"[O]utput and requirements contracts involving a particular or peculiarly available source or market present today the typical commercial specific performance situation." O.R.C. §1302.90, Off. Cmt. 2. Although the statute does not exclude non-requirements contracts from its scope, practically speaking, a buyer to a non-requirements sales contract may well face difficulties of proof in seeking specific performance. As one court put it, "[o]utput and requirements contracts, explicitly cited as examples of situations in which specific performance may be appropriate, by their nature call for a series of continuing acts and an ongoing relationship." Copylease Corp. of Am. v. Memorex Corp., 408 F. Supp. 758, 760 (S.D.N.Y. 1976). And it is "where a contract calls for continuing sale of unique or 'noncoverable' goods" that the Official Comment "contemplate[s] that at least in some circumstances specific performance will issue contrary to the historical reluctance to grant such relief in these situations." Id.

Sunpower argues that because the Supply Agreement is not a requirements contract, Mirion can prevail only if the goods are unique. That is, Sunpower would remove the "other proper circumstances" prong of the statute as a way in which Mirion could show it is entitled to specific performance. If Mirion did not obligate itself to refrain from obtaining cryocoolers from another supplier, so the argument goes, then Mirion has the contractual ability to obtain cover. The court, however, has not found any authority to support Sunpower's categorical proposition that a buyer to a non-requirements contract cannot avail itself of the "other proper circumstances" prong of the statute. A buyer might have the contractual freedom to obtain cover, but the statute and case law look to the commercial feasibility of finding cover and whether the buyer has the ability to go to the marketplace and actually obtain a replacement.

The focus of the court's inquiry, therefore, is twofold: whether Sunpower's cryocoolers are unique and, even if they are not unique, whether Mirion is able to obtain cover.

Courts have said that a good is unique if it is rare, "one of a kind," or nearly impossible to replace. See, e.g., King Aircraft Sales, Inc. v. Lane, 68 Wash. App. 706, 711, 717, 846 P.2d 550, 553, 556-57 (Wash. Ct. App. 1993). Other courts look to the "uncertainty of valuing" the good, in keeping with the precept that specific performance is available only when there is no adequate remedy at law. Van Wagner Advert. Corp. v. S & M Enterprises, 67 N.E.2d 186, 193, 492 N.E.2d 756, 760 (N.Y. 1986). The U.C.C. provides that "test of uniqueness ... must be made in terms of the total situation which characterizes the contract." O.R.C. §1302.90, Off. Cmt. 2.

The court finds no support for Mirion's claim that Sunpower's CryoTel GT cryocooler is unique. It may be that high-purity germanium detectors are one of a kind, in comparison to other radiation detectors, in their sensitivity to radioactivity. It may be that hybrid cryostats are the best option available for cooling germanium crystals. And it may be that cryocoolers, which make the detectors and cryostats operational, are devices which reflect sophisticated design and technology. But within the nuclear energy industry in which the parties operate, cryocoolers are not unique or rare goods, nor are they incapable of being valued. Mirion's own witness, James Colaresi, testified that when Sunpower terminated the prior supply agreement with Canberra in 2013, Canberra "came up with a fairly long list of potential companies" with whom it could approach about supplying a cryocooler for Canberra's Cryo-Cycle II. Canberra "pared down that list to about five and then ultimately selected two [Twinbird and Thales] out of the five." He further testified that cost was the consideration that drove Canberra's selection of Twinbird. During the hearing, the court heard of no material changes in the marketplace from 2013 to present day. Sunpower remains one of many potential suppliers of cryocoolers. (Hearing Exs. 12, 13) (charts listing at least six more manufacturers beyond those named in this Opinion and Order). The value of these goods—as expressed by their cost—is ascertainable to Mirion. Indeed, the reason Mirion pursued Sunpower over Thales in early 2017 was not the uniqueness of Sunpower's product but the higher costs associated with Thales.

Mirion argues that cryocoolers have a number of important features and that reliability is one of them. The court agrees that in evaluating uniqueness, it should view the totality of the situation and consider the characteristics or attributes of a good which are important to the parties and to others in the relevant marketplace or industry. See *King Aircraft Sales*, 68 Wash. App. at 711, 846 P.2d at 553 (examining the claim that two aircraft were "rare in terms of their exceptional condition"); Sedmak v. Charlie's Chevrolet, Inc., 622 S.W.2d 694, 699-700 (Mo. Ct. App. 1981) (examining the "mileage, condition, ownership and appearance" of a collectible automobile). Sunpower does not dispute, and common sense dictates, that reliability is an important feature of a machine or a scientific instrument.

According to Mirion, Sunpower is uniquely able to produce a cryocooler that drops into the Cryo-Cycle II and performs reliably. This claim has slim factual support. Though Webb and Colaresi testified that Lihan's product is generally less reliable than Sunpower's, Mirion failed to produce documents or data regarding the respective reliability of Lihan's and Sunpower's cryocoolers. This leaves the court without specific information from which it could determine, for instance, the comparative failure rates of the two makes of cryocoolers, the average lifespan of a Lihan cryocooler before it fails and whether the failure rate or lifespan of Lihan devices has improved over time.

The court finds that Mirion has shown only that the Sunpower cryocooler perhaps is better than Lihan's on the reliability front, not that the Sunpower device is unique. Lihan's device is not so unreliable that Mirion is unable to sell its Cryo-Cycle II, as was the case when Canberra attempted to work with Twinbird. Mirion/Canberra has sold its product with the Lihan cryocooler since December 2014 and has addressed the reliability issues with Lihan's product through a warranty return program. As Webb and Colaresi testified, Mirion has a "fairly large" service team that is equipped to "immediately" replace defective cryocoolers with new ones.

For the same reasons that Mirion has not shown that Sunpower's product is unique, Mirion has not established that it is unable to obtain cover. See

Kaiser Trading Co. v. Associated Metals & Minerals Corp., 321 F. Supp. 923, 932 (N.D. Cal. 1970) (noting that cover can refer to the "scarcity of goods" or to "when the goods contracted for cannot be purchased on the open market"). Mirion's experience with Lihan proves that it is commercially feasible for Mirion to obtain an alternative supply of cryocoolers. Mirion has access to enough of a supply from Lihan to produce the Cryo-Cycle II and fill warranty returns.

Again, numerous potential suppliers exist for Mirion. Bounds testified that while Mirion negotiated with Sunpower in May 2017, Mirion looked at "multiple options," including staying with Lihan, switching to Thales, proceeding with Sunpower and various combinations thereof. Bounds emphasized that Mirion "wanted those options" and wanted the opt-out provision in the Supply Agreement—"knowing the history with Sunpower, I wanted to make sure that we would have the agility or the option to find another source if this agreement failed and . . . I would then be able to adjust and go find another supplier."

Webb similarly testified that Mirion "knew that there was some risk associated with the agreement with Sunpower" and that they were considering their options with Lihan and Thales because they wanted to avoid relying on a single source for cryocoolers. According to Webb, Mirion viewed Sunpower as "the best solution without a lot of engineering effort and design work." The court finds that Sunpower is simply Mirion's preferred supplier among many options and that any extra engineering and design costs associated with choosing another supplier are quantifiable and redressable by monetary damages.

Now that the relationship with Sunpower has indeed failed, Mirion remains able to obtain cryocoolers from Lihan, including during any interim period in which Mirion would seek to work with Thales or another potential supplier on research and development.

Accordingly, the court finds that Mirion has not established a strong likelihood of success on its claim for specific performance. . . .

VI. CONCLUSION

For the reasons stated above, Mirion's motion for a preliminary injunction (doc. 2) is denied.

An important buyer remedy is found in §2-712, where the buyer is authorized to *cover* — that is, purchase substitute goods. If a buyer covers properly, the damages are measured by a comparison of the original contract price and the cost of the cover. Read §2-712.

PROBLEM 87

Mr. and Mrs. Transient ordered a 2020 Blocklong model mobile home for $8,000 from the Home on Wheels Sales Corporation, delivery to be made on May 20. The Transients planned on spending an additional $500 to build a foundation that the Blocklong trailer had to have for maximum utility. Due to widespread industry strikes, the price of trailers rose dramatically in the early spring, and on May 10 Home on Wheels informed the Transients that the deal was off. The Transients shopped around and on September 25 bought a 2020 Behemoth model mobile home for $15,000 from another dealer. The Behemoth was larger than the Blocklong model (it had a basement and a laundry room), but it did not require a foundation. The Transients then brought suit. Home on Wheels defended by offering to show that (a) the Behemoth was selling for $10,000 up to September 5 when the price rose to $15,000, and (b) the Behemoth always sells for $2,000 more than the Blocklong since the former is a snazzier trailer. What damages can the Transients get under §2-712? See Official Comment 2 of that section; White & Summers §7-3; Annot., 79 A.L.R.4th 844.

Hughes Communications Galaxy, Inc. v. United States

United States Court of Appeals, Federal Circuit, 2001, 271 F.3d 1060

RADER, Circuit Judge.

Following a trial on damages for breach of contract, the United States Court of Federal Claims awarded Hughes Communications Galaxy, Inc. $102,680,625. Hughes Communications Galaxy, Inc. v. United States, 47 Fed. Cl. 236 (2000) (*Hughes V*). Because the Court of Federal Claims did not abuse its discretion in calculating damages, this court affirms.

I.

This case has received extensive factual analysis in prior opinions. . . . This appeal addresses only the Court of Federal Claims' breach of contract damage determination in *Hughes IV* and *Hughes V*.

In December 1985, NASA and Hughes entered into a Launch Services Agreement (LSA), which required NASA to use its "best efforts" to launch ten of Hughes' HS-393 satellites on space shuttles. The LSA required NASA to continue using its best efforts to launch Hughes' HS-393s until it launched all ten HS-393s or until September 30, 1994, whichever was earlier. NASA compiled "manifests" of all shuttle payloads scheduled for launch on shuttles. NASA reissued these manifests periodically to account for changed circumstances. The manifests listed commercial payloads in order of their planned or firm launch dates and scheduled a shuttle for each launch. After NASA and Hughes entered the LSA, NASA assigned Hughes' satellites specific slots on a manifest.

In January 1986, the space shuttle Challenger exploded. Following the Challenger explosion, NASA suspended operation of the shuttles until September 1988. Further, in August 1986, President Reagan announced that NASA would no longer launch commercial satellites on shuttles. On July 10, 1986, NASA completed the last manifest before President Reagan's announcement. It projected that NASA would launch eight Hughes satellites on shuttles by September 1994. Thereafter, NASA compiled a new manifest that only included "shuttle unique" and "national security and foreign policy" payloads. That manifest did not list any Hughes satellites. Later NASA informed Hughes that it would almost certainly not launch any Hughes satellites on shuttles.

After 1986, Hughes launched three of its HS-393s on expendable launch vehicles (ELVs), one of which was the JCSAT-1. Hughes also launched several similar satellites on ELVs, including six HS-601 satellites. The HS-601s are similar to the HS-393s, except they are more powerful and better suited for ELV launches. While the ELV launches provided an alternative to shuttle launch services under the LSA, Hughes incurred more costs by launching satellites on ELVs rather than on shuttles.

Hughes sued the United States Government for breach of contract and for taking its property without providing just compensation. The Court of Federal Claims granted summary judgment to the Government on both claims based on the sovereign act defense. *Hughes I*, 26 Cl. Ct. at 144-46. This court reversed that summary judgment and remanded. *Hughes II*, 998 F.2d at 959. On remand, the Court of Federal Claims granted summary judgment for Hughes for breach of contract. *Hughes III*, 34 Fed. Cl. at 634. Before holding a trial on damages, the Court of Federal Claims ruled that the Government could not produce evidence to reduce its damages by the amount Hughes had passed on to its customers in increased prices. *Hughes IV*, 38 Fed. Cl. at 582.

At the damages trial, Hughes sought to prove damages by showing its increased costs in launching satellites on ELVs, rather than on shuttles. Hughes presented two main methods for calculating the increased costs. The first method, the Ten HS-393 Satellites Method, compared the costs of launching ten HS-393s on shuttles under the LSA with the costs of launching ten HS-393s on ELVs. Because Hughes had actually launched only three HS-393s on ELVs, the method based the ELV launch costs on the actual costs of launching the three HS-393s. The second method, the Primary Method, compared Hughes' actual costs of launching ten satellites on ELVs with the costs that Hughes would have incurred by launching ten satellites on shuttles under the LSA. The ten satellites included the three HS-393s, the six HS-601s, and one HS-376.

The Court of Federal Claims used the Ten HS-393 Satellites Method to calculate Hughes' increased costs of "cover." *Hughes V*, 47 Fed. Cl. at 244. However, the court modified the method in several important respects. First, the court found that even using its best efforts, NASA would have only launched five HS-393s under the LSA. Accordingly, the court only awarded Hughes increased costs for five satellites, rather than ten. Id. Second, the court averaged the costs of launching on shuttles the three HS-393s that were actually launched on ELVs and used that average for the fourth and fifth satellites, rather than individually calculating the cost of launching each satellite on a shuttle, as Hughes' expert had done. Id. at 244 n.12. Third, in calculating the ELV launch costs for the fourth and fifth satellites, the court escalated the costs using the midpoint between March 1989 and September 1994, rather than the midpoint between March 1989 and December 1995, as Hughes' expert had done. Id. at 244. Fourth, the court refused to award Hughes prejudgment interest on its damages. Id. at 244-45. Fifth, the court refused to award Hughes reflight insurance costs and increased launch insurance costs for the five satellites. Id. at 245-46.

Based on its modified HS-393 method, the court awarded Hughes $102,680,625 in damages for its increased launch costs. Id. at 247. Hughes and the Government both appeal. This court has jurisdiction under 28 U.S.C. §1295(a)(3) (1994).

II. . . .

"The general rule in common law breach of contract cases is to award damages sufficient to place the injured party in as good a position as he or she would have been had the breaching party fully performed." San Carlos Irrigation & Drainage Dist. v. United States, 111 F.3d 1557, 1562-63 (Fed. Cir. 1997). Thus, "[a] plaintiff must show that but for the breach, the damages alleged would not have been suffered." Id. Moreover, the damages must have been foreseeable at the time the parties entered the contract, which requires that they "be the natural and proximate result of the breach." Locke v. United States, 151 Ct. Cl. 262, 283 F.2d 521, 526 (Ct. Cl. 1960). The LSA itself further limits damages to "direct damages only" and excludes consequential damages from any recovery.

The Court of Federal Claims awarded Hughes its increased costs of "cover." If a seller breaches a contract for goods, the buyer may "cover" or, in other words, obtain substitute goods from another seller. U.C.C. §2-712 (1997); E. Allan Farnsworth, Farnsworth on Contracts, §12.11 (2d ed. 1998). Additionally, courts often award an analogous remedy for breach of service contracts such as the LSA. Farnsworth, supra, §12.11. While the cover remedy of the Uniform Commercial Code does not govern this analogous remedy under the LSA, the Uniform Commercial Code provides useful guidance in applying general contract principles. Because both parties and the Court of Federal Claims have referred to this remedy as a "cover" remedy, this court will also use this term to refer to the remedy for Hughes' increased costs of obtaining substitute launch services.

The substitute goods or services involved in cover need not be identical to those involved in the contract, but they must be "commercially usable as reasonable substitutes under the circumstances." U.C.C. §2-712 cmt. 2. Whether cover provides a reasonable substitute under the circumstances is a question of fact. Bigelow-Sanford, Inc. v. Gunny Corp., 649 F.2d 1060, 1065 (5th Cir. 1981) (stating that whether cover is reasonable is a "classic jury issue" (quoting Transammonia Export Corp. v. Conserv, Inc., 554 F.2d 719, 724 (5th Cir. 1977))).

When a buyer of goods covers, the buyer's remedy for the seller's breach as to those goods equals the difference between the cost of the replacement goods and the contract price plus other losses. U.C.C. §2-712; Farnsworth, supra, §12.11. Similarly, if the seller breaches a contract for services, the buyer's remedy for cover equals the difference between the cost of the substitute services and the contract price plus other losses. Farnsworth, supra, §12.11 (where a building contractor breaches a first contract and the owner obtains substitute performance under a second contract, the owner can recover "any additional amount required by the second contract beyond what the owner would have had to pay under the first").

The Government cross appeals, arguing that Hughes should only be able to recover damages for the three HS-393s that it actually launched. While Hughes did not actually launch the fourth and fifth HS-393s that the Court of Federal Claims used to calculate damages, Hughes did incur costs in launching the HS-601s. The Court of Federal Claims found that Hughes developed the HS-601s to replace the HS-393s because the HS-601s were better suited for ELV launches, and that Hughes would have launched ten HS-393s on shuttles, given the opportunity. *Hughes V,* 47 Fed. Cl. at 240-41. The Government disputes these findings, asserting that Hughes developed the HS-601s for independent business reasons, specifically, the more powerful HS-601s were more marketable. On this point, however, the Court of Federal Claims specifically credited testimony of Hughes' witnesses that Hughes would not have developed the HS-601 if the Government had not breached the LSA and that Hughes could have designed the HS-393 to accommodate the additional power of the HS-601. Id. at 240. This testimony directly supports the Court of Federal Claims' finding that "the HS-393 could have been used in place of the HS-601" for HS-601 launches during the contract period. *Hughes V,* 47 Fed. Cl. at 240. Thus, the trial court found that the HS-601 launches were reasonable substitutes under the circumstances of this breach.

Additionally, the Court of Federal Claims specifically found that no credible evidence supported the Government's attack on the HS-601 as a reasonable substitute. Specifically, the Government argues that at the time of contracting, the Government could not have foreseen "the demise of the HS-393" as a result of its breach. However, the Court of Federal Claims' damages method does not compensate Hughes for the "demise of the HS-393." Rather it compensates Hughes for increased launch costs. Had Hughes kept using the HS-393s, it would likely have incurred the same damages that the Court of Federal Claims awarded.

In sum, the Court of Federal Claims hinged its determination of this issue on credibility. Such determinations are virtually never clear error. First Interstate Bank v. United States, 61 F.3d 876, 882 (Fed. Cir. 1995). Furthermore, while the damages calculation might have been easier if Hughes had kept launching HS-393s on ELVs, ease of proof in potential future litigation is not sufficient justification to require Hughes to continue launching satellites that were ill-suited for ELV launches. As the victim of the breach, Hughes was within its rights to obtain commercially reasonable substitute launch services even if the substitute services were not identical to those covered by the LSA. The Court of Federal Claims thus did not clearly err in holding that Hughes successfully covered by launching HS-601s on ELVs. Accordingly, this court rejects the Government's cross appeal.

The Court of Federal Claims' use of increased HS-393 launch costs provided reasonable certainty in calculating damages. The trial court compared the costs of launching HS-393s on ELVs with the costs of launching the same HS-393s on shuttles. That comparison provided a basis for assessing Hughes' increased costs in launching the HS-601s. Under this method, the Court of Federal Claims accounted for any measurable difference in value to Hughes between the HS-393 launches and the HS-601 launches. See Farnsworth, supra, §12.11 ("[A]ny measurable difference in quality [of a substitute] can be compensated for by a money allowance."). Accordingly, the Court of Federal Claims used the increased costs for HS-393s as a reasonable approximation of the increased costs incurred by Hughes in launching the substitute HS-601s. Under this method, the trial court did not abuse its discretion. See S.W. Elecs. & Mfg. Corp. v. United States, 228 Ct. Cl. 333, 655 F.2d 1078, 1088 (Ct. Cl. 1981) (the trial court need only "make a fair and reasonable approximation").

The LSA states that damages "shall be limited to direct damages only and shall not include any loss of revenue, profits or other indirect or consequential damages." As discussed above, the increased costs represent direct damages incurred by Hughes in obtaining substitute launch services. Additionally, the damages do not include any lost revenues or profits, only increased costs. Finally, the damages are not consequential. The Uniform Commercial Code is instructive on this point. It allows recovery of the difference between the cost of cover and the contract price "together with any incidental and consequential damages," U.C.C. §2-712 (emphasis added), thereby distinguishing between consequential damages and the direct cost of cover. In sum, the Court of Federal Claims did not abuse its discretion by awarding Hughes damages for its increased costs incurred by obtaining substitute launch services for two HS-601s in addition to the three HS-393s.

Hughes decided to launch the JCSAT-1 satellite, a particular HS-393, on an ELV several months before President Reagan's announcement in 1986 that NASA would no longer launch commercial satellites on shuttles. NASA only breached its best efforts obligation after President Reagan's announcement. *Hughes III,* 34 Fed. Cl. at 630-34; *Hughes V,* 47 Fed. Cl. at 243. However, the LSA is not limited to launching particular satellites, such as the JCSAT-1. Rather, the LSA specifies a particular type of satellite (HS-393) in its preamble, and refers to the ten satellites as "HC-9 through HC-18." Thus, Hughes could have substituted another HS-393 for JCSAT-1, and Hughes still would have launched ten HS-393s on shuttles if NASA had provided those services under the LSA. Accordingly, the Court of Federal Claims did not abuse its discretion by awarding Hughes damages for the increased costs of launching the JCSAT-1.

III.

The Court of Federal Claims found that NASA could have launched five HS-393s during the LSA contract period using its best efforts. The Court of Federal Claims based this finding on the July 1986 manifest, but credited a report by Barrington Consulting Group that unexpected delays beyond NASA's control reduced the number of shuttle launches below the projections in the July 1986 manifest. *Hughes V,* 47 Fed. Cl. at 243. Under the priorities in the July 1986 manifest, the Barrington report concluded that NASA would have launched five HS-393 satellites.

If NASA had given commercial satellites priority over NASA satellites, Hughes asserts, NASA would have launched ten HS-393s. However, before President Reagan's statement, NASA did not elevate commercial launches above its other priorities. NASA did not breach its best efforts obligation before President Reagan's statement. The priorities before President Reagan's statement gave approximately equal priority to commercial and NASA payloads. As the Court of Federal Claims correctly reasoned, Hughes could not have reasonably expected NASA priorities to elevate commercial satellites above other goals for the remainder of the contract period.

Similarly, the LSA's best efforts requirement did not obligate NASA to use the 1984 policy announced in a House sub-committee hearing. In the event of shuttle scheduling conflicts, the 1984 policy gave commercial satellites priority over NASA research and development missions. Under this policy, Hughes asserts, NASA would have launched all ten HS-393s. The LSA itself specifically included a 1982 listing of priorities, but said nothing about the 1984 policy. Without the 1984 policy in the contract, the LSA did not incorporate those priorities into NASA's best efforts obligation.

The Court of Federal Claims also correctly found that circumstances prevented NASA from increasing its launch rates to include all ten HS-393s. In testimony to Congress in 1992, NASA asserted its ability to launch more shuttles than its budget allowed. According to Hughes, the Government chose to limit the number of launches by limiting NASA's budget. The record amply supports the trial court's finding that the post-Challenger investigation and technical problems prevented NASA from launching more shuttles. *Hughes V,* 47 Fed. Cl. at 242-43. The record shows that, in all years except 1994, the Government budgeted for more shuttle launches than NASA was able to launch. In 1994, the Government budgeted for eight launches and NASA actually launched eight. Thus, the Court of Federal Claims did not clearly err in finding that technical obstacles, rather than budget choices, prevented NASA from launching more shuttles during the LSA contract period.

Additionally, Mr. Kiraly, the Government's expert, estimated the number of HS-393s that NASA's best efforts could have launched at between one and six. The variance in this estimate does not undercut the Court of Federal Claims' finding. The Court of Federal Claims relied on the Barrington report, which specifically concluded that NASA's best efforts would have launched five HS-393s. Id. at 243. Thus, the Court of Federal Claims did not clearly err in finding that NASA's best efforts would have produced five HS-393 launches.

IV.

Because Hughes actually launched only three HS-393s, the Court of Federal Claims calculated the average costs of launching those three satellites on shuttles. Then, using the report of Hughes' expert, Mr. Hammer, the trial court applied that average to project the shuttle launch costs of the fourth and fifth satellites. Id. at 244. Hughes asserts that the Court of Federal Claims should have used the shuttle launch costs for each individual satellite shown in Mr. Hammer's report. However, the trial court's method is symmetrical with its calculation of the costs of ELV launches. For ELV launch costs, the trial court averaged the actual ELV launch costs for the three HS-393s and applied that average to project the ELV launch costs of the fourth and fifth satellites. Id. at 244. Hughes does not disagree with the method of calculating ELV launch costs; the Court of Federal Claims merely did the same thing with the shuttle launch costs. The trial court reasonably exercised its discretion in using this symmetrical approach in calculating damages. . . .

IX.

The Government sought to reduce Hughes' damages by the amount Hughes recouped by increasing prices to customers, in other words, by the amount Hughes "passed through" to its customers. The Court of Federal Claims did not allow the Government to assert this defense at the damages trial. *Hughes IV,* 38 Fed. Cl. at 582. According to the Court of Federal Claims, this type of mitigation is too remote to consider. Id.

Although not in the breach of contract context, the Supreme Court has addressed this issue. In Southern Pacific Co. v. Darnell-Taenzer Lumber Co., 245 U.S. 531, 38 S. Ct. 186, 62 L. Ed. 451 (1918), a railroad overcharge case, the Court addressed the reduction of damages because the damaged party allegedly passed the unreasonable charge on to its customers. The Court stated: "The answer is not difficult. The general tendency of the law, in regard to damages at least, is not to go beyond the first step. As it does not attribute remote consequences to a defendant so it holds him liable if proximately the plaintiff has suffered a loss." Id. at 533-34, 38 S. Ct. 186. In an antitrust case, the Court noted that calculating pass-through damages reductions would present "the nearly insuperable difficulty of demonstrating that the particular plaintiff could not or would not have raised his prices absent the overcharge or maintained the higher price had the overcharge been discontinued." Hanover Shoe, Inc. v. United Shoe Mach. Corp., 392 U.S. 481, 493, 88 S. Ct. 2224, 20 L. Ed. 2d 1231 (1968). Similarly, allowing a pass-through damages reduction in a breach of contract action would destroy symmetry between reduction and escalation of damages. Moreover a standard for pass-through reductions would entail extremely difficult burdens for the trial court. Thus, the Supreme Court's reasoning also applies to this breach of contract action. The Court of Federal Claims did not abuse its discretion by disallowing pass-through damages reductions.

CONCLUSION

Because the Court of Federal Claims did not abuse its discretion in determining Hughes' damages for the Government's breach of the LSA, this court affirms.

———————————

Technically, a buyer does not have to cover. See, e.g., Turner v. NJN Cotton Company, 485 S.W.3d 513 (Tex. App. 2015) (buyer may choose between cover damages under §2-712 and market differential damages under §2-713). If a buyer fails to cover in an appropriate situation, however, consequential damages that could have been avoided are denied. See

§2-715(2)(a). If a buyer decides to cover, the legal effect of the steps taken, as well as when cover should be effectuated, is measured against a standard of reasonableness in the given factual situation. Financial inability is an excuse for non-cover. See REB, Inc. v. Ralston Purina Co., 525 F.2d 749, (10th Cir. 1975). One practical test by which to gauge the reasonableness of the buyer's covering actions is to ask if the buyer would have made the same arrangements if there was no prospect of a successful suit against the breaching seller. See White & Summers §7-3, at 287-288.

If the buyer does not cover, damages may be measured under the next section, §2-713, a much criticized provision. See Childres, Buyer's Remedies: The Danger of Section 2-713, 72 Nw. U. L. Rev. 837 (1978). Read §2-713.

PROBLEM 88

The Student Bar Association (SBA) of the Gilberts Law School decided to hold a mammoth wine-and-cheese-tasting party for the students, faculty, staff, and alumni. The SBA ordered the wine from Classy Caterers. They agreed to pay $1,000 for it; the wine to be delivered on March 30, the day of the party. Classy Caterers ordered the wine from Grapes Vineyards in California, "F.O.B. San Francisco" for $750, but Grapes Vineyards went bankrupt on March 25. Classy Caterers was able to find identical wine in its own city for $750, and it bought the wine on March 25 for that amount. On March 25, the price of similar wine in San Francisco was $900. The cost of transporting the wine from San Francisco to the site of the party would have been $100. The SBA paid Classy Caterers $1,000 for the wine. Classy Caterers filed claims for damages in the bankruptcy proceeding of its defaulting supplier.

(a) Compute the damages due Classy for the failure to deliver the wine under §2-712. Now do it under §2-713. See Official Comment 5 to §2-713; White & Summers §7-4.

(b) What role does the $100 transportation cost play in computing damages? Note the definition of "market place" in §2-723.

Tongish v. Thomas

Supreme Court of Kansas, 1992, 251 Kan. 728, 840 P.2d 471

McFarland, Justice:

This case presents the narrow issue of whether damages arising from the nondelivery of contracted-for sunflower seeds should be computed on the basis of K.S.A. 84-1-106 or K.S.A. 84-2-713. That is, whether the buyer is entitled to its actual loss of profit or the difference between the market price and the contract price. The trial court awarded damages on the basis of the buyer's actual loss of profit. The Court of Appeals reversed the judgment, holding that the difference between the market price and the contract price was the proper measure of damages (Tongish v. Thomas, 16 Kan. App. 2d 809, 829 P.2d 916 [1992]). The matter is before us on petition for review.

The pertinent facts are as follows. Denis Tongish entered into a contract on April 28, 1988, with the Decatur Coop Association (Coop) where Tongish agreed to grow 160 acres of sunflower seeds, said crop to be purchased by Coop at $13 per hundredweight for large seeds and $8 per hundredweight for small seeds. By agreement, the acreage was subsequently reduced to 116.8 acres. The crop was to be delivered in increments of one-third by December 31, 1988, March 31, 1989, and May 31, 1989.

Coop had a contract to deliver the seeds purchased to Bambino Bean & Seed, Inc. Coop was to be paid the same price it paid the farmers less a 55 cent per hundredweight handling fee. Coop's only anticipated profit was the handling fee.

In October and November 1988, Tongish delivered sunflower seeds to Coop. In January, a dispute arose over the amount of dockage charged against Tongish's seeds. Tongish's seeds were of higher quality than those of many other farmers selling to Coop, and Coop's practice of commingling seeds prior to sampling was disadvantageous to Tongish. This was resolved by Coop issuing an additional check to Tongish reflecting a lower dockage charge.

Due to a short crop, bad weather, and other factors, the market price of sunflower seeds in January 1989 was double that set forth in the Tongish/ Coop contract. On January 13, Tongish notified Coop he would not deliver any more sunflower seeds.

In May 1989, Tongish sold and delivered 82,820 pounds of sunflower seeds to Danny Thomas for approximately $20 per hundredweight. Tongish was to receive $14,714.89, which was $5,153.13 more than the Coop contract price. Thomas paid for approximately one-half of the seeds. Tongish brought this action to collect the balance due. Thomas paid the balance of $7,359.61 into court and was ultimately dismissed from the action.

Meanwhile, Coop intervened in the action, seeking damages for Tongish's breach of their contract. Following a bench trial, the district court held that Tongish had breached the contract with no basis therefor. Damages were allowed in the amount of $455.51, which was the computed loss of handling charges. Coop appealed from said damage award. The Court of Appeals reversed the district court and remanded the case to the district court to determine and award damages pursuant to K.S.A. 84-2-713 (the difference between the market price and the contract price).

The analyses and rationale of the Court of Appeals utilized in resolving the issue are sound and we adopt the following portion thereof:

"The trial court decided the damages to Coop should be the loss of expected profits. Coop argues that K.S.A. 84-2-713 entitles it to collect as damages the difference between the market price and the contract price. Tongish argues that the trial court was correct and cites K.S.A. 84-1-106 as support for the contention that a party should be placed in as good a position as it would be in had the other party performed. Therefore, the only disagreement is how the damages should be calculated.

"The measure of damages in this action involves two sections of the Uniform Commercial Code: K.S.A. 84-1-106 and K.S.A. 84-2-713. The issue to be determined is which statute governs the measure of damages. Stated in another way, if the statutes are in conflict, which statute should prevail? The answer involves an ongoing academic discussion of two contending positions. The issues in this case disclose the problem.

"If Tongish had not breached the contract, he may have received under the contract terms with Coop about $5,153.13 less than he received from Danny Thomas. Coop in turn had an oral contract with Bambino to sell whatever seeds it received from Tongish to Bambino for the same price Coop paid for them. Therefore, if the contract had been performed, Coop would not have actually received the extra $5,153.13.

"We first turn our attention to the conflicting statutes and the applicable rules of statutory construction. K.S.A. 84-1-106(1) states:

'The remedies provided by this act shall be liberally administered to the end that the aggrieved party may be put in as good a position as if the other party had fully performed but neither consequential or special nor penal damages may be had except as specifically provided in this act or by other rule of law.'

"If a seller breaches a contract and the buyer does not 'cover,' the buyer is free to pursue other available remedies. K.S.A. 84-2-711 and 84-2-712. One remedy, which is a complete alternative to 'cover' (K.S.A. 84-2-713, Official comment, ¶5), is K.S.A. 84-2-713(1), which provides:

'Subject to the provisions of this article with respect to proof of market price (section 84-2-723), the measure of damages for nondelivery or repudiation by the seller is the difference between the market price at the time when the buyer learned of the breach and the contract price together with any incidental and consequential damages provided in this article (section 84-2-715), but less expenses saved in consequence of the seller's breach.'

"Neither party argues that the Uniform Commercial Code is inapplicable. Both agree that the issue to be determined is which provision of the UCC should be applied. As stated by the appellee: 'This is really the essence of this appeal, *i.e.,* whether this general rule of damages [K.S.A. 84-1-106] controls the measure of damages set forth in K.S.A. 84-2-713.' However,

Tongish then offers no support that K.S.A. 84-1-106 controls over K.S.A. 84-2-713. The authority he does cite (M & W Development, Inc. v. El Paso Water Co., 6 Kan. App. 2d 735, 634 P.2d 166 [1981]) is not a UCC case and K.S.A. 84-2-713 was not applicable.

"The statutes do contain conflicting provisions. On the one hand, K.S.A. 84-1-106 offers a general guide of how remedies of the UCC should be applied, whereas K.S.A. 84-2-713 specifically describes a damage remedy that gives the buyer certain damages when the seller breaches a contract for the sale of goods.

"The cardinal rule of statutory construction, to which all others are subordinate, is that the purpose and intent of the legislature govern. State ex rel. Stephan v. Kansas Racing Comm'n, 246 Kan. 708, 719, 792 P.2d 971 (1990); Cedar Creek Properties, Inc. v. Board of Johnson County Comm'rs, 246 Kan. 412, 417, 789 P.2d 1170 (1990); and Stauffer Communications, Inc. v. Mitchell, 246 Kan. 492, Syl. ¶1, 789 P.2d 1153 (1990). When there is a conflict between a statute dealing generally with a subject and another statute dealing specifically with a certain phase of it, the specific statute controls unless it appears that the legislature intended to make the general act controlling. State v. Wilcox, 245 Kan. 76, Syl. ¶1, 775 P.2d 177 (1989). The Kansas Supreme Court stated in Kansas Racing Management, Inc. v. Kansas Racing Comm'n, 244 Kan. 343, 353, 770 P.2d 423 (1989): 'General and special statutes should be read together and harmonized whenever possible, but to the extent a conflict between them exists, the special statute will prevail unless it appears the legislature intended to make the general statute controlling.'

"K.S.A. 84-2-713 allows the buyer to collect the difference in market price and contract price for damages in a breached contract. For that reason, it seems impossible to reconcile the decision of the district court that limits damages to lost profits with this statute.

"Therefore, because it appears impractical to make K.S.A. 84-1-106 and K.S.A. 84-2-713 harmonize in this factual situation, K.S.A. 84-2-713 should prevail as the more specific statute according to statutory rules of construction.

"As stated, however, Coop protected itself against market price fluctuations through its contract with Bambino. Other than the minimal handling charge, Coop suffered no lost profits from the breach. Should the protection require an exception to the general rule under K.S.A. 84-2-713?

"In Panhandle Agri-Service, Inc. v. Becker, 231 Kan. 291, 292, 644 P.2d 413 (1982), a farmer agreed to sell 10,000 tons of alfalfa to the buyer for $45 per ton. At the time the seller breached the contract, the market price was $62 per ton. 231 Kan. at 293 [644 P.2d 413]. The court found, pursuant to K.S.A. 84-2-713, that the damages amounted to $17 per ton or the difference between the market price and the contract price. The court stated: 'We find nothing which would justify the trial court in arriving at damages using loss of business profits which are consequential damages.' 231 Kan. at 298 [644 P.2d 413].

"In Baker v. Ratzlaff, 1 Kan. App. 2d 285, 564 P.2d 153 (1977), the seller contracted to sell all the popcorn planted on 380 acres for $4.75 per hundredweight. The seller breached, and the trial court found that the market price for popcorn was $8 per hundredweight when the buyer learned of the breach. The court held that the proper measure of damages would be the difference between the market price and the contract price as provided in K.S.A. 84-2-713. 1 Kan. App. 2d at 290 [564 P.2d 153].

"Neither Panhandle nor Baker involved a conflict between the two UCC provisions. The difference between the market price and the contract price placed the nonbreaching party in as good a position as that party would have been if the contract had been performed. The decisions can be distinguished from this case, however, in that Coop protected itself against market price fluctuations with the Bambino contract.

"There is authority for appellee's position that K.S.A. 84-2-713 should not be applied in certain circumstances. In Allied Canners & Packers, Inc. v. Victor Packing Co., 162 Cal. App. 3d 905, 209 Cal. Rptr. 60 (1984), Allied contracted to purchase 375,000 pounds of raisins from Victor for 29.75 cents per pound with a 4% discount. Allied then contracted to sell the raisins for 29.75 cents per pound expecting a profit of $4,462.50 from the 4% discount it received from Victor. 162 Cal. App. 3d at 907-08 [209 Cal. Rptr. 60].

"Heavy rains damaged the raisin crop and Victor breached its contract, being unable to fulfill the requirement. The market price of raisins had risen to about 80 cents per pound. Allied's buyers agreed to rescind their contracts so Allied was not bound to supply them with raisins at a severe loss. Therefore, the actual loss to Allied was the $4,462.50 profit it expected, while the difference between the market price and the contract price was about $150,000. 162 Cal. App. 3d at 908-09 [209 Cal. Rptr. 60].

"The California appellate court, in writing an exception, stated: 'It has been recognized that the use of the market-price contract-price formula under section 2-713 does not, absent pure accident, result in a damage award reflecting the buyer's actual loss. [Citations omitted.]' 162 Cal. App. 3d at 912 [209 Cal. Rptr. 60]. The court indicated that section 2-713 may be more of a statutory liquidated damages clause and, therefore, conflicts with the goal of section 1-106. The court discussed that in situations where the buyer has made a resale contract for the goods, which the seller knows about, it may be appropriate to limit 2-713 damages to actual loss. However, the court cited a concern that a seller not be rewarded for a bad faith breach of contract. 162 Cal. App. 3d at 912-14 [209 Cal. Rptr. 60].

"In Allied, the court determined that if the seller knew the buyer had a resale contract for the goods, and the seller did not breach the contract in bad faith, the buyer was limited to actual loss of damages under section 1-106. 162 Cal. App. 3d at 915 [209 Cal. Rptr. 60].

"The similarities between the present case and Allied are that the buyer made a resale contract which the seller knew about. (Tongish knew the seeds eventually went to Bambino, although he may not have known the details of the deal.) However, in examining the breach itself, Victor could not deliver the raisins because its crop had been destroyed. Tongish testified that he breached the contract because he was dissatisfied with dockage tests of Coop and/or Bambino. Victor had no raisins to sell to any buyer, while Tongish took advantage of the doubling price of sunflower seeds and sold to Danny Thomas. Although the trial court had no need to find whether Tongish breached the contract in bad faith, it did find there was no valid reason for the breach. Therefore, the nature of Tongish's breach was much different than Victor's in *Allied*.

"Section 2-713 and the theories behind it have a lengthy and somewhat controversial history. In 1963, it was suggested that 2-713 was a statutory liquidated damages clause and not really an effort to try and accurately predict what actual damages would be. Peters, *Remedies for Breach of Contracts Relating to the Sale of Goods Under the Uniform Commercial Code: A Roadmap for Article Two*, 73 Yale L.J. 199, 259 (1963).

"In 1978, Robert Childres called for the repeal of section 2-713. Childres, *Buyer's Remedies: The Danger of Section 2-713*, 72 Nw. U. L. Rev. 837 (1978). Childres reflected that because the market price/contract price remedy 'has been the cornerstone of Anglo-American damages' that it has been so hard to see that this remedy 'makes no sense whatever when applied to real life situations.' 72 Nw. U. L. Rev. at 841-42.

"In 1979, David Simon and Gerald A. Novack wrote a fairly objective analysis of the two arguments about section 2-713 and stated:

'For over sixty years our courts have divided on the question of which measure of damages is appropriate for the supplier's breach of his delivery obligations. The majority view, reinforced by applicable codes, would award market damages even though in excess of plaintiff's loss. A persistent minority would reduce market damages to the plaintiff's loss, without regard to whether this creates a windfall for the defendant. Strangely enough, each view has generally tended to disregard the arguments, and even the existence, of the opposing view.' Simon and Novack, *Limiting the Buyer's Market Damages to Lost Profits: A Challenge to the Enforceability of Market Contracts*, 92 Harv. L. Rev. 1395, 1397 (1979).

"Although the article discussed both sides of the issue, the authors came down on the side of market price/contract price as the preferred damages theory. The authors admit that market damages fly in the face 'of the familiar maxim that the purpose of contract damages is to make the injured party whole, not penalize the breaching party.' 92 Harv. L. Rev. at 1437. However, they argue that the market damages rule discourages the breach of contracts and encourages a more efficient market. 92 Harv. L. Rev. at 1437.

"The *Allied* decision in 1984, which relied on the articles cited above for its analysis to reject market price/contract price damages, has been sharply criticized. In Schneider, *UCC Section 2-713: A Defense of Buyers' Expectancy Damages*, 22 Cal. W. L. Rev. 233, 266 (1986), the author stated that *Allied* 'adopted the most restrictive [position] on buyer's damages. This Article is intended to reverse that trend.' Schneider argued that by following section 1-106, 'the court ignored the clear language of section 2-713's compensation scheme to award expectation damages in accordance with the parties' allocation of risk as measured by the difference between contract price and market price on the date set for performance.' 22 Cal. W. L. Rev. at 264.

"Recently in Scott, *The Case for Market Damages: Revisiting the Lost Profits Puzzle*, 57 U. Chi. L. Rev. 1155, 1200 (1990), the *Allied* result was called 'unfortunate.' Scott argues that section 1-106 is 'entirely consistent' with the market damages remedy of 2-713. 57 U. Chi. L. Rev. at 1201. According to Scott, it is possible to harmonize sections 1-106 and 2-713. Scott states, 'Market damages measure the expectancy ex ante, and thus reflect the value of the option; lost profits, on the other hand, measure losses ex post, and thus only reflect the value of the completed exchange.' 57 U. Chi. L. Rev. at 1174. The author argues that if the nonbreaching party has laid off part of the market risk (like Coop did) the lost profits rule creates instability because the other party is now encouraged to breach the contract if the market fluctuates to its advantage. 57 U. Chi. L. Rev. at 1178.

"We are not persuaded that the lost profits view under *Allied* should be embraced. It is a minority rule that has received only nominal support. We believe the majority rule or the market damages remedy as contained in K.S.A. 84-2-713 is more reasoned and should be followed as the preferred measure of damages. While application of the rule may not reflect the actual loss to a buyer, it encourages a more efficient market and discourages the breach of contracts." Tongish v. Thomas, 16 Kan. App. 2d at 811-17 [829 P.2d 916].

At first blush, the result reached herein appears unfair. However, closer scrutiny dissipates this impression. By the terms of the contract Coop was obligated to buy Tongish's large sunflower seeds at $13 per hundredweight whether or not it had a market for them. Had the price of sunflower seeds plummeted by delivery time, Coop's obligation to purchase at the agreed price was fixed. If loss of actual profit pursuant to K.S.A. 84-1-106(1) would be the measure of damages to be applied herein, it would enable Tongish to consider the Coop contract price of $13 per hundredweight plus 55 cents per hundredweight handling fee as the "floor" price for his seeds, take advantage of rapidly escalating prices, ignore his contractual obligation, and profitably sell to the highest bidder. Damages computed under K.S.A. 84-2-713 encourage the honoring of contracts and market stability. . . .

The judgment of the Court of Appeals reversing the district court and remanding the case for the determination and award of damages pursuant to the provisions of K.S.A. 84-2-713 is affirmed. The judgment of the district court is reversed.

―――――――――

Remedies Under the CISG Treaty. The damages provisions in the CISG for the international sale of goods are modeled after the similar provisions of the UCC and should look reassuringly familiar to you. Read Articles 74 to 78. There are some new words that the treaty must teach American ears. One is the concept of "fundamental breach," an idea that comes from the civil law. Read Articles 46(2) and 25. Fundamental breach is roughly equivalent to "material breach" (the opposite of "substantial performance"). The Restatement (Second) of Contracts §241 states:

Section 241. Circumstances Significant in Determining Whether a Failure Is Material
In determining whether a failure to render or to offer performance is material, the following circumstances are significant:
(a) the extent to which the injured party will be deprived of the benefit which he reasonably expected;
(b) the extent to which the injured party can be adequately compensated for the part of that benefit of which he will be deprived;
(c) the extent to which the party failing to perform or to offer to perform will suffer forfeiture;
(d) the likelihood that the party failing to perform or to offer to perform will cure his failure, taking account of all the circumstances including any reasonable assurances;
(e) the extent to which the behavior of the party failing to perform or to offer to perform comports with standards of good faith and fair dealing.

Another new concept is *Nachfrist* (German for "extension"). It is illustrated in the following Problem.

PROBLEM 89

Experimental Transportation, Inc., of Los Angeles designed an all-terrain vehicle for rugged hill country travel (called the "Clod Jumper") and agreed to sell one for $30,000 to Dingo Ranch of Australia. Neither party was willing to be bound by the laws of the other's country, so they agreed to adopt the law of the CISG. Experimental Transportation was supposed to deliver the Clod Jumper by December 1, but it had problems with Customs and that date came and went with no activity. Dingo Ranch sent a letter to Experimental Transportation proposing that the date of delivery be moved to February 1. Having sent such a letter, is Dingo Ranch now bound to wait until that date before suing? See Article 47. Is Dingo Ranch bound to wait even if Experimental Transportation's reply is "Go to hell!"? What if instead of the buyer proposing the *Nachfrist,* the seller, Experimental Transportation, is the one to propose a grace period? Can this be done? Compare Articles 48 and 63. If the machine is delivered and then fails to work, can Dingo Ranch force Experimental Transportation to fix it? See Article 46(3). Is this remedy available in American law? See Uniform Commercial Code §2-716.

The treaty has a strong presumption in favor of specific performance. See Articles 46 and 62. However, Article 28 does not require specific performance if the court that would be asked to grant it would not do so if its own law applied. For example, in the United States there are major limits on equitable remedies (there must be no adequate remedy at law — i.e., damages; the court must not become involved in undue supervision of the resulting performance; etc.), and an American court might use these rules to duck an order for specific performance.

IV. ANTICIPATORY REPUDIATION

Ever since the classic case of Hochster v. De La Tour, 2 El. & Bl. 678, 118 Eng. Rep. 922 (Q.B. 1853), it has been settled that if one party to a contract makes a definite repudiation of the contract before the date set for performance, the other party could treat the repudiation as a breach and sue immediately. But the common law also permitted the innocent party to ignore the repudiation and await the performance date to see if the repudiator would retract the repudiation. As long as the innocent party had not changed position in reliance on the repudiation (say, by covering), the repudiator was free to retract the repudiation, reinstate the contract, and perform as originally agreed.

To what extent has the Code changed these common law rules? Read §§2-610 and 2-611. These sections do not define *repudiation,* which is, of course, their triggering event. A repudiation must be a definite refusal to perform; mere equivocation is not enough. See Official Comment 1 to §2-610; White & Summers §7-2; Copylease Corp. of Am. v. Memorex Corp., 403 F. Supp. 625 (S.D.N.Y. 1975). The equivocating party can be forced into performance or repudiation by use of the procedure outlined in §2-609 (Right to Adequate Assurance of Performance).

Unfortunately, in the process of drafting the Code's damages sections, the drafters became careless when dealing with the time for measuring damages in an anticipatory repudiation situation, and the UCC sections simply do not fit together. The following Problem should help you see the difficulty.

PROBLEM 90

The United States Army contracted with the Hawaiian Cattle Company for the purchase of 1,000 pounds of beef. Delivery was set six months later, on October 8, the agreed price to be $5,000. Shortly thereafter, the price of beef rose sharply, and Hawaiian Cattle repudiated the contract on July 10, when the price was $6,000. The Army's procurement officer scrambled around and on July 15 discovered it was possible to cover by buying similar cattle from Texas at a cost of $7,000. Instead, the Army sent Hawaiian Cattle a telegram stating that it did not accept or recognize the repudiation and expected performance on October 8. By October 8 the price had risen to $8,000. The Army decided not to cover at all and instead served the troops beans. As general counsel for the Army, advise the Army of the amount it can recover from Hawaiian Cattle. Read §§2-610, 2-713, and 2-723(1). Does it help reconcile these sections to know that the drafters of §2-713 were thinking of a buyer who learns of the repudiation *after* the date set for the original performance, not (as in this Problem) *before* the due date?

V.   THE STATUTE OF LIMITATIONS

The Code drafters decided that it was important to have a uniform statute of limitations for transactions in goods, and they chose four years "as the most appropriate to modern business practice. This is within the normal commercial record keeping period." Official Comment to §2-725. Read §2-725, and note that the four-year period begins to run at the *accrual* of the cause of action (the moment a suit could be brought). The parties may reduce the period by agreement down to one year, but they may not extend it beyond four. One court has decided that an agreement so reducing the limitation period need not be conspicuous to be enforced. Jandreau v. Sheesley Plumbing & Heating Co., 324 N.W.2d 266 (S.D. 1982). In most jurisdictions the statute of limitations is an affirmative defense and is waived if not pleaded and proved. See, e.g., Mysel v. Gross, 70 Cal. App. 3d 10, 138 Cal. Rptr. 873 (1977).

PROBLEM 91

Four years and two days after delivery of his new car, Joe Suburb came out of his house to discover he had a flat tire. He changed it and, for the first time, put on the spare tire. That afternoon as he was driving on the interstate, the tire burst due to a manufacturing flaw. Joe was killed. Has the statute of limitations run under these situations?

(a) The tire warranty read: "These tires are merchantable." If this were a lease of goods, would Article 2A reach a different result? See §2A-506.

(b) The tire warranty read: "These tires have a lifetime guarantee." See Kelleher v. Lumber, 152 N.H. 813, 891 A.2d 477 (2005); Rawls v. Associated Materials, LLC, 2011 WL 3297622 (S.D.W. Va. 2011); Annot., 93 A.L.R.3d 690.

(c) The sales material said with regard to the tires: "Many tires are still on the road after five years." See Jones & Laughlin Steel Corp. v. Johns-Manville Sales Corp. v. Brown & Kerr, Inc., 626 F.2d 280 (3d Cir. 1980) (a statement of future performance is "explicit" if it does not arise by implication, but is instead "distinctly stated; plain in language; clear; not ambiguous; express; unequivocal").

(d) The tire warranty read: "These tires are warranted for seven years from date of purchase." If a tire first malfunctioned at the beginning of the third year, when would the statute of limitations expire? See Joswick v. Chesapeake Mobile Homes, Inc., 765 A.2d 90 (Md. 2001).

(e) There were no express warranties given with regard to the tires; there were also no warranty disclaimers. See Note, When Does the Statute of Limitations Begin to Run on Breaches of Implied Warranties?, 30 Baylor L. Rev. 386 (1978).

Mydlach v. DaimlerChrysler Corporation

Supreme Court of Illinois, 2007, 226 Ill. 2d 307, 314 Ill. Dec. 760, 875 N.E.2d 1047

Justice FITZGERALD delivered the judgment of the court, with opinion:

BACKGROUND

On June 20, 1998, plaintiff purchased a used 1996 Dodge Neon, manufactured by defendant, from McGrath Buick-Nissan (McGrath) in Elgin, Illinois. The vehicle was originally put into service on June 24, 1996, with a three-year/36,000-mile limited warranty. The warranty provided, in relevant part, as follows:

The "Basic Warranty" begins on your vehicle's Warranty Start Date which is the earlier of (1) the date you take delivery of your new vehicle, OR (2) the date the vehicle was first put into service. . . .

The "Basic Warranty" covers the cost of all parts and labor needed to repair any item on your vehicle (except as noted below) that's defective in material, workmanship, or factory preparation. You pay nothing for these repairs.

The "Basic Warranty" covers every Chrysler-supplied part of your vehicle, EXCEPT its tires and cellular telephone.

. . .

These warranty repairs or adjustments (parts and labor) will be made by your dealer at no charge using new or remanufactured parts.

. . .

The "Basic Warranty" lasts for 36 months from the vehicle's Warranty Start Date OR for 36,000 miles on the odometer, whichever occurs first. (Emphasis in original.)

At the time of plaintiff's purchase in 1998, the car's mileage was 26,296. Thus, the warranty had approximately one year or 10,000 miles remaining.

Beginning July 7, 1998, plaintiff brought the car to McGrath and another authorized dealership several times for a variety of problems, including a recurring fluid leak. Plaintiff claimed that the dealerships' repair attempts were unsuccessful and, as a result, she could not use the vehicle as intended. Plaintiff ultimately filed suit against defendant on May 16, 2001, seeking legal and equitable relief, as well as attorney fees and costs, under the Magnuson-Moss Act. . . .

III

Although the Magnuson-Moss Act provides a private right of action for breach of a written warranty, the Act does not contain a limitations provision for such an action. Where a federal statute fails to specify a limitations period for suits under it, "courts apply the most closely analogous statute of limitations under state law." Del Costello v. International Brotherhood of Teamsters, 462 U.S. 151, 158, 103 S. Ct. 2281, 2287, 76 L. Ed. 2d 476, 485 (1983); accord Wilson v. Garcia, 471 U.S. 261, 268, 105 S. Ct. 1938, 1942, 85 L. Ed. 2d 254, 261 (1985); Teamsters & Employers Welfare Trust v. Gorman Brothers Ready Mix, 283 F.3d 877, 880 (7th Cir. 2002). In suits brought under the Magnuson-Moss Act, our appellate court, as well as courts in other jurisdictions, generally consider the UCC to be the most closely analogous statute and have borrowed the limitations provision contained therein. See, e.g., Nowalski, 335 Ill. App. 3d at 628, 269 Ill. Dec. 781, 781 N.E.2d 578 (collecting Illinois cases); Hillery v. Georgie Boy Manufacturing, Inc., 341 F. Supp. 2d 1112, 1114 (D. Ariz. 2004); Poli v. DaimlerChrysler Corp., 349 N.J. Super. 169, 181, 793 A.2d 104, 111 (2002); Murungi v. Mercedes Benz Credit Corp., 192 F. Supp. 2d 71, 79 (W.D.N.Y. 2001); Keller v. Volkswagen, 1999 PA Super. 153, ¶5, 733 A.2d 642. We agree with the foregoing authorities and will look to the limitations provision contained in the UCC to determine the timeliness of plaintiff's complaint. Specifically, we will look to article 2 of the UCC, which applies to "transactions in goods." 810 ILCS 5/2-102 (West 2006).

Section 2-725 of the UCC, titled "Statute of limitations in contracts for sale," generally provides a four-year limitations period:

> (1) An action for breach of any contract for sale must be commenced within 4 years after the cause of action has accrued. By the original agreement the parties may reduce the period of limitation to not less than one year but may not extend it.
>
> (2) A cause of action accrues when the breach occurs, regardless of the aggrieved party's lack of knowledge of the breach. A breach of warranty occurs when tender of delivery is made, except that where a warranty explicitly extends to future performance of the goods and discovery of the breach must await the time of such performance the cause of action accrues when the breach is or should have been discovered.

810 ILCS 5/2-725 (West 2006).

Preliminarily, we note that the future-performance exception to the four-year limitations period, set forth in subsection (2) above, is not at issue in this case. As will be discussed in greater detail below, a repair or replacement warranty like the one issued by defendant here "has nothing to do with the inherent quality of the goods or their future performance." *Cosman,* 285 Ill. App. 3d at 261, 220 Ill. Dec. 790, 674 N.E.2d 61. See also C. Reitz, Manufacturers' Warranties of Consumer Goods, 75 Wash. U. L.Q. 357, 364 n.24 (1997) ("Promises to repair or replace refer to future performance of sellers, not to future performance of goods"); L. Lawrence, Lawrence's Anderson on the Uniform Commercial Code §2-625:129, at 332 (3d ed. 2001) (discussing difference between a warranty of future performance and a covenant to repair or replace). Accordingly, we turn our attention to the balance of the statute and the parties' arguments relative thereto.

Defendant argues that section 2-725 should be applied as written. Thus, because the statute provides that a "breach of warranty occurs when tender of delivery is made," and tender of delivery of the Dodge Neon was first made in June 1996, plaintiff's suit, filed in May 2001, was untimely. See *Nowalski,* 335 Ill. App. 3d at 632, 269 Ill. Dec. 781, 781 N.E.2d 578 (holding that cause of action for breach of three-year/36,000-mile limited warranty accrued when the vehicle was delivered and not when defendant failed to successfully repair the vehicle). Plaintiff argues that a repair warranty cannot be breached until the manufacturer fails to repair the vehicle after a reasonable opportunity to do so, and that the appellate court did not err in finding her complaint was timely filed. See *Cosman,* 285 Ill. App. 3d at 260, 220 Ill. Dec. 790, 674 N.E.2d 61 (holding that breach of six-year/60,000-mile limited power-train warranty "cannot occur until Ford refuses or fails to repair the powertrain if and when it breaks"); Belfour v. Schaumburg Auto, 306 Ill. App. 3d 234, 241, 239 Ill. Dec. 383, 713 N.E.2d 1233 (1999) (following *Cosman* and holding that breach of three-year/50,000-mile repair warranty "cannot occur until Audi refuses or fails to repair the defect"); *Cogley*, 368 Ill. App. 3d at 96-97, 306 Ill. Dec. 243, 857 N.E.2d 336 (following *Cosman* and holding that suit for breach of three-year/36,000-mile repair warranty filed within four years of repair attempt was timely).[7]

We begin our analysis by turning to the language of article 2 of the UCC. Section 2-725(2) plainly states that "[a] breach of warranty occurs when tender of delivery is made." 810 ILCS 5/2-725(2) (West 2006). The *Nowalski* opinion, on which defendant relies, concluded that once article 2 of the UCC is chosen as the analogous state statute from which to borrow the statute of limitations, the analysis begins and ends with the "tender of delivery" language quoted above. *Nowalski*, 335 Ill. App. 3d at 632, 269 Ill. Dec. 781, 781 N.E.2d 578. We disagree.

Although courts generally consider article 2 of the UCC to be the statute most closely analogous to the Magnuson-Moss Act, the two enactments are not identical. For example, article 2 addresses warranties that are created by the "seller." See 810 ILCS 5/2-312, 2-313, 2-314, 2-315 (West 2006). The Magnuson-Moss Act, however, addresses warranties from a "supplier" or "warrantor" who may or may not be the immediate seller. See 15 U.S.C. §§2301(4), (5), (6) (1994). In addition, the term "warranty," as used in the two enactments, is not the same. As discussed above, the Act speaks of implied warranties and written warranties, the latter of which may be either full or limited. 15 U.S.C. §§2301(6), (7), 2303 (1994). In contrast, the UCC speaks of express warranties (which may be oral or written), implied warranties, and warranty of title. 810 ILCS 5/2-312, 2-313, 2-314, 2-315 (West 2006).

Although the parties agree that defendant's warranty is a "written warranty" under the Magnuson-Moss Act, they disagree as to whether the warranty is an "express warranty" under the UCC. Defendant argues that the repair warranty qualifies as an express warranty and that plaintiff's claim is therefore governed by the tender-of-delivery rule in section 2-725(2). Plaintiff argues that it does not qualify as an express warranty and that her claim is not subject to the tender-of-delivery rule.

Section 2-313 of the UCC explains how express warranties are created.

---

7. The same divergence of opinion on the limitations issue that is exemplified by *Nowalski* and *Cosman* exists among our sister states. See generally L. Garvin, Uncertainty and Error in the Law of Sales: The Article Two Statute of Limitations, 83 B.U. L. Rev. 345, 377-81 (2003) (discussing the split among state courts in their approach to repair or replacement promises).

Express warranties by the seller are created as follows:

(a) Any affirmation of fact or promise made by the seller to the buyer which relates to the goods and becomes part of the basis of the bargain creates an express warranty that the goods shall conform to the affirmation or promise.

(b) Any description of the goods which is made part of the basis of the bargain creates an express warrant

(c) Any sample or model which is made part of the basis of the bargain creates an express warranty that the whole of the goods shall conform to the sample or model." 810 ILCS 5/2-313(1) (West 2006).

The UCC makes plain that an express warranty is related to the quality or description of the goods. See Moorman Manufacturing Co. v. National Tank Co., 91 Ill. 2d 69, 78, 61 Ill. Dec. 746, 435 N.E.2d 443 (1982) (observing that UCC warranty rules "determine the quality of the product the manufacturer promises and thereby determine the quality he must deliver"); Alloway v. General Marine Industries, L.P., 149 N.J. 620, 630, 695 A.2d 264, 269 (1997) (stating that "the U.C.C. provides for express warranties regarding the quality of goods"); Allis-Chalmers Credit Corp. v. Herbolt, 17 Ohio App. 3d 230, 233, 17 OBR 496, 479 N.E.2d 293, 297 (1984) (identifying UCC express warranties as one of the "warranties of quality"); 1 W. Hawkland, Uniform Commercial Code Series §2-313.4, at 546 (2002) ("express warranties relate exclusively to quality, description and title of the goods and have nothing to do with the other terms of the contract").

In other words, an express warranty, for purposes of the UCC, obligates the seller to deliver goods that conform to the affirmation, promise, description, sample or model. If a seller delivers conforming goods, the warranty is satisfied. If the seller delivers nonconforming goods, the warranty is breached at that time. Even if the buyer is unaware that the goods, as delivered, do not conform to the seller's affirmation, promise, description, sample or model, the warranty has been breached. Under this scenario, the statutory pronouncement that "[a] breach of warranty occurs when tender of delivery is made" (810 ILCS 5/2-725(2) (West 2006)) makes perfect sense, and the four-year limitations period commences at that time. See M. Klinger, The Concept of Warranty Duration: A Tangled Web, 89 Dick. L. Rev. 935, 939 (1985) ("Section 2-725(2) presumes that all warranties, expressed or implied, relate only to the condition of the goods at the time of sale" and "[a]s a result, the period of limitations begins to run at that time"); L. Garvin, Uncertainty and Error in the Law of Sales: The Article Two Statute of Limitations, 83 B.U. L. Rev. 345, 379 (2003) ("Article Two defines a range of express and implied warranties" which "[a]ll go to the quality of the goods at tender").

The warranty in the present case, however, is not related to the quality or description of the goods at tender. It does not warrant that the vehicle will conform to some affirmation, promise, description, sample or model. Rather, the warranty promises only that the manufacturer will repair or replace defective parts during the warranty period. As defendant made clear in its brief before this court:

> DaimlerChrysler's limited warranty was not a promise that the vehicle would be defect free and in the event of a breach of warranty, Plaintiff would be limited to repair or replacement of the vehicle. Rather, DaimlerChrysler's limited warranty promised to cover the cost to repair or replace defective parts in the automobile for the time period covering 36 months or 36 thousand miles.

Although defendant's warranty qualifies as a "written warranty" under the Act, it is not an "express warranty" under the UCC, and is thus not the type of warranty that can be breached on "tender of delivery" (810 ILCS 5/ 2-725(2) (West 2006)). See *Cogley*, 368 Ill. App. 3d at 96, 306 Ill. Dec. 243, 857 N.E.2d 336; *Cosman*, 285 Ill. App. 3d at 258-60, 220 Ill. Dec. 790, 674 N.E.2d 61; C. Dewitt, Note, Action Accrual Date for Written Warranties to Repair: Date of Delivery or Date of Failure to Repair, 17 U. Mich. J.L. Reform 713, 722 n.35 (1984) (promise to repair "relates not to the goods and their quality, but to the manufacturer and its obligation to the purchaser," and thus "a repair 'warranty' falls beyond the scope of . . . the on-delivery rule"); C. Reitz, Manufacturers' Warranties of Consumer Goods, 75 Wash. U. L.Q. 357, 364 n.24 (1997) (tender-of-delivery date for commencement of four-year UCC limitations provision is "completely inappropriate to promises to repair or replace goods that are later determined to be defective"). Accordingly, we reject defendant's argument that the four-year limitations period for breach of the repair warranty commenced upon delivery of the Dodge Neon in 1996, and we overrule the *Nowalski* opinion on which defendant relies.

Our conclusion that the repair warranty is not a UCC express warranty, and thus not subject to the tender-of-delivery rule set forth in the second sentence of section 2-725(2), does not render section 2-725(2) irrelevant for purposes of determining when the limitations period began on plaintiff's claim under the Magnuson-Moss Act. The first sentence of section 2-725(2) remains applicable. The first sentence states: "[a] cause of action accrues when the breach occurs, regardless of the aggrieved party's lack of knowledge of the breach." (Emphasis added.) 810 ILCS 5/2-725(2) (West 2006). Although the UCC does not expressly state when the breach of a repair promise occurs, we may refer to the law that exists outside of the UCC. See 810 ILCS 5/1-103 (West 2006) ("Unless displaced by the particular provisions of this Act, the principles of law and equity . . . shall supplement its provisions"); L. Lawrence, Lawrence's Anderson on the Uniform Commercial Code §2-725:99, at 301 (3d ed. 2001) (because the UCC provides no assistance as to when a nonwarranty breach of contract "occurs" for purposes of computing the limitations period, "it is necessary to resort to the general non-Code law of contracts," which "has not been displaced by the Code and therefore continues in force").

Generally, "[w]hen performance of a duty under a contract is due any non-performance is a breach." Restatement (Second) of Contracts §235, at 211 (1979). Performance under a vehicle manufacturer's promise to repair or replace defective parts is due not at tender of delivery, but only when, and if, a covered defect arises and repairs are required. In that event, if the promised repairs are refused or unsuccessful, the repair warranty is breached and the cause of action accrues, triggering the four-year limitations period. See *Cosman*, 285 Ill. App. 3d at 260, 220 Ill. Dec. 790, 674 N.E.2d 61 (holding that breach of six-year/60,000-mile limited power-train warranty "cannot occur until Ford refuses or fails to repair the power train if and when it breaks"); *Belfour*, 306 Ill. App. 3d at 241, 239 Ill. Dec. 383, 713 N.E.2d 1233 (holding that breach of three-year/50,000-mile repair warranty "cannot occur until Audi refuses or fails to repair the defect"); *Cogley*, 368 Ill. App. 3d at 96-97, 306 Ill. Dec. 243, 857 N.E.2d 336 (holding that suit for breach of three-year/36,000-mile repair warranty filed within four years of repair attempt was timely). See also Monticello v. Winnebago Industries, Inc., 369 F. Supp. 2d 1350, 1356-57 (N.D. Ga. 2005) (under Georgia law, a written warranty that provides for repair or replacement of parts is breached when the purchaser returns the product to the dealer for repair and repair is refused or unsuccessful); *Poli*, 349 N.J. Super. at 180, 793 A.2d at 110-11 (under New Jersey law, cause of action for breach of seven-year/70,000-mile power-train warranty would not have accrued when the car was delivered, but rather when persistent problems appeared or when DaimlerChrysler was unable to repair the defect); Long Island Lighting Co. v. Imo Industries Inc., 6 F.3d 876, 889-90 (2d Cir. 1993) (under New York law, cause of action for breach of a repair promise accrued when the generator malfunctioned and the seller refused to make the necessary repairs).

This is the approach advocated by some commentators. For example, in his discussion of the appropriate treatment of a manufacturer's express warranty to repair or replace defective parts, Professor Lawrence states:

> The sounder approach is to recognize that the failure to repair or replace is merely a breach of contract and not a breach of warranty, and therefore no cause of action arises until the seller has refused to repair or replace the goods. This is because until the seller has failed or refused to make the repairs or provide a replacement, the buyer, not being entitled to such a remedy, has no right to commence an action for damages. As a result, the action is timely if brought within four years of the seller's failure or refusal.

L. Lawrence, Lawrence's Anderson on the Uniform Commercial Code §2-725:101, at 303 (3d ed. 2001). Accord L. Garvin, Uncertainty and Error in the Law of Sales: The Article Two Statute of Limitations, 83 B.U. L. Rev. 345, 381 (2003).

The correctness of this approach is manifest when we consider consumer claims for breach of repair warranties that run for periods longer than the three years/36,000 miles at issue here. For example, consider the case of a consumer who purchases a vehicle carrying a five-year/50,000-mile repair warranty. If the four-year limitations period commences at "tender of delivery," the limitations period for a breach of the repair promise occurring in year five will expire before the breach even occurs, thus rendering the repair warranty unenforceable during its final year. Statutes of limitations, however, are intended "to prevent stale claims, not to preclude claims before they are ripe for adjudication." Guzman v. C.R. Epperson Construction, Inc., 196 Ill. 2d 391, 400, 256 Ill. Dec. 827, 752 N.E.2d 1069 (2001). Even a four-year warranty could be rendered unenforceable if breach of the repair promise occurred near the end of the warranty period. In that case, the buyer would have only the briefest of periods in which to file suit. See Nationwide Insurance Co., 533 Pa. at 434, 625 A.2d at 1178.

Defendant argues that concerns about the enforceability of longer-term repair warranties are inapplicable to the facts of this case and without merit. We disagree. Although the repair warranty at issue here ran for three years, our holding in this case will apply equally to longer-term warranties. Such warranties are common in the automobile industry. Adoption of defendant's position would be an invitation to manufacturers and sellers of automobiles, as well as other goods, to engage in misleading marketing. That is, a manufacturer or seller could use the marketing advantage of a longer repair warranty, yet escape the accompanying obligations of that warranty by pleading the statute of limitations in defense. C. Williams, The Statute of Limitations, Prospective Warranties, and Problems of Interpretation in Article Two of the UCC, 52 Geo. Wash. L. Rev. 67, 105 (1983). Such a result is contrary to the very purpose of the Magnuson-Moss Act: "to improve the adequacy of information available to consumers" and "prevent deception." 15 U.S.C. §2302(a) (1994).

Defendant also argues that unless the tender-of-delivery rule in section 2-725 is given effect, the limitations period for breach of limited warranty actions will be "limitless" and "uncertain." This argument is without merit. Because the promise to repair or replace defective parts is only good during the warranty period, the latest a breach of warranty can occur is at the very end of that period. Accordingly, the statute of limitations will expire, at the latest, four years after the warranty period has run. If breach of a repair warranty occurs earlier in the warranty period, the limitations period for that breach will expire sooner, but in no event will the warrantor's exposure extend beyond the warranty period, plus four years. Thus, contrary to defendant's argument, commencing the four-year limitations period from the date the warrantor fails or refuses to repair the vehicle does not result in a limitless limitations period.

We recognize, of course, that a fact question may arise as to the date on which a repair warranty was breached which, in turn, would create some uncertainty as to when the four-year limitations period should commence. Fact questions of this nature, however, frequently arise in cases where the statute of limitations has been pled in defense. Resolution of this type of uncertainty is a classic function of the trier of fact. See, e.g., County of Du Page v. Graham, Anderson, Probst & White, Inc., 109 Ill. 2d 143, 153-54, 92 Ill. Dec. 833, 485 N.E.2d 1076 (1985) (remanding the matter to the circuit court for a factual determination as to when the statute of limitations began to run against the county on its claims for defective design and construction of the county's administration building); Knox College v. Celotex Corp., 88 Ill. 2d 407, 417, 58 Ill. Dec. 725, 430 N.E.2d 976 (1981) (holding that trier of fact must determine when the plaintiff had sufficient information as to the roof defect to start the running of the limitations period); Witherell v. Weimer, 85 Ill. 2d 146, 156, 52 Ill. Dec. 6, 421 N.E.2d 869 (1981) ("In many, if not most, cases the time at which an injured party knows or reasonably should have known both of his injury and that it was wrongfully caused will be a disputed question to be resolved by the finder of fact"). We therefore reject defendant's argument that commencing the limitations period when the warrantor fails or refuses to repair the defect — rather than at tender of delivery — will create unacceptable uncertainty in the limitations period.

Turning to the facts of this case, the record indicates that plaintiff brought her vehicle to McGrath and another authorized dealer on several occasions beginning in July 1998. At that point, assuming the alleged defects were covered defects, defendant was obligated (through its authorized dealer) to make good on its repair promise. Plaintiff's lawsuit, filed in May 2001, is therefore timely. Accordingly, we affirm that portion of the judgment of the appellate court which reversed the grant of summary judgment in favor of defendant as to count I of the complaint.

Affirmed in part and reversed in part; cause remanded.

PROBLEM 92

If the manufacturer of a vehicle sold it to the dealership, and the dealership then resold the vehicle to a consumer, would the four-year period on the manufacturer's *implied* warranty start running on the date of delivery to the dealership or on the date of the sale to the ultimate consumer? See Wilson v. Class, 605 A.2d 907 (Del. Super. 1992). Would we reach the same result on an *express* warranty given by the manufacturer?

PROBLEM 93

Painter Sally Smock had no luck selling her own works, but made good money by creating phony works supposedly by Salvador Dali, signing Dali's name to them, and selling them to DaDa Gallery. In 2020, DaDa Gallery unwittingly sold two of Smock's forgeries to Mr. and Mrs. America, tourists who paid $150,000. The Americas proudly exhibited the supposed Dalis in their Cincinnati living room, until 2025 when Smock made the national news as she went to jail for art forgery. The Americas then sued DaDa Gallery for breach of express warranty, only to be met with the argument that the statute of limitations under §2-725 had run out. How should this come out? See Balog v. Center Art Gallery, 745 F. Supp. 1556 (D. Haw. 1990); Doss, Inc. v. Christie's, Inc., 2009 WL 3053713 (S.D.N.Y. 2009) (holding that a cause of action for selling a painting, which had been stolen by the Nazis from a Paris art dealer, accrued in 1991 when the painting was sold by Christie's, not in 2006 when there was a challenge to the buyer's ownership); Equinox Gallery Ltd. v. Dorfman, 306 F. Supp. 3d 560 (S.D.N.Y. 2018).

PROBLEM 94

In 2015, Notheby's Auction Company sold Max Collector a painting expressly warranted to be by Degas for $1 million. Experts hired by Notheby's had all agreed it was created by Degas in 1886. In 2032, Max Collector sold the painting to Grandiose Museum for $5 million, making an express warranty that it was by Degas. Two years later, the museum learned conclusively that the painting was in fact a forgery created in 1923. It sued Max Collector for return of the purchase price. Does Max Collector have an indemnification action against Notheby's, or has the statute of limitations expired on that claim? See §2-725 and the following case.[8]

Central Washington Refrigeration, Inc. v. Barbee

Supreme Court of Washington, 1997, 133 Wash. 2d 509, 946 P.2d 760

SANDERS, Justice.

We are asked whether a buyer of goods may bring an indemnity action against the seller for liability incurred to a third party for a defect in the goods, and, if so, when the statute of limitations begins to run. We hold a

---

8. Some states regulate art authenticity problems by special statute; see L. Garvin, Uncertainty and Error in the Law of Sales: The Article Two Statute of Limitations, 83 B.U. L. Rev. 345, 371 n.116 (2003), citing Fla. Stat. Ann. §686.504; Mich. Comp. Laws Ann. §442.322; N.Y. Arts & Cult. Aff. Law §13.01; R.I. Gen. Laws §5-62-9(1).

buyer may maintain such indemnity action and that the statute of limitations begins to run when the buyer pays damages to the third party or the third party obtains judgment against the buyer, whichever is first in time.

In 1987 petitioner Central Washington Refrigeration, Inc. (Central) contracted with a Yakima orchard to install a set of cold storage rooms to store apples and other fruit. Central in turn contracted with respondent McCormack Engineering (McCormack) to purchase the refrigeration coils which Central was to install. Pursuant to the sales agreement McCormack specially manufactured the coils according to Central's specifications and timely delivered them in August 1987 at which time Central installed the coils in the cold storage rooms.

From the start, however, the orchard experienced problems with the cold storage rooms. After several repair attempts and an intervening bankruptcy by the orchard, the orchard defaulted on payments for the cold storage rooms and Central subsequently sued for payment. In March 1989 the orchard counterclaimed for damages asserting Central misdesigned the cold storage system, used poor workmanship in building it, installed improper components, and failed to repair the system.

On May 22, 1992 — over four-and-a-half years after McCormack delivered the coils — Central filed a third-party complaint against McCormack alleging the coils were defective and caused all the problems, seeking contribution and/or indemnity from McCormack for any damages due the orchard from Central. [The court below held that] to the extent Central's claim was either contractual or for indemnity, it was barred by the four-year U.C.C. statute of limitations governing contracts. Central Washington Refrigeration, Inc. v. Barbee, 81 Wash. App. 212, 220, 223-24, 913 P.2d 836 (1996). We granted review to determine whether a buyer may maintain an indemnity action against the seller based on breach of warranty, and, if so, when the applicable statute of limitations commences to run. . . .

Indemnity in its most basic sense means reimbursement (Black's Law Dictionary 769 (6th ed. 1990)) and may lie when one party discharges a liability which another should rightfully have assumed. Stevens v. Security Pac. Mortgage Corp., 53 Wash. App. 507, 517, 768 P.2d 1007, *review denied,* 112 Wash. 2d 1023 (1989) ("Indemnity requires full reimbursement and transfers liability from the one who has been compelled to pay damages to another who should bear the entire loss.").[9]

---

9. See also McDermott v. City of New York, 50 N.Y.2d 211, 406 N.E.2d 460, 462, 428 N.Y.S.2d 643 (1980) ("Conceptually, implied indemnification finds its roots in the principles of equity. It is nothing short of simple fairness to recognize that '[a] person who, in whole or in part, has discharged a duty which is owed by him but which as between himself and another should have been discharged by the other, is entitled to indemnity' (Restatement, Restitution, §76). To prevent unjust enrichment, courts have assumed the duty of placing the obligation where in equity it belongs.").

While indemnity sounds in contract and tort it is a separate equitable cause of action. The variety of indemnity relevant to this case is implied contractual indemnity, also referenced to as "implied in fact" indemnity. Such arises when one party incurs a liability the other party should discharge by virtue of the nature of the relationship between the two parties. . . . The nature of the relationship between the parties gives rise to the right of implied indemnity. . . .[10] The question here is whether the contractual relationship between buyer and seller under the U.C.C. is sufficient to give rise to an implied right of indemnity when a defect in the good causes damage to a third party user and such defect constitutes breach of seller's warranties.

A minority of courts addressing the issue under comparable facts has found the contractual relationship between buyer and seller under the U.C.C. insufficient to give rise to an indemnity action. See, e.g., Perry v. Pioneer Wholesale Supply Co., 681 P.2d 214, 219 (Utah 1984). Jurisdictions following this minority rule are Utah, Idaho, and South Dakota. The minority rule would view Central's claim as nothing more than a claim for damages under a sales contract between merchants for breach of implied warranties resulting in consequential damages owed to a third party.[11] Use of the label "indemnity" would not alter the perception that the action still sounds in contract. The claim would be governed in whole by the U.C.C. Under the U.C.C. actions for breach of contract must be commenced within four years of date of delivery of goods regardless of when the buyer discovers the defect. Because Central failed to bring its claim against McCormack within four years of delivery, its suit would be time-barred under the minority rule. The Court of Appeals chose to follow the minority rule.

Central, however, argues the minority rule errs in failing to recognize an indemnity claim here. We agree. Central points to the majority of courts addressing the issue which have ruled the contractual relationship between buyer and seller under the U.C.C. is a sufficient relationship to give rise to an

---

10. See 42 C.J.S. Indemnity §31, at 121 (1991) ("A right to indemnity, while not implied in every contract or contractual relationship, may be claimed on the basis of an implied contract, which can arise either from the conduct of the parties or be implied from the nature of their relationship, whether it be a contractual or other legal relationship, and from given warranties and covenants, or be otherwise implied from unique special factors indicating the parties' intent that the party from whom indemnity is sought should be ultimately liable.") (citations omitted).

11. Two legal commentaries argue the minority rule has it right. See Paul J. Wilkinson, An Ind. Run Around the U.C.C.: The Use (or Abuse?) of Indemnity, 20 Pepp. L. Rev. 1407, 1438 (1993) (such "indemnity" actions are nothing more than actions for consequential damages resulting from breach of contract and there is no reason to treat consequential damages paid to a third party any differently from any other damages incurred as a result of a breach of contract); Thomas A. Leggette, When Can an Implied Indemnity Cause of Action Be Used to End-Run a Limitations Bar?, 42 Fed'n Ins. & Corp. Couns. Q. 33, 33 (1991) (a party should not be able to end-run the strict four-year U.C.C. statute of limitations period for suing on contracts by simply denominating the action one for "indemnity").

implied right of indemnity. Jurisdictions following the majority rule include California, Maine, Michigan, Minnesota, Missouri, Nebraska, New Hampshire, New York, North Carolina, Pennsylvania, and Virginia.

A clear statement of the majority rule appears in Bellevue South Assocs. v. HRH Constr. Corp., 78 N.Y.2d 282, 579 N.E.2d 195, 574 N.Y.S.2d 165 (1991). In Bellevue a subcontractor installed defective floor tiles in an apartment complex and was sued by the apartment complex owner. The subcontractor eventually sued the tile manufacturer for indemnity, seeking to shift the entire liability, alleging the manufacturer breached the implied warranties. The manufacturer argued the suit was nothing more than one on the contract and thus the U.C.C. four-year statute of limitations must govern to bar the suit. The New York high court rejected the manufacturer's argument, concluding the contractual relationship and the U.C.C.'s implied warranties provided "the requisite basis for an indemnification claim." Id., 574 N.Y.S.2d at 171, 579 N.E.2d at 201.

We adopt the majority rule and hold a contractual relationship under the U.C.C., with its implied warranties, provides sufficient basis for an implied indemnity claim when the buyer incurs liability to a third party as a result of a defect in the goods which would constitute a breach of the seller's implied or express warranties. In so holding we acknowledge "[t]here is a substantial difference between an instance where a product simply fails as opposed to a situation where the product fails and causes damage to a third party." Carrier Corp. v. Detrex Corp., 4 Cal. App. 4th 1522, 6 Cal. Rptr. 2d 565, 569 (1992). We also understand our decision to join the majority camp comports with the equitable principles underlying indemnity.[12]

The remaining question is when the statute of limitations commences to run on the indemnity claim. Indemnity actions are distinct, separate causes of action from the underlying wrong and are governed by separate statutes of limitations. It is settled law that indemnity actions accrue when the party seeking indemnity pays or is legally adjudged obligated to pay damages to

---

12. See, e.g., City of Willmar v. Short-Elliott-Hendrickson, Inc., 512 N.W.2d 872, 874 (1994) (indemnity is an equitable action and "is not based on contract or tort, although either may secondarily be involved, but on one party paying more than its fair share."); City of Clayton v. Grumman Emergency Prods., Inc., 576 F. Supp. 1122, 1127 (E.D. Mo. 1983) ("A party who buys and then resells a product is not in a position to discover the latent defect within the warranty's limitation period because the product is in the hands of the consumer during that time. Only when the consumer sues the retailer does the retailer gain notice of the latent defect."). We note indemnity may not be available when equity does not so require. See Sheehan v. Morris Irr., Inc., 460 N.W.2d 413, 417 (S.D. 1990); Farmers Nat'l Bank v. Wickham Pipeline Constr., 114 Idaho 565, 759 P.2d 71, 75 (1988) (equity does not require an indemnity action to be recognized where parties could have sued at law but slept on their rights). As the parties have not so requested, we refrain from assessing the particular equities in this case.

a third party. The statute of limitations on the indemnity action therefore begins to run at that point. . . .

Thus, the statute of limitations on Central's alleged indemnity claim began to run when Central paid the orchard to settle the orchard's claims. Because Central brought suit at the same time it settled, we hold its indemnity action is not time barred. Central's indemnification suit must be determined on its merits. The Court of Appeals is reversed, the case is remanded for trial and Central shall recover its costs on appeal.

GUY, Justice (dissenting).

Article 2 of the Uniform Commercial Code (U.C.C.) establishes one general law governing all commercial sales for the purpose of providing predictability and consistency for all commercial sales transactions. In my view the majority opinion is inconsistent with this purpose. By holding contract-based indemnity claims are outside the U.C.C.'s four-year statute of repose, RCW 62A.2-725, the majority leaves commercial retailers susceptible to indemnity claims indefinitely.[13] Therefore, I dissent.

The transaction between Central and McCormack was a sale of goods. I would hold that any claim stemming from this commercial sales transaction, including one for indemnity, is governed by article 2 of the U.C.C. and its four-year statute of repose. Further, I would hold that Central's claim for indemnity was time barred since it was raised after the four-year time period had expired.

The majority is compelled by the belief that this court must follow the lead of other jurisdictions and find that when commercial buyers have paid damages to a third party due to defective products purchased from a commercial retailer, the buyer has two avenues for compensation. The jurisdictions on which the majority relies found that such commercial buyers not only have a breach of warranty claim against the commercial retailer under article 2 but also have an implied right of indemnity against the retailer founded in common law and governed by general statutes of limitations. The majority does not thoroughly discuss why this policy decision is correct but instead places great importance on the fact that a "majority" of other jurisdictions follow it. Contrary to the majority's conclusion, there is no majority/minority view on whether indemnity claims are independent of the U.C.C. Rather, there exists a split of authority. Four states, South Dakota,

---

13. Although a third party's claim against a commercial buyer for breach of warranty continues to be bound by the four-year time period, under the majority opinion there is no predictability as to how long a commercial retailer will be held liable for indemnity. Because accrual of an indemnity claim against a commercial retailer does not occur until a judgment is entered against a commercial buyer or when a commercial buyer pays damages to a third party, a commercial retailer cannot predict on what date an action for indemnity will accrue against it.

Idaho, Utah and Georgia, find that such claims fall exclusively under the U.C.C. Courts in six states, Minnesota, California, New York, Nebraska, New Hampshire and Maine, hold indemnity claims may be raised independent of the U.C.C. Therefore, there exists authority from other jurisdictions to support both sides of this policy debate as to whether all contract-based claims, including those of indemnity, are bound by the U.C.C. I would hold that a decision finding contract-based indemnity claims are governed by the U.C.C. is correct because it creates a policy consistent with the purpose of the U.C.C. — one of predictability and uniformity.

Although the jurisdictions cited by the majority claim fairness requires that a commercial buyer who pays out-of-pocket damages to a third party has a remedy unrestricted by a statute of repose, I believe at some point the law must recognize commercial practices and concepts, including the concept of bargained-for risk. Commercial buyers do not purchase items with the notion they are receiving an implied lifetime guarantee. They know products may not last forever. However, there does exist an implied warrantability that lasts for four years after delivery, in order to create a balance between fairness and bargained-for risk. The U.C.C. has identified this four-year period, commencing at the time of delivery, as a fair period of time for a commercial buyer to expect guaranteed warrantability and a commercial retailer to expect to be held liable.

Section 2-725 was adopted to "[take] sales contracts out of the general laws limiting the time for commencing contractual actions and selects a four-year period as the most appropriate to modern business practice. This is within the normal commercial record keeping period." RCWA 62A.2-725 U.C.C. cmt. at 415 (Purposes). Section 2-725 provides "a time when [a merchant] ought to be secure in his reasonable expectation that the slate has been wiped clean of ancient obligations, and he ought not to be called on to resist a claim when 'evidence has been lost, memories have faded, and witnesses have disappeared.' " Paul J. Wilkinson, Comment, An Ind. Run Around the U.C.C.: The Use (or Abuse?) of Indemnity, 20 Pepp. L. Rev. 1407, 1412 (1993) (quoting Developments in the Law, Statutes of Limitations, 63 Harv. L. Rev. 1177, 1185 (1950)). These comments illustrate the U.C.C.'s goal to establish an across-the-board governing law for all commercial sales transactions that adequately addresses fairness and bargained-for risk. By allowing a common law remedy in a commercial sale relationship, the majority contradicts this goal. In order to remain consistent with the purpose of the U.C.C., I would hold that Central's action against McCormack is governed by article 2 and that section 2-725 applies.

I would also hold that Central's action, under article 2, is barred under section 2-725. In my view, section 2-725 is a statute of repose, not a statute of limitation. A statute of limitation bars plaintiffs from bringing an already accrued claim after a specified period of time; a statute of repose terminates a right of action after a specified time, even if the injury has not yet occurred. . . .

The language of U.C.C. §2-725 unambiguously creates a statute of repose. Because it is unambiguous, the meaning of the statute is derived from the words of the statute. State v. McDougal, 120 Wash. 2d 334, 350, 841 P.2d 1232 (1992); State v. Olson, 47 Wash. App. 514, 516, 735 P.2d 1362 (1987). The statute states a claim must be made within "four years after the cause of action has accrued." RCW 62A.2-725(1). According to the statute "[a] cause of action accrues when the breach occurs," and "[a] breach of warranty occurs when tender of delivery is made. . . ." RCW 62A.2-725(2). Therefore, all claims must be made no more than four years after delivery, whether or not the buyer is aware of the product's defect. Based on this clear language, I would hold that Central's contractual indemnity claim, based on the breach of an implied warranty, was barred when the action was filed in May 1992, since the coils were delivered more than four and a half years earlier — in August 1987.

Section 2-725 actually "poses few problems: it simply bars a buyer from bringing an action for breach of warranty more than four years after tender of delivery. This straight-forward rule forces buyers to sue when evidence is most readily available and allows sellers to continue with their businesses without fear of suit after a reasonable definite period." Debra L. Goetz et al., Project, Article Two Warranties in Commercial Transactions: An Update, 72 Cornell L. Rev. 1159, 1324-29 (1987).

I would find that Central's claim is governed by U.C.C. §2-725, a statute of repose, and was properly dismissed by the trial court. I would affirm the decision of the Court of Appeals.

CHAPTER 7 REVIEW QUESTIONS

When is a seller entitled to reclaim the goods?

Is a penalty clause for nonperformance enforceable?

When is a breaching buyer entitled to restitution?

Why is the measure of remedies different depending on whether the goods were accepted?

Can buyer be liable for the price if seller breached?

Can seller be liable if buyer has effectively rejected the goods?

Can *buyer* be liable if buyer has effectively rejected the goods?

What is the difference, in seller's remedies, between market price damages, resale damages, and lost profits damages?

When is a party liable for consequential damages?

How might buyer's damages differ for breach of warranty and for failure to deliver?

ASSESSMENT: MULTIPLE CHOICE QUESTIONS

1. Cold Feet Labs entered into a contract to purchase a popular genetic sequencing machine from Precision Devices. The machine was delivered on time and met all the contract specifications. The manager of Cold Feet Labs inspected the machine and found no problems, but refused to take delivery. The manager cited budgetary concerns. The market price for the machine had become lower than the contract price, so it would be cheaper to buy the machine elsewhere. How much is the liability of Cold Feet Labs to Precision Devices?
   a. Cold Feet Labs is liable for the contract price, because the seller tendered conforming goods in timely fashion.
   b. Cold Feet Labs is liable for the market price of the machine.
   c. Cold Feet Labs is not liable for anything, because Precision Devices still has the machine.
   d. Cold Feet Labs could be liable for the difference between the contract price and the market price.

2. Pursuant to contract, Gdansk Boats delivered a wooden sailing ship to Historic Cruises. The purchasing agent for Historic Cruises inspected the ship, and quickly noted that many of the fixtures were mahogany rather than the promised teak, that various repairs and adjustments would be required in some of the cabins, and that several sails were missing. Historic Cruises indicated they would take the ship but sue for breach of contract, listing the defects. Is Gdansk Boats liable to Historic Cruises?
   a. No. Historic Cruises accepted the goods and must pay the contract price.
   b. Yes. Historic Cruises is liable for the price, but has a counterclaim for damages for breach of warranty, which could be the difference between the value of the boat promised and the boat delivered, and possible consequential damages.
   c. Yes. Gdansk Boats did not deliver the boat promised, so Historic Cruises is not liable for the price unless all the shortcomings are cured.
   d. No. Gdansk Boats is not liable for defects of which Historic Cruises was aware.

3. Gdansk Boats delivered a defective boat to another customer, Tolerant Harbor. The buyer noted quite a list of defects in the boat, but took it and paid without complaint. After a year, however, Tolerant Harbor realized the defects substantially impaired the value of the boat and resulted in higher repair and service costs. Can Tolerant Harbor recover for breach of contract?
   a. No, because it accepted the boat with defects.
   b. No, because the statute of limitations has run.

    c. Yes, because the statute of limitations has not yet run.

    d. No, because it did not give timely notice of breach.

4. Pemulis Auto had a contract to sell a 2016 Fireworks Rambler to Suzie Sousa for $35,000. On the agreed day of delivery, Pemulis Auto notified Suzie Sousa that they would not be able to perform their obligations. Suzie Sousa shopped around, and found the market price for the car had risen to $40,000. After some thought, she decided to stick with her current automobile. Is Pemulis Auto liable to Suzie Sousa?

    a. Yes, for the $35,000 contract price.

    b. Yes, for the $5,000 difference between the contract and market price.

    c. No, because she did not purchase a substitute.

    d. No, because they gave timely notice of nondelivery.

5. Gdansk Boats sold a fishing boat to Olivier Robeson, an actor. Not long afterwards, the boat's defective engine left Robeson floating for several hours. As a result, he missed a call offering a juicy part, which was quickly offered to a rival. Is Gdansk Boats liable for damages for Robeson's lost role?

    a. Yes, the damages were caused by their breach and Gdansk Boats knew that the boat needed an engine to travel.

    b. No, a breach of sales contract results in damages only for a lost bargain or diminished value.

    c. No, because the damages were not caused by a requirement known to the seller.

    d. Yes, because the breach was a but-for cause of the lost role.

ANSWERS

1. *D* is the best answer. Cold Feet Labs has breached the contract. But Cold Feet Labs is not liable for the price of the machine. The buyer becomes liable for the price under §2-709 if the buyer accepts the goods, but Cold Feet Labs did not accept the goods. The buyer can be liable for the price if the goods cannot reasonably be resold, §2-709(1)(b), but the machine is popular, not a unique product for the buyer. The buyer is also liable for the price of goods destroyed while the risk of loss is on the buyer, §2-709(1)(a), but that likewise does not apply here. Rather, Cold Feet is liable for nonacceptance under §2-708, which could be market differential damages under §2-708(1) or lost profits under §2-708(2). Contrary to *C*, Precision Devices is entitled to damages even though it still has the machine, because it lost the benefit of the bargain.

2. *B* is the best answer. If the buyer accepts the goods, the buyer is liable for the price under §2-709, even if the goods do not conform to the contract.

But such a buyer may have a claim for breach of warranty under §2-714, provided the buyer gives notice under §2-607(3)(a), which the buyer did here.

3. *D* is the best answer. A buyer who accepts the goods may still recover for breach of warranty, but only if the buyer gives notice of breach to the seller within a reasonable time. §2-607(3)(a). Tolerant Harbor knew of the breaches for a year before giving notice, which would not be a reasonable time (absent unusual circumstances). So, contrary to *C*, the statute of limitations is not the key limit on time in such sales cases. Rather, buyers may lose their right to sue much more quickly if they fail to give timely notice of breach.

4. *B* is the best answer. Where a seller fails to deliver, a buyer may recover for the loss of the benefit of the bargain. If the buyer purchases the goods elsewhere, the buyer may seek damages calculated by the cover price under §2-712. But the buyer is not required to cover, and may also seek damages for loss of the bargain under §2-713, measured by the difference between the contract price and the market price. Notice of nondelivery is not required, as opposed to where the buyer has accepted the goods and must give notice of any breach. The seller is the one who did not deliver so seller would not need notice.

5. *C* is the best answer. A buyer may recover consequential damages (contrary to *B*), including "any loss resulting from general or particular requirements and needs of which the seller at the time of contracting had reason to know and which could not reasonably be prevented by cover or otherwise." §2-715. The damages here do not fall within that description. Where seller delivers a machine that seller knows buyer needs to operate a factory, seller could be liable if the defective machine shuts down the factory. But the seller of a boat would not reasonably expect that failure of an engine could result in missing a telephone call that in turn would result in loss of an acting role. Mere but-for causation is insufficient, contrary to *A* and *D*.

DOCUMENTS

OF TITLE

If you open up your pantry, or closet, or look around the things on your desk you'll discover item after item that came there from far away — not just from other states but even from the other side of the globe: apples from New Zealand, shirts from Malaysia, numerous gadgets from China. How did they all get from there to here? Some might have been mailed or specially delivered by hand, but almost all were boxed up, put in shipping containers, and carried vast distances by plane or cargo ship or truck. The paperwork for these transactions consists of invoices and identification tags, but the primary item is a "document of title," usually a "bill of lading," which describes the goods and the details of carriage, particularly to whom they will be delivered and what conditions exist before that delivery will occur. There are international agreements about bills of lading, and a federal statute on point, and, most importantly for our purposes, Article 7 of the Uniform Commercial Code entitled "Documents of Title." Millions of these transactions take place each year and they usually go off without complications. But when the paperwork gets lost, or the goods are destroyed, or the buyer has committed fraud and the seller wants the transaction halted prior to delivery, the lawyer's phone will ring with legal questions. This chapter should give you some help with that call.

Article 7 of the Code deals with these documents of title (defined in
§1-201(b)(16)) — items (whether tangible paper or electronic records)
issued for the purpose of actually representing title to goods. The two primary types of documents of title are bills of lading (§1-201(b)(6)) and warehouse receipts (§1-201(b)(42)).[1] Article 7 was revised in 2003,[2] primarily to
allow the creation of electronic forms of documents of title, and §§7-106 and
7-105 (in that reverse order) deal with such creatures.[3]

The creation of paper representing the right of ownership of the goods
became inevitable as soon as merchants wanted to borrow money and pledge
goods that they owned as collateral. If the goods were large enough to store
in a warehouse, the money lender was normally unwilling to take physical
possession of the goods. The money lender was also normally unwilling to
give the borrower possession of the collateral for fear the goods would be
sold to someone else or taken by the buyer's other creditors. The solution
to the problem was to store the goods with a bailee and have the bailee
issue a paper stating that the goods belonged to the owner of the paper. In
this fashion, the paper, representing the obligation of the bailee to deliver
the goods to the holder, could be freely transferred, discounted, and redis-
counted without the necessity of moving the goods into the physical control
of each new owner. Any holder of the paper could surrender it and require
the bailee (*issuer*) to turn over the goods. Read §7-403 carefully. Note that
under subsection (c) the person claiming the goods *must* (except in the
§7-503 situation discussed later) surrender the negotiable document of title
for cancellation in order to receive the goods. If the document has been
lost, the holder can get the goods only by procuring a court order directing the bailee to turn over the goods. Read §7-601. Documents of title are
negotiable or nonnegotiable depending on whether they contain order or
bearer language (§7-104). Since under §7-403(c) the bailee can demand
only the surrender of negotiable paper, only negotiable documents of title
truly represent absolute ownership of the goods. Nonnegotiable paper simply evidences the contract between the bailor and the bailee, which is to
do whatever the contract says. Nonnegotiable documents normally state
exactly to whom the bailee will deliver the goods and under what conditions.
Therefore, for reasons of safety, lenders prefer to loan money against negotiable documents. With nonnegotiable documents, lenders run the risk that
there has already been a delivery of the goods to someone else.

1. For treatises on point, see W. Towle, Warehousing Law (2d ed. 2001), and R. Henson,
Documents of Title Under the Uniform Commercial Code (2d ed. 1990).
2. Citations in this chapter referencing Article 7 refer to the 2003 version, which has
been adopted by all fifty states and the District of Columbia.
3. For an article on point, see Susan Beecher, Can the Electronic Bill of Lading Go
Paperless?, 40 Intl. Law. 627 (2006).

I. *WAREHOUSE RECEIPTS*

A. *Form*

The front of a *negotiable* warehouse receipt states the name of the warehouse that is issuing the receipt and states in large type that:

This is to certify that we have received in storage for the account of _____ in apparent order, except as noted hereon (contents, condition, and quality being unknown), the following described property, subject to all of the terms and conditions on the front or back of this contract, such property to be delivered to _____ or order, upon payment of all storage, handling, and other charges and the surrender of this Warehouse receipt properly indorsed.

Following this statement usually there are the following:

(1) a space for listing the goods stored,
(2) a statement of the warehouse company's intention to claim a lien against the goods until the storage charges are paid,
(3) a statement as to the amount of the storage charge, and
(4) the official signature of the warehouse company.

The back of the warehouse receipt contains a space in which the agent of the warehouse can note *partial* deliveries to the holder of the document (later holders can claim only the amount of goods the document shows were not delivered to prior holders). The back also has the *standard contract terms* in small print (these standard terms were adopted by a 1926 conference of experts and approved by the Department of Commerce); the terms cover the fact that the storage is on a month-to-month basis and spell out in detail the warehouse company's position as to insurance, limitation of liability, right to move the goods, etc.

A nonnegotiable warehouse receipt looks substantially the same except:

(1) It is not made deliverable to anyone. The warehouse engages to deliver the goods as per instructions received from the person storing the goods (the bailor). *Order* language is not used.
(2) There is no space on the back for notation of partial deliveries. This is because surrender of the document is not required to take out all or part of the goods. Section 7-403(c) applies only to *negotiable* documents.

Negotiable warehouse receipts normally have the word *NEGOTIABLE* stamped across their face in large letters (and the documents tend to have fancy and ornate borders, designed to make counterfeiting more difficult). Nonnegotiable documents have *NONNEGOTIABLE* stamped on the front.

Glance through §7-202.

As can be seen from the above, the warehouse receipt plays three roles: it is (1) a *receipt* for the goods, (2) a *contract* for storage, and (3) if negotiable, a *physical embodiment* of the concept of *title* to the goods.

B.   Basic Bailment Law

All document-of-title situations start with the bailment of the goods and the issuance of a receipt by the bailee. Bailment law is relevant to fill in the gaps in Article 7 and the federal statutes. The most important bailment concept needed to supplement the Code is that the bailee is required to make proper delivery of the goods to the bailor when the bailment ends or is to be responsible for nondelivery. Section 7-403(a) gives very few excuses for nondelivery. An *unauthorized* delivery of the goods by a bailee is conversion. Restatement (Second) of Torts §234; cf. §7-601(b). Read §7-404. A "bailee is absolutely liable for misdelivering cargo, unless his mistake as to the person entitled to receive the goods was induced by the bailor." David Crystal, Inc. v. Cunard Steam-Ship Co., Ltd., 339 F.2d 295, 298 (2d Cir. 1964); Met-Al, Inc. v. Hansen Storage Co., 828 F. Supp. 1369 (E.D. Wis. 1993) ("Equitable defenses to allegations of misdelivery are disfavored."); Singer Co. v. Stott & Davis Motor Express, Inc., 79 A.D.2d 227, 463 N.Y.S.2d 508 (App. Div. 1981) ("Once a plaintiff establishes delivery of goods and the failure of the bailee to return them on demand, a prima facie case of negligence is made and the burden of coming forward with evidence tending to show due cause shifts to the bailee. . . ."); People v. Wallace, 2011 WL 1662860 (N.Y. App. Div. 2011) ("A person need not knowingly or intentionally act wrongfully for a conversion to occur"). These principles are best illustrated by one of the cases rising out of the famous Salad Oil scandal.

Procter & Gamble Distributing Co. v. Lawrence American Field Warehouse Corp.

Court of Appeals of New York, 1965
16 N.Y.2d 344, 213 N.E.2d 897, 266 N.Y.S.2d 765 21 A.L.R.3d 1320

Van Voorhis, J.

This is an action against a warehouse corporation based upon the non-delivery of the merchandise for which it issued its warehouse receipts. The theory of action is conversion. Plaintiff (hereafter called P & G) asserts that in the absence of any explanation of the disappearance of these goods, the defendant (hereafter called Field) is liable for the market value of this merchandise at the times when it was delivered to the warehouse. Plaintiff is correct in these contentions, we have concluded, and is entitled to summary judgment in this amount. We agree with the Appellate Division that no triable issue is presented concerning the liability of defendant, but consider that the Appellate Division erred in directing an assessment of damages and in not awarding to plaintiff the undisputed market value of the merchandise delivered to defendant at the time of its delivery, which was as high as at any subsequent time or times prior to notification to plaintiff of its disappearance. The basic issue is simple, but it has been encrusted with a complex of fact and legal argument which makes it necessary to discuss the case in more detail.

Allied Crude Vegetable Oil Refining Corp. (hereinafter called Allied) is not a party to this action, but this cause of action against defendant arose through a course of dealings between plaintiff and Allied, which traded in vegetable oils manufactured by various producers including plaintiff. Originally plaintiff sold such merchandise outright on sight draft with bill of lading attached. In the early Fall of 1962, however, in order more fully to utilize its working capital, Allied persuaded plaintiff to engage in a practice known as field warehousing. Allied had leased oil storage tanks at Bayonne, New Jersey, formerly owned by the Tidewater Associated Oil Company. These were sublet to Field, a wholly owned subsidiary of American Express Company (hereafter called Amexco), which thereupon operated as an independent warehouse company. When Allied purchased vegetable oils from plaintiff, and other producers, as it did f.o.b. seller's plant or warehouse, Bayonne, New Jersey, the oil would be shipped to Bayonne to the seller's order, and stored for the seller's account in Field's warehouses. Down payments were made, described in the contract as "Margin Requirements on Consigned Shipments," amounting to about 20% of the purchase price, at the time of receipt of the oil at Field's warehouse, and the balance by sight draft with bill of lading attached, or cash in advance of shipment to buyer, as Allied disposed of the oil.

In accordance with this procedure, plaintiff shipped 9,206,740 pounds of fully refined soybean oil under bills of lading to plaintiff itself as consignee at Bayonne, New Jersey, which was delivered for storage and safe keeping to Field at said warehouse for plaintiff's account. Field, the defendant, issued five warehouse receipts for this oil dated March 22, April 1 and April 9, 1963. Each warehouse receipt recited the number of the bill of lading for the tank car in which it had been contained, amounting in total to 151 tank carloads. Not only was the presence of this oil in defendant's tanks attested by these nonnegotiable receipts issued in plaintiff's name, but also by a series of month-end statements, issued by defendant indicating that the oil was in the warehouse. Both the warehouse receipts and these month-end statements, based on defendant's books, are evidence that the oil was received by defendant at its tank warehouse in Bayonne, New Jersey. In the absence of any evidentiary facts showing that defendant did not receive the oil in the suit, its warehouse receipts, month-end statements and books of account are conclusive against defendant on this point. Mere suspicion that the oil was stolen before reaching defendant's tanks is not sufficient to overcome this documentary evidence. . . . The usual measure of damage, in event of non-delivery of goods by a bailee, is the market value on the date of the conversion . . . not the date when the bailor learns of the loss or presents his warehouse receipt and demands his merchandise. Where, as here, the date of the conversion has not been identified, the Appellate Division has held that the value should be fixed as of the date when the bailor received notice of the loss. This, we think, was error. The circumstances regarding the loss of bailed property are more likely to be known by the bailee than by the bailor, and, where the time and manner of the loss is unknown, it ought not lie in the power of the bailee to choose the date for determining market value by electing when to notify the bailor that the goods have disappeared and cannot be accounted for. The rule that the loss is to be measured as of the time of the conversion, when the conversion date is known, should not be reshaped to designate the date when the bailor is notified of the conversion if the conversion date is unknown. That would place the bailee in a better legal position by pleading ignorance of the circumstances of the loss than if he knew or revealed the circumstances. . . .

[I]t follows that the bailor should be awarded damages measured by the highest value of the property between the date when the bailment commenced and the date when the bailor has received notice that the property has been lost. . . .

On its appeal defendant (Field) contends that there is a triable issue respecting whether it exercised reasonable care as bailee of this oil. Defendant points to section 7-204 of the Uniform Commercial Code, in effect in New Jersey at the time, providing that a warehouseman is liable for damages for loss or injury to the goods "caused by his failure to exercise such care in regard to them as a reasonably careful man would exercise under like circumstances but unless otherwise agreed he is not liable for damages which could not have been avoided by the exercise of such care." Section 7-403 of the same statute provides that the bailee must deliver the goods to a person under the document unless and to the extent that the bailee established "damage to or delay, loss or destruction of the goods for which the bailee is not liable."

These sections of the Uniform Commercial Code appear not to have altered for present purposes the prior law . . . that a warehouseman shall not be liable for loss or injury to the goods which could not have been avoided by the exercise of reasonable care, and section 8 (General Business Law, former §95), like section 7-403 of the Uniform Commercial Code, stated that a warehouseman is liable for nondelivery of bailed goods "in the absence of some lawful excuse provided by this article." Citing these sections, the Appellate Division correctly stated . . . that a warehouseman "has the burden of explanation for any loss or disappearance of the property bailed. . . . It is not enough to assert that care was taken, describing the practices used, when the disappearance of the oil remains wholly unexplained." . . . In the opinion by the present Chief Judge the rule applicable here was stated in the form of a quotation from Claflin v. Meyer (75 N.Y. 260, 264):

> If he [the bailor] proves the demand upon the warehouseman and his refusal to deliver, these facts unexplained are treated by the courts as prima facie evidence of negligence; but if, either in the course of his proof or that of the defendant, it appears that the goods have been lost by theft, the evidence must show that the loss arose from the negligence of the warehouseman. . . .

The Appellate Division well said that it is self-contradictory for a warehouseman simultaneously to assert due care and total lack of knowledge of what happened, and that it would establish an unwise rule to place a bailee in better position to be excused if he knew less about the disappearance of the goods than if he knew more. That is the underlying reason for the time-honored law of New York and New Jersey requiring a warehouseman to make an explanation of injury or loss in the case of bailed merchandise, which has been continued and not abolished by the Uniform Commercial Code.

The other points raised on the appeal by defendant Field merit but passing mention. One is that plaintiff should be obliged to accept a proportionate share of the conglomerate found on hand in the tanks of these subsidiaries of Amexco. This consisted mostly of acid soap stock, fish oil and water. These mixed fluids were not the edible fully refined vegetable oil delivered to Field by plaintiff. An argument is made that the warehouse receipts showed plaintiff's refined vegetable oil to be fungible, and granted permission to mix it with similar oil owned by other depositors. From that it is said that a warehouseman need do no more than take the word of other customers concerning the nature of the fluids which are being placed in the tanks of the warehouseman, and that if it be soap acid or fish oil then that is plaintiff's misfortune. It is a sufficient answer to that contention that plaintiff is not required to acquit the warehouse in whole or in part by taking in return a commodity or blend of commodities of a different nature from that which was deposited. . . .

No one has ever discovered exactly what happened to the missing salad oil (which was the collateral for millions of dollars worth of loans). N. Miller, The Great Salad Oil Swindle (1965).

As this case indicates, a warehouse company that issues a warehouse receipt is liable to good faith holders even if the warehouse never received the goods. Read §7-203. It is also liable if the goods are incorrectly described. A warehouse is required to keep goods separate unless they are fungible. See §7-207. If the goods are fungible, a "buyer in the ordinary course of business" can purchase the goods and get good title even though there is an outstanding negotiable warehouse receipt (§7-205).

A bailee's duty of care is that which "a reasonably careful person would exercise under similar circumstances." See, e.g., Global Strategies, Inc. v. Harbor Freight Transport Corp., 2015 WL 6737024 (D.N.J. 2015) (holding that freight storage company would be liable for its negligent failure to release, relocate, or otherwise safeguard the goods as storm approached). Read §7-204 and the following case.

Admiralty Island Fisheries, Inc. v. Millard Refrigerated Services, Inc.

United States District Court, District of Nebraska, 2007
2007 WL 4051649

LAURIE SMITH CAMP, District Judge.

This matter is before the Court on cross-motions for partial summary judgment. The Plaintiff National Fire Insurance of Hartford as subrogee of Suram Trading Corporation filed a motion for partial summary judgment (Filing No. 67 reviving Filing No. 35), in which Admiralty Island Fisheries has joined. (Filing No. 68). The Defendant, Millard Refrigerated Services, Inc. ("Millard") has filed a motion for partial summary judgment against those Plaintiffs (Filing No. 70 and 72), and Plaintiffs Certain Underwriters at Lloyd's of London as subrogee of Icicle Seafoods, Inc., and Hartford Casualty Insurance Company, as subrogee of Global Fishing, Inc. (Filing Nos. 69 and 71) (hereafter the subrogees and subrogors will be referred to collectively as the "Plaintffs"). The cross-motions ask the Court to determine the legal effect of relevant limitation of liability clauses.

FACTUAL BACKGROUND

Millard operates cold storage warehouses throughout the country. Suram, Icicle, Global, and Admiralty have all stored seafood products in a Millard warehouse. It is undisputed that, as each truckload of seafood was delivered by the Plaintiffs to Millard warehouse, Millard issued a warehouse receipt. The warehouse receipts contain the parties' agreement regarding the storage of the seafood product.

Sometime in March 2006, Millard discovered that several pounds of seafood that were owned by the various Plaintiffs were missing. Millard conducted an internal investigation into the loss and determined that at least some of the seafood had been stolen by some of its employees. Millard ultimately terminated five of its employees for theft of seafood that was supposed be stored in the warehouse. The five employees admitted to stealing only small quantities of the seafood, which was a sufficient basis for terminating their employment. National Fire contends that Millard's former employees stole more than 94,000 pounds of seafood with a fair market value of $455,000. Millard contends that its liability for the loss is limited to 50 cents per pound, or $47,000. The issue presented on these cross-motions for partial summary judgment is whether the limitation of liability clause is enforceable, assuming that the former employees were responsible for the theft.

ANALYSIS

Consistent with the UCC, warehouse receipts may contain a limitation of liability provision that limits the warehouse operator's liability for the stored products in the case of loss or damage. Millard's warehouse receipts include a limitation of liability clause. The Plaintiffs seek a declaration from the Court that the limitation of liability clause contained on the back of the warehouse receipt is of no effect if the Plaintiffs succeed in demonstrating that Millard employees stole the seafood. The Defendant, on the other hand, asks the Court to conclude as a matter of law that the parties' contract permits Millard to limit its liability for the loss of the seafood to 50 cents per pound, regardless of whether the disappearance of the seafood is attributable to theft by the Millard employees.

THE WAREHOUSE RECEIPT

The front of the warehouse receipts in question contain the following provision, in all capital lettering:

> Limitation of liability: Unless the depositor declares a valuation higher than $.50 per pound or $12.00 per cubic foot for stored goods and such declared higher value is agreed to in writing by the warehouseman, the warehouseman's liability for loss or damage thereto shall be expressly limited as specifically set forth in Section 10(e) of the standard contract terms on the reverse side hereof.

The front of the warehouse receipt also provides:

> The goods listed hereon in apparent good order [sic], except as noted hereon (contents, condition and quality unknown) subject to all terms and conditions herein and on the reverse hereof. Such property to be delivered to the Depositor upon the payment of all storage, handling and other charges.

On the back of the receipt is Section 10(e), copied below in the same manner that it appears in the receipt, states:

> IN THE EVENT OF LOSS, DAMAGE OR DESTRUCTION TO STORED GOODS FOR WHICH COMPANY IS LEGALLY LIABLE, STORER DECLARES THAT COMPANY'S LIABILITY FOR DAMAGES SHALL BE LIMITED TO THE LESSER OF THE FOLLOWING AMOUNTS: (1) THE ACTUAL COST TO DEPOSITOR OF REPLACING OR REPRODUCING THE DAMAGED GOOD TOGETHER WITH TRANSPORTATION COSTS TO THE WAREHOUSE, (2) THE FAIR MARKET VALUE OF THE GOODS ON THE DATE DEPOSITOR IS NOTIFIED OF LOSS, DAMAGE OR DESTRUCTION, (3) 50 TIMES THE MONTHLY STORAGE CHARGE APPLICABLE TO SUCH LOST, DAMAGED, OR DESTROYED GOODS OR (4) THE GREATER OF (I) $.50 PER POUND NET WEIGHT OF THE GOODS, EXCLUSIVE OF TARE, OR (II) $12.00 PER CUBIC FOOT, PROVIDED, HOWEVER, THAT WITHIN A REASONABLE TIME AFTER RECEIPT OF THIS WAREHOUSE RECEIPT, DEPOSITOR MAY, UPON WRITTEN REQUEST, INCREASE WAREHOUSEMAN'S LIABILITY ON PART OR ALL OF THE GOODS STORED UNDER THE WAREHOUSE RECEIPT, IN WHICH CASE AN INCREASED CHARGE WILL BE MADE BASED UPON SUCH INCREASED VALUATION; FURTHER PROVIDED THAT NO SUCH REQUEST SHALL BE VALID UNLESS MADE BEFORE LOSS, DAMAGE OR DESTRUCTION TO ANY PORTION OF THE GOODS STORED UNDER THIS WAREHOUSE RECEIPT HAS OCCURRED.

Section 10(f) states:

> The limitation of liability referred to in paragraph (e) above shall be Depositor's exclusive remedy against Warehouseman for any claim or cause of action whatsoever relating to loss, damage and/or destruction of the stored goods and shall apply to all claims including inventory shortage and mysterious disappearance claims unless Depositor proves by affirmative evidence that Warehouseman converted the good to its own use. Depositor waives any right to rely upon any presumption of conversion imposed by law. In no event shall Depositor be entitled to incidental, special, punitive or consequential damages.

(See e.g., Filing No. 69, Ex. 5).

APPLICABLE PROVISIONS OF THE UNIFORM COMMERCIAL CODE

The Court finds that Uniform Commercial Code §7-204 applies to the facts presented. Section 7-204, captioned *Duty of Care; Contractual Limitation of Warehouse's Liability,* states:

> (a) A warehouse is liable for damages for loss of or injury to the goods caused by its failure to exercise care with regard to the goods that a reasonably careful person would exercise under similar circumstances. Unless otherwise agreed, the warehouse is not liable for damages that could not have been avoided by the exercise of that care.
>
> (b) Damages may be limited by a term in the warehouse receipt or storage agreement limiting the amount of liability in case of loss or damage beyond which the warehouse is not liable. *Such a limitation is not effective with respect to the warehouse's liability for conversion to its own use.* On request of the bailor in a record at the time of signing the storage agreement or within a reasonable time after receipt of the warehouse receipt, the warehouse's liability may be increased on part or all of the goods covered by the storage agreement or the warehouse receipt. In this event, increased rates may be charged based on an increased valuation of the goods.

PLAINTIFFS' MOTION FOR PARTIAL SUMMARY JUDGMENT

Because a warehouse operator would not be liable at all absent a failure of due care, a failure of due care by Millard must be established before the enforcement of the limitation of liability clause even becomes an issue. The Plaintiffs ask the Court to assume that they can prove their seafood disappeared due to employee theft. The Court might assume, for purposes of this motion, that Millard was negligent in hiring the former employees without checking their backgrounds for criminal history or in failing to maintain security over the seafood after it was deposited at the warehouse. These assumptions relate to the threshold issue of Millard's lack of due care. For purposes of this motion only, the Court will assume that Millard was negligent in failing to prevent the former employees' theft of the Plaintiffs' property.

Under Nebraska law, conversion is "any unauthorized or wrongful act of dominion exerted over another's personal property which deprives the owner of his property permanently or for an indefinite period of time." Roth v. Farmers Mutual Insurance Company of Nebraska, 371 N.W.2d 289, 291 (Neb. 1985). Under this definition, there is no dispute that the former Millard employees committed an intentional conversion of the Plaintiffs' property. Assuming Millard's liability arising out ordinary negligence under Section 7-204(a), the limitation of liability provision applies according to Section 7-204(b), unless the warehouse operator's liability arises out of a conversion "for its own use." The Court agrees with the observation of the commentators that "conversion for it[s] own use" as used in Section 7-204(a) must mean something more and different than simple conversion. See Comment Note No. 4, UCC §7-204 (2005) (explaining that "[c]onversion to its own use" is narrower than the idea of conversion generally" and disapproving "[c]ases such as Lipman v. Peterson, 575 P.2d 19 (Kan. 1978) holding to the contrary. . . .")

The limitation of liability provision applies in the presence of ordinary negligence unless there is proof that the former employees' theft, the conversion, was for the purpose of advancing Millard's interests. Enforcement of a limitation of liability clause is not a complete defense to liability, but it must be raised as would an affirmative defense because it benefits the defendant. For that reason, the Court concludes that the burden of proof should be on the warehouse operator to demonstrate that the conversion of the bailor's property was not for its own use. In reaching this legal conclusion, the Court acknowledges its rejection of Millard's attempt to place the burden on the Plaintiffs as stated in the warehouse receipts' paragraph 10(f). To place the burden of proof on the Plaintiffs, as bailors, would ignore the policy arguments that support the enforcement of limitation of liability provisions in commercial contracts.[4]

Millard has come forward with evidence that the conversion was not for its own use. Millard's general manager, Michael McTier, conducted an investigation into the Plaintiffs' losses. As a result of the investigation, five employees were fired for theft. McTier believes, based on the investigation, that all losses were caused by the former employees' theft. (Filing No. 79, McTier Dep. 159). At least one of the former employees has stated that the seafood was sold to a third party. McTier has testified that Millard did not benefit in any way from the theft.

The Plaintiffs have not come forward with any evidence to create a genuine issue of material fact regarding whether the conversion — the theft — was for Millard's own use. Plaintiffs argue that the conversion was

---

4. According to at least one commentator, there are good reasons to place the burden of proof on the warehouse operator. First, the warehouse operator is in the best position to explain the loss because the operator has taken control of the goods and has determined the manner in which they are stored. Second, placing the burden on the warehouse operator to show that it acted with due care will encourage warehouse operators to act with care and caution in the handling and storage of bailed goods and to maintain adequate tracking systems that will withstand judicial scrutiny. Third, placing the burden on operators will also have a beneficial effect on the industry because those warehouses that are unable to establish that their storage practices are reasonable will incur increased operating costs, eventually forcing poorly run facilities out of business. Last, placing the burden on the warehouses will give the operators incentive to procure insurance on all bailed goods entrusted to them which the operators can procure, presumably at a lower cost than would be incurred if each bailor had to procure its own insurance. "A Warehouse's Burden of Proof," Ralph Anzivino, UCC Law Journal (Spring 2004).

for Millard's own purposes because it 1) was committed within the authorized space and time of the employees' employment, 2) was committed while they were performing duties for which they were hired, and 3) "was actuated, at least in part, by a purpose to serve the master [Millard]." (Filing No. 82, p. 12). The crux of Plaintiffs' argument is that Millard's interests were furthered by the conversion because Millard was paying the former employees to work while they were also stealing; the former employees used Millard's equipment, including pallets, forklifts, and trucks, to accomplish the theft; and the former employees conducted the theft during hours when they were "also" working. I do not agree that these facts are evidence that the conversion was to Millard's own use. The former employees' abuse of their employment position does not automatically transform their conversion to a conversion for Millard's own use. Absent undisputed facts that the conversion was for Millard's own use, the Court concludes that the Plaintiff's motion for partial summary judgment is denied.

MILLARD'S MOTION FOR PARTIAL SUMMARY JUDGMENT

Millard also moves for partial summary judgment asking the Court to confirm the enforceability of the limitation of liability clauses in its warehouse receipts. Because there are genuine issues related to the degree of Millard's negligence, Millard's motion will be denied. The Court, assuming ordinary negligence on the part of Millard, has found that the Plaintiffs have failed to come forward with evidence to create a genuine issue regarding whether the former employees stole the seafood to further Millard's own interests. There is no evidence that the conversion was to Millard's own use. It would seem to follow that the limitation of liability clause is enforceable to limit the damages that Millard may owe to the Plaintiffs.

This case does not present a relationship involving a monopoly or parties of unequal bargaining power that might make the contract unenforceable. Where ordinary commercial relationships exist, the Eighth Circuit Court has upheld "the strong public policies of recognizing parties' liberty to contract and enforcing contracts as written." Sander v. Alexander Richardson Investments, 334 F.3d 712, 719 (8th Cir. 2003). The Plaintiffs had an opportunity to negotiate for a higher price per pound to be paid under the limitation of liability clause in the event of loss, but Plaintiffs did not. As a result, they were not obligated to pay the higher storage costs that likely would have come with a limitation of liability clause that was more advantageous to them. Rather, the parties agreed that the risk of loss greater than 50 cents per pound would be borne by the Plaintiffs.

However, in opposition to Millard's motion, the Plaintiffs argue that the limitation of liability clause should not be enforced as against public policy. The Plaintiffs contend that it will show at trial that Millard acted with gross negligence in failing to prevent the theft. If the Plaintiffs are able to demonstrate at trial that the failure of due care on the part of Millard constitutes gross negligence, not just ordinary negligence, then enforcement of the limitation of liability clause may be contrary to public policy. See New Light Company, Inc. v. Wells Fargo Alarm Services, 525 N.W.2d 25, (Neb. 1994) (holding that exculpatory clause in parties' agreement was void as against public policy to the extent that it purported to relieve fire alarm company from liability for its own gross negligence or willful and wanton misconduct). "Whether a particular exculpatory clause in a contractual agreement violates public policy depends upon the facts and circumstances of the agreement and the parties involved." Id. (noting that the greater the risk to human life and property, the stronger the argument in favor of voiding attempts by a party to insulate itself from damages caused by that party's gross negligence or willful and wanton misconduct.) "Gross negligence" has been defined as:

> [G]reat and excessive negligence; that is, negligence in a very high degree. It indicates the absence of slight care in the performance of a duty. . . . Willful and wanton misconduct exists where a defendant had actual knowledge that because of its actions, a danger existed to the plaintiff and the defendant intentionally failed to act to prevent a harm that was reasonably likely to result.

Id. at 30. Both the Plaintiffs and Millard have offered evidence relative to the degree of care exercised by Millard in connection with the seafood. There is some evidence that Millard knew of the thefts or should have known of them several months before Millard did anything about it. Because there are genuine issues of fact regarding the reasonableness of the security steps Millard took and did not take, whether Millard's conduct rises to the level of gross negligence is an issue for the jury. Accordingly, Millard's motion for partial summary judgment will also be denied.

IT IS ORDERED:

1. The Plaintiffs' Motions for Partial Summary Judgment . . . are denied; and

2. The Defendant's Motions for Partial Summary Judgment as to the Plaintiffs . . . are denied.

QUESTIONS

1. Would the court have reached the same result if the limitation was buried in the fine print on the receipt? See Keefe v. Bekins Van & Storage Co., 540 P.2d 1132 (Colo. App. 1975) (limitation effective even though not called to customer's attention); Sanfisket Inc. v. Atlantic Cold Storage Corp., 347 So. 2d 647 (Fla. Dist. Ct. App. 1977) (inconspicuous limitation held

effective); Jasphy v. Osinsky, 834 A.2d 426 (N.J. Super. 2003) (limitation of liability to one dollar held unconscionable).

2. Could the bailee depend on a clause in the receipt that completely disclaimed liability for its own negligence? See §1-302; and the *XL Specialty Insurance* case below; Blue Valley Co-op. v. National Farmers Organization, 600 N.W.2d 786 (Neb. 1999) (disclaimer in crop storage); Gonzalez v. A-1 Self Storage, Inc., 795 A.2d 885 (N.J. Super. 2000) (disclaimer in consumer goods storage).

XL Specialty Insurance Co., as Subrogee of Chowaiki & Co., Fine Art Ltd. v. Christie's Fine Art Storage Services, Inc.

Supreme Court of New York, Appellate Division, First Department, 2016
137 A.D.3d 563

TOM, J.P., SWEENY, ANDRIAS, GISCHE, JJ.
Opinion
Order, Supreme Court, New York County (Saliann Scarpulla, J.), entered September 24, 2014, which, to the extent appealed from, granted defendant's motion to dismiss the complaint, unanimously reversed, on the law, without costs, and the motion denied.

Plaintiff is the insurer for Chowaiki & Co. Fine Art Ltd., a private fine art gallery. In February 2011, Chowaiki entered into a one-year managed storage agreement with defendant, Christie's Fine Art Storage Services, Inc., wherein defendant was to provide secure storage for certain of Chowaiki's fine art works at its facility in the Red Hook section of Brooklyn.

Pursuant to the terms of the agreement, Chowaiki had the option to either (a) have defendant "accept liability for physical loss of, or damage to, the Goods," or to (b) "sign a loss/damage waiver," under which Chowaiki accepted that defendant "shall not be liable for any physical loss of, or damage to, the Goods." In the event Chowaiki opted to sign the waiver, it was required to "effect and maintain adequate insurance in respect of the Goods deposited." The agreement further provided for an additional limitation of liability, stating that "even if," despite the aforementioned language, defendant was found "liable for any loss of, or damage to, the Goods," liability was not to exceed the lower of $100,000 or the market value of the goods.

Chowaiki elected to sign the waiver, which provided that Chowaiki was responsible for obtaining an "against All Risks of loss or physical damage" insurance policy covering the goods deposited with defendant. This insurance was provided by plaintiff. The waiver also absolved defendant of all responsibility for loss or damage to Chowaiki's goods, and required Chowaiki to notify its insurer of the waiver and "arrange for them to waive any rights of subrogation" against defendant with respect to any loss or damage to Chowaiki's goods while in defendant's custody.

The agreement and waiver were renewed for a second year in February 2012. In October 2012, "Superstorm Sandy" struck the New York City metropolitan area, causing major damage throughout the region.

Prior to Sandy striking, defendant notified Chowaiki via email that "extra precautions" were being taken with respect to Chowaiki's goods, specifically, that "all property on the first floor" of the building where Chowaiki's artwork was stored would be "checked to ensure all items are raised off the floor," or, if necessary, the goods would be removed to empty rooms on the upper floors of defendant's storage facility. During a prior storm (Hurricane Irene), defendant's facility flooded; however, defendant had taken measures at that time to protect Chowaiki's goods from damage. This time, however, when the facility flooded, Chowaiki's goods were damaged, apparently because the goods were left on the first floor. Plaintiff insurer reimbursed Chowaiki for its losses and commenced this action as Chowaiki's subrogee, as the policy between plaintiff and Chowaiki did not waive plaintiff's right to subrogation against defendant. Plaintiff's complaint asserted causes of action for gross negligence, breach of bailment, negligence, breach of contract, negligent misrepresentation and fraudulent misrepresentation. In lieu of an answer, defendant moved to dismiss pursuant to CPLR 3016(b), 3211(a)(1), (3), and (7), asserting four grounds for dismissal: (a) that the waiver signed by Chowaiki contained both a waiver of subrogation clause and a limitation of liability, both of which barred plaintiff's claims; (b) that even if its waiver of liability was deemed to be invalid, the agreement nonetheless limited plaintiff's damages to $100,000; (c) that plaintiff's breach of bailment claim must fail because the agreement created a lessor/lessee relationship, not bailor/bailee; and (d) that Sandy was an Act of God, which, as a matter of law, excused defendant's liability.

The motion court correctly found that the agreement between Chowaiki and defendant created a bailor/bailee relationship under article 7 of the Uniform Commercial Code and that the agreement's limitation of liability was unenforceable because it purported to exempt defendant from all liability, in contravention of then UCC 7-204(2) (UCC 7-204[b], as amended by L. 2014, ch. 505, §23, eff. Dec. 17, 2014]).

UCC 7-204(a) provides that a "warehouse is liable for damages for loss of or injury to the goods caused by its failure to exercise care with regard to the goods that a reasonably careful person would exercise under similar circumstances" and "is not liable for damages that could not have been avoided by the exercise of that care." UCC 7-204(b) provides that "[d]amages may be limited by a term in the warehouse receipt or storage agreement limiting the amount of liability in case of loss or damage beyond which the warehouse is not liable." However, such limitations on liability are limited by UCC 7-202(c), which provides that such terms must not "impair its ... duty of care under Section 7-204. Any contrary provision is ineffective."

Here there is a question of fact concerning whether defendant, in failing to move Chowaiki's goods to either another floor, or to a location above ground level on the floor they were on, was reasonable under the circumstances. If the trier of fact finds that defendant did not act reasonably, then defendant may be liable for damages to Chowaiki's goods (*see e.g.* Modelia v. Rose Warehouse, Inc., 1968 WL 9201 [Sup. Ct., New York County 1968], *affd.* 36 A.D.2d 582, 317 N.Y.S.2d 735 [1st Dept. 1971]).

However, the court erred in finding that the waiver of subrogation contained in the agreement's loss/damage waiver is enforceable and bars this action.

Provisions purporting to exempt the bailee from liability for damage to stored goods from perils against which the bailor had secured insurance, even when caused by the bailee's negligence have been held to run afoul of the statutory scheme of UCC Article 7.

In Kimberly-Clark Corp. v. Lake Erie Warehouse, Div. of Lake Erie Rolling Mill, 49 A.D.2d 492, 375 N.Y.S.2d 918 (4th Dept. 1975), *appeal dismissed* 39 N.Y.2d 888, 386 N.Y.S.2d 393, 352 N.E.2d 580 (1976), the Court found such an exculpatory clause to be invalid. In that case, the agreement between the bailee and bailor provided that the bailor "waives any and all right of recovery from the warehouseman for losses caused by the perils covered by fire and extended coverage insurance and caused by any other perils against which customer has insured" (id. at 493, 375 N.Y.S.2d 918). In invalidating this clause, the Court noted that while UCC 7-204 permits a warehouseman to limit the *amount* of liability, it cannot completely exempt itself from liability as imposed by UCC Article 7 (id. at 494-495, 375 N.Y.S.2d 918). Quoting *Modelia,* supra, the Court stated that a warehouseman "may not contract away or lessen his responsibility except in such manner as the statute provides. ... Any other attempted exoneration or limitation would defeat the statute and must be held void" (id. at 495, 375 N.Y.S.2d 918). It should be noted that the exoneration clause at issue in *Kimberley-Clark* was not as broad as the provisions in this case in that it did not contain an express waiver of subrogation clause or a requirement that the bailor obtain a waiver of subrogation from its insurer. The *Kimberley-Clark* Court did note that the implied waiver of subrogation in that case was nothing more than another attempt by defendant to exempt itself from all liability, which "would defeat the statute and must be held void" (see Kimberly-Clark, 49 A.D.2d at 495, 375 N.Y.S.2d 918). . . .

We have considered defendant's remaining arguments and find them unavailing.

QUESTION

Would the result be different if the clause had read: "The warehouse-man shall not be liable for loss, damage, delay or demurrage caused by acts of God, ... or by ... flood, wind, storm, ... or by any other cause beyond the control [of] the warehouseman, or by any cause not originating in the warehouse"? See HDI Gerling Industrie Versicherung AG v. Continental Terminals, Inc., 2017 WL 4776757 (D.N.J. 2017).

C. Bailee's Lien

All bailees (including warehousemen and carriers) are given a statutory lien in the bailed goods to the extent of the charges for storage and expenses incident to the bailment contract (expenses necessary to preserve the goods, for instance). For warehouses, this lien is described in §§7-209 and 7-210; for carriers, §§7-307 and 7-308. These bailee's liens are possessory liens only; the bailee loses its lien if it voluntarily surrenders the goods (or wrongfully refuses to surrender them). See Darby v. Baltimore & Ohio Ry. Co., 259 Md. 493, 270 A.2d 652 (1970). If the lien is contested, the bailee must have evidence of the failure to pay. See Thompson v. T & G Relocation Systems, Inc., 2018 WL 1440683 (N.Y. Sup. Ct. 2018). If the bailor does not pay the bailee's charges, the latter may foreclose its lien by public or private sale (the rules of which are described in the above-named sections). The Code primarily requires the foreclosure sale to be held in a "commercially reasonable manner." The bailee must give the bailor proper notice of the sale. See OEC Freight (NY) v. KT Superwin Corp., 2014 WL 3887744 (S.D.N.Y. 2014). For a case exploring the details of a bailee lien foreclosure on stored household goods, see Bradford v. Muinzer, 498 F. Supp. 1384 (N.D. Ill. 1980).

D. Delivery Orders

You will remember that if the goods are stored under a nonnegotiable warehouse receipt, the bailee can deliver the goods without requiring surrender of the warehouse receipt. Many nonnegotiable warehouse forms state that delivery will be made "on *detached written authority without* the return of this receipt." When the owner (bailor) wants the order delivered, the owner simply sends a letter (called a *delivery order*) to the bailee, explaining to whom the goods are to be delivered.

Storing goods in bulk under a nonnegotiable warehouse receipt and then breaking them up into smaller units by separate delivery orders is a convenient way to merchandise commodities. The delivery orders, which need take no particular form, can be negotiable or nonnegotiable. A delivery order is negotiable if it directs the bailee to deliver the goods to someone, "or his order," or "to bearer"; otherwise, it is nonnegotiable. In many ways a delivery order is directly analogous to an Article 3 draft, only it is an order to deliver goods instead of to pay money. Like a draft, it imposes no liability on the bailee until the bailee *accepts* the order (no liability to the holder of the delivery order, that is; the bailee who refuses to accept a delivery order may be in breach of the bailment contract and, if so, is liable to the bailor). See §7-502(a)(4), especially the last sentence.

All of this ties in with how a seller of bailed goods makes *tender* to the buyer under Article 2 of the Code. Read §§2-509(2) and 2-503(4) carefully. Where a *negotiable* document of title is involved, both §§2-509(2) and 2-503(4)(a) make it clear that the risk of loss shifts to the buyer on delivery of the document if the goods conform to the contract (if not, §2-510 applies). However, these sections do *not* apply to negotiable delivery orders, which are lumped in with the rules governing nonnegotiable documents in §§2-509(2)(c) and 2-503(4)(b) ("record directing the bailee to deliver" means a delivery order). Where no documents are involved (say, a pet dog is boarded at a kennel and sold while still there), §2-509(2)(b) passes the risk of loss to the buyer on the bailee's acknowledgment of the buyer's right to possession. See Whately v. Tetrault, 29 Mass. App. Dec. 112 (1964).

PROBLEM 95

Fred Bandanna, a farmer, took two truckloads of his cotton to Rural Warehouse for storage. The first truckload of 80 bales he stored under a negotiable warehouse receipt issued by Rural. For the second truckload of 80 bales, he obtained a nonnegotiable warehouse receipt. Fred took the documents to the offices of Harold Fastbuck, a commodity merchant. Harold bought both the negotiable receipt covering the first truckload and the nonnegotiable receipt covering the second truckload of cotton from Fred. Harold asked, however, that Fred divide the 80 bales represented by the nonnegotiable receipt into two equal lots so that Harold could resell them more easily. Fred sat down and wrote out two delivery orders addressed to Rural, each requiring the warehouse to turn over 40 bales to "Harold Fastbuck or order." As soon as Fred left his office, Harold sold one of the delivery orders to another commodity merchant, Sue Fourthparty. He indorsed on the back of the delivery order "Deliver to Sue Fourthparty or order, (signed) Harold Fastbuck." Sue phoned Rural Warehouse and said that she was the owner of 40 bales of the Fred Bandanna cotton under a delivery order. The warehouse agent agreed that Sue could pick up the bales the next day. That night lightning struck the warehouse, and all the cotton burned. Who took the risk of loss as to each segment of the cotton? See §§2-509(2), 2-503(4)(b), 7-502(a)(4).

E.   Terminology: The Issuer

Under the Code, the person primarily liable on a document of title is the *issuer* of the document. Since the *bailee* (warehouse or carrier) is almost always the person who *issues* (creates) the document, there is a temptation to think of *issuer* as synonymous with *bailee*. This would be correct except for the fact that the issuer of a delivery order (which *is* a document of title according to §1-201(b)(16)) is the *bailor.* Read §§7-102(a)(5) and 7-102(a)(8). This fact will become important later on when we get to talking about *due negotiation* and the duties of the issuer. Question: who was (were) the issuer(s) in Problem 95?

II.   BILLS OF LADING

Just as warehouses issue negotiable or nonnegotiable receipts for bailed goods, carriers (such as railroads, airlines, ocean liners, and trucking firms) issue similar documents on the receipt of goods for transportation across the country or the world. These documents, called *bills of lading,* may be negotiable or nonnegotiable (depending on whether order or bearer language is used). As with warehouse receipts, the bill of lading is, simultaneously, a receipt for the goods, a contract of transportation, and tangible evidence of ownership of the bailed goods.

A.   Federal Law

Article 7 of the Code covers only intrastate shipments. If the goods are to cross state lines, the documents issued by the carrier are governed by the Federal Bills of Lading Act (the Pomerene Act of 1916), 49 U.S.C. §81 et seq. If the goods are to cross water, they will be governed by a host of federal statutes including the Shipping Act, 46 U.S.C. §801 et seq.; the Intercoastal Shipping Act, 46 U.S.C. §843 et seq.; and (most important) the Carriage of Goods by Sea Act, 46 U.S.C. §1300 et seq. (For those of you who will have commercial bailees as clients, note at this point that all interstate carriers and warehouses are subject to federal regulation of their trade. The Federal Aviation Administration, for example, formulates rules and regulations for the airlines involved in interstate and foreign air carriage. The Department of Agriculture regulates warehouses storing agricultural products. See the United States Warehouse Act, 7 U.S.C. §241 et seq. There will also be special state statutes and regulations that deal with warehouses and carriers.)

Fortunately, the basic law set out in the Federal Bills of Lading Act is more or less the same as that in Article 7, and unless the wording is particularly crucial, language of the federal act will not be mentioned. What is important is that you remember that Article 7 does *not* apply (except by analogy) to any bill of lading issued for goods that are to leave the state. For such a bill you need to refer to the exact language of the relevant federal statutes.

B. The Basic Idea

Do not confuse *shipper* with *carrier* or *issuer.* The *shipper* is the original owner (bailor) of the goods who turns them over to the carrier for transportation. The *carrier* then issues a bill of lading (thus becoming an *issuer*) to the shipper. If the bill is negotiable, the carrier (issuer) will not turn over the goods at the destination until the negotiable bill of lading is surrendered (§7-403(c) applies to carriers as well as warehouses). This means that the shipper must send the bill of lading to the person who is to receive the goods (normally the buyer) before the latter can get possession of the goods. Often the shipper will not surrender the bill of lading to the buyer until the latter has paid for the goods (or has *accepted* a draft drawn on it; see the discussion below); this is called requiring *payment against documents.* As soon as the buyer pays the seller (or seller's agent), the buyer gets possession of the negotiable bill of lading and can claim the goods from the carrier. A carrier that delivers the goods to the buyer without demanding surrender of an outstanding negotiable bill of lading has converted the goods and is liable to the holder of the negotiable bill. See BII Finance Co. v. U-States Forwarding Serv. Corp., 115 Cal. Rptr. 2d 312 (Cal. App. 2002). Review §7-403(c) and read §§7-404 and 7-601(b).

C. Form

1. Negotiable

The word *consign* means to send or hand over goods to another. A negotiable bill of lading is called an *order bill of lading* because the goods are consigned to the "order of _____."

In bill of lading terminology, the goods are entrusted to the carrier by the *consignor* (the shipper) for delivery to the *consignee* (the person to whom the goods will belong at the end of their journey, normally the buyer). The consignee is *not* the carrier-bailee. If Sam Seller in Toledo sells goods to Betty Buyer in Atlanta via the Monopoly Railroad, using a negotiable bill of lading issued by the railroad, then Sam is the consignor, Betty is the consignee, and the Monopoly Railroad is the carrier-issuer (the agent of the consignor who carries out the consignment contract). Order (negotiable) bills of lading are yellow in color, as required by Interstate Commerce Commission (ICC) regulations.

An order bill states that the goods have been received in apparent good order, except as otherwise indicated, and states the contract of transportation (including rates), incorporating all the fine print on the back of the contract. On the front is space for describing the goods covered by the document and blanks to be filled in showing, among other things,

(1) shipper's (consignor's) name and address,
(2) to whose order the goods are consigned,
(3) the destination of the goods, and
(4) whom the carrier is to notify when the goods arrive (normally the buyer).

A negotiable bill also contains sentences like this one in large print on the front: "Surrender of this original order bill of lading properly indorsed is required prior to the delivery of the property. Inspection of such property will not be permitted by anyone prior to delivery unless permission is indorsed hereon or given in writing by the consignor." (As to inspection rights, see note §2-513(3), which agrees with this language.)

2.   Nonnegotiable

A nonnegotiable bill of lading is called a *straight* bill of lading because the goods are delivered straight to the consignee whether or not the nonnegotiable bill is surrendered. Straight bills are to be printed on white paper by ICC regulation. The carrier will take the goods to their destination, notify the consignee of their arrival, and await instructions as to whom the goods are to be delivered.

Frequently the consignor consigns the goods to *itself,* thereby making the consignor and the consignee the same entity. This happens on negotiable as well as nonnegotiable bills. The reason that this is often done is to make it clear that the consignor is at all times the owner of the goods, and for that reason it is called a "shipment under reservation" (meaning a reservation of *title*). When the buyer pays for them, the seller will indorse a negotiable bill over to the buyer or, if a nonnegotiable bill is used, will issue a *delivery order* (the same as with warehouse receipts) to the carrier telling it to deliver the goods to the buyer. In effect, consigning the goods to itself gives the seller a security interest in the goods until the purchase price is paid. The Code recognizes that the *equitable* interest is in the buyer even though the legal title is in the seller. Read §2-505 carefully.

PROBLEM 96

Homer Widget, of South Bend, Indiana, the inventor of the three-dimensional widget, contracted to sell 5,000 widgets to Ned's Novelty Store in Evansville, Indiana. Homer delivered the goods to the Overnight Trucking Company, consigning the goods to himself but writing "Notify Ned's Novelty Store on arrival" on the straight bill of lading. (The carrier keeps a duplicate copy of the bill of lading with the goods; the original is, of course, turned over to the consignor.) Homer mailed the original bill to his cousin Wilbur Widget, who lived in Evansville. Along with the bill he sent a delivery order signed by himself and addressed to the trucking company telling the company to deliver the goods to Ned's Novelty Store. Homer's cover letter to his cousin stated that Wilbur should take the delivery order down to Ned at the store and turn it over to Ned only if Ned paid Wilbur cash for the goods. Wilbur did present the delivery order as Homer directed, but Ned was short on funds and could not pay. Wilbur, confused, mailed all the documents back to Homer with a letter saying Ned would not pay. Meanwhile, the goods arrived at Evansville, and John ("Slow") Burly, the company's truck driver, had to decide what to do with the widgets. Reading the bill of lading, he discovered that the consignee lived in South Bend. By checking the phone book, he learned that Homer Widget had no address in Evansville. Then the truck driver noticed that he was to notify Ned's Novelty Store, which did have an Evansville address, so he delivered the widgets to Ned.

(a) Was the carrier's delivery to Ned improper? Read §7-303 carefully; see Mistletoe Express Serv. v. Sanchez, 721 S.W.2d 418 (Tex. App. 1986).

(b) If the widgets were destroyed in an auto accident prior to Ned's refusal to pay, who would have had the risk of loss if the contract was "F.O.B. truck South Bend"? See §2-509(1). See also Sternheim v. Silver Bell of Roslyn, Inc., 66 Misc. 726, 321 N.Y.S.2d 965 (Cty. Ct. 1971). As to the carrier's duty of care, read §7-309(1).

(c) Would the result with regard to the risk of loss or proper delivery change if the bill of lading had been an order bill? See §§7-403(c), 2-509.

PROBLEM 97

Blue Skies Air Lines was about to deliver a shipment of frozen fish to the buyer to whom it was consigned under a straight bill issued by the airline when the phone rang. The seller-consignor was on the phone, and she forbade the delivery, telling Blue Skies to return the fish to her, since she had learned that the "buyer is a bum." If Blue Skies returns the goods to the seller, is it risking liability to the buyer? See §§7-303, 2-505, 2-705 (plus Official Comment 1 to §2-705); Clock v. Missouri-Texas R.R., 407 F. Supp. 448 (E.D. Mo. 1976).

In re TSAWD Holdings, Inc.

United States Bankruptcy Court, District of Delaware, 2017
574 B.R. 482, 2017 WL 4179817

MARY F. WALRATH, United States Bankruptcy Judge

Before the Court is a Joint Motion for Summary Judgment filed by TSA Stores, Inc. ("TSA Stores") and Yusen Logistics (Americas) Inc. ("Yusen") (collectively, the "Movants") in an adversary proceeding brought by O2Cool, LLC ("O2Cool"). In its Complaint, O2Cool seeks a determination that, inter alia, certain goods that were shipped to TSA Stores from O2Cool were not property of the estate and have, consequently, been converted. The Movants contend that they are entitled to a ruling that these goods are property of the estate. Because the Court finds that the Movants have satisfied their burden that there is no genuine dispute of material fact and that they are entitled to a finding in their favor, the Court will grant the Motion for Summary Judgment for the reasons set forth below.

I. BACKGROUND

A. FACTUAL HISTORY

On March 2, 2016, TSA Stores and its affiliates (the "Debtors") filed voluntary chapter 11 petitions under the Bankruptcy Code. The Debtors were in the sporting goods and retail apparel business and had their principal place of business in Colorado. O2Cool designs, manufactures, and distributes specialized consumer items involving hydration, cooling, patio, and beach solutions. In 2015, one of the Debtors, TSA Stores, purchased products (the "Goods") from O2Cool pursuant to a 2015 Import Vendor Deal Sheet (the "Vendor Deal Sheet"). TSA Stores and O2Cool agreed to F.O.B. origin shipping terms in a Vendor Relationship Guide (the "Vendor Guide") that was incorporated by reference into the Vendor Deal Sheet.

(Adv. D.I. 1-2, Ex. B, at 3.) Pursuant to their agreement, the Goods, which originated in China, were delivered to a freight forwarder in Yantian, China, and transported to distribution centers in the U.S. (Adv. D.I. 70, Ex. 1.)

TSA Stores hired several parties—Yusen, Yusen Logistics (Hong Kong) Inc. ("YL Hong Kong"), Shenzen Yusen Freight Service Company Limited–OCM ("Shenzen"), OOCL, and Orient Overseas Container Line Limited ("Orient Overseas")—to transport goods purchased from various vendors. Yusen provided logistics and supply chain management that included origin cargo management and customs house brokerage services. Vendors were required to notify TSA Stores and Yusen about impending shipments to TSA Stores. YL Hong Kong was the freight forwarder in Yantian for TSA Stores. Shenzen consolidated the goods into containers and delivered them to their designated carriers.

Pursuant to the agreement with TSA Stores, O2Cool delivered several shipments to YL Hong Kong in Yantian between January 13 and February 3, 2016. (Adv. D.I. 70, Ex. 1.) Upon receipt, YL Hong Kong issued forwarder cargo receipts, and Shenzen consolidated and delivered the Goods to their designated carriers. Orient Overseas was one carrier that received the Goods for shipment and issued non-negotiable seaway bills or bills of lading. (Adv. D.I. 70, Ex. 3.) The bills of lading issued by Orient Overseas did not list O2Cool, but instead stated that the shipper was Shenzen. Orient Overseas' vessels departed with the Goods between February 1 and February 10, 2016.

Between February 12 and February 26, 2016, O2Cool sent Yusen five Stop Shipment Notices, pursuant to section 2-705 of the Uniform Commercial Code (the "UCC"). At the time Yusen received the Stop Shipment Notices, the Goods were not in Yusen's possession. Yusen subsequently notified O2Cool that it was not a carrier for the Goods.

O2Cool forwarded the Stop Shipment Notices to OOCL on or about February 26, 2016, and OOCL acknowledged receipt thereof. However, Shenzen, YL Hong Kong, Orient Overseas and none of the other designated carriers were sent the Stop Shipment Notices from O2Cool, and the Goods were delivered to TSA Stores at their distribution centers.

B.   PROCEDURAL BACKGROUND

O2Cool commenced this adversary proceeding against TSA Stores, Yusen, and others in the Debtors' chapter 11 bankruptcy case on June 21, 2016. In Count I, O2Cool seeks a determination that the Goods are not property of the estate and that certain parties are required to complete an accounting of such Goods and proceeds derived therefrom. (Adv. D.I. 1.) In Count II, O2Cool requests a judgment stating that it has rights to the Goods superior to certain lenders. Id. In Count III, O2Cool seeks a determination that the Defendants have converted its property, namely, the Goods. Id.

Yusen and TSA Stores filed answers to the Complaint. On March 3, 2017, they jointly moved for summary judgment on all counts pursuant to Rule 56. Briefing is now complete, and the matter is ripe for consideration. . . .

III.   DISCUSSION . . .

B.   PARTIES' ARGUMENTS

1.   *Title Passed to the Debtor*

It is the Movants' position that summary judgment should be granted on Counts I (Determination of Property of the Estate) and Count III (Conversion) as a matter of law because O2Cool's right to stop delivery ceased when title to the Goods passed to TSA Stores. Their contention rests on the terms of the Vendor Guide, which provided that title to the Goods passed to TSA Stores when O2Cool delivered them to YL Hong Kong for shipment.

O2Cool disagrees and asserts that it had the right to stop the Goods' shipment regardless of whether TSA Stores had title because the Goods were still in the carriers' possession.

The UCC states that a seller may stop goods from being delivered to a buyer when the seller discovers that the buyer is insolvent and the goods are still in a carrier's or bailee's possession. Del. Code Ann. tit. 6, §2-705(a) (West 2017). This right to stop shipment exists until the buyer receives the goods. Id. at §2-705(b). "Receipt" occurs when the buyer or the buyer's designated representative takes actual physical possession of the goods. Id. at §2-103(1)(c) & §2-705 cmt. 2. Goods that are in a common carrier's possession for delivery to the buyer have not been received by the buyer. Montello Oil Corp. v. Marin Motor Oil, Inc. (In re Marin Motor Oil, Inc.), 740 F.2d 220, 222 (3d Cir. 1984). A seller's right to stop goods from being delivered persists until the goods reach their final place of delivery. Del. Code Ann. tit. 6, §2-705 cmt. 2.

Because the Goods were not yet in the physical possession of TSA Stores when O2Cool sent the Stop Shipment Notices, the Court concludes that O2Cool still had the right to stop shipment of the Goods. . . .

2.   *Effectiveness of Stop Shipment Notices*

a.   ~~Parties Served with Stop Shipment Notices~~

Alternatively, the Movants argue that the Stop Shipment Notices that O2Cool sent to Yusen and OOCL were ineffective because they were not sent to the proper party, i.e. the bailee of the goods. They assert that Yusen was neither a bailee nor a carrier in possession of the Goods and that OOCL was neither a carrier nor acting as an agent for one.

The UCC states that a seller has the right to stop delivery of goods upon discovering that a buyer is insolvent. Del. Code Ann. tit. 6, §2-702(1) (West 2017). Under section 2-705, a seller may stop shipment by notifying the bailee so as to "enable the bailee by reasonable diligence to prevent delivery of the goods." Id. §2-705(3)(a). The UCC defines a bailee as "a person that by a warehouse receipt, bill of lading, or other document of title acknowledges possession of goods and contracts to deliver them." Id. §7-102(a)(1). Carriers are bailees. Id. §7-102(a)(2).

In this case, Yusen was not listed as a carrier on the bills of lading, only Orient Overseas was listed as the carrier. Moreover, after it received the Stop Shipment Notices, Yusen notified O2Cool that it was neither a carrier nor in possession of the Goods. (Adv. D.I. 70, Ex. 5.)

O2Cool admits this. (Adv. D.I. 77, at 5.) However, O2Cool asserts that OOCL was a proper party to receive the Stop Shipment Notices because OOCL was an agent for the carrier, Orient Overseas, and, thus, Orient Overseas received the notice.

The Court agrees with O2Cool and concludes that Overseas Orient did receive the Stop Shipment Notices when they were delivered to its agent, OOCL. See Restatement (Second) of Agency §268 cmt. a (Am. Law. Inst. 2017) (stating that "the notice of stoppage in transit" must be "directed to the party to be affected, to his agent authorized to receive it[,] or to a person upon whom the notifier has a right to rely as one so authorized" to receive such a notice); David Frisch, Lawrence's Anderson on the Uniform Commercial Code §2-705:33 (3d ed. 2016) (stating that "notice may be given to an agent of the carrier or bailee who has actual custody of the goods" and, "[i]f the seller [can] determine which agent of the carrier or bailee has the goods in actual custody[] and can reach that agent," then a seller may "notify that agent").

b. Consignors Listed on Bill of Lading

The Movants contend, however, that even if OOCL was an agent for Orient Overseas, the Stop Shipment Notices were still not effective to prevent the Goods from being shipped by the carriers or received by the Debtors because O2Cool was not listed as the consignor on the bills of lading. The Movants argue that section 2-705(3)(d) of the UCC only requires compliance with a stop shipment notice when it is received from the consignor listed on the non-negotiable bills of lading that were issued.

According to O2Cool, the mere fact that its name does not appear on the bills of lading as the consignor is inconsequential because it was the actual owner and seller of the Goods that were shipped.

The Court agrees with the Movants on this point. Section 2-705(3)(d) of the UCC states that "a carrier who has issued a non-negotiable bill of lading is *not obliged to obey* a notification to stop received from a person other than the consignor." Del. Code Ann. tit. 6, §2-705(3)(d) (emphasis added). Consignor is defined as "a person named in a bill of lading as the person from which the goods have been received for shipment." Id. §7-102(a)(4).

Here, Orient Overseas issued non-negotiable bills of lading showing Shenzen as the "the person from which the goods have been received for shipment." Thus, the Court concludes that OOCL was not required to obey O2Cool's Stop Shipment Notices under section 2-705(3)(d). See generally Oak Harbor Freight Lines, Inc. v. Sears Roebuck & Co., 420 F. Supp. 2d 1138, 1148 (W.D. Wash. 2006) ("The bill of lading is the basic transportation contract between the shipper-consignor and the carrier; its terms and conditions bind the shipper and all connecting carriers." (citing S. Pac. Transp. Co. v. Commercial Metals Co., 456 U.S. 336, 342, 102 S. Ct. 1815, 72 L. Ed. 2d 114 (1982))).

Therefore, the Court concludes that summary judgment in favor of the Movants on Count I is warranted because the Stop Shipment Notices were not effective to stop shipment and the Goods became property of the estate when they were delivered to TSA Stores. See 11 U.S.C. §541(a) (West 2014) (defining estate property as including "all legal or equitable interests of the debtor in property as of the commencement of the case" and "[a]ny interest in property that the estate acquires after the commencement of the case").

3.   Right to Reclamation

The Movants assert that the Goods remained property of the Debtors' estates and could be sold by them because O2Cool failed to exercise its reclamation rights after TSA Stores received the Goods. Therefore, they ask for judgment on Count III (conversion).

A seller's right to stop goods from being delivered to a buyer ceases once the buyer receives the goods. Del. Code Ann. tit. 6, §2-05(2)(a). Instead, a seller has only the right of reclamation once a buyer takes possession of the goods. Id. §2-702(2). UCC section 2-702 states that "[w]here the seller discovers that the buyer has received goods on credit while insolvent he or she may reclaim the goods upon demand made within ten days after the receipt." Id.

O2Cool admits that it did not timely seek to reclaim the Goods. As a result, the Court concludes that TSA Stores and Yusen are entitled to summary judgment on Count III of the Complaint.

4.   Priority of Rights in the Goods

The Movants also argue that because the Stop Shipment Notices were ineffective, O2Cool did not retain any rights in the Goods that are superior to the Lenders. They therefore ask for summary judgment on Count II (Determination of Lien Priority) of the Complaint.

O2Cool argues that it holds superior rights to the Goods relative to the secured lenders in the Debtors' bankruptcy case. That argument is based on the *Cargill* case. See Cargill Inc. v. Trico Steel Co., L.L.C. (In re Trico Steel

Co. L.L.C.), 282 B.R. 318, 327-30 (Bankr. D. Del. 2002). The Court in *Cargill* explained that a seller that properly exercises its right to stop shipment is not subject to a buyer's secured creditors' rights in the goods. *Cargill*, 282 B.R. at 329-330.

The Court concludes, however, that the *Cargill* case is inapplicable because the Court has found that O2Cool's Stop Shipment Notices were not effective to prevent TSA Stores from obtaining title or possession of the Goods.

While O2Cool asserts that there is a factual dispute as to when TSA Stores received actual possession of the Goods, the Court finds that dispute is not material because the Stop Shipment Notices never became effective. Therefore, the Court concludes that the Movants are entitled to summary judgment on Count II of the Complaint as well.

IV. Conclusion

For the reasons set forth above, the Court will grant the Joint Motion for Summary Judgment filed by TSA Stores and Yusen and enter judgment in their favor on all Counts of the Complaint.

PROBLEM 98

Jane Pitchfork, a southern Iowa farmer, had an excellent pumpkin crop (1,700 pumpkins) this year. She stored 1,000 pumpkins with the Pumpkin Warehouse, Inc., located in Des Moines, taking a negotiable warehouse receipt for 500 and a nonnegotiable receipt for the other 500. She also contracted to sell 700 other pumpkins to Peter P. Pumpkineater, who lived in Sioux City, Iowa. The terms of the contract required her to ship Pumpkineater 700 stemless pumpkins "F.O.B. railroad car Fort Madison, Iowa." Jane was too lazy to cut off the stems, but she thought Pumpkineater really would not care, so she loaded 700 pumpkins on board an Iowa Pacific Railroad car at Fort Madison, Iowa. She received a negotiable bill of lading consigned to her own order and made a proper contract for carriage of the pumpkins to Sioux City. She sold the 1,000 warehouse pumpkins to Mom's Pies, Inc., of Cedar Rapids. She indorsed the negotiable warehouse receipt over to Mom's Pies for the first 500 stored pumpkins and gave them a nonnegotiable delivery order for the other 500 stored pumpkins. Before Mom's Pies could contact the warehouse, the Iowa Pacific Railroad train carrying the pumpkins passed through Des Moines and derailed (due to the negligence of the train's engineer). The train ran off the track and went through the center of the Pumpkin Warehouse, destroying all 1,700 pumpkins. Jane Pitchfork, a dejected woman, comes to you. The railroad is, of course, going to be liable to whoever took the risk of loss as to the pumpkins. Advise Jane as to where the risk of loss is placed for each of the pumpkin transactions. See §§2-503, 2-509, 2-510, 2-601, 2-319.

D. Misdescription

Consider this problem. The bill of lading states that the boxcar contains 42 cartons of widgets. When the goods are delivered to buyer, there are only 32 cartons, or the cartons contain peanuts, or the boxcar (which was loaded and sealed by the shipper) is empty. Is the carrier liable for wrong information (misdescription) on the bill of lading if the shipper furnished the carrier with the information? The problem frequently comes up because carriers (particularly railroads) often permit the shipper to load the goods itself and then to fill out the descriptive section of the bill of lading, which the carrier then signs. Carriers defend this practice by saying that as a practical matter it is impossible for the carrier's agents to police the shipper's loading or to inventory the goods loaded. To guard against possible liability for resulting misdescription, the carrier normally states SHIPPER'S WEIGHT, LOAD, AND COUNT on the bill of lading in order to indicate that the carrier makes no warranties as to these matters. Is this language effective to eliminate the carrier's liability for misdescription? Study §7-301.

The corresponding federal law is the Federal Bills of Lading Act §22, which follows. This section has been much litigated:

> If a bill of lading has been issued by a carrier or on his behalf by an agent or employee the scope of whose actual or apparent authority includes the receiving of goods and issuing bills of lading therefor for transportation in commerce among several States and with foreign nations, the carrier shall be liable to (a) the owner of goods covered by a straight bill subject to existing right of stoppage in transit or (b) the holder of an order bill, who has given value in good faith relying upon the description therein of the goods, or upon the shipment being made upon the date therein shown, for damages caused by the nonreceipt by the carrier of all or part of the goods upon or prior to the date therein shown, or their failure to correspond with the description thereof in the bill at the time of its issue.

GAC Commercial Corp. v. Wilson

United States District Court, Southern District of New York, 1967
271 F. Supp. 242

BRYAN, J.
[The St. Lawrence Pulp & Paper Corp. borrowed money from plaintiff G.A.C., which took as collateral straight bills of lading, both interstate and intrastate, issued by defendant Norwood & St. Law. Railroad. The bills of lading indicated that St. Lawrence, as consignor, had shipped various

amounts of paper products to different consignees and the plaintiff took the bills with the understanding that the goods had not yet been delivered. Plaintiff loaned St. Lawrence $254,173.42 against the bills of lading, but St. Lawrence went bankrupt anyway. To the great surprise of everyone but some of St. Lawrence's employees, the railroad cars proved to be empty. Plaintiff brought this action against St. Lawrence's officers and the Norwood Railroad.]

The method by which the alleged fraudulent scheme was carried out appears for purposes of this motion to be as follows: the bankrupt St. Lawrence, as part of its facilities in Norfolk, New York, maintained a railroad siding connected with the lines of defendant carrier which had a freight office approximately 1/8th of a mile from the siding. St. Lawrence was permitted to load freight at its spur track in preparation for shipments on defendant's line. The railroad cars were sealed by St. Lawrence with seals provided by the railroad. St. Lawrence also prepared the bills of lading on blanks furnished in quadruplicate by defendant Norwood. The bills thus prepared were then presented to Norwood's agent who signed the original and one copy without inspecting the contents of the cars. No notation such as "contents of packages unknown" or "shipper's weight, load and count" was written on the bills. The signed copies were returned to St. Lawrence and forwarded with the invoices to G.A.C. which made advances on the goods described, which, as it turned out, had not been shipped.

Since sixty of the bills of lading were issued by a common carrier for the transportation of goods in interstate commerce, the issues as to these bills are controlled by the provisions of the Federal Bills of Lading Act, 49 U.S.C. §81. This statute stands as "a clear expression of the determination of Congress to take the whole subject matter of such bills of lading within its control." . . .

Prior to the passage of the Federal Bills of Lading Act "the United States courts held that a carrier was not liable for the act of its agent in issuing a bill of lading for goods where no goods had in fact been received." Josephy v. Panhandle & S.F. Ry., 235 N.Y. 306, 310, 139 N.E. 277, 278 (1923); see, e.g., Clark v. Clyde S.S. Co., 148 F. 243 (S.D.N.Y. 1906). The liability of carriers for acts of their agents was expanded, but not drastically, by the passage of the federal legislation which draws a sharp distinction between order bills of lading and straight bills where in fact the goods are never received for shipment by the carrier. Under §22 of the Act, 49 U.S.C. §102, "[i]f a bill of lading has been issued by a carrier or on his behalf by an agent or employee . . ., the carrier shall be liable to . . . the holder of an order bill, who has given value in good faith, relying upon the description therein of the goods, . . . for damages caused by the nonreceipt by the carrier of all or part of the goods upon or prior to the date therein shown." However, the liability of the carrier for nonreceipt extends only to "the owner of goods covered by a straight bill," provided, of course, he also gives value in good faith in reliance upon the description of goods contained in the bill. See Strohmeyer & Arpe Co. v. American Line S.S. Corp., 97 F.2d 360, 362 (2d Cir. 1938).

It is clear that a party in the position of Norwood is not included within the narrow category of those liable on a straight bill under the federal legislation. In the first place there is no question that the straight bills of lading here involved are non-negotiable. [Citations omitted.] As a consequence plaintiff G.A.C., as apparent transferee of bills and invoices representing accounts receivable under the agreement with St. Lawrence, upon notification to the carrier of the transfer, could only "become the direct obligee of whatever obligations the carrier owed to the transferor of the bill immediately before the notification." 49 U.S.C. §112; see id. §109. Norwood obviously owed St. Lawrence nothing because no goods in fact were received. There was therefore no outstanding obligation to G.A.C. . . .

By no stretch of the imagination does G.A.C. qualify as an "owner of goods covered by a straight bill" who can sue the carrier under §22 of the Federal Bills of Lading Act, 39 U.S.C. §102, for representing that goods in fact had been received. The reason for this is that it is completely illusory to attempt to assign an "owner" to non-existent goods. R. Braucher, Documents of Title 23 (1958); 2 S. Williston, Sales §419a, at 576-77 (rev. ed. 1948). While the consignee is generally deemed to have title to goods shipped under a straight bill of lading, see George F. Hinrichs, Inc. v. Standard Trust & Sav. Bank, 279 F. 382, 386 (2d Cir. 1922), even he cannot sue the carrier for representing in a straight bill that non-existent goods had in fact been received. Martin Jessee Motors v. Reading Co., 87 F. Supp. 318 (E.D. Pa.), aff'd, 181 F.2d 766 (3d Cir. 1950). The rationale applied in *Martin Jessee Motors* — that the consignee can prevail against the carrier "only by proving its title to specific property," 181 F.2d at 767 — applies a fortiori to bar the claim of G.A.C. Plaintiff's interest in the "aggregate face value of the accounts receivable pledged as security" under no conceivable reading of the statute can be deemed an "[ownership] of goods covered by a straight bill." G.A.C. is not one of the favored few who can recover under the Federal Bills of Lading Act. . . .

Plaintiff G.A.C. fares no better with respect to the two bills of lading representing intrastate shipments in New York. . . . Although the awkward term "owner" in 49 U.S.C. §102 has been replaced by the word "consignee" in the Uniform Commercial Code §7-301 . . . the change is immaterial for purposes of this case. Plaintiff, perhaps an assignee, transferee or pledgee of the non-negotiable bills, though it claims not to be, is certainly not a "consignee," which is the only party protected. 2 Anderson, Uniform Commercial Code 261 n.9 (1961); see R. Braucher, Documents of Title 23-24 (1958). Contrast

U.C.C. §7-203. Thus, as with the sixty interstate bills, G.A.C. cannot success-fully sue on the two intrastate bills. . . .

It is true that the result dictated by the federal legislation may lead to some inequities. A straight bill under the Federal Bills of Lading Act is obvi-ously not a good security risk. Casenote, 63 Harv. L. Rev. 1439, 1440 (1950). The fraud of the shipper by failing to deliver goods to the carrier can result, as it did here, in misleading statements on the bills of lading, which operate to the detriment of banks and other commercial financers making advances on the basis of the bills. See Oliver Straw Goods Corp. v. Osaka Shosen Kaisha, 27 F.2d 129, 134 (2d Cir. 1928) (A. Hand, J.). Moreover, the carrier can readily prevent such a situation from arising by inserting "in the bill of lading the words, 'Shipper's weight, load, and count,' or other words of like purport" to "indicate that the goods were loaded by the shipper and the description of them made by him." 49 U.S.C. §101.

But the overriding policy considerations in the Act look the other way on the issue of liability. First, "[t]here is nothing in the statute to indicate that the mere omission of the words 'Shipper's weight, load, and count' in and of itself makes the carrier liable for damages to goods improperly loaded. The omission of the statutory words merely serves to shift upon the carrier the burden of proving that the goods were improperly loaded by the ship-per, and that the damage ensued from that cause." (D.N.J. 1951); see UCC §7-301(4).[5] According to the allegations the true culprits in this case were the shipper and its agents; there is no reason to saddle defendant Norwood with liability simply because it did not insert the "Shipper's weight, load, and count" language in the bills. In addition, practicality demands loading arrangements such as those here, where the shipper places his goods aboard and seals the railroad car which the carrier has provided. Section 21 of the Act, 4 U.S.C. §101, anticipates that shippers are expected to do much of the counting and loading on their own sidings or spur tracks. The rapid flow of commerce might well be hindered if the carrier in every instance were charged with ascertaining whether in fact there were goods behind every one of its straight bills.

Moreover, denying security value to a straight bill of lading does not work a hardship upon banks and other commercial institutions. G.A.C., as a knowledgeable lender, is fully aware of the risks inherent in straight bills, and could well have required order bills to protect itself. See Chicago & Northwestern Ry. v. Stevens Natl. Bank, 75 F.2d 398 (8th Cir. 1935). It never-theless chose to rely upon straight bills to lend money to the now bankrupt St. Lawrence at a profitable rate of interest. Wiser now, G.A.C. seeks to shift its loss to Norwood, an undoubtedly solvent defendant. The Federal Bills of

---

5. Now §7-301(d). — Ed.

Lading Act protects against this type of hindsight by requiring the lender to accept this kind of security subject to the defenses between the carrier and the shipper.

The motion of defendant Norwood for Judgment on the pleadings treated as a motion for summary judgment is granted.

It is so ordered.

Read §7-301.

In the *GAC* case, which involves a straight bill of lading, §22 of the Federal Bills of Lading Act (FBLA) does not protect GAC because there are no goods, and hence there can be no owner. Professor Robert Riegert argues that the protection given owners of straight bills by the FBLA is thus illusory and that Congress did not intend the *GAC* result. See Riegert, Rights of a Transferee of Document of Title Who Is Not Holder by Due Negotiation, 9 Cumb. L. Rev. 27 (1978). The UCC in §7-301 gives protection on a straight bill to the consignee. Is the *GAC* court right in saying that plaintiff is not protected by §7-301? See §7-102(a) (3).

Both the FBLA and §7-301 protect holders by due negotiation of order bills. Both acts also allow the carrier to disclaim liability under certain circumstances. For a case involving an order bill where the disclaimer did not work, see Chicago & Nw. Ry. Co. v. Stephens Natl. Bank of Fremont, 75 F.2d 398 (8th Cir. 1935). Liability for nonreceipt or misdescription under bills of lading, either negotiable or nonnegotiable, is a tricky subject. See J. White & R. Summers, 3 Uniform Commercial Code §§28.10-28.14 (6th ed. Practitioner Treatise Series 2014).

PROBLEM 99

Harry Thief went to the offices of Monopoly Railroad to see his old prison cellmate, Phillip ("Forger") Copy. Copy, under an assumed name, was currently employed by Monopoly as chief shipping clerk. Harry asked Phillip to make out some phony negotiable bills of lading representing nonexistent shipments by Harry to a buyer in California. Harry wanted to sell the bills to a bank and split the money with Phillip. Phillip made out the bills, which Harry discounted at the Octopus National Bank, and the two of them left town. When the bank sued the railroad, the latter defended on the grounds that the phony bills contain the words "Shipper's weight, load, and count." Is this defense good? See §7-301 and its Official Comment 3; Gleason v. Seaboard Air Line Ry. Co., 278 U.S. 349 (1929); cf. Societe Generale v. Federal Ins. Co., 856 F.2d 461 (2d Cir. 1988).

III. DUE NEGOTIATION

A. The Basic Concept

The word *negotiable* in our law always means that if a piece of paper is in the proper form (a typical requirement is that it be made out either to *bearer* or to the *order* of a named individual), is transferred in the proper manner, and reaches the hands of a bona fide purchaser (BFP) who has no knowledge of problems with the paper, then the BFP may enforce the paper as written and does not take subject to the usual claims or defenses. In Article 3 of the Uniform Commercial Code, the BFP who gets these extraordinary rights is called a *holder in due course*. In Article 7, the BFP is given the jaw-breaking designation of a "holder to whom a negotiable document of title has been duly negotiated" (§7-502). Note well that the whole concept applies only to *negotiable* documents and hence excludes nonnegotiable warehouse receipts and straight bills of lading. Holders of such documents get no special rights and are subject to all the usual defenses (§7-504).

Negotiation of a negotiable document of title (whether warehouse receipt, bill of lading, or delivery order) is accomplished by indorsement and delivery under rules that are virtually interchangeable with the rules for the negotiation of Article 3 drafts and notes: §§7-501(a), 7-501(b) (providing for negotiation of electronic documents of title), 7-501(c) ("Indorsement of a nonnegotiable document of title neither makes it negotiable nor adds to the transferee's rights" (emphasis added)), §7-501(d).

A person cannot become a §7-502 holder until the document has been *duly negotiated*. Due negotiation is a term of art. It is defined in §7-501(a)(5) and (b)(3), which should be read carefully at this point.

Cleveland v. McNabb

United States District Court, Western District of Tennessee, 1970
312 F. Supp. 155

Brown, C.J.

The plaintiffs here, Dr. W.B. Cleveland and his wife, Katherine Cleveland, are owners of lands situated in Fayette County, Tennessee. On January 17, 1967, these plaintiffs entered into a written lease with the defendant Jack McNabb which lease provided that, for a period of five years, the tenant McNabb would pay the landlord an annual rental amounting to fifty dollars per acre for all acreage allotted to cotton by the government and ten dollars per acre for all acreage actually planted in soybeans. (This lease is attached to the Amended and Supplemental Complaint as Exhibit A). In this action the plaintiffs sue the defendant McNabb for rent allegedly due and owing from the 1968 crop year. Further, the plaintiffs sue the defendants TFC Marketing Service, Inc., John S. Wilder and W.W. Wilder, individually and as partners doing business as Longtown Supply Company, the Commodity Credit Corporation and the United States of America to enforce landlord's liens for the value of purchased crops to the extent that such liens are necessary to satisfy any unpaid rent. It is undisputed that each of this group of defendants received crops raised by the defendant McNabb on the plaintiffs' lands. (The United States is named as a defendant because the Commodity Credit Corporation is a branch of the United States Department of Agriculture. The named defendant Ralston Purina Company has by consent been dismissed.) . . .

As stated previously, the plaintiffs also seek in this action to enforce landlord's liens for the value of crops raised on their lands in 1968 to the extent that such liens are necessary to satisfy any unpaid rent. In this connection it is stipulated that the defendant Commodity Credit Corporation made a loan on and later acquired ownership of cotton grown on the plaintiffs' lands in 1968 and that this cotton had a value of $27,155.40. . . .

To support their contention that they are entitled to liens on all crops grown on their lands in 1968, the plaintiffs rely on the Tennessee Crop Liens Statute, T.C.A. §§64-1201 to 64-1214. In particular the plaintiffs rely on the following sections: [The court quotes the statute that gives landlords a lien on all crops grown on their land to the amount of rent due, and further provides that the landlord can enforce this lien against a purchaser of the crop "with or without notice." — Ed.].

It is next contended by the defendant United States that the plaintiffs are not entitled to a lien upon crops purchased by the Commodity Credit Corporation because the Commodity Credit Corporation was a good faith purchaser for value of negotiable warehouse receipts. As a result of such negotiation, the United States contends, the Commodity Credit Corporation acquired title to the crops in question free of the plaintiffs' crop lien.

Article Seven of the Uniform Commercial Code, as adopted in Tennessee, provides that, with limited exceptions, a holder to whom a negotiable document of title has been "duly negotiated" thereby acquires title to the goods described in such documents. §7-502. The term "duly negotiated" is defined in the preceding section, §7-501, as follows: [the court quoted the version of §7-501 in effect at the time].

In addition, §1-201[6] provides in part:

_____

6. Now §1-202. — Ed.

(25) A person has "notice" of a fact when . . . (c) from all the facts and circumstances known to him at the time in question he has reason to know that it exists.

The United States contends that the Commodity Credit Corporation received the warehouse receipts in question "duly negotiated." The plaintiffs, on the other hand, contend that the negotiation in question was not in the regular course of business and that the Commodity Credit Corporation, from all the facts and circumstances known to it, had reason to know of the plaintiffs' lien. Consequently it is the plaintiffs' position that the Commodity Credit Corporation did not acquire title, through due negotiation, to the crops it purchased.

The proof shows that the defendant McNabb delivered the cotton he had raised on the plaintiffs' lands and later sold to Commodity Credit Corporation to a cotton gin. After the cotton was ginned it was taken directly to a warehouse which issued a negotiable warehouse receipt for each bale of cotton it held. McNabb later received these receipts which were issued in his name as producer at the cotton gin and took them to the Agricultural Stabilization and Conservation Service office, which is the government office administrator of the cotton loan program in Somerville, Tennessee. McNabb left the warehouse receipts at this office and in return ultimately received a "loan." [Under the system, if the loan is not paid, the cotton becomes the property of the government. — Ed.]

A clerk from the ASCS office, Mrs. Sally Pat McNeil, testified that she had made no inquiry as to where the defendant McNabb had grown his cotton. The loan papers executed by this clerk show in the space designated for information concerning liens that there was no lien on the cotton grown by McNabb. Mrs. McNeil testified that she obtained this information from McNabb himself. McNabb testified that a copy of his lease with the plaintiffs was on file in the ASCS office. Further, the proof shows that the warehouse receipts referred to cotton gin tickets which in turn indicate that the cotton delivered by McNabb was grown on the plaintiffs' lands.

On this record we find that the warehouse receipts were not "duly negotiated" to the Commodity Credit Corporation so as to cut off the plaintiffs' lien. First, as the plaintiffs point out, the Department of Agriculture's own regulations, specifically 7 C.F.R. 1427.1364, require that cotton going into the loan program be lien-free. This regulation, we think, indicates that some inquiry is to be made by the local ASCS office to determine if there is a lien on cotton which is to be put into the government loan program. McNabb, as a tenant farmer (albeit a large one) could not reasonably be expected to be fully familiar with the Tennessee Lien statutes and therefore limited inquiry from him alone, even if it might reasonably be assumed that he would give an honest answer, was not sufficient, especially since Mrs. McNeil only asked McNabb whether there was a lien on the cotton he had grown, and not whether his farm land was leased. Also, as indicated, the information that McNabb was a tenant farmer was readily available to the ASCS office. Either the government office disregarded the Tennessee Lien statute or was unfamiliar with it. At any rate, we think from all the facts and circumstances known to it, the Commodity Credit Corporation had reason to know of the plaintiffs' lien. Further, we do not believe that the existence of the above-mentioned custom and usage should lead us to the conclusion that the government through its representatives had no reason to know that the lien existed.

In *McNabb*, Commodity Credit Corp. was denied §7-502 holder status because it "had reason to know." Not all courts agree on the amount of knowledge of a claim or defense that is sufficient to deprive one of the §7-502 status. Compare R.E. Huntly Cotton Co. v. Fields, 551 S.W.2d 472 (Tex. Civ. App. 1977) ("access to information sufficient to put [transferees] on notice of claims . . . is immaterial unless defendants had actual knowledge of facts and circumstances that would amount to bad faith").

Under §7-501, the negotiation must also be in the regular course of business or financing to be a due negotiation. Official Comment 1 to §7-501 provides in part:

> There are two aspects to the usual and normal course of mercantile dealings, namely, the person making the transfer and the nature of the transaction itself. The first question which arises is: Is the transferor a person with whom it is reasonable to deal as having full powers? In regard to documents of title the only holder whose possession appears, commercially, to be in order is almost invariably a person in the trade. No commercial purpose is served by allowing a tramp or a professor to "duly negotiate" an order bill of lading for hides or cotton not his own, and since such a transfer is obviously not in the regular course of business, it is excluded from the scope of the protection of subsection (a)(5) or (b)(3).
>
> The second question posed by the "regular course" qualification is: Is the transaction one which is normally proper to pass full rights without inquiry, even though the transferor itself may not have such rights to pass, and even though the transferor may be acting in breach of duty? In raising this question the "regular course" criterion has the further advantage of limiting the effective wrongful disposition to transactions whose protection will really further trade. Obviously, the snapping up of goods for quick resale at a price suspiciously below the market deserves no protection as a matter of policy: it is also clearly outside the range of regular course.
>
> Any notice on the document sufficient to put a merchant on inquiry as to the "regular course" quality of the transaction will frustrate a "due negotiation." Thus irregularity of the document or unexplained staleness of a bill of

lading may appropriately be recognized as negating a negotiation in "regular" course.

A §7-502 holder gets the rights listed in that section. The FBLA is similar. Read §7-502 carefully and do the next Problem.

PROBLEM 100

Wonder Warehouse issued a negotiable warehouse receipt to "bearer" that covered 40 drums of oil. The bailor was Bonanza Petroleum Company. The receipt was pledged by Bonanza to the Octopus National Bank as collateral for a $5,000 loan. While in the bank's possession, the receipt was stolen by the bank's credit manager, Claude McStuffy, who gave it to his cousin Al McStuffy, a disreputable oil products salesman. Al presented the receipt at the warehouse, and the new agent on duty delivered the drums to him. The agent, however, also stupidly returned the receipt to Al. Al sold the drums through his business. He then took the old warehouse receipt to the Antitrust National Bank, where he pledged it as collateral for a $5,000 loan. Al and Claude then skipped town. When both banks make demand on the warehouse for the goods, does the warehouse have any defenses? Remember §7-403? Consider it; then read §7-404.

B.   The §7-503(a) Owner

Go back to Article 2 (Sales), and read the *entrusting rule* found in §§2-403(2) and 2-403(3), which we considered when we talked about the warranty of title; see Simson v. Moon, 137 Ga. App. 82, 222 S.E.2d 873 (1975); Annot., 59 A.L.R.4th 567. An understanding of what constitutes an entrusting is essential to understand the Problem and discussion that follow.

PROBLEM 101

Albert Collector took his favorite antique grandfather clock down to the Antique Clock Store to be cleaned. The proprietor assured him it would be ready on Friday. On Thursday, Betty Shopper wandered into the store, saw the clock, and became entranced by it. She made the proprietor an offer he couldn't refuse, so he sold her the clock and she took it home. Albert Collector was furious. He consults you. Can he replevy the clock from Betty? See Lindholm v. Brant, 283 Conn. 65, 925 A.2d 1048 (2007) (reprinted in Chapter 4). Can he sue the proprietor? Using what theory (or theories)? If the proprietor had stored the clock in a warehouse, received a negotiable warehouse receipt therefor, and pledged the receipt to Last National Bank in return for a loan, could Albert Collector retrieve the clock from the warehouse? Compare §§7-403, 7-502, and 7-503.

What *real* defenses are available against a §7-502 holder? The only ones that the Code sets out are listed in §7-403(a): proper delivery to a superior claimant, nonnegligent destruction of the goods, sale to enforce bailee's lien, and "any other lawful excuse" (not further defined in the Code). Who is the *superior claimant* that §7-403(a) permits to get the goods from the bailee even though there is an outstanding negotiable document of title? The answer: a §7-503(a) owner.

A §7-503(a) owner is a person who had a legal interest or perfected security interest in the goods *prior to* the bailee's issuance of a document of title and who was in no way responsible for the creation of a situation permitting a negotiable document of title to come into existence. Read §7-503(a) carefully along with Official Comment 1. Essentially, §7-503(a) means that if the owner of goods *entrusts* them (or documents covering them) or delivers them to anyone so that that person has the *apparent* authority to deal with the goods, the owner is estopped to assert ownership against a subsequent §7-502 holder. See In re Jamestown Farmers Elevator, Inc., 49 Bankr. 661 (Bankr. D.N.D. 1985).

Where the owner has entrusted and is thus estopped, *ownership* becomes a *personal* defense, meaning it is only available against persons who do not qualify as a §7-502 holder, but is not assertable against such a holder. *But* when the owner of goods has had them, in effect, *stolen* by someone other than the owner's agent, then the owner is the very person §7-503(a) was meant to protect. A §7-503(a) owner has a superior right to the goods even against a §7-502 holder. In this case, ownership is a *real* defense (one that can be asserted against all parties, including a §7-502 holder), and the true owner can force the bailee to turn over the goods to the §7-503(a) owner without surrendering the negotiable document (though, as a practical matter, the owner will probably either have to get a court order or sign an indemnity agreement with the bailee before the latter will turn over the goods).

The policy here is that — since one of two innocent parties must bear a loss — if the owner has been even slightly at fault by permitting someone else to have the goods (and therefore apparent authority to ship or store them) or the documents, the owner should bear the loss. The owner must learn not to be so trusting in the future — or to insure against employee defalcation. But if the owner has had the goods stolen by someone not permitted to hold onto the goods, then the owner should be able to trace the goods and recover them even if they are found in the possession of a bailee.

The following case involves electronic documents of title. These are allowed by §§7-105, 7-106, and 7-501(b).

Agricredit Acceptance, LLC v. Hendrix

United States District Court, Southern District of Georgia, 2000
82 F. Supp. 2d 1379

Nangle, District Judge.

Before the Court is defendant Hohenberg Bros. Co., Loeb & Company, Inc., Weil Brothers-Cotton, Inc., and the Montgomery Company, Inc.'s (the merchants') motion for summary judgment (Doc. 80). For the reasons that follow, defendants' motion is denied.

I. Background . . .

The defendant merchants buy cotton stored in warehouses and resell it to textile mills. Br. Supp. Defs.' Consolidated Mot. Summ. J. at 1 (Doc. 81). These transactions are generally electronic in nature, involving electronic warehouse receipts (EWRs) maintained in the central operating systems of various EWR providers. Id. at 1-2. The sale typically begins with the merchants' receipt of a recap sheet from a prospective seller, which describes a number of bales being offered for sale by grade, quantity and warehouse in which the bales are stored. Id. at 2. The merchant then telephones the seller and submits an offer involving either a fixed price or an "on call" price which is based on the price of cotton futures on the New York market. Id. Once an agreement is reached between the merchant and the seller, the seller transfers the EWRs for the bales sold into the name of the merchant, and the merchant receives a confirmation of this transaction from the EWR provider. Id. When the EWRs are in the name of the merchant, the merchant is able to obtain a list of the bales by receipt number from the central filing system by downloading the list into the merchant's computers. Id. The sale is completed when the merchant pays the seller for the cotton represented by the EWRs. Id.

These sales can also be accomplished via contract for future delivery. Id. at 5. These contracts involve the seller promising to provide some specific number of bales in the future at a provisional price. After the seller acquires the bales, it transfers the EWRs for the bales into the name of the merchant and the process proceeds as above. Id.

Thomas Hendrix's 1997 cotton crop was financed by a loan from plaintiff Agricredit Acceptance Corporation (AAC). Order dated Dec. 21, 1998, at 2. The loan was secured by the cotton crop. Id. AAC's security interest was properly perfected by filing the Security Agreement in the real estate records of the counties wherein the cotton was grown and with the County clerks' offices. Id. at 3. Sea Island Cotton Trading was designated as a selling agent through which Hendrix would sell the cotton crop, and AAC notified Sea Island of its security interest in accordance with the provisions of the Food Security Act (FSA), 7 U.S.C. §1631. Id. Hendrix's cotton crop was ginned, baled, and stored in various warehouses, including Collins Gin & Warehouse, Candler Gin & Warehouse, Goldkist, Inc., Growers Gin & Warehouse, Inc., and Bulloch Gin. Id.; Br. Supp. Defs.' Mot. Summ. J. at 3. The warehouses issued EWRs for the cotton in the central filing system of the EWR provider to which they were subscribed. Br. Supp. Defs.' Mot. Summ. J. at 3. These receipts were eventually placed in the name of Sea Island. Id. at 4; Order dated Dec. 21, 1998, at 3.

All of the defendant merchants purchased large quantities of cotton from Sea Island in 1997 and 1998, including many bales from Hendrix's 1997 crop. The merchants paid Sea Island for these bales, and the EWRs representing the bales were transferred by Sea Island into the names of the purchasing merchants. Br. Supp. Defs.' Mot. Summ. J. at 4-15. Sea Island never paid AAC or Hendrix for the cotton in violation of its obligations under the FSA notice. Order dated Dec. 21, 1998, at 4. Consequently, plaintiff AAC filed suit against the defendant merchants and others seeking foreclosure of its security interest in the Hendrix cotton, a writ of possession against anyone in possession of the cotton, and a finding of conversion and an award of damages against the cotton merchants, among other things. Id.

The defendant merchants assert that because the EWRs representing the Hendrix cotton were duly negotiated to them by Sea Island and because AAC entrusted the cotton to Hendrix with apparent authority to sell it, the cotton is no longer subject to AAC's security interest. That is, the merchants assert that duly negotiated EWRs have priority over a prior perfected security interest, especially when the secured party entrusts the collateral to the borrower. As this Court found in its Order dated December 21, 1998, the resolution of these issues depends on this Court's interpretation of the Georgia Uniform Commercial Code and its application to the facts of this case. Id. at 13-14.

II.　Analysis . . .

In Georgia, a security interest in crops can only be perfected by the filing of a financing statement. O.C.G.A. §11-9-302(1)(h).[7] Generally, a perfected security interest takes priority over other liens, claims or rights to property and to security interests perfected at a later date. O.C.G.A. §§11-9-310, -312.[8] This general rule is of course subject to exception. For example, a buyer in the ordinary course of business takes free of a security

7. Section 9-310(a) in the 1999 revision of Article 9. — Ed.
8. Section 9-334 in the 1999 revision of Article 9. — Ed.

interest created by his seller, O.C.G.A. §11-9-307(1). Furthermore, nothing in Article 9 of the UCC limits the rights of "a holder to whom a negotiable document of title has been duly negotiated . . . and such holders . . . take priority over an earlier security interest even though perfected," O.C.G.A. §11-9-309.[9]

A warehouse receipt is a negotiable document of title if it provides by its terms that the goods are to be delivered to bearer or to the order of a named person. O.C.G.A. §11-7-104(1)(a).[10] These receipts may be in an electronic format. O.C.G.A. §10-4-19(e). A negotiable document running to order is negotiated by indorsement and delivery. O.C.G.A. §§11-7-501(1).[11] A negotiable document running to bearer is negotiated by delivery alone. O.C.G.A. §11-7-501(2).[12]

To be duly negotiated, a document of title must be negotiated "to a holder who purchases it in good faith without any notice of any defense against it or claim to it on the part of any person and for value, unless it is established that the negotiation is not in the regular course of business." O.C.G.A. §11-7-501(4).[13] Good faith is defined by reference to O.C.G.A. §11-1-201(19) as "honesty in fact in the conduct or transaction concerned." "A person has 'notice' of a fact when: (a) He has actual knowledge of it; or (b) He has received a notice or notification of it; or (c) From all the facts and circumstances known to him at the time in question he has reason to know that it exists." O.C.G.A. §11-1-201(25). Finally, in general, a person gives value for rights if he acquires them "in return for any consideration sufficient to support a simple contract." O.C.G.A. §11-1-201(44). Section 11-7-502 provides that a holder to whom a negotiable warehouse receipt has been duly negotiated acquires title to the document, title to the goods, and the direct obligation of the warehouse to deliver the goods, except as provided in O.C.G.A. §11-7-503.

Section 11-7-503[14] provides that:

> (1) A document of title confers no right in goods against a person who before issuance of the document had a legal interest or a perfected security interest in [the goods] and who neither:
>   (a) Delivered or entrusted [the goods] . . . to the bailor or his nominee with actual or apparent authority to ship, store, or sell . . .; nor
>   (b) Acquiesced in the procurement by the bailor or his nominee of any document of title.

---

9. Section 9-331 in the 1999 revision of Article 9. — Ed.
10. Now §7-104(a). — Ed.
11. Now §7-501(a)(1). — Ed.
12. Now §7-501(a)(2). — Ed.
13. Now §7-501(b)(3). — Ed.
14. The same rule is continued with slight wording changes in §7-503.

Neither Article 1 nor Article 7 defines the term "entrusted." This term is used elsewhere in the UCC, however. Section 11-2-403(3) defines it as "any delivery and any acquiescence in retention of possession regardless of any condition expressed between the parties." However, Georgia courts have found that this provision only applies to owners of goods, because one cannot entrust goods one does not own. Sunnyland Employees' Fed. Credit Union v. Fort Wayne Mortgage Co., 182 Ga. App. 5, 354 S.E.2d 645, 647 (1987) (holding that party with security interest in mobile home could not be the entruster of it because party was not the owner of the home); United Carolina Bank v. Sistrunk, 158 Ga. App. 107, 279 S.E.2d 272, 274 (1981) (holding party with security interest in car could not be the entruster of it because party was not the owner of the car); McConnell v. Barrett, 154 Ga. App. 767, 270 S.E.2d 13, 15-16 (1980) (holding that non-owners cannot be entrusters and citing Adams v. City Nat'l Bank & Trust Co., 565 P.2d 26, 29 (Okla. 1977)). Acquiescence is not defined anywhere in the UCC.

C.   INTERPRETATION AND APPLICATION OF THE UCC

Defendants' motion for summary judgment is based on two theories: (1) that the EWRs were duly negotiated to the merchants and pursuant to O.C.G.A. §§11-9-309, the merchants' interest in the cotton has priority over AAC's interest, Br. Supp. Defs.' Mot. Summ. J. at 16-19; Defs.' Objections to Dep. Testimony Offered by Pl. at 2-4, 6, 7-8 (Doc. 123); and (2) that AAC waived the priority of its security interest by entrusting the cotton to Hendrix pursuant to O.C.G.A. §§11-7-503, Br. Supp. Defs.' Mot. Summ. J. at 20; Defs.' Objections to Dep. Testimony Offered by Pl. at 7-8; Defs.' Resp. Opp'n AAC's Objection to Affs. at 9-12 (Doc. 120).

1.   Due Negotiation and §11-9-309[15]

For the EWRs to be duly negotiated to the merchants, the merchants must be purchasers in good faith without notice of claims or defenses to the receipts and for value. O.C.G.A. §11-7-501(4).[16] It is undisputed that the merchants purchased the EWRs for value. Consequently, the Court must determine whether the merchants also purchased the EWRs in good faith and without notice.

Good faith as defined in Article 1[17] means "honesty in fact." Plaintiff does not dispute that the merchants acted with honesty in fact in this transaction.

---

15. Now §9-331. — Ed.
16. Now §7-501(b)(3). — Ed.
17. In the revised version of Article 1 (now the law in most jurisdictions), §1-20(b)(20) defines "good faith" as "honesty in fact and the observance of reasonable commercial standards of fair dealing," thus adding an objective component to the mix. — Eds.

Rather, relying on an improper definition of good faith, AAC asserts that good faith requires the merchants to perform a lien check on the cotton before purchase. The Court finds that the "honesty in fact" definition does not require the merchants to perform a lien check on the cotton prior to purchase. Consequently, the Court holds that the merchants are purchasers in good faith as a matter of law.

However, this finding does not end the inquiry. The merchants must also be purchasers without notice of any defenses or claims to the EWRs. Plaintiff relies on the third prong of Article 1's definition of notice in arguing that the merchants' experience with the cotton industry and its willful ignorance as to the existence of liens on the cotton constitute reason to know that plaintiff's defense to the EWRs existed. Pl's Resp. Opp'n Defs.' Mot. Summ. J. at 22-24 (Doc. 93). While some jurisdictions have required the existence of suspicious circumstances for a finding of "reason to know"; Colin v. Central Penn Nat'l Bank, 404 F. Supp. 638, 640-41 (E.D. Pa. 1975); others hold that willful or deliberate indifference to or ignorance of information is a basis for a finding of "reason to know;" Demoulas v. Demoulas, 428 Mass. 555, 703 N.E.2d 1149, 1167 (1998) ("If a person confronted with a state of facts closes his eyes in order that he may not see that which would be visible and therefore known to him if he looked, he is chargeable with 'knowledge' of what he would have seen had he looked.") (citations omitted); New Bedford Inst. for Savings v. Gildroy, 36 Mass. App. Ct. 647, 634 N.E.2d 920 (1994) ("Further, a holder has no duty to inquire unless 'the circumstances reveal a deliberate desire by the holder to evade knowledge of claims made by the maker.'") (citations omitted).

The Court finds that the evidence in the record indicates that a genuine issue of fact exists concerning the merchants' notice of AAC's claims to the cotton. The merchants testified in deposition that they do not perform lien searches on cotton bought from merchants or gins. Dep. Hohenberg Bros. Co. through John D. Mitchell at 25-27 (Doc. 91); Dep. Weil Brothers-Cotton, Inc. through James A. Wade at 18-19 (Doc. 90); Dep. Loeb & Co., Inc. through James L. Loeb at 24 (Doc. 87); Dep. Montgomery Co. through Jack D. Atkins at 27-28, 42-43 (Doc. 89). However, when buying directly from the producer or when buying in a state with a central lien filing system, most of the merchants do perform lien searches. Dep. Mitchell at 25-26; Dep. Loeb at 24; Dep. Atkins at 28, 42-43. Further, when dealing with sales via contract for future delivery, the merchants include a clause in the contract requiring the seller to warrant that there are no liens on the cotton. Dep. Mitchell at 68-72. These facts imply that the merchants certainly knew of the possibility of the existence of liens. Whether their failure to search for liens amounts to deliberate indifference or ignorance to their existence, however, is less than clear from the facts presently in the record. The Court finds that this issue is one for a jury to decide.

Even if the Court finds that the merchants had no notice of AAC's claims to the cotton, this finding would not automatically provide superiority to the merchants' claims to the cotton. O.C.G.A. §11-9-309[18] provides that "Nothing in this article limits the rights . . . of a holder to whom a negotiable document of title has been duly negotiated . . . and such holders take priority over an earlier security interest even though perfected." Defendants urge the Court to hold that this Section provides that any duly negotiated EWR automatically trumps a prior perfected security interest in the goods covered by that EWR. Defendants' interpretation of §11-9-309 is in error. Such an interpretation would eviscerate the provisions of O.C.G.A. §11-7-503, which expressly provide that EWRs confer no rights in the goods covered by the EWRs against security interests existing and perfected prior to the issuance of the EWR where there has been no entrustment or acquiescence on the part of the secured party. The proper interpretation of §11-9-309 is that the Section only applies when the negotiable document holder and the secured party are both claiming an interest in the document. Farmers State Bank of Somonauk v. National Bank of Earlville, 230 Ill. App. 3d 881, 172 Ill. Dec. 894, 596 N.E.2d 173, 174-76 (1992). That is, §11-9-309 addresses disputes between competing interests in a negotiable document whereas §11-7-503 covers disputes between competing interests in the underlying goods. Accordingly, even if the EWRs were duly negotiated to the merchants, disposition of the cotton covered by those EWRs depends upon the application of O.C.G.A. §11-7-503.

2.   Entrustment

Defendants argue that despite the Georgia courts' interpretation of §11-2-403, this Court is free to find that AAC entrusted the cotton to Hendrix by leaving it in his possession and allowing him to sell it through Sea Island. However, because Article 1 and Article 7 provide no definition for the term "entrusted," this Court must look to the Georgia courts' interpretation of that term as it is used in other sections of the UCC. Banks v. Georgia Power Co., 267 Ga. 602, 481 S.E.2d 200, 202 (1997) (stating that court is required to construe statute with reference to other statutes and decisions of the courts); Poteat v. Butler, 231 Ga. 187, 200 S.E.2d 741, 742 (1973) ("All statutes are presumed to be enacted by the General Assembly with full knowledge of the existing condition of the law . . . and their meaning and effect is to be determined in connection . . . with reference to other statutes and decisions of the courts."). Because the Georgia courts have held in the context of §11-2-403 that a secured party who does not own the goods cannot

---

18. Now §9-331. — Ed.

entrust them; *Sunnyland*, 354 S.E.2d at 647; *United Carolina Bank*, 279 S.E.2d at 274; *McConnell*, 270 S.E.2d at 15-16; this Court must hold similarly in the context of §11-7-503.[19] Consequently, the Court finds that plaintiff did not entrust the cotton to Hendrix as a matter of law.

Plaintiff may, however, have acquiesced in the procurement of a document of title in the cotton (namely the EWRs) pursuant to §11-7-503(1)(b).[20] When a bank knows that a farmer is attempting to sell his collateral and it acquiesces in his procurement of documents of title to that collateral, the bank has waived its right to assert its security interest in the collateral. Mercantile Bank of Springfield v. Joplin Regional Stockyards, Inc., 870 F. Supp. 278, 283 (W.D. Mo. 1994). The evidence presently before the Court is not sufficient to support a ruling on this issue as a matter of law. Consequently, the question of plaintiff s acquiescence is better left to a jury.

III.   CONCLUSION

Because genuine issues of material fact exist,

IT IS HEREBY ORDERED that defendants' motion for summary judgment is denied.

C.   *Other Transfers*

Section 7-504, which you should read as soon as you finish this paragraph, sets out the rights acquired by a transferee of a document when there has been no *due negotiation*. Section 7-505 goes on to provide that the indorser of a document of title does not make any *contract* that the bailee will honor the document, but §7-507 (which you should also glance at) provides that any transferor makes the warranties listed there. In addition, since a sale of goods is involved in the transfer of any document of title, a transferor also makes the Article 2 warranties, discussed in the earlier part of this book.

It is a basic rule of all commercial law that a transferee gets whatever legal rights the transferor had. This rule is called the shelter rule because the transferee is said to take shelter in the status of the transferor. In Article 2 (Sale of Goods) the shelter rule is found in §2-403; read it.

---

19. This interpretation does not make the use of the term "entrusted" superfluous in the context of §11-7-503. Rather, that Section also applies to any persons with any legal interest in the goods which was created prior to the issuance of the document of title. When such persons are the owners of the goods, the entrustment provision would apply.

20. Now §7-503(a)(2). — Ed.

In Article 3 (Commercial Paper) the rule turns up in §3-203(b), and in Article 8 (Investment Securities) it is reflected in §8-301. For Article 7 the rule is codified in §7-504(a). Read it, and use it to work the following Problem.

PROBLEM 102

The shipping agent for the King Cotton Manufacturing Company wrongfully took for himself 90 bales of cotton that had come under his control and stored them in the Rural Warehouse, which issued to him a negotiable warehouse receipt. This receipt he took to Octopus National Bank (ONB) and gave as security for a loan. He indorsed the receipt over to ONB. King Cotton discovered the bales were missing and investigated; the shipping agent was arrested. Shortly thereafter, ONB sold the warehouse receipt to Antitrust National Bank (ANB), which bought the document with full knowledge of the above facts. Both ANB and King Cotton made a demand on Rural Warehouse for the cotton. Rural calls you, its attorney, for advice. What do you say? Note §§7-403(c), 7-501 through 7-504, 7-603.

IV. COLLECTION THROUGH BANKS

A. "Payment Against Documents"

If the seller and buyer deal with each other on a face-to-face basis, delivery of the goods and payment of the price normally occur at the same moment, and neither party need trust the other. Where seller and buyer are separated by great distances, a seller must either trust the buyer to live up to the contract (a sale on *open account* with trust on both sides) or figure out a way to make certain that the buyer cannot get the goods until they are paid for. The easiest way to do this would be to have an agent in the buyer's city who could present the bill of lading covering the goods to the buyer but not turn it over to the buyer until cash was paid for the goods. In effect, this is the solution that sellers have adopted. See §2-503(5)(b). The *agent that sellers typically use* is a bank in the buyer's city. And, instead of a letter of instruction telling the bank-agent what to do, the seller simply draws an Article 3 draft (§3-104(e)) on the buyer (so that the buyer is the drawee) and attaches it to the bill of lading.

A draft is similar to a check; it is an instruction of payment. The seller is the drawer, and the buyer is the drawee. A simple draft will look like this:

```
┌─────────────────────────────────────────────────────────────┐
│                                           _____         │
│                                            (Date)             │
│                                                               │
│   To:  _____               _____         │
│        (Buyer's Name)                      (Amount)           │
│   At sight pay to the order of _____  │
│                               (Payee's Name)                  │
│   _____ dollars and _____ cents.         │
│                                                               │
│                                           _____ │
│                                           (Seller's Signature)│
└─────────────────────────────────────────────────────────────┘
```

The payee will be whomever the seller nominates: the seller's bank, one of the seller's creditors, or even the seller itself. The only difference between this draft and your typical check is that the drawee is the buyer and not a bank.

Now that the seller has created the draft, it is combined with other papers for delivery to the buyer. The papers (which will normally include the bill of lading, a sales invoice, and, occasionally, an inspection certificate) along with the seller's draft on buyer are indorsed over to the seller's local bank for collection. Then the normal bank collection machinery in Article 4 is put into motion. Eventually, a bank in buyer's vicinity makes a formal Article 3 *presentment* of the draft (§3-501), and the buyer must either pay or dishonor. In any event, the buyer cannot get the documents (especially the bill of lading) until payment, so the seller is protected from having to trust a buyer in an arm's length transaction. If the buyer dishonors, the seller is notified by the collecting bank. The seller will then give instructions to the bank as to what to do with the goods when they arrive (the bank will be able to claim them from the carrier because it has the bill of lading; §7-403(c)).

Any draft accompanied by sales documents like those mentioned above is called a *documentary draft*. See §4-104(a)(6). The normal rules for negotiable instruments in Articles 3 and 4 apply to such drafts, but occasionally the sections make special rules for documentary drafts, e.g., §4-202(a)(2) (providing that after dishonor a collecting bank need not return a documentary draft to its transferor).

Sometimes the seller does not demand that the buyer actually pay prior to receiving the documents. Under some contracts, it is enough that buyer *accept* the draft and incur the obligation of an *acceptor* (§3-413), thus becoming primarily liable on the draft (the draft is now commonly called a *trade acceptance*). Typically, these are *time drafts* (as opposed to *sight drafts*, whereby payment is required as soon as buyer sees the draft) because they require payment in 30, 60, or 90 days after "sight" (presentment to buyer). The business reason why this is frequently done is so that the buyer can take the goods during the grace period, by manufacturing transform them into other goods, and resell them. In these transactions the seller sends the draft and documents through the banks and asks the collecting bank to call the buyer and make a presentment for acceptance. Read §4-212. The buyer shows up and accepts by writing the buyer's signature on the draft (if the buyer does not show up, the draft is dishonored). After acceptance, the draft is returned to the presenter and may be further negotiated. On acceptance by the buyer, the bank turns over the documents, and in 30, 60, or 90 days (or whatever time period the draft provides) the buyer is required to pay the draft or is in breach of the acceptor's contract. If the buyer fails to pay or accept the draft (which happens about 10 percent of the time) notice of that must immediately be sent back up the line. For an article spelling out *payment against documents* in detail, see Farnsworth, Documentary Drafts Under the Uniform Commercial Code, 22 Bus. Law. 479 (1967).

PROBLEM 103

Sam Seller in Dallas signed a sales contract to sell one ton of tennis balls to Beth Buyer in Indianapolis, "FOB truck in Dallas," $800 to be paid by a 60-day time draft on the buyer. Sam boxed the tennis balls and filled out a packaging invoice describing the goods. He drew a draft as follows:

To: Beth Buyer

Sixty days after sight pay to the order of *Sam Seller* $800.

(Signed) *Sam Seller*

He took the tennis balls down to the Texas Trucking Company and asked for a negotiable bill of lading consigned to his own order, with the instructions "notify Beth Buyer on arrival." The trucking company issued the negotiable ("order") bill to Sam.

Sam then took the bill of lading, the invoice describing the goods, and the draft on Buyer down to his local bank, the Lone Star National Bank. He asked Lone Star to collect the draft. On agreeing to the bank's collection charge, Sam indorsed both the draft and the bill of lading over to the bank. Lone Star Bank then forwarded the draft and the documents to the Indianapolis State Hoosier Bank for collection. The Hoosier Bank called Beth Buyer and told her to come by the bank and get the papers. Beth came down that afternoon, wrote her name diagonally on the draft (which the bank dated and kept), and received the other documents. Read §2-514. Two days later the Texas Trucking Company showed up with the goods and promptly notified Buyer of their arrival. Buyer went down to the truck depot and surrendered the bill of lading (as required by §7-403(c)), whereupon she received the tennis balls. Now, to see how Article 2 and Article 7 fit together like one glorious puzzle, answer the following questions:

(a) Can Beth Buyer *inspect* the goods? If so, when? See §2-513.

(b) If the tennis balls are defective (Seller has breached one of his Article 2 warranties), can Buyer reject (§2-602) or revoke her acceptance (§2-608) and refuse to pay?

(c) If the cartons are empty (Sam is a crook), can Buyer sue the Texas Trucking Company, since the bill of lading states that the goods shipped are "ONE TON TENNIS BALLS"?

(d) Can Buyer sue the collecting bank because the documents did not conform to the goods shipped? Read §7-508 to answer this one.

B. *Liability of the Collecting Bank*

Sometimes a seller in the position of Sam (above) will sell (*discount*) the draft and documents to a local bank. This generally makes no difference in the resulting rights (see, for example, the last sentence of §7-508), but it does give the collecting bank a security interest in the draft and documents (§4-210(a)(3)) and therefore permits it to become a holder in due course (§4-211). Read §2-506.

The last Part of Article 4 contains four sections that deal specifically with the collection of documentary drafts. Read §§4-501 to 4-504 to see how these sections link the sale under Article 2 with the use of Article 7 documents of title.

Rheinberg Kellerei GmbH v. Brooksfield National Bank of Commerce

United States Court of Appeals, Fifth Circuit, 1990
901 F.2d 481

GARZA, J.

American bank did not notify German bank of difficulty in payment on international collection order which came due on arrival of goods in Houston; the collection order was eventually dishonored. The district court held that the American bank did not know, and had no duty to inquire, whether goods had arrived, and entered take nothing judgment. Because we find that the American bank was on notice of the possibility of dishonor and should have told the German bank of the problem in collection, we reverse.

FACTS

In January of 1986, J & J Wine, an American company, ordered a shipment of wine from a German firm, Rheinberg Kellerei GmbH, through an importer, Frank Sutton & Co.[21] Payment was to be made through an international letter of collection handled by Edekabank in Germany and Brooksfield National Bank of Commerce Bank in San Antonio ("NBC Bank").[22] On March 27, NBC Bank received the letter of collection, bill of lading and invoices from Edeka.[23] The letter of collection noted that payment was due "on arrival of goods in Houston harbor," and called for NBC Bank to notify Sutton "in case of any difficulty of lack payment." The invoices noted an estimated time of arrival: April 2, 1986. NBC Bank then presented the documents to J & J Wine on March 27.

There is some dispute as to what, exactly, J & J Wine told NBC Bank about its financial situation at the time, but it is sure that J & J Wine did not pay the amount due, and instead asked NBC Bank to hold the letter for a time while J & J Wine worked to raise the money for payment. NBC Bank did not notify Edeka or Sutton of J & J Wine's failure to pay on presentment. In fact, NBC Bank did nothing further until early May, when Sutton informed them that the wine was still at the Houston port and NBC Bank cabled Edeka for further instructions.

The wine had arrived in Houston on March 31, but NBC Bank did not receive notice of that. Because J & J Wine had not taken delivery of it, the wine sat, exposed, at Houston harbor in metal containers until it had deteriorated completely. U.S. Customs agents eventually sold it at auction. J & J Wine subsequently went out of business, and Rheinberg Kellerei was never paid for the wine.

Rheinberg Kellerei then brought this suit, alleging that NBC Bank had negligently failed to inform it of J & J Wine's failure to pay, and that because of that negligence, the wine had spoiled at Houston harbor. After a bench trial, the district court entered a take-nothing judgment for NBC Bank. The court reasoned that, because payment was not due until the wine's arrival,

---

21. The "GmbH" designation means "Gesellschaft mit beschrankter Haftung," or "company with limited liability." GmbH is a common form of corporate organization in Germany and is similar to the "Inc." designation in the American corporate system.

22. In a case like this one, international letters of collection are issued by the seller's bank (Edeka) and sent to the buyer's bank (NBC Bank), which in turn presents the letter and its documents to the buyer. To receive the documents and collect the goods, the buyer pays the amount due to its bank, which then forwards the funds to the seller's bank. Enforcement of these letters is governed by the International Chamber of Commerce's International Rules for Collection.

23. The bill of lading called for notification of Sutton and M.G. Maher & Co., the customs broker, on arrival of the goods in Houston. NBC Bank was not listed on the Bill of Lading or the invoices.

and NBC Bank had no notice of that arrival and no duty to inquire further, NBC Bank had no knowledge that J & J Wine was in breach of the payment terms. For that reason, the district court held that NBC Bank could not be held liable for failure to inform Edeka of J & J Wine's default.

Complaining that the district court improperly applied the requirements of the International Rules for Collection (the "Rules") and erred in construing the letter of collection itself, Rheinberg Kellerei brought this appeal.

DISCUSSION

I. DUTY TO INFORM

NBC Bank presented the letter of collection and the other documents to J & J Wine for payment on March 27, 1986, before the wine had arrived and before the payment was due. Rheinberg Kellerei argues that, regardless of whether NBC Bank knew when the wine had arrived, once NBC Bank presented the documents, it had a duty to inform Edeka of any problem in collecting J & J Wine's payment. We agree. That duty arises both from the Rules and the collection letter itself.

A. *Letter of Collection*

The letter, which is the primary source of responsibility in this case, instructs NBC Bank to notify Sutton "in case of any difficulty of lack payment."[24] The district court found that section demanded notice only if there were a "lack of payment or failure to pay." Likewise, NBC Bank emphasizes that the trigger for notice is a *lack* of payment. What the court below and NBC Bank ignore is the word "difficulty." The letter did not instruct NBC Bank to notify Sutton only if there were a default, or a failure to pay, or a lack of payment. Rather, NBC Bank was called on to act also if there were any *difficulty* in collecting payment. And the request that NBC Bank hold the letter while J & J Wine sought financing certainly posed a difficulty in collection. Once NBC Bank knew that J & J Wine had asked for time to come up with the money, it should have notified Sutton in accordance with the letter's instructions.

The Rules specify that any special instructions posted on a letter of collection should be "complete and precise." General Provisions, §C. While the instructions given on this letter could have been in clearer language, they are sufficiently precise to make NBC Bank aware of its duty to notify Sutton once difficulty arose in the collection.

---

24. Sutton was Rheinberg Kellerei's agent in this sale.

B.   International Rules for Collection

Article 20(iii)(c) of the Rules provides that the "collecting bank [NBC Bank] must send without delay advice on non-payment or advice of non-acceptance to the bank from whom the collecting order was received [Edeka]." The court below and NBC Bank submit that section called on NBC Bank to notify Edeka if J & J Wine had not paid on the letter at the time it came due: on arrival of the goods in Houston harbor. And, they argue, since NBC Bank had no actual notice of the arrival of the goods, it did not breach that duty to notify.

The issue, it seems, is the definition of "non-payment" as it is used in Art. 20(iii)(c). Does it refer to a failure to pay on presentment? Does it require an affirmative statement of intent not to pay? Must the due date have arrived? No court has yet defined the term and its attendant duties, so we must look for guidance elsewhere.

The Rules were adopted to aid in "defining, simplifying and harmonizing the practices and terminology used in international banking." I.C.C. Banking Commission, Statement of Services to Business. They serve, for the international banking community, the same function as the Uniform Commercial Code does for domestic players. There is no reason, then, to ignore the UCC as an advisory source.

Section 4-502 of the UCC governs payment of "on arrival" drafts, such as were presented in our case. Tex. Bus. & Com. Code Ann., §4-502 (Tex. UCC) (Vernon's 1968). Under that section, a bank such as NBC Bank may, but need not, present the documents to the buyer before the goods arrive. But if the buyer does not pay at that time, the bank must notify the seller's bank: "Refusal to pay or accept because the goods have not arrived is not dishonor; *the bank must notify its transferor of such refusal* but need not present the draft again. . . ." UCC §4-502 (emphasis added). The UCC imposes on the presenting bank a duty to notify the seller's bank of any delay or failure to pay on presentment of an "on arrival" draft, *whether or not the draft is yet due.*

If §4-502 were applied to our case, NBC Bank would have a duty to notify Edeka of J & J Wine's failure to pay the letter of collection when it was presented on March 27, even though the goods were not yet in Houston harbor and the payment was not yet due. This is not to say that J & J Wine was in default at that time or had dishonored the letter. Rather, the notice is an act of prudence, an exercise in due care. And, as the aims of the Rules and the UCC are more than consistent, and both demand the exercise of due care, we find that the Rules impose the same duty. NBC Bank should have notified Edeka of J & J Wine's failure to pay at presentment, as that failure constituted a "non-payment" under Art. 20(iii)(c).

NBC Bank and the court below rely heavily on the fact that NBC Bank had no actual knowledge of the wine's arrival in Houston, and had no duty to inquire further. We agree with those premises, but do not feel they affect NBC Bank's duty to notify. That duty arose — under both the Rules and the letter itself — when J & J Wine failed to pay on presentment and asked for time. Arrival of the wine did not trigger it. And NBC Bank cannot avoid liability by hiding from knowledge of arrival and claiming that ignorance as a defense.

II.   DAMAGES

State law governs the measure of damages in a case such as this one. Gathercrest, Ltd. v. First American Bank & Trust, 805 F.2d 995, 997 (11th Cir. 1986). Tex. Bus. & Com. Code Ann. §2-709(1) (Tex. UCC) (Vernon's 1968) gives the relevant standard: "the seller may recover, together with any incidental damages under the next section, the price (1) of goods accepted or of conforming goods lost or damaged . . . after risk of their loss has passed to the buyer." Risk of loss had passed to J & J Wine when the goods arrived at Houston harbor and were available for J & J Wine to take delivery. Tex. Bus. & Com. Code Ann., §2-509(1)(b) (Tex. UCC) (Vernon's 1968). The district court found that because the wine was exposed for such a long period in Houston harbor, it was "'over cooked' and had deteriorated, lost its original flavor, freshness, was flat and should not be sold into the market that it was intended." Since the goods were so damaged, Rheinberg Kellerei is entitled to the contract price plus the unpaid freight costs, as provided in UCC [§2-709(1)(a)].

NBC Bank is entitled to a credit for the net proceeds of any resale of the damaged wine. UCC §2-709(2). Customs agents sold the wine at auction, but we have no evidence before us of the price paid or the net amount remaining after customs fees, wharfage, and the costs of the auction were paid. For that reason, we remand this case to the district court for the limited purpose of calculating that net amount. After finding that net amount, the district court should enter judgment for Rheinberg Kellerei for the contract price plus freight charges, less the net proceeds of the customs auction.

Conclusion

NBC Bank had a duty to notify Edeka or Sutton, which was triggered when J & J Wine failed to pay the letter of collection on presentment and asked for more time. That duty arose from two sources: the Rules and the letter itself. Though payment was not due until the wine arrived in Houston harbor, that arrival was not a triggering event for the duty to arise, and lack of knowledge of it is no defense. The judgment of the district court is, therefore, reversed, and this cause is remanded for calculation of damages.

It is so ordered.

Up to this point, the text has mostly dealt with sales transactions within the United States. To understand sales of goods between sellers and buyers in different countries, Article 5 (Letters of Credit) must now be mastered. In international sales, most sales are carried out through the use of documents of title, with the added complication that letters of credit are also used. International collection of documentary drafts is regulated by Brochure 600 of the International Chamber of Commerce (2007 revision), which the banks regard as "the law." The relevant UCC Articles — 4, 5, and 7 — are similar to its provisions.

CHAPTER 8 REVIEW QUESTIONS

How do we distinguish negotiable and nonnegotiable documents of title?

Should a bailee surrender goods to their owner if the owner does not present the negotiable document of title?

Why do lenders prefer negotiable documents of title as collateral?

What are the consequences of unauthorized delivery of goods by bailor?

If the goods are lost without negligence of the bailor, is bailor liable for nondelivery?

When can the owner of goods recover goods that were entrusted to a merchant who then sold them?

Is a carrier liable to the consignee if the goods delivered do not match the description of the goods in the bill of lading?

ASSESSMENT: MULTIPLE CHOICE QUESTIONS

1. Frankie Knuckles operated several warehouses in Chicago. Derrick May delivered several dozen boxes of robotics equipment for storage. Knuckles issued a negotiable warehouse receipt to May. A few weeks later, despite Knuckles's state-of-the-art security and safety technology, the equipment was destroyed in an earthquake, rare for Chicago. May subsequently showed up with the warehouse receipt and demanded the equipment. Is Knuckles liable for nondelivery?

    a. Yes. A warehouse that issues a negotiable warehouse receipt is strictly liable to deliver the goods upon presentation of the receipt.

    b. Yes. A warehouse is obliged to protect against loss by carrying insurance.

    c. No. A warehouse is not liable for damage to goods, where the damage was not caused by failure to take reasonable care of the goods.

d. No. A warehouse is not liable for loss unless the parties agree so in writing, under the doctrine of "buyer beware."

2. Jamie Principle arrived at another of Knuckles's warehouses with a truckload of printer ink for storage. The warehouse manager issued Principle a negotiable receipt for the ink. However, Principle drove away without unloading the ink. Principle later duly negotiated the receipt to Alison Limerick, who presented the receipt to Knuckles. Is Knuckles liable to Limerick for nondelivery of goods that Knuckles never received?
   a. No. Knuckles is not obliged to deliver goods that he never received.
   b. Yes. Nondelivery of the goods to the warehouse is not a defense that can be raised against a holder to which a negotiable document of title has been duly negotiated.
   c. No. The negotiable document is fraudulent and so not enforceable.
   d. Yes. Knuckles is liable as the agent for Principle.

3. Mundy burglarized Levan's home and stole a painting, *Introspective*. Mundy stored the painting in a warehouse of Knuckles, receiving a negotiable warehouse receipt. Mundy sold the painting to Collector, who gave value in good faith. Levan learned of the painting's whereabouts and claimed it. Between Levan and Collector, who is entitled to the painting?
   a. Levan, who owns the painting.
   b. Collector, who owns the receipt covering the painting and has priority to the painting.
   c. Collector, because the painting was entrusted to a bailee.
   d. Levan, because Collector dealt directly with the thief.

4. Larchwoods Devices shipped 600 set top boxes on Reading Railroad, with a straight bill of lading consigning the goods to Bolcast Cable. Before delivery, Larchwood Devices sent an electronic message to Reading Railroad, cancelling the shipment, because of a separate dispute with Bolcast Cable about industry standards. Reading Railroad returned the goods to Larchwood Devices. Is Reading Railroad liable to Bolcast Cable for nondelivery?
   a. Yes, because with a straight bill of lading, the seller may only stop delivery if the buyer is insolvent, repudiates the contract, or otherwise gives the seller the right to withhold delivery.
   b. Yes, because seller no longer had title to the goods.
   c. No. The shipper may cancel a shipment and the carrier is obliged to comply.
   d. No. Bolcast Cable has rights under the sales contract only against the seller.

5. Sneaky Sneakers delivered a shipment of running shoes to Reading Railroad. The bill of lading listed the goods as "1,000 pairs of running shoes, Shipper's Load Weight and Count." The buyer paid for the goods after inspecting the bill of lading, but on delivery determined that only 400 pairs of shoes were shipped. Is Reading Railroad liable to the buyer?
   a. No. The carrier is never liable for the sales contract between buyer and seller.
   b. No. The carrier may be liable for misdescription, but not where the bill of lading indicates that the carrier makes no warranty about the description.
   c. Yes. The carrier is bound by the bill of lading and cannot disclaim liability for its own misrepresentations.
   d. Yes. The carrier is always strictly liable to deliver the goods promised.

ANSWERS

1. *C* is the best answer. Under §7-403(a)(2), a bailee is not liable for non-delivery on account of "damage to or delay, loss, or destruction of the goods for which the bailee is not liable." Under §7-204, "A warehouse is liable for damages for loss of or injury to the goods caused by its failure to exercise care with regard to the goods that a reasonably careful person would exercise under similar circumstances. However, unless otherwise agreed, the warehouse is not liable for damages that could not have been avoided by the exercise of that care." So a bailee is not liable for damages to the goods unless caused by the bailee's failure to be reasonably careful. Frankie Knuckles did take reasonable care, with state-of-the-art security and safety technology, so is not liable for the goods. There is no strict liability, contrary to *A*, or a requirement to have insurance, contrary to *C*.

2. *B* is the best answer. None of the defenses good against "a holder to which a negotiable document of title has been duly negotiated" apply here. See §7-403. There was no damage to the goods, or delivery to a party with superior rights, or sale to enforce a lien, or any of the other reasons listed in §7-403. Rather, Knuckles made the error of issuing a negotiable document, which represents the right to goods, without having the goods delivered.

3. *A* is the best answer. Levan owns the painting and nothing has happened that would give Collector priority. It would be different if Levan had entrusted the painting to a dealer, who sold it contrary to Levan's agreement. In that case, entrustment would apply to give the buyer priority over the entrusting owner, Levan. But Levan did not entrust the painting. Rather, it was stolen by Mundy, who sold it to Collector.

4. *A* is the best answer. When a straight bill of lading is issued to the buyer as consignee, the buyer has the right to the goods. The seller may stop

delivery in transit, but only for specified reasons, such as buyer's insolvency, failure to pay, or repudiation of the contract. §2-704(1). In turn, such a justified stoppage would excuse the carrier from its obligation to deliver. §7-403(a)(4). None of those applies, here, so Reading Railroad would be liable for nondelivery.

5. *B* is the best answer. Section 7-301(a) imposes liability on the bailee for misdescription, but allows the bailee to avoid that liability with a disclaimer such as "Shipper's Load Weight and Count," which indicates that the issuer does not know whether the description of the goods is accurate.

LETTERS OF
CREDIT

Perhaps, upstanding citizen, you have such splendid credit that anyone would instantly grant you credit if asked, but, if so, you are a rare individual (or organization). However, the only entities whose credit *is* that trustworthy are banks themselves. If someone with unknown credit wants to deal with an unknown person, the whole transaction would be easier if the credit-seeker could, in effect, have a bank back up any credit extension involved. Better yet, why not have the bank itself be the primary party making the payment promise? This concept was the impetus behind the creation of a "letter of credit," which is just what it sounds like: a letter from a bank promising credit to a stranger in a business transaction. This chapter explores the situations in which a bank might issue such a letter and explains the law governing the transaction.

There are two primary sources for this law: Article 5 of the Uniform Commercial Code and the Uniform Customs and Practice for Documentary Credits, 2007 Revision (Brochure 600 of the International Chamber of Commerce, hereinafter, the UCP). The letter of credit may effectively state that it is governed by the UCP. See, e.g., ACR Systems, Inc. v. Woori Bank, 2017 WL 532300 (S.D.N.Y. 2017). Since the two are not significantly different, we shall look primarily to the Code for study purposes. If you should get involved in a letter of credit case, however, remember to study the UCP carefully — it is recognized as a complete statement of prevailing international banking practices in the field; for the relationship of Article 5 to the UCP, see Official Comment 2 to §5-103. The leading treatise on Article 5 is J. Dolan, The Law of Letters of Credit (4th ed. 2007).

I.   THE BASIC PROBLEM

Assume you are the proprietor of a business in Detroit, Michigan that makes and sells men's shirts. One day you get a letter from Germany saying: "I want to buy 50,000 shirts at $7 each United States currency, FOB Frankfurt. (Signed) *Hans Goldschnitt.*" Since you have never heard of Hans Goldschnitt, you are reluctant to ship him 50,000 shirts and risk nonpayment after the shipping costs are incurred. There are no satisfactory credit bureaus similar to Dun and Bradstreet on an international basis. How can you avoid a credit risk? The answer devised by the law merchant is for you to write Herr Goldschnitt and tell him that you will ship the goods only to a *bank* of international repute that is willing to write a letter to you making itself *primarily* and *irrevocably* liable for the payment of the contract price. If Hans Goldschnitt agrees and you agree on the other contract terms, he will go to a major German bank — say, the National Volksbank of Frankfurt (NVF) — and establish credit with the bank. Shortly thereafter you will receive a letter from the bank more or less in the following form:

NATIONAL VOLKSBANK OF FRANKFURT
Credit no. 829-411
November 20, 2018

Dear Detroit Seller:

We hereby establish our **IRREVOCABLE CREDIT** in your favor for the account of Hans Goldschnitt, our customer, up to the aggregate amount of $350,000, U.S. dollars, available by your sight draft on us, to be accompanied by the following documents:

(1) full set of clean bills of lading issued by German Ocean Lines to the order of National Volksbank of Frankfurt, notify Hans Goldschnitt;

(2) signed commercial sales invoices describing the goods;

(3) customs certificates;

(4) packing lists;

(5) inspection certificate by Grey Goods Inspection Service of New York.

Bills of lading must be dated not later than August 1, 2019; drafts must be negotiated within ten days of shipment; all drafts must be marked "Drawn

Under Credit No. 829-411." Subject to UCP rules (Brochure 600). This credit will expire on October 1, 2019. We hereby agree with drawers, indorsers, and bona fide holders of drafts drawn under and in compliance with the terms and conditions of this credit to honor the same on due presentation of draft to the drawee.

Yours very truly,

National Volksbank of Frankfurt

The German bank will probably forward this letter of credit to you through a local Detroit bank (which has translation facilities and better international commercial paper routing procedures than you do). The Detroit bank will give you the letter and tell you that it is willing to transmit the documents and drafts to the German bank at the proper time. In this situation the Detroit bank is called an *adviser*.

On July 6, 2019, per your contract with Hans Goldschnitt, you draw up the packing lists, invoices, and certificates required by the letter of credit and put the goods on board a German Ocean Lines ship. In return you get a *clean* (free of carrier's notation indicating a defect in the goods or packaging) bill of lading to the order of the German bank and draw a draft payable to yourself on the NVF (that is, the German bank will be the drawee). You clip all these documents together and take them down to the Detroit bank, which forwards them to the German bank and makes an Article 3 presentment for you. If the German bank decides that you have complied with the terms of the letter of credit, it will honor the draft (pay it — the money is then remitted to you by the Detroit bank) and receive all the documents. The German bank then calls Hans Goldschnitt and tells him to come pay if he wants the documents he will need to get the goods off the ship. He does so. When the goods arrive, German Ocean Lines notifies Hans pursuant to instructions on their copy of the bill of lading. He presents the bill of lading and receives the goods.

Several variations on the above are possible. If you are unwilling to wait to get your money, you may be able to sell (*discount*) the drafts to the Detroit bank. Or, as part of your initial contract with the buyer, you may have required him to get a *Detroit bank* to issue the letter of credit to you. He can do this as follows: he establishes credit with the NVF; the NVF issues a letter of credit to you through the Detroit bank and asks the Detroit bank to *confirm* it. If the Detroit bank decides to do so (and it will first investigate the credit reputation of the German bank), it will notify you that the NVF has issued a letter of credit to you and that the Detroit bank "hereby confirms it." This makes the Detroit bank a *confirmer* and liable in exactly the same fashion as the issuer. The confirming letter of credit will state that the Detroit bank will honor drafts under the letter of credit if accompanied by the listed documents. The transaction then proceeds as above, except the drafts you draw are drawn on and presented to the Detroit bank for payment. (*Note:* it is possible to draw a *time* draft on the issuing bank whereby it is given 30, 60, or 90 days — as determined by contract — following formal *acceptance* in which to pay. Such a time draft is commonly called a *banker's acceptance*.) The issuing bank may require that the draft be presented for payment not to itself but to another entity with whom it has a contractual arrangement (called a *nominated person* — see §5-102(a)(11), defining the term, and §5-107(b) and its Official Comment 4, explaining the legal status of a nominated person). This is often done, for example, when the issuer does not carry sufficient amounts of the currency called for by the credit or when the issuing bank wants a more experienced institution to examine the documents presented by the beneficiary.

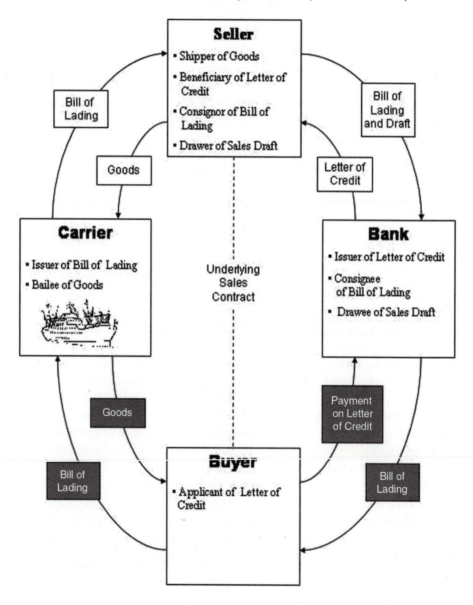

To be distinguished from the above *documentary credit* is the so-called *standby letter of credit*. A standby credit is issued by a bank to be honored only if there is default in an unrelated contract. For example, assume that a contractor agrees to build 50 apartment buildings for the owner of the lots on which the construction will occur. The owner might require the contractor to have its bank issue a standby credit in favor of the owner, to be drawn on only in the event that the contractor does not fulfill its contractual obligation. A standby credit differs from a documentary credit in that the beneficiary of the credit is not required to produce documents along with its draft against the letter of credit; instead, it typically just gives a written notice of breach. Thus, a standby credit is similar to a surety obligation (though not the same).[1] Standby letters of credit are much in use nowadays; in 2018, according to the Federal Reserve, standby letters of credit in the United States totaled over $550 billion. In the case that follows the letter of credit was for $1 million.

Kirchhoff-Consigli Construction Management, LLC v. DeLuxe Building Systems, Inc.

United States District Court, Middle District of Pennsylvania, 2017
WL 3601981

MATTHEW W. BRANN, United States District Judge
BACKGROUND

Plaintiff, Kirchhoff-Consigli Construction Management, LLC (hereinafter "KCCM") filed this action against Defendant, Deluxe Building Systems, Inc., a subcontractor (hereinafter "Deluxe"); KCCM is the general contractor for Pace University's expansion of its Pleasantville, New York campus. KCCM subcontracted with Deluxe to build modular dormitories at its Berwick, Pennsylvania facility and deliver those units to the Pace campus. . . .

II. DISCUSSION

As part of the subcontract between the parties (hereinafter "the contract" or "the subcontract"), Deluxe was required to secure an Irrevocable

---

1. It is *ultra vires* for a bank to act as a surety, so the courts have been careful to draw distinctions between suretyship and the issuance of a standby letter of credit, typically pointing to the fact that a surety is secondarily liable on the contract between the principal and the creditor, but that a bank's liability on a standby letter of credit is an independent obligation. See, e.g., State ex rel. Missouri Highway & Transp. Commn. v. Morganstein, 703 S.W.2d 894 (Mo. 1986).

Standby Letter of Credit in the amount of one-million dollars, naming KCCM as beneficiary. On July 28, 2016, KCCM sent the bank a drawing certificate requesting a withdrawal of the entire one-million dollars. The bank duly authorized the withdrawal of one-million dollars to KCCM (hereinafter "the draw").

Deluxe now moves to amend Counts I and II of its counterclaims to include the draw in its breach of contract and unjust enrichment claims, respectively. Deluxe also seeks to add a third counterclaim to allege breach of warranty under the Uniform Commercial Code. . . .

C.   TERMS OF THE SUBCONTRACT RELEVANT TO THE IRREVOCABLE STANDBY LETTER OF CREDIT

Attachment E to the subcontract between KCCM and Deluxe required that Deluxe obtain the irrevocable standby letter of credit. I set it forth in its entirety below:

Attachment E

To the Subcontract between Kirchhoff-Consigli Construction Management (KCCM) and DeLuxe Building Systems (DBS), for KCCM Project # 421, Pace University Master Plan Phase 1A

1. As security for its faithful performance of all of its obligations under the Subcontract, DBS shall furnish an irrevocable standby letter of credit in the amount of One Million Dollars ($1,000,000), in the form attached hereto, within ten (10) days of the execution by both parties of this Subcontract. The failure to furnish this letter of credit shall be deemed a material breach of this Subcontract, and grounds for immediate termination after ten (10) days' notice to DBS and the failure of DBS to so furnish the letter of credit within that ten (10) day period. Upon such termination, KCCM shall be entitled to all remedies provided for in the Subcontract, as well as any other remedies available at law or in equity.

2. DBS's principal Donald E. Meske shall execute a Personal Guaranty of the form attached hereto, simultaneously with DBS's execution of this Subcontract.

3. DBS shall execute the FIRST AMENDMENT TO SUBCONTRACT attached hereto simultaneously with its execution of this Subcontract.

4. Should DBS fail to meet any of the scheduled milestones identified in Exhibit E, Project Schedule Requirements, of this Subcontract, provided KCCM is current in its payments to DBS pursuant to the terms of the Subcontract, KCCM may assess liquidated damages against DBS as follows:

   a. Five Thousand Dollars ($5,000) per day for each of the first thirty (30) days past the schedule milestone that DBS has failed to complete the task associated with the scheduled milestone.

    b. Ten Thousand ($10,000) per day starting on the thirty-first (31st) day and for every day thereafter that DBS has failed to complete the task associated with the scheduled milestone.

KCCM shall be entitled to withhold such liquidated damages from amounts otherwise due to DBS under the Subcontract. In the event that DBS shall recover the Subcontract schedule and ultimately meet the completion date, the amount of liquidated damages withheld shall be restored to the Subcontract price, less the sum of any and all costs incurred by KCCM in connection with maintaining and/or recovering the Subcontract schedule by reason of the failure of DBS to meet milestones, and paid to Subcontractor with its payment for its next regularly scheduled requisition; it is expressly agreed and acknowledged that in its sole discretion KCCM may expend any and all amounts reasonably necessary to mitigate the impacts of any DBS delay to the Project.

    The amounts set forth above are fixed and agreed on by and between the KCCM and DBS because of the impracticability and difficulty fixing and ascertaining the true value of the damages KCCM will sustain by failure of the DBS to complete its Work in accordance with the scheduled milestones, such as loss of revenue, interest charges, liquidated damages assessed by the project Owner against KCCM, delays caused to other contractors, and other damages. Said amounts are agreed to be a reasonable estimate of the amount of damages which KCCM will sustain and said amount shall be deducted or withheld from any monies due or that may become due to DBS, and if said monies are insufficient to cover said damages, then DBS shall pay the amount of the difference.

    The right of KCCM to assess liquidated damages as provided for herein is independent of KCCM's right to backcharge DBS for liquidated damages assessed against KCCM by the Owner that result from delay or other actions or inactions on the part of DBS.

5. In addition to the rights and remedies afforded it under applicable law and under other provisions of this Subcontract, should DBS fail to meet any of the scheduled milestones identified in Exhibit E associated with its modular manufacturing, or should DBS otherwise breach a material condition of this Subcontract while it is engaged in the modular manufacturing for this Project, then KCCM or its designee shall be entitled to enter into DBS's facilities to inspect the work and the manufacturing process, and shall be afforded direct access to any/all DBS executive leadership, management, and production supervisory personnel for the purpose of communicating about the status and completion of the work. During the course of such communication, DBS personnel shall truthfully and accurately answer all questions by KCCM or its designee about the status of and plans for completion of its work, DBS's financials for the project, and other topics relevant to DBS's successful completion of its work, and shall receive any suggestions or guidance that KCCM or its designee may offer.

D.   TERMS OF THE IRREVOCABLE STANDBY LETTER OF CREDIT

The text of the revised irrevocable standby letter of credit at issue, dated October 2, 2014 is also set forth, in full.

Ladies & Gentlemen:

We, First Keystone Community Bank (the "Bank"), hereby establish and issue in favor of Beneficiary, Kirchhoff-Consigli Construction Management, LLC ("Beneficiary") this Amended Irrevocable Standby Letter of Credit No. 224 (the "Letter of Credit") in the aggregate amount not exceeding One Million Dollars and No Cents ($1,000,000.00) in support of the liabilities and obligations of the Account Party, DeLuxe Building Systems, Inc. and Donald E. Meske to the Beneficiary, which will be available upon presentment of the Beneficiary's draft effective immediately and expiring on the Expiration Date (as hereinafter defined), providing Kirchhoff-Consigli has no default toward DeLuxe Building Systems or Donald E. Meske. This Amended Irrevocable Letter of Credit replaces and supersedes the original version dated September 29, 2014.

Each draft drawn by the Beneficiary must be marked "Drawn under First Keystone Community Bank Irrevocable Standby letter of Credit No. 224" and be accompanied by the original of this letter, or if the original has been returned to the Bank, a certified copy thereof, and a statements signed by an authorized representative of the Beneficiary that the amount of the draft does not exceed the amount due and owing to the Beneficiary from the Account Party, and there has been a default by Account Party under the terms of a Subcontract between Deluxe Building Systems, Inc. ("Subcontractor") and the Beneficiary dated June 10, 2014, together with any amendments thereto or personal guarantees thereof ("Subcontract") beyond any applicable cure period or failure by Subcontractor to perform or pay for any of the obligations required by the Subcontract or to pay to the Beneficiary any damages or other amounts which the Subcontractor or Account Party is required to pay to the Beneficiary under the terms of the Subcontract provided therewith. This Letter of Credit shall be released and the original returned to the Bank by the Beneficiary within 10 days of the date that the final payment of retainage under the Subcontract becomes due to the Subcontractor.

Beneficiary under the terms of the Subcontract provided therewith. This Letter of Credit shall be released and the original returned to the Bank by the Beneficiary within 10 days of the date that the final payment of retainage under the Subcontract becomes due to the Subcontractor.

The Bank is not to be called upon to resolve issues of law or fact between the Beneficiary and Account Party. Any draft(s) drawn hereunder and in compliance with the terms of this Letter of Credit will be duly honored if drawn and presented to our office at the above address prior to the expiration of this Letter of Credit. Partial drawings are permitted. The Beneficiary hereby agrees to endorse of the reverse side of the original Letter of Credit the amount(s) of any such partial draft(s) which Beneficiary is paid, and to surrender the original Letter of Credit to the Bank together with any draft which exhaust the amount available under this Letter of Credit.

E.   TEXT OF THE DRAWING CERTIFICATE AND ACCOMPANYING CERTIFICATION

Anthony M. Consigli, the Chief Executive Officer of KCCM[,] signed and issued a drawing certificate to the bank. That drawing certificate is also set forth in pertinent part:

> The undersigned, Kirchhoff-Consigli Construction Management, LLC, now known as Consigli Construction NY, LLC (the "Beneficiary"), hereby certifies to First Keystone Community Bank as follows:
>
> The Beneficiary is entitled to draw upon the Letter of Credit in the amount of $1,000,000.00, pursuant to that certain Subcontract between DeLuxe Building Systems, Inc. (the "Account Party") and the Beneficiary dated June 10, 2014, together with any amendments thereto or personal guarantees thereof (the "Subcontract").
>
> Pursuant to the Letter of Credit, this Drawing Certificate is accompanied by the following documents:
>
> 1. An original of the Letter of Credit; and
> 2. A statement signed by an authorized representative of the Beneficiary.
>
> The attached certification signed by Mr. Consigli is additionally noted as follows:
>
> The undersigned Anthony M. Consigli, Chief Executive Officer of Kirchhoff-Consigli Construction Management, LLC, now known as Consigli Construction NY, LLC, does hereby certify to First Keystone Community Bank, as follows:
>
> 1. I am the duly elected Chief Executive Officer of Kirchhoff-Consigli Construction Management, LLC, now known as Consigli Construction NY, LLC, the beneficiary ("Beneficiary") under that certain Irrevocable Standby Letter of Credit Number 224, as amended by Amendment to Irrevocable Standby Letter of Credit Number 224 (the "Letter of Credit"), and I am authorized to submit this certification on behalf of the Beneficiary.
> 2. The Beneficiary is now known as Consigli Construction NY, LLC, as evidenced by the certificate issued by the Secretary of State of the State of New York on July 26, 2016, a copy of which is attached as Exhibit A.
> 3. I am making this certification pursuant to the terms of the Letter of Credit and that certain Drawing Certificate dated July 28, 2016 (the "Drawing Certificate"), pursuant to which the Beneficiary is drawing on the Letter of Credit in the amount of One Million Dollars ($1,000,000.00) (the "Draw").
> 4. DeLuxe Building Systems, Inc. (the "Account Party") is in default beyond any applicable cure period of its obligations to the Beneficiary under that certain Subcontract between the Account Party and the Beneficiary dated June 10, 2014, together with any amendments thereto or personal guarantees thereof (the "Subcontract"). The Account Party has failed to perform its obligations and pay amounts due to the Beneficiary under the Subcontract.

5. As of the date of this certification, the Account Party owes at least $1,180,566 to the Beneficiary for failure to perform its obligations under the Subcontract, and such amount owed by the Account Party continues to increase because the Account Party's scope of work is not completed and the Account Party ceased performing all services under the Subcontract.

6. The amount of the Draw does not exceed the amount due and owing to the Beneficiary from the Account Party.

This certification was dated July 28, 2016 and signed by Mr. Consigli.

F.   AMENDMENT TO COUNT I, BREACH OF CONTRACT

As written presently, Count I of Deluxe's counterclaims against KCCM is a claim entitled "Breach of Contract—Failure to Pay." Deluxe originally asserted in this claim that "KCCM was required to . . . make prompt payments to Deluxe . . . [and that] KCCM breached the Subcontract by . . . failing and refusing to make payment for work performed by Deluxe." The demand in Count I is for damages "in excess of $1,500,000."

The proposed amendment to Count I changes the title to succinctly "Breach of Contract." The amended counterclaim contains the language quoted above but adds the following: "Further the Letter of Credit could only be drawn upon if KCCM was not in default of its obligations under the Subcontract and if sums were owed to KCCM." Deluxe also proposes to add language that "KCCM breached the Subcontract and the Letter of Credit by drawing on the Letter of Credit at a time when it was in default of its obligations under the Subcontract and at a time when sums were not owed to KCCM." Finally, Deluxe proposes to change the damages demand to read "As a result of the breaches of the Subcontract and Letter of Credit, Deluxe has incurred, and continues to incur, damages in excess of $1,000,000."

G.   AMENDMENT TO COUNT II, UNJUST ENRICHMENT

Count II, Unjust Enrichment, presently reads in part, "KCCM has been enriched, at Deluxe's expense, by the services and products provided by Deluxe, which have not been paid for by KCCM." Deluxe seeks to amend this sentence to add the following concluding language: "and by the funds received by the wrongful Draw under the Letter of Credit."

H.   ADDING COUNT III, BREACH OF WARRANTY UNDER THE UNIFORM COMMERCIAL CODE

Finally, Deluxe seeks to add a third counterclaim, Count III, Breach of Warranty under the Uniform Commercial Code to allege, in relevant part: "Pursuant to section 5-110 of the Uniform Commercial Code, as codified in Pennsylvania at 13 Pa. C.S.A. §5110, if a letter of credit is presented and honored, the beneficiary (KCCM), among other things, warrants to the applicant (Deluxe) that the drawing on the letter of credit does not violate any agreement between the applicant and beneficiary or any other agreement intended by them to be augmented by the letter of credit (the "UCC Letter of Credit Warranty"). "KCCM's draw on the Letter of Credit is in breach of the UCC Letter of Credit Warranty because KCCM has defaulted under the Subcontract, sums were not owed by Deluxe to KCCM and KCCM violated the provisions of the Letter of Credit."

I.   AMENDMENT WILL BE PERMITTED AS TO COUNTS I AND II

[The court allowed these amendments to be added.]

J.   DELUXE WILL NOT BE PERMITTED TO ADD COUNTERCLAIM COUNT III

KCCM next argues that "Deluxe's motion to amend is also procedurally deficient to the extent that the amended complaint fails to state a claim against KCCM for Breach of Warranty under the Uniform Commercial Code." Pennsylvania's codification of the commercial code states:

(a) Warranties generally.—If its presentation is honored, the beneficiary warrants:
   (1) to the issuer, any other person to whom presentation is made and the applicant that there is no fraud or forgery of the kind described in section 5109(a) (relating to fraud and forgery generally); and
   (2) to the applicant that the drawing does not violate any agreement between the applicant and beneficiary or any other agreement intended by them to be augmented by the letter of credit.

The Uniform Commercial Code defines a letter of credit as "a definite undertaking that satisfies the requirements of the Section 5-104 by an issuer to a beneficiary at the request or for the account of an applicant or, in the case of a financial institution, to itself or for its own account, to honor a documentary presentation by payment or delivery of an item of value."[2]

The Westlaw annotations to the statue state "this warranty has primary application in standby letters of credit or other circumstances where the applicant is not a party to an underlying contract with the beneficiary." "It is not a warranty that the statements made on the presentation of the documents presented are truthful nor is it a warranty that the documents strictly comply under Section 5-108(a)." "It is a warranty that the beneficiary has performed all the acts expressly and implicitly necessary under any underlying agreement to entitle the beneficiary to honor." "If, for example, an underlying sales contract authorized the beneficiary to draw only upon 'due performance' and the beneficiary drew even though it had breached the underlying contract by delivering defective goods, honor of its draw would break the warranty." "By the same token, if the underlying contract

---

2. U.C.C. §5-102.

authorized the beneficiary to draw only upon actual default or upon its or a third party's determination of default by the applicant and if the beneficiary drew in violation of its authorization, then upon honor of its draw the warranty would be breached." "In many cases, therefore, the documents presented to the issuer will contain inaccurate statements (concerning the goods delivered or concerning default or other matters), but the breach of warranty arises not because the statements are untrue but because the beneficiary's drawing violated its express or implied obligations in the underlying transaction."

"An 'irrevocable standby letter of credit,' is different from a standard commercial letter of credit." "The latter is a simple payment mechanism." "Rather than a buyer promising to pay seller, a buyer/account party has issuer promise to pay a seller/beneficiary; payment is expected to occur through the issuer." "In contrast, the standby letter of credit is merely a backup." "The beneficiary makes proper demand upon the issuer only if the account party fails to pay or perform." "The Uniform Commercial Code makes no distinction between these different uses of a letter of credit." "The standby letter of credit differs from the traditional letter of credit in that the beneficiary may draw on the standby letter of credit only after the customer defaults on the underlying contract." "[U]nder the standby letter of credit, the beneficiary usually generates all of the necessary documents himself (usually a simple statement that the customer is in default)." "The standby letter of credit allows the beneficiary to recover damages simply by asserting that the customer has defaulted on the contract; except where the fraud in the transaction exception applies, the issuer is not permitted to refuse payment based either on its belief that the beneficiary's assertion is false or on the existence of any defenses that the customer may have on the underlying contract."

"Letters of credit serve international commerce by providing assurance of prompt payment at minimal cost." "In the ordinary letter of credit transaction, there are at least three distinct agreements: 'the underlying contract between the customer and the beneficiary which gave rise to their resort to the letter of credit mechanism to arrange payment; the contract between the bank and its customer regarding the issuance of the letter and reimbursement of the bank upon its honoring a demand for payment; and the letter of credit itself, obligating the bank to pay the beneficiary.'" "Customer also bears the risk that Beneficiary will demand payment without justification—that is, that Beneficiary will assert that Customer has defaulted when it knows that Customer has complied with the terms of the contract."

KCCM argues that to state a claim under the UCC, Deluxe must have alleged that the draw is violative of the subcontract, as opposed to violative of the letter of credit itself. I agree.

The subcontract between KCCM and Deluxe states very little regarding the irrevocable standby letter of credit. The only reference to the irrevocable standby letter of credit merely states that Deluxe must obtain one. The subcontract places no limits on KCCM's ability to draw. The sole reference in the subcontract to the irrevocable standby letter of credit states, in pertinent part:

> As security for its faithful performance of all of its obligations under the Subcontract, DBS shall furnish an irrevocable standby letter of credit in the amount of One Million Dollars ($1,000,000), in the form attached hereto, within ten (10) days of the execution by both parties of this Subcontract. The failure to furnish this letter of credit shall be deemed a material breach of this Subcontract, and grounds for immediate termination after ten (10) days' notice to DBS and the failure of DBS to so furnish the letter of credit within that ten (10) day period. Upon such termination, KCCM shall be entitled to all remedies provided for in the Subcontract, as well as any other remedies available at law or in equity.

The UCC itself notes, as relevant to the parties here, "if its presentation is honored, the beneficiary [here, KCCM,] warrants to the applicant [here, Deluxe] that the drawing does not violate any agreement between the applicant [Deluxe] and beneficiary [KCCM] or any other agreement intended by them to be augmented by the letter of credit."

KCCM argues that "in order to state a claim under the statute, a claimant must demonstrate that a draw is violative of some extraneous agreement, as opposed to the letter of credit itself." The footnote to the *Al Makaaseb Gen. Trading Co.* case KCCM cited to this position states:

> In its motion for reconsideration, plaintiff argues that the revised 2001 version of the Article V is incompatible with the holding in the PNC case. This Court disagrees with plaintiff's assertions and finds that the PNC case remains good law and that the revised Section 5110 does not create a "warranty of veracity." Revised Section 5110 states that a document required for presentation neither be forged or materially fraudulent, nor should it violate any agreement between the applicant and the beneficiary or any other agreement intended by them to be augmented by the letter of credit. As explained below, the Court finds that there is no evidence that the document was forged or materially fraudulent, nor was there evidence that the letter of credit violated any other agreement between USSI and plaintiff or the contracting parties, USSI and VG.

[Al Makaaseb Gen. Trading Co. v. U.S. Steel Intl., Inc., 412 F. Supp. 2d 485, 495 n.6 (W.D. Pa. 2006).]

Here, KCCM is correct that "Deluxe has not identified any contract provision that prohibited the draw." Without allegations of how KCCM's draw on the letter of credit violates the subcontract between the parties, proposed amended counterclaim III fails to state a claim.

By obtaining the irrevocable standby letter of credit, Deluxe undertook precisely the risk the document contemplated—that KCCM would draw on it. It would seem that Deluxe's proposed addition of counterclaim III is merely an attempt to replead Count I—KCCM should not have taken what is in effect, one-million dollars in liquidated damages because it asserts that KCCM was in default of the subcontract. But a breach of warranty claim would only apply if KCCM had warranted in the subcontract that it would only draw if certain conditions applied. The text of the subcontract noted above cites no conditions on the draw; in fact, it gives KCCM unfettered discretion to draw. "It is not a warranty that the statements made on the presentation of the documents presented are truthful nor is it a warranty that the documents strictly comply under Section 5-108(a)." "It is a warranty that the beneficiary has performed all the acts expressly and implicitly necessary under any underlying agreement to entitle the beneficiary to honor."

Because the subcontract does not specify any acts that either entitle or disallow the beneficiary (here KCCM) to make a draw, Deluxe cannot state a claim under the UCC for breach of warranty.

III. CONCLUSION

For the foregoing reasons, Deluxe's motion is granted in part and denied in part. Deluxe will be permitted to file an amended answer with counterclaims amending Counts I and II. It may not add its proposed Count III.

PROBLEM 104

The U.S. Army wanted to order uniforms for its soldiers from Khaki Clothing, Inc., agreeing to pay a set amount on delivery. The Army, however, had had major problems in past dealings with Khaki, which was always very late at meeting delivery schedules. The purchasing officer for the Army asked the Army's attorney if the contract could contain a penalty clause, imposing a huge penalty on Khaki if it did not deliver the uniforms by the required date. The attorney, mindful of basic contracts law, opined that penalty clauses (even if disguised as liquidated damages clauses) are invalid as a matter of common law, but then he had an idea. He put a clause in the purchasing contract requiring Khaki to get a standby letter of credit in favor of the Army and requiring the issuing bank to pay a huge penalty sum to the Army in the event that Khaki did not deliver the uniforms on time. Octopus National Bank issued such a credit, but when Khaki missed the delivery deadline and the Army tried to collect the penalty specified in the credit, the bank balked and in its defense pointed to the common law rule forbidding penalty clauses in contracts. Will this succeed? See Balboa Ins. Co. v. Coastal Bank (S.D. Ga. 1986); Telenois, Inc. v. Village of Schaumburg, 628 N.E.2d 581 (Ill. App. 1993); McLaughlin, Standby Letters of Credit and Penalty Clauses: An Unexpected Synergy, 43 Ohio St. L.J. 1 (1982).

II.   DEFINITIONS AND SCOPE OF ARTICLE 5

Section 5-102(a)(9) addresses itself to the question of who can issue a letter of credit. Section 5-104 describes the formal requirements of such a letter (note that electronically generated letters of credit are clearly allowed; see Official Comment 3 to §5-104).

Letters of credit *not* requiring the presentation of documents are called *clean credits* because normally only drafts are tendered. See Housing Sec. Inc. v. Maine Natl. Bank, 391 A.2d 311 (Me. 1978). Perhaps the most startling use of such a letter of credit occurred in 1963, when the Royal Bank of Canada, the Morgan Guaranty Trust Co., and the Bank of America issued letters of credit totaling $106 million as security for the ransom of prisoners from the Cuban Bay of Pigs invasion. See Gerald T. McLaughlin, Remembering the Bay of Pigs: Using Letters of Credit to Facilitate the Resolution of International Disputes, 32 Ga. J. Intl. & Comp. L. 743 (2004).

Now read the definitions in §5-102. In the above hypothetical you were the *beneficiary* of the letter of credit; Hans Goldschnitt was the *applicant* (the former version of Article 5 called Hans the *customer*); the German bank was the *issuer;* and the Detroit bank was the *advisor* or *confirmer,* depending on which part of the hypothetical you are looking at. Read §5-107. Do not get these terms confused.

Now go back and reread §5-102(a)(10), which defines *letter of credit*. Note that a letter of credit can be "revocable" or "irrevocable," which means just what it sounds like. With a revocable letter of credit, the issuing bank can escape from its obligation easily. Article 7 of the UCP states that an "issuing bank is irrevocably bound to honour as of the time it issues the credit." By contrast, §5-106(a) *presumes* (if not otherwise stated) that a letter of credit is irrevocable. Remember this: *no one wants a revocable letter of credit.* To understand why, see §5-106(b); Official Comment 1 to that section comments that "revocable letters of credit offer unhappy possibilities for misleading the parties who deal with them." See Beathard v. Chicago Football Club, Inc., 419 F. Supp. 1133 (N.D. Ill. 1976). Article 2 of the UCC decrees that in sale of goods contracts, a clause requiring a letter of credit means an *irrevocable* letter of credit. Read §2-325. Circle the word *irrevocable* in subsection (3).

III.   THE ISSUER — DUTIES AND RIGHTS

When the applicant comes to the issuing bank and asks to establish credit so that the bank will issue a letter of credit to the seller, the bank normally makes the applicant sign an airtight contract absolutely binding the applicant to reimburse the bank *or else*. Cf. §5-108(i)(1). When a bank issues an irrevocable letter of credit, it is under a duty to honor a draft properly drawn there under §5-108(a), so it wants to protect itself and make sure of reimbursement from the applicant. A bank owes corresponding duties to its applicant when performing its duties under the credit. Read §5-108 carefully. It is important to understand that if the issuer honors a draft that it should have dishonored, *the issuer may not seek reimbursement from its applicant*.[3] See Brenntag Intl. Chemicals, Inc. v. Norddeutsche Landesbank GZ, 70 F. Supp. 2d 399 (S.D.N.Y. 1999). An issuer in this predicament has a potential remedy in the warranty section, §5-110.

The moment of truth for the issuer occurs when the beneficiary presents a draft drawn on the issuer for the amount of the credit, accompanied by all the other items listed in the credit to be presented with the draft. In making the decision whether to pay the credit or to dishonor it (which could lead to a lawsuit alleging wrongful dishonor, with damages measured under §5-111) the issuer is only allowed to consider the documents presented by the beneficiary. What is called the "independence principle" flatly forbids the issuer to bring up matters having to do with the underlying transaction between the beneficiary and the applicant; read §5-103(d); see, e.g., Societe Anonyme Marocaine de l'Industrie du Raffinage v. Bank of America N.A., 2016 WL 488665 (Sup. Ct. N.Y. 2016) (bank not required to determine facts of the underlying transaction, where beneficiary's presentation did not conform to the requirements in the letter of credit).

PROBLEM 105

At the request of its applicant, Greenbaum Construction Company, the Last National Bank issued a letter of credit to Latek Steel Company, obligating itself to pay drafts drawn against it, reflecting steel shipped to Greenbaum

---

3. Failure of the applicant to reimburse the issuer is irrelevant as far as the beneficiary is concerned. In this situation, the beneficiary is not liable to the issuer in quasi-contract under a theory of unjust enrichment. See City Natl. Bank v. Westland Towers Apartments, 152 Mich. App. 136 (1986). The usual explanation is that the beneficiary has not in any way been unjustly enriched; it was paid for goods delivered. Section 5-108 (i)(4) clearly bars a restitution action in any situation where the defect was apparent on the face of the documents presented.

Construction under "Invoice #0046." Two weeks after the letter of credit was issued, the buyer and seller changed the shipment dates on the underlying contract and issued a new invoice, this one being "Invoice #0060." Latek Steel Company shipped the steel to Greenbaum Construction Company as agreed and was disturbed to learn that the buyer had filed for bankruptcy two days later. However, it was reassured by the terms of the letter of credit. On Friday, March 27, it submitted a draft to Last National, accompanied by Invoice #0060, and was turned down for payment on April 1. Answer these questions:

(a) Label the parties: who is the *issuer,* the *beneficiary,* the *applicant?*

(b) What is the effect of the bank holding onto the presented draft until April 1? See §5-108(b).

(c) Remembering the doctrine of *de minimis non curat lex* ("the law does not notice small defects"), the attorney for Latek Steel argued that it had substantially complied with the letter of credit, so the bank was guilty of wrongful dishonor and ought to respond in damages under §5-111. Is this right? See Dubose Steel, Inc. v. Branch Banking & Trust Co., 72 N.C. App. 598, 324 S.E.2d 859 (1985); Dolan, Strict Compliance with Letters of Credit: Striking a Fair Balance, 102 Banking L.J. 18 (1985).

(d) Does the seller have any other remedy? See §2-702; Bankruptcy Code §546(c).

(e) What should Latek Steel have done to avoid all this? See §5-106(b). See also BasicNet S.p.A. v. CFP Services Ltd., 127 A.D.3d 157, 4 N.Y.S.3d 27 (N.Y. App. Div. 2015).

Voest-Alpine Trading Co. v. Bank of China

United States District Court, Southern District of Texas, 2000
167 F. Supp. 2d 940

GILMORE, District Judge.

On February 16-17 and 21-23, 2000, a bench trial was held in the above-styled case. Having considered the evidence in this case and the applicable law, the Court enters the following findings of fact and conclusions of law.

On June 23, 1995, Plaintiff Voest-Alpine Trading USA Corporation ("Voest-Alpine") entered into a contract with Jiangyin Foreign Trade Corporation ("JFTC") to sell JFTC 1,000 metric tons of styrene monomer at a total price of $1.2 million. To finance the transaction, JFTC applied for a letter of credit through Defendant Bank of China. The letter of credit provided for payment to Voest-Alpine once the goods had been shipped to Zhangjiagang, China and Voest-Alpine had presented the requisite paperwork to the Bank of China as described in the letter of credit. The letter of credit was issued by the Bank of China on July 6, 1995 and assigned the number LC9521033/95. In addition to numerous other typographical errors, Voest-Alpine's name was listed as "Voest-Alpine USA Trading Corp." instead of "Voest-Alpine Trading USA Corp." with the "Trading USA" portion inverted. The destination port was also misspelled in one place as "Zhang-jiagng," missing the third "a." The letter of credit did indicate, however, that the transaction would be subject to the 1993 Uniform Customs and Practice, International Chamber of Commerce Publication Number 500 ("UCP 500").

By the time the product was ready to ship, the market price of styrene monomer had dropped significantly from the original contract price between Voest-Alpine and JFTC. Although JFTC asked for a price concession in light of the decrease in market price, Voest-Alpine declined and, through its agents, shipped the styrene monomer on July 18, 1995. All required inspection and documentation was completed. On August 1, 1995, Voest-Alpine presented the documents specified in the letter of credit to Texas Commerce Bank, the presenting bank. Texas Commerce Bank found discrepancies between the presentation documents and the letter of credit which it related to Voest-Alpine. Because Voest-Alpine did not believe that any of the noted discrepancies would warrant refusal to pay, it instructed Texas Commerce Bank to forward the presentation documents to the Bank of China.

Texas Commerce Bank sent the documents via DHL courier to the Bank of China on August 3, 1995. According to the letter of credit, Voest-Alpine, the beneficiary, was required to present the documents within fifteen days of the shipping date, by August 2, 1995. As the documents were presented on August 1, 1995, they were presented timely under the letter of credit. Bank of China received the documents on August 9, 1995.

On August 11, 1995, the Bank of China sent a telex to Texas Commerce Bank, informing them of seven alleged discrepancies between the letter of credit and the documents Voest-Alpine presented, six of which are the subject of this action. The Bank of China claimed that 1) the beneficiary's name differed from the name listed in the letter of credit, as noted by the presenting bank; 2) Voest-Alpine had submitted bills of lading marked "duplicate" and "triplicate" instead of "original"; 3) the invoice, packing list and the certificate of origin were not marked "original"; 4) the date of the survey report was later than that of the bill of lading; 5) the letter of credit number in the beneficiary's certified copy of the fax was incorrect, as noted by the presenting bank; and 6) the destination was not listed correctly in the certificate of origin and the beneficiary's certificate, as noted by the presenting bank. The telex further stated. "We are contacting the applicant of the relative discrepancy [sic]. Holding documents at your risks and disposal."

On August 15, Texas Commerce Bank faxed the Bank of China, stating that the discrepancies were not an adequate basis to refuse to pay the letter of credit and requested that the bank honor the letter of credit and pay Voest-Alpine accordingly. The telex identified Voest-Alpine as the beneficiary in the transaction. Voest-Alpine also contacted JFTC directly in an effort to secure a waiver of the discrepancies but was unsuccessful.

On August 19, 1995, the Bank of China sent another telex to Texas Commerce Bank further explaining what it believed to be discrepancies between the letter of credit and the documentation presented by Voest-Alpine according to the UCP 500. In relevant part, the telex provided: "You cannot say [the discrepancies] are of no consequence. The fact is that our bank must examine all documents stipulated in the credit with reasonable care, to ascertain whether or not they appear, on their face, to be incompliance [*sic*] with the terms and conditions of the credit. According to Article 13 of UCP 500. An irrevocable credit constitutes a definite undertaking of the issuing bank, providing that the stipulated documents are complied with the terms and conditions of the credit according to Article UCP 500. Now the discrepant documents may have us refuse to take up the documents according to article 14(B) of UCP 500."

The Bank of China returned the documents to Voest-Alpine and did not honor the letter of credit.

I.

The commercial letter of credit is a payment device often used in international trade which permits a buyer in a transaction to substitute its financial integrity with that of a stable credit source, usually a bank. Alaska Textile Co., Inc. v. Chase Manhattan Bank, N.A., 982 F.2d 813, 815 (2d Cir. 1992).

"[A letter of credit] transaction usually comprises three separate contracts: '[f]irst, the issuing bank enters into a contract with its customer to issue the letter of credit. Second, there is a contract between the issuing bank and the party receiving the letter of credit. Third, the customer who procured the letter of credit signs a contract with the person receiving it, usually involving the sale of goods or the provision of some service.'" Resolution Trust Corporation v. Kimball, 963 F.2d 820, 820 (5th Cir. 1992) (quoting East Girard Sav. Ass'n v. Citizens National Bank, Etc., 593 F.2d 598, 601 (5th Cir. 1979)). The underlying principle of the letter of credit transaction is the independence of the three contracts. Philadelphia Gear Corp. v. Central Bank, 717 F.2d 230, 235 (5th Cir. 1983). The issuing bank does not verify that all the terms of the underlying contract have been fulfilled and must pay on a draft properly presented by a beneficiary, without reference to the rights or obligations of the parties to the contract. Tex. Bus. & Comm. Code Ann §5.108(a), (f)(1) (Vernon's 2000). The issuing bank need only make a facial examination of the presenting documents to determine whether the beneficiary has complied with the terms of the letter of credit, however, the bank bears the risk of any misinterpretation of the beneficiary's demand for payment. Tex. Bus. & Comm. Code Ann. §5.108(i)(4) (Vernon's 2000).

Prior to the amendments to the Texas Business and Commercial Code in 1999, a beneficiary was not required to make its presentation documents strictly comply with the letter of credit, but to present documents that on their face "appear[ed] to comply" with the letter of credit in order to receive payment. Tex. Bus. & Comm. Code Ann. §5.109(b)[4] (Vernon's 1998); see also Vest v. Pilot Point Nat'l Bank, 996 S.W.2d 9, 12 (Tex. Civ. App. 1999) (finding that the language in section 5.109 did not mandate strict compliance). The current statutory law requires an issuer to honor a presentation that, as determined by standard practice of financial institutions that regularly issue letters of credit, "appears on its face strictly to comply with the terms and conditions of the letter of credit." Tex. Bus. & Comm. Code Ann. §5.108(a), (e) (Vernon's 2000). Determination of what constitutes standard practice of financial institutions is a "matter of interpretation for the court." Tex. Bus. & Comm. Code Ann. §5.108(e) (Vernon's 2000).

The Uniform Customs and Practices for Documentary Credits, first issued in 1930 by the International Chamber of Commerce and revised approximately once every ten years since, is a compilation of internationally accepted commercial practices which may be incorporated into the private law of a contract between parties. Banco General Runinahui, S.A. v. Citibank Int'l, 97 F.3d 480, 482 (11th Cir. 1996) (citing *Alaska Textile*, 982 F.2d at 816). In this case, the parties expressly adopted the UCP 500 as the governing authority in the letter of credit. Where parties explicitly refer to the UCP 500 in their contracts, the UCP has been interpreted to apply to the transaction. *Vest*, 996 S.W.2d at 15. Accordingly, the Court will look to the UCP for guidance in analyzing whether the actions of the Bank of China were in conformity with "standard practice" of financial institutions.

The Bank of China claims that its August 11, 1995 telex to Texas Commerce Bank constituted notice of refusal under the UCP 500 because it contained the required elements listed in Article 14(d). Voest-Alpine argues that the telex did not constitute notice of refusal because there is no clear statement of refusal and because the portion of the telex that indicated that the Bank of China was contacting JFTC to seek a waiver rendered the communication ambiguous.

Article 14(d) of the UCP 500 provides:

> i. If the Issuing Bank . . . decides to refuse the [presentation] documents, it must give notice to that effect by telecommunication or, if that is not possible, by other expeditious means, without delay but no later than the close of the seventh banking day following the day of receipt of the documents.

---

4. The prior version of Article 5. — Ed.

Such notice shall be given to the bank from which it received the documents, or to the Beneficiary, if it received the documents directly from him.

ii. Such notice must state all discrepancies in respect of which the bank refuses the documents and must also state whether it is holding the documents at the disposal of, or is returning them to, the presenter.

International Chamber of Commerce, ICC Uniform Customs and Practice for Documentary Credits, ICC Publication No. 500 20 (1993).

According to Article 14(d), if the issuing bank elects not to honor the presentation documents, it must provide a notice of refusal within seven banking days of receipt of the documents and the notice must contain any and all discrepancies and state the disposition of the rejected documents. The section requires that if a bank wishes to reject a presentation of documents, it "*must give notice to that effect.*" (emphasis supplied)

Here, the Bank of China's notice is deficient because nowhere does it state that it is actually rejecting the documents or refusing to honor the letter of credit or any words to that effect. While it is true that under the UCP 500 the notice must contain a list of discrepancies and the disposition of the documents and the Bank of China's telex of August 11, 1995 does indeed contain these elements, this only addresses the requirements of Article 14(d)(ii). A notice of refusal, by its own terms must actually convey refusal, as specified in Article 14(d)(i). This omission is only compounded by the statement that the Bank of China would contact the applicant to determine if it would waive the discrepancies. As Plaintiff's expert, Professor James Byrne, testified, within the framework of Article 14, this additional piece of information holds open the possibility of acceptance upon waiver of the discrepancies by JFTC and indicates that the Bank of China has not refused the documents.

In the August 19, 1995 telex, the Bank of China stated, "Now the discrepant documents *may have us refuse* to take up the documents according to article 14(B) of UCP 500" (emphasis supplied). This is the bank's first mention of refusal and it is tentative at best. The use of "now" further indicates that the documents were not previously refused in the August 11, 1995 telex. Even if this second telex was sent as a notice of refusal, it came too late. The Court finds that the evidence establishes that the telex was sent on August 19, 1995. Seven banking days, the refusal period allotted by the UCP 500 Article 14(d), would have expired on August 18, 1995. International Chamber of Commerce, ICC Uniform Customs and Practice for Documentary Credits, ICC Publication No. 500 21 (1993). Accordingly, the Court finds that the Bank of China did not provide a notice of refusal within seven banking days of receipt of the presentation documents as required by Article 14(d) of the UCP 500. The Bank of China's failure to formally refuse the documents before the deadline precludes the bank from claiming that the documents are not in compliance with the terms and conditions of the credit, according to Article 14(e) of the UCP 500. Id. Although the Court could properly conclude its analysis here, the Court will analyze the discrepancies listed by the Bank of China in the August 11, 1995 telex.

II.

Voest-Alpine claims that the six remaining discrepancies cited by the Bank of China are mere technicalities and typographical errors that do not warrant the rejection of the documents. Voest-Alpine argues for a "functional standard" of compliance, contending that if the whole of the documents obviously relate to the transaction covered by the credit, the issuing bank must honor the letter of credit. The Bank of China argues that the discrepancies were significant and that if the documents contain discrepancies on their face, it is justified in rejecting them and is not required to look beyond the papers themselves.

Section 13(a) of the UCP 500 provides:

> Banks must examine all documents stipulated in the Credit with reasonable care, to ascertain whether or not they appear, on their face, to be in compliance with the terms and conditions of the Credit. Compliance of the stipulated documents on their face with the terms and conditions of the Credit shall be determined by international standard banking practice as reflected in these Articles. Documents which appear on their face to be inconsistent with one another will be considered as not appearing on their face to be in compliance with the terms and conditions of the Credit.

International Chamber of Commerce, ICC Uniform Customs and Practice for Documentary Credits, ICC Publication No. 500 19 (1993).

The UCP 500 does not provide guidance on what inconsistencies would justify a conclusion on the part of a bank that the documents are not in compliance with the terms and conditions of the letter of credit or what discrepancies are not a reasonable basis for such a conclusion. The UCP 500 does not mandate that the documents be a mirror image of the requirements or use the term "strict compliance."

The Court notes the wide range of interpretations on what standard banks should employ in examining letter of credit document presentations for compliance. Even where courts claim to uphold strict compliance, the standard is hardly uniform. The first and most restrictive approach is to require that the presentation documents be a mirror image of the requirements. See Banco General Runinahui, S.A. v. Citibank Int'l, 97 F.3d 480, 483 (11th Cir. 1996) ("This Court has recognized and applied the 'strict compliance' standard to requests for payment under commercial letters of credit. . . . '[T]he fact that a defect is a mere technicality' does not matter.") (quoting

Kerr-McGee Chem. Corp. v. FDIC, 872 F.2d 971, 973 (11th Cir. 1989)); Alaska Textile Co. v. Chase Manhattan Bank, 982 F.2d 813, 816 (2d Cir. 1992) (Noting that documents that are nearly the same as those required by the letter of credit are unacceptable for presentation in a letter of credit transaction).

Second, there are also cases claiming to follow the strict compliance standard but support rejection only where the discrepancies are such that would create risks for the issuer if the bank were to accept the presentation documents. See Flagship Cruises Ltd., v. New England Merchants Nat'l Bank of Boston, 569 F.2d 699, 705 (1st Cir. 1978) ("We do not see these rulings as retreats from rigorous insistence on compliance with letter of credit requirements. They merely recognize that variance between documents specified and documents submitted is not fatal if there is no possibility that the documents could mislead the paying bank to its detriment"); Crist v. J. Henry Schroder Bank & Trust Co., 693 F. Supp. 1429, 1433 (S.D.N.Y. 1988) (where a party who has succeeded by operation of law to the rights of the beneficiary of a letter of credit, refusal was improper, even though the terms of the credit provided for payment only to the beneficiary); Bank of Cochin, Ltd. v. Manufacturers Hanover Trust Co., 612 F. Supp. 1533, 1541 (S.D.N.Y. 1985) (even under the strict compliance standard, a variance is permitted between the documents specified in a letter of credit and the documents presented thereunder where "there is no possibility that the documents could mislead the paying bank to its detriment"); *Vest,* 996 S.W.2d at 14 (noting that strict compliance does not demand "oppressive perfectionism").

A third standard, without much support in case law, is to analyze the documents for risk to the applicant. See Int'l Chamber of Commerce, Comm'n on Banking Technique and Practice, Publication No. 511, UCP 500 & 400 Compared 39 (Charles del Busto ed. 1994) (discussion of a standard that would permit "deviations that do not cause ostensible harm" to the applicant); see also Breathless Assoc. v. First Savings & Loan Assoc., 654 F. Supp. 832, 836 (N.D. Tex. 1986) (noting, under the strict compliance standard, "[a] discrepancy . . . should not warrant dishonor unless it reflects an increased likelihood of defective performance or fraud on the part of the beneficiary").

The mirror image approach is problematic because it absolves the bank reviewing the documents of any responsibility to use common sense to determine if the documents, on their face, are related to the transaction or even to review an entire document in the context of the others presented to the bank. On the other hand, the second and third approaches employ a determination-of-harm standard that is too unwieldy. Such an analysis would improperly require the bank to evaluate risks that it might suffer or that might be suffered by the applicant and could undermine the independence of the three contracts that underlie the letter of credit payment scheme by forcing the bank to look beyond the face of the presentation documents.

The Court finds that a moderate, more appropriate standard lies within the UCP 500 itself and the opinions issued by the International Chamber of Commerce ("ICC") Banking Commission. One of the Banking Commission opinions defined the term "consistency" between the letter of credit and the documents presented to the issuing bank as used in Article 13(a) of the UCP to mean that "the whole of the documents must obviously relate to the same transaction, that is to say, that each should bear a relation (link) with the others on its face. . . ." Int'l Chamber of Commerce, Banking Comm'n, Publication No. 371, Decisions (1975-1979) of the ICC Banking Commission R. 12 (1980). The Banking Commission rejected the notion that "all of the documents should be *exactly* consistent in their wording." Id. (emphasis in original).

A common sense, case-by-case approach would permit minor deviations of a typographical nature because such a letter-for-letter correspondence between the letter of credit and the presentation documents is virtually impossible. See Int'l Chamber of Commerce, Comm'n on Banking Technique and Practice, Publication No. 511, UCP 500 & 400 Compared 39 (Charles del Busto ed. 1994) (noting the difficulty in attaining mirror-image compliance). While the end result of such an analysis may bear a strong resemblance to the relaxed strict compliance standard, the actual calculus used by the issuing bank is not the risk it or the applicant faces but rather, whether the documents bear a rational link to one another. In this way, the issuing bank is required to examine a particular document in light of all documents presented and use common sense but is not required to evaluate risks or go beyond the face of the documents. The Court finds that in this case the Bank of China's listed discrepancies should be analyzed under this standard by determining whether the whole of the documents obviously relate to the transaction on their face.

First, the Bank of China claimed that the beneficiary's name in the presentation documents, Voest-Alpine Trading USA, differed from the letter of credit, which listed the beneficiary as Voest-Alpine USA Trading. While it is true that the letter of credit inverted Voest-Alpine's geographic locator, all the documents Voest-Alpine presented that obviously related to this transaction placed the geographic locator behind "Trading," not in front of it. Furthermore, the addresses corresponded to that listed in the letter of credit and Texas Commerce Bank's cover letter to the Bank of China identified Voest-Alpine Trading USA as the beneficiary in the transaction with JFTC. The letter of credit with the inverted name bore obvious links to the documents presented by Voest-Alpine Trading USA. This is in contrast to a misspelling or outright omission. See Beyene v. Irving Trust Co., 762 F.2d 4 (2d Cir. 1985) (listing beneficiary as "Soran" rather than "Sofan" was sufficient basis for refusal); Bank of Cochin, Ltd. v. Manufacturers Hanover Trust Co., 612 F. Supp. 1533 (S.D.N.Y.

1985) (omitting "Ltd." from corporate name justified rejection). In contrast with these cases, the inversion of the geographic locator here does not signify a different corporate entity. The expert testimony of Professor Byrne supports the finding that this is not a discrepancy that warrants rejection of the presentation documents because the UCP 500 does not impose a standard of exact replication.

Second, the Bank of China pointed out that the set of originals of the bill of lading should have all been stamped "original" rather than "original," "duplicate" and "triplicate." It should be noted that neither the letter of credit nor any provision in the UCP 500 requires such stamping. In fact, the ICC Banking Commission expressly ruled that "duplicate" and "triplicate" bills of lading did not need to be marked "original" and that failure to label them as originals did not justify refusal of the documents. Int'l Chamber of Commerce, Banking Comm'n, Publication No. 565, Opinions of the ICC Banking Comm'n 1995-1996 38 (Gary Collyer ed. 1997). While it is true that this clarification by the ICC came after the transaction at issue in this case, it is clear from the face of the documents that these documents are three originals rather than one original and two copies. The documents have signatures in blue ink [*sic* — that?] vary slightly, bear original stamps oriented differently on each page and clearly state on their face that the preparer made three original bills. Further, one possible definition of duplicate is "[t]o make or execute again" and one definition of triplicate is "[o]ne of a set of three identical things." Webster's II New Riverside University Dictionary 410, 1237 (1994). While the "duplicate" and "triplicate" stamps may have been confusing, stamps do not make obviously original documents into copies.

Third, the Bank of China claimed that the failure to stamp the packing list documents as "original" was a discrepancy. Again, these documents are clearly originals on their face as they have three slightly differing signatures in blue ink. There was no requirement in the letter of credit or the UCP 500 that original documents be marked as such. The ICC's policy statement on the issue provides that, "banks treat as original any document that appears to be hand signed by the issuer of the document." (Int'l Chamber of Commerce, Comm'n on Banking Technique and Practice, The determination of an "Original" document in the context of UCP 500 sub-Article 20 (b) July 12, 1999). [https://www.iccmex.mx/uploads/banca/posturas/The-determination-of-an-Original-document-in-the-context-of-UCP-500-sub-Article-20-b-.pdf]. The failure to mark obvious originals is not a discrepancy.

Fourth, the Bank of China argues that the date of the survey report is after the bill of lading and is therefore discrepant. A careful examination of the survey report reveals that the survey took place "immediately before/after loading" and that the sample of cargo "to be loaded" was taken. The plain language of the report reveals that the report may have been issued after the bill of lading but the survey itself was conducted before the ship departed. The date does not pose a discrepancy.

Fifth, the Bank of China claims that the letter of credit number listed in the beneficiary's certified copy of [*sic*] fax is wrong. The letter of credit number was listed as "LC95231033/95" on the copy of [*sic*] fax instead of "LC9521033/95" as in the letter of credit itself, adding an extra "3" after "LC952." However, adding the letter of credit number to this document was gratuitous and in the numerous other places in the documents that the letter of credit was referenced by number, it was incorrect only in one place. Moreover, the seven other pieces of information contained in the document were correct. The document checker could have easily looked to any other document to verify the letter of credit number, or looked to the balance of the information within the document and found that the document as a whole bears an obvious relationship to the transaction. Madame Gao, the document checker who reviewed Voest-Alpine's presentation documents for the Bank of China, testified that she did not look beyond the face of this particular document in assessing the discrepancy. The cover letter from Texas Commerce Bank, for example, had the correct number.

Finally, the Bank of China claims that the wrong destination is listed in the certificate of origin and the beneficiary's certificate. The certificate of origin spelled Zhangjiagang as "Zhangjiagng" missing an "a" as it is misspelled once in the letter of credit, making it consistent. The beneficiary's certificate, however, spelled it "Zhanjiagng," missing a "g" in addition to the "a," a third spelling that did not appear in the letter of credit. Madame Gao first considered the discrepancy a "misspelling" rather than an indication of the wrong port, according to her notes. There is no port in China called "Zhangjiagng" or "Zhanjiagng." "Gng" is a combination of letters not found in Romanized Chinese, whereas "gang" means "port" in Chinese. The other information contained in the document was correct, such as the letter of credit number and the contract number, and even contained the distinctive phrase "by courie lukdt within 3 days after shipment," presumably meaning by courier within three days after shipment, as in the letter of credit. The document as a whole bears an obvious relationship with the transaction. The misspelling of the destination is not a basis for dishonor of the letter of credit where the rest of the document has demonstrated linkage to the transaction on its face.

Based on the foregoing, the Court finds in favor of the plaintiff, Voest-Alpine.

NOTES

1. This case was decided under the UCP 500, where the so-called *strict compliance* requirement was less markedly pronounced than it currently is in the Uniform Commercial Code. Indeed, in the more recent UCP 600

things get even murkier. Article 14(d) states that "Data in a document, when read in context with the credit, the document itself and international standard banking practice, need not be identical to, but must not conflict with, data in that document, any other stipulated document or the credit." For the tests under the UCC, read §§5-103(d) and 5-108(a) and the following Official Comments: Official Comment 3 to §5-102 and Official Comment 1 to §5-108. Using the tests therein (which have changed since the above case), would the court have reached the same result? In determining whether there is strict compliance with the credit, §5-108(a) refers to "standard practice," as does (e). The International Chamber of Commerce has promulgated a guide as to that called "International Standard Banking Practice for the Examination of Documents Under Documentary Credits" (ICC Publication 645).

One court held that the beneficiary complied with a letter of credit requiring presentation of the original letter of credit by presenting a true copy of the letter of credit, which had been issued by the issuer itself. Ladenburg Thalmann & Co., Inc. v. Signature Bank, 2015 WL 1239293 (N.Y. App. Div. 2015). The court looked to the purpose of the strict compliance rule:

> In the matter before us, there is no possibility that the presentation of a true copy of amendment 2, instead of the original, could mislead defendant to its detriment. Indeed, this copy had been prepared by defendant itself, and was provided to plaintiff by defendant's own attorney. Its accuracy was not in dispute, and there is no dispute regarding the content of the document, which merely extended the expiration date of amendment 2 and which had since been superseded by subsequent amendments. Since the submission of a true copy of amendment 2 would not compel any inquiry by the bank into the underlying transaction, the rationale for the strict compliance rule, "to protect the issuer from having to know the commercial impact of a discrepancy in the documents" (E & H Partners, 39 F. Supp. 2d at 284), has no applicability here.

2. As to the waiver issue in the above case, see §5-108(c); Arch Specialty Insurance Company v. First Community Bank of Eastern Arkansas, 2016 WL 4473438 (E.D. Ark. 2016) (where bank failed to give beneficiary timely notice of alleged discrepancies in presentation under letter of credit, bank was precluded from relying on those discrepancies to justify failure to pay).

3. In letter of credit transactions, it should be emphasized that banks issuing the credits do not charge a great deal and therefore should be exposed to a minimum risk. If a bank is going to dishonor the credit, it should make sure that it is playing fair with all the parties involved so that in any ensuing litigation the commercial reasonableness of its actions will attract the sympathy of the court.

PROBLEM 106

Assume in the last Problem that the letter of credit issued by Last National had required that the bill of lading representing the goods be given not to Greenbaum Construction Company, the applicant, but presented to the bank itself. Assume also that Latek Steel has completely complied with all of the terms of the credit, but Last National, knowing of the applicant's bankruptcy, wrongfully refuses to pay the credit as agreed. You are the attorney for Latek Steel, and the vice president in charge of marketing calls you with some questions. The market for steel is falling rapidly. Must Latek Steel resell the steel involved in this transaction immediately, or may it wait, hoping the bank will change its mind and pay what it owes? If it does resell, does that reduce the amount it can claim as damages from Last National? As to both these matters, see §5-111(a).

PROBLEM 107

At the request of its applicant, Octopus National Bank (ONB) issued an irrevocable letter of credit to Warren Crook, the beneficiary. The credit's terms required a bill of lading showing that the goods were loaded on board the *S.S. Titanic* by April 1, 2014. Crook cleverly drew up a phony bill of lading supposedly issued by the *Titanic* and presented it along with a draft on the bank to the issuer. ONB paid the draft. Can it collect from its applicant? See §5-108; also note §§5-110 (warranties on transfer and presentation), 5-111 (presenter's right to damages on wrongful dishonor of a draft), and 5-117 (subrogation rights of the parties). Could the applicant use the §5-110 warranties to sue the beneficiary?

PROBLEM 108

Luddite Technologies, Inc. wanted to build a new company headquarters. It hired Weekend Construction Company to do the job, requiring a standby letter of credit of $80,000 to be paid if Weekend failed to keep to the required schedule for completion of the building. At Weekend's request, Last National Bank issued such a credit in favor of Luddite, payable, according to the terms of the credit, "on default by Weekend Construction Company in meeting the attached completion schedule and the beneficiary's presentation of an affidavit to that effect along with a draft drawn on us for $80,000." Weekend Construction dutifully performed its contractual duties, but the president of Luddite, needing money, sent the required draft and affidavit to Last National, wrongfully asserting that Weekend had missed timely completion of a part of the project. Last National paid the draft without investigating the truth of the assertions in the affidavit and now seeks reimbursement from the applicant, Weekend Construction. Can Weekend resist paying under the theory that Last National did not verify the default as the letter of credit required? See §5-108(g) and its Official Comment 9. White & Summers explain: "Where the documents commit the issuer to assess facts and events outside the documents presented, they disable the independence principle and topple the wall that separates presented documents from beneficiary-applicant disputes"; §21-6-g at 1112. If Weekend Construction has gone bankrupt since the bank honored the draft, can Last National pursue Luddite Technologies to get its money back? See §§5-108(i)(4), 5-110. How quickly must it act? See §5-115.

IV. FRAUD

Sztejn v. J. Henry Schroder Bank Corp.

Supreme Court of New York, 1941
177 Misc. 719, 31 N.Y.S.2d 631

SHIENTAG, J.

This is a motion by the defendant, the Chartered Bank of India, Australia and China, (hereafter referred to as the Chartered Bank), made pursuant to Rule 106(5) of the Rules of Civil Practice to dismiss the supplemental complaint on the ground that it fails to state facts sufficient to constitute a cause of action against the moving defendant. The plaintiff brings this action to restrain the payment or presentment of payment of drafts under a letter of credit issued to secure the purchase price of certain merchandise, bought by the plaintiff and his coadventurer, one Schwarz, who is a party defendant in this action. The plaintiff also seeks a judgment declaring the letter of credit and drafts thereunder null and void. The complaint alleges that the documents accompanying the drafts are fraudulent in that they do not represent actual merchandise but instead cover boxes fraudulently filled with worthless material by the seller of the goods. The moving defendant urges that the complaint fails to state a cause of action against it because the Chartered Bank is only concerned with the documents and on their face these conform to the requirement of the letter of credit.

On January 7, 1941, the plaintiff and his coadventurer contracted to purchase a quantity of bristles from the defendant Transea Traders, Ltd. (hereafter referred to as Transea) a corporation having its place of business in Lucknow, India. In order to pay for the bristles, the plaintiff and Schwarz contracted with the defendant J. Henry Schroder Banking Corporation (hereafter referred to as Schroder), a domestic corporation, for the issuance of an irrevocable letter of credit to Transea which provided that drafts by the latter for a specified portion of the purchase price of the bristles would be paid by Schroder upon shipment of the described merchandise and presentation of an invoice and a bill of lading covering the shipment, made out to the order of Schroder.

The letter of credit was delivered to Transea by Schroder's correspondent bank in India, Transea placed fifty cases of material on board a steamship, procured a bill of lading from the steamship company and obtained the customary invoices. These documents describe the bristles called for by the letter of credit. However, the complaint alleges that in fact Transea filled the fifty crates with cowhair, other worthless material and rubbish with intent to simulate genuine merchandise and defraud the plaintiff and Schwarz. The complaint then alleges that Transea drew a draft under the letter of credit to the order of the Chartered Bank and delivered the draft and the fraudulent documents to the "Chartered Bank at Cawnpore, India, for collection for the account of said defendant Transea." The Chartered Bank has presented the draft along with the documents to Schroder for payment. The plaintiff prays for a judgment declaring the letter of credit and draft there under void and for injunctive relief to prevent the payment of the draft.

For the purpose of this motion, the allegations of the complaint must be deemed established and "every intendment and fair inference is in favor of the pleading." . . . Therefore, it must be assumed that Transea was engaged in a scheme to defraud the plaintiff and Schwarz, that the merchandise shipped by Transea is worthless rubbish and that the Chartered Bank is not an innocent holder of the draft for value but is merely attempting to procure payment of the draft for Transea's account.

It is well established that a letter of credit is independent of the primary contract of sale between the buyer and the seller. The issuing bank agrees to pay upon presentation of documents, not goods. This rule is necessary to preserve the efficiency of the letter of credit as an instrument for the financing of trade. One of the chief purposes of the letter of credit is to furnish the seller with a ready means of obtaining prompt payment for his merchandise. It would be a most unfortunate interference with business transactions if a bank before honoring drafts drawn upon it was obliged or even allowed to go behind the documents, at the request of the buyer and enter into controversies between the buyer and the seller regarding the quality of the merchandise shipped. If the buyer and the seller intended the bank to do this they could have so provided in the letter of credit itself, and in the absence of such a provision, the court will not demand or even permit the bank to delay paying drafts which are proper in form. . . . Of course, the application of this doctrine presupposes that the documents accompanying the draft are genuine and conform in terms to the requirements of the letter of credit. . . .

However, I believe that a different situation is presented in the instant action. This is not a controversy between the buyer and seller concerning a mere breach of warranty regarding the quality of the merchandise; on the present motion, it must be assumed that the seller has intentionally failed to ship any goods ordered by the buyer. In such a situation, where the seller's fraud has been called to the bank's attention before the drafts and documents have been presented for payment, the principle of the independence of the bank's obligation under the letter of credit should not be extended to protect the unscrupulous seller. It is true that even though the documents are forged or fraudulent, if the issuing bank has already paid the draft before receiving notice of the seller's fraud, it will be protected if it exercised reasonable diligence before making such payment. . . . However, in the instant action Schroder has received notice of Transea's active fraud before it accepted or paid the draft. The Chartered Bank, which under the allegations of the complaint stands in no better position than Transea, should not be heard to complain because Schroder is not forced to pay the draft accompanied by documents covering a transaction which it has reason to believe is fraudulent.

Although our courts have used broad language to the effect that a letter of credit is independent of the primary contract between the buyer and seller, that language was used in cases concerning alleged breaches of warranty; no case has been brought to my attention on this point involving an intentional fraud on the part of the seller which was brought to the bank's notice with the request that it withhold payment of the draft on this account. This distinction between a breach of warranty and active fraud on the part of the seller is supported by authority and reason. As one court has stated: "Obviously, when the issuer of a letter of credit knows that a document, although correct in form, is, in point of fact, false or illegal, he cannot be called upon to recognize such a document as complying with the terms of a letter of credit." Old Colony Trust Co. v. Lawyers' Title & Trust Co., 2d Cir., 297 F. 152 at page 158, *certiorari denied*, 265 U.S. 585, 44 S. Ct. 459, 68 L. Ed. 1192. . . .

No hardship will be caused by permitting the bank to refuse payment where fraud is claimed, where the merchandise is not merely inferior in quality but consists of worthless rubbish, where the draft and the accompanying documents are in the hands of one who stands in the same position as the fraudulent seller, where the bank has been given notice of the fraud before being presented with the drafts and documents for payment, and where the bank itself does not wish to pay pending an adjudication of the rights and obligations of the other parties. While the primary factor in the issuance of the letter of credit is the credit standing of the buyer, the security afforded by the merchandise is also taken into account. In fact, the letter of credit requires a bill of lading made out to the order of the bank and not the buyer. Although the bank is not interested in the exact detailed performance of the sales contract, it is vitally interested in assuring itself that there are some goods represented by the documents. Finkelstein, Legal Aspects of Commercial Letters of Credit, p. 238; O'Meara v. National Park Bank of New York, 239 N.Y. 386, 401, 146 N.E. 636, 39 A.L.R. 747, opinion of Cardozo, J., dissenting; Thayer, Irrevocable Credits in International Commerce, 37 C.L.R. 1326, 1335.

On this motion only the complaint is before me and I am bound by its allegation that the Chartered Bank is not a holder in due course but is a mere agent for collection for the account of the seller charged with fraud. Therefore, the Chartered Bank's motion to dismiss the complaint must be denied. If it had appeared from the face of the complaint that the bank presenting the draft for payment was a holder in due course, its claim against the bank issuing the letter of credit would not be defeated even though the primary transaction was tainted with fraud. . . .

Accordingly, the defendant's motion to dismiss the supplemental complaint is denied.

Is *Sztejn* still good law? Read §5-109 and its Official Comments carefully; see Mid-America Tire, Inc. v. PTZ Trading Ltd. Import and Export Agents, 2000 WL 1725415 (Ohio App. 2000).

Note well that it has always been the law that if the draft is held by a holder in due course, the bank that issued the letter of credit is not allowed to allege the defense of fraud; see §5-109(a)(1) (expanding this idea to protect all innocent parties); Daiwa Products, Inc. v. NationsBank, N.A., 885 So. 2d 884 (Fla. Dist. Ct. App. 2004).

PROBLEM 109

Just as Octopus National Bank was about to honor a draft drawn on it by the beneficiary of its letter of credit, the bank's applicant called and demanded that the bank dishonor the draft because the beneficiary was guilty of "out-and-out fraud" on the underlying transaction between them. The bank calls you, its attorney, for advice. The documents presented along with the draft exactly match the terms of the credit, and the bank officials are sure that there is no fraud in the documents. Look at §§5-108 and 5-109, and tell the bank what you think it should do.

Cf. Emery-Waterhouse Co. v. Rhode Island Hosp. Trust Natl. Bank, 757 F.2d 399 (1st Cir. 1985) (punitive damages of $1,397,000 awarded against beneficiary who fraudulently drew against a letter of credit). If ONB dishonors the draft and this causes the beneficiary to lose millions of dollars on the underlying transaction, is ONB ever liable for *more* than the amount of the letter of credit? See §5-111.

In §5-109(a) the bank is given the option to honor or not as it wishes. As you can well imagine, banks tend to pay more attention to the applicant's request to dishonor if his name is Donald Trump than if her name is Jane Doe. The bank will not be entitled to reimbursement if it does not act in good faith. See Zeeco, Inc. v. JPMorgan Chase Bank, National Association, 2018 WL 1414119 (N.D. Okla. 2018). If the bank decides to honor the draft, the applicant has two causes of action against the seller-beneficiary: the underlying obligation (normally the contract of sale, see Article 2) and the §5-110(a)(2) warranty.

Hook Point, LLC v. Branch Banking and Trust Company

Supreme Court of South Carolina, 2012
397 S.C. 507, 725 S.E.2d 681

Justice PLEICONES.

Respondent Hook Point, LLC (Hook Point) was granted a preliminary injunction preventing Appellant Branch Banking and Trust Company (BB & T) from drawing on, and defendant First Reliance Bank (First Reliance) from honoring, a $1.5 million letter of credit. BB & T appeals. We reverse.

FACTS

In late 2007, Hook Point sought a loan from BB & T for the purpose of developing a subdivision on property Hook Point owned on Lake Murray called Panama Pointe. BB & T issued a commitment letter to Hook Point in September 2007 indicating that it would loan the company $5.1 million and establish a $2 million line of credit to enable Hook Point to develop the subdivision. Security for the loan included a first mortgage on the Panama Pointe property, personal guarantees of Hook Point's four principals, and a $1.5 million standby letter of credit issued by First Reliance in favor of BB & T.

Hook Point applied to and obtained a letter of credit (LC) from First Reliance that named BB & T as beneficiary. The LC was secured by a cash deposit at First Reliance of approximately $310,000, several real properties owned by a Hook Point affiliate, and personal guarantees of the Hook Point principals. Under the terms of the LC, BB & T was permitted to make draws upon presentation of a draft accompanied by

1) The original letter of credit.
2) A notarized, sworn statement by the Beneficiary, or an officer thereof, that:

   a) The Borrower has failed to perform its obligations to the Beneficiary under the Loan Agreement and Promissory Note dated November 16, 2007, executed by and between [Hook Point and BB & T];

   b) The amount of the draft does not exceed the amount due to the Beneficiary under the obligations; and,

   c) The signer has the authority to act for the Beneficiary with regard to the Letter of Credit.

The loan from BB & T to Hook Point was finalized in a loan agreement on the same day the LC was issued. Hook Point proceeded to complete infrastructure work in the development and began construction on the first home before determining that market conditions had become unfavorable to the project as originally contemplated. Hook Point defaulted on the Loan Agreement and related notes and loan documents by, among other things, failing to pay property taxes, to make interest payments due under the notes, or to pay the principal due under one note. BB & T gave Hook Point notice of default in September 2010 and accelerated the loans under the terms of the Loan Agreement on December 21, 2010. On the same day, BB & T tendered a demand letter to First Reliance, seeking to draw the full amount of the LC.

On December 23, Hook Point filed suit alleging several causes of action against BB & T, including for fraudulent misrepresentation by which BB & T induced Hook Point to enter the loan agreement. Hook Point admitted to being $70,000 in arrears on interest but argued that the terms of the agreement did not permit BB & T to draw the full amount of the LC if that exceeded the amount of interest due. It also sought an *ex parte* temporary restraining order preventing First Reliance from honoring a draft on the LC by BB & T, which the court granted. After a hearing, the court also granted a preliminary injunction against drafts on or honor of the LC beyond amounts of accrued interest, requiring extension of the LC for one year, and requiring Hook Point to post a $50,000 bond with the court. This appeal followed, and the case was transferred to this Court pursuant to Rule 204(b), SCACR.

ISSUE

Did the circuit court err when it granted a preliminary injunction? . . .

DISCUSSION

BB & T contends that the circuit court erred when it granted the preliminary injunction. We agree.

"A preliminary injunction should issue only if necessary to preserve the status quo ante, and only upon a showing by the moving party that without such relief it will suffer irreparable harm, that it has a likelihood of success on the merits, and that there is no adequate remedy at law." Poynter Investments, Inc. v. Century Builders of Piedmont, Inc., 387 S.C. 583, 586-87, 694 S.E.2d 15, 17 (2010).

On the second element, likelihood of success on the merits, BB & T argues that the grounds for refusing to honor a letter of credit are exceedingly narrow and that Hook Point has failed to show it is likely to succeed on the merits under that standard. Thus, BB & T argues that the circuit court erred when it found that Hook Point had sufficiently established this element. We agree.

A letter of credit is a financial instrument designed to reduce the need for counterparties in a transaction to trust one another by adding an intermediary bank to the transaction. This intermediary bank extends credit to one party (typically the buyer in a sales transaction[2]) so that the other need not do so. In a sales transaction, the letter of credit typically requires a seller to represent that he has shipped goods under a sales contract and to document this representation with a bill of lading in order to draw on the LC provided by the buyer. This arrangement entails risk to the buyer, who is vulnerable to loss should the seller present fraudulent documents or deliberately ship nonconforming goods. Nevertheless, the usefulness of a letter of credit depends on its being the virtual equivalent of cash. The judicial doctrine that has developed around letters of credit reflects courts' understanding of this background and the importance to commerce of respecting the terms of this financial instrument so that it remains available as a reliable means of shifting financial risk.

Specifically, this understanding is embodied in the independence principle, under which courts recognize that the obligations created in the letter of credit are independent of the obligations of the underlying contract. *See, e.g.,* Intraworld Industries, Inc. v. Girard Trust Bank, 461 Pa. 343, 357, 336 A.2d 316, 323 (Pa. 1975) ("The primary purpose of a letter of credit is to provide assurance to the seller of goods . . . of prompt payment upon presentation of documents. A seller who would otherwise have only the solvency and good faith of his buyer as assurance of payment may, with a letter of credit, rely on the full responsibility of a bank. Promptness is assured by the engagement of the bank to honor drafts upon the presentation of documents. The great utility of letters of credit flows from the independence of the issuer-bank's engagement from the underlying contract between beneficiary and customer. Long-standing case law has established that, unless otherwise agreed, the issuer deals only in documents. If the documents presented conform to the requirements of the credit, the issuer may and must honor demands for payment, regardless of whether the goods conform to the underlying contract between beneficiary and customer."); Itek Corp. v. First Nat'l Bank of Boston, 730 F.2d 19 (1st Cir. 1984) (Breyer, J.) ("Parties to a contract may use a letter of credit in order to make certain that contractual disputes wend their way towards resolution with money in the beneficiary's pocket rather than in the pocket of the contracting party. Thus, courts typically have asserted that such letters of credit are 'independent' of the underlying contract. . . . And they have recognized that examining the rights and wrongs of a contract dispute to determine whether a letter of credit should be paid risks depriving its beneficiary of the very advantage for which he bargained, namely that the dispute would be resolved while he is in possession of the money." (citations omitted)); *Roger J. Johns and Mark S. Blodgett,* Fairness at the Expense of Commercial Certainty: The International Emergence of Unconscionability and Illegality As Exceptions to the Independence Principle of Letters of Credit and Bank Guarantees, 31 N. Ill. U. L. Rev. 297, 309 (2011) ("[T]he common concern among all stakeholders is that as the ease with which letters of credit . . . can be enjoined increases their commercial utility decreases.").

Nevertheless, courts have carved out a very narrow exception to the independence principle. Aside from permitting the intermediary bank to refuse to honor forged documents presented in order to draw on the letter of credit, courts enjoin the payment of LCs for "fraud in the transaction" when "the beneficiary's conduct has so vitiated the entire transaction that the legitimate purposes of the independence of the issuer's obligation would no longer be served." *Itek,* 730 F.2d at 25 (internal quotation marks and citations omitted).

Put simply, the cases in which the "fraud in the transaction" exception has been applied are those in which the underlying transaction or the demand for payment is clearly a sham, and it is apparent that rigid adherence to the independence principle would facilitate what amounts to a scheme to defraud. In the case that established the fraud in the transaction exception, the beneficiary made an actual shipment so that the shipping documents were real, but substituted "rubbish" in place of salable bristles. Sztejn v. J. Henry Schroder Banking Corp., 177 Misc. 719, 31 N.Y.S.2d 631 (Sup. Ct. 1941). In another leading case, the beneficiary was not permitted to collect on the LC because the fall of the Iranian government so altered conditions that the contract for military equipment could not be completed, and thus there was no possibility that the original purpose of the transaction of which the LC was a part could be accomplished. In addition, no other legal recourse was available to the applicant, and the applicant had cancelled the underlying contract in compliance with its force majeure provisions, which called for cancellation of the LC upon cancellation of the underlying contract. *Itek,* supra.

Several other cases also illustrate the narrowness of the fraud in the transaction exception. *See* Intraworld Industries, Inc. v. Girard Trust Bank, 461 Pa. 343, 357, 336 A.2d 316, 325 (Pa. 1975) ("We conclude that, if the documents presented by [the beneficiary of the LC] are genuine in the sense of having some basis in fact, an injunction must be refused. . . . [N]either the trial court nor this Court may attempt to determine [the beneficiary's] actual entitlement to payment under the lease."); *see also* Roman Ceramics Corp. v. Peoples Nat. Bank, 714 F.2d 1207, 1209 (3d Cir. 1983) (permitting issuing bank to dishonor LC when it knew underlying invoice had been paid and that contrary certification was false); Dynamics Corp. of Am. v. Citizens & S. Nat. Bank, 356 F. Supp. 991, 999 (D.C. Ga. 1973) (describing court's role as limited to ensuring that the defendant could not "run off with plaintiff's money on a *pro forma* declaration which has absolutely no basis in fact"); Mid-America Tire, Inc. v. PTZ Trading Ltd., 95 Ohio St. 3d 367, 392, 768 N.E.2d 619, 641 (Ohio 2002) (affirming injunction against honor of LC where defendants repeatedly lied to and misled plaintiffs about the tires available for sale in order to pressure them into making the LC available before they "could discover the truth").

The Uniform Commercial Code (UCC) incorporated this judicially developed doctrine into Article 5, the UCC formulation of the law governing letters of credit. Thus, South Carolina's adoption of the UCC incorporated into South Carolina law the same independence principle and narrow exception limiting the enjoinment of payment of LCs to instances of egregious fraud that operates to vitiate the entire transaction. In particular, UCC Article 5, S.C. Code §§36-5-101 through-119, governs letters of credit. S.C. Code Ann. §36-5-109(b) (2003) sets forth the conditions under which a court may enjoin honor of a letter of credit as follows, in relevant part:

> If an applicant claims that a required document is forged or materially fraudulent or that honor of the presentation would facilitate a material fraud by the beneficiary on the issuer or applicant, a court of competent jurisdiction may temporarily or permanently enjoin the issuer from honoring a presentation or grant similar relief against the issuer or other persons only if the court finds that:
>
>   . . .
>   (3) all of the conditions to entitle a person to the relief under the law of this State have been met; and
>   (4) on the basis of the information submitted to the court, the applicant is more likely than not to succeed under its claim of forgery or material fraud. . . .

For purposes of a preliminary injunction, subsection (3) effectively incorporates the requirements of the common law related to injunctions generally: that the movant show that irreparable harm will result and that no adequate remedy at law exists if the court refuses the injunction. *Poynter Investments,* supra.

Subsection (4) codifies not only the general common law requirement that the movant show a likelihood of success on the merits but also the special rule for letters of credit allowing only a narrow exception for fraud in the transaction, as discussed above. The Official Comment makes this codification explicit.

In the present case, Hook Point argues that BB & T is not entitled to draw on the LC because the commitment letter described the LC as "to be used as last resort for interest carry." Hook Point also seeks to construe as fraudulent BB & T's demand on the LC. The LC, however, by its terms requires only that BB & T represent that "[t]he Borrower has failed to perform its obligations . . . under the Loan Agreement and Promissory Note" and that "[t]he amount of the draft does not exceed the amount due to the Beneficiary under the obligation." Thus, contrary to Hook Point's arguments, the plain language of the LC permitted BB & T to use it if Hook Point defaulted under any obligation of the loan agreement and note, including an acceleration clause. Furthermore, no term in the loan agreement or note to which the LC refers limits BB & T's use of the LC to interest due. Thus, it is incontrovertible that BB & T had some basis in fact for the representations it made when it drew on the LC.

If there is any validity to Hook Point's argument that the commitment letter limited the utilization of the LC exclusively to interest, that is an ordinary contract dispute that raises no implication of fraud by BB & T sufficient to trigger the narrow fraud exception. *Dynamics Corp.,* supra. In fact, $500,000 had been reserved by BB & T from the original $5.1 million loan for the purpose of drawing down interest carry. A more plausible explanation for the "last resort" language in the commitment letter is that it was intended merely as an accommodation to the principals that BB & T would not seek to draw on the LC for interest until the reserve had been exhausted. That language, whatever it meant, is a red herring in this case as the draw on the LC was sought not only to recoup interest but as a result of multiple defaults that caused BB & T to invoke the acceleration of the entire debt.

Indeed, Hook Point's admission that BB & T was entitled to any draw on the LC for past due interest was conclusive as to the issue whether honor of the LC should be enjoined, since BB & T's entitlement to past due interest is alone some basis in fact on which BB & T could demand payment under the LC. Moreover, the strict standard required under §36-5-109(b)(4) is that the alleged fraud vitiate the entire transaction, that is, it deprives Hook Point of any benefit from the transaction. In this case, there is no dispute that Hook

Point received $5.1 million from BB & T. These facts hardly parallel the receipt of "rubbish" instead of bargained-for salable bristles. *See Sztejn v. J. Henry Schroder Banking Corp., supra.*

Thus, there is no evidence Hook Point is more likely than not to succeed on a claim of material fraud so egregious as to vitiate the entire transaction as required under §36-5-109(b)(4), and the circuit court failed to evaluate the evidence under the strict standard required for injunctions against the honor of LCs. Under the proper standard, it is clear that BB & T had a sufficient basis in fact upon which to demand payment under the LC. Thus, the circuit court's finding was based upon an error of law.

Because this issue is dispositive of the case, we need not address BB & T's remaining issues. Rule 220(b), SCACR; *e.g.,* Futch v. McAllister Towing of Georgetown, Inc., 335 S.C. 598, 613, 518 S.E.2d 591, 598 (1999).

CONCLUSION

The standard under which a fraud in the transaction claim must be measured when deciding whether to enjoin honor of a letter of credit requires that the beneficiary have no colorable claim or basis in fact for asserting its rights under the letter of credit. In this case BB & T has, in our view, not only a colorable claim but an undeniable basis in fact for asserting its rights under the letter of credit. Therefore, the circuit court erred when it granted the preliminary injunction. **REVERSED.**

NOTE

In deciding the liability of an issuer who refuses to honor a credit, the courts have placed great emphasis on the "real" reason the issuer wants out. If that reason is that the applicant is bankrupt, so that the issuer fears no reimbursement will be forthcoming, the courts will stretch to hold the issuer liable; see ACE American Ins. Co. v. Bank of the Ozarks, 2014 WL 4953566 (S.D.N.Y. 2014). After all, fear of applicant insolvency was the very reason the seller wanted a letter of credit in the beginning. On the other hand, where the issuer hesitates because it is afraid that honoring will violate §5-108, and the issuer will lose the right to seek reimbursement from its applicant, the issuer's conduct is more likely to receive favorable treatment from the court. Cf. In re Factory Sales & Engineering, Inc., 2017 WL 4570813 (E.D. La. 2017) (beneficiary made fraudulent presentation by submitting false statement that it had terminated underlying contract). For a fascinating example of these considerations at work, compare the district and appellate court opinions in Courtaulds N. Am., Inc. v. North Carolina Natl. Bank, 387 F. Supp. 92 (M.D.N.C. 1975), *rev'd,* 528 F.2d 802 (4th Cir. 1975).

V. ASSIGNMENT

PROBLEM 110

Octopus National Bank issued a $50,000 letter of credit to Grey Goods of New York, payable to Grey Goods on presentation of a draft and certain documents demonstrating shipment of clothing to Ohio Wholesalers, the bank's applicant. Grey Goods needed money to finance its operations, so it borrowed $30,000 from Midwest State Bank, giving MSB a security interest in the proceeds of the letter of credit, and assigning the right to those proceeds to MSB, which promptly notified ONB of the assignment. Grey Goods had trouble filling the Ohio Wholesalers order, so those two parties agreed to lower the amount shipped and the price to $10,000 worth of clothing, and the letter of credit was amended to reflect this lower amount. When the clothing was shipped and the draft presented under the letter of credit, ONB was only willing to pay $10,000 to MSB. MSB calls you, its attorney. What are its rights here? See §§5-114, 5-106, and Official Comment 2 to the latter.

VI. SUBROGATION

PROBLEM 111

Ebenezer Scrooge was the sole shareholder of Scrooge and Marley, Inc., a corporation that sold coal. In early 2019, the corporation signed a $2 million contract to buy mineral rights in a new coal tract in Pennsylvania from Frederick Bean, the owner of the land, agreeing that he would allow Scrooge and Marley to mine the coal in the summer of 2019, sell it to others, and then pay the $2 million to Bean. In the meantime Scrooge and Marley signed a promissory note for this amount payable to Bean, guaranteed personally by Ebenezer Scrooge, due June 1, 2022. Bean also required Scrooge and Marley to get a standby letter of credit in his favor for the amount of $2 million, payable if the corporation defaulted on its promissory note. The corporation had Dickens National Bank issue such a letter of credit, with Bean as the beneficiary. The transaction went as planned until the market for coal collapsed after Scrooge and Marley had mined the Bean tract and found itself unable to sell that coal at a profit. When the promissory note was not paid when it came due in 2022, Bean drew a draft on the bank under the letter of credit.

Dickens National Bank has this draft in hand, and calls you, the bank's attorney. Scrooge and Marley has just filed for bankruptcy, and has no assets. Must it pay the letter of credit? If it does so, can it subrogate itself to Bean's rights against Ebenezer Scrooge? See §5-117;[5] JP Morgan Chase Bank v. Cook, 318 F. Supp. 2d 159 (S.D.N.Y. 2004). Can it go after Scrooge *before* it pays Bean's draft? See §5-117(d).

CHAPTER 9 REVIEW QUESTIONS

Would the seller of goods more likely be the applicant or the beneficiary of a letter of credit?

Why is a revocable letter of credit of little value?

When is an issuer entitled to reimbursement from its applicant for paying a letter of credit?

Is a beneficiary entitled to payment, if it substantially, but not strictly, complies with the terms of the letter of credit?

How is the requirement of strict compliance related to the independence principle?

How does the independence principle insulate the issuer bank from the underlying transaction?

If the seller has substantially, but not strictly, complied with its obligations in the underlying sales transaction, would it be fraud for the seller to draw on the letter of credit?

ASSESSMENT: MULTIPLE CHOICE QUESTIONS

1. Desktop Solutions ordered 1,000 video controllers from Larchwood Devices. Desktop Solutions arranged to have Octopus National Bank (ONB) issue a letter of credit to Larchwood Devices for the amount of the contract price. Larchwood Devices shipped the video controllers and presented to ONB the documents specified in the letter of credit (a bill of lading, an invoice, and a certificate of inspection from Ida Tech). By this time, however, Desktop Solutions had run into financial problems and would not be able to reimburse ONB if the letter of credit was paid. May ONB dishonor the presentation, for lack of sufficient funds?

---

5. In reading that section you should know that the Restatement (Third) of Suretyship and Guaranty calls sureties and similar parties "secondary obligors," and has complicated rules explaining under what circumstances they are entitled to subrogation. See the Official Comments to §5-117.

   a. Yes. The letter of credit is not properly payable, just like an overdrawn check.

   b. Yes. ONB has no obligation to Larchwood Devices, rather only an obligation to its customer Desktop Solutions, who would be unable to perform its own obligations.

   c. No. ONB's obligation to pay is independent from its right to reimbursement.

   d. No. By issuing the letter of credit, ONB guaranteed the quality of the set top boxes.

2. Would ONB have the right to dishonor, if it could show that the video controllers did not meet the warranties that Larchwood Devices made about them in the sales contract?

   a. Yes. Larchwood Devices would not be entitled to payment if it shipped nonconforming goods.

   b. Yes, but ONB could only set off the amount of damages from the breach of warranty.

   c. No. ONB's obligation to pay is independent from the underlying contract.

   d. No. By issuing the letter of credit, ONB guaranteed the quality of the set top boxes.

3. Would ONB have the right to dishonor if it could show that the bill of lading showed shipment of only 500 video controllers, as opposed to the 1,000 video controllers specified in the letter of credit?

   a. Yes. Larchwood Devices would not be entitled to payment if it failed to present a bill of lading that conformed to the letter of credit.

   b. Yes, but ONB could only set off the amount of damages from the breach of contract (presumably half the contract price).

   c. No. ONB's obligation to pay is independent from the underlying contract.

   d. No. By issuing the letter of credit, ONB guaranteed the delivery of the set top boxes.

4. ONB had issued another letter of credit to Sneaky Sneakers, who presented the letter of credit along with the specified documents (a bill of lading, an invoice, customs documents, and a certificate of inspection from Footles Inspections). ONB's customer, however, notified ONB that the boxes delivered contained not the promised sneakers, but only empty plastic bottles, some inscribed with "Size 11" and a smiley face. An ONB vice president visited the buyer's warehouse and verified the facts. May ONB dishonor the letter of credit?

   a. Yes. ONB may dishonor the letter of credit if the buyer has breached the underlying contract.

     b. Yes. ONB may dishonor the letter of credit in the case of fraud.

     c. No. ONB's obligation to pay is independent from the underlying contract.

     d. No. By issuing the letter of credit, ONB guaranteed the delivery of the set top boxes.

5. ONB also issued a $500,000 letter of credit to Gdansk Boats, in connection with the sale by Gdansk Boats of two custom-made yachts. Gdansk Boats assigned the letter of credit to Factor Finance, for a payment of $400,000. Factor Finance and Gdansk Boats notified ONB of the assignment. Gdansk Boats later modified the sales contract, making it a single custom-made yacht for $250,000. ONB, with the agreement of Gdansk Boats and the buyer, amended the letter of credit to be payable for $250,000. When the boat was delivered, Gdansk Boats presented the letter of credit to ONB, along with the required documentation (its signed certification that it had performed under the contract). How much should ONB pay, and to whom?

     a. Gdansk Boats, $250,000, because letters of credit are not assignable.

     b. Gdansk Boats, $500,000, because letters of credit are not assignable or amendable.

     c. Factor Finance, $500,000, because it did not agree to the amendment and the letter of credit had been assigned to it before the amendment.

     d. Factor Finance, $250,000, because an assignee is subject to amendment of the letter of credit.

ANSWERS

1. *C* is the best answer. The bank's obligation to pay a letter of credit is independent of its right to reimbursement. Indeed, the whole purpose of a letter of credit is for the beneficiary to be able to rely on the bank, not on the applicant, for payment. Contrary to *A*, a letter of credit is quite different from a check, which a bank may dishonor if there are insufficient funds. Contrary to *B*, and again unlike a check, a bank does have a direct obligation to the beneficiary to pay the letter of credit.

2. *C* is the best answer. A bank's obligation to pay a letter of credit is also independent of the underlying contract between the applicant and the beneficiary. Whether the beneficiary is entitled to payment on the underlying contract does not determine whether the beneficiary is entitled to payment on the letter of credit, contrary to *A* and *B*. Note that it works in the other direction as well: if the beneficiary has performed the contract, but does not present the required documents for payment on the letter of credit, it is not entitled to payment on the letter of credit.

3. *A* is the best answer. ONB could dishonor because the specified documents have not been presented. Contrary to *C*, this result is consistent with the independence principle. ONB can dishonor not because Larchwood Devices has not performed under the contract, but because Larchwood Devices has not presented the documents specified by the letter of credit. The question illustrates how the buyer should protect itself, by specifying documents for presentation that require performing under the contract.

4. *B* is the best answer. This question illustrates the exception to the independence principle. In the case of fraud, the bank is not obliged to honor a letter of credit. It must be true fraud, not just breach of contract. But here there was fraud, delivering empty plastic bottles instead of shoes, along with taunting messages indicating knowing deception.

5. *D* is the best answer. The right to proceeds of a letter of credit may be assigned, but the assignee is subject to any amendment of the letter of credit.

533